The Complete Book

Illustrations by Donna Wright

# of Natural Foods

by Fred Rohé

 Shambhala • Boulder & London

SHAMBHALA PUBLICATIONS, INC.
1920 13th Street
Boulder, Colorado 80302

9 8 7 6 5 4 3 2 1
First Edition

Distributed in the United States by Random House
and in Canada by Random House of Canada Ltd.
Distributed in the United Kingdom by Routledge & Kegan Paul Ltd.,
London and Henley-on-Thames

Printed in the United States of America

LIBRARY OF CONGRESS CATALOGING IN PUBLICATION DATA

Rohé, Fred
      The complete book of natural foods.
      Bibliography: p.
      Includes index.
      1. Food, Natural.   2. Nutrition.   3. Diet.   I. Title.
II. Title: Complete book of natural foods.
TX741.R63   1983   641.5′637   82-5082
ISBN   0-87773-230-2 (pbk.)
ISBN   0-394-71240-4 (Random House: pbk.)

Dedicated to the memory of my mother,

Jeanne Marie Rohé

Acknowledgments

My gratitude to

Gail Hartman for the books she loaned, her ideas and criticisms, and her loving support.

Susan Roth for her patience, culinary skills, and loving spirit.

Dick Roth for his unfailing faith in our project.

Anna Hawken, Thom Hamilton, and Sandy Scott for their patience in reading rough drafts and coming through it all with helpful criticisms.

Lindy Hough, Julie Runk, and Emily Hilburn for perceptive editorial contribution above and beyond the call of duty.

Donna Wright for more than delightful illustrations—for being a delight to work with.

Janet McCandless for her reliability and serenity and efficient word processing.

Jonathan King, Jacob Collier, Steve and Deb Terre, for providing a firm moral support base.

The entire Sunburst community for friendship and hospitality.

Contents

Recipe Directory   xi

Prologue   1

Introduction   7

PART I: THE NEW AMERICAN DIET   19

1. The New Way to Eat   21
   *Diets, Broadly Speaking—The Four Historical Phases of the
   Grain/Meat Cycle—A Vegetarian or a What?*

2. Considering Protein   27
   *Where Do I Get My Protein?—Complementarity Reconsidered—
   High Protein/Low Protein: Which is Best?—Conservation*

3. The Water Story   34
   Trouble at the Tap—Water Questions

4. Sugar and Salt   43
   The Sugar Story—Honey vs. Sugar—Fructose—The Salt Story

5. Milk and Eggs   58
   Milk: A Most Controversial Food—Cheese—The Egg Business

6. Most Controversial of All—Fats!   70
   Cholesterolphobia—The Alternatives

7. To: Pregnant and Nursing Women, Teenagers, the Middle-   80
   Aged and Elderly, Athletes
   *Pregnancy and Lactation—Dear Teenager—The Middle and
   Later Years—What Athletes Should Eat—Concluding Words*

8. Knowing What to Eat   91
   *Metabolic You—Metabolic Profiles—Dysplasia—Metabolic
   Profiles and the Dietary Connections*

9. "Balanced Diet" Redefined   102
   *Metabolic-Dietary Guidelines—Metabolic Categories and Food
   Affinities—An Overview of Acid-Alkaline Balance—Your
   Metabolism and Choosing Food—Other Factors Influencing
   Balance—Vegetarianism and Other Ideal Diets—Listening*

10. New American Meal Planning   112
    The Elements of Meal Planning—Variety Revisited—In Case
    You're Stuck—Planning Around Restaurants
11. Natural Weight Control   121
    Overweight but Undermotivated—When the Real Calories Stand
    Up to Be Counted—Dieting—Balanced Eating for Permanent
    Normal Weight—Moderation
12. Vitamins and Minerals   134
    Natural vs. Synthetic: A Bogus Issue?—Minerals—Excipients—
    Timed Release Vitamins—Shopping for Vitamins—Supplementa-
    tion and Metabolic Individuality
13. A Folk Medicine Sampler   148
    Folk Remedies for Common Problems—Iatrogenic Diseases—
    Self-Help and Degenerative Diseases
14. New and Future Natural Foods   162
    Soy Foods—Vegetable Gels and Thickeners—Future Foods from
    the Sea—Other Future Foods

PART II: THE NEW AMERICAN CUISINE   171
15. Making the New American Cuisine Work   173
    A Cuisine for Everybody—In the Marketplace—In Your
    Home— Our Costly Favorites
16. Saving Money, Finding Time   182
    The Major Fundamentals—The Minor Fundamentals—Finding
    the Time
PHASE ONE: SIMPLE STEPS TOWARD EATING BETTER
FOR LESS   191
17. Breakfasts   193
    Cold Cereals—Hot Cereals—Pancakes and Baked Goods—
    Potatoes
18. Lunch and Dinner   201
    Lunch—Dinner—Potatoes—Pasta and Sauces
19. Vegetables   210
    About Salads—Cooking Vegetables
20. Beans, Nuts, and Seeds   222
    Beans—Cooking with Soybeans—Nuts and Seeds
21. The Animal Proteins   237
    Meat—Poultry—Fish

22. Snacks and Beverages   251
    *Snacking—Natural Readymades—Ice Cream—Beverages—
    Alcohol: Pros and Cons*
23. Babies and Children   264
    *Breast Milk—What's in Baby's Bottle—First Foods—Teething
    Foods—Allergies—Beyond Babyhood*
24. What to Buy   274
    *Buying Bread—Buying Grains, Beans, Nuts, and Seeds—
    Buying Produce—Buying Meat—Fish—Generics*

PHASE TWO: GOING FURTHER   289
25. Natural Convenience Foods   291
    How to Make Your Own Mixes—Soups
26. Indoor Gardens   298
    Sprouts—Growing Herbs Indoors
27. Making Dairy Products   304
    *Making Yogurt—Making Kefir—Making Buttermilk, Sour
    Cream, and Cottage Cheese—Making Butter*
28. Baking Bread, Making Pasta   311
    Baking Bread—Substitution—Making Pasta
29. Desserts from Scratch   323
    *Summary of Baking with Natural Ingredients—Ice Cream—
    Pies, Cakes, Cookies, and Candies*

PHASE THREE: MOVING TOWARD SELF-SUFFICIENCY   333
30. Juicing   335
    The Juices—The Juicers
31. Becoming a Miller   343
    Storage—How to Choose Wheat—Other Grains—Grinding
32. Small-Scale Canning and Pickling   353
    *Canning in General—Water-Bath Canning of Tomatoes,
    Fruits, and Pickled Vegetables—Pressure Canning—Sweet
    Spreads—Questions about Canning—Spoilage*
33. Freezing   368
    *What to Freeze and How to Freeze It—Freezing Fruits—
    Freezing Vegetables—Freezing Meat, Fish, and Poultry—TV
    Dinners—Miscellanea*
34. Drying Food   381
    *Methods of Drying—Drying Fruit—Drying Vegetables—Drying
    Herbs—Some Unusual Dried Foods*

35.   Machinery and Miscellany   389
      Food Processors—To Buy or Not to Buy—Cooking Equipment
36.   Beyond the Phases   396
      The Backyard Level—The Homesteader—Interconnections

Epilog: Organically Grown—Big Words or Buzz Words?   400

APPENDICES AND INDEX   419

ONE: Where to Find Pure American Spring Waters   421
TWO: A Look at Food Additives   423
THREE: Vitamin and Mineral Profiles   427
FOUR: A Cost Analysis of America's Most Popular Fast Foods   447
FIVE: Natural Foods by Mail   455
SIX: Herbs and Spices   457
SEVEN: Food Supplements and Supplementary Foods   462
EIGHT: Recommended Reading List   471
Index   480

RECIPE DIRECTORY

The Complete Book of Natural Foods establishes the facts behind and the principles underlying the New American Diet and Cuisine. Where diet is concerned, this is done by reference to experience with theory and research; where cuisine is concerned, this is done by reference to experience in the kitchen—recipes. Recipes, then, demonstrate the progression of lessons that lead to mastery of the New American Cuisine, a cuisine that is as nutritious as it is delicious.

THE NEW AMERICAN CUISINE: PHASE ONE

Chapter 17: Breakfasts

Cold cereals	193
Granola	194
Muesli	194
Instant Muesli	195
Powerful Breakfast	197
Hot Cereals	195
Porridge	195
Seasoned grains	196
Pre-preparation	196
Cereal creams	197
Polenta	197
Indian Pudding	197
Whole grain flour	198
French toast (2 kinds)	198
Basic Muffins	199
Pan Bread	199
Basic Pancakes	199
Walnut Coffee Cake	200
Home fries and hash browns	200

Chapter 18: Lunch and Dinner

Sandwiches without nitrates	201
5 kinds of sandwiches	202
Improvised lunches	203
Dinner	204
4 ways to make fluffy brown rice	205
Millet Cheese	205
Vegetable Bulgur	205
Refried Rice	205

Chicken Rice Casserole 206
Lentil Kasha 206
Soy Burgers 206
Wheat Balls 207
Potatoes 207
 French fries 207
 Potatoes boiled, etc. 207
Pasta 207
 4 basic steps 208
 The basics of sauces 208
Improvisational cooking 209

Chapter 19: Vegetables
Salad fundamentals 211
 Bulgur Salad 212
Salad dressing fundamentals 212
 French-Style Piquant 213
 California Green 213
 Thousand Island 214
 Mayonnaise 214
 Sesanaise 214
Steaming 216
Vegetable sauces 217
 Cream Sauce 217
 Curry Sauce 217
 Sweet 'n' Sour Sauce 217
Sautéing and stir-frying 217
 Quiche 218
 Vegetable Burritos 219
 Winter Vegetable Stir Fry 219
 Egg Foo Yung 219
Baking vegetables 219
Cooking in milk 220
More vegetable ideas 220
 Ploughman's Share 220
 Stroganoff 220
 Eggplant Parmigiana 221

Chapter 20: Beans, Nuts, Seeds
Preventing flatulence from beans 223
Cooking beans 223
 (Table) 227
 Garbanzo Spread 227
 Hearty Pea Soup 228
 Lentil Nut Loaf 228
Pressure cooking 228

Cooking with soybeans	229
Tofu	229
Tofu combinations	230
Tofu "fillets"	230
Tofu Enchiladas	230
Roasting nuts and seeds	232
Nut and seed butter	232
Peanut Butter Cookies	233
Peanut-Cheddar Spread	233
Peanut Butter Frosting	233
Peanut Butter Sauce	233
Peanut Butter Bars	234
Making butters	234
Gorp and other mixes	234
Ground Seed Dressing	235

Chapter 21: The Animal Proteins

Tenderizing	238
Sukiyaki	238
Basic theme in using meat	239
All Purpose Marinade	239
Sweet 'n' Sour Marinade	239
Meat in Fresh Vegetable Sauce	240
Shepherd's Pie	241
Poultry	241
A bit of butchering	241
The bird in the oven	243
Simmered Chicken	243
Reversing a trend	244
[Chicken] Chop Suey	244
Chinese Sauce	244
Fish	245
Cooking fish	247
Fish soups	248
Boiling or steaming	248
Poached Fish	248
Fish Sticks, etc.	248
Baked Fish in Herb Butter Sauce	249
Broiled Fillets or Steaks	249
Barbecue Sauce	249
Seafood Salad	249
Eating raw fish	250

Chapter 22: Snacks and Beverages

Food combining   253
Turning desserts into snacks   253
Simple dessert snacks   253
    Gelatin-Apple Salad   253
    Baked Apples   254
Natural readymades   254
Beverages   256

Chapter 23: Babies and Children

First foods   266
    Fruits   267
    Vegetables   267
    Honey   268
    Grains and beans   268
    Dairy   269
    Eggs   269
    Baked Custard   269
    Meat . . .   269

THE NEW AMERICAN CUISINE: PHASE TWO

Chapter 25: Natural Convenience Foods

How to make your own mixes   291
    Pancake mix   291
    Muffin mix   292
    Herb dressing mix   293
    Spaghetti sauce mix   293
    Chili Powder   294
    Curry Powder   294
Soups   295

Chapter 27: Making Dairy Products

Making yogurt   304
    Yogurt Salad Dressing   307
    Yogurt Spaghetti Sauce   307
    Yogurt Cream Cheese   307
    Raw Milk "Yogurt"   308
    Making Kefir   308
Making buttermilk, sour cream, and cottage cheese   309
Making butter   310

Chapter 28: Baking Bread, Making Pasta

Bread   311
    Sponge Method WW Bread   312
    Pita Bread   314

About Yeast 315
Unyeasted breads 315
    Corn Bread 315
Unleavened bread 316
    Sesame Crackers 316
Natural sourdough 317
    Sourdough Bread 317
The simplest bread of all 318
    Sprouted Wheat Bread 318
Substitution 318
Making Bulgur 319
Making Pasta 320
    Basic Pasta 320
    Egg Pasta 320
    Variations 320

Chapter 29: Desserts From Scratch
Summary on baking with natural ingredients 323
    Ice Cream 325
    Frozen Yogurt 326
    Flaky Pie Crust 326
    Cracker Crust 328
    Basic Honey Cake 328
    Variations on Honey Cake 329
    Butter Cookies 330
    Almond Cookies 330
    Date or Fig Bars 331
    Carob Crunchies 332
    Dried Fruit & Nut Balls 332

THE NEW AMERICAN CUISINE: PHASE THREE
Chapter 32: Small-Scale Canning & Pickling
Making tomato juice, fruit juices, fruit purees 360
    Fresh-Pack Dill Pickles 360
    Sauerkraut 361
    Green Tomato Relish 361
    Catsup 362
Sweet spreads 363
    Strawberry Preserves 364
    Apple Butter 364
    Blueberry Jam 365

Chapter 33: Freezing
Methods of freezing fruit 373
    Honey Syrups 374
TV dinners 379

Chapter 34: Drying Food

    Fruit Jerky   386
    Beef Jerky   388
    Salmon Jerky   388

APPENDIX 4: A Cost Analysis of America's Most Popular Fast Foods—Hamburger, Fried Chicken—and How to Do Them Better

    The Burger   452
    Fried Chicken   452
    Pizza   453

The Complete Book
of Natural Foods

Prologue

In 1964, at the ripe old age of twenty-seven, not only was I overweight, I was also tired, susceptible to colds, and rapidly losing my hair. There wasn't anything seriously wrong, but I had been burning the candle at both ends since my early teens and my body was sending me a clear message: Clean up your act or get old before your time.

Drinking; smoking; eating big meals with lots of refined carbohydrates, fats, sugar, and chemical additives; a sedentary lifestyle—they were doing to me what they'll do to anybody. I didn't feel good, I didn't look good, and I didn't like it. It was time to do something about it. Adelle Davis became my guru and Thom Hamilton—the health foods store owner who sold me *Let's Eat Right to Keep Fit*—became my mentor.

At that age it doesn't take long to turn things around. Weight dropping off, energy flooding my system—within a few months I was well on my way to being a renewed young man. It was enough to make me enthusiastic.

So in 1965 I bought a small health food store in the Sunset district of San Francisco. One category in the inventory I inherited didn't interest me: dietetic foods, whose sole virtue was the absence of salt and sugar but which were nevertheless low quality or even junk foods. I realized that a "health food" store was not really the type of food store I wanted, but it was a good place for me to start since it wasn't clear yet what I did want.

I did see clearly that my first task was to clear the shelves of junk and fill the space with real food. The junk disappeared in various directions—given away, thrown away, returned to suppliers, sold at discount. As my inventory dwindled and available space grew, a vision of my future store began to form. An important element of the vision came from photos, drawings, and descriptions of old-fashioned grocery stores—stores where people's genuine needs were fulfilled without seductive advertising and promotional gimmickry. Those stores pre-dated the food business as an *industry*: there were no marketing experts and packaging wasn't an end in itself. In fact, there were a lot of barrels, crocks, jars, and drawers in those old stores where foodstuffs and related items were kept in bulk because packages were unnecessary. Those were key elements in my developing vision: information rather than hype; bulk instead of packaging. People wouldn't have to pay for packaging, advertising, and promotion if I could find and present bulk foods in a self-service format.

I began to search for sources of bulk food, for barrels and crocks, and to redesign the store to accommodate them. I was evolving away from my health food store, which had been a source for specialty foods, discovering my interest was really in old-fashioned groceries—basic stuff, traditional, simple, whole food. As the vision materialized, I became uncomfortable with "Sunset Health Foods," the name I'd inherited, because it didn't reflect my vision or my purpose or the changes that had taken place. What was evolving was a modern version of an old-fashioned grocery store, with

1

emphasis on food rather than food supplements, a store where people could find unadorned natural food as well as the nutritional supplements to augment it. I renamed the store "New Age Natural Foods."

This book is not designed to be the story of my career as a natural foods merchant, but to share some of what I learned during those years and in subsequent years as a participant in the natural foods industry. My career as a retailer ended in 1973, after eight years. New Age Natural Foods had served as a model for what were called in those days "hippie food stores." It is credited as being the prototype natural foods store, as distinct from a health food store. Whatever my store's little role in history might be, I learned a lot as a retailer and since 1973 have continued to work in the natural foods industry, sometimes working in salaried management positions, sometimes working as an independent consultant. It was in my capacity as a consultant that I met the people of Sunburst Farms, who have been my collaborators on this book.

Sunburst is the realization of a vision experienced in 1951 by its founder, Norm Paulsen, while he was living as a student monk studying yoga at the Self-Realization Fellowship in Los Angeles. He foresaw a group of people living communally under spiritual principles in the mountains above Santa Barbara. Norm moved to the Santa Barbara area and, while operating a construction business, remained faithful to his vision for fifteen years. Finally, in 1968, it was time to share the vision and bring it into being. He found people from every part of the country ready to join hands to help materialize it.

They pooled their resources, bought 160 acres of land in the mountains above Santa Barbara and went to work. Their "farm" was littered with a crop of debris, having served as an unofficial dump for people who couldn't be bothered to use an official one. The ground under the garbage was shale—no topsoil. They bought a dump truck, and for months hauled the litter down the mountainside and topsoil—350 tons of it—back up. Growing food organically was part of the vision, so if the land didn't have soil, soil had to be brought to the land.

To integrate themselves with the town, provide a meaningful service compatible with their chosen lifestyle, and earn money for support of their community, Sunburst opened a natural foods store in Santa Barbara in 1970. Both the community—Sunburst Farms—and the community-owned business—Sunburst Natural Foods—flourished. The community now included a second ranch, growing organic vegetables and avocadoes on a commercial scale (this ranch came with topsoil included) and grew to a membership of over 200 people. The business came to include manufacturing and wholesaling as well as retailing. There are now five Sunburst Farmer's Markets, two of them—in Goleta and Ventura—large, complete natural foods supermarkets. Sunburst also owns and operates a natural foods restaurant, "The Farmer and the Fisherman," thirty-five miles north of Santa Barbara along the coastal highway.

Prospering with their diversified natural foods enterprises, nobody would have guessed it was all to be uprooted and dispersed. But so it was. Norm envisioned a new direction and the community responded. What he saw was a completely self-sufficient community totally integrated with its ecosystem. It meant leaving behind the Southern California coastal environment with balmy climate and year-round vegetables, citrus, and avocadoes. Their 6,000 acre coastal ranch was traded for northeastern Nevada land totaling over 500,000 acres. Now they are in the high desert and mountain country, with long, hard winters. It could hardly have been a more radical change. But the soil is rich in minerals and there is abundant water from artesian wells. They are responding strongly to the challenge of, as they say, "making the desert bloom as a rose."

HOW THE BOOK BEGAN

My association with Sunburst began in autumn of 1979 when they hired me to make a store survey and marketing recommendations for their products in Northern California. That done, I began to think seriously of collaborating with them on a book. I had done some writing on natural foods over the years and they had a successful cookbook to their credit, *The Sunburst Farms Family Cookbook*. I remembered the kinds of questions people had asked in my stores and were still asking in Sunburst Farmer's Markets. There is never enough time nor enough staff to answer all the questions. It would be wonderful to have a book available that would serve as a guidebook from store to kitchen to table for the natural foods consumer. Such a book could never be as personal and complete as one-to-one consultation, but it would cover ground that just could not be covered otherwise. It would be invaluable to the beginner as well as to the already convinced and converted.

It wasn't the first time I had considered writing a book on natural foods, but I had never felt the necessary urgency to begin until I read the results of a mid–1979 Gallup Poll that found that "65 percent of the American people want pure food."

My Sunburst friends and I knew the interest in natural food was significant and had been growing rapidly for more than a dozen years; but the strength of the majority surprised us. While we had been going about our business, the attitudes of over 140 million people toward their food supply had changed.

There have been hundreds of books published on nutrition, on making natural foods taste good, on selecting foods according to nutritional needs, and on home food processing. But, until now, there has not been one book that brought all these aspects together into a comprehensive whole. I proposed to Sunburst that we were well qualified to produce such a book, with Sunburst providing research, advice, illustrations, and financial support, while I acted as writer and project director. Sunburst didn't just decide to back my proposal—they decided to back it *enthusiastically*.

The way I envisioned it, if there were such a thing as a course you could take to learn both why and how to switch to natural foods, *The Complete Book of Natural Foods* could serve as the textbook—a kitchen workbook for the new American kitchen. And this kitchen workbook would be completely practical because it would wrap the how-tos of natural foods in cost considerations. No other general book about natural foods has adequately addressed the economic aspect; most have, in fact, ignored the issue entirely. Sunburst and I saw that it is not just health that demands natural foods, but economics, on the weekly-food-budget level.

We all want pure foods but, by all reports, if we make the switch to natural foods it will cost us more money. Even without inflation, most of us would pause in the face of a higher food budget. But what if switching to natural foods didn't require a bigger food budget? What if, in fact, you could switch to natural foods and *save* money? You may be thinking it's just a rhetorical question, leading somewhere else. But it *is* possible—you can eat better (more purely, more naturally) for less. A natural foods diet can be so inexpensive as to make sense on the basis of economics alone. Collectively, the people responsible for this book have hundreds of years of experience as buyers, sellers, cooks, and consumers of natural foods. Time and time again, we have said or heard words to this effect: "Once I learned my way around, I was amazed at how much money I saved eating natural foods."

Considerations of food purity, costs, and methodology cannot be separated from nutritional considerations. Medical statistics prove that Americans are overfed but undernourished. Basic whole food staples wouldn't be such outstanding bargains if it weren't for their nutritional properties. From the beginning, an integral part of the vision for this book was that it provide the facts required to include nutritional needs in the process of grocery shopping.

And while this book presents an in-depth discussion of the economic advantages of natural foods, it would be misleading to ignore the method of payment you must use to gain those advantages. It is a trade-off in time—the more food processing responsibilities you take on, the more money you save. It is not, however, an all-or-nothing situation. There are basic responsibilities we all have time for and from that point a logical progression allows you to find the level of involvement that suits you. So a key feature of *The Complete Book of Natural Foods* is the progressive rendering of home food processing principles and methods that allows you to choose the degree of kitchen self-sufficiency appropriate to your circumstances.

When they think about natural foods, people commonly imagine themselves stocked up with unfamiliar staples, mealtimes coming and going with bowls of inedible glop left behind. Having natural foods in your kitchen is one thing; knowing what to do with them is another. *The Complete Book of Natural Foods* is a *how to* book, covering not only how to plan and shop, but how to assure the results will taste good and how to discover the intangible rewards in the process.

You may have the impression by now that I think *The Complete Book of Natural Foods* is a book for everybody. Well, almost. I make no claim to be unbiased. You can't be unbiased and be an advocate and I strongly advocate kitchen self-sufficiency built on a foundation of natural foods, for both health and economic reasons. My friends at Sunburst and I have virtually eliminated medical expenses and greatly reduced food costs in our own lives. Since we see ourselves as being much like everybody else in most respects, we believe that the lessons we have learned have truly broad applicability. In the broadest sense, this book is about how to live safely and sanely in harmony with our planet—surely not the whole story but just as surely a significant part of it.

SOME BASIC DEFINITIONS

Natural Foods. To know whether or not a food qualifies as natural, one must look at two aspects: its origin and its processing. "Existing in or formed by nature" is the dictionary definition describing the origin of natural foods. This means that it may be a product of human *intervention* (agriculture is human intervention with natural processes), but not of human *invention* (industrial synthesis is human invention utilizing natural laws). Thus, the origin of a natural food is the field, not the factory; a plant or animal, not a lifeless synthesis of chemicals.

Whereas natural foods must originate with life, they may well pass through industrialized processing before they reach you. So in looking at their processing you must look at two aspects: subtraction and addition. Nothing that is edible and nutritious is removed from a natural food. Thus, brown rice can be termed a natural food, white rice cannot. And a natural food is combined only with other natural substances. Thus, whole wheat bread sweetened with honey and shortened with unrefined safflower oil is still a natural food; whole wheat bread sweetened with sugar and preserved with calcium propionate cannot be called a natural food.

The word "natural" is being grossly misused and maligned in the food business. A sure-fire way to boost the sales of an unnatural food product is to call it natural. The inevitable result of seemingly inevitable labeling dishonesty is that a few companies having the real thing have concluded that the word natural has been rendered useless and have gone looking for an alternative. The most popular choice has been "whole" foods.

Whole is a good word, but it is not a good synonym for natural, because wholeness is just one aspect of naturalness. Here, then, is the definition:

Natural foods originate in the life of plants and animals, have nothing edible and nutritious removed and nothing unnatural added.

The key to the term natural foods is understanding what it means. By the time you are through with this book, there will be no doubt in your mind about what a natural food is. The misuse of the term will not guarantee sure-fire sales, but rather will surely backfire.

Diet and Cuisine. The reader will find that I frequently refer to the New American Diet and the New American Cuisine. To be sure we understand the distinction between the two terms, let's return to the dictionary. Diet is "food considered in terms of its qualities, composition, and effects on health." Cuisine is "a style or quality of cooking." So in the part of this book dealing with information about natural foods, I refer to the New American Diet. Where I deal with the practical work done in the kitchen with natural foods, I refer to the New American Cuisine.

New American. When I got into the business in 1965, the term "natural foods store" had not been coined, and less than half of one percent of Americans counted themselves users of "health foods." Natural foods stores, cousins to health food stores, came into being to distinguish the emphasis on food from the emphasis on vitamins and food supplements that characterizes health food stores. Many observers during the sixties viewed the natural foods movement as a hippie phenomenon that would fade. But it has not faded; rather, it has grown steadily and continues to do so. Since the mid-sixties, the natural foods business has grown from something virtually infinitesimal into a billion-dollar industry, with over 10 per cent of Americans considering themselves regular purchasers of natural foods products. Natural foods are *the* New American Diet and will continue to grow in popularity because they are an integral part of the search for quality in American life.

Phases One, Two, and Three. Throughout the book, I have used the terms, "Phase One," "Phase Two," and "Phase Three" to describe certain stages of involvement with a natural foods diet. These terms represent a progressively greater investment of time with substantially reduced expenditures of food budget money:

Phase One: This phase requires the least investment of time. It basically involves knowing what to eat and what to avoid, how to cook and shop for natural foods. It can be undertaken immediately, with little equipment.

Phase Two: Phase Two includes phase one involvement, *plus* additional time invested in such activities such as cultivating an indoor garden, growing sprouts, baking bread, activities suitable for the full-time homemaker who wishes to invest his or her time for greater food budget savings.

Phase Three: Phase three will suit those who want to invest even more time for a more self-sufficient lifestyle at a great savings. Activities here include juicing, freezing, milling, and canning.

The phases are a logical structural form introduced to simplify organization and understanding. Don't feel limited by them. The first twenty-four chapters of the book are for everybody; you will find the rest of the book useful for occasional reference if you are, say, a phase one bachelor who happens to enjoy a phase two activity like baking bread, or a phase two homemaker who likes to can or freeze the garden's bounty. Or you may find the whole book extremely useful as straight reading, if you are out to establish a more self-sufficient lifestyle in which you invest more time but less money for a deliciously wide range of healthful foods.

Introduction

THE CASE AGAINST REFINED FOOD

The verdict has been in since 1939. That was the year Weston Price published *Nutrition and Physical Degeneration,* a little-read classic on the relationship between diet and health. Dr. Price, a dentist, undertook to test the hypothesis that dental abnormalities could be directly linked to what he termed "the absence of essential factors" in refined foods. Price declined to follow the customary procedure of analyzing the symptoms of experimental rats and mice. With the sort of straightforward clarity that always characterizes scientific genius, he conducted a systematic search for groups of human beings to use as controls.

In Switzerland, the Hebrides, Alaska, Canada, the U.S., the South Pacific, Australia, New Zealand, Malaysia, Africa, and South America, Price found groups of people still relying on primitive natural food for sustenance. These he contrasted with others of their group who had become "civilized" and changed to refined foods. Fourteen separate examples widely scattered around our planet were analyzed by Price. His book describes each of those contacts, in every case finding them "rapidly declining in health and numbers at their point of contact with our modern civilization." One hundred and thirty-four photographs vividly illustrated his findings. He was not talking about susceptibility to communicable diseases for which people had no immune defenses. He was literally chronicling physical *degeneration*—malformed teeth and bones, arthritis, osteoporosis and other physical deformities, unknown to the primitives and commonplace among their civilized counterparts. What had begun as a specialized study expanded into one of the broadest as well as one of the most penetrating nutritional studies ever executed.

> While a primary quest was to find the cause of tooth decay, which was established quite readily as being controlled directly by nutrition, it rapidly became apparent that a chain of disturbances developed in these various primitive racial stocks starting even in the first generation after the adoption of the modernized diet and rapidly increased in severity with expressions quite constantly like the characteristic degenerative processes of our modern civilization of America and Europe . . . Applying these methods of study to our American families, we find readily that a considerable percentage . . . show this same degeneration in the younger members . . .

Forty years after the publication of *Nutrition and Physical Degeneration,* we have accumulated much of the same knowledge by other means. What we need now is the courage to face certain facts. Nature alone knows how to make complete, live, wholly perfect food. Man is wise only when he cooperates with nature. Working against nature is usually a direct road to disaster.

Refining food makes the food easier to handle: Refined food is not lumpy or sticky, and does not spoil or get bugs in it. Yet the very lumpiness, stickiness, ability to spoil, and attractiveness to bugs are all due to the presence of essential nutritional elements. It may be convenient and profitable to eliminate nutritional value, but in the long run good health is eliminated as well.

BANKRUPTING THE FOOD BANK

White wheat flour is our most popular refined grain product. As the bran and germ are discarded in milling, here is a partial list of what we lose nutritionally:

Nutrient	Loss Before Enrichment	Loss After Enrichment
Vitamin B1	89%	20%
Vitamin B2	58%	0%
Vitamin B6	60%	60%
Pantothenic Acid	69%	69%
Folic Acid	79%	79%
Niacin	89%	19%
Vitamin E	100%	100%
Calcium	60%	60%
Chromium	40%	40%
Cobalt	89%	89%
Copper	74%	74%
Iron	76%	12%
Magnesium	85%	85%
Manganese	86%	86%
Molybdenum	48%	48%
Phosphorus	71%	71%
Potassium	77%	77%
Sodium	78%	78%
Selenium	16%	16%
Zinc	78%	78%
Protein	22%	22%

An old health food taunt regarding "enrichment" goes, "If a thief held you up for a hundred dollars, then gave you back one, would you be enriched or impoverished?" We are looking at twenty-one food elements in the above table, four of which are replaced, three of them only partially, representing an "enrichment" score of 14 percent. And this table covers only part of the story: it says nothing about the invaluable fiber and trace minerals in the bran, B vitamins, and amino acids in the germ, for which I can find no figures. Dr. Henry A. Schroeder of Dartmouth Medical School, an expert on trace elements, told the U. S. Senate Subcommittee on Energy, Natural Resources and the Environment, "Most of the trace elements essential for health are removed from processed foods. Unfortunately, they are not restored . . ."

Wheat is only one example of the nutritional folly represented by refining processes. Another example is brown rice compared with white. Brown rice has twelve percent more protein, 33 percent more calcium, five times more vitamin B1, 67 percent more vitamin B2, three times as much niacin, and more than twice as much potassium and iron. (*Composition of Foods*, USDA.) The tale is only partially told by easily-found statistics. Vitamin E, for example, present in brown rice, is absent in white, since the rice germ has been removed.

There is a tricky but important aspect to the refining of foods, because of the presence of *unidentified food factors*. We don't even know all that we're throwing away when we fractionate and discard parts of food. As the U.S. Senate Select Committee on Nutrition said in *Dietary Goals for the United States*:

> . . . it is important to understand the degree of our ignorance about what constitutes food value. Out of more than fifty known nutrients, Recommended Dietary Allowances have been established for only seventeen. In addition, there is no definitive evidence that food composition described solely in terms of all known nutrients would be an accurate measure of total food value.

About the unknown nutrients, Dr. Hamish Munro of the Massachusetts Institute of Technology, speaking to the 1977 Convention of Food Technologists said:

> There is insufficient information about requirements for a number of essential trace elements. We must also recognize that other essential nutrients may be discovered in the future, and in consequence we cannot guarantee that RDA's (Recommended Daily Allowances) represent the whole of nutrient needs . . .

In contrast to refined and processed foods, whole foods grown in mineral-rich soil provide a wide variety of vitamins, minerals, enzymes, and other essential nutritional elements—both known and unknown. This book has been written to show you how to make the switch from a diet of nutritionally bankrupt foods and heavy dependence on essentially non-nutritive substances like salt and sugar to a wholesome diet based on delicious, nutritious, and inexpensive natural foods.

Dietary Goals For The United States

The U.S. Senate Select Committee on Nutrition, spurred into action, perhaps, by the prolific incidence of degenerative disease in the United States, suggested these seven steps towards a healthier country in its report, *Dietary Goals for the United States*:

1) To avoid overweight, consume only as much energy as expended; if overweight, decrease energy intake and increase energy expenditure.
2) Increase consumption of complex carbohydrates and "naturally occurring" sugars.
3) Reduce consumption of refined and processed sugars.
4) Reduce overall fat consumption.
5) Reduce saturated fat consumption.
6) Reduce cholesterol consumption.
7) Limit the intake of sodium.

Dr. D. M. Hegsted, professor of nutrition, Harvard School of Public Health, supervised the drafting of *Dietary Goals*. He said:

WHEN WHITE BECAME RIGHT

In *The Book of Whole Foods*, Karen MacNeil suggests that we can look back thousands of years for the genesis of refining folly. And what do we find? Snobbery. Unleavened, whole wheat bread was the mainstay of the peasants.

By the twelfth century B.C., however, rich Egyptians, nobles, and priests distinguished themselves from the poor by eating raised breads and cakes baked in as many as forty different varieties. Some were baked with honey, some with milk or eggs; all shaped into lavish forms: cones, braids, and twists. The poor looked on enviously. And the stage was set. Bread was too important a food for the wealthy to give up. The solution was to eat a bread the peasants didn't.

When the flour that was used in raised breads became plentiful and inexpensive enough for the poor to purchase, the wealthy found themselves needing a new bread to set them apart. The answer was white bread.

The history of white bread indicates that there was no reason, other than a political one, for flour to be milled until it was white. White bread was less tasty and more expensive than whole-grain bread. White flour took inordinately more time to produce. But because white bread was neither common, easily affordable, nor the same color as whole-grain bread, it became a convenient wedge that once again could separate rich and poor. By eating white bread, a Roman citizen silently but conclusively elevated himself over those around him.

And the symbol stuck. White bread became associated with those in power; dark bread with the common man. By the thirteenth century, in the most lavish and extravagant Arabian courts, white bread, along with roast kid and wine, was considered a supreme mark of self-indulgence. A few hundred years later Paris bakeries would be kept under constant pressure filling the long lists of orders for white bread that came regularly from the households of French monarchs.

In modern America we have a further ironic twist, now a sort of reverse snobbery. Whole wheat bread is the choice of the intelligentsia, and so certain members of the lower classes snub it as "intellectuals' food," for what self-respecting working man wants to be associated with *those* snobs?

The diet of the American people has become increasingly rich—rich in meat, other sources of saturated fat and cholesterol, and in sugar. We might be better able to tolerate this diet if we were much more active physically, but we are a sedentary people.

It should be emphasized that this diet which affluent people generally consume is everywhere associated with a similar disease pattern—high rates of [arterial] heart disease, certain forms of cancer, diabetes and obesity. These are the major causes of death and disability in the United States.

Dietary Goals goes on to say:

Most of all the health problems underlying the leading causes of death in the United States could be modified by improvements in diet. . . . Death rates for many of these conditions are higher in the U.S. than in other countries of comparable economic development. . . . The use of high [complex] carbohydrate diets by civilized man has an historical basis, is economically sound and has every implication of causing less, rather than more, disease. . . . especially heart disease.

We could summarize the seven dietary goals proposed by the Senate Committee in one sentence: To avoid overweight, increase the consumption of complex carbohydrates and "naturally occurring" sugars, and reduce the consumption of refined and processed sugars, fat, and salt. That one sentence could also be used to summarize the background motif for the New American Diet and Cuisine presented here.

Overweight

The first dietary goal is, "*To avoid overweight, consume only as much energy as expended; if overweight, decrease energy intake and increase energy expenditure.*" On the surface, that sounds like good old common sense. If you are fat, eat less and exercise more, right? Yes and no. The problem of overweight has a great deal to do not only with how *much* we eat, but also *what* we eat, and how our body metabolizes it. The calories in a meal centered on meat, with refined and processed foods as accompaniments, may be the same as the calories in a meal of natural foods. Yet the way your body absorbs and utilizes those calories will be entirely different. A meal of natural foods contains trace elements which have been shown to play an invaluable part in the metabolism of other nutrients. It contains fiber that will help your body absorb the nutrients in the food and keep your entire digestive system active. It provides a slow, steady stream of food fuel (glucose) for your system, as opposed to the quick flash of energy provided by refined foods that can leave you unable to produce the insulin necessary for glucose metabolism (perhaps contributing to diabetes, one of our major degenerative diseases).

You may find that by paying more attention to good nutrition based on natural foods and exercising regularly, you are able to lose weight without effort, while increasing your state of overall health as well. See Chapters Eight through Eleven for a complete discussion of metabolism, natural foods, and weight control.

Complex Carbohydrates

The second dietary goal is, "*Increase consumption of complex carbohydrates and 'naturally occuring' sugars.*" If there were a theme song for the New American Diet and Cuisine, this would be it. It is interesting to see that this one goal exercises controlling influence over all the others.

Selection of complex carbohydrates stresses choices of natural foods, automatically eliminating the sugar, fat, salt, and additives so ubiquitous in refined, processed, and junk foods. Emphasis on complex carbohydrates also tends to reduce calorie consumption—in short, it alters the entire dietary pattern. The Senate Committee recognized the influence of the complex carbohydrate goal, saying " . . . by following the Report's recommendation to increase the consumption of whole grains, fruits, and vegetables . . . an alteration in the ratio between animal and vegetable proteins will occur."

The Senate recommended that we eat approximately 60 percent carbohydrates, 30 percent fat, and 10 percent protein. But I agree with the many nutritional experts who feel that the reduction from 40 percent fat to 30 percent was not nearly severe enough. And the percentages are not practically useful, since complex carbohydrates are made complex by having protein, fiber, fat, vitamins, and enzymes, and "protein" food is equally complex. It is much more useful to translate the percentages into *types* of food. In the broad approximation of this dietary system below, complex carbohydrates are found in the first four types of food, representing roughly 75 percent, with fat being roughly 15 percent and protein 10:

Types of Food	Percent (%)
Whole grains	30.0
Fresh vegetables	25.0
Fresh and dried fruit	10.0
Beans, nuts, seeds	10.0
Yogurt, cheese, milk, eggs	10.0
Fish, poultry, lean meat	10.0
Vegetable oil (baking, cooking, salads)	2.5
Sweeteners (honey, molasses, maple syrup)	2.5

As you read this book, it will become clear that the above figures are a truly broad approximation of the New American Diet. The percentages given here aren't rigid; they can be loosely applied to everyone. Regard them as a roadsign with a name and an arrow, which tells you nothing about distance, terrain, road conditions, turns and intersections, or the sights along the way.

Sugar

The third dietary goal is, "*Reduce consumption of refined and processed sugars.*" Describing "the dramatic increase in the use of refined sugar added outside the control of the consumer," *Dietary Goals* quotes a report published by the Nutrition Foundation showing that more than two-thirds of the refined sugar consumed is accounted for by processed foods. The astonishing figures show that direct sugar purchases per capita went *down* between 1910 and 1970 from 52 to 25 pounds per year. Yet our sugar consumption went *up* from 76 pounds to 102 (130 pounds in 1981). This is because the *sugar we consumed in processed foods went from 19 pounds to 70 per year for each person.*

By concentrating on a diet of complex carbohydrates in the form of whole, natural foods, you will find that your sugar intake naturally decreases. And as you make the gradual switch from processed to natural foods, you will also discover that your body's craving for sweets may naturally subside. The calm, steady stream of energy that results from a diet of natural foods is fortunately even *more* addictive than the energy provided by a "quick fix" of sugar. See Chapter Four for the details.

Fats

The third, fourth, and fifth dietary goals set by the Senate Committee all concern the reduction of fat in our diet, particularly saturated fat and cholesterol. Again, the New American Diet accomplishes this goal naturally and deliciously. You will find it much leaner—because the emphasis on complex carbohydrates demotes meat from a primary food to a secondary food.

YOUR DAILY SUGAR

When you're told the average American consumes 130 pounds a year of sugar, you know it's a lot. But to give it more reality, look what it means on a daily basis: one third of a pound, or thirty-two teaspoons, every day, and most of it comes already packaged. Here are some examples:

Source	Teaspoons of sugar
Soft drink, 6 oz.	4
Chocolate milk, 8 oz.	6

Source	Teaspoons of sugar
Fruit cocktail, 1 cup	10
Doughnut, plain	4
Ice cream, cup	11
Banana split, 3 scoop	24
Chocolate bar, 2 oz.	14
—some popular breakfast cereals—	
Sugar Smacks, 3 oz.	10
Fruit Loops, 3 oz.	8.6
Super Sugar Crips, 3 oz.	8.3
Frosted Rice Krinkles, 3 oz.	7.9
Sugar Frosted Flakes, 3 oz.	7.4
Frosted Rice, 3 oz.	6.7
Raisin Bran, 3 oz.	5.2

but are they cereals or candy?

adapted USDA figures

However, I challenge the "cholesterolphobia" that is sweeping our country, spurred on by millions of advertising dollars from food processors that might benefit from it. It is time to put cholesterol and fats in their proper perspective (see Chapter Six).

Salt

The final goal proposed by the Senate Committee is, *"Limit the intake of sodium."* Dr. Mark Hegsted, author of *Dietary Goals,* said of salt, "Indeed, if salt were a new food additive, it is doubtful that it would be classified as safe and certainly not at the levels most of us consume. The relationship of salt to high blood pressure (hypertension) and fluid retention (edema) are well proven."

The salt intake level recommended by the Senate's report amounts to five grams or about a teaspoon per day. This translates into about four and one half pounds of salt a year; the average per capita American salt consumption is currently fifteen pounds a year. Dealing in averages can only give indicators: how much salt you need depends on such factors as your individual metabolic type, your level of activity, the climate, and the season. You may not need to add any salt at all to your food, not even in cooking. The goals above really answer the question of how much salt is a safe margin of error. You will find that switching to the New American Diet keeps you within that margin of error naturally by greatly reducing the consumption of processed foods, by using flavorings other than salt for variety at the dinner table, and by cooking with less salt. You may also discover that whole, natural foods have their own delicious flavors that have no need to be either enhanced or masked by the use of salt. See Chapter Four for more on salt.

Additives

Although no mention of additives is made in the dietary goals set by the Senate, our current diet, based on processed, refined foods is full of inadequately tested synthetic ingredients such as artificial colorings and flavorings. Poet Diane Di Prima sums it up well:

SALT IN A TYPICAL DAY OF PROCESSED FOODS

		Sodium, mg:
Breakfast:	2 slices white bread toast	355
	2 ounces corn flakes	640
Morning snack:	Danish pastry	540
Lunch:	5 ounces tomato soup	525
	sandwich with 2 slices white bread	355
	two slices bologna	450
	one ounce American cheese	235
	a teaspoon of mustard	75
	one dill pickle	1100
	½ cup chocolate pudding	480
Afternoon snack:	3 sandwich cookies	240
Dinner:	8 crackers	250
	1 ounce cheddar cheese	190
	turkey TV dinner	1735
	tablespoon of dressing on salad	315
	slice of apple pie	400
Evening:	1 cup of hot chocolate	100
	Total milligrams of sodium	7985

There are 2132 milligrams of sodium in a teaspoon of salt, therefore the equivalent of salt in the meals above is 3.75 teaspoons, at least 95 percent of it added by the manufacturers.

What if you asked them to leave out the salt? "It wouldn't taste good," would be the answer. Exactly right . . .

REVOLUTIONARY LETTER #5

It takes courage to say no

No to canned corn & instant
mashed potatoes. No to rice krispies.
No to Special K. No to margarine
mono- & di-glycerides, NDSA
for coloring, causing cancer. No to
white bread, bleached w/nerve gas (wonder
bread). No to everything fried
in hardened oil w/silicates. No to
once-so-delicious salami, now red
w/sodium nitrate.
No to processed cheeses, No
no again to irradiated bacon, pink
phosphorescent ham, dead plastic
pasteurized milk. No to chocolate pudding
like grandma never made. No thanx
to coca-cola. No to freshness preservers,
dough conditioners, no
potassium sorbate, no
aluminum silicate, NO
BHA, BHT, NO
di-ethyl-propyl glycerate

No more ice cream? not w/embalming fluid.
Goodbye potato chips, peanut butter, jelly, jelly
white sugar! No more DES
all-American steaks or hamburgers either!
Goodbye, frozen fish! (dipped & coated w/
aureomycin) Fried eggs over easy w/
hormones, penicillin & speed.
Carnation Instant Breakfast Nestle's Quik
Fritos, goodbye! Your labels are very confusing

All I can say
is what my daughter age six once said to me:
"if I can't pronounce it
Maybe I shouldn't eat it." . . .

REVOLUTIONARY LETTERS ETC. 1966–1978
Diane Di Prima, City Lights Books

The New American Diet, you will find, automatically eliminates many food additives simply by emphasizing whole unprocessed foods. For more information on the additives you will be saying "no" to by switching to natural foods, see Appendix Two.

Summary

The following table summarizes the direction of the New American Diet and Cuisine:

More	*From*
Complex Carbohydrate	Whole grains, fresh fruits and vegetables
Vitamins and Minerals	Whole and fresh foods of all types
Protein	Whole grains, beans, nuts and seeds
Fiber	Whole grains, fresh fruits and vegetables

Less	*From*
Calories	White flour, white sugar, junk foods in general
Sugar	Soft drinks, candy, pastry, breakfast cereals, canned fruits and vegetables
Salt	Salty snacks, processed foods in general
Saturated Fat	Meat, lard, butter, margarine, snacks
Additives	Processed foods in general

PART ONE: The New American Diet

1   The New Way to Eat

DIETS, BROADLY SPEAKING

Diets come and go and return again under other names year after year. Most of us have tried one or another of these diets, fallen off them, tried again, or tried a new one, and so on, an altogether familiar pattern. We learn that what we eat certainly affects the way we feel and how much we weigh—no problem accepting those facts. The problem is that the diets all make promises, either plainly explicit or heavily implied, and too often they fail to deliver. The diet may deliver for someone you know, but for you and a couple of other people you know, it doesn't. For an initial period it probably looked promising, but after awhile, you just couldn't keep it up—hard to say why, really, it just felt like there was something in you that wasn't being satisfied.

Having fallen off the diet, many of us suffer from guilt . . . *That diet was supposed to be good for me and it actually was doing me some good. Or at least it did for a while. What's wrong with me? Don't I have enough will power? Am I self-destructive? Masochistic? . . .* However, the fault more often lies with the diet.

Usually the people promoting the diets genuinely want to help us. They have had successes with their diet, with others as well as themselves. The fault lies in the belief that what is good for a few will necessarily be good for all. Most diet promoters would readily admit that a strict way of eating satisfactory for *everybody* is a faulty concept—except for *this* diet, that is. This diet is different because . . . The fact is that the stricter, the more rigid, the diet is, the fewer people will be satisfied by it. They key word here is *satisfy*. The way we eat has to be more than just good for us in order to satisfy. And what will satisfy you may not satisfy me. (More on nutritional individuality in Chapter 8.) Most diets are narrow, inflexible, restricted, unexciting. The Parsnip and Brussel Sprout Weight Loss Regime and the Heavy Cream and Soybean Weight Gain Program have built-in revulsion for most people, no matter how much weight they lose or gain during the first two weeks.

There is no strict way of eating that is good for *everybody*. The New American Diet is strict in one way only: no junk food. No foodless, plastic, non-food. There may be hardly any change in the types of food you choose to eat, but it is certain you will choose much higher quality food after you become strict on this point.

The New American Diet is more a *system of food selection*, a diet only in the broadest sense. Within this system you will be able to discover your own diet, the diet that works for you. If your diet is strict it will be because you make it that way; it suits your needs, satisfies you. The flexibility within the system allows you any changes any time, as your needs change. There are numerous influences that might need to be reflected in dietary changes: changes of season, geographic location, schedule, physical activities, emotional stress, social requirements, change for the sake of change, change to combat or prevent illness, or to experiment—these are merely a sampling of the many kinds of events and processes that often need to be joined by food changes.

The system I am proposing is not hypothetical or theoretical. I have been living within it for over ten years. Many of my friends and acquaintances live comfortably within it. When I visit my friends at Sunburst I am right at home breaking bread with them in their dining rooms; they live within the same dietary system.

It might be useful for someone interested in this subject and with a flair for the empirical method of compiling facts to study Sunburst. The data regarding health would be quite different from national averages. They don't get sick much. At Sunburst, over a twelve-year period, with more than 200 people representing all age groups, the only case of cancer was cured without radiation, chemotherapy, or surgery. The incidence of obesity is minor; other degenerative diseases are unknown.

When I and most of the people I know fill out a form that asks for the name of our family doctor, the question is left blank. The need for regular visits to a doctor doesn't exist. When we encounter a health problem we can't handle ourselves, we tap into the grapevine for advice on good medical people to bail us out. But that is seldom necessary. And usually the medical people we see are utilizing the same dietary system we are. They are practitioners of holistic medicine and proponents of the New American Diet because it is an essential element of preventive medicine.

It has been only since I undertook the project of sharing what we've learned about low-cost natural food that I realized it is possible to call what we do a dietary system. We've never thought of what we are doing in that way; it's been an unorganized evolution grown out of shared experiences with diets having names like "macrobiotic," "vegan," "lacto-vegetarian," "fruitarian." The result in common of our various individual experiments was to break old dietary patterns, and to broaden our dietary horizons with new knowledge and new experiences.

The people of my generation all came out of the same supermarket culture, highly dependent on meat and processed foods based on refined carbohydrates, white flour, and white sugar. There was no other way to eat; Mother knew best. But by the time we were mothers and fathers ourselves, we questioned whether Mother really did know best. It began to appear that our diet had begun to wander off the best path starting somewhere back there with Mother's mother, that many technological advances had really been one step forward, two steps back.

Whatever the individual idiosyncrasies, the new pattern that has emerged for us is a reduced consumption of animal protein, replaced by a variety of vegetarian protein sources, and virtual abandonment of refined carbohydrates, replaced by complex carbohydrates. When the Senate Committee published their seven dietary goals, we saw that we had already accomplished them. Where we found ourselves was healthier and less expensive than our old ways.

Dr. Hegsted, the Harvard professor who wrote *DIETARY GOALS* for the Senate, said:

> . . . the diet we eat today was not planned or developed for any particular purpose. It is a happenstance related to our affluence, the productivity of our farmers and the activities of our food industry. The risks associated with eating this diet are demonstrably large. The question to be asked, therefore, is not why should we change our diet but why not? What are the risks associated with eating less meat, less fat, less saturated fat, less cholesterol, less sugar, less salt, and more fruits, vegetables, unsaturated fat and cereal products—especially whole grain cereals? There are none that can be identified and important benefits can be expected.

THE FOUR HISTORICAL PHASES OF THE GRAIN/MEAT CYCLE

First Phase

One hundred years is not much on the human evolutionary time scale. If you go back that far, or 150 years at most, into the ancestry of any American, whether those ancestors be European, Asian, or African, you find people whose diet was centered around grains and tubers. European staples were wheat, rye, barley, oats and, since the discovery of the Americas, potatoes. African staples were wheat, millet, and yams. Asian staples were rice, millet, and wheat. In Central and South America, the staples of the great Indian civilizations were corn and potatoes. On a global scale, then, we see complex carbohydrates as the center of people's diets—grains the major staple, tubers the minor. This state of affairs began in the dawn of prehistory when mankind first turned to agriculture and continued wherever we switched from hunting and foraging to farming.

Second Phase

Most immigrants to this country never dreamed of eating meat every day in the old country, much less at every meal. But early settlers arrived on the shores of an untamed continent teeming with wild game and, with lessons from the Native Americans, we quickly became a nation of hunters. As long as we had a western frontier the supply of game guaranteed meat at every meal—a dietary revolution for peoples who had previously killed precious livestock to celebrate special events, perhaps not eating meat from one month to the next. The second phase established one of the unique features of the American way of life: meat as a staple food. As the New World staple, meat claimed a special status: it was the food of promise, one of the chief differences between the poverty of the old country and the richness of America. Meat signified the promise of affluence to come, the reward for exploiting the inexhaustible resources of the New World.

Third Phase

Land was cheap. You paid nothing for it and invested your labor, or, if you paid for it, you paid very little. Cheap land meant cheap food. Food was so cheap that what had principally been human food—grains—could principally become animal food. It didn't matter that it took anywhere from four to twenty pounds of grain to produce one pound of meat. The cheapness of the land plus the fertility of the soil made grain production such a low-cost proposition that grains could economically be fed to animals and Americans could go on eating meat. In this phase, meat was elevated to a higher level than a mere staple: meat was synonymous with the realization of affluence. The promise of the second phase was realized in the third phase and meat graduated to the level of *status symbol*.

Acquiring a taste for meat is easy for most people. Since it takes a long time to digest, it gives a long-lasting satisfaction to hunger and almost everybody can afford it—often. The third phase was entrenched by the turn of the century and reached its peak during the unparalleled post-World War II economic boom.

Fourth Phase

Food isn't cheap any more. The margin between net income and cost of living is shrinking; we are not as affluent as we were. The last economic surge went so high and lasted so long that we believed it would last forever. We forgot that everything in life is cyclical. In the ups and downs of economic cycles, we are sliding from a peak that may never be reached again. What we took to be ordinary affluence was, relatively speaking, excess affluence. In other words, we are returning from the days of excess affluence to the days of ordinary affluence. Some fear that we will keep sliding from ordinary affluence down into substandard affluence; others see that as inevitable, a matter of equilibrium, compensation necessary to create balance.

Either ordinary affluence or substandard affluence requires a review of the role of meat in the American diet. Let me make it clear at this point that I am not proposing we become a nation of vegetarians. What I am proposing is that we demote meat from its status as *the* American staple for two simple reasons: it will improve our health and lower the cost of our food. I am suggesting, furthermore, that to demote meat is so eminently sensible that it will become a widespread practice and we will fully enter phase four of the grain/meat cycle, having already entered the early stages of it. As Colin Tudge puts it in *Future Food*:

> . . . it is in the spirit of twenty-first century cooking to use meat as sparingly and flavorsomely as possible . . . In practical terms, this means demoting meat from its present *prima donna* role in Western cuisine to the role of garnish, as in the cooking of modern China and as in the peasant cooking of all the world through most of history. There is no hardship implied, for Chinese and traditional European cooking scale the gastronomic heights.

In phase four, more people will become vegetarians because it will suit their metabolisms, their tastes, their lifestyles, their budgets. Most of the rest of us will eat meat less often. The movement is away from being mainly carnivorous to truly omnivorous. This change of emphasis will accompany a broadening of our dietary base that will make eating more fun, as well as healthier and less expensive. The phase four change of emphasis regarding meat is a chief feature of the New American Diet.

If being an omnivarian were all there is to the New American Diet, it would suffice to say, "Well, back to phase one." But what is new, what creates a new phase, is *choice*. Not only can we choose to be an omnivarian or a vegetarian but we can choose from types, varieties, and forms of food inconceivable to our ancestors.

A VEGETARIAN OR A WHAT?

Perhaps you noticed a new word above: omnivarian. You won't find it in your dictionary because it's a word adaptation I'm introducing here. Heretofore, we have been amused but also a bit nonplussed to hear ourselves saying something like, "Well, I'm sort of a vegetarian," or "I'm kind of a semi-vegetarian," or "I don't eat meat except fish and poultry." If we wanted to communicate on the subject, we found ourselves hampered by self-contradictory, awkward, ineffectual terminology. The question of whether or not you are a vegetarian should simply yield a yes or no answer. If you're not, there should be a word for what you are.

Well, what's wrong with omnivore? I've heard the word come up in conversations—tentative, somehow unsatisfactory. It invariably gets rejected, I think because it fails to communicate any of the sense of quality so important in the New American Diet. The word omnivore carries the connotation of indiscriminate eating—no judgment, whatever turns up when hunger makes the stomach gurgle. A baby learning what is edible by putting everything it can pick up into its mouth is an omnivore. A vegetarian, on the other hand, is an adult using discrimination, chewing some foods and eschewing others. The word vegetarian carries connotations of judgment, decisions, the process of thinking; it also has the utilitarian beauty of being both a noun and an adjective.

I coined the word omnivarian for three reasons:

1. to imply the decision-making process;
2. to imply the qualitative considerations;
3. to have a noun/adjective word to juxtapose against the word vegetarian.

With the hope that this new word fulfills a need and is graceful enough to earn a place in your vocabulary, here is its definition: *omnivarian* (om'ni·var'i·an) *n*. 1. a person who eats natural foods with an emphasis on plant foods, with complex carbohydrates as the principal foods, supplemented by all other types of food, including or excluding meat and animal products according to individual discretion or circumstances.—*adj.* 2. of or pertaining to omnivarianism or omnivarians. 3. consisting of a complex carbohydrate as principal ingredient, meat as one secondary ingredient: *an omnivarian casserole.*

In talking with people about dietary change, I've often encountered two opposite extremes: "I'd like some help in becoming a vegetarian," and, "You're not going to tell me I should become a vegetarian, are you?" Our new word makes it clear that there are two equally legitimate approaches to the New American Diet. When the roots of this diet were being set in the sixties, almost everybody got into it via the vegetarian route. But the message filtered back from the pathfinders that vegetarianism isn't for everybody and these days omnivarians outnumber vegetarians by far, perhaps by 3 to 1, because within the omnivarian approach there is a broad range of choices.

The absence of a principal, or foundational, food in the old American cuisine was pointed out by George Ohsawa, the Japanese scientist-philosopher who brought the macrobiotic diet to the West in the 1950s. Colin Tudge, in *Future Food* (Harmony Books), refers to principal and secondary foods as "food of the first kind" and "food of the second kind." "Food of the third kind" includes everything we use to lend character to our cooking, and "self-indulgent food . . . eaten precisely because it is unnecessary; for when nutrition has been taken care of, gastronomy comes into its own."

Conventional American Diet

First: the "main dish," a protein food, usually some form of flesh, i.e., beef, lamb, pork, poultry, fish.

Second: the "filler," a staple in the form of a simple or refined carbohydrate, i.e., white rice, white pasta, potatoes cooked without skins.

Third: the vegetable, often frozen or canned.

Omnivarian Diet

First: a "principal food" as a staple in the form of complex carbohydrates, i.e., brown rice, millet, bulgur, whole grain bread, whole potatoes.

Second: secondary foods to complement the principal foods. The secondary foods are protein foods i.e., all forms of flesh, dairy products, beans, nuts, seeds, and, equally important, vegetables both raw and cooked.

2   Considering Protein

WHERE DO I GET MY PROTEIN?

The above question is a common first reaction to the proposition of eliminating or greatly reducing the role of meat in the diet. A common American assumption is that every meal will be centered around some kind of flesh; without it we won't get our protein. That assumption is either the product of a "four basic food groups" instruction that was supposed to suffice as our nutritional education or simply what we absorbed as just another of those cultural norms of the world we live in. Bacon for breakfast, beef for lunch, chicken for dinner—really, if we don't eat that way, where do we get our protein? We grow up thinking that if we haven't eaten meat, we haven't eaten a "good" meal, no matter how good it tasted.

In explaining the New American Diet, it would not be necessary to concern myself much with questions about protein if it weren't for the fact that we as a nation have allowed ourselves to become preoccupied by protein considerations. We equate protein intake with healthy eating, and this against respectable scientific advice:

> . . . the average American eats daily almost twice as much protein as the Food and Nutrition Board of the National Academy of Sciences recommends for meeting the needs of most healthy people. There is no known nutritional need for our current high level of protein intake. (DIETARY GOALS)

I am a typical enough omnivarian practitioner of the New American Diet to serve as an example of how the protein question is answered. My protein requirements are met in only a minor way by fish, chicken, and red meat, because I seldom eat them. They are met in a major way by a broad variety of plant proteins including nuts, seeds, beans, and *whole grains*, and dairy protein foods such as yogurt and cheese. I emphasized whole grains because they are not usually considered a protein source. But as the following chart illustrates, whole grains are really significant enough in protein to be counted. In fact, grains account for almost half of the protein consumed worldwide. I could easily switch off the animal protein sources—I did for eight years—without suffering any protein shortage.

PROTEIN VALUE AND PERCENTAGE COMPARISONS
(Adapted from the *Diet for a Small Planet* chart "Protein Cost Comparisons", Appendix C)

Rank	Item/Price (1980)	Cost*	Protein Content	Protein Category
1	Soybeans @ .59/lb	.27	34.1%	Vegetable—legume
2	Split peas @ .35lb	.35	24.1%	Vegetable—legume
3	Whole wheat flour @ .35/lb	.39	13.3%	Vegetable—grain
	Oatmeal @ .39/lb	.39	14.2%	Vegetable—grain
4	Eggs @ .79/dozen	.41	12.4%	Animal—eggs
5	Nonfat dry milk @ 1.95/lb.	.50	35.9%	Animal—dairy
6	Cottage cheese @ 1.05/lb	.64	17%	Animal—dairy
7	Cornmeal @ .33/lb	.65	9.2%	Vegetable—grain
8	Sunflower seeds @ 1.09/lb	.75	24%	Vegetable—seed
9	Milk, whole @ .47/qt.	.80	3.5%	Animal—dairy
10	Brown rice @ .45/lb	.81	8%	Vegetable—grain
11	Peanuts, raw @ .95/lb	.82	26%	Vegetable—legume
12	Kidney beans @ .75/lb	.83	22.5%	Vegetable—legume
13	Peanut butter @ .99/lb	.87	25%	Vegetable—legume
14	Navy beans @ .89/lb	1.01	27.8%	Vegetable—legume
15	Cod @ 2.39/lb	1.05	17.6%	Animal—fish
16	Turbot @ 1.99/lb	1.06	19.5%	Animal—fish
	Lentils @ .79/lb	1.06	24.7%	Vegetable—legume
17	Cheddar cheese @ 1.99/lb	1.09	25%	Animal—dairy
18	Perch @ 1.79/lb	1.12	19.3%	Animal—fish
19	Hamburger @ 1.49/lb	1.21	24.2%	Animal—meat
20	Chicken @ 1.49/lb	1.34	32.5%	Vegetable—seed
21	Sesame seeds @ 1.39/lb	1.35	18.6%	Vegetable—seed
22	Swordfish @ 5.00/lb	2.15	19.2%	Animal—fish
23	Pork, loin chop w/bone @ 2.19/lb	2.31	24.5%	Animal—meat
24	Lamb, rib chop w/bone @ 2.59/lb	3.15	20.1%	Animal—meat
25	Salmon @ 4.98/lb	3.42	22.5%	Animal—fish
26	Cashews, raw @ 3.85/lb	3.82	17.2%	Vegetable—nut
27	Steak, Porterhouse, choice w/bone @ 3.79/lb	4.01	19.7%	Animal—meat

* Cost of 1.52 ounces of *usable* protein, the daily allowance for an "average" American male weighing 154 pounds. "Usable" protein is defined as the percentage that is actually available to the body, considering the amino acid patterns and digestibility (technically known as NPU-*net protein utilization*). The variance between price and cost is due to the fact that different sources of protein consist of different percentages and quality of protein.

Note: I chose to compare thirty familiar protein sources from the original table. In the ten years following publication, prices on those thirty items rose an average of 254 percent; vegetable protein rose an average 203 percent, animal protein an average 305 percent. The breakdown is as follows:

Protein Type	Price Rise from 1970 to 1980
Grains	154%
Nuts and Seeds	183%
Meat and Poultry	214%
Dairy and Eggs	264%
Legumes	272%
Seafood	438%

The above chart illustrates two important facts: (1) that other sources of protein such as dairy and legumes are comparable to meat on both cost and protein percentage and (2) that grains are lower in percentage of protein while being far less expensive than meat.

Logic would dictate that we would complement the lower percentage protein grains with higher percentage foods such as dairy and legumes to make the overall protein percentage more comparable to meat. The New American Diet does this, not so much out of concern about protein but more as a consequence of overall dietary and culinary balance.

COMPLEMENTARITY RECONSIDERED

The law of complementarity was brilliantly introduced by Frances Moore Lappé in her landmark book, *Diet for a Small Planet*. What Lappé explained so well is that many individual plant proteins are incomplete and must be complemented by the presence of other protein sources, plant or animal to be completely utilized.

There are twenty-two amino acids which in combination form our body protein. Completeness refers to the presence of eight "essential" amino acids—essential because they cannot be synthesized within our bodies, therefore must be obtained from our food. Most animal protein—flesh structured similarly to our own flesh—has all the essential amino acids; it is complete protein. Many plant proteins are *incomplete* because they are limited in one or two of the eight essential amino acids. So if the amino acid pattern of a food matches our own in seven but the eighth essential amino acid only matches human protein at a rate of 50 percent, the limiting factor on the other seven essential amino acids is 50 percent. It's like having a hundred bricks for building a wall, but only enough mortar to cement fifty bricks together. The other fifty bricks are useless until you are able to double your supply of mortar.

Limiting factors in the law of complementarity are absolutely rigid biochemically speaking, but in practice complementarity becomes flexible because we never eat just one kind of food at a meal. And every incomplete protein has a different pattern of amino acids; where one food is short, another will be fuller or even full. So if our 50 percent food is complemented by other foods containing the short amino acid, its efficiency can be raised to 100 percent. Incomplete non-meat protein becomes complete through complementarity, utilized for our protein requirements just as effectively as meat.

During the '70s, after Lappé explained complementarity, many people focused their attention on *Small Planet* meal planning charts and recipes, particularly people trying to be vegetarians without protein deficiencies. But after working with the law for a while, people realized that the urge to eat a variety of foods is so universally natural to us that we don't need to think about complementarity unless we want to. During the '80s, therefore, complementarity has become an element in our storehouse of knowledge, rather than our guiding light.

The prevailing attitude towards complementarity has also been reoriented by advances in research techniques. Until quite recently it was thought that *all* plant protein was incomplete, but more recent research has proved otherwise:

> According to outdated and erroneous thinking, only animal foods, such as meat, fowl, fish, milk, and eggs, contain complete high quality proteins, but proteins in vegetable foods are inferior or incomplete. The newest nutritional research has now completely disproved the validity of such thinking. Studies made at the most respected nutrition research center in the world, the Max Planck Institute in Germany, show that the earlier beliefs about the biological superiority of animal proteins were unsubstantiated, and that many vegetable protein foods are "just as good or better than animal proteins." Vegetable foods which contain all eight essential amino acids and, therefore, are complete protein foods, are soybeans, peanuts, almonds, buckwheat, sunflower seeds, pumpkin seeds, potatoes, avocadoes, and all green leafy vegetables. [Paavo Airola, N.D., Ph.D., a leading writer and lecturer on health and nutrition, writing in *Hypoglycemia: A Better Approach*, pub. Health Plus Publishers.]

HIGH PROTEIN/LOW PROTEIN: WHICH IS BEST?

DIETARY GOALS told us that most Americans get twice as much protein as they need. To explain why, let's look at some average figures, not forgetting that there's no such thing as an average person and that these figures only give us a rough idea.

Let's say we have a couple named John and Mary. John weighs 180 pounds and Mary weighs 130. According to the Food and Nutrition Board of the National Academy of Sciences, John and Mary both need 0.36 grams or 0.126 ounces of protein for each pound of body weight. So John should get 64.8 grams or 2.27 ounces of protein per day; Mary should get 46.8 grams or 1.64 ounces.

Now let's say that they ate all their meals together yesterday and that Mary only ate 72 percent as much as John since she only weighs 72 percent as much. John's main sources of protein were a cup of oatmeal at breakfast (4.8 grams or .168 ounces or protein), a turkey sandwich with 3 ounces of meat at lunch (32 grams of 1.12 ounces of protein) and a 3 ounce portion of flounder (25.5 grams or .89 ounces of protein) with a cup of brown rice (4.9 grams or .172 ounces of protein) for dinner.

So John got 67.2 grams or 2.35 ounces of protein, 4 percent more than he needed, not even counting the other food he ate. Eating 72 percent as much, Mary got 48.4 grams or 1.69 ounces of protein, also close to 4 percent more than she needed.

Now consider that they also had vegetables, some yogurt for dessert, a handful of nuts for a snack: for John that's about 24 grams or .84 ounces of protein, for Mary 17.3 grams or .61 ounces. Their totals for the day: John, 91.2 grams or 3.19 ounces; for Mary, 65.7 grams or 2.3 ounces. So, even though they weren't eating particularly high on the protein hog by American standards, they both got more than 40 percent more protein than the averages call for.

But wait, not so fast . . . A doctor friend of mine with a practice given over entirely to nutritional counseling finds that virtually all of his patients are protein deficient. John and Mary, with all their "extra" protein, are probably protein deficient just like almost everybody else. This seemingly murky riddle is explained by an extremely important aspect of the protein picture that is frequently overlooked:

> Raw proteins have a higher biological value than cooked proteins. Cooking makes all proteins less assimilable. You need only about one-half the amount of proteins if you eat raw vegetable proteins instead of animal proteins, which are, as a rule, cooked. [Paavo Airola in *Hypoglycemia: A Better Approach.*]

Six of the eight essential amino acids are at least partially destroyed by cooking. Roughly half of the amino acids in John's and Mary's protein foods never reached the cells of their bodies. While they seem to be eating too much protein, they are intuitively responding to a need for more amino acids. High protein or low protein, then, is not the issue. The real issue is the *quality* of the protein. (See also page 28 on protein quality.)

Cooking protein *denatures* it—reduces its quality. John and Mary could simultaneously correct their overconsumption and their deficiency by eating less cooked protein and more raw protein. That translates into more raw greens and sprouted beans, raw nuts and seeds, raw milk and raw milk cheese.

Symptoms of protein deficiency include:

—undue weight loss;
—poor condition of skin, nails, and hair;
—inordinately slow healing of cuts and bruises.

Protein deficiency is a general condition, so the more of those symptoms that exist simultaneously, the more likely that there is protein deficiency.

The first response to a suspected protein deficiency should not be to assume you need more meat but to focus on protein quality. Increasing meat consumption is the answer if and when an increase of raw plant proteins fails to solve the problem. The reason for this order of priority is that overconsumption of meat, which is very common, has significant health disadvantages. They include:

Calcium deficiency. Meat contains up to twenty times more phosphorus than calcium, but they are needed in about equal amounts in the diet. Since the body needs the calcium to balance the high phosphorus content of the meat, high meat consumption can be accompanied by calcium deficiency. If the diet is deficient in calcium-rich foods, which is common, the body may even remove stored calcium in an effort to offset the high phosphorus ratio; this can lead to conditions related to calcium deficiency, such as osteoporosis, osteoarthritis, tooth decay, and periodontal disease.

Excess uric acid. Uric acid is a metabolic by-product found in particularly high concentrations in red meat and in our own bodies. We must rid ourselves of both the uric acid we produce and that which we consume; what we are unable to excrete can crystalize into stones and the painful deposits of gout.

Biochemical imbalance. Excess animal protein can lead to intestinal sluggishness and overacidity. It can also lead to intestinal putrefaction and the formation of ammonia. Ammonia is a proven carcinogen and a major cause of cancer of the colon. Too much meat is invariably associated with fat, which is frequently associated with the heart/circulatory problems/obesity syndrome.

Kidney stress. Nitrogen is the vital element supplied by protein, not present in either carbohydrate or fat. But it is relatively easy to get more nitrogen than we need. Excess nitrogen is excreted by the kidneys; therefore, excess meat consumption can put undue stress on the kidneys.

Another perspective on excess meat consumption is that it is a waste of money. The meat that cannot be utilized for growth or the replacement of cells because the amino acids have been denatured by cooking can still be utilized for energy or stored as fat. But protein utilized for energy or fat production is akin to breaking up your furniture and burning it in your fireplace or throwing it on your firewood pile: it will burn well enough but it's an expensive way to use furniture.

Vegetarian or omnivarian diets which don't consciously load up on protein foods, but just let a variety of cooked and raw proteins fall where they may, have the consequence of dropping protein consumption levels to a lower, healthier, less expensive level. They do this by either eliminating or lowering the ratio between animal and vegetable protein. This in turn brings us closer to the goal of lower fat consumption.

Another health aspect of reducing flesh consumption is that it results in lowering our involuntary ingestion of pesticide residues. Far more pesticide residues are found in meat and fish (36 percent) as compared to grains and legumes (19 percent) (1964–1968 figures, Appendix E, *Diet for a Small Planet.*)

CONSERVATION

American hogs, cattle, chickens, and turkeys eat more grains and soybeans than American people do. You can see the gross inefficiencies of this situation by a quick glance at the protein conversion ratios of these creatures. The protein conversion ratio means the amount of plant protein in pounds that is required to produce one pound of protein as a constituent of flesh.

	Amount of Feed*	Amount of Plant Protein	Animal Protein Produced**
Beef	107.0 lbs	21.4 lbs	1 lb
Pork	41.5 lbs	8.3 lbs	1 lb
Poultry	27.5 lbs	5.5 lbs	1 lb

*Feed taken as a corn/soybean mix at 20 percent protein.
**Animal protein taken as 20 percent of the flesh.

Your protein needs could be covered for three months by the corn and soybeans it takes to produce a pound of beef protein (five pounds of beef). Ironically, however, it isn't so much the protein we're after in feeding grains and beans to cattle—it's the fat! We have acquired a taste for beef that is highly marbled with fat; in fact, the more fat in it, the higher we grade it. A carcass trimmed to retail level is "Standard" when 18 percent fat, "Good" when 22 percent fat and "Choice" when 25 percent fat.

It's obviously an inefficient and unhealthy use of our resources to have so many cattle standing around in feedlots getting so fat. What really is efficient is to have the cattle out on the range eating grass that we can't eat instead of grains and beans we *can* eat. Cattle are the obvious means for rendering otherwise unproductive range land into land capable of producing food. Grass-fed beef is efficient and it is also healthier—leaner, lower in fat and cholesterol. It's tougher and gamier but it would be worthwhile to learn to cook it and develop a taste for it. A person who didn't become a vegetarian or omnivarian, and whose only major change was to grass fed beef, could lower cholesterol consumption by approximately 12 percent.

Other ways of measuring the efficiency of livestock production are in terms of acreage and water. According to *Diet for a Small Planet*, grains can produce *five times* more protein per acre than livestock, beans *ten times* more and leafy vegetables *fifteen times* more. An estimated *eight times* more water is required to support a beef and grain diet compared to one without beef.

Quite clearly, a shift toward vegetarian and omnivarian diets can lead to much wiser utilization of our agricultural resources. Lappé sums up:

> Thus, in a single year through [the present American] consumption pattern, 18 million tons of protein becomes inaccessible to man. This amount is equivalent to 90% *of the yearly world protein deficit*—enough protein to provide 12 grams a day for every person in the world!

By redeploying our staples, we have the agricultural potential to be the breadbasket of the world to a far greater degree than we are now—*if*, that is, we also get off our farm dependence on petroleum and switch to an agricultural system that conserves our rapidly vanishing topsoil. (Food is the ultimate resource; our topsoil is the *penultimate* resource—see Epilogue.)

Our agricultural resources represent far more economic power than the limited foreign oil reserves. If it is really true that we are losing economic battles to OPEC, we can still win the war because we are food exporters, while they are food importers. The favorable economic influence of the New American Diet on your personal food budget translates into a favorable influence on the national economic future because it fosters more efficient resource utilization. If that fails to inspire you, just remember that reducing your consumption of meat leads to a lowering of food costs, leaving you more money for other purposes. *Inflation Fighters* (Judith Klinger; Fawcett Columbine Books) puts it this way:

> In the growing movement away from meat protein dependence and processed foods, whole grains and whole-grain flours, seeds, legumes, and nuts are being rediscovered. For much of the world they have always been staple foods on which diets are based. For inflation fighters, these foods stretch the budget farther than any other food category.

3 *The Water Story*

TROUBLE AT THE TAP

We have all heard about the dangers of drinking municipal tap water in third and fourth world countries—water that can spread a host of diseases from dysentery to typhoid. By comparison, few of us realize our own waters are dangerous, though for different reasons. Since most of our municipal waters are chlorinated, and therefore don't spread infectious diseases, we think of them as being safe. But infectious diseases, as we have already noted more than once, are not the primary cause of illness and death in the United States—degenerative diseases are. And our municipal water supplies are contributing to physical degeneration; the two major contributors are chlorine and industrial pollutants.

The Chlorine Problem

Most of us have always assumed that chlorine is a solution, not a problem. After all, doesn't it kill germs? Yes, it does. But one problem occurs when municipal water comes from surface water, instead of from underground. (Roughly half of municipal waters are from lakes and rivers.)

Surface water comes into contact with organic matter as humus in soil, silt, and mud, dead leaves, and various forms of effluent. The interaction of organic matter and water produces humic acids. The interaction of humic acids and chlorine produces compounds called trihalomethanes (THMs) a prominent one being chloroform. Chloroform and other THMs such as carbon tetrachloride have been shown to be carcinogens. A study conducted by the Columbia University School of Public Health, which compared women who drank municipal water in seven upstate New York counties with those who drank from home wells, found the death rate from gastrointestinal and urinary tract cancers to be 44 percent higher among the chlorinated water drinkers. And you cannot assume that the THM problem only exists in the water of the town down the road. A 1978 EPA report stated that every chlorinated water supply tested contained THMs. Commenting on this situation, Douglas Costle, then head of the EPA, said, "The lifetime exposure of our population to these chemicals poses a serious threat to public health. We are especially concerned about the increase in cancer risk."

Drinkers of water from underground are not protected from the chlorine problem because it has another aspect: the chlorine itself. Significant research has linked chlorine to high blood pressure, anemia, and diabetes (see *Water Fit to Drink*, Carol Keough, Rodale Press). It is also indicted as a contributor to heart disease by Richard Passwater, Ph.D. (*Supernutrition*, Pocket Books) and Richard Kunin, M.D. (*Mega-Nutrition*, New American Library). Says Kunin, "Even in the minute quantities sufficient to kill germs, chlorine can undermine the body's defenses against atherosclerosis. Chlorine creates electrically charged molecules called free radicals, which can combine with alpha tocopherol (vitamin E) and eliminate it from your system. In addition, free radicals can directly damage the [lining] of blood vessels and so create the environment for the formation of plaque."

Industrial Pollution

In *The Coming Water Famine*, Congressman Jim Wright said,

Pollution from ordinary sewage and related organic substances is perhaps the worst with which we have to contend. There are fifty-nine million Americans living in approximately two thousand cities who use sewer systems which are either partly or totally inadequate in the treatment of human wastes before those wastes are dumped into rivers and streams. Among these are some of our very largest cities. We have never attacked this, one of the most primitive problems of civilization, with sufficient boldness and forethought.

A 1978 report by the General Accounting Office of the United States reported that "the nation's water supplies are threatened by the careless use of hundreds of chemical compounds and the heedless disposal of toxic wastes." There have been more than 600 such contaminants discovered in municipal drinking water, more than half of them proven toxic, fifty-five of them pesticides. Those figures merely scratch the surface of the problem. There are 60,000 industrial chemicals now in use; by 1990 the number will probably be 70,000. Do such numbers sound impossible to monitor? The EPA hears them that way, saying in their November, 1979, report: "Because the chemicals thus far identified in drinking water account for only a small fraction of the total organic content, the possibility, and indeed the probability, exists that additional substances of equal or greater toxicological significance may be present but remain undetected by present monitoring capabilities . . ."

What we don't know might hurt us. Love Canal will long stand as a gruesome reminder: 237 homes of the nearly 800 built on the filled-in canal near Niagara Falls had to be bought by the state and condemned. Why? Because their drinking water was contaminated by the landfill, laced with eleven known or suspected carcinogens and a witch's brew of more than seventy other industrial pollutants, the dangers of which are still unknown.

An Industrial Solution

We will begin to get safe drinking water when we begin applying pressure at two points. First, the industrial polluters must be shut off at the source. "But the price of our products will go up if we have to remove all the pollutants," the industrialists warn us. So what? If it's a good and necessary product, we'll pay more for it. A basic responsibility of business is to help keep our environment clean. If there is a risk that consumers will not be willing to pay the price, the ethical route for the business person is to decide whether the possible reward is worth the risk. When we are told that a manufacturer can't make cheap products without dumping chemical wastes in the river, we need to tell the company not to make cheap products.

Municipal Solutions

The second place on which to apply pressure is our municipal water company. Filter beds of granular activated carbon (GAC), are a method that has been proven effective by thirty-five years of use in Europe. Activated carbon filtration removes a broad spectrum of chemicals, including THMs. "That would be too expensive," water treatment professionals protest. Is a 40 percent higher rate of bladder cancer cheap? We have vastly underrated the care required to deliver safe drinking water; chloroform in your bloodstream is only appropriate when you're ready to be embalmed. Other alternatives to chlorine are aeration, treatment with ultraviolet radiation, and treatment with ozone. Ozone treatment is another purification procedure used successfully in Europe but criticized here as too expensive.

Seventy percent of our bodies are water, 92 percent of our blood plasma; does anyone doubt that our drinking water should be pure? Yet qualified observers have concluded that three-fourths of American municipal water is unfit for human consumption. Apart from THMs and industrial chemicals, other significant water contaminants are heavy metals such as lead and cadmium, PCBs, nitrates, asbestos, and radioactivity. My personal opinion is that three-fourths as an estimate for unfit water is too conservative—my hunch is that virtually *all* municipal water is unfit to drink.

Home Solutions

One barrier to discovering that our water is unsafe is that we are accustomed to it. But most of us have had the experience of going to a different locale, drinking the water and noticing that it tastes "funny." We usually assume that the funny taste is due to different minerals. It may be, but it is also just as likely to be different contaminants than the ones you've become accustomed to. Somebody drinking *your* tap water for the first time might accuse it of tasting or smelling weird: that could be caused by any or all of those things mentioned above.

Even if you're used to it and therefore can't depend on your nose or tastebuds, you can look at it. Is there any trace of color? Pure water is colorless. Is it all cloudy, foamy, or murky? Pure water is clear. Your state public-health agency will probably test your water if you are in doubt.

"Well then," people ask, "what do I do while we're waiting for our water to be cleaned up?" Wash with it, brush with it, flush with it, but don't drink it or cook with it. For fifteen years I have been drinking and cooking with water filtered by granular activated carbon (GAC) or, more often, bought bottled spring water. A few places I've lived have been near springs from which I could fetch my water every week.

The inexpensive filters that attach to the end of your faucet are comparatively ineffective; the bigger units are comparatively effective but expensive. I've heard the argument that you can pay for a good filtration unit with the money you would spend on five-gallon bottles of spring water in one year. That depends on whether you buy a unit for $300 or $500 and on how much water you use; but in any case, the filtration unit will not give you the top quality water of a good spring. Water is too important to focus on saving money; better to go for the best possible quality and focus on the many ways to save money that can benefit your health. Those interested in learning about filtration devices should write the Environmental Protection Agency, Washington, D.C. 20460. See also *Consumer Reports*, February, 1983, for a rating of seventeen brands of activated carbon water filters.

Good quality bottled spring water is not available everywhere. (See Appendix One for sources.) You may live where the only bottled water is "reconditioned" municipal water. Then you have to know what you are being guaranteed by the bottler. It should be certified by laboratory analysis, copies of which are available to the consumer, to be free of THMs, pesticide residues, PCBs, nitrates, heavy metals, asbestos, and chlorine. Terminology such as "bottled at the springs" may not mean what you assume it means: it can mean that municipal water is being bottled at the site of a natural spring. "Natural spring water" should mean the water comes directly from a spring, perhaps filtered, but with nothing added. Take nothing for granted, however; insist on the same guarantees for spring water as for reconditioned municipal water.

You might feel you just cannot handle the additional expense of bottled water. In that case, the least expensive, effective alternative is the coffee filter method, as described by Carol Keough in *Water Fit to Drink* (Rodale Press). You need four things: some granulated activated carbon, a large funnel, a large collecting container with a narrow neck to hold the funnel, and coffee filter paper. (At the time of writing, a six-month supply of GAC costs around four dollars. Write Walnut Acres, Penns Creek, PA 17862 for their mail order catalog.) The steps:

1. Wash the GAC by putting it in a jar full of water and allowing it to settle to the bottom. Then pour off the water and repeat as often as necessary to get clear water.
2. Fill paper-lined funnel about one-fourth with washed GAC and cover it with another piece of filter paper.
3. Pour water into the funnel in a steady trickle—*slowly*, because you want all the water to come into contact with the carbon.
4. Boil the water for twenty minutes at a simmer level to kill any bacteria that may have passed through.

The carbon should be replaced every three weeks. It should also be replaced after processing 200 gallons, but if you require anything close to that amount of water, you should consider building a filtration unit that doesn't have to be hand-operated. The EPA has designed one, called the Self-Leveling Activated Carbon Column, that made water from the Ohio River at Cincinnati drinkable. It can fit under most kitchen sinks and be built with fifty dollars worth of materials; plans can be had from Walnut Acres, the GAC supplier, or from the EPA.

Your homemade GAC filter will remove THMs, pesticides, industrial chemicals, PCBs, and PBBs. I don't recommend any of the expensive filtration units because of what they can't remove: fluoride, nitrates, and asbestos. For a similiar investment, a more complete cleaning can be done by reverse osmosis, a method capable of turning salt water into fresh water. Reverse osmosis (RO) appears to be the water-purifying method of the future. Carol Keough, in *Water Fit to Drink*, describes it like this:

> Reverse osmosis is a simple process, both in concept and practice. All you need is the reverse osmosis membrane and the normal water pressure present in the service line. No additional energy is required to operate the unit. . . . RO is similar to filtration, but will remove not only the matter in water, but unlike a filter, also the *dissolved* matter. . . . RO is also an excellent way to remove asbestos from water. . . . In terms of ordinary tap water, RO will remove chlorides, fluoride, calcium, magnesium, manganese, nitrates, silica, silicates, sodium, sulphates, and copper. Detergents, organic matter, tannins (which can hide iron compounds), chlorinated compounds, and many toxic chemicals are also removed. . . . RO removes turbidity, particulate and colloidal matter, ionized and nonionized dissolved solids, bacteria, viruses, and pyrogens (fever-causing substances). . . . It will remove aromatic hydrocarbons, most pesticides, and other complicated chemicals . . .

Keough reports that the only weakness of RO is that "it will not remove simple compounds like chloroform and phenol." But a household RO unit called the Aqua-Cleer corrects that weakness by adding a carbon filter. The Aqua-Cleer seems to offer the most thorough kind of home water-treatment system. It costs about $500 or rents for about $14 a month at the time of writing, and is made by Culligan Water Conditioning Company of Northbrook, Illinois.

People with their own wells would be wise to submit a sample of their water for laboratory analysis. There are farmers who can't drink their own well water because huge reservoirs of underground water have been poisoned by nitrate fertilizers gradually percolating down through the soil substrata over the years. As many as 80 percent of home wells may be contaminated by industrial waste. The source of contamination is usually many miles from the individual well; the well becomes contaminated because it draws from a vast underground aquifer system. The little hole in the yard appears to be local and private but in reality is another example of broad ecological connectedness.

WATER QUESTIONS

Is soft water better than hard water?

Softness/hardness in water refers to mineral content, the hardest water having the most minerals. We are naturally equipped to utilize minerals dissolved in water and, since we are even more apt to be mineral deficient than vitamin deficient (most of our food is grown on mineral-depleted farmland), drinking water can be a good source of vital nutrients. Fear of minerals in water is unreasonable: throughout all of human history almost all of man's drinking water has been mineralized by nature.

When the hardness of water is due to calcium and magnesium, its drinkers suffer a far lower death rate from heart disease (*Supernutrition for Healthy Hearts*, Richard Passwater, Dial Press). Calcium is used by the heart muscle for contraction; magnesium is used to produce the relaxation of the heart muscle between beats.

Soft water, however, is generally proportionately high in sodium, which can disrupt the balance between sodium and potassium, interfering with the electrical impulse responsible for a regular heartbeat. It is prudent for soft-water drinkers to supplement their diets with calcium (aiding heart relaxation) and magnesium (aiding heart contraction). Carbon and other types of home filtration units remove minerals. If you don't know whether your water is soft or hard, make ice cubes from it. Hard water makes clear cubes with a white spot in the middle where the minerals concentrate; soft water makes cloudy ice cubes.

Some people are afraid that minerals in water will lead to kidney stones. Actually, it seems that metabolic imbalance is responsible; in one experiment, approximately 80 percent of sufferers from chronic kidney stone formation found protection by taking vitamin B6 and magnesium (*Journal of Urology*, October, 1974). Magnesium can act as a preventive rather than a cause of kidney stones.

We have been endowed with the ability to assimilate the minute traces of minerals found in water, just as other forms of life do. Of course our ability to assimilate inorganic minerals is limited. Eating powdered rocks, which some people do for minerals, is asking too much of your body. Even water can be overmineralized—too hard—but in such cases we generally don't like the way it tastes.

What effects do pipes have on water?

It depends on what kind of pipes. Hypertension, nervous and immune system disorders, and cancer have all been linked to contaminants leached from pipes made with materials such as galvanized iron, plastic, copper, lead, zinc, and asbestos-containing cement. The effects are more drastic where the water is soft, because soft water is more acidic than hard. Pipes are another reason for not drinking or cooking with water as it comes from the tap.

Is distilled water good to drink?

Distilled water is the softest water possible, all minerals having been removed by mechanical evaporation and condensation. In other words, distilled water has been artificially emptied; it doesn't exist in nature. Water is the universal solvent and naturally contains life-supporting elements wherever it is found. It is this quality we describe when we compare the experience of drinking distilled water to the water from a high mountain wilderness stream. The first, we say, is "dead" when compared with the second, which is "alive."

Some people explain the difference in terms of minerals. But it is more than that because you can add minerals back to distilled water without achieving that lifelike quality. It is also more than the oxygenation and ultraviolet light that enlivens water running down mountainsides, because underground water can transmit that lifelike quality too. We may be talking about electromagnetism. Whatever the reason, when we come across certain spring waters we say they taste good, something we never say about distilled water. So in this sense, distilled water is not good to drink.

However, it is vital to remember that uncontaminated water is extremely hard to find. Some people say that there is no clean water left on the planet, just as there is no completely clean air. In these times, the status of distilled water is elevated enormously. Distilled water should be the choice whenever pure spring water is unavailable: though dead and tasteless, distilled water is pure.

What's better for home water purification—reverse osmosis or distillation?

I prefer reverse osmosis. The water seems to have a little life to it, the unit is easier to maintain, does not waste water, and uses no extra energy. However, the important thing is not the choice but the pure water you get either way. If you decide in favor of distillation, be sure that your unit is a *fractional* distillation type; otherwise, contaminants with a lower boiling point than water will wind up recondensed right back in your distilled water. Two makers of fractional distillers are New World Distiller Corporation, Box 476, Gravette, AR 72736 and Pure Water, Inc., 3725 Touzalin Ave., Lincoln, NE 68506.

Won't distilled water leach minerals out of my blood and bones?

No. As soon as you drink water you begin mixing your body fluids into it and impregnating it with your own electromagnetic energy. In other words, it quickly stops being just water; and when it passes through your intestinal walls, it becomes one of the elements of your blood. It does not rob anything from your blood and bones; it has been transformed. The distilled water is no more; it is river water now, with sugars and salts, nutrients and waste products born along in it. The function of blood in a normal body is to carry nutrients *to* the bones, not leach them out.

What about fluoridated water?

You can't shut up a vocal health minority just by calling them "quacks." The anti-fluoridation quacks have not been silenced and it might be good for your health to listen to them.

On the plus side of the fluoride ledger, it has been definitely proved that when it is taken before the formation of the permanent teeth, it protects against tooth decay. That is, it protects if taken by pregnant women and children through seven years of age. There is also solid evidence that it has a preventive effect, though not as pronounced, for older children through the teens. And though it cannot be proved to afford dental protection to adults, it may help protect adults against osteoporosis and heart attacks. Fluoride, like all other nutrients, is a preventive medicine.

The preventive effect of fluoride, however, must be qualified: it is one of the *trace minerals*, meaning that is a preventive medicine in *minute quantities*. And like most things that are good in small amounts, too much is poison. Fluoride is the most powerful of a group of compounds called *halogens*. Halogens inhibit enzymes by binding the metal ions they need to function properly; enzymes are catalysts for every single one of our body processes. Furthermore, fluoride has been proved to be mutagenic by research at Columbia University and the University of Missouri. Finally, fluoride is another of the long list of things suspected of being carcinogenic.

There is no way to control how much fluoride you are getting when it is in the water, and, just as important, you should be able to control more than just the amount of fluoride: you should be able to choose whether or not you even take the medicine. And that you cannot do when your water is medicated. Medicated water is no more ethical than medicated food. What powerful, wealthy special interest group will next propagandize some other medicine, or tranquilizer, or contraceptive, into your water?

Fluoride is not basically different from other nutrients. I am sure that we would all have fewer colds if vitamin C were added to the water but I don't advocate doing it. Being against the fluoridation of water does not equate with being for the decay of your children's teeth. I have a son, eighteen years old at the time of writing, who has far better dental health than either his mother or I had—not because of fluoride but due to lifelong better nutrition than either of us had. That nutrition resulted in his being healthier than we were in *all* respects.

If I were raising Jason now, I would do nothing to artificially increase the amount of fluoride in his diet because I suspect it might make him grow to seven foot two instead of his mere six foot four. Here is how that might work: fluorine, the most active halogen, would replace iodine, a less active halogen, in the thyroid gland. He would then be deprived of his normal growth control mechanism, allowing his bones to become elongated. This can be accomplished experimentally with laboratory animals and may explain the correspondence of fluoridated water with giantism. In the fifties, the tallest man in the National Basketball Association was six foot ten; now every team has a couple of seven footers.

It would be prudent for us to remember that the fluoridation of water is a massive experiment that has already been banned in ten European countries. The long-term health effects of fluoride may turn out to be as negative as the ethics of mass medication.

Doctor George Waldbott was one of medicine's first allergy specialists. An outspoken critic of fluoridation, he has identified a condition called "chronic fluoride toxicity syndrome." Some of its symptoms are chronic fatigue, headaches, excessive water consumption, frequent urinaton, arthritic-like pain in muscles and bones, gastrointestinal disturbances, and depression. In *Fluoridation, the*

Great Dilemma, Waldbott points out that "today many scientists suspect that fluoridated water causes or increases chromosome damage, birth defects, and even cancer." Such a wide range of side effects is due, says Waldbott, to the fact that fluoride interferes with enzyme function and mineral balance—"authoritative assurances notwithstanding."

Isn't it better to chlorinate water than to spread disease in it?

Yes—*if* the chlorinated water itself does not cause diseases. A process co-developed by Army, EPA, and university scientists in Virginia monitors the breathing rate of fish to detect water pollutants, which cause them to breathe shallower and to cough. Chlorine in water causes the shallow breathing–coughing pattern. To the creatures living in water, chlorine is just another poison.

We need to pay attention to the fact that in this century our plague is degenerative, not communicable, diseases. Beyond the carcinogenic chlorine-related THMs, there is evidence to link chlorine with heart disease and diabetes.

In *Coronaries, Cholesterol, Chlorine*, Dr. Joseph Price draws the parallel between the spread of chlorination and the increasing incidence of heart attacks in this century. In *Supernutrition for Healthy Hearts*, Dr. Passwater agrees that there is a link between chlorinated water and heart disease, observing that Japan abandoned chlorination after World War II and has one-sixth the heart-disease rate of the United States.

The National Center for Health Statistics reported in 1980 that there are 300,000 cases of diabetes each year. It has multiplied by 600 percent during the last forty years, and at the current rate of increase, by the turn of the century roughly 10 percent of the population will have diabetes. Chlorine is implicated in the development of diabetes because it reacts internally to produce *alloxan*. Alloxan appears to contribute to diabetes in two ways. First, by destroying the reproductive capacity of the cells in the pancreas that produce insulin, alloxan is related to degeneration of the pancreas. Second, alloxan inhibits the function of the insulin because it is an oxidizing agent that deactivates zinc, and zinc is involved in the function and storage of insulin.

Chlorine is also an oxidizing agent for iron. Since iron is the nucleus of each blood cell, it appears that chlorine also threatens the structure of your blood. *Water Fit to Drink* cites studies at the University of Minnesota linking chlorinated water to anemia.

What if the only water I can get is chlorinated?

Fortunately, we know there are safer methods than chlorination to purify water; unfortunately, we have not yet begun to employ those methods. If you have no alternatives, drink chlorinated water for a short time without worrying about it—degenerative diseases develop over years, not months. But if you're not going to be able to escape the chlorinated water within months, choose between bottled spring or distilled water, home filtration or home distillation.

Is it worth the hassle?

I can understand that you would rather not be bothered and also that fiddling with your water smacks of fanaticism. But it is necessary. You can't clean up your diet without clean water. Food is only 50 percent of the equation; it should be as simple and inexpensive as the water half. Whatever you do to guarantee yourself pure water is an integral part of a healthy lifestyle.

How much water should I drink?

How much other fluid—tea, juice, wine, beer—which are almost all water, are you drinking? Then, how big are you? How active? What's the weather like? At one extreme, a big person working hard in hot weather could easily consume more than a gallon of fluids in a day. At the other extreme, a small inactive person in the dead of a cold winter might drink a quart of fluids and be fulfilling needs exactly.

It would be nice if we could trust thirst to settle the whole matter. Unfortunately, it is not quite that simple. Dr. David Costill, Director of the Human Performance Laboratory at Ball State University, says that human beings are unlike animals, who have a reliable thirst mechanism. Ours, he says, is "sluggish." We can depend on thirst to tell us *when* to drink but not how much: drink when thirsty but drink more than thirst bids you, when the drink is water. The familiar old advice to drink four glasses of water a day is really not bad advice, if you keep in mind that it is not an absolute, but a safe generality—safe when the water is pure.

4 *Sugar and Salt*

THE SUGAR STORY

If the FDA posted "Wanted" flyers in food stores as the FBI does in post offices, sugar (alias "sucrose") would be Public Enemy Number One. "Murderer, Thief, Extortionist, and Con Man," the poster would warn us. Sugar is the original and worst "foodless food," really not a food at all, and we should all understand how its dirty work is done.

Sugar The Murderer

Sugar is murder on teeth. Statistically, dental disease is the number one health problem in America, and sugar is the universally recognized culprit where dental decay is concerned. Ask any dentist what you can do to prevent your teeth from rotting and he will tell you to avoid sugar. It reacts with saliva to form acids that dissolve the enamel of your teeth and forms an ideal medium for the growth of bacteria that cause decay.

Yet, an extreme irony about sugar is that natural sucrose—raw sugar cane as you would cut it down in the field—has a factor that actually strengthens teeth. Cane workers who regularly chew raw sugar cane, regardless of what else they eat, are virtually free of tooth decay. Called "the Wulzen factor" after the professor who isolated it over twenty-five years ago, this nutritional oddity is not found in any other form of sugar. It is apparently extremely heat-fragile, appearing only in raw cane.

Sugar is also murder on the blood sugar level. Blood sugar should enter your circulatory system in a steady flow; eating sugar causes it to leap and plunge. Tragically, most of us have been experiencing a leaping and plunging blood sugar level all our lives and assume it to be normal. But escaping this form of murder can lead to some of life's most dramatic improvements, particularly in how we deal with stress. We all realize that what is stressful one time is not at some other time, and what is stressful for one person is not so for another. Dr. Cheraskin, in *Psychodietetics*, promises his readers that greatly reducing sugar intake leads to "incredible" personality changes, particularly the ability to handle stress without anger and impatience.

Blood sugar murder is accomplished with the aid of the sugar con game, which is so important that I will expose it separately, after a look at sugar as thief and extortionist.

Sugar The Thief

Sugar has accomplices who testify that it's a carbohydrate, that all carbohydrate eventually becomes sugar, ergo sugar is okay. Such testimony would not constitute perjury, but a little judicious cross-examination would expose it as a half-truth (often even more misleading than an outright lie).

The vital missing fact: sugar is a *simple* carbohydrate. It is totally devoid of vitamins, minerals, and enzymes. It is 99.96 percent sucrose. The duplicity is often accentuated in sugar propaganda using the term "pure sugar," as if it were something virtuous. It is exactly that purity that makes sugar a thief.

Vitamins, minerals, and enzymes are essential for digestion, assimilation, and utilization. But analysis of molasses, the by-product of sugar refining, reveals six B vitamins and eight minerals detached from the sugar; these are just a portion of the nutrients your system must somehow provide to metabolize sugar. The missing elements must be stolen from the real food in your diet, from the nutrients in your blood that were intended for other functions, even from the reserves stored in your bones. Only by theft can a simple carbohydrate imitate a complex one and act like a food.

By contrast, a complex carbohydrate (real food) has its sugars accompanied by fiber, vitamins, minerals, enzymes, protein, and fat—everything necessary to complete the metabolic activities that will be fired by the sugars. The sugars of complex carbohydrates are chains of glucose molecules (*polysaccharides*). The glucose chains are separated by the digestive process, sent through the walls of the small intestine to the liver for storage as glycogen. As we need energy, the liver releases glucose into the bloodstream: smooth, even, balanced. Complex carbohydrates supply our cells with a slow, steady, stream of blood sugar and none of the companion essentials are missing. Nothing needs to be stolen. This is natural sugar metabolism.

Sugar has been tried for stealing nutrients like vitamin B6 and chromium and its conviction has been well publicized. But hardly anyone knows that it has also been convicted of stealing the ability of your white blood cells to destroy bacteria. White blood cells are technically known as "phagocytes" and phagocytic tests show that a couple of teaspoons of sugar can sap the strength of white blood cells by 25 percent. The sugar in a big helping of pie a la mode can render your white blood cells virtually 100 percent helpless. The effect lasts about four hours—about enough time to make room for another dose of sugar, enough time for your white blood cells to regain their ability to fight disease, only to have it stolen again.

Sugar can reduce your resistance to everything from colds to cancer. Recently I saw a demonstration of the weakening effect of sugar. The demonstrator called for a skeptic to come forward from the audience. The skeptic who stepped up was perfect for his role, about six foot four and 230 pounds. He was asked to hold his arm out to the side, horizontal to the floor, and resist the pressure of the demonstrator pulling down. The demonstrator was able to move the massive arm no more than an inch; one had the feeling he could have swung from it like the limb of a tree. Then he put a cube of sugar under the volunteer's tongue. Down went the arm like it was made of mush. The demonstrator was approximately half the size of the volunteer. "Isn't that amazing?" he asked. "Yup," answered the giant.

Sugar The Extortionist

One dictionary definition of extortion is "the wrongful taking of a person's property with his consent but by the use of threat." Your property in this case is insulin; the threat is that your blood sugar will get out of control. To pull this job off, sugar works through the pancreas. Sucrose extortion is somewhat more complex than its murder and thievery.

One of the many key functions of the liver is to remove excess glucose from the blood. In order to perform that function it requires insulin: enter the pancreas. Scattered throughout the pancreas, wrapped by pancreatic tissue but separate from it, are a group of endocrine glands collectively known as the *islands of Langerhans* (the name of their discoverer), or beta cells. Endocrine glands produce hormones and differ from other glands by not having ducts to carry their secretions to a specific locale, so they are often referred to as "ductless" glands. The blood or lymph passes directly through the endocrine glands, in that way picking up the hormones and carrying them to wherever they are needed.

Beta cells produce insulin, the hormone responsible for controlling the metabolism of carbohydrates. Beta cells read the signals carried by the blood about how much carbohydrate we've consumed, send the necessary insulin, and the liver then is able to convert the glucose into the storage form, glycogen. Later, as glucose is needed for energy, other hormones are sent from the adrenals to break the glycogen back into glucose, which is then released into the bloodstream as "blood sugar."

The accomplices of sugar take the stand and say, "Sugar is sugar." But different kinds of sugar are metabolized differently, involving differing enzymes. It is an extremely misleading oversimplification to say that all forms of sugar are the same, another attempt to mislead us with half-truths. It is true that your body cells will use any kind of sugar for energy, just like it is true that a fireplace will burn any kind of wood. But not all kinds of wood burn alike. Blood sugar is like the hard, seasoned wood stacked neat and dry in a woodshed: with just a little kindling, it crackles into a clean-burning, long-lasting, hot and steady fire. Sucrose is like wood shavings thrown on the fire.

Extortion is the name of the crime here because the metabolic requirements of sucrose cause a sudden leap in the level of sugar in your blood. "More insulin," it threatens, "or your blood sugar level will shoot out of control." To make sure you respond fully, a bit of pressure will be applied in the form of a brief, mild form of diabetes; but more on that when we get to the sucrose con game.

The Many Aliases Of Sugar

Since other kinds of sugar are accepted into the bloodstream as a substitute form of blood sugar, they should be judged by their effect, using glucose as the norm. In the following table, the rise in blood sugar caused by the release of glucose by your liver represents the value of 1.

OTHER SUGARS AT A GLANCE

Kind of Sugar	Common Name	Sweetening Power*	Source	Blood Sugar Rise
Lactose	Milk Sugar	16%	milk	2
Maltose	Malt Sugar	32%	sprouted grain	2
Fructose	Fruit Sugar	173%	fruit	3
Dextrose	Grape Sugar, Corn Sugar	74%	starch	4
Sucrose	Table Sugar	100%	sugar cane, sugar beets	5

*calculated with sucrose representing 100%

When you see *ose* or common name equivalents listed as ingredients you can be sure you are looking at a refined sugar and they all murder and steal about as much as sucrose. It is as an extortionist that sucrose surpasses all the others. And of all the forms of refined sugar, sucrose is by far the most often used for commercial purposes because of its abundance and cheapness. When you know all the aliases sucrose uses, you begin to learn how ubiquitous it really is.

ALIASES THAT DISGUISE THE PRESENCE OF SUCROSE

Cane sugar	Corn syrup
Raw sugar	Invert sugar
Kleenraw sugar	Invert sugar syrup
Light & dark brown sugar	Blackstrap molasses
Turbinado sugar	Barbados molasses
Barbados sugar	Cane syrup
Muscovado sugar	Ribbon cane syrup
Maple sugar	Maple syrup
	Sorghum syrup

Some of the above differ from common white sugar in having flavor as well as sweetness, some even have minor (extremely minor except for blackstrap molasses) amounts of nutrients, but in all cases what makes them sweet is sucrose.

Newcomers to the New American Diet are often unpleasantly surprised to learn about brown or "raw" sugar. It is merely white sugar in disguise, wearing a brown mask. Dark brown sugar ("yellow-D") is 87% white sugar, light brown is 88%, "Kleenraw" is 95%, turbinado is 99.5% white. The word "raw" means nothing; no such thing as raw sugar exists in the American marketplace. "What it means," the argument goes, "is that the brown sugar has vitamins and minerals." Nonsense. Or, as Phil Levy (*Sugar and How It Gets That Way*) concedes: "If a man strips off all his clothing except his socks you could argue that he was still dressed, and you might win on a technicality." All you can really claim for brown sugar is that it's brown, which means nothing.

The following sweeteners do not depend on sucrose for their sweetening power:

Sweetener	*Kind of Sugar*	*Sweetening Power**
Rice syrup	Maltose	20%
Barley malt syrup	Maltose	40%
Date sugar	Fructose	100%
Honey	Glucose & Fructose	140%

*calculated with sucrose representing 100%

Of the above, only date sugar is a solid, and it is the only one that is a whole food: dates that have been pitted, dried, and ground. Its sugar is actually fructose. "Date sugar" is a misnomer, but a harmless one. It is suitable for sprinkling on things, but does not mix well and dissolve easily, and therefore can be a problem in baking and cooking. The liquids are easier to work with in baking and cooking, but all recipes that are being converted from a solid-form sucrose sweetener need to have their liquid content adjusted to compensate for the liquid of the syrup and/or honey. (See p. 319.) Blending barley malt syrup and honey is a good way to lighten the malt flavor and lessen the sweetness of honey; a fifty-fifty blend has roughly the sweetening power of sucrose.

Sugar And The Con Game

Beta cells naturally gear their production of insulin to the pace of glucose traveling through the walls of the small intestine from the digestion of complex carbohydrates. With that clearly in mind, you have the key to the sugar con game.

When you have eaten complex carbohydrates, the first glucose that reaches the liver passes through largely unaltered to the pancreas as a messenger. The rise in blood sugar represented by the presence of this messenger gives the beta cells their signal for how much insulin to produce. And it gives sucrose the opportunity to play its con game. For the sad fact is, the beta cells don't know how to discriminate between glucose and other forms of sugar; the innocent beta cells see sucrose as if it were glucose. Beta cells only know how to respond to natural foods, because that's all we've been programmed for during many centuries of evolution. The game is on and we're much the worse for it.

Sucrose gets its best opportunity to give us the shuck and jive routine when we eat a candy bar or drink a soda pop between meals—that good old "quick energy." To the beta cells the leap in blood sugar from that candy bar or soda pop means there must be half a loaf of whole wheat bread back there in the small intestine: better get into high gear, the liver needs a tankful of insulin so it can store all that glucose. Meanwhile, the sucrose goes speeding madly through the bloodstream, like a getaway car roaring past stop signs and red lights, ripping through 25-miles-per-hour speed zones at 100 . . . only to run out of gas and sputter lamely into a ditch.

About the time the sucrose joy ride has fizzled out, the big load of insulin begins arriving at the liver, looking for the stream of glucose that was supposed to be pouring through from the small intestine. But there is no such thing—the small intestine is, in fact, quite empty. Now what?

Insulin is energetic, like all good hormones, and simple-minded. It only knows one thing to do: take glucose out of the blood so the liver can store it away as glycogen. No glucose is coming over from the small intestine, so it just latches on to all the blood sugar that should be heading out to the cells, and packs it away as it has been programmed to do.

Down plunges your blood sugar level; after the sugar buzz, you feel the letdown—tired, irritable, depressed. You have what William Dufty calls *The Sugar Blues* (Warner Books). You remember the lift you felt while the sugar was scorching your arteries and capillaries: another dose will bring you out of it. And you've been conned again. Up, down, up, down, your blood-sugar level pitches and plunges, the beleaguered beta cells of your pancreas puffing along in an exhausting effort to keep up. This is why sugar is an addiction and we speak of "sugar freaks" and "sugar junkies." It also explains why diabetes, the ultimate failure of the beta cells to produce adequate insulin, is now a leading killer disease, having become so as the American diet became whiter and sweeter during this century.

Food-industry executives and scientists are not the only accomplices to sugar's life of crime. Many members of the medical establishment fail to recognize the causal relationship between sugar consumption and adult onset diabetes. They are waiting for proof positive. Eventually they will get it, if only because what goes up always comes down, and as sugar consumption comes down, so will the incidence of diabetes.

People want to know what to do when they feel hunger pangs between meals. Sometimes the hunger pangs are accompanied by weakness, faintness, shakiness, headache, confusion—the symptoms of low blood sugar (*hypoglycemia*; diabetes is *hyperglycemia*). You might benefit from frequent small meals, rather than infrequent big ones. There is nothing wrong with snacking and nibbling as long as two rules are followed: (1) that you snack and nibble on wholesome, natural food; (2) that your snacks and nibbles are not *extra* food.

A Final Accusation

Doctor John Yudkin, emeritus professor of nutrition at London University, is one of the world's foremost researchers, lecturers, and writers on nutrition (*This Nutrition Business; This Slimming Business; Pure, White and Deadly: The Problem of Sugar*). In *This Nutrition Business*, Professor Yudkin presents us with a list of biochemical disturbances, identified as increases of

—fats in blood
—uric acid in the blood
—glucose in the blood
—the stickiness of blood platelets
—the concentration of insulin and cortisol (another hormone active in carbohydrate metabolism).

This list, which has also been confirmed by the research of others, delineates characteristics of people who develop coronary disease and of people who have "fairly large" amounts of dietary sugar. It is not a list of disturbances caused by diets high in fat and/or cholesterol; therefore, Professor Yudkin believes that *sugar* is the chief dietary factor producing coronary disease.

He has no problem seeing the sugar/diabetes link and observes that sugar is linked to gout and duodenal ulcers, and that people suffering diabetes, gout, and duodenal ulcers are also predisposed to coronary disease. Professor Yudkin believes in the sugar/coronary link based on circumstantial evidence; for the unconvinced, he lists "certain advantages" accruing to those who eliminate or curtail sugar consumption:

—reduction of dental decay, especially in children
—aid in control of weight, an indirect link to coronary disease
—improvement of digestion
—improvement or correction of the blood abnormalities listed above

We have already seen that the U.S. Senate, the USDA, and the Surgeon General all consider it imperative that we reduce sugar consumption. Many years earlier, J. I. Rodale, founder of *Prevention* magazine, said: "We receive many letters from readers asking what kind of sugar to use. So far as we are concerned, the answer is none . . . if you would be healthy, omit all sugar and just get accustomed to doing without it."

HONEY VS. SUGAR

In natural food circles, honey is usually advocated as the ideal sweetener. The argument thrown up against it is that honey is just another form of sugar. That argument is partially true: honey is approximately 98 percent sugar, a combination of fructose and glucose. But the 2 percent of enzymes, minerals and vitamins makes a big difference in appearance, flavor, and consistency. Asking us to believe that honey is just another form of sugar is asking us to deny our senses. Honey

SUGAR VOTED MOST LIKELY TO CAUSE DISEASE

W.D. Ringsdorf, D.M.D., M.S., (with E. Cheraskin, D.M.D., M.D., co-author of *Psycho-dietetics*, Bantam Books), said of sugar in a San Francisco lecture, "It enters in, probably, to more disease production, more different kinds of problems than any other single factor in our nutritional lifestyle." He went on to trace the degenerative effects of sugar from the mouth to the stomach and thence throughout the body. A summary:

Mouth: cavities and gum disease.

Stomach: increase of gastric acidity, leading to indigestion, with possible link to peptic ulcers.

Heart and circulatory system: raises blood pressure. Mixed with animal fats, leads to atherosclerosis. By increasing the stickiness (viscosity) of the blood, increases possibility of blood clots.

Pancreas: fatigue of this organ linked to hypoglycemia and adult-onset diabetes.

Bowel: transit time of 4–5 days (sugar and other refined foods) versus 1–1½ days (natural foods) linked with diverticulitis and colon cancer.

Vagina: the fungus *candida albicans*, naturally present in most women, can multiply disproportionately with excessive sugar consumption, leading to infection.

Bones: excretion of calcium in urine, caused by sugar, linked to osteoporosis.

Blood: extraction of B vitamins, phosphorus, magnesium, and other minerals, necessary to metabolize sugar, linked to malnutrition.

Blood pressure: the sugar link to hypertension is particularly strong. Dr. Richard Ahrens, at the University of Maryland, has been able to raise blood pressure simply by feeding sugar to human volunteers.

Immune system: small amounts of sugar decrease effectiveness of white blood cells, while large amounts can totally paralyze them. White cell normalization takes 4–5 hours, weakening defenses against disease. (Remember, there is usually not much more than 4–5 hours between most Americans' sugar-laden meals, leaving them with almost constantly ineffectual white blood cells.)

I vote with Ringsdorf for sugar as the biggest of all disease-producers and so, it seems, does Vincent Calli, D.D.S., author of *The New, Lower-Cost Way to End Gum Trouble Without Surgery* (Warner Books). Says Calli, "If I had three words, and three words only, to explain to you how to improve your diet, your life expectancy and your overall physical and mental health, I would say, 'Don't eat sugar.' "

is another example of the fact that there is more to whole, natural foods than can be described by mere chemistry. Honey, a complex carbohydrate, is food; sugar, a simple carbohydrate, is foodless food.

Honey has the interesting characteristic of being antiseptic, meaning that bacteria cannot survive in it. Dr. Jarvis, in *Folk Medicine*, explains this characteristic by the presence of potassium in honey, which draws the moisture necessary for survival from bacterial cells. Dr. Jarvis also lists numerous therapeutic uses of honey, calling it the one sweetener with "life-giving qualities." Yet just because honey is a natural food does not mean we should use it without restraint. Bears who regularly plunder the hives of wild honey bees are the only animals in nature with decayed teeth.

It is also important to observe the purpose of honey: it is designed to feed tiny creatures whose wings flap so fast they whine and who exhaust their lives within a year. Thus seen for its purpose in nature, one would logically assume that eating large quantities of honey would be quite unbalancing to the human system. And one would be right: although a whole food, it enters the bloodstream rapidly, as sugar does, and can cause the same kind of blood-sugar race, causing the same kind of strain on the pancreas. Since honey has the complexity of a whole food, the blood-sugar race it triggers will be conducted at a slower speed than the one triggered by sugar. But prudent dietary practices require discipline regarding *all* concentrated sweeteners, including honey.

There are quality considerations in selecting honey. Different kinds of blossoms produce different flavors and colors. The lighter colored honeys are mildest in flavor. Darker honeys have more minerals and richer flavors. Good honey should be unfiltered and uncooked. Filtering removes the pollen and it is pollen that gives good honey its cloudiness and valuable nutrients. Straining through cheesecloth is sufficient to remove extraneous material such as the occasional wing or leg of a bee. In this regard, Grade C is actually superior to Grade A, called such because of its clarity.

The word "uncooked" on a honey label should tell us what temperature was employed during the processing. Temperatures up to 145° F can be used with "uncooked" still permitted as a description. To be meaningful, however, the word should mean not heated over 104° F, just enough to encourage free flowing but not high enough to destroy vitamins and enzymes. Truly uncooked honey begins to crystallize—become solid—at room temperature within several weeks after bottling. To reliquify it, set the jar or can into a pan of hot water.

People often ask about what to do with those recipes that just won't work with honey substituted for sugar. The first thing to consider is not to make the recipe. But if it's irresistible, the next option is to use brown sugar, a little better than white because of its molasses content. The objection to brown sugar is sometimes that very molasses flavor, however, and that brings us to the final option: use white sugar. This, in turn, brings us to the crux of the whole sugar problem: *over*consumption. If we consumed a few pounds of sugar a year, it would cause little or no problem. But sugar is not just the most widely used sweetener, it is the most widely used food additive. Average consumption is currently 130 pounds per person a year; nobody can even approach that level of sugar consumption and expect good health to last.

FRUCTOSE

During the last few years, fructose (fruit sugar) has been appearing more and more often in so-called natural foods. First of all, it should be understood that fructose is *not* an exception to the admonition to restrict the use of sweeteners. Fructose—like sucrose, dextrose, glucose and lactose—is a simple, not a complex, carbohydrate. It is generally manufactured from corn syrup, another simple carbohydrate. Corn syrup is a liquid form of sucrose; sucrose is actually two even simpler sugars— fructose and glucose—bonded together. So fructose is obtained by splitting apart the two components of corn syrup.

The advocates of fructose point out that it is a *mono*saccharide, whereas sucrose is a *di*saccharide. These prefixes indicate that the molecular structure of fructose only has a single bond whereas sucrose is double-bonded between the atoms of carbon, hydrogen, and oxygen. This means that fructose is easier to break down: fructose does not require large charges of insulin to be released from the pancreas, whereas sucrose does (to split the glucose from the fructose). Fructose advocates are right in claiming it is easier to metabolize than sucrose, even safe for some diabetics. They admit that it is a simple carbohydrate; they also claim that its sweetening power is twice that of sucrose. Therefore its superiority also lies in being able to achieve the same degree of sweetening with half the amount. They are right in that too.

The big problem with fructose as a substitute for sucrose is looseness in labeling. There is pure fructose, 90 percent fructose, and "high-fructose corn solids," which may be as much as 55 percent sucrose. But it is permissible to identify all of them simply as "fructose." It could be deadly to a diabetic who thinks he is buying fructose and is really getting half sucrose. This officially sanctioned duplicity should be eliminated immediately by food manufacturers voluntarily telling us what they mean when they use the word "fructose." And we should use fructose as we would any other sweetener—extremely lightly. It may not be quite the extortionist and con man that sucrose is, but it is still a murderer and thief, as are all refined sugars.

The best place to get fructose is in fruit; lactose in milk; maltose in sprouted grain; dextrose in grapes and raisins; sucrose in raw sugar cane. Glucose, the perfect human energy food, comes from your liver, which gets it from complex carbohydrates. You may feel some lack of energy while weaning yourself from a sweet, white diet; but once the weaning is over (from two weeks to two months), you'll find the New American Diet produces the most effective, efficient energy available. From a diet based on complex carbohydrates, you get your internal energy in a steady, strong, clean stream.

THE SALT STORY

The state of Oregon has made the term "sea salt" illegal, charging that the implication of superiority is groundless, that the term is merely an excuse to charge more money for regular salt. That's a bit cynical, but fundamentally Oregon is right: the term is an exercise in meaningless language.

If there were such a thing available as unrefined sea salt, it would be gray in color, approximately 58 percent chloride, 33 percent sodium, 4 percent magnesium, 3 percent sulphur, one percent calcium, one percent potassium, and traces of all other known minerals. (The concentration of minerals in salt water is not uniform everywhere in the oceans and seas.)

Sea salt production is entirely the business of large-scale facilities—thousands of acres of collection ponds, huge kilns, long packaging lines, big storage facilities, rail car sidings—the sort of endeavor done massively or not done at all. A company that wants to sell something they can legally call sea salt has to buy it from companies that actually evaporate sea water to obtain salt. Two in my region are Leslie Salt and Morton Salt, who both extract salt from the waters of San Francisco Bay. The would-be sea salt seller would agree to buy so much salt at such and such a price, establish credit, supply his own label design, and enter the sea salt business. The big difference between Leslie or Morton and their private label customer would be the package. And the price—the manufacturer's price structure would guarantee that the private label sea salt price would be higher. Another difference is that the manufacturers don't bother to call it "sea salt" when selling under their own labels.

Whatever this salt is called, the processing is the same. When you visit the producer you see mammoth piles of salt that have been collected from miles of ponds. When these piles are ready for processing, the salt is dissolved in water and treated with lime and soda ash to remove impurities. The water is then evaporated off by kiln drying at temperatures up to 1200° F. I have seen the term "solar evaporated" applied to this kind of salt. You might feel like granting it half-truth status because the sun is the evaporator *before* it gets to the kiln, but calling it solar evaporated is really as meaningless as calling it sea salt.

If the salt really were solar evaporated, meaning *only* sun dried, it might be worth attention. True sun-dried salt dissolves quicker and stays in solution longer than salt subjected to high kiln temperatures. I reason that the solubility difference must be caused by a molecular alteration caused by the high evaporating temperature of kiln-dried salt, and that the more natural molecular structure of the sun-dried salt would be easier for my body to metabolize.

Simple solubility tests could establish what temperatures have what effects on salt and would thereby give some meaning to the term "low-temperature kiln-drying". It could be that salt dried at less than 400°F, for example, is just as soluble and stays in solution as long as solar evaporated salt. But if such information exists, it is certainly not widely circulated. As things stand, the label of the most natural salt you might find would read something like this: "The color of this salt is due to naturally occurring minerals. This salt is not kiln-dried and has nothing added. It is packaged exactly as it comes from the ground." A few obscure sources of mined or "rock" salt are unheated, and have solubility characteristics similar to genuinely solar-evaporated sea salt. They are usually off-white in color and are probably the most natural salts available. (The 2.5 percent of allowable trace minerals will produce red salt if one of the minerals is iron.)

Salt mines are deposits from prehistoric sea beds, which is what is meant by the statement, "All salt is sea salt." Salt springs, resulting from fresh water flowing over such underground salt deposits, yield over half of the salt produced in this country. Brine from salt springs is dried at similar kiln temperatures and receives the same additives as so-called sea salt.

The usual additives to salt are potassium iodide as a source of iodine to prevent goiter, dextrose to keep the iodine from oxidizing, sodium bicarbonate to keep the iodine from turning the salt purple, and sodium silico aluminate or calcium carbonate to keep it free-flowing. Private labelers of sea salt usually choose to add only calcium carbonate, since it is a common, naturally occurring mineral compound, and leave out the others.

Nutrition In Salt And Sodium-Potassium Balance

No matter where the salt is from, sodium and chlorine are important minerals to the human body. Deficiency of sodium causes muscle shrinkage and weakness, nausea, loss of appetite, and flatulence. Sodium maintains our cellular fluid level and the health of our nervous, muscular, blood, and lymph systems. Deficiency of chlorine causes hair and tooth loss, weak muscles, and poor digestion. Chlorine regulates our acid/alkaline balance, enhances osmosis, stimulates production of hydrochloric acid and helps maintain joints and tendons.

However, the importance of sodium and chlorine should not be interpreted to mean that we're caught in a damned-if-we-do-or-don't, eat-salt/don't-eat-salt trap. Both minerals abound as sodium chloride in a wide variety of foods: fish, sea vegetables, carrots, celery, beets, swiss chard, lentils, olives, pickles, cheese, and soy sauce. Sea vegetables are a particularly good source of natural sodium chloride because they also contain the abundant trace minerals held in solution in sea water, including iodine. I refer to kelp and dulse as well as such Japanese varieties as *hiziki, wakame, nori,* and *arame* (more on sea vegetables in Chapter 14).

Since sodium and chlorine are so widely distributed in natural foods, it is almost never nutritionally essential to salt food. Salted food is an acquired, not an inborn taste. Most of us acquired it back in the days when our mothers spooned baby foods into our mouths. As explained previously, the real nutritional problem is not salt, but the overconsumption of it. Too much salt destroys the balance between sodium outside of cell walls and potassium inside them. Working together, potassium and sodium are major participants in regulating blood and urine pH, water balance, conduction of nerve impulses, and muscle contractions.

Sodium-potassium balance is particularly fascinating as energy transference. In lightning-like

---

HIDDEN SODIUM

It is not just the salt from the shaker that transports two and a half teaspoons of salt into each American every day. Sodium "sneaks" into unreformed diets in processed foods and additives at great cost to sodium-potassium balance.

PROCESSED FOODS

3½ oz. of	mg sodium	mg potassium
Salmon, raw	48	391
Salmon, canned	522	344
Oysters, raw	73	121
Oysters, frozen	380	210
Pork, raw	70	285
Pork, hot dog	1100	340
Green peas, raw	2	316
Green peas, frozen	196	150
Green beans, raw	7	243
Green beans, canned	236	95
Whole wheat flour	3	370
White flour	2	95
White flour, self-rising	1079	90

ADDITIVES

Additive	Purpose
Monosodium glutamate (MSG)	flavor enhancer
Sodium bicarbonate	leavening agent
Sodium nitrite	meat curing agent
Sodium benzoate	preservative
Sodium propionate	mold inhibitor
Sodium citrate	acidity controller

Hidden sodium also is transported by such medicines as antibiotics, alkalizers, cough preparations and sedatives.

exchanges, the energy impulses in nerve and muscle fibers flash back and forth across cell walls. These exchanges are achieved by sodium and potassium as electrolytes, whereby sodium zips into the cell, potassium zips out, and then they immediately flash back into the original sodium-outside, potassium-inside conformation. Too much salt outside the cell walls may reduce the efficiency of energy exchanges in the nerve and muscle fibers.

This type of salt-induced decrease in metabolic efficiency might also occur if your diet had an excess of potassium, because, again, the ideal sodium-potassium ratio would be upset. But excesses of potassium are rare because your kidneys tend to conserve sodium while excreting potassium. This inborn tendency is compensated for by most natural foods having more potassium than sodium—when, that is, little or no salt is added.

Iodized Salt

Iodine is essential to the development and maintenance of the thyroid gland and is a major component of the hormone thyroxine, produced by the thyroid. Thyroxine plays a major role in energy production and is one of the master hormones involved in a multiplicity of metabolic functions. Three ways to prevent iodine deficiency are: (1) eating seafood, both fish and sea vegetables; (2) taking mineral supplements, such as kelp or dulse tablets, or multi-vitamin/mineral supplements; (3) using iodized salt in preference to other kinds. With options one and two at hand, one should not feel pushed to use salt in order to prevent iodine deficiency.

Mushrooms are a reasonable source of food iodine if they are not grown in iodine-deficient soil—such as the "Goiter Belt" of the midwest. Home gardeners, there or anywhere, can prevent iodine deficiency by using kelp or fish emulsion fertilizers.

Sodium, Potassium, And Hypertension

Hypertension, or high blood pressure, refers to the tenseness of your blood vessel walls. Too much tension in your blood vessels can be associated with nervous tension. It can also be related to sodium and the balance between sodium and potassium. Dr. Naosuke Sasaki, a Japanese researcher, studied two northern Japanese villages where the people ate large amounts of salt, but one village had a much higher rate of hypertension. The dietary difference was that the villagers with the lower blood pressure ate a lot of high-potassium apples.

Lowering hypertension can be acccomplished simply by reducing salt consumption. Primitive people living without salt consistently have little or no hypertension and researchers in countless experiments dating from the earliest days of this century have been able to lower blood pressure by reducing salt. (Other dietary factors may be too much alcohol, too much fat, and too little calcium. For a comprehensive review, see "Nutrition Action," December, 1982, CSPI, 1755 S St. NW, Washington DC 20009.)

Heart attack, stroke, and kidney failure all represent some type of blood vessel rupture associated with hypertension. All are preventable and, since 25 percent of the population suffers hypertension (50 percent of those 65 years or older), the argument for low sodium consumption is quite strong.

Salt Without Sodium

Many of the recipes in this book call for small amounts of salt. The purpose of the salt is usually for flavoring; it is seldom necessary to make a recipe "work." In following those recipes, feel free to

INTERPRETING BLOOD PRESSURE READINGS

When your blood pressure is taken, the force of your blood against the walls of your arteries is measured in degrees (as, for example, mercury being pushed up a glass column). The first number read to you is your *systolic* blood pressure, which is at the peak of your heart's contraction. The second number is your *diastolic* blood pressure, when your heart is relaxing between beats. The diastolic number is usually given more significance because it can indicate tense blood vessel walls even between beats, whereas nervousness about having your blood pressure checked can raise the systolic number. High numbers indicate that your heart is forced to work extra hard to push blood through your circulatory system.

	When Heart Beats (Systolic)	Between Heart Beats (Diastolic)	Risk
Normal	120	80 or less	low
Above normal	130	81–89	intermediate
Borderline high	140	90–94	high
High	160	95 and over	dangerous

simply leave the salt out. Or else, use a little less each time you make a recipe, substituting herbs and spices (see Appendix Six for suggestions).

Things acquired—like the taste for salt—can be surrendered. A salt shaker was always on the table when I was a kid, just as there was one on the tables of everyone I knew. I salted most everything before I even tasted it because that's the way things were done—salt it, then eat it. I don't even have a salt shaker any more; my salt tooth went the way of my sweet tooth and I know a lot more about the real flavors of food now. When adapting recipes, I automatically reduce the salt by at least half. (All recipes in this book have had the salt content adjusted down.)

Enhancing Flavor Without Salt

To enhance food flavors I use garlic, herbs, and little squirts of soy sauce here and there. Natural foods stores have various herbal seasoning mixes, some with salt as one ingredient, some without. You can buy bulk ingredients for making your own herbal seasoning. Try this formula:

—3 parts kelp powder
—2 parts parsley powder (parsley flakes reduced to powder in a blender)
—1 part garlic powder
—1 part cayenne pepper

This seasoning will do a better job of enhancing flavors than plain salt and has a far more beneficial effect nutritionally.

Most salt substitutes replace 80 percent or more of the sodium chloride with potassium chloride. Potassium chloride looks and tastes like ordinary table salt, although some people find it has a slightly bitter flavor, absent in sodium chloride. Dr. Carl Pfeiffer, writing in *Zinc and Other Micro-Nutrients* (Keats Publishing, Inc.), indicates that whether sodium or potassium chloride tastes best is only a matter of what you are accustomed to. He tells of an African village where the people have a natural source of potassium chloride which they use for seasoning, preferring it to white man's salt.

Potassium chloride salt substitutes are like sodium chloride in that they have no accompanying trace minerals. For trace minerals you can substitute magnesium chloride in the form of *bitterns* (English name), or *nigari* (Japanese name).

Nigari is the traditional coagulant with which truly natural tofu is made. When sodium chloride is removed from sea salt, nigari is left; it is all the other minerals found in sea water. Use it carefully and experimentally as a salt substitute in order to learn how it differs from sodium chloride. Nigari is available in some natural foods stores, soyfoods delicatessens, or by mail from Gem Cultures, 30301 Sherwood Rd., Ft. Bragg, CA 95437.

Potassium chloride salt substitutes are an inexpensive way to supplement your diet with potassium. Nigari is an excellent magnesium supplement. Since magnesium must be present for the body to retain potassium, you would create an intelligent salt substitute by mixing potassium chloride with nigari. The best single natural food source for all three of these highly associated minerals—magnesium, potassium, and sodium—is seafood.

Sodium High And Low

Sodium chloride is 39 percent sodium; therefore, one teaspoon of salt, which contains 5000 mg of sodium chloride, represents 1950 mg of sodium. Compare that with the statement, "a separate supply of salt in addition to that present in the food is not essential for man"—the consensus of academic nutritionists (*Human Nutrition and Dietetics*, Sir Stanley Davidson et al. Churchill Livingstone). It would seem that even a teaspoon of salt a day may be "high" sodium consumption.

What, then, about people who eat 2–3 teaspoons of salt a day (the national average according to the U.S. Dept. of Health and Human Services)? That can mean as much as 5850 mg of sodium. Perhaps the word for that level of salt consumption is "astronomical," even though it seems normal to most people. Faced with the huge disparity between usage and need, most nutritionists choose the realistic rather than the idealistic, advising one to cut salt back to a teaspoon a day, even though Dr. Mark Hegsted, chief of the USDA Human Nutrition Center, said ". . . if salt were a new food additive, it is doubtful that it would be classified as safe . . ."

The only circumstances in which it is actually necessary to add salt to your diet is when you do long, strenuous exercise in hot weather to which you have not had a chance to acclimatize. Then the recommendation is: above a six-pound weight loss due to sweating, add roughly a half teaspoon of salt for each pound lost (Food and Nutrition Board of the National Academy of Sciences). That can be reduced to a quarter teaspoon after eight days because, says Dr. David Costill, Ball State University's expert on sports medicine, that's how long it takes for the body to acclimatize. Sodium excreted through sweat is then reduced by from one half to two thirds.

Ordinary activity, even in very hot climates, should not require added salt in any great amount. What "acclimatization" means in reference to sodium, is that your kidneys and sweat glands adapt by conserving sodium and water. The Bedouin of the Sahara use no salt. Thoroughly acclimatized, they barely sweat, so that even the hottest weather poses no threat of sodium deficiency. Symptoms of sodium deficiency are nausea, diarrhea, extreme weakness and dizziness, and severe muscle cramps.

It should be obvious that the answer to the question, "How much salt should I use?" is not much different from the answer to the same question about sugar. Prudence demands reduced salt in cooking and either "go lightly" or "hands off" the salt shaker. The answer is: Use as little salt as possible.

5 Milk and Eggs

MILK—A MOST CONTROVERSIAL FOOD

Questions about milk abound in natural foods stores: Is milk really a healthy food? Should adults drink milk? Is raw milk better than pasteurized? Does milk cause excess mucus? What's different about cultured milk products?

Milk was designed to feed calves, infants that weigh seventy pounds at birth. At first it is their only food. Then, as they begin to nibble grass, it becomes their principal food. As they grow, they feed less from the udder, more from the ground. By the time their weight has increased tenfold, the infants have gone through childhood to adolescence—become heifers or bulls—and grass has become their only food.

Such simplicity was never intended for man. The mothers of our species were not intended to nurse their children through a tenfold increase in body weight. It is natural for us to seek out a wide variety of foods, including the specialties of other species, such as eggs, honey, and milk. The problems with milk come not so much from people using it but from (1) the wrong people using it; (2) using the wrong form; (3) using too much of it.

The Wrong People

Many people who drank milk with pleasure in childhood are not attracted to it as adults, an understandable response to what is basically a "growth food." Other adults are still attracted to it, but find it gives them digestive problems. This is because the enzymes—particularly lactase for digesting lactose, or milk sugar—are no longer produced in sufficient quantity by the adult to handle milk efficiently. So one kind of wrong person for milk is the adult who responds to it with indigestion and flatulence.

Some children are also the wrong people for milk. A widely used measurement for this condition is *lactose intolerance*. Lactose intolerance can be as low as 5 percent in white children of North European extraction and, in vivid contrast, as high as 70 percent in black American children. Statistics prove that children descended from cultures with a long heritage of milk and dairy product consumption digest and assimilate milk best.

Knowing whether someone is a wrong person for milk is easy to determine by the presence of marked symptoms. These symptoms are excessive mucus, indigestion, and a high degree of susceptibility to colds and sinus problems.

The Wrong Form

Right up through the early years of this century it was common for dairy cows to have tuberculosis. A related problem was that the methodologies of hygiene were poorly understood and developed. Pasteurization was developed to kill tuberculosis and other disease-causing bacteria. Pasteurization of milk is accomplished by heating the milk to 161°F for fifteen seconds (the most common method) or to 145°F for thirty minutes. Since either temperature is far below the boiling point, pasteurized milk can be thought of as half-boiled. This half-boiling leaves milk in a halfway state between raw and boiled milk which is harder to digest than either. Here is a probable explanation, offered by Dr. Rudolph Ballentine in *Diet and Nutrition*:

In large protein molecules, the amino acid chain is coiled or bent into limbs; these in turn fold upon each other in intricate but very important ways. The folding and coiling is maintained by relatively weak bonds between the amino acids. These bonds must be strong enough to hold the molecule's shape, but not so strong as to make it rigid, for the high protein molecules often depend for their function on the ability to change their shape. These delicate limbs which shift are very fragile, and heat can alter them. Then the shape of the molecule is changed and its ability to function is impaired. This is called denaturing the protein, i.e., its basic nature is disrupted. If too many of the weak bonds are broken, the complex molecule collapses into a broken tangle which may present great difficulties for the digestive enzymes, which are hard put to "get a handle on it" so as to break it down. In this case, further heating may, under some circumstances, complete the denaturation to the point of breaking it into shorter chains, or even down to single amino acid links, in which case digestion is actually facilitated. Something of this sort may happen with milk.

Experiments have shown that when milk is partially heated (pasteurized), it tends to coagulate into a tight mass when exposed to stomach acid. Many dairy farmers know from experience with their children that pasteurized milk constipates them whereas raw milk does not. If pasteurizing milk tangles the large and complex coils of the protein molecule, making them difficult to digest, boiling breaks it down more completely. Fifty years ago it was observed that children who were given milk that had been quickly brought to the boiling point and cooled were healthier and gained more weight than those taking pasteurized milk.

Pasteurization: an outmoded solution. Pasteurization is an outmoded solution to the problem of clean milk, a case where commercial interests heavily promote turn-of-the-century technology because they are convinced the public won't pay the price for good food. I disagree. I think people would pay the price if they knew the facts. The facts are that pasteurization causes

—loss of all the vitamin A
—loss of 6 percent of the calcium, while the rest is altered into a form that is more difficult to assimilate
—loss of 20 percent, or more, of the iodine
—loss of approximately 40 percent of the B vitamins
—loss of enzymes that make the milk more digestible and assimilable
—loss of an unidentified food factor responsible for promoting growth
—loss of most or all of the vitamin C
—reduction of protein biological value by 17 percent

(Figures obtained from The International College of Applied Nutrition and Alta Dena Dairy.)

But, people ask, how will we get milk that's clean enough to drink if we don't pasteurize? The technology is really simple and it starts on the farm. I've been on dairy farms that were incredibly sloppy—urine and feces and flies could splash into the milk, but it didn't matter because the dairy was going to pasteurize the milk anyway. In extreme contrast, I've visited Alta Dena Dairy, a producer of certified raw milk in California, which is so clean you could literally eat off the floor. The barnyard and feedlot are kept clean so that the cows come into the milking parlor clean. Their flanks, udders, and teats are washed and the milk is pumped through equipment which is kept scrupulously clean, untouched by anything that would contaminate it. The milk is held cold and promptly bottled to prevent the multiplication of undesirable bacteria. Fifty years ago we didn't have the technology to handle milk like this. There should be a term "drinking milk" and this is the way it should all be handled. The farmers producing this certified raw or drinking milk would be backed by equally efficient handling on the part of the dairies and be paid a premium for their care. Pasteurized milk would still be produced for making certain kinds of cheeses and for other manufacturing purposes.

Whereas fully boiled milk is more digestible than half-boiled (pasteurized) milk, clearly the most nutritious drinking milk is not heated at all. As it comes from the cow, milk contains a natural germicide; the secret from that point onward is to keep it clean and cold. Alta Dena has proved that raw milk can be produced successfully on a large scale. I expect that widespread consumer demand will eventually make certified raw milk much more widely available. When I was a teenager, I drank raw milk for two glorious summers working on a Vermont farm. Then I had to return to the city and pasteurized milk—from milk sweet and sparkling to milk dull and flat. When you are able to obtain it, you might discover that whereas pasteurized milk is not a good food for you, raw milk is. Until such time, I recommend quick boiling of pasteurized milk to improve its digestibility.

There are also differences between raw and pasteurized buttermilk. Raw buttermilk is the by-product of churning raw milk to make raw butter; pasteurized buttermilk is "cultured," meaning that a bacterial culture has been added to sour it. The souring process, because it uses up the lactose, makes cultured buttermilk more digestible than pasteurized milk; but again, raw buttermilk is more nutritious. Where pasteurized cream and pasteurized butter are concerned, they too have been denatured by heat and, if nothing else is different, the taste of raw cream and raw butter is decidedly superior. Most people also prefer the taste of raw milk cottage cheese, which has the same kind of nutritional advantages as raw milk.

Homogenized milk. The big advantage of homogenizing milk is that it saves us the work(?) of shaking the milk to disperse the cream. What an advance—just think of all the tired arms homogenization prevents. This wonder is achieved by breaking the fat globules into such tiny fragments that they can't regroup, therefore stay dispersed. The problem with this is that they also don't get properly acted upon by digestive secretions and pass through the intestinal walls unaltered. The bloodstream then has undigested milk fat to contend with—one more reason so many people are allergic to milk.

Research conducted by Dr. Kurt Oster, Chief of Cardiology at Park City Hospital, Bridgeport, Connecticut, explained why the tiny undigested fat fragments of homogenized milk pose a serious health problem. One element of milk is *xanthine oxidase* (XO), an enzyme that attacks heart arteries, leading to deterioration of heart function. Dr. Kurt Esselbacher, chairman of the Department of

Medicine at Harvard Medical School, agreed with Dr. Oster's findings, saying "Homogenized milk, because of its XO content, is one of the major causes of heart disease in the U.S." When milk is raw or merely pasteurized, leaving the fat globules their normal size, XO does not pass through the intestinal walls. Failing to reach the bloodstream, it is harmlessly excreted. (See *Healthview Newsletter no. 14*, "The Truth About Milk," an interview with Dr. William Ellis.) Like many "primitive" practices, shaking milk is much healthier. And it's really not terribly hard work.

Low-fat milk. Other undesirable forms of milk could well be nonfat and low-fat. These have become popular as we have become more conscious of fats in our diets. But there are more effective ways of reducing dietary fat. The problem created by reducing or eliminating the fat in milk is that the more fat you remove, the less calcium can be assimilated. The fat of milk—butterfat—is an integral element in the calcium metabolism of milk, a chief purpose for using milk as food. Milk is also intended to be a source of vitamins A and D, both fat-soluble vitamins. It is at least a little futile to add vitamin D to milk after removing the fat which would have carried it into the bloodstream, somewhat like putting gas in a car without wheels.

The current flap over cholesterol causes many people to shudder when they hear the word "butterfat." But for all but a very few, their fears are unfounded. The fat in milk has dozens of fatty acids, 26 percent of them *unsaturated*. Unsaturated or not, when these fatty acids are unaltered by heat, they perform vital functions in human nutrition. Writing in *Nutriton Against Disease*, Dr. Roger Williams informs us that butterfat *protects* us against atherosclerosis. African herdsmen tribes such as the Masai, Somalis, and Samburus, live on a milk and meat diet, with as much as 65 percent of their calories coming from *raw* butterfat. These tribesmen are virtually free of heart disease, as well as cancer, diabetes, and our other degenerative diseases. Dr. Williams also cites extensive studies showing that *nonfat* dry milk fed to rats produced atherosclerosis but full-fat milk did not.

Recently, Dr. George Mann of Vanderbilt University discovered that drinking whole milk actually *lowers* cholesterol in the blood (and fermented milk products such as yogurt and kefir lower it considerably more). Nobody has ever told me they preferred the taste of low-fat milk. As we come to appreciate more and more the wisdom of using our food in natural forms, low-fat milk will prove to be another of those fads that faded away. Reducing the fat reduces both food value and pleasure. Why do it?

Too Much Of It

Sometimes the symptoms of milk intolerance can be sufficiently alleviated simply by reducing the amount being consumed. Teenage boys, especially in hot weather, often drink a quart of milk at a sitting. Afterwards, they can't honk fast enough to keep their nasal passages clear. This overconsumption can be reduced by drinking a glsss of water before sitting down, so that milk isn't used to slake thirst. Milk is a food, not a beverage.

Another side-effect of overconsumption of milk is over-growth. Milk contains growth hormones intended for animals that usually weigh well over a thousand pounds. It also contains the calcium to support the stimulation provided by the hormones. Americans have become bigger people during this century, coinciding with the mass-marketing of milk made possible by pasteurization. Invariably, when the next generation assumes the American milk-consumption pattern, they outgrow their parents substantially. This growth is generally considered to be a good thing. But is it? There is more to strength than muscle and bone; another way of measuring strength is resistance to disease. Measured thus, growth stimulation sometimes produces weaker members of a species. For example, the runty varities of Indian corn withstand wind, drought and disease far better than the huge hybrid varieties. And, while 130 pounders are crossing the finishing lines of marathon races, 200 pounders are dropping from exhaustion miles behind. Bigger is not always better; in fact, sometimes smaller is greater. Our love affair with bigness produced cars that guzzle too much gas and gigantic oranges and apples that hardly taste like oranges and apples, two kinds of size-related weakness. Are our big milk-fed bodies unnaturally susceptible to degenerative disease because our defensive mechanisms haven't kept up with our bulk?

The milk issue is interesting from the perspective of the question, "Are all natural foods good for me?" It depends on who you are and how much of it. Milk, natural or not, might be bad for you, good for me. A pint a day might be too much for you, while a half pint is beneficial. A common recommendation regarding milk is a quart a day for children and adolescents, a pint for adults. But that's a poor generalization. No milk at all is the best quantity for some. If your kids' noses are always runny or stuffy and they get colds three or more times a year, try cutting back or eliminating milk. Where will they get their calcium? Here are some good sources of calcium, compared to milk:

Foods	Portion	Mg. of Calcium
Milk, cows'	1 cup	291
Yogurt, whole milk, plain	1 cup	274
Goats' milk	1 cup	326
Buttermilk	1 cup	285
Nonfat dry milk (1 cup to make 1 quart liquid)	1 cup	377
Dulse	3.5 ounces*	567
Hiziki (sea vegetable)	3.5 ounces	1400
Kelp	3.5 ounces	1100
Kombu (sea vegetable)	3.5 ounces	800
Wakame (sea vegetable)	3.5 ounces	1300
Nori (sea vegetable)	3.5 ounces	260
Agar-agar (sea vegetable gelatin)	3.5 ounces	400
Sockeye salmon, canned	3.5 ounces	259
Mackerel, canned	3.5 ounces	185
Almonds, raw	3.5 ounces	234
Filberts (hazelnuts)	3.5 ounces	209
Brazil nuts	3.5 ounces	186
Black-eyed peas, cooked	1 cup	270
Kale, cooked	1 cup	206
Mustard greens, cooked	1 cup	284

Foods	*Portion*	*Mg. of Calcium*
Turnip greens, cooked	1 cup	267
Dandelion greens, raw	3.5 ounces	187
Torula yeast	3.5 ounces	429
Mustard	1 Tbsp. (15 grams)	150
Cheese:		
Cheddar	1 oz. (28 grams)	211
Colby	1 oz. (28 grams)	194
Gouda	1 oz. (28 grams)	198
Gruyere	1 oz. (28 grams)	287
Monterey jack	1 oz. (28 grams)	212
Muenster	1 oz. (28 grams)	203
Parmesan	1 oz. (28 grams)	320
Provolone	1 oz. (28 grams)	214
Ricotta, part skim	1 cup	669
Swiss	1 oz.	272

*100 grams

Calcium is also available from such calcium supplements as bone meal, calcium lactate, calcium gluconate, and dolomite.

Goats' Milk

Those unable to tolerate cows' milk even when it's raw can usually get along with goats' milk. The milk of goats is intended for an infant goat, which usually weighs about the same as the average human baby. The fat and protein molecules are much smaller, so goats' milk is much easier to digest than cows' milk. The approximate time in the human digestive tract for cows' milk is two hours; for goats' milk it is twenty minutes. "But," people protest, "it smells and tastes goatty." That's true when it's more than a day old; if you can find a source of really fresh, raw goats' milk, you will find its taste and odor just as mild as cows' milk.

The Yogurt Alternative

The culturing of milk, as in yogurt, is an excellent way of improving the digestibility of pasteurized milk. In the case of yogurt, milk is actually transformed into an entirely different food. (For how to make yogurt, see page 304). The bacterial culturing agent consumes most of the lactose, which is, as we have noted, a major reason for intolerance to milk, particularly in adults. The bacteria also act on the milk protein, so that it becomes in effect predigested. The changes to the lactose and protein of milk in yogurt render it easily digestible, even to people unable to tolerate raw milk. Yogurt is so nourishing and digestible that it is an excellent food for invalids. *Kefir* is a cousin to yogurt, a liquid form with otherwise similar characteristics.

Commercial yogurt has various forms of gelatin and vegetable gums added for thickness; they all denature the yogurt whether they be gelatin, agar agar, or guar gum.

We are also seeing more and more fruited yogurts, whose sugar, artificial colors and flavors turn yogurt from a superior food into a dubious one. A common ruse with fruited yogurts is the phrase "no sugar added," which disguises the fact that the fruit preserves bought by the yogurt manufacturer to flavor his yogurt already had the sugar and corn syrup added by the fruit preserve manufacturer. The yogurt manufacturer might not have a grain of sugar on the premises; he really doesn't *add* any sugar, but his yogurt may still be loaded with it. You don't know whether or not you're getting sugar in your fruited yogurt unless the label specifies not just how the yogurt was sweetened but how the fruit was as well.

CHEESE

Cheese, being coagulated milk with most of the water (whey) removed, is a highly concentrated food, therefore doesn't provoke overconsumption as readily as milk. However, the same symptoms that arise from excessive milk-drinking arise from excessive cheese-eating. Similarly, many people find raw milk cheeses easier to digest than pasteurized. But raw-milk cheese is not lower in butterfat than pasteurized and should be eaten moderately. The more room given in your diet to grains and vegetables and the less to meat, the more room there is for the butterfat of cheese.

The natural color for cheese is white (like milk) or off-white. The yellow or orange colors associated with some of our popular cheeses are achieved with additives. Carotene or beta-carotene (*pro-vitamin A*, from which our bodies make vitamin A) is often used and this is not only harmless but may be beneficial. In other cases, artificial color, which should be avoided, is used.

Raw-Milk Cheese—Which Often Is Not

There is an imprecision regarding raw-milk cheese that leaves room for unscrupulous manufacturers to stretch the truth. We have seen that the pasteurization temperatures are 161°F for fifteen seconds or 145°F for thirty minutes. Unless milk reaches those temperatures, for those times, technically it is not pasteurized. It is at this point that we are vulnerable: when milk is technically

---

FROZEN YOGURT: SIMPLE OR SYMBOL?

In *The Book of Whole Foods*, Karen MacNeil points out that commercial frozen yogurt is not simply yogurt that has been frozen; it is, in most cases, merely a symbol of a natural food, related to yogurt in name only. The list of non-yogurt ingredients that may be found lurking in frozen yogurt mixes includes sugar, corn syrup, sodium citrate, polysorbate 80, vegetable gum, gelatin, carboxymethal cellulose, mono- and diglycerides, artificial flavors, and artificial colors. Were you looking for a healthy alternative to ice cream? There are a few decent quality frozen yogurt mixes. The conscientious owner of a frozen yogurt machine can be expected to post the ingredients of the yogurt mix being used; you certainly should know what you are eating, particularly if you are hoping that your treat is relatively pure. The word "yogurt" allows you to assume nothing: commercial frozen yogurt, particularly the thickest, creamiest versions, may not even have any live yogurt culture.

not pasteurized, the law allows it to be called "raw" for cheesemaking purposes, even if it has been heated to 160°F. And that is what your favorite "raw-milk" cheese maker may be doing.

The Sacramento Bee, Wednesday, February 24, 1982:

> Leland Lockhart, chief of the State Bureau of Milk and Dairy Foods Control told the *Bee* that state analyses of raw-milk cheeses over the past three months found that a "high percentage" hadn't been made with raw milk. He wouldn't speculate about how much of the raw-milk cheese might constitute misrepresentation. Lockhart said the state review of raw-milk cheese was prompted by complaints from retailers concerned that they might be misleading customers.

This situation is not unique to California. My inquiries lead me to believe that there may be as few as six manufacturers in the entire country making "raw-milk" cheese from genuine raw milk. The reason? By exploiting the weakness in the definition (and us), they can make a cheaper product.

It works like this: instead of using Grade A raw milk with a low bacteria count, they use Grade B manufacturers class milk, which is cheaper by perhaps ten cents a pound. The Grade B milk is then "heat treated" to reduce the bacteria count; some technologists refer to this as "underpasteurized" milk. Since it hasn't been pasteurized, it is "raw-milk" cheese by default, not because it qualifies as such. When such cheese is packaged, the packager usually protects himself with an ingredients list that reads something like, "Made from unpasteurized milk and . . .". Then he can defend himself by saying, "Raw milk is just part of the *name* of the cheese. We tell you that it is made from unpasteurized milk, which is true."

But that's cheating us. We're looking for cheese made from milk that hasn't had its protein denatured and its vitamins and enzymes altered or destroyed by high temperatures. Instead, we're usually getting cheese that can't possibly give us the nutritional value we have mistakenly assumed we're paying for. I saw figures from an independent California state-approved laboratory revealing that of ten brands of "raw milk" cheese tested, only one was made entirely of raw milk. Of the other nine, three had a small percentage of cheese varieties made of raw milk. The other six brands, representing more than thirty varieties of cheese, were all made from either pasteurized or heat-treated milk. Each of these boldly identified "raw milk" cheeses was a counterfeit.

When we buy raw milk cheese, the procedure should have gone approximately like this: The milk came from the cow at about 101.5°F. It was immediately chilled to 50°F or less and held at that temperature, to prevent the multiplication of bacteria, until it was dumped into the cheese vat. Then it was heated to 88–90°F to activate the starter, then to 99–103°F to separate the whey from the curd and to produce the proper moisture levels. Since certain amino acids are destroyed at 104°F, we know the milk was never heated above 103.5°F. We also know that certain types of cheese, like Swiss that needs to be heated to around 130°F for the starter to work, will never be called raw-milk cheese because that's impossible. We know exactly what we're getting because the regulations require that the manufacturer tell us; so we see statements such as this on the label: "This cheddar cheese is made from cultured Grade A raw milk and was not heated above 103.5°F during its manufacture." And "Aged sixty days" so that any stray coliform bacteria will have died. This may be fantasy now, but an informed public can pressure it into reality.

Rennet

Traditionally, rennet is the enzyme employed to coagulate milk for cheese. The traditional form of rennet is derived from calves' stomachs. It is both expensive and objectionable to some lacto-vegetarians. Hence, rennet is being replaced by a vegetable-derived enzyme, sometimes described by the misnomer "vegetable rennet." If it is rennet, it does not come from a vegetable source; what matters is to know what is meant by the term.

In Conclusion

Being associated so closely with infancy, childhood and adolescence, milk has more emotional reverberations than any other food. A critic of cows' milk as human food appears to some a more sinister figure than the big, bad wolf. Yet, milk is the most common of all food allergies; it may or may not be a healthy food. It should not be assumed that milk is *necessary*, even for children. The symptoms of milk intolerance are:

—excessive mucus
—susceptibility to colds and sinus problems
—indigestion accompanied by flatulence

The remedies for milk intolerance are:

—raw milk
—boiled milk
—yogurt, kefir, buttermilk
—reduced milk
—no milk

Protein and calcium are the chief nutritional features of milk, but the many alternatives for both should be considered by people who experience its negative aspects. Vegetarian and omnivarian diets can be exciting to the palate and more than adequate nutritionally with milk and dairy products occupying a minor niche. For most of us, total elimination of dairy products is not necessary, or even desirable, but it is certainly possible. There is no such thing as a sacred food, not even milk.

THE EGG BUSINESS

About ten years ago I had a business venture called the New Age Egg Ranch. My idea was to produce old-fashioned barnyard-quality eggs in commercial quantities. I began by finding a professional poultry man to manage the operation. What kind of birds would we raise? Our manager didn't know whether one kind of egg was really better than another, but he knew that the hens that laid brown eggs were bigger, ate more food, laid fewer eggs, and were stronger birds than the chickens that laid white eggs. Because we intended to keep our birds healthy by natural means, obviously stronger birds would be preferable, so we chose to produce brown eggs.

Next we considered how to raise our birds. To understand our choices it is helpful to have a mental outline of the modern egg factory farm—an outline is all that is really possible, because the reality is unimaginable. Picture a windowless building in which there are 30,000 hens, each in a cage. You might see a hen standing but you won't see her turning around—the cage isn't big enough for that. She's been de-beaked to prevent her from cannibalizing her neighbors. The lights never go off in her house so that there won't be any such thing as night, because hens don't lay eggs while they're sleeping. She lays on wire in a relentless light while medicated food and water pass by endlessly and her eggs roll away onto a conveyor belt as soon as she squeezes them out.

We bought 30,000 chicks and when they were old enough, we put them on the ground, walking here and there for food, roosting when the sun went down, laying their eggs in nests that had soft beds made of rice hulls. The objective wasn't to see how humane we could be to chickens; rather, humane treatment allowed them to live robustly, and made the commercial practice of medicating their feed with antibiotics unnecessary.

Where chicken feed was concerned, once again what we didn't do was as important as what we did. Antibiotics weren't the only thing we didn't feed our hens: we also didn't feed them arsenic compounds, or any other stimulants; slaughterhouse by-products; synthetic vitamins; chemical preservatives; hormones; phosphates; chemical dyes. What we did feed them was soy beans and corn meal fortified with wheat germ, bone meal, kelp, and cod liver oil; we also recycled waste greens back from our stores and our wholesale produce business. Laboratory analysis showed that our green feeding program yielded eggs with three or four times the vitamin A content as ordinary commercial eggs. The birds thrived; they were vigorous; their feathers had a lustrous sheen. We had visiting hours Tuesday and Thursday afternoons so that people could see what a beautiful flock we had.

When you saw our flock, you saw roosters as well as hens—in fact, one rooster for every ten hens. We regularly tested our eggs for fertility and they always checked out well over 90 percent fertile. Fertile eggs contain growth and reproductive hormones and steroids beneficial to nerves and glands, none of which are found in sterile eggs.

At the New Age Egg Ranch we had a healthy flock of chickens that produced the quality of product we were after: success, but only a very partial success because we failed the ultimate test. We failed to make a profit. In fact, the only way we could sell our eggs was at a loss; the retail price was twice as high as it was for ordinary commercial eggs. That quality on that scale is being done successfully now; there are enough people willing to pay the price of good eggs. We were ahead of the times and behind on market research—expensive lessons.

But Are Eggs A Good Food?

The amino acid pattern of eggs is so well proportioned that they are a reference point for judging the quality of protein in other foods. They are particularly high in methionine, an amino acid in which grains are low. They are a good source of vitamin A and one of the few food sources of vitamin D. Eggs are also a rich source of B vitamins and of highly assimilable minerals. Of particular interest in eggs are the strong presence of inositol, choline, and lecithin, all involved in balanced cholesterol metabolism.

The membrane next to the shell of the egg contains *avidin,* an enzyme which interferes with the biotin in the egg, essential for proper cholesterol metabolism. Avidin can be neutralized simply by soaking the egg in hot water (140°–160°F) for five minutes, after which it can be eaten raw. All the usual methods of cooking also neutralize avidin, but the less the egg is cooked, the more valuable it is nutritionally. Frying an egg to the hardness of a tire patch not only destroys amino acids but makes the protein difficult to assimilate.

It is the cholesterol content of eggs that has made them controversial. Some researchers say their studies show that eating eggs does not raise blood cholesterol levels; others say the opposite. We can only conclude that the contradictory evidence must allow the battle to rage on. And if we apply a little logic, we will become disinterested in which side wins the argument. It is illogical to believe that any food that has been an important part of human nutrition for centuries suddenly, in this century, began to cause people to have heart attacks, unless it might have some relationship to a drastic change in the *quality* of eggs.

When care is taken to produce eggs whose quality is as good as the eggs our great-grandparents ate, the answer to the question of whether or not eggs are a good food is "yes." In spite of cholesterol? Yes, providing the quantity is reasonable—two a day as a reasonable upper limit. In a February, 1972, letter to *Chemical and Engineering News*, Dr. C.W. Carlson, professor of animal science at South Dakota State University, pointed out that for a cholesterol-*reducing* diet, many physicians recommend an egg a day. In *Vitamin C and the Common Cold*, Dr. Linus Pauling called the idea that heart disease could be controlled by not eating foods such as eggs "oversimplified" and "dangerous." Remember that any good food can become a liability if consumed excessively. It is possible that eating cholesterol may have nothing at all to do with heart and circulatory problems (See page 70).

The Good Egg

Good eggs come from chickens that have freedom, fresh air, daylight and darkness, and are fed only pure natural foods.

Good eggs are fresh, indicated by the grade: AA (Fresh Fancy), A, and B, with B the oldest. Freshness in eggs is critical because eggshell is permeable—fluid can evaporate out and the air and bacteria responsible for rotting can get in. Refrigeration helps to maintain freshness, but freshness is poorly simulated in cold storage, where eggs are kept for six months or more by dipping them in a liquid plastic sealing compound to prevent the white from shrinking. A shrinking white means the egg is losing weight as moisture leaves through the shell, and eggs are sold by weight:

Sizes	Ounces (Doz.)
Jumbo	30
Extra Large	27
Large	24
Medium	21
Small	18
Peewee	15

Theoretically, you could have peewee eggs in a jumbo carton as long as the dozen weighed 30 ounces. Size tells you nothing about quality.

Good eggs will have dark yellow yolks, almost orange. But the deep color will not be achieved by putting dye in the chicken feed, a common commercial practice. The shell of a good egg will be thick and strong, a little bit hard to crack. The white will be thick, not runny. And the yolk will set up in a high mound without flattening out.

Good eggs will be fertile and described as "natural" or "naturally produced" or a similar term. There should be at least a brief explanation of the methods used so you know why the eggs deserve to be called natural. They should not be called "organic" unless everything they were fed was organically grown, which is highly unlikely, nearly impossible.

If you can find such eggs, consider yourself fortunate. They will cost more money, but natural eggs are worth more money. Factory farm eggs are an example of how the effort to produce cheap food can turn ugly, no matter what the original intention.

6 Most Controversial of All—Fats!

CHOLESTEROLPHOBIA

The controversy surrounding fat is related to cholesterol and the notion that eating fat/cholesterol causes plaque which leads to heart attacks and strokes. A Ph.D. biochemist published a book in 1977 which attacked this theory, issuing the following challenge on the book's cover: "No one has ever shown that eating cholesterol causes heart disease. If anyone can step forward and prove that eating cholesterol causes heart disease, I will donate all the proceeds from this book to the American Heart Association." The author is Richard Passwater, the book *Supernutrition for a Healthy Heart*, and six years later the American Heart Association is still not collecting his royalties, despite their fear of cholesterol.

Dr. Passwater calls fear of cholesterol needless and unfounded, "the worst form of food faddism." He has coined a word for it, "cholesterolphobia," which he believes has its genesis in blatant commercialism designed to create a market for manufactured nonfoods such as margarines and other dairy substitutes, egg and meat substitutes. David Reuben, M.D., in his book *Everything You Always Wanted to Know About Nutrition*, calls the cholesterol flap "the greatest swindle in the history of nutrition." To Dr. George Mann, of the Vanderbilt University School of Medicine, fear of cholesterol is "the nutritional disaster of the century" foisted on us by "food companies that employ cholesterol-scare tactics in their advertising."

We got swindled and caught cholesterolphobia because cholesterol is a major constituent of the plaque that causes heart attacks and strokes. The picture we got was of excess, fat-laden cholesterol getting stuck on the walls of our arteries, attracting more and more cholesterol, becoming bigger and bigger piles of plaque, finally breaking off, and, if we were one of the unlucky, causing a heart attack or stroke. To prevent this scenario from being enacted, the commercial juggernaut has created an obsession that is supposed to be a counterbalancing force: *polyunsaturates.**

There are reams of data from studies of rats, rabbits, pigs, and dogs which purport to prove that cholesterol is a problem and polyunsaturates are the solution. But we are not laboratory animals and if you look at people, the evidence begins to look quite unconvincing. A fine example is the contrast between the Indians of Northern Udaipur and Southern Madras. The northerners eat over fifteen *times* more saturated fats, yet have fifteen times *less* heart disease. (*Nutrition Against Disease*, Williams, Bantam Books).

The food industry has capitalized on shallow and dubious scientism and created a flood of oily propaganda. Tiny voices—like those of Williams, Passwater, Mann, and Reuben—have been raised

---

*For a description of fatty acid structure, see page 73.

70

against the tidal wave of polyunsaturated products, but their voices have been drowned. For the sake of your personal and our national health, we cannot allow their protests to go unheeded. The core of their message is this: the increase in American fat consumption during the twentieth century, which corresponds to the enormous increase of heart attacks and strokes, has been primarily an increase of eating *polyunsaturates.* In the twenty years from 1950 to 1970, American polyunsaturate use tripled, from 2 percent to 6 percent of our diet (National Heart and Lung Institute).

Plaque is not debris catching on the walls of our arteries, like rust piling up inside a pipe. The walls of our arteries are constructed of four sheaths wrapped around each other like the layers making up the walls of a tire. Before there is any plaque, there is an eruption within the arterial walls, causing a bulge. The bulge contains cholesterol and the lesion that builds up on top of the bulge contains cholesterol. Does that mean the root of the problem is cholesterol?

The ooze from a boil contains a lot of white blood cells, but a boil is not a matter of too many white blood cells. Their presence is symptomatic of a more profound problem. Likewise, accumulated cholesterol is just a symptom. First there was some kind of metabolic aberration within the arterial wall, then there was a bulge, then there was a lesion of accumulated plaque.

The liver manufacturers up to a cup of cholesterol a day. Realizing that, most Americans would wish for an *off* switch, so much bad publicity has cholesterol received. But let's not assume we have been badly designed; let's assume our designer had a perfect plan and try to move as close as we can to an understanding of cholesterol.

If you don't eat cholesterol, your body will produce it; if you eat it, your production of it will slow down. Therefore, over long periods of time, eating polyunsaturates doesn't permanently reduce the amount of cholesterol in your blood. Furthermore, many people have extremely high levels of cholesterol compared to others and are none the worse for it.

You can think of cholesterol as being analogous to a good coat of wax on your car: the wax protects your car's paint with a coating that causes air and water to flow across the surface without damaging the paint. But the wax itself is constantly being eroded and so it should be replaced periodically. Cholesterol is a yellow-white hydrocarbon (as wax is a hydrocarbon) with an oily surface. It gives a protective coating to the membranes of all our cells so that fluids such as blood flowing over the surface will not erode them. Cholesterol is the wax of our innards, and, like car wax, gradually wears off and needs to be periodically replaced.

It is also a constituent of the sheaths that protect our nerve fibers, a constituent of our hormones, of vitamin D, and of bile. Dr. Reuben, in his acidly satiric manner, suggests that if food manufacturers had spotted cholesterol as a potential money maker, we would be paying a high price, victims of an ad campaign touting it as a solution for all our problems including sex. But the profit potential is poor, because you can hardly contrive to be deficient in cholesterol. Your liver is wisely churning it out and so vital is it that each individual cell also contributes to cholesterol production for its own needs. At this cellular level of cholesterol production within arterial walls the metabolic derangement that causes the bulge occurs, according to Dr. Earl Benditt, who has done extensive research at the University of Washington School of Medicine.

Even more recent research has been focusing on the material responsible for transporting cholesterol, called lipoproteins—literally "fatty proteins." It has been discovered that cholesterol travels in the bloodstream by latching on piggyback style to protein molecules. You will probably be hearing more and more about good lipoproteins (HDLs, for high-density lipoproteins) and bad lipoproteins (LDLs and VLDLs, for low- and very low-density). It seems that the HDLs actually protect against the formation of plaque, while the LDLs and VLDLs are associated with plaque formation. Therefore, it is not total cholesterol levels that are scrutinized, but the proportion of HDL to LDL. "You cannot generalize about cholesterol," says Neil Solomon in *High Health Diet & Exercise Plan.* "Different kinds of cholesterol must be distinguished between, because they act in very different ways: one kind does good and another does harm." The lipoproteins are no doubt an element in the cholesterol picture. But we should not stop trying to see the whole picture because we have seen a part of it. It is likely that there are not only good and bad lipoproteins but good and bad cholesterol. More than fifteen years ago Dr. Henry Bieler proposed in *Food Is Your Best Medicine* that one kind of bad cholesterol is made by our liver, turning out bad because we give our liver bad raw materials to work with. Dr. Bieler's findings deserve our consideration because they illustrate a principle we have all been able to observe in life: *the quality of a product depends on the quality of the raw materials it is made from* (and, of course, the quality of the workmanship).

Dr. Bieler maintained that as long as fats and oils are in their natural state, they do not lead to arterial disease. Eating natural fats, whether they be saturated animal fats or unsaturated vegetable fats, provides the liver with the high-quality raw materials it needs to manufacture good cholesterol. Studies of primitive peoples with diets high in natural animal fats (Eskimos, Masai) and high in natural vegetable fats (Italian and Greek peasants) have revealed virtually no arterial disease. The trouble arises, said Dr. Bieler, only from ingesting unnatural fats and natural fats which have been overheated. Unnatural fats or natural fats that have been overheated provide bad raw materials and badly made cholesterol is the inevitable result.

Dr. Bieler's further observation is that the worst harm is done by fats that have been overheated in combination with starch, no matter whether the fat is natural or not, animal or vegetable. What are under attack here are foods like deep fried foods, pastries, and snack foods such as potato chips. It is impossible for the liver to upgrade the quality of this stuff; it can only go ahead with cholesterol manufacturing to the best of its ability, making through no fault of its own the worst possible grade of cholesterol. This shoddy cholesterol has characteristics we are familiar with in other low-grade products: it doesn't last as long as it should, corrodes easily, and therefore sloughs off.

If Dr. Bieler is right, and I believe he is, we have a vital clue to the metabolic derangement behind the fat/cholesterol/ lipoprotein symptoms. Poor-quality raw materials not only produce shoddy cholesterol, they are a strain on the cholesterol-producing machinery itself. In time, the quality of the workmanship begins to break down too. A protective coating of cholesterol is most critical where blood rushes unceasingly every moment of our lives; a production crisis is reached, arterial cells can no longer cope with the stress, and they erupt. The eruption is like the bulge in a weakened tire wall; a lesion begins.

The peoples who have eaten high-fat diets and been immune from the problems we associate with fat have been different from us in this respect: they have eaten natural fats. Most of the fat they have eaten has been wrapped in the protective structures of grains, beans, seeds, nuts, fish, milk, eggs, or meat. Whatever extracted fat they have used has been produced at low temperatures. Fat, in natural, forms, has been their friend.

OPPOSING THE POLYUNSATURATE DOGMA

Conventional wisdom has been that if you up polyunsaturates, cholesterol will come down. The more recent version is that if you up polyunsaturates, LDL levels will go down and HDL levels will go up. And as Ross Hume Hall points out in *Food for Nought*, "All research out of line with the official dogma is thrown away or discredited."

Yet, "when we study the effects of a primitive diet in almost every civilization on this planet, we find that there are no heart attacks. They occur only when the time-tested native diet, whatever its particular form, is replaced by a diet more suitable to mass production, ease of distribution, and shelf life than to the needs of the human body" (Richard Kunin, M.D., in *Mega-Nutrition*).

And, "in its enthusiasm to switch from animal fats to vegetable oils, the orthodoxy has failed to note that polyunsaturates are chock-full of free radicals which may hasten the aging and degeneration processes and increase our requirements for vitamin E" (Robert Atkins, M.D., in *Dr. Atkins's Nutrition Breakthrough*).

While, "Over the last twenty years, people have trimmed fats from their meat, eaten less fried foods, and consumed more polyunsaturated fats than ever. Dietary fat has been reduced by nearly one-third of what it was. Our intake of polyunsaturated fat is at an all-time high . . . Yet, heart disease increases, in epidemic proportions" (Richard Passwater, Ph.D., in *Supernutrition*).

It is usually difficult to wrench one's self away from belief in dogma. But the polyunsaturate dogma is worth the effort because it is not working. In opposition to the dogma, what the words quoted above suggest is this: It is not the *kind* of dietary fat—saturated or unsaturated, animal or vegetable—that is truly significant, but the *quality* of the fat.

We, in contrast, particularly during the last forty years, have been eating more and more solvent-extracted vegetable oil, more and more oil that gets hydrogenated after extraction. Pick up food products in your local supermarket and see how ubiquitous the terms "vegetable oil," "vegetable shortening," and "hydrogenated" are. These words sound innocent enough; but a look behind the bland facade shows you why most of that vegetable fat has been turned from friend to foe.

Polyunsaturates

There are three types of fatty acids. We can understand them by picturing them as looking like microscopic clusters of grapes. An *unsaturated* cluster has no grapes missing, a *monosaturated* cluster has a couple of grapes missing, and a *polyunsaturated* cluster has twice as many missing grapes. The grapes represent atoms of hydrogen; we will see the significance of the missing grapes below.

To be good for you, we are being told these days, oil just needs to be polyunsaturated. This is not true. As with most of everything else, there is vegetable oil and there is vegetable oil. Dr. Williams points out in *Nutrition Against Disease* that vegetable oils can promote good health *if* such vital nutrients as vitamin E and lecithin have not been removed by refining. Yes, another version of the same story: refining vegetable oil is exactly analogous to refining wheat or sugar cane—the end result falls somewhere in the range between devitalized and dangerous. Just as the bran and germ are removed when wheat is refined, refining oil removes waxes, resins, stearines, and phosphatides.

When they are eliminated, chlorophyll, lecithin, pro-vitamin A, vitamin E, copper, iron, magnesium, calcium, and phosphorus all disappear. The industrial oil technician sees these nutrients as "impurities," largely because he doesn't think of vegetable oil as food but as grease. He doesn't want impurities in his grease because the product the public has been propagandized into accepting is bland, virtually free of color, odor and flavor.

The absence of color, odor, and flavor should serve us as primary warning signals. We have senses of sight, smell, and taste to help us recognize what is good to eat. And this oil has nothing we can respond to because its molecules have been profoundly and irreparably damaged. To understand how the damage is inflicted, look at how oil-bearing materials are treated:

Most of the oil is usually pressed out mechanically, then solvent is added to the leftover meal to extract the remaining oil. At some refineries, the mechanical step is eliminated and solvent alone is used. Hexane is the solvent used most frequently; benzene, ethyl ether, carbon disulphide, carbon tetrachloride, methylene chloride, and gasoline could also do the job. The solvent frees the oil, then the solvent and oil are boiled to drive off the solvent, leaving extracted oil. (Oil processors, when asked how much solvent residue remains in the oil, have answered, "Very little," meaning up to 100 ppm. These solvent residues are proven or suspected carcinogens.)

Next comes the massive assault against impurities: color and flavor are whipped with lye first, then caustic soda, then filtration. Then all but the faintest whiff of odor is removed by heating it at temperatures in the range of 400°F for twelve hours. Before bottling this bedraggled and woebegone grease, a preservative like BHA, BHT, or propyl gallate is usually added. You will understand why the preservative is necessary when I explain unrefined oils a few pages along.

When I learned how oil molecules were brutalized by processing, I wondered if perhaps it were not even more dangerous than white sugar. I'm still wondering, but we don't need to know which is worse. We know enough to appreciate why Dr. Williams concluded that commercial polyunsaturated vegetable oils are dangerous and "should be avoided by the consumer." Dr. Passwater agrees, citing these possible dangers connected to a diet high in refined polyunsaturated oil: iron-deficiency anemia, weight gain, liver disease, intestinal damage, hypertension, abnormal waxy deposits, gallstones, raised levels of uric acid in the blood, and the promotion of the release of *free radicals*, which accelerate aging, and cause cancer and mutation.

Free radicals are a rare case of a chemical term being almost poetically literal. The name connotes a sort of renegade gang roaming around the body with nothing to do, spoiling for action, preferably violent and destructive action. They play no positive role in human metabolism and Dr. Passwater believes they are responsible for the arterial eruptions of atherosclerosis. They may even be a factor in the two varieties of cellular aberration, atherosclerosis and cancer, though it is not acknowledged that they have anything in common.

Hydrogenation

It is commonly assumed that the term "plastic food" is figurative language and so it is, when broadly used to describe highly processed, industrialized food. Plastic food can, however, be quite literal in one particular instance. The term was actually coined to describe hydrogenated vegetable oil. Hydrogenation is a next step after refining in which hydrogen gas is introduced to the liquid oil in the presence of a metallic catalyst, usually nickel or cadmium. This succeeds in bonding hydrogen ions onto the oil molecules, saturating them, transforming them from a liquid to a solid. "Plastic" is an accurate description for hydrogenated oil because when you examine its molecular structure under a microscope, plastic is what it looks like.

There are a couple of problems attached to eating this stuff. The first is that it is what it looks like—plastic. Not food. I once conducted an experiment because I suspected margarine, whose main ingredient is hydrogenated oil, is not really food. I placed a cube of margarine on a saucer on a windowsill that caught afternoon sun. I knew what would happen if it were butter: the heat of the sun through the glass would melt it down, it would begin to stink, mold would grow, bugs would find it—it would be an ugly mess until the forces of nature could manage to draw all the life from it. If margarine is really food, I reasoned, it will get attacked in the same way.

Two years later I gave up waiting for anything alive to attack that margarine. It had only about half melted in all that time, it was quite dusty, but no stink, no mold, no bugs, *no sign of life.* Long before I officially terminated the experiment I stopped selling margarine because I was in the *food* business. "Good" margarine is really a contradiction in terms.

The other problem connected with hydrogenated oil is that it gives manufacturers another opportunity to swindle us. HIGH IN POLYUNSATURATES says one label, HIGHEST IN UNSATURATES answers another. But read their labels and you see that they are both made from some kind of hydrogenated oil and you have just learned that hydrogenation is a saturation process. Translation: the oil was high in polyunsaturates before we hydrogenated it so we could make margarine from it . . . heh-heh, uh, sorry. . . .

Continuing in their spirit of duplicity, both labels blithely say CONTAINS NO CHOLESTEROL. Right, and the night sky does not contain the sun. Axle grease does not contain cholesterol either.

"But," people protest, "you're saying butter is better than margarine." That's right. Butter is saturated and has cholesterol. But it is food. And it tastes good. And it is not a shameless boondoggle, which margarine is for even posing as food.

Partially Hydrogenated or *Specially Processed* vegetable oil: synonyms for oil that is only partially saturated—liquid plastic instead of solid. This is the choice when the manufacturer wants a shortening that will liquify quickly. Do you want to prevent rancidity, spattering, and foaming? Simple: add propyl gallate, methyl silicone, and citric acid. You name the problem, there is an additive for it.

Vegetable Shortening is another term that misleads almost everybody. It is often headlined on food packages—CONTAINS VEGETABLE SHORTENING—expecting that we will assume it is a polyunsaturated improvement over lard, which is an animal fat. But in fact it may be even worse. Like margarine, vegetable shortening is an artificially saturated fat made from refined oil. The difference between them is that margarine is imitation butter, while vegetable shortening is imitation lard. It is a little simpler to imitate lard; you don't, for example, need to color it yellow. As usual, however, the real is preferable to the ersatz; at least lard is real food and nobody is making false claims about it.

THE ALTERNATIVES

Cold Pressed

There are vegetable oils in health food stores, in some natural food stores and a few supermarkets labeled "cold pressed" in different varieties such as corn, peanut, safflower, avocado, walnut—as many as a dozen varieties, some commonplace, some exotic. They are all virtually the same color and if you were blindfolded you wouldn't be able to tell one from another by odor and taste. They are just about as tasteless as the familiar nationally advertised bland brands. The words "cold pressed" are meaningless to us in our search for good oil. A friend of mine, Paul Hawken, tells an interesting anecdote regarding that term as used by a certain "health-food" company:

> I once met the owner-representative of one of these large companies and asked him what was meant by the term "cold-pressed" that appeared on his labels. He answered that "It means nothing at all," and that it was put there because his biggest competitor also called his oil "cold-pressed." Shocked, because I had been selling his products in my store, I asked how he could do such a thing. He said that in a way it did mean something because, after all, the oils were cold processed—that is, chilled and filtered; and were processed and extracted. Some, he said, were solvent extracted, and all were chemically refined. I asked him why he was telling me all this, since it was so damaging to his reputation. He said that it wasn't all that damaging because he had worked for his competitor for several years and they bought their oil from the same sources.

This flagrant misuse of the term is possible because there is no legal definition of cold-pressed. If the term were to become widely popular, there would be nothing to stop the big name bland brands from grabbing it. Soon all oils would be "cold-pressed" just as everything these days from beer to shampoo is "natural." But "cold-pressed" is pure deception; on a commercial scale it *couldn't* be true, as I will soon explain. Offered as alternatives to mass-merchandised refined oils, they are not—they also are refined.

Unrefined Oils

As we saw above, it is common for oil manufacturers to extract most of it mechanically, the balance with solvent. Next, they usually mix the two types of oil before refining. This has afforded a few small natural foods manufacturers an opportunity to interrupt the procedure, buying the mechanically extracted oil before it gets mixed with the solvent-extracted oil and refined.

The machinery is variously called an "expeller," "auger," or "screw" press, expeller being most common. There are no legal definitions for this mechanically extracted oil, resulting in labeling imprecision. However, the terminology that indicates a genuine alternative to refined oil includes the words *pressed* or *expeller-pressed,* accompanied by the statement *no preservatives.* The words "crude" or "unrefined" can describe a mixture of pressed and solvent-extracted oil, and therefore do not guarantee the pure alternative. The clearest labeling says something like "Unrefined Corn Oil—100% expeller pressed."

Unrefined, pressed oil is dark in color, sediment will accumulate on the bottom of the bottle, and the odors and flavors will be strong and distinctive. Each type will be easy to distinguish from the others, for those infamous "impurities" have been saved.

Rancidity

A rancid oil is one which has been acted on by oxygen. Oxidation leads to the formation of free radicals, whose damaging effects were noted earlier. Vitamin E, present in unrefined oil, prevents both oxidation and the formation of free radicals. Vitamin E and other natural antioxidants are in unrefined oil simply because they have not been subjected to mistreatment with lye, caustic soda, and filtration. The lecithin, chlorophyll, minerals, and pro-vitamin A are still there too. Like whole wheat flour, it is better because of what is *not* done to it.

Unrefined oils will keep for six months or longer at 65°F, even longer at lower temperatures. Rancid oil has an unmistakable bitter, biting flavor and aroma: the smell is rank and the taste will curl your tongue.

Your senses, however, will probably not be able to detect the slighter degrees of rancidity and you should take precautions to deter the process. Heat encourages rancidity, so keep your unrefined oil cold before and after opening. Light accelerates rancidity, so keep it dark. Unfortunately, most of the bottlers of unrefined oils use clear bottles; perhaps we can persuade them to use dark glass, even though that will hide the different shades of the oils. Once the oil is in the dark of your refrigerator you have the best conditions for preventing rancidity.

The potential for rancidity is also related to the amount of unsaturated fat naturally found in the oil. To understand this you need to return to our model of fatty acids looking like clusters of grapes. The grapes represent hydrogen and the missing grapes represent places where oxygen can move in to replace hydrogen. It is oxygen that causes rancidity. Therefore, unsaturated fatty acids are quite unstable and polyunsaturated fatty acids are quite volatile.

For this reason, the amount of polyunsaturated fat in an oil is not a good measure of its desirability. Safflower oil, touted so highly because it is the highest in polyunsaturates, is really the least desirable because it is the hardest to keep fresh. Dr. Ballentine confirms this in *Diet and Nutrition*, telling us that in ancient India they systematically classified oils according to their effects and found that safflower oil was excessively irritating.

Another factor often mentioned as affecting the stability of vegetable oils is the heat used to extract them. High heat affects the molecular structure, denaturing it, making it more unstable, more prone to oxidation. The question here is, how high is high heat? My research indicates these probabilities: the molecular structures begins to break down at around 200°F and once the temperature passes around 400°F, it is complete. The smoking point—that point at which the oil gives off thin, bluish smoke—probably indicates the point of no return, but that point is not reached in pressing, only in restaurants and at home when cooking *too hot*.

Pressing temperatures in a range between 105°F and 230°F are reached due to the intense pressure and the steam-jacketed pipes used to speed the flow of oil from the mash. The higher the pressure, the more oil is extracted, and the higher goes the temperature. But it is impossible to say what oils are produced at what temperatures—different producers follow somewhat different procedures, and the same producer will vary somewhat from one week, month, or season, to another. An oil technician I interviewed on this subject said that about 170°F would be a reasonable average production temperature for all expeller-pressed oils, saying there is no incentive to go for high extraction rates, since they will get the oil missed by the press with solvents. You can assume, generally speaking, that expeller-pressed oils have not had their stability impaired by pressing temperatures.

At some refineries, oil-bearing material is cooked before it is pressed. Temperatures may go over 200°F, but once again, there is considerable variation for reasons similar to the factors that influence pressing temperatures. You can assume, however, that sesame and olive oils are not cooked before pressing (see below).

Using Unrefined Oils

A big problem with unrefined oils is that people are unaccustomed to them. The rich aromas and flavors can be a bit overwhelming when all you've ever experienced is blandness. It is important to remember that color, aroma, and flavor are inseparable and that these qualities are inseparable from food value. Not just oil, but all types of food are aromatic and flavorful because those qualities are imparted by *nutrients*. When you become accustomed to them, they taste delicious because they are nutritious. The descriptions that follow are of seven oils, the only ones to be found unrefined in commercial quantities.

CHARACTERISTICS AND USES OF UNREFINED OILS

Light in color, aroma, and flavor:		*Stability*
Safflower	versatile—cooking, baking, salads	poor
Sesame	versatile—cooking, baking, salads	excellent
Medium in color, aroma, and flavor:		
Corn	Baking, salads	good
Peanut	Frying, salads	good
Sunflower	Baking, sautéing, salads	good
Dark in color; heavy aroma, and flavor:		
Soy	Baking	poor
Olive*	Salads, sauces, and sautéing	excellent

*There is quite a lot of variation and confusion regarding olive oil. This is due to the general misuse of the word "virgin," another term with no legal definition. The term originated when small-scale hydraulic pressing was the only extraction method in use and referred to the first pressing, that which came most easily. This first, or virgin, pressing was darker and more aromatic and flavorful than subsequent pressings (which were sometimes aided by heat), therefore most desirable. You have probably never had real virgin olive oil where the word used on the bottle or can was "pure." Pure olive oil may have some virgin mixed in to improve flavor (5 percent to 20 percent), but otherwise can be second pressings extracted at high temperature, perhaps even solvent-extracted.

Virgin olive oil comes in three grades of quality:
First—"extra virgin"
Second—"fine virgin"
Third—"virgin"
The higher the grade, the better the flavor and aroma, the lower the acidity.

Olive oil and sesame oil are really the only two kinds that could *be* cold pressed on any sort of commercial scale. They are the only oily substances that will yield their oil by simple, low-intensity pressure, as could be accomplished at home with a hand-operated hydraulic press. Olive and sesame are the oils of antiquity. All the other vegetable oils have appeared in the marketplace during this century, riding the waves of the industrial revolution. Olive and sesame oils have low polyunsaturated values, making them stable. The ancient Indians rated sesame oil the most stable; this has been underscored by the modern discovery of its unique antioxidant, *sesamol.* Expeller-pressed sesame oil is the premier vegetable oil choice for all cooking purposes.

How Much Unrefined Oil?

People who select food according to some scary advice about fat are quite likely to wind up with an unbalanced diet that fails to meet their needs. We are establishing guidelines which say, in effect:

A SURPRISE ALTERNATIVE

It is known by three names: ghee (the Indian name), clarified butter, or butter oil.

Ghee (pronounced with a hard g, as in great) has many virtues. Made from sweet butter, which has a very low melting point, it is produced at a very low temperature. It is extremely stable, at least the equal of sesame oil in this respect, having 30 percent polyunsaturated fat compared to sesame oil's 44 percent. It has a way of enhancing food flavors as no vegetable oil can, and, as Dr. Roger Williams has pointed out, butterfat has a mysterious ability to protect against atherosclerosis. Perhaps best of all, you can easily make it yourself at home in small quantities without special equipment. Here is how you do it:

Bring a pound of sweet butter to the boil, then lower the heat to simmer. The white foam is a combination of water and milk solids boiling out of the butterfat, and must be skimmed off. Some of the milk solids will also sink to the bottom as the water that holds them is driven off. The sinking milk solids should be allowed to accumulate undisturbed, turning a golden brown. If the heat is too high, they will scorch, ruining the flavor of the ghee.

The sound of boiling changes to the hissing sound of frying when all the water has evaporated and the bubbling has stopped (about 20 minutes). The ghee should now be removed from the burner. Let the ghee cool, then pour it off, leaving the sediment behind. Stored in a covered container that keeps light out—a small, crock, for example—it will not get rancid and need not be refrigerated. *Yield:* about 1¾ c. (Thanks to *Diet and Nutrition,* Dr. Ballentine, for the lesson.)

The method for making clarified butter, quite common to French cooking, is somewhat different. "Melt any desired amount of unsalted butter slowly over low heat in a saucepan. When the last of the butter is melted, remove from the heat and carefully skim off the foam with a spoon. Strain the pure yellow oil through a fine sieve into a container, being certain to leave all the milky residue in the bottom of the pan." (Thanks to the *Judith Ets-Hokin Culinary Institute* of San Francisco for the lesson.)

don't allow your diet to be dominated by fatty foods, then just let the fats fall where they may. Don't avoid raw dairy products and fertile eggs because of bad advice about cholesterol and fat. Eat them if you like them, in moderation, as part of a balanced diet.

The amount of vitamin F (essential fatty acids) needed daily is roughly the amount to be found in a tablespoon of sesame oil. When the staple foods of your diet are whole grains supplemented by the other rich sources of unsaturated fat, that tablespoon shrinks to a teaspoon or less for most people. Almost every American on refined and devitalized foods tests deficient in vitamin F, while showing excess dietary fat. The solution to that problem is more whole natural foods, not big doses of vegetable oil.

The parts of food we remove from the whole form become more volatile because we have removed them from complex relationships that anchored them. We do not find butter, or lard, or vegetable oils in nature. They are not whole foods, but food fractions produced by man. The rule of thumb in answering the *how much* question about any food fraction is almost always *very little.* The corollary to that rule is that we should obtain most of the fractions as part of the whole: our fats should come wrapped in the protective structures of grains, beans, seeds, nuts, fish, milk, eggs, and meat.

7 To: Pregnant and Nursing Women; Teenagers; The Middle-aged and Elderly; Athletes

PREGNANCY AND LACTATION

"You don't have to worry about the fetus," I have often heard people say. "It always obtains the nutrition it needs." According to this theory, Mother Nature protects fetuses, insuring that they don't suffer nutritional diseases, whether the mother likes it or not. The way it supposedly works is that if the mother is eating a deficient diet, the fetus will draw what it needs from the mother's organs and bones. If this were true, there would never be any such thing as diet-related birth defects. But there *are* diet-related birth defects (*Nutrition Today*, Vol. 9, 1974). Brain damage, bone abnormalities, growth retardation, cleft palate, and more subtle problems such as behavioral and learning problems and hyperactivity have all been linked to dietary deficiencies during pregnancy. Some of these deficiencies have, in turn, been linked to the consumption of caffeine and alcohol during pregnancy (see *Jane Brody's Nutrition Book*).

There is some truth to the Mother Nature's Insurance Policy theory. It is common for poorly nourished mothers to give birth to healthy babies. The problem is that the insurance policy gives uncertain coverage. With this kind of policy, it's as if the insurance agent were to tell you, "Well, if something goes wrong, you might get paid and you might not." That's because the mother/fetus nutritional street carries traffic both ways: not only do mothers compensate for fetal deficiencies, fetuses also compensate for maternal deficiencies. At the end of nine months, maybe baby will end up deficient, maybe mother will, perhaps both will. What you thought was an insurance policy turns out to be a crap shoot.

Weight Gain During Pregnancy

Nutritionally speaking, pregnant women need more of everything, particularly protein, vitamins, and minerals. This is symptomized by an increase of appetite, recognized as necessary by most—"I'm eating for two now"—and feared by many—"I can't eat too much or I'll put on fat I'll never get rid of."

Experts generally agree that fetal needs are approximately 150 extra calories per day during the first three months, resulting in about three pounds of weight gain for that period. During the next six months, the approximate need is for 200 more calories per day, totaling 350, resulting in a gain of about three-quarters of a pound per week. The nine-month total comes to roughly twenty-one pounds of added weight.

There are many variables that would cause the actual ideal weight gain to be more or less than the twenty-one pound average: your body type and size, your metabolism, whether you are overweight or underweight at the start of pregnancy, and by how much. It might be reasonable for one woman to gain thirty pounds during pregnancy, and for another to gain fifteen, but keep in mind that either too much or too little weight gained during pregnancy endangers the fetus.

Weight reduction diets pose a two-way threat to the fetus. First, they virtually guarantee there will not be enough nutrients for both mother and fetus; second, during weight loss toxins are discharged into the bloodstream, and can be transferred to the fetus, potentially causing birth defects.

So you might give birth to an eight-pound baby but gain three times eight pounds in weight and be told by your doctor that it is not just normal but desirable. While you can accept that it is healthy to gain a lot of weight while you are pregnant, still you may fear that some of those pounds will never come off again. We have all known women who became heavier after giving birth and got heavier and heavier after succeeding births. You don't want to gain thirty-five pounds and find that ten of them seem to have become permanent. How can this be avoided?

The New American Pregnancy Diet

The best things are always most reliable when you need them most. And nowhere does the nutritional beauty of the New American Diet shine as brightly as when a pregnant woman is relying on it to maintain her own health while providing the necessities for a healthy baby. During pregnancy you need perhaps 20 percent more food in terms of calories, simultaneously requiring up to twice as much protein and folic acid, 50 percent more iron and calcium, and at least 25 percent more of all the other vitamins and minerals. There are two requirements for achieving this kind of super nutrition:

1. Apply the principles of the New American Diet as strictly as possible, totally eliminating junk foods.
2. Stress nutrient-dense foods even more than you normally would. (Nutrient-dense foods are those that concentrate the most nutrition into a serving.)

As a first step to finding nutrient-dense foods, let's look briefly at the ways three of the specific nutrients mentioned in the paragraph above help to create your healthy baby:

Calcium: bone and tooth formation; muscle growth; control of heart rhythm; the ability of blood to clot; the transmission of nerve impulses.

Iron: formation of red blood cells; disease resistance; stress resistance; regularity of elimination.

Folic acid: growth and reproduction of all cells; formation of red blood cells; increased appetite; stimulation of production of hydrochloric acid.

For the second step, let's see what foods are good sources of those nutrients:

Calcium: dairy products; green leafy vegetables; fish; sea vegetables; molasses.

Iron: molasses; eggs; fish; organ meats; wheat germ; sea vegetables.

Folic acid: nutritional yeast; organ meats; green leafy vegetables; fish; dairy products; whole grains. The final step is to consolidate the foods above into a list of

NUTRIENT-DENSE FOODS

Fish	Dairy Products
Organ Meats	Sea Vegetables
Nutritional Yeast	Wheat Germ
Whole Grains	Molasses
Green Leafy Vegetables	Eggs

An analysis of those foods reveals that they comprise a list high in protein and cover the entire range of vitamins and minerals. An emphasis of those nutrient-dense foods combined with the elimination of junk foods provides for a healthy weight gain—one that is enough to guarantee the health of mother and fetus but not so much that it leaves the mother worried about obesity.

A good way to insure an emphasis on nutrient-dense foods is with the

PREGNANCY COCKTAIL

2 c. yogurt (or, if your yogurt is thick, 1 c. yogurt & 1 c. whole, raw milk)	1 T. honey
2 t. nutritional yeast	1 raw egg yolk
2 t. molasses	1 T. wheat germ
	¼ t. kelp

Mix the above in your blender as the base. Add fruit in season according to preference. Other variations can be made with a dash of vanilla; ¼ teaspoon of ground coriander seed or cinnamon or cardamom; fruit concentrates. Make the cocktail early in the day, keep refrigerated, and drink when hunger strikes between meals.

For nutritional insurance, I recommend a high quality, natural vitamin/mineral supplement (see Chapter 12).

The Nursing Mother

"The same only more so" describes the nursing mother's diet compared to her pregnancy diet. You need more food: from 500 to 1,200 more calories per day than your normal diet, or 150 to 850 more than the last six months of pregnancy, depending on how long you continue nursing. You also need more liquids: a rule of thumb is twice what you're accustomed to. If your milk production falls off, increase your fluid intake even more. In all fluid consumption, of course, avoid sugar, artificial colors and flavors, caffeine and alcohol.

The Pregnancy Cocktail is also valuable to nursing mothers, as is a vitamin/mineral supplement. In short, nutrient density is just as important to nursing as it is to pregnancy.

DEAR TEENAGER:

If you're eating like most Americans, there's something wrong with your diet. But millions of Americans have changed to a more natural way of eating. Many more are ready to start changing, and this book is meant to give them the help they need.

What's been happening in America during the twentieth century is that we have all been part of a gigantic experiment. It looked like there were a number of ways in which we could improve on nature. We could make things last longer on grocery store shelves by refining certain elements out of food and adding newly invented chemical preservatives; we could make things look and taste natural or even better than natural by adding newly invented colorings and flavorings; we could even alter certain natural things, and add synthetic things. None of this happened all at once. It was gradual, step-by-step, just like all the other advancing technology you've learned about.

Now that we've entered the tail-end of the twentieth century, we finally have the perspective to see some of the results of our gigantic dietary experiment. Some of the results have been good. We know how to handle food so that it is clean, is not a breeding ground for dangerous bacteria, and doesn't spread infectious diseases. But where nourishment is concerned, we're seeing that nature knows best; she has secrets we haven't unraveled and will probably never be able to duplicate. The experiment has had some negative consequences. Where people often died of infectious diseases in the old days (typhoid, tuberculosis), these days they often die of degenerative diseases (heart attacks, cancer, diabetes).

Many links between degenerative diseases and the quality of the food we eat have been established, and reputable scientists are investigating other strong evidence. The U.S. Senate, the U.S. Department of Agriculture, and the Surgeon General have all agreed that we need to change to a more natural way of eating. They became convinced because of the testimony of doctors, biochemists, nutritionists, and other scientifically trained people working at universities and independent laboratories and research organizations.

What's wrong with your diet is too much junk food and not enough fresh vegetables, fruits, and whole grains. It sounds simple because it is simple. You're no stranger to the term "junk food" and you know what you mean when you use the term: soda pop, doughnuts, potato chips, candy. You don't even think about it when you call it junk. Your instincts tell you the nutritional truth even while you're enjoying the taste. You may not experience the same sort of pleasure eating a salad, an apple, or a piece of whole wheat toast, but your instincts also tell you that natural foods have a lot more nutrition to offer you than the junk.

You've been around long enough to know that the quality of any product depends on the quality of the raw materials and the quality of the workmanship. Your body is one of nature's great wonders, it has been programmed to produce an excellent product. What your body requires for making that excellent product is the high quality raw materials. Of course diet isn't the whole story, but it's a large and important part of it that you can't ignore if being healthy and attractive is important to you.

The problem with junk food is that it doesn't build strong muscle and bone, clear skin, shining eyes and hair, immunity to sickness and disease. On the other hand, natural foods do those things. You can only eat so much food in any one day, so the more of it that is junk, the less of it will be good. I'm not saying drink another bottle of pop and you'll drop dead. What I am saying is that you should cut way back on the junk and replace it with whatever kinds of natural foods you find appealing. Give yourself a chance to tune into your own body wisdom on an intuitive level: probably most of the time but not all the time, you know what's right for you.

I started my own switch to natural foods back in 1963. My son Jason was born in 1964, so he's been eating natural foods all his life. It might interest you to know what's different for a teenager for whom natural foods are completely integrated into daily life.

I'm sure you've observed that people can become snobbish about almost anything. But Jason is no food snob; for him natural foods are simply a sensible part of life. But there's no kind of junk food you know about that he hasn't tasted. He's not afraid of junk; he knows it won't kill him. But he also knows it doesn't make sense for junk to dominate his diet. He eats all kinds of food. When he encounters something for the first time, he reads the label so he knows what he's getting. He doesn't have to be encouraged to eat salads, fruits and fruit juices, whole-wheat bread and pancakes, corn tortillas—he's accustomed to such things and likes them. He asks me questions about food because it's practical in a way not too different from knowing how to fix his motorcycle.

Another thing about Jason in relation to natural food is that he eats a lot of it. I get a real kick out of seeing the way a growing boy can put the food away. We're about the same size and I get at least as much exercise as he does, but I almost seem dainty in comparison. And that's exactly as it should be—while you're growing up you need good raw material and you need plenty of it.

That leads me to a subject that disturbs me deeply: *anorexia nervosa.* In anorexia nervosa, dieting and/or fasting is pursued so intensely and persistently that the body loses its ability to digest food. Appetite for food is replaced by nausea; dieting/fasting is replaced by starvation. Many teenage girls have had it or have it by the time they reach college age.

One of the primary motivations behind the condition is no secret: the desire to be attractive to boys. I think girls should be attractive to boys, and vice versa. But I've never met a member of my sex yet who was attracted by an emaciated bag of bones. Some of us are attracted by great big ladies, some of us aren't, but all of us want to see enough flesh on your bones to know you're really there. If you weren't made to be skinny, the only way you can make yourself that way is to starve yourself to death, and the threat of death is very real in anorexia nervosa. Everybody, including boys, is attracted by vigor, sparkle, vitality—by *health.* You may have inherited the predisposition to have a sturdy, or heavy, body; then be sturdy or heavy and *healthy.* If you think you have a problem with your weight, check out Chapter 11. There's no way you can change your basic body type. But you can control your weight naturally and help yourself become a healthy version of yourself. And that's the real secret of being attractive.

If you have friends who are falling into the anorexia nervosa trap or are already in it, remember that they need help. Once they're into it, it's unlikely that they'll get out by themselves. So encourage them to seek medical help before they do damage to themselves that will leave them weakened for the rest of their lives.

But getting back to the main matter, when you heard that natural foods should replace most of the junk you've been eating, you got the essential message. There's a lot of other reading in this book in Part One, if this subject interests you and you want to give yourself enough background to make knowledgeable choices. If you want to read more widely, check Appendix Eight, which contains recommended reading. I'm not suggesting you become some kind of fanatic, but only that you learn the basics of eating right. Afraid your friends will call you a natural foods freak? Well, it makes a lot more sense than being a junk foods freak. Why are so many actors, actresses, and athletes natural foods freaks? Because natural foods help them look and perform at their best.

THE MIDDLE AND LATER YEARS

As you grow older, the amount of food you need to maintain your ideal body weight decreases by approximately 5 percent each decade past the age of twenty. Expressed in pounds, a person who needed two pounds of food a day at the age of twenty only needs a pound and a half at the age of seventy. But there is no correlative lessening of the need for protein, vitamins, and minerals. So junk foods (*empty calorie* foods) proportionately rob you of nutrition more and more as you grow older, even if you don't increase the amount of them you consume.

The mineral calcium is a good example of a much-needed nutrient that becomes widely deficient as people grow older. A simple fall that might produce a bruise for a twenty-year old produces a broken hip for an eighty-year-old woman. Year by year she's been losing calcium from her bones; they've been getting more and more porous, brittle, less dense (*osteoporosis*). Simultaneously, her body has been depositing calcium at the joints to protect weakening bones where they are most vulnerable (*arthritis* and a plausable theory to explain arthritis). Not only did her need for calcium never diminish, but she mistakenly thought she was getting *too much* calcium when she started to suffer from arthritis, so she consciously avoided foods she knew to be rich in calcium (see page 440). She has been doing just the opposite of what she should have been doing where calcium is concerned. And, living on saltines and canned soup and vegetables, she has been undoing herself in all the other nutrients too.

There is a unique difficulty for older people presented by many years of devitalized foods: the older one is, the more time it may take to adjust to a new regimen of natural foods. The primary adjustment takes place in the intestines. If you have been eating white flour and white sugar products, canned and frozen vegetables, then suddenly switch to whole grains, salads, and fresh fruits and vegetables, they are likely to give your digestive tract fits. With the wisdom that comes with age, it would be best to make your changes gradually, somewhat like this:

In the first week you might make the switch to whole-grain baked goods, choosing only those that are made without sugar and preservatives. By the time you are into your second week you might also have used up your supply of crackers, replacing them with whole-grain crackers made without salt.

In the third week you might begin to make a small salad to accompany the big meal of the day, and *in the fourth week* start making the salads a little bigger. You may find that, try as you may, you cannot accustom yourself to eating more than a few salads a week. If so, try to add other raw (uncooked) foods. Ideally, your diet would be in the range of 30 to 50 percent raw foods. Other possibilities: carrot sticks, celery stalks, and other vegetable "finger food"; nuts; sunflower and other seeds; raw-milk dairy products.

In the fifth week you might begin making the switch to all fresh vegetables, having used up your supply of canned or frozen vegetables. In the future, when the quality or variety of fresh vegetables is poor, use frozen vegetables to fill in, avoiding canned vegetables as much as possible.

In the seventh week you might turn your attention to your sweet tooth. You've already eliminated white flour and white sugar desserts. Now you might start getting tough on the whole dessert category, eliminating most of them and substituting fresh fruit for desserts and snacks that formerly were such things as pastry, pudding, and candy.

In other words, you're making the transition to natural foods over a couple of months or more. Your intestines will greatly appreciate the gradual approach.

If you have become addicted to laxatives over the years, your new natural foods regimen should allow you to quit them. Try cutting back on them as you get into the salads, working your way out of the laxative habit by the time you're a couple of months into the New American Diet. Bran can be very helpful for the elimination problem. Begin by taking just a pinch at a time and gradually increasing over about a month, but don't exceed a couple of tablespoons a day because excess bran causes nutritional imbalances.

A lot of older folks complain about lack of appetite. Much of that is attributable to lack of exercise. Swimming and walking are both excellent for older folks. But again, if you're not used to it, easy does it. Build up your stamina very gradually, so as not to tax your heart unduly. If you aim to be able to swim for half an hour, start with five minutes; if you aim to be able to walk for an hour and a half, start with fifteen minutes. Proper exercise will not only improve your appetite, it will improve your digestion, assimilation, and muscle tone, be good for your heart and lungs, and help prevent osteoporosis. The tendencies to get flabby and gain weight that start in our middle years, or even sooner, can be virtually blocked by a program of regular, vigorous exercise begun before the aging process makes too many inroads and maintained throughout middle age. A person who does so is not refusing to age gracefully but insisting on aging healthfully. And few things are more graceful than a strong, supple body, no matter what its age, size, or shape.

As we age, eating less and assimilating less efficiently, a good, natural vitamin/mineral supplement makes even more sense than it did when we were younger (see Chapter 12). As with so many other things, a gradual approach would be best for older folks here too. Start out with half doses for the first few weeks, giving your body a chance to get accustomed to the new high level of nutrients.

Sociological statistics inform us that we are in transition from a society dominated by youth to one dominated by the middle-aged and elderly. We need to take steps to insure that those statistics don't mean we will also be a society dominated by degenerative diseases. We also need to wean ourselves from the habit of expecting such improvements to arrive magically as a pill, potion, miracle food, or wonder drug. Futuristic gerontologists predict tremendous breakthroughs in longevity during the next few decades. But their hopes are always pinned to a substance, some sort of chemical magic wand due to poof from a test-tube any day now. There's something a bit illogical about that: we're not getting so sick and dying so young because we're missing some one single substance. Why should we believe that one single substance will be invented that will make everything right? I might be a believer if what went into the test tube were clean air and water, natural foods and exercise, and world peace . . .

Furthermore, why should we even be interested in living longer if vigor, alacrity, and joy don't accompany our years? Write on my tombstone, "He could have lived longer, but he couldn't have lived fuller." The New American Diet may not help you to reach one hundred and twenty but it will help you enjoy whatever you have coming. And it's not too late to start, no matter how old you are.

WHAT ATHLETES SHOULD EAT

Before sitting down to write this I went to a nearby pool and swam sixty-five 100-foot laps. While I was swimming I was thinking about what to write here. I've been interested in athletics most of my life, played a lot of basketball when I was a kid, and these days do a lot of running and swimming. As I churned through the water, some of the questions athletes commonly ask began breaking through.

Shouldn't I be on some sort of special diet?

No. All the advice in this book about what to eat applies to athletes. Just as much as everybody else, athletes need to eat a balanced diet attuned to individual needs. But, depending on what your activity is, how much time you spend at it, and what your body type is, you will need *more* of the foods that everybody should eat than nonathletes. Let's look at the difference between moderate and strenuous exercise, expressed as expended calories per hour. Moderate exercise means the equivalent of normal walking, strenuous means all the things that cause you to sweat freely and pant for air.

CALORIES EXPENDED PER HOUR

Body Type	Moderate exercise, women	Strenuous exercise, women	Moderate exercise, men	Strenuous exercise, men
Thin	170	330	205	400
Sturdy	185	365	220	425
Heavy	205	400	240	450

Fat is 75 percent richer in calories than either protein or carbohydrate, but that does not mean you should be on a high fat diet to get those extra calories. Get them from bigger portions or more frequent portions of everything—an unbalanced diet or one that is not suited to your metabolic individuality will cause you to under-perform.

Are there some special foods that will help me perform better?

I suggest you do what I've done and am still doing: experiment. The same thing that gives you that extra zing might make me feel dopey. For example, vitamin E: vitamin E has been proven to enhance the oxygenation of the blood, so I expected to feel its effects on my running. I tried doses from 200 units to 1200 units with negligible results until I added wheat germ oil. Wheat germ oil, from which vitamin E is crystalized, has *octocosanol*, which has been proven to encourage energy production in muscle cells. They are able to claim on the label, "increases endurance, stamina, and vigor."

I found that neither wheat germ oil nor E works for me as well alone as in combination. These days the ideal dose for me seems to be 400 units of vitamin E with 1700 mg of wheat germ oil (5 capsules of 6 minims); larger or smaller doses don't seem as effective. Experimentation was the only way I could establish what combination of E and octocosanol worked best for me. It could be quite different for you, and different for me some other time in some other circumstances.

I've heard people tout such things as kelp, pollen, ginseng, honey, royal jelly, chia seeds, and cayenne pepper as aids to high performance. None of those things will harm you if they are supplements to a balanced diet. They work for some ("it's great stuff") and not for others ("it's bunk") because we all have different needs.

Does carbohydrate loading work?

Yes. It works because carbohydrates break down into glycogen, which is your main muscle fuel for roughly the first half hour of strenuous exercise, after which you switch to burning fat. The extra store of carbohydrates extends the time of burning glycogen. You get into the stored fat later, and the result is increased endurance.

To do carbohydrate loading you first deplete your muscles of glycogen, combining a few days of low carbohydrate intake with a strenuous workout four days before the event. Then for the next three days you work out lightly, or even not at all, cramming as many high-carbohydrate foods as you can—loading up on such things as bread, pasta, and pancakes. The improvement for the athlete on the New American Diet is that all the high carbohydrate foods are whole grains or made from whole grains.

Playboy (March, 1981) reported a bonus to men loading carbohydrates. They described experiments showing that increased libido attributed to running is actually derived from carbohydrate loading. The experiments involved impotent men, men who had difficulty achieving orgasm, and normal men, none of whom were runners. The men with sexual problems improved an average of 67 percent, the normal men 13 percent. Don't run, *Playboy* concluded, just eat like a runner.

Should I take vitamin/mineral supplements?

I think you should, but not because you're an athlete. A natural vitamin/mineral supplement is simply a form of nutritional insurance. It's unlikely to give you any sort of competitive advantage.

Are there any foods I should avoid?

Just like everyone else, you should avoid all junk foods. Interestingly, though, the high degree of regular and strenuous exercise you get gives you more latitude about what you eat than more sedentary people can allow themselves. I don't advise anyone to trash out; but athletes can get away with it better than anyone else. As much as I advocate natural foods, I rate diet behind exercise in its importance to good health (though there is no earthly reason anybody should have to make a choice between them). Beyond that, don't eat anything that doesn't agree with you, no matter what you've heard about it being some kind of superfood.

Do I need extra protein?

No, no more than you need extra carbohydrate and fat. You need more of everything together—balance. If you're a muscle builder, a high-fat diet will put the pounds on you faster than anything. But you may also be laying the ground for a heart attack or cancer—not worth it.

Keep in mind, however, that balance is somewhat redefined by the New American Diet. Compared to the old way of eating, it has a higher proportion of carbohydrates, less of animal protein. This works perfectly for athletes—high-carbohydrate diets have been proved much more effective for athletic endurance than normal diets and vastly more so than high-protein diets. A study reported in *Progress in Human Nutrition* (Margen, Avi Publishing Co.) stated that skiers rated for endurance did 50 percent worse than normal on a high-protein diet, 46 percent better than normal on a high-carbohydrate diet.

How long before an event or workout can I eat?

You should allow at least three hours to digest any major meal, and more if it contains meat. It's even better not to have a major meal before an event because the excitement of competition is not conducive to good digestion. But there usually is no problem with very simple, light eating shortly before a workout. This morning I had a piece of toast and a cup of herb tea about a half hour before going swimming. I can eat a piece of fruit shortly before going for a run without any problem. The things to load up on are fluids; but not during the final prior hour—you want to start with an empty bladder.

What sort of things should I drink?

Thin, watery things. Remember that liquids such as milk, juice, and soup are really foods and that milk in particular takes a long time to digest. The main things needed by working muscles are glycogen, fat, and water. Every pound you lose during a workout or event represents the loss of a pint of water. Water is the best drink for athletes; drink plenty of it.

Sugar in any concentrated form can make you nauseated and give you intestinal cramps, so stay away from soft drinks. Here is a formula for a slightly sweet, watery drink you might find energizing during long, hot exercise. To make it you need a bottle of *Bioplasma* one-grain tablets containing all twelve tissue salts, made by Standard Homeopathic Company, Los Angeles. *The drink:*

3 pints of water
1 pint of apple juice
36 *Bioplasma* tablets (that's not as much as it sounds, because they're tiny)

Put the tablets into a pint jar of water and shake until dissolved, then add the other two pints of water and the pint of apple juice. You can substitute any other fruit juice you like; the point is to have it very diluted and just slightly sweet, so it will energize you, not make you feel sick. There are, of course, those preparations made especially for athletes to drink, but their labels reveal them to be water, sugar, and a string of artificial ingredients—I wouldn't expect much help from them.

Some athletes say they perform better if they drink coffee before an event. I've tried it and it works for me; but it's a two-edged sword. On the one side, the caffeine in coffee or tea tends to lessen muscle fatigue somewhat; on the other side, it overstimulates the heart, kidneys, and nervous system. Having satisfied my curiosity, I don't drink coffee or tea before a workout. My aim is to be good to my body, and there's nothing to prove anyway. If coffee belongs in this context at all, it's on the morning of the big event.

These are probably the most unnecessary three words in this book, but just to be sure: alcohol is out. Both your muscle efficiency and your judgment will be impaired by alcohol before or during any workout or event. That is not to say that athletes should all be absolute teetotalers; a drink or two in the evening can be just as relaxing for an athlete as anyone else.

Should I take salt tablets?

Jane Brody calls salt tablets "dangerous," explaining that they distort the natural ratio between water inside the cells and sodium in the fluids outside of the cells. When the body fluids are too salty, water is drawn from inside the cells in order to dilute the excess sodium; the word for this process is *dehydration*. In other words, salt tablets may contribute to a process they are supposed to prevent. The best way to replace excess weight loss from strenuous exercise is to drink copious amounts of water. Brody cites Dr. Gabe Mirkin, a specialist in sports medicine and a competitive athlete, who co-authored *The Sportsmedicine Book* (Little, Brown, publisher), who holds that hot-weather athletic performance is improved by salt *restriction*. No, you shouldn't take salt tablets.

CONCLUDING WORDS

The principles of the New American Diet apply equally to all, whether you are old or young, an athlete, trying to gain, maintain, or lose weight. About ten years ago I wrote some dietary advice for *The Zen of Running*, and I'll quote myself here because the advice is as appropriate now as it was then.

The XYZ of eating:
X — eat pure, whole foods
Y — eat simply, according to appetite
Z — eat slowly, gratefully, joyfully.

8 Knowing What to Eat

A person who reaches the age of 100 is always asked how he did it. One person credits his long life to never having smoked or drunk alcohol; another will attribute her years to a drink of whiskey each night.
Roger J. Williams

METABOLIC YOU

I saw it over and over among people shopping in my stores: they would read a book touting a diet guaranteed to make them feel great and would feel lousy instead; or they'd feel better at first, then start losing it; or a couple's guru would put them on his enlightenment diet and she would feel great, he would feel awful. The inevitable question was, what's wrong with this diet? Dr. George Watson supplied the answer in *Nutrition and Your Mind*, telling us that an ideal diet right for everyone is "impossible to specify."

We know we each have different fingerprints, look different, smell different, think different, sound different. We know we're all different; why do we entertain the notion that one diet will be good for all of us? It really would be easier that way, wouldn't it? Like one religion, one political system, one blanket to cover us all. I fell into the trap myself in my early days as a natural foods merchant. I'd feel good as a result of some dietary experiment and be surprise when a customer/friend would tell me, "I feel rotten on that diet of yours, Fred." Experience taught me that broad general advice like, "Everyone should eat natural foods," was safe but more specific advice like, "You should be a vegetarian," was not. What I was learning was how to take responsibility for my own health by reading, listening to the experiences of others and experimenting. I soon realized that I wasn't becoming an expert on anything but that I was becoming a repository for ideas that could help others become responsible for themselves. I could tell you about something that worked for me, something else that worked for somebody else and another thing that reputedly works for a lot of people: take your choice, or try them all. As Roger J. Williams says, "Individuals have some inescapable responsibilities for the way they conduct their lives. Among them is learning something about nutrition."

Williams is a member of the National Academy of Sciences and was the only biochemist to hold the post of president of the American Chemical Society. He discovered the B vitamin *pantothenic acid* and supplied the name for the B vitamin *folic acid*. A noted author as well as researcher, Williams was director of the University of Texas Clayton Foundation Biochemical Institute in Austin, a center for nutritional research, from 1941 to 1963. He is responsible for the *genetotrophic* theory of disease, suggesting that "every individual has, because of his genetic make-up, distinctive nutritional needs . . ." which predispose him to certain diseases. We all recognize, for example, that some people are *constantly* plagued by colds, others *never* get them, while most of us fall somewhere between the extremes.

It is easy enough to recognize the external differences between people, yet somehow we tend to assume the internal differences are not as great. But they are. Williams observes that individuality "pervades every part of the body. From birth, human beings are highly distinctive in both microscopic and gross anatomy, in the functioning of their organs, the composition of body fluids and in nutritional requirements." These distinctions are permanent because they are genetically determined, extending "to the structure and metabolism of every cell." The genetic individualities are profound, for they "determine the speed and efficiency with which cells perform their essential functions."* While the genetotrophic theory extends from our inherited predispositions for certain disease to our inherited nutritional requirements for preventing those diseases, genetic individually determines how each of us functions, guaranteeing that this "how" will be at least a little different from one of us to another.

Long before GOALS was published, Williams was saying that degenerative diseases such as cancer, heart disease, arthritis and diabetes are caused by "cellular malnutrition." In his book *Nutrition Against Disease*, Williams wrote

> That malnutrition—unbalanced or inadequate nutrition—at the cellular level should be thought of as a major cause of human disease seems crystal clear to me. It is the inevitable conclusion to be drawn from the facts produced by decades of biochemical research.
>
> What do these facts suggest in terms of practical application? We need to develop techniques for identifying far more accurately than is now possible the inherited pattern of susceptibilities and resistances that is unique to each individual. Call it a "metabolic profile" or any other name you wish, but plainly it represents a necessary precondition for making rational programs of nutrition tailored to fit each individual's special requirements.

We need to know who we are—of course! But how to find out? How to draw that profile?

Early clues were provided by George Watson in his book, *Nutrition and Your Mind* (Harper & Row, 1972). Watson, formerly professor of philosophy of science at the University of Southern California, has devoted years of research to correlating the fields of biochemistry and psychology. He has been able to demonstrate that many mental and emotional disorders can be traced to poor nutrition resulting from choosing foods not suited to an individual's metabolism. He identified three metabolic categories: slow, fast and normal oxidizers, where oxidation referred to the rate at which blood sugar was metabolized.

But it wasn't until I stayed for a couple of months in early 1976 with a Christian community named Shiloh Farms in Sulphur Springs, Arkansas, that I really began to find out about metabolic profiles. Shiloh Farms has been in existence for almost forty years, supporting itself by manufacturing and distributing natural foods. One member is Warren Clough, a chemist by profession, who operates a laboratory and is always investigating the latest promising theories, diets, and products in the field of nutrition. Warren introduced me to the work of Dr. William Donald Kelley.

Dr. Kelley earned B.S., B.A., M.S. and D.D.S. degrees from Baylor University in Texas. He is a

---

* Williams quotes from "Nutritional Individuality", courtesy of *Journal of the Nutritional Academy*, Vol. 11, No. 11, 1238 Hayes, Eugene, OR 97402.

member of the International Academy of Preventive Medicine, the International Academy of Metabology and a fellow of the International College of Applied Nutrition. Dr. Kelley has engaged in nutritional research for over twenty-five years, having designed nutritional programs for well over 30,000 people, many of them seriously ill. The International Association of Cancer Victims and Friends awarded Dr. Kelley its Humanitarian Award in 1975.

Dr. Kelley cured himself of liver-pancreas cancer with a dietary approach (see *Metabolic Ecology: A Way to Win the Cancer War*, Rohé, Wedgestone Press, Box 175, Winfield, KS 67156.) When his wife Suzi developed serious health problems, she tried the diet and supplement program that had saved her husband's life. But in her case the results were almost disastrous. I quote Dr. Kelley in *Metabolic Ecology* saying, "Since I had been so successful, I mistakenly thought it would work on everybody."

After her false start copying her husband's program, Suzi improved dramatically when the diet and supplements that matched her metabolism were determined. Dr. Kelley wrote in his own book, *One Answer to Cancer*, now out of print,

> It was through this experience with Suzi that I began to reformulate many of my ideas. I began listening intently to patients who would tell me that certain vitamins, minerals and foods made them feel better or worse. My eyes just hadn't been open to it before—some supplements and foods worked well for some people while the same supplements and foods caused other people to feel terrible. From close observation and clinical experiments with many disease conditions, I began to classify people into different types.

The work of creating "metabolic profiles" that had been called for by Williams was undertaken by Dr. Kelley.

To understand Dr. Kelley's work we need a rudimentary understanding of the human nervous system. It is one system with two components, often described as if they were two separate systems. There is the somatic (voluntary) component, governing all *conscious* movement, all action that proceeds from a decision. I pick up this pen to write these words—somatic nervous system. There is also the *autonomic* (involuntary) nervous system, governing all *unconscious* movement, actions that proceed automatically. While I am writing these words, food is being assimilated, I am breathing, my heart is beating—autonomic nervous system. It is the autonomic nervous system that is the master regulator of the body's metabolism.

The autonomic nervous system has, in turn, two branches, the *sympathetic* and the *parasympathetic*, sending electrical impulses to our glands and organs. The basic message of our sympathetic branch is "speed up." The basic message of our parasympathetic branch is "slow down." To greater or lesser degrees everyone is (1) dominated by the sympathetic branch or (2) the parasympathetic branch or (3) in relative balance between the two. This phenomenon is the basis for what Dr. Kelley calls "the science of metabolic typing." The three basic states relative to the autonomic nervous system translate into three general categories of metabolism. People who are dominated by their sympathetic branch receive comparatively more nerve stimulation in the glands responsible for energy production and comparatively less in the organs of digestion; this type Dr. Kelley identifies as having a sympathetic, or "vegetarian" metabolism. Where blood sugar is concerned, these people are "slow oxidizers."

Those dominated by the parasympathetic branch of their autonomic nervous system receive comparatively more nerve stimulation in the digestive organs, less in the energy-producing glands;

this type has a parasympathetic, or "meat-eating" metabolism. Where blood sugar is concerned, these people are "fast oxidizers."

Less than half of us are vegetarian and meat-eating types. More than half have "balanced" metabolisms. Where blood sugar is concerned, these people are "normal oxidizers."

Dr. Kelley has identified degrees of efficiency within the three categories, establishing ten metabolic types. A single chapter could not do justice to this subject, but for most of us it will suffice to know our category. That alone prevents many serious errors, the kinds of errors that leave people feeling "lousy," "wiped out," "dead," even though they are following all the rules for choosing the "right" foods.

When my friend Warren Clough introduced me to Dr. Kelley's work he said, "This is just the beginning in this field. I think we'll get much more sophisticated about metabolic types in the future; but it's a very good beginning." For me it was more than a good beginning, it was a giant second step. I had been standing on the first step during most of the eight years I owned natural foods stores. I had often seen people struggling with some diet, *believing* in the diet so much that it was difficult or impossible to suggest that the diet might be *incapable* of supplying their needs. There was really little help I could offer, though it was obvious they weren't eating the kinds of food right for them . . . All right, what should I be eating? I don't know; experiment . . . Sometimes the failing diet was undertaken with a switch to natural foods, resulting in naturalness getting the blame for failure: "I feel lousy; natural foods are bunko."

Some of the saddest cases I saw were people following some guru's instructions about what to eat. Most commonly the guru would be Hindu, from India, with centuries of a vegetarian tradition behind him. It is immoral to kill animals, the devotee would have been told, ignoring the fact that something always dies in order that we live. You cannot advance spiritually, the devotee would have been told, unless you are a vegetarian. I have seen some of them doing just fine physically on the guru's diet; but I have seen others *dragging* themselves around, some of them struggling on for years with no strength, little energy. "This is a good diet for meditation," they would say, brainwashing themselves or being brainwashed by others into believing their poor health was serenity, bliss, "spiritual advancement."

There is no such thing as a "spiritual" diet. Diet and spirit are not separate; what is spiritual about diet is to know yourself, be in harmony with who you are, to have a feeling of gratitude towards food, and to be free of greed and eager to share.

Testing Yourself

For a seminar I give called "How to End the Search for the Perfect Diet," I devised the following test combining material received from Dr. Kelley with adapted material from Dr. Watson's *Nutrition and Your Mind*. It is called the "Autonomic Nervous System (ANS) Equilibrium Self Test" and yields a profile showing whether you are predominantly sympathetic, parasympathetic, or in between.

Answer all the questions to the best of your ability according to how things are with you in *this* period of your life. "When I was a kid" or "back in my school years" should be ignored if your preferences have changed since then—answer for *now*. (But one exception: If you have recently become a vegetarian, answer the questions as if you were still eating meat, according to your preferences at the most recent time before becoming a vegetarian. If you have been a vegetarian for years and can no longer relate to non-vegetarianism, you are not the one exception—answer for *now*.)

AUTONOMIC NERVOUS SYSTEM EQUILIBRIUM SELF TEST

Answer each question

    a) always or often

    b) sometimes

    c) rarely or never. *Circle a or b or c in the parentheses.*

1. I could eat a steak for breakfast. (a b c)
2. I prefer a light breakfast. (a b c)
3. I like butter on my soft-boiled eggs. (a b c)
4. I can skip breakfast without feeling hungry or tired. (a b c)
5. I feel better when I have bacon and eggs for breakfast. (a b c)
6. I feel hunger between meals and satisfy it with something sweet. (a b c)
7. I feel a bit weak if I go without food for two or three hours. (a b c)
8. I drink a lot of water. (a b c)
9. I could eat beef every day, even twice a day. (a b c)
10. I like raw onions. (a b c)
11. I get hungry between meals and like to snack on salty nuts, cheese and crackers, maybe even a hot dog. (a b c)
12. I crave sweets. (a b c)
13. I like olive oil. (a b c)
14. I find the vegetables that go with a steak or roast more interesting than the meat. (a b c)
15. I prefer liver with bacon to liver with onions. (a b c)
16. I prefer liver with onions to liver with bacon. (a b c)
17. I like a lot of salt on my food. (a b c)
18. I like salads and raw vegetables and they agree with me. (a b c)
19. I don't like cooking smells, even though the food tastes okay at the table. (a b c)
20. I like lettuce, cottage cheese, and fruit for lunch. (a b c)
21. I like a lot of lean salt pork in baked beans. (a b c)
22. I eat something sweet like fruit, pastry, or candy, and it picks me right up when my energy gets low. (a b c)
23. I like steak and lobster together for dinner. (a b c)
24. I like soft drinks. (a b c)
25. I feel tired during the day but snap out of it after eating a big portion of meat for dinner. (a b c)
26. I like to drink a large glass of fruit juice. (a b c)
27. I find candy or cake too sweet. (a b c)
28. I would prefer carrot and celery sticks to olives and sardines for appetizers. (a b c)

29. I want something like cheese or nuts after dinner. (a   b   c   )
30. I prefer to eat hamburgers with a lot of catsup and/or tomatoes. (a   b   c   )
31. I get hunger pains. (a   b   c   )
32. I look forward to fresh fruit season and like to make a whole meal of fresh fruit.
    (a   b   c   )
33. I like pickles. (a   b   c   )
34. I like meatless meals. (a   b   c   )
35. I like fatty meats like ham and pork chops. (a   b   c   )
36. I eat small portions. (a   b   c   )
37. I like potatoes. (a   b   c   )
38. I forget to eat meals, or would if someone didn't remind me. (a   b   c   )
39. I would choose some nuts over an apple for a snack. (a   b   c   )
40. I prefer wine over beer. (a   b   c   )

Count the number of "a" answers to odd-numbered questions _____
Count the number of "c" answers to even-numbered questions _____
Add them together for your "P" score   P: _____

Count the number of "a" answers to even-numbered questions _____
Count the number of "c" answers to odd-numbered questions _____
Add them together for your "S" score   S: _____
Count the number of "b" answers for your "B" score   B: _____

  Your ANS Equilibrium profile is
PARASYMPATHETIC if your highest score is P.
SYMPATHETIC if your highest score is S.
BALANCED is your highest score is B.
  Enter your ANS Equilibrium profile here _____

If the results of the self test are inconclusive, or you want to cross-check them, Tests 2 and 3 are offered courtesy of Dr. Kelley.

Test 2: Swallow 50 mg. of niacin with water on an empty stomach. If your skin turns red within a half-hour, and you feel hot and itchy, you have a parasympathetic metabolism. You have a balanced metabolism if you feel warmer and have a better color in your face. You have a sympathetic metabolism if you don't feel anything.

Test 3: Take 8 grams of ascorbic acid a day for three days in a row. If you're a woman and experience vaginal irritation, or if you feel depressed, lethargic, exhausted and irritable, then you have a parasympathetic metabolism. You have a balanced metabolism if you don't notice any change at all. You have a sympathetic metabolism if you feel an improvement in how you feel—more energy, more alert, and better quality sleep.

Dr. Kelley says the tests are not infallible. But they are quite accurate a great majority of the time. If two or three of the tests say you have a balanced metabolism, you can feel pretty certain that you do, and the same holds true for sympathetic and parasympathetic metabolisms. (See page 146 for more on Tests 2 and 3.)

For the sick or seriously unhealthy, knowing your metabolic category may not be sufficient to get you out of trouble. For a moment I'll return to the story of Dr. Kelley and his wife Suzi. What had worked for him was a strict vegetarian diet combined with an internal cleansing regimen and extensive nutritional supplementation. His program was a disaster for her, they learned the hard way, because Suzi has a parasympathetic metabolism, needing meat four or five times a week. They also had to learn by trial and error what supplements worked for her.

As a result of her experience, Suzi founded the International Health Institute to train doctors and lay people in the practical application of metabolic typing. Through doctors and lay counselors who have completed the educational seminars conducted by the International Health Institute, individuals can be connected with its highly detailed computer analysis facility, operated by a company named Nutritional Counseling Service (NCS). The computer analysis will go beyond ascertaining your metabolic type, identifying the relationship between your type and your condition and recommending a specific nutritional program, including kinds and amounts of both foods and nutritional supplements. The lay counselors work only in affiliation with doctors; this service can be acquired only under the supervision of a licensed medical practitioner. For the names of doctors and lay counselors nearest you, contact Nutritional Counseling Service, P.O. Box 402607, Dallas, TX 75240, telephone 1-800-527-0453. If you are a resident of Alaska, Hawaii, Texas, or a foreign country, telephone (214) 241-3414.

METABOLIC PROFILES

With the aid of computer technology, Dr. Kelley has been developing the science of metabolic typing for over twenty years. In the data banks are the results of nutritional counseling with more than 30,000 people. Skimming the surface of this enormous amount of information provides us with recognizable outlines of metabolic profiles, manifested according to the equilibrium of the autonomic nervous system. The variations in the state of balance between the branches of the autonomic nervous system are, of course, infinite. The far end of the spectrum is absolute metabolic individuality—no two people exactly alike. The near end of the spectrum, however, allows us to observe generalities. It has been an empirical process, the facts accumulating until the patterns have emerged.

A Sympathetic Profile

The sympathetic system stimulates the adrenalin-producing portion of the adrenals, the cardiovascular, muscular, and skeletal systems, as well as the arteries, veins, and capillaries. These are the components of the "fight or flight" mechanism, which raises blood pressure and increases blood flow to the muscles and brain. The word here is *action*. People who are sympathetically dominated are action people, receiving comparatively more nerve stimulation in the systems responsible for energy production and comparatively less for such passive activities as digestion and assimilation.

Sympathetics are strongly intellectual, prone to hyperactivity, tension, constipation, insomnia, and have a tendency towards a rapid heartbeat and being underweight. They may have firm muscle tone, bright white teeth, pale gums, dilated pupils, thick eyebrows, and their face and ears are usually pale.

This "fast" metabolism emphasizes the *catabolic* aspect of metabolism—that is, the processes of breaking down complex substances into simpler ones. Catabolic processes are *anaerobic*—take place in the absence of oxygen—so the sympathetic oxidizes blood sugar slowly, has a tendency towards toxicity due to relatively high levels of cellular waste products, and has a markedly acidic body chemistry.

Sympathetics are prone to anxiety, nervous strain, and irritability, but are seldom depressed. They are ambitious, with a high energy level, take the initiative, and like to make decisions. They are left-brain dominant, with a decided rational bent, exhibitors of "type A" behavior. They have good powers of concentration and enjoy exercise. They can even become fanatical about it. (The enforced oxygenation of aerobic exercise overcomes the sympathetic metabolizer's natural inefficiency of oxygen utilization, burning up toxins and causing a feeling of well-being bordering on euphoria.)

A Parasympathetic Profile

The systems responsible for digestion, assimilation, and excretion are all parasympathetically stimulated. These are the components of rest and repair, the exact opposite of fight or flight. The word here is *inaction*. Parasympathetics tend to be slow, generating comparatively more energy for vegetative functions and less for action.

Parasympathetics have strong appetites, are prone to lethargy, fall asleep easily, have a strong energy reserve, and a tendency towards being overweight. They may have oily skin and hair, droopy eyelids, scanty eyebrows, dark-colored gums, and their complexion is ruddy.

This "slow" metabolism emphasizes the *anabolic* aspects of metabolism—that is, the processes of synthesizing substances from simpler ones. Anabolic processes are *aerobic*—take place in the presence of oxygen—so the parasympathetic metabolism oxidizes blood sugar rapdily, is not highly susceptible to toxicity because of relatively low levels of cellular wastes, and has a comparatively alkaline body chemistry.

Parasympathetics act on intuition more often than reason, being right-brain dominant. Their actions are relaxed and calm, they seldom get angry, but are subject to depression. They have poor powers of concentration, seldom worry, and tend to be charming talkers. They dislike exercise, find it hard to get out of bed and get going in the morning, but can keep going late into the night.

A Balanced Profile

Balanced descriptions border on nondescriptions—few extremes, characterized by words like "normal," "average," "medium." However, balanced metabolisms can manifest some of the extremes typical of both other categories, while being predominantly between the extremes. This moderately-paced metabolism is in the middle ground between catabolic/anaerobic and anabolic/aerobic processes. Therefore, the balanced metabolism oxidizes blood sugar at an intermediate rate and has a more acidic body chemistry than the parasympathetic, but less so than the sympathetic.

The person with a balanced metabolism does not get excited easily nor tend to worry. Balanced metabolizers are not heavily dominated by either hemisphere of the brain. With a fair amount of drive and less likelihood to manifest extremes, the balanced personality is less predictable than the others, displaying occasional impulsiveness, anger, and other emotional upsets. Balanced metabolizers are fairly easy to get started in the morning, with normal alertness, occasional fatigue and need for extra sleep. The balanced metabolizer has a "take it or leave it" attitude towards exercise—less likely to be fanatical about it as a sympathetic but more likely to do it for health reasons than a parasympathetic.

DYSPLASIA

The metabolic profiles sketched above are what might be considered "classic", offered here to give you a feel for the subject, not to provide your definitive metabolic portrait. What if your self-test results don't match the profile? What if you see yourself reflected in more than one profile? The answer could by *dysplasia*, meaning displacement.

Dr. William Sheldon used this term to describe the mixing of characteristics he found in somatotyping, the classification of people according to body types (endomorphs, mesomorphs, ectomorphs). Sheldon found that people often had mixtures of the characteristics of all three somatotypes. Dr. Kelley finds this to be equally true in analyzing people metabolically, saying that there is no such thing as a pure type.

To be a pure type would mean that one branch of the autonomic nervous sytem would not be functioning at all, which would result in death. In scoring the forty questions on pages 95–96, notice that you did not answer all the questions with absolute consistency. You fall into one category or another because of the equilibrium between the two branches of your autonomic nervous system—not an either/or situation, but a both/and.

METABOLIC PROFILES AND THE DIETARY CONNECTIONS

Sympathetic

Since blood sugar is oxidized slowly, a little food goes a long way. Sympathetics often experience food as a heavy feeling in the stomach, suffer sour stomach and heartburn. About this category, Dr. Kelley says, "These people, for social reasons and because of American eating traditions, have accustomed themselves to eating steaks; but they really don't do well on them because meat is acid-forming. With their acidic body chemistry, they need alkaline foods like fruits and vegetables to balance their pH. These people do really well on the Pritikin program."

Following their natural inclinations, sympathetics crave fruits, enjoy vegetables, and dislike fatty or oily foods. The tendencies towards eating fruits and vegetables and eating lightly counter the tendency towards having high levels of cellular waste products. It is important for sympathetics to match food to their metabolic profile in order to avoid cellular toxicity.

Parasympathetic

Since blood sugar is oxidized rapidly, large quantities of food are required to keep the blood sugar level up. Parasympathetics experience energy gain after eating meat, energy loss after eating sweets, and a jittery feeling after eating fruit. About parasympathetics, Dr. Kelley says, "These people tremble at the thought of becoming vegetarians and they are right to do so. Their body chemistry tends towards alkalinity, so they need acid-forming foods such as meat and fish to keep balanced. These people do well on the high-protein Atkins program."

Following their natural inclinations, parasympathetics crave butter, cream sauces, fatty, salty, and acidic foods. The tendency to like fats is allied with their high energy (calorie) value, supplying ample blood sugar. It is important for parasympathetics to match food to their metabolic profile in order to avoid fatigue.

Balanced

The balanced metabolizer has a naturally wider latitude in food selection and tends to like a wide variety of foods, including both meat and fruit and all kinds of vegetables and salad dressings. The familiar advice to eat widely from a great variety of foods is especially appropriate for these people because that is the way they match food to their metabolic profile. Otherwise, by adhering to too narrow a diet, they are subject to either of the major weaknesses of the other categories, cellular toxicity or fatigue. Dr. Kelley says about the balanced metabolizer, "Although these people can eat a variety of foods and thrive, poor nutrition and other improper lifestyle patterns will cause them to crash." In the "crashed" condition (meaning the person has spun down the metabolic spiral into a state of depressed metabolic efficiency), the person with a naturally balanced profile may find himself functioning as either an unwell sympathetic or an unwell parasympathetic.

In Pritikin versus Atkins terms, balanced metabolizers would get the best results by modifying both diets and synthesizing them into a wide selection of foods with the only heavy emphasis being on naturalness. Dr. Kelley uses the Pritikin and Atkins programs as excellent examples of how confusion has been perpetuated by dietists, who are often qualified and sincere, with valuable information to share. Problems arise from not appreciating the metabolic limitations of their advice—trying to jam a left shoe onto a right foot.

The program created by Nathan Pritikin is a good low-protein, low-fat regimen. Dr. Robert Atkins' regimen is also good, but diametrically opposed—high-protein, high fat. You can find people who have become healthier, even cured diseases, following one or the other diet. While both "work," the implication of either is that is *the* way to eat, and yet they could hardly be more dissimilar. How, the confused neophyte wants to know, can such dissimilar diets both be right?

Having read this far, you now understand that they *are* both right—for different people. If you are sympathetic-dominant, Atkins' diet is wrong, Pritikin's is right. And, obviously, the opposite is true if you are parasympathetic. Balanced metabolizers would get along in the range between marginally well and reasonably well, depending on their metabolic vigor.

Everybody is familiar with the observation that the United States is a genetic melting pot, but few have appreciated that the pot has cooked up a stew of metabolic-dietary ramifications. Some of our ancestors came from northern countries where generation after generation lived on high animal-protein diets, including much meat, fish, and dairy products. Others came from centuries of reliance on wheat, rye, barley and oats. Some came from Mediterranean countries, where the climate provided more fruits and vegetables. Others came from rice-growing areas and places where tropical fruits fall from trees. Generations of life supported by these indigenous foods made different genetic imprints on the local peoples. And then in America, we have mixed and remixed all these genetic influences in countless ways.

Beyond all other nations, we require a diversified approach to diet. I think we have responded to this on an intuitive level, for there is no nation on earth that is even close as a marketplace for diet books. "Eat a balanced diet," we have heard all our lives, and each year a new diet book takes its place on the bestsellers list, replacing last year's bestselling book; both are, of course, entirely different. To know whether or not you can or should dance to the new tune, you first need to know who you are metabolically. Next you need to know how that should affect your food choices. Or, in other words, what is a balanced diet?

9 "Balanced Diet" Redefined

Your metabolic profile (see Chapter 8) should affect your food choices according to two major biochemical variables:

(1) The equilibrium of your autonomic nervous system influences your body chemistry: sympathetic dominance tends to push body chemistry towards acidity; parasympathetic dominance tends to push body chemistry towards alkalinity.

(2) Food is either acid, alkaline, or neutral, as determined by measuring the pH of its ash after it has been burned. Therefore, different foods have different effects on body chemistry.

The interaction of these two variables means that the acid-alkaline balance will be affected differently in different metabolic categories by the same foods. Phrased conversely, it takes different foods to maintain the same optimum acid-alkaline balance in different people. Choosing food according to your metabolic category is synonymous with choosing food appropriate to your body chemistry.

Conventional nutritional wisdom has been that everybody should favor alkaline-forming foods. This would be true if everybody were metabolically alike. It is good advice for balanced metabolizers and particularly good advice for sympathetics. But for parasympathetics it is an injustice, since their body chemistry has a strong natural alkaline bias. Too many fruits and vegetables can make the already alkaline parasympathetic even further alkaline, creating the condition known as *alkalosis*. Symptoms of alkalosis include bleeding gums, bloating, diarrhea, foul intestinal gas, headaches, joint pain, lethargy, rashes, scalding rectum, excessive sneezing and sweating, and teeth sensitivity. Disease conditions of alkalosis include allergies, arrhythmia, and edema.

Excessive protein foods, which are acid-forming, produce the same kind of disorder for sympathetics. In their case, however, it is in the opposite direction: *acidosis*, the unbalancing of an already acid system. Symptoms of acidosis include dehydration, dry, hard stools, heartburn, sweet tooth, sour stomach, rapid heartbeat, white spots under fingernails, constipation, muscle cramps, and insomnia. Disease conditions of acidosis include acne, arthritis, duodenal ulcers, hemorrhoids, and hyperactivity.

"The perfect diet for your [category]," says Dr. Kelley, "should be determined by knowing which foods will best stimulate the weaker division of your autonomic nervous system to produce a balancing effect. Or, if the two divisions are in relative balance, knowing how to maintain that balance." The foods he has found best are so because of their nutritional content *and* their effect on acid-alkaline balance. For sympathetic and balanced metabolizers, he recommends more than half alkaline-forming foods; for parasympathetics he recommends more than half acid-forming foods.

FOODS AND BODY CHEMISTRY

Alkaline-forming	*Neutral*	*Acid-forming*
Fruits*	Milk	Meat
Vegetables	Cream	Fish
Sea Vegetables	Butter	Eggs
Millet	Buttermilk	Beans, dried
Seeds	Vegetable oils	Grains (including bread,
Most herbs & spices	Honey	crackers, pasta,
Salt	Sugar	excepting millet)
Soy sauce		Nuts
Miso		Cheese
Wine		Vinegar
Tea, coffee, most		Beer, whiskey, fortified
herbal teas		wine (port, sherry)
Mineral waters		Most food additives &
		most drugs

*There is a great deal of confusion regarding "acid" fruits, such as the citrus family, which Dr. Kelley cleared up for me. Their tartness is due to the presence of various acids which are "burned" by the body, forming carbon dioxide and water. The mineral ash that remains has an alkaline reaction in the body tissues. This rule concerning acid fruits does not apply to plums, cranberries, and prunes. These contain benzoic acid, which is not broken down by the body, hence causing an acid reaction.

METABOLIC-DIETARY GUIDELINES

Sympathetic

This category needs alkalinizing diets low in purines and high in potassium (supportive of the parasympathetic system). Proteins should come mainly from vegetarian sources and poultry and fish rather than red meat. Sympathetics do well on all vegetables and fruits, whole grains, and seeds. Dairy products may tend to be mucus-forming for sympathetics, but they tolerate coffee, alcohol, and sweeteners well.

Parasympathetic

This category needs acidifying diets high in purines and high in calcium (supportive of the sympathetic system). Much of their protein should come from organ and red meats. Parasympathetics do well on root vegetables, not so well on leafy greens. They also do well on whole grains and legumes, not as well on fruit. The best fruits for parasympathetics are apples, pears, plums, peaches, nectarines, cranberries, and avocados. Citrus and bananas should generally be avoided. Parasympathetics do well on cream, butter, and cultured dairy products.

Balanced

Reading the emphases for the other categories gives this category an idea of what not to do. Balanced metabolizers maintain balance by eating broadly through a wide range of natural foods.

Protein can come from vegetarian or animal sources. Dr. Kelley recommends switching back and forth on alternate days.

(The above guidelines were condensed and paraphrased from Dr. Kelley's training manuals, *Metabolic Technology 1 and 2*, published by International Health Institute of Dallas, TX.)

METABOLIC CATEGORIES AND FOOD AFFINITIES

Fruits

Sympathetics have a natural affinity for fruit. It is sustaining for them because they do not burn the easily-digested fruit sugars rapidly. Parasympathetics may enjoy eating fruit, but, since they utilize carbohydrates rapidly, their intuition leads them to generalize, "Fruit doesn't have enough *substance* to it." They may even dislike it because they burn up the fruit sugars so quickly that it makes them feel jittery.

Vegetables

Sympathetics also handle all kinds of vegetables well. Green leafy vegetables, having a high potassium content, stimulate the parasympathetic system, so sympathetics are inclined by intuition to be enthusiastic salad eaters. Because of that very same high potassium level, parasympathetics are generally not enthusiastic salad eaters. They are more drawn to root vegetables, which are not as alkalinizing.

Grains

The body converts grain into blood sugar more slowly than fruit but more rapidly than fat or protein. Having this in-between status, grains are the class of foods where the natural affinities of sympathetics and parasympathetics come closest to overlapping. The sympathetic finds them more sustaining than the parasympathetic; on the other hand, grains strike the parasympathetic as having more substance than fruits and vegetables.

Grains are acid-forming, but not strongly so. They are therefore relatively closer to a middle ground than fruits, vegetables, and protein foods, whose effects on body chemistry are more pronounced.

Proteins

To understand how the different metabolic classes respond to protein foods, one needs to understand the roles of three related substances: nucleoproteins, purines, and ATP.

Nucleoproteins are proteins found in plant and animal cells, formed in the nucleus of the cells by combining protein with nucleic acid. *Purines* are a class of nucleoproteins, one of which—adenine—is the major constituent of *ATP* (adenosine triphosphate). ATP is the principal energy carrier at the cellular level. The relationship of these substances to one another can be represented by these three greatly simplified equations:

$$\text{protein} + \text{nucleic acids} = \text{purines (adenine)}$$
$$\text{adenine} + \text{phosphate} = \text{ATP}$$
$$\text{ATP} = \text{energy transference}$$

The purine adenine can either by synthesized within the body or obtained ready-made in food. Apparently, sympathetic metabolizers synthesize adenine more effectively then parasympathetics, as evidenced by the high energy level of the sympathetic. Therefore, parasympathetics are comparatively more attracted by protein foods with a high purine content—organ meats, anchovies, caviar, herring, mussels, sardines.

Sympathetics are more attracted to low-purine protein foods such as nuts, seeds, eggs, milk, cheese.

Medium purine protein foods are meat, fish, fowl, whole grains, dried legumes, nutritional yeast. Within this category, red meat has more purines than fish or fowl. Therefore, parasympathetics are more apt to be steak lovers; sympathetics are more apt to favor chicken and fish.

A by-product of the oxidation of purines is uric acid. Uric acid crystals are the irritant in gout. Dr. Kelley has observed that sympathetic metabolizers are prone to gout. This demonstates why a high protein diet—particularly if it is high in "rich" high-purine proteins—can be devastating to sympathetics. For parasympathetics, on the other hand, high purine foods can transform lethargy into vitality.

Not appreciating the physiological basis for these natural predilections for certain foods is the basis for many bitter memories of protracted wars around family dinner tables. "I don't know what's wrong with Johnny, I just can't get him to eat enough salad, no matter what I do." Or, "I don't know what's wrong with Mary—no matter what I do with her she just pecks at her meat like a little bird." Of course, nothing is wrong with Johnny or Mary. They should be allowed to eat small portions of salad or meat and fill up on the types of food they are intuitively drawn to. The concerns of the meal planners and cooks should be to make certain that the quality is as high (natural and fresh) as possible, and that it is as tasty and nicely presented as possible.

This does not necessarily mean cooking three entirely different meals at one time because there are three different metabolic categories represented within a family (there may not be). It means that the sympathetic sharing the same meal with the parasympathetic will eat comparatively more of the salad and less of the meat. If they are sharing a beef stew together, the sympathetic will fish more for pieces of potato and carrot while the parasympathetic stirs around hoping to find chunks of meat. They both intuitively seek a balancing influence on the autonomic nervous systems in the food they select, but "balance," being relative, means something at least slightly different for everybody.

AN OVERVIEW OF ACID-ALKALINE BALANCE

The International College of Applied Nutrition describes the human body as "an acid-making factory" continually emptying acids into the bloodstream each moment of the day and night. Acids are the by-products of a wide range of activities and influences, including beating of the heart, breathing, and other involuntary movement of the muscles; both positive and negative emotions; exercise; stress of all kinds, including such forms of pollution as radiation, pesticide residues, and food additives.

The word "balance" is used in reference to acidity and alkalinity because there is not one pH in the body, but many. (The *pH* number measures acidity and alkalinity, with 7 being neutral, less than 7 being acid, more than 7 being alkaline.) Thus, if we view the body as if it were an onion, each layer has a different optimum pH value, or range of values: skin and saliva are slightly acid; the stomach is much more acid; the small intestine is alkaline; the large intestine is slightly acid; blood and cells are slightly alkaline; urine is somewhat acid.

The blood, recipient of acids from many sources, seeks to preserve its slightly alkaline status at all costs, buffering the acids with calcium. While the blood is preserving its status, the various other pH values are fluctuating. Dr. Kelley (who knows more about this subject than anyone I've met, yet calls acid-alkaline balance "very poorly understood") describes its periodicity thus:

> In every 24-hour cycle, the human body has two peak periods of alkalinity. These are periods of cellular repair, lasting two and a half to three hours, peaking at about 3:30 A.M. and 2:30 P.M. The fluctuations between these eleven- and thirteen-hour peaks is known as the acid-alkaline cycle.

To speak of your acid-alkaline balance, then, is to speak about many things and to speak about them relatively. You are more alkaline at some times than others, relative to all the acid-making influences and the time of day. You are also more alkaline than somebody else relative to the functioning of your autonomic nervous system. The approximate optimum stomach pH range is 4 to 4.5. Optimum function for a sympathetic will be in the low end of that range, the parasympathetic will function best in the high end, and the balanced metabolizer will function most efficiently between the extremes. This is one good perspective from which to see how the same diet effects different people in different ways—to see why optimum functionality means relatively more alkaline-forming foods for the sympathetic (preventing acidosis), and more acid-forming foods for the parasympathetic (preventing alkalosis).

YOUR METABOLISM AND CHOOSING FOOD

Having at least a workable notion of who you are, metabolically speaking, and how that influences acid-alkaline balance, is an essential and giant step towards choosing the foods right for you. But it still leaves questions unanswered: "Okay, I need a lot of meat; but I can't eat just meat." Or, "I don't handle meat well but I can't just eat salads." Or, "Sure I can eat widely, but what's best?" We have these kinds of questions because we still have only part of the equation. The other part is the intrinsic properties of food—its *dynamics*; having a working knowledge of these allows us to match who *we* are with what *food* is.

We are accustomed to hearing food talked about in terms of its vitamins, minerals, protein, fat, etc. Chemists pass on statistical data to us with such terminology. This information is the language of specialists; it's much more useful to them than it is to us. We're generalists, looking at stores full of food, trying to make some practical sense of it all. Time and again I've seen people with their heads full of the chemist's language looking around one of my stores with an air of bewilderment, knowing what is high in iron, what is high in vitamin A, and not knowing what to eat.

"For a balanced diet," we have also been told, "eat from each of the four basic food groups each day." That advice is as oversimplified as the diets that are supposed to be good for everybody. It also doesn't make any allowances for who you are, or give you any means of measuring quality, nor does it recognize that different kinds of food produce different reactions after you consume them. (See Chapter 10 for more on food groups).

There are three broad classifications of food that correspond to the metabolic categories based on the rate at which food is digested, assimilated and utilized. There are foods that digest quickly (light foods); foods that digest slowly (heavy foods); and foods that digest at a medium rate between the extremes.

FOOD DYNAMICS

	Light Food	Medium Food	Heavy Food
		Direct Relationships	
Digestion Rates	fast	moderate	slow
Food Groups:	fruits & their juices, vegetables & their juices; beer, wine	whole grains	meats, nuts, seeds, beans, dairy products
Colors:	vivid	neutral	somber
Flavors:	sharp, sweet	bland	savory, rich
Textures:	airy	firm	dense
Nutritional emphasis:	cellulose, minerals	carbohydrate fiber	protein, fat
Chemical characteristics:	alkaline	slightly acid	acid

Indirect Relationships

	Light Food	Medium Food	Heavy Food
The seasons in which these foods are preferred:	summer	all seasons	winter
The geographical/genetic influences are from:	tropics	temperate zone	northern latitudes
Emanations:	active	neutral	passive
Energy:	expansive	balancing	contractive
Electrical:	positive charge		negative charge
Body Polarity:	right side—positive top of spine— positive		left side—negative bottom of spine— negative
Ayurvedic nutrition:	vata (subtle) rajasic	pitta (active) sattvic	kapha (dense) tamasic
Classical Chinese medicine:	yang	tao	yin
People who are:	slow oxidizers	normal oxidizers	fast oxidizers
Most harmonious to the dietary inclinations:	vegetarian	omnivarian	carnivorian
People whose ANS are dominated:	sympathetic	double domination	parasympathetically

A discerning reader might note exceptions to the above generalities and also be able to expand them further. We are not dealing in scientific exactitudes, particularly regarding the indirect relationship. We don't have to be chemists to know there is far more to food than chemistry; we begin to become intelligent regarding our food choices when we begin to look at it in a comprehensive manner—broadly, from an overview, like generalists, not specialists.

OTHER FACTORS INFLUENCING BALANCE

The metabolic-dietary guidelines given earlier in this chapter were extremely broad. This is because there is an almost infinite variety between people within any metabolic category. There are a host of additional factors to consider as well. You may feel a need for a few days of a very unbalanced diet for cleansing purposes—for example, nothing but cooked brown rice, or nothing but raw fruits. What is balancing for you in broad, general terms cannot be determined apart from the general state of your health.

Other important factors are the season and the environment you live in. The season should have a strong influence on your food choices. As you will see in the second part of this book, eating according to the flow of the seasons is a major principle of the New American Cuisine. The same is true of eating according to what is natural to your environment: it is folly in more ways than one to try to live on bananas in Alaska or caribou in Florida.

Everything you read, here or elsewhere, about diets balanced or unbalanced, should be interpreted flexibly. Change is a constant and variability is the rule. Warnings such as the following two should be understood as being *generally* true. If you have a sympathetic metabolism, it is important to avoid fatty meats, excess fats of all kinds, and to avoid organ meats and anchovies, sardines, and herring, foods rich in purines. If you have a parasympathetic metabolism, it is even more important to avoid refined carbohydrates, *especially* sugar. For the fast oxidizer, sugar is so taxing to the pancreas as to be poisonous, rather than merely bad.

No matter what your metabolism, the feeling of "needing a drink" or "needing some sugar" is a misreading of the body's signal. What you need is energy, derived from the acetone resulting from the breakdown of blood sugar, or glucose. The only natural mechanism we have for this process is designed to process glucose coming from two primary sources: complex carbohydrates and protein. Sweet drinks, alcoholic drinks, and coffee are debilitating, but particularly so for those with parasympathetic metabolisms.

Metabolic profile is just as important in food selection for children as for adults. Some children need far less food than others their age and size because of metabolic differences. Forcing children to eat is unwise; their appetites are dependable measures of their needs *if* they are offered the kinds of food right for them. It is rarely advisable to *load* children with milk, protein or any so-called "growth" foods. The caloric needs of growing children are met by the fact that they consume more food as a percentage of body weight than adults.

Unconsciously, we all seek to establish biochemical equilibrium with our food choices. Because of the foods commonly and habitually eaten, balance for most of us is attempted by juggling extremes. Sugar in all its forms, as found in pop, desserts and processed foods; colorings, flavorings, preservatives and other synthetic additives; caffeine, alcohol, marijuana, cocaine and other drugs—these form the extreme on the side of erratic, expansive energy. Salt and meat and other heavy protein foods form the opposite extreme of stolid, contractive energy. When we drink coffee and eat sugared snacks between meals, we gravitate more towards meat at mealtime. When we drink cocktails before meals we hunger for meat, then after eating a lot of meat we hunger for a sweet dessert. Back and forth, we push ourselves between extremes in our instinctual effort to achieve balance. It always requires more force to achieve balance when pushing at extremes, creating more stress on the organism (another perspective from which to view our national epidemic of degenerative disease).

Occupational, environmental, sociological, emotional, and psychological sources of stress are commonly recognized; dietary sources of stress go virtually unrecognized because we have an extremely narrow way of looking at food. "Food is just chemicals," we are told. I like to simplify things, but that gross oversimplification just doesn't work. If we were merely plumbing systems piping food in one end and out the other, dietary balance could be reduced to simple mechanics and the opposition of extremes would work just fine. It doesn't work just fine because the instrinsic properties of foods can cause violent internal fluctuations, enervating us; constant enervation—exhaustion of resistance—is what degeneration is all about.

Your metabolic profile is not chiseled in granite. It often changes as general health improves over time. No matter what metabolism you are, the ideal direction to move in is towards more balance and greater efficiency. This leads us once again to whole grains, the principal balancing food. It is precisely the need for a *principal food* of a *balanced nature* that is the heart of the modern American dietary problem. Professor Paul C. Mangelsdorf, agronomist and former director of the Harvard Botanical Museum, wrote in *Scientific American*, July 1963:

> No civilization worthy of the name has ever been founded on any agricultural basis other than the cereals. The grain of cereal grasses, a nutlike structure with a thin shell covering the seed, contains not only the embryo of a new plant, but also a food supply to nourish it . . . They represent a five-in-one food supply which contains carbohydrate, proteins, fats, minerals and vitamins. A whole grain cereal, if its food values are not destroyed by the over-refinement of modern processing methods, comes closer than any other plant product to providing an adequate diet.

We can consciously move ourselves in the direction of more metabolic balance by consciously selecting whole grains as our principal food.

VEGETARIANISM AND OTHER IDEAL DIETS

There has been a great surge of interest in vegetarianism in recent years, spurred by the superior health statistics regarding degenerative diseases in Seventh Day Adventists and other vegetarian groups. This has occurred because only about six in 20 people have parasympathetic metabolisms and perhaps only two of those will be extremely inefficient metabolizers. So any large group of people will be healthier overall as vegetarians but as many as 30 percent will do poorly with it and for perhaps ten percent vegetarianism represents disaster.

The same kind of observation applies to all of the so-called "ideal" diets, usually described something like, "The original before-the-fall natural diet for Man." It may be all fruit and nuts, or all uncooked, or all fruit, or all meat, depending on what ideas are filling the heads of the promoters. Invariably, this all-world diet will be right for a few, and feeling so good on it fills them with fervor. But you can be sure that the narrower the range of foods, the less ideal it will be for most people.

The promoters of vegetarianism have the most confidence, feeling that their position is the most reasonable. But there is no instance in recorded history of a purely vegetarian society. As to pre-recorded history, *Science 81* (July/August 1981) reported on 8,000 year old well-preserved intestinal contents in Peru: the remains of flowers, deer, fish bones, sea lions, peanuts, squash, and peppers. Our close relatives in the ape family are not pure vegetarians either; though they are mostly vegetarian, all of them seek small amounts of animal protein when they are free in their natural habitats. Writing in the *Journal of Applied Nutrition* (Spring, 1982), H. Leon Abrams, Jr. professor of anthropology at the University of Georgia, Swainsboro, said, "Until recently, it was taken for granted that all monkeys and apes were vegetarians, but ethological studies revealed that all primates, in their natural habitat, also eat small animals. These studies have necessitated the reclassification of all apes and monkeys from herbivores to omnivores."

Personally, I get along fine on either vegetarian or vegan diets. But it is clear to me that they are not for everybody. Omnivarianism is more broadly applicable and is as close as you can get to an ideal diet for human beings.

LISTENING

We all possess an intuitive ability to discern our own needs. For most of us that ability is more latent than active; it is loosely connected if connected at all. The connection can be made, however, and it can be tightened. We can learn to tune in to ourselves, to feel out our internal states. The term I like to use for the process is "listening to one's inner voice," a general term describing an experience connected with every aspect of life.

There is a more precise term, *quasi*-scientific, really, because so little is known about it: *appestat.* The dictionary simply describes it as "the region responsible for controlling the appetite." It is a function of the hypothalamus, and it should tell us what to eat, when, and how much. The appestats of wild animals work perfectly; those of domesticated animals work more or less well according to how tightly they are controlled by man; the appestats of human beings are more or less atrophied depending on how civilized we are. We have the potential for connecting our appestats. How well they work will, again, be an individual matter.

You might ask, "What good does it do to listen if my appestat is atrophied? I can't assume my food cravings are all manifestations of body wisdom." Most of us would be right about that. As Dr. George Watson points out, people "choose foods which have bad effects on them . . . *liking* something is not sufficient grounds for also eating it."

But we would not be right to be discouraged because our appestats have been inoperative for so long. There is a great difference between the process that led to the shut-down of your appestat and the process that can lead to its regeneration. It shut down because you created a dependence on industrially and chemically adulterated foods. You were thus deprived of certain nutrients you would have got from natural foods; or you got those nutrients in altered ratios, quantities, and forms (as in the fortification of refined foods with synthetic vitamins). The unnatural and unbalanced diet resulted in your appestat sending screwy signals in the form of unnatural food cravings, faint or unreadable signals, or no signals at all.

The process that can make your appestat dependable, probably for the first time within memory, begins with ending your dependency on industrially and chemically adulterated foods. In a sense, it begins to talk to you because you are talking to it in a language it comprehends. This regeneration is accelerated by *consciousness*—knowing where you are going and how to get there.

No, you can't interpret the craving for chocolate ice cream as a message from your appestat that your vital organs need a big dose of chocolate, sugar, fat, and chemical emulsifier. You can't even expect that you will eventually hear messages like, "flounder," "corn meal," "spinach". What you can expect is that in time, confronted with a variety of natural foods, you will intuitively find yourself choosing the ones that are appropriate for your nutritional requirements.

For some people, even more useful than reading books like this is to meditate on the nature of food: drawing on all your experience with and observation of food, there is a wealth of knowledge directly applicable to you, asleep in your unconscious mind. Whether you call it meditation, connecting your appestat, tuning in to body wisdom, or listening to your inner voice, the point is that intuition is a quality inborn to every one of us. We need to reach for it. That's how each of us, for ourselves, can become an expert on what to eat.

10 New American Meal Planning

Everybody has to eat, and more and more people want to get the best nutrition for their food dollar. But there are a lot of questions . . . and it's hard to find answers because leading authorities don't agree. Faced with these dilemmas, many consumers are unwilling to wait for all the experts to agree. They want to understand the facts as best we know them, so they can decide for themselves what actions to take
         —From *Food*, published by the Science and Education Administration of the U.S.D.A.

THE ELEMENTS OF MEAL PLANNING

The twin themes of food quality and economy are interwoven throughout the pages of this book. Those themes form the background for all meal planning. Participants in the New American Cuisine look for naturalness and freshness, buy as much bulk food as possible, and undertake as much of their own food processing as is compatible with individual lifestyles.

The objective of economy will stand without need of further comment. Quality, however, has two aspects of equal importance—nutritional value and taste. These two aspects are so tightly locked together that an emphasis on one tends to fulfill the requirements of the other. Choosing food in order to fulfill the wide variety of your nutritional requirements will automatically bring you a wide variety of tastes; choosing food to satisfy a wide variety of tastes will automatically fulfill many of your various nutritional requirements (when those tastes are for fresh, natural food).

Taste brings another important meal-planning consideration into view: We Americans share the privilege of eating for pleasure as well as for sustenance. This raises taste to the level of a major objective in meal planning. Consequently, the three major objectives behind planning New American Cuisine meals are *quality, economy, variety.*

The Food Groups Reoriented

What little most of us remember from a woefully deficient nutritional education has something to do with four basic food groups and the necessity to eat something from all of them every day. They were: the vegetable and fruit group; the bread and cereal group; the milk and cheese group; the meat, poultry, fish, beans group (which also included eggs). Since the official recognition in 1977 that Americans eat too much fat and sugar, the U.S.D.A. has created a fifth group: the fats, sweets, alcohol group ("a basic number of servings is not suggested for this group"—*Food*, U.S.D.A.).

The New American Cuisine has *seven* food groups:

1. The whole grain and potato group (complex carbohydrates);
2. The vegetable group;
3. The beans, seeds, nuts group (vegetable protein);
4. The meat, fish, poultry group (animal protein);
5. The dairy and eggs group;
6. The fruit group;
7. The fats, sweets, salt, spices group (including vegetable oils, honey, molasses, etc.)—for the sake of convenience, the *miscellaneous* group.

NOTE: A reminder that the food groups are greatly oversimplified—a clam has a little carbohydrate, an apple has a little protein, a grain of wheat has significant percentages of protein and fat.

DAILY FOOD GROUP SERVINGS
ADJUSTED FOR METABOLIC CATEGORIES

Food Groups		Metabolic Types— Servings Per Day				
	Vegetarian		Balanced		Meat-eating	
1. Whole grain & potato group	7		6		5	
2. Vegetable group	6		5		3	
3. Beans, nuts, seeds, group*	1		2		3	
4. Meat, fish, poultry group*	1	3*	2	6*	4	10*
5. Dairy and eggs group*	1		2		3	
6. Fruit group	3		2		1	
7. Miscellaneous group	traces		traces		traces	

*These three groups—the protein groups—are combined to suit necessity or a preference such as vegetarianism.

SERVINGS DEFINED

Food Group	Amounts in Servings
1. Whole grain & potato	1 slice of bread
	½ c. cooked pasta
	½ c. cooked grain
	1 oz. dry breakfast cereal
	1 medium potato
2. Vegetables	½ c. cooked vegetable
	1 c. raw vegetable
	1 bowl salad
3. Beans, nuts, seeds	½ c. cooked beans
	½ c. raw nuts, seeds
	4 T. nut, seed butter
	5 oz. tofu
	4 oz. tempeh
4. Meat, fish, poultry	3 oz. cooked, boneless

5. Dairy and eggs	8 oz. milk
	8 oz. yogurt
	4 oz. cottage cheese
	2 oz. hard cheese
	1 egg
6. Fruit	1 apple
	1 orange
	1 banana
	½ melon
7. Miscellaneous	"traces" for example, a T. of vegetable oil, a tp. of honey, ⅛ tp. salt

NOTES: (1) In assaying the relative acid-alkaline-forming characteristics of the above table and the Daily Food Guide Frameworks drawn from it (pages 115–116), it should be remembered that whole grains are only slightly acid-forming. The major adjustments between metabolic categories are made by varying groups 2, 4, and 6.

(2) The numbers of servings represent an "average" person, meaning a statistical rather than a real one. These figures should not be interpreted as rigid dietary guidelines, but as illustrative of the fact that "balance" is achieved differently by different metabolic categories. Even people within the same metabolic category achieve balance differently, although there the differences are usually not as great.

Children's Servings

Since children are smaller than adults, their servings should be smaller, even though they will normally eat proportionally more food than adults. The following rule of thumb is gaining favor with nutritionists: *one tablespoon for each year of age.* Thus, four tablespoons is a serving for a four-year-old, and so forth. When children reach their teens, their serving size has usually drawn even with adults; thus, any children thirteen or older can generally be counted as adults for meal planning purposes.

It is important to bear in mind that these suggestions are rough guidelines and specifically where planning is concerned, you shouldn't feel obligated to have "X" number of servings of anything each and every day. Not only is balance a highly individual matter, it is also not achieved from scratch each day but in the ebb and flow of day connected with day.

As pointed out in Chapter 8, it is simple enough to find out what metabolic category you belong in, but if you haven't found out yet, haven't found out regarding other people you are planning for, or don't want to be bothered finding out, I suggest you assume everybody you are planning for is a balanced type unless they express a strong intuitive feeling to the contrary regarding themselves. Over time, such feelings will either be confirmed or refuted by making experimental deviations on both sides of the balanced median and observing any significant reactions.

DAILY FOOD GUIDE FRAMEWORK
(see Chapters 17–23 for recipe ideas)
Balanced Metabolism

Meal	*Framework*
Breakfast	2 servings *Whole grain and potato group*
	2 servings *Dairy and egg group*
Lunch	2 servings *Whole grain and potato group*
	2 servings *Meat, fish, poultry group*
	2 servings *Vegetable group*
Afternoon Snack	1 serving *Fruit group*
Dinner	2 servings *Whole grain and potato group*
	3 servings *Vegetable group*
	2 servings *Beans, nuts, seeds group*
Evening Snack	1 serving *Fruit group*

Sympathetic Metabolism

Meal	*Framework*
Breakfast	2 servings *Whole grain and potato group*
	1 serving *Dairy and egg group*
	1 serving *Fruit group*
Lunch	2 servings *Whole grain and potato group*
	1 serving *Beans, nuts, seeds group*
	3 servings *Vegetable group*
Afternoon Snack	1 serving *Fruit group*
Dinner	3 servings *Whole grain and potato group*
	3 servings *Vegetable group*
	1 serving *Meat, fish, poultry group*
Evening Snack	1 serving *Fruit group*

Parasympathetic Metabolism

Meal	*Framework*
Breakfast	2 servings *Whole grain and potato group*
	2 servings *Dairy and egg group*
Lunch	1 serving *Whole grain and potato group*
	1 serving *Beans, nuts, seed group*
	2 servings *Meat, fish, poultry group*
	2 servings *Vegetable group*
Afternoon Snack	1 serving *Fruit group*

Meal	*Framework*
Dinner	2 servings *Whole grain and potato group*
	1 serving *Beans, nuts, seed group*
	2 servings *Meat, fish, poultry group*
	1 serving *Vegetable group*
	1 serving *Dairy and egg group*
Evening Snack	1 serving *Beans, nuts, seeds group*

VARIETY REVISITED

Focusing on variety brings four key features on the New American Cuisine into view; that it

1. is widely international,
2. makes broad application of the principles of protein complementarity,
3. stresses the use of inexpensive cuts of meat, less meat, or no meat at all,
4. may frequently use one-pot meals.

This approach employs "principles already laid down by the best traditional French, Italian and Chinese cuisines, nations which have perfected the art of making a little luxury go a long way . . ." These peoples, says Dorothy Hollingsworth, Director-General of the British Nutrition Foundation, "have learned how to juxtapose a few simple ingredients so as to achieve the best of flavor and visual appeal."

Using internationalism as a primary motif, the following examples illustrate how the four themes interweave.

Entrée	*Nationality*	*Major Ingredients*
Meatballs	Italian	Ground beef, sauce, whole wheat pasta or brown rice
	German	
	Swedish	
	Hawaiian	
Enchiladas	Mexican	Corn meal, meat, cheese
Egg foo young	Chinese	Eggs and vegetables with brown rice
Moussaka	Greek	Eggplant, lamb, sauce, with brown rice
Lasagne	Italian	Whole wheat pasta with meat and/or cheese
Sukiyaki	Japanese	Meat, vegetables, brown rice
Chicken pot pie	English	Chicken, vegetables, whole wheat crust
Beef stroganoff	Hungarian	Beef, sour cream, whole wheat noodles
Couscous	Moroccan	Meat in sauce on whole wheat (bulgur)
Curry	Indian	Beans, vegetables, brown rice
Chilis rellenos	Mexican	Peppers, eggs, brown rice
Sloppy Joe	American	Ground beef, sauce, whole wheat bread
Paella	Spanish	Shellfish, vegetables, brown rice
Stew	International	With or without meat or fish; vegetables, grain or potato

Many of the above dishes can be made in both meat and meatless versions, with beans an almost universal substitute for meat. Made either way, the laws of complementarity provide excellent protein values. Following my practice of using recipes to illustrate cooking principles, I have not included recipes for the above dishes. There are many excellent full-length books devoted to international cooking; the common flaw in them is the use of refined rather than natural ingredients. With the understanding gleaned from this book, however, that flaw usually is easily remedied.

IN CASE YOU'RE STUCK

The work of Anna Gordon, dietician at Columbia-Presbyterian Medical Center, makes casseroles particularly worthy of mention. *Eating Better For Less* (Rodale Press) called it "an amazing piece of work" (and I agree), and reports, "Anyone who says meatless eating is boring should take a look at this chart. Using only thirty ingredients, it has an unbelievable, 7,776 possible meals." In my adaptation, columns 1, 2, 3, and 5 provide four-way protein complementarity, yielding extremely high protein values.

THE CASSEROLE MIXMASTER

2 cups cooked (1)	1 cup cooked (2)	Sauce* (3)	Vegetables to make 1 ½ c. (4)	3–5 T. topping (5)
Brown rice	Pinto beans	Cream of tomato	Sauteed celery & green onions	Wheat germ
Whole wheat macaroni	Lima beans	Cream of potato	Mushrooms & bamboo shoots	Slivered almonds
Millet	Peas	Cream of mushroom	Sauteed green pepper & garlic	Soy grits
Whole wheat spaghetti	Kidney beans	Cream of celery	Cooked green beans	Grated cheese
Bulgur wheat	Black beans	Cream of leek (or onion)	Cooked carrots	Nutritional yeast
Whole wheat noodles	Garbanzos (chickpeas)	Cream of pea	Sauteed onion & pimento	Sunflower seeds

*Sauce: Ms. Gordon recommends the sauce be made from a can of soup and ¾ c. of water. I recommend making your own with ¾ c. of the cooked vegetable named in the sauce column, ¾ c. of water and 2 T. of noninstant dry milk powder, whizzed together in the blender. This also gives you the opportunity to try a wide variety of spices, e.g., basil, oregano, cumin, sage, chili and curry powders. My way is purer and more interesting, Ms. Gordon's quicker—your choice.

Directions for using The Casserole Mixmaster:

1. Select five ingredients, one from each column.
2. Mix the ingredients selected from the first four columns.

3. Pour the mixture into a one-quart, oiled casserole dish and bake thirty minutes at 375°F.
4. Select one ingredient from column 5 for topping, bake for fifteen minutes more at 325°F.
5. Season with salt to taste at the table, serve with salad and whole-grain bread.

You can also substitute and/or add your own ideas in all columns. You really can't go wrong where nutritional quality is concerned, though you will certainly like the tastes of some combinations better than others. The Casserole Mixmaster can be turned into an omnivarian tool by adding meat, fish and poultry in column 2; many other sauces and vetetables can find a home in columns 3 and 4. The Casserole Mixmaster is a handy tool to have around for those times when you run dry of ideas or haven't had time to plan ahead.

PLANNING AROUND RESTAURANTS

"I eat in restaurants a lot. So how can I follow a good diet?" Don't eat in restaurants so often. "But I have to; I travel a lot, and then there are all the business lunches and the social occasions." There are undoubtedly occasions when you will not be able to avoid restaurant food. Although we are talking about establishing a quality level that is relatively easy to establish at home and nowhere to be found in restaurants, we don't want to sit at every restaurant table with knots in our stomachs, feeling we are being attacked, if not poisoned outright. The best course is to make the best of it when you order, then relax and enjoy yourself.

The general formula for setting prices in restaurants is to multiply the cost of ingredients by 3 or 4 times; so $2 worth of ingredients will be priced from $5.95 to $7.95, depending, as they say, on what the traffic will bear. Most of the other costs in a restaurant are fixed, and the main variable expense is the food itself. So if costs are going to be held down, it will be by saving on the ingredients. The most common way for restaurants to keep the cost of ingredients down is to buy assembly-line factory food from the army of companies whose business is supplying restaurants, then heat, garnish, and serve.

Most of the factory food that is set in front of you on restaurant tables is highly refined, very fat, too salty, and laced with additives. The healthiest thing to know about restaurants is how to avoid factory food.

Beware Of:

—*Long menus filled with complicated dishes.* If these are to be made on the premises, a large and highly skilled staff is required. Most likely to come from a factory are those dishes involving rich, complex sauces, and puffy, flaky pastry crusts. Examples: stuffed cabbage, lasagne, shrimp or lobster or crab Newburg, chicken Kiev, coq au vin, coquilles Saint-Jacques, beef Wellington, beef Stroganoff, veal Cordon Bleu, quiche, chicken or beef pot pie, all kinds of dessert pastry. A short menu with sometimes sold-out specials of the day is much more likely to represent good ingredients.

—*The word "fresh,"* which ought to mean what it implies but is often deliberately misleading. "Fresh baked bread" or "homemade" or "baked on the premises" usually means frozen dough made "fresh" at the factory, perhaps in some vague imitation of a homemade loaf. The restaurant simply finished it off in its oven. "Fresh vegetables" usually means vegetables that were frozen when they were fresh. Fresh fish is often older than anything you would buy. Is it today's catch? Yesterday's? If it isn't either, you'd be better off if it were IQF (individually quick frozen). The usual ploy with old fresh fish is to float it in a pool of sauce. Sauces often mean white flour, lard, and salt as major ingredients.

—*Deep-fried anything, no matter what.* The oil is the poorest quality to begin with, held at 400°F or more, filtered to remove bits and scraps, added to as the food soaks up this carcinogenic liquid plastic, and used over and over. Truly dangerous!

—*Salad bars with big bowls of shredded iceburg lettuce,* soupy coleslaw, soupy mixes of canned beans and vegetables, creamy looking dressings. The dressings? Fat, salt, artificial. The beans and vegetables? Overcooked, salty, preserved. The shredded lettuce and cabbage? Old, vitamins and minerals oxidized and leached out by excessive water, preserved at the factory to keep it looking decent until you see it at the salad bar two days later.

You ought to be able to eat liberally at a salad bar, but, as with everything, there are salad bars and there are salad bars. Look for greens that have been hand torn, sprouts that are not brown, a maximum of things fresh, nothing canned, simple dressings.

Stick with dishes prepared by the simple, direct cooking methods: sautéed, stir-fried, poached, grilled. The fewer ingredients in your entrée, the better. Ask for whole wheat bread instead of white, butter instead of margarine, milk or half-and-half instead of nondairy creamer. Order baked potato in preference to any other kind; it is one of the most wholesome foods available in most restaurants.

Desserts are usually made mostly of white flour, a lot of some kind of fat, and a lot of sugar. "Homemade" or "our own special" are usually meaningless in the search for good desserts. The question is, was it made from scratch on the premises? They rarely are. Resist if you can.

Coffee

Waiters and waitresses in many restaurants are trying to pour coffee for you even before you start reading the menu. Just out of habit, most of us hardly notice and automatically start sipping. It is much healthier to wait until after you have finished eating, healthier yet to skip it entirely. It would be far more compatible with the pleasure of eating to order wine. (See Chapter 22 for more on coffee.)

Wine

Wine is closer to the composition of your gastric juices than any other natural beverage. Therefore it enhances the flavors and digestion of the food it accompanies. Drunk moderately, wine is also reputedly healthy because it has both vitamins B and P, all the major minerals, and some of the trace minerals. Not the least of its virtues is its mellowing effect, which can help you relax and enjoy your restaurant meal even though you suspect, probably rightly, that everything is not as good as it could be in the kitchen.

But everything might not be as you like it at the winery either. According to *Chemicals In Booze* ($4.95 from CSPI, 1755 S St. NW, Washington DC 20009), the government allows over eighty additives for winemaking, none of which are required to be listed on the label. Sulphur dioxide is called the "essential" wine additive. Winemakers say it has been used for over 2,000 years as a preservative for wine and that without it wine spoils within a few months. It is also used to halt fermentation and to kill bacteria on grapes and in winemakers' equipment. There is, in other words, no way for wine drinkers to avoid sulphur dioxide or its substitutes, potassium and sodium metabisulfite.

Sulphur dioxide and related chemicals are still under study to determine their effects on health. However, there is one class of people for whom there is no doubt about the risk: asthmatics. *Chemicals In Booze* notes that allergists have reported severe reactions to sulphur dioxide—wheezing, chest constriction, loss of breath and consciousness.

Other common additives in winemaking are acids, water, and sugar; regulations allow up to 53 percent of water and/or sugar. Substances such as egg white, gelatin, diatomaceous earth, bentonite, and cellulose are used for clarification and filtration, but are presumably removed from the finished product. Winemakers come closest to making a pure product when they bottle it unfiltered. Consumers avoid acids, water, and sugar in wine by not buying cheap, nonvarietal wines bottled with screw caps instead of corks.

11 Natural Weight Control

Goal 1. To avoid overweight, consume only as much energy (calories) as is expended; if overweight, *decrease energy intake and increase energy expenditure.*   GOALS

OVERWEIGHT BUT UNDERMOTIVATED?

Obesity is tolerated, even condoned, as is no other disease: fat and jolly Santa Claus, the epitome of generosity, for example—fatness is not only associated with joy and generosity but with contentment, wealth, and opulence. How can I call anything so good as fat a disease? The first definition of "disease" by Webster reads, "A condition of the body in which there is incorrect function resulting from the effect of heredity, infection, diet or environment . ." If it were not an "incorrect function" to be too fat, there would be no such term as *overweight.* Technically, you become *obese* once you are more than 20 percent above your normal or optimum weight.

Someone who would like to argue against their fatness being a disease can raise such arguments as, "I feel fine," and "My doctor says I'm in good health, just says I could lose a few pounds," and finally "Who knows what my normal weight should be, anyway?" But people in the early stages of cancer and heart disease often feel "fine" too. Obesity increases blood cholesterol, blood sugar, and blood pressure. Each 10 percent increase in weight results in a 30 percent increase in the risk of heart disease. Your doctor might have a complacent attitude towards obesity simply because he has a hundred other patients suffering from the disease. It's different from diseases that kill you directly; the effects of fat are indirect. The risk factor in seven out of ten of the leading causes of death is raised dramatically by being overweight and the risk goes higher and higher the fatter you get.

Each extra pound of fat represents one more mile of capillaries you heart has to pump blood through. You can't defend obesity by saying you don't have a heart problem; long-term obesity is a virtual guarantee you will develop one. Degrees of overweight correspond to degrees of sickness and if you're obese, you have a serious illness. It is also a curable disease.

What Is Overweight?

Perhaps even more common than undermotivation is its opposite, particularly in those women who are perpetually frustrated because they don't have the figure of a fashion model. The only way out for most of them is to *abandon* the fashion model self-image simply because it is unrealistic. It is as if I fancied myself as the world's fastest human: unrealistic and, if I remain stuck on such a self-image, perpetually frustrating. If, however, my expectations match my potential, I have a chance at fulfillment. Sure, it would be an exhilarating ego trip to be the world's fastest human or to have the figure of a fashion model; but really, let's face it, that's not me and that's not you.

Your normal weight? There are tables with average male and female height and weight figures but of course you are right in protesting that you are not an average person. It's not only your sex and height that determine how much you should weigh but your skeletal structure, metabolic rate, and whether you have the innate musculature of an ectomorph, mesomorph or endomorph. One woman five-foot-seven-inches tall should weigh 115 pounds; another the same height should weigh 135 pounds. One man six feet tall should weigh 160 pounds, another six-footer, 190. It is useless to try to judge whether or not you are overweight from tables that are not categorized according to body typology. The basic body types are as follows:

Ectomorphic: *thin* body build
Mesomorphic: muscular or *sturdy* body build
Endomorphic: *heavy* body build

BODY TYPES AND ACCEPTABLE WEIGHT RANGES

HEIGHT		MEN Small Frame	Medium Frame	Large Frame
Feet	Inches			
5	2	128–134	131–141	138–150
5	3	130–136	133–143	140–153
5	4	132–138	135–145	142–156
5	5	134–140	137–148	144–160
5	6	136–142	139–151	146–164
5	7	138–145	142–154	149–168
5	8	140–148	145–157	152–172
5	9	142–151	148–160	155–176
5	10	144–154	151–163	158–180
5	11	146–157	154–166	161–184
6	0	149–160	157–170	164–188
6	1	152–164	160–174	168–192
6	2	155–168	164–178	172–197
6	3	158–172	167–182	176–202
6	4	162–176	171–187	181–207

Weights at ages 25–59 based on lowest mortality.
Weight in pounds according to frame (in indoor clothing weighing five lbs., shoes with one-inch heels).

Source: 1979 Build Study, Society of Actuaries and Association of Life Insurance Medical Directors of America, 1980

	HEIGHT	WOMEN Small	Medium	Large
Feet	Inches	Frame	Frame	Frame
4	10	102–111	109–121	118–131
4	11	103–113	111–123	120–134
5	0	104–115	113–126	122–137
5	1	106–118	115–129	125–140
5	2	108–121	118–132	128–143
5	3	111–124	121–135	131–147
5	4	114–127	124–138	134–151
5	5	117–130	127–141	137–155
5	6	120–133	130–144	140–159
5	7	123–136	133–147	143–163
5	8	126–139	136–150	146–167
5	9	129–142	139–153	149–170
5	10	132–145	142–156	152–173
5	11	135–148	145–159	155–176
6	0	138–151	148–162	158–179

Weights at ages 25–59 based on lowest mortality.
Weight in pounds according to frame (in indoor clothing weighing three lbs., shoes with one-inch heels).

Source: 1979 Build Study, Society of Actuaries and Association of Life Insurance Medical Directors of America, 1980

I've never yet met anyone who didn't have an intuitive feeling for what he or she should weigh. Truly, as soon as you really want to know and are therefore ready to be honest with yourself, you know roughly how much you should weigh. Furthermore, nobody knows better than you. Tables such as the one above are mere objectification of intuitive knowledge you can have simply by reaching for it; their primary utility is to confirm that your expectations are realistic.

How Weight Is Gained And Lost

Assuming you are ready to join the army of Americans who have declared war on fat, I'll also assume that once you've won the war you won't want to fight it again. Therefore it's important to know how weight is gained in order to prevent what you lose from coming back. There are two critical factors:

1. Potential energy consumed in the form of food.
2. Actual energy expended in the form of exercise.

If potential energy consumed exceeds actual energy expended, the result is added weight. Conversely, if actual energy expended exceeds potential energy consumed, the result is lost weight.

Food > Exercise = Weight gain
Exercise > Food = Weight loss

Diet should almost never be considered apart from exercise (a faulty heart, for example, might constitute an exception). Convinced as I am of the value of natural food, I am even more convinced of the importance of exercise. Unquestionably, a major reason .for the American epidemic of obesity is our sedentary lifestyle. The way out is to reverse directions; we must improve both our eating *and* our exercise habits.

The potential energy in food is measured in calories. It can be useful to get a calorie counter and measure the energy value of the food you eat. After you've worked with it for a while, you'll develop a feel for how much of certain kinds of food is too much and you can drop the use of the device. Some people use the device with enough dedication to lose weight significantly. By cutting back caloric intake severely for long enough, weight will be lost. But this method wins the battle, not the war. As soon as you relax a bit too much or too long, weight begins to reappear—the war goes on; you must engage in battle yet again.

However, you can never win a war if you don't know who the enemy is. Calorie counters win battles but lose wars because the enemy is not calories. In the war against fat the enemy is a lifestyle. That lifestyle has a front and a back that can't be separated: excess food and insufficient exercise.

Exercise is the way out of endless warfare. Generally speaking, you meet two kinds of people who have lost weight: "But I really have to watch my calories"—these people are not exercising. "Now I can pretty much eat what I want"—these people are exercising.

I like the various forms of walking such as hiking and mountain climbing; I like cycling and running. In my book, *The Zen of Running*, I tried to make three points:

—You don't have to be an athlete to run; anybody with two legs can do it.
—If you have the right attitude—that is, if you're good to yourself—you can enjoy it.
—Once you're enjoying it, running can even be a form of meditation.

Even so, I don't think running is for everyone. But there is *some* form of exercise for everyone, something you can enjoy doing. If I'm wrong about that, you should do something anyway, perhaps whatever it is you hate the least. Exercise is just too critical not to do it. The minimum we need is four half-hour sessions a week of something rigorous enough to make us pant and sweat (but build up to it slowly).

Debilitating as it is, obesity also represents a great opportunity. Winning the war by utilizing both diet and exercise, we transform negative disease symptoms into the virtues of positive health. We feel better and everybody who knows us can tell because we look better. It's not just that we're thinner; we *glow*, we radiate health.

OBESITY IN CHILDREN

When I was a kid thirty-some years ago, few of my peers were fat; sure, there were some who were on the chubby side, but as for obesity, I can't remember a single case. Jane Brody, the nutrition writer for *The New York Times*, contends that children are obese these days because of lack of exercise, not, usually, from overeating. I agree with her. While I was growing up there was no TV to watch. There were radio programs for kids but they didn't come on until evening. So we were much more active than kids have been during the past twenty-five years. The same relationship that applies to normal weight and exercise in adults applies to children.

There are more reasons than obesity to turn off the TV and send your children out for some good, hard exercise. Where TV is concerned, there is the constant bombardment of radiation; nobody knows fully yet what the long-range results of that particular form of pollution have been and will be. Beyond that, there's the invaluable building of strength and coordination that comes from prolonged, vigorous exercise in childhood. It lays down a foundation for the rest of life that cannot be duplicated in the adult years, no matter how much you exercise. You can strengthen the foundation of a standing house but it can never be quite as solid as the foundation that was properly laid down before the house was built. Get those kids off their backsides, on their feet, then get them moving.

WHEN THE REAL CALORIES STAND UP TO BE COUNTED

An understanding of the significance of calories can be extremely useful, particularly if it is an understanding of calories as they relate to physical activity. There are three essential elements to your working knowledge of calories:

1. The generality that a pound of fat contains 3,500 calories. Therefore, using 3,500 more calories of energy than you consume results in the loss of a pound.
2. You need one of the many available tables that tells you the calorie values of various foods.
3. You need to know how the expenditure of energy translates into calories, as in the following table:

CALORIE EXPENDITURES PER HOUR

	Women		Activity		Men	
Thin	*Sturdy*	*Heavy*		*Thin*	*Sturdy*	*Heavy*
80	85	90	*Sedentary*	90	95	100
			(reading, writing, watching TV)			
110	120	135	*Light*	135	145	160
			(walking slowly, washing dishes, driving a car)			
170	185	205	*Moderate*	205	220	240
			(normal walking pace, shopping)			

	Women		*Activity*		*Men*	
Thin	Sturdy	Heavy		Thin	Sturdy	Heavy
250	275	300	*Vigorous*	300	325	350

(walking fast, bowling, golfing without cart, gardening)

330	365	400	*Strenuous*	400	425	450

(all the activities that cause you to sweat freely and pant for air,
like running, swimming and cycling)

The calorie numbers above are approximations. The exact number of calories you expend in any given activity depends on your weight and body condition. The heavier you are the more calories you expend to perform any given activity. The better the conditioning of your body, the fewer calories it takes to perform any given activity (for this reason once you get into "good shape," you stop losing weight, and your activities maintain the body weight that's right for you).

There are two ways the above table can be useful. One way is illustrated, for example, when you know there are 400 calories in that chocolate milkshake you just had. You also know your general body type is heavy, so, since you're a woman, it will take an hour of strenuous activity, an hour and twenty minutes of vigorous activity, a bit less than two hours of moderate activity, and so forth, to work off those calories. The formula for making this kind of calculation is to

1. Divide the number of calories per hour for the type of activity you are interested in by 60 minutes:

$$\frac{300 \text{ calories (of vigorous activity)}}{60 \text{ minutes}} = 5 \text{ calorie minutes}$$

2. Divide the number of calories in the food by the answer obtained in step 1:

$$\frac{400 \text{ calories (in the chocolate milkshake)}}{5 \text{ calorie minutes}} = 80 \text{ minutes of vigorous activity}$$

Calculating calorie quotients is another use for the calorie expenditure table, meaning that you can get an approximation of the calories you burn up each day. First you have to approximate the amount of time you spend at various levels of activity. For this you also include sleep, rated at half of your sedentary expenditure. If you are a sturdily built woman, for example, you would multiply the figures in that column by the amount of time averaged in that type of activity:

Activity	*Hours*	*×Calorie Expenditure*	*= Calories*
Sleep	8	42.5	340
Sedentary	11	85	935
Light	2	120	240
Moderate	1	185	185
Vigorous	1	275	275
Strenuous	1	365	365
Total			2340

This assumes your body weight is in the "acceptable" range (see pages 122–123); it also assumes you are of average height (5'5", 126 lbs., is the composite). To make the calorie expense account more useful to you personally, it should be adjusted from the average as follows:

Male Heights		Female Heights
5'2"–5'4"	multiply average by 80%	4'10"–5'0"
5'5"–5'7"	multiply average by 90%	5'1"–5'3"
5'8"–5'10"	use the average	5'4"–5'6"
5'11"–6'	multiply average by 110%	5'7"–5'9"
6'2"–6'4"	multiply average of 120%	5'10"–6'0"

So, the sturdy woman calorie expense account looks different, though these sturdy women are all following the same activity schedules, because they are all different heights and weights:

Height	Calorie Expense Account
4'10"	1870
5'2"	2105
5'5"	2340
5'8"	2575
6'0"	2810

Calorie counting is much too dull an affair to incorporate permanently. Its major application is to weight loss, not proper weight maintenance. In the latter regard, it can be useful in gaining an understanding of how much of what types of exercise are required for you to maintain an acceptable body weight. The important thing in all this is not to lose sight of the diet/exercise relationship.

The diet/exercise connection is the essence of natural weight control, because eating *and* exercising are natural for human beings. A sedentary lifestyle, in which more energy is consumed than expended, is unnatural and should be compensated for by regular, vigorous exercise. Everything related to physical human health benefits from vigorous exercise performed regularly.

To various degrees, just about everybody experiences a tendency towards laziness. To begin with, you may only have promises to use against laziness: I'll do it because it will make me feel better. Once you have managed to push yourself into reasonable condition, you may be one of the fortunate ones who not only enjoys the way you feel afterwards, but even enjoys the walking, running, swimming, tennis, or whatever, while you're doing it.

Compulsion is the ultimate countermeasure to laziness—want to or not, you do it because you are *compelled* to, knowing it makes the greatest contribution to your ultimate well-being. It is another form of enlightened self-interest. Food is really the lesser value in the weight loss equation; exercise is the greater value because it imparts muscle tone and overall internal efficiency by stimulating digestion, absorption, circulation, oxygenation, detoxification, and elimination.

DIETING

We hear people say they are "on a diet" when they decline the hors d'oeuvres and dessert and we understand that it is only a temporary state of affairs. They will win this battle but after a bit the war will start to go against them again and they will be back on that diet, or the latest one, again. How many times can they fight the battle before they give up, and sink into lifelong corpulence, knowing their sedentary ways doom them in warfare? Diets are not the answer. Of them, GOALS says,

The evergrowing list of diets are an affirmation of the fact that no diet yet described is by itself a solution to the problem of obesity. The truth of this statement is reflected in the fact that new diets appear yearly, each claiming to be the "ultimate solution." The list of diets include low-carbohydrate diets, high-protein diets, high-fat diets, and diets which contain mainly a single food. . . ."

None of these battle plans could get to the point of being called "a diet" if they weren't somewhat successful. GOALS goes on to observe,

Obesity experts differ as to the reasons for the general failure of many obese people to maintain weight loss. However, the obesity treatments which are the most successful over time tend to modify the total diet in a balanced manner.

True as far as it goes, but the obesity treatments that are even more successful modify the *total lifestyle* in a balanced manner.

The most recent research indicates that the least effective approach to *permanent* weight loss is the use of diet pills, which have dangerous side effects and have never had FDA approval. The most effective are methods that succeed in modifying behavior. The defect in most behavior modification programs is that they are an immature sort of self-manipulation. You give yourself a reward every time you lose X number of pounds, playing games with yourself as if you were a child. No doubt this works better than pills; but it is not the *release* into permanent weight loss *and* boundless vitality that real change can effect. Obesity is intricately connected with habits surrounding excess food and insufficient exercise. Real change consists of developing new habits to replace old ones.

Old Food Habits To Replace

The three food types to replace in a weight-loss program are:

—Refined carbohydrates
—Fatty foods
—Alcoholic beverages

Refined Carbohydrates. White bread, white rice, white pasta, and potatoes that have been cut and peeled before cooking must be listed along with soft drinks, pastries, candies, presweetened breakfast cereals and canned fruits.

The two main culprits are white flour and white sugar—the "empty calorie" or "foodless" foods. Here we are dealing with the fact that a calorie is only an expression of quantity, and tells us absolutely nothing about quality. A cup of white flour has the same number of calories as a cup of whole wheat flour but, as we saw in the Introduction, it is not the same cup of nutritional value—the white cup is empty by comparison, emptied of most of the vitamins, minerals, and fiber, and much of the enzymes and protein.

The metabolic mechanisms at work to make empty-calorie foods fat producers are not clearly understood. Certainly it has something to do with the absence of fiber, discouraging peristalsis in the intestine, and allowing food to linger longer than it should (also a causative factor in diverticulitis and cancer of the bowel). Beyond that one ventures into the realm of theory. I call it "the theory of metabolic complexity," explained thus:

The needs of the body that must be supported by nutrition are complex. Every cell of our bodies is replaced in a continuous process within seven years. We are constantly building bone, connective tissue, muscle, and fatty tissue. We are maintaining and repairing circulatory, nervous, and lymphatic systems, growing hair and nails, replacing and building energy reserves. All these needs and others are met by the process of metabolism, defined as the sum of the physiochemical processes by which protoplasm is produced, maintained, and destroyed, and by which energy is made available.

Complex foods—whole, unrefined, natural foods—have the greatest potential for matching our complex metabolic needs. The more a food is refined, the more nutrients are removed, the less potential that food has for matching our complex metabolic requirements. Due to its complexity, the unrefined food might be able to contribute to a dozen functions; due to its lack of complexity, the refined food might be able to contribute to only a few different functions.

Furthermore, we are looking at more than just a failure to deliver; we are looking at *deprivation*. A nourishing food cannot occupy the place already occupied by the empty food. Our metabolic needs must remain unsatisfied until the food bearing the required nutrients finally arrives. We may feel hungry most of the time and nothing seems to fully appease our appetites. Therefore, food that has been devitalized by refining processes is a metabolic *liability* to a degree corresponding to the degree of refinement and the amount consumed. A nutritionist friend of mine refers to refined foods as "negative nutrients."

The ultimate example of negative food value is the completely refined carbohydrate that literally has nothing left to measure except calories—white sugar. We are all aware that eating sweets produces fat. Why? Sugar is too lacking in complexity to fulfill any need but immediate energy. Chemically, sugar is nothing but carbon, hydrogen, and oxygen and that's all fat is too: from sugar we get fat.

So my theory of metabolic complexity states: (1) complex metabolic needs cannot be met by foods lacking complexity; (2) ingesting foods lacking in complexity leads to metabolic imbalances; (3) the most common response to metabolic imbalance is the creation of fat.

Fatty Foods and Alcohol. Fatty foods and alcohol should be limited in a natural weight-control diet because they are extremely high in calories compared to carbohydrate and protein: fat averages 225 percent more calories and alcohol 1759 percent more than equal amounts of either carbohydrate or protein. Recent USDA studies indicate that the amount of calories from food in the average American diet has actually gone down since 1965. During the same time, however, the amount of calories from alcohol has gone up and obesity has become a greater problem than ever before.

Eating Habits

Besides the food habits, there are habits surrounding the way food is eaten that have a bearing on obesity. Consider these:

1. Slow down. It takes less food to appease hunger when you eat slowly. Perhaps the best way to cultivate the habit of eating slowly is to count the number of times you chew each mouthful of food—say twenty times. Three or four weeks of this is usually enough to establish a slower eating pace, automatically reducing intake. This also improves digestion and assimilation, so that lesser quantities have an equal or even greater nutritional impact.

2. Think smaller. Having worked your way slowly through a meal, that meal will also have consisted of smaller portions. Cook less, but don't be too drastic, to avoid feeling deprived; reducing the amounts you cook by 25 percent is a reasonable approach. This is also essential to making the next point fully effective.

3. Avoid seconds. Almost always, the first helping is the food you need, the second helping is the food you don't need.

4. Avoid desserts. The sweet at the end of the meal is also almost always extra food. It is also usually chemically incompatible with the food that preceded it, causing indigestion, heartburn, and flatulence.

5. Encourage your own maturity. Many of our parents inadvertently created a bad habit pattern by using food as a reward—"If you're a good boy, you can have a lollipop." The food-as-reward syndrome has much to do with adult attachments to immature foods such as soft drinks, candy, and other junk foods. We often resist entering into the pleasures of eating wholesome foods because they replace lifelong favorites. We are not conscious of the childhood roots tying us to childish foods. Natural foods seem "weird," while unhealthy fabrications seem normal. An impartial, mature appraisal of the chemistry and biology of junk foods, however, clearly show them to be the weird ones—extremely weird, whether we remember childhood fondly or not.

BALANCED EATING FOR PERMANENT NORMAL WEIGHT

One of the best foods in natural weight control is bread, ironic because bread has the reputation of being a fat producer. GOALS comments on the incorrect view of bread as a fattening food:

Bread is of intermediate caloric density, and a relatively good protein source. Professor Olaf Mickelsen of Michigan State University, reports in *Cereal Foods World* of July, 1975: "Contrary to what most people think, bread in large amounts is an ideal food in a weight-reducing regimen. Recent work in our laboratory indicates that slightly overweight young men lost weight in a painless and practically effortless manner when they included twelve slices of bread per day in their program.

THE WRONG KIND OF DIET FOR LOSING WEIGHT

Jane Brody's Nutrition Book points out that the human body is made to use *glucose* (blood sugar) for energy, and that glucose is the by-product of carbohydrate metabolism. If you deprive yourself of carbohydrates, you force your body to use protein and fat for energy—somewhat analogous to trying to make a gasoline engine run on kerosene or diesel fuel, either of which causes severe problems in gasoline engines.

Fat is the wrong fuel, she explains, because it burns inefficiently without the carbohydrates to accompany it, polluting the blood with a waste product called *ketones*, which can cause nausea, fatigue, apathy, and brain damage. Further, they put an undue burden on the kidneys, which must assume the task of ridding the bloodstream of the pollutants as fast as possible.

Protein is the wrong fuel for the same general reason: inefficiency. In this case there is the formation of excess nitrogen as a pollutant in the bloodstream. All blood pollutants have the characteristic of causing fatigue, apathy, and a general weakening of your system. Like fat, protein for energy stresses the kidneys.

What kind of diet does Jane Brody think you should follow in order to lose weight? A balanced diet.

That bread was eaten with their meals. As a result, they became satisfied before they consumed their usual quota of calories. The subjects were admonished to restrict those foods that were concentrated sources of energy; otherwise, they were free to eat as much as they desired. In eight weeks, the average weight loss for each subject was 12.7 pounds." That translates into about 83 pounds over a year. The eight-week weight-loss average for white bread was 13.7 pounds; for whole wheat bread it was 19.4 pounds—whole wheat bread was 42 percent more effective.

Colin Tudge in *Future Food* agrees with GOALS:

In short, the nutritionists' traditional attitude to carbohydrate has been completely reversed. . . . [According to the old approach] the first thing fat people cut down on is potatoes. . . . Yet the diet of the demonstrably svelte, even thin, rural African is very high in carbohydrate. And of course the enemy of the slimmer is not carbohydrate itself, but refined carbohydrate—the white flour which is pure starch, and, in particular, the pure sugar that is 100% sucrose (and brown sugar is just as bad as white). If you ate carbohydrate only in unrefined form—whole wheat flour, lashings of fruit and vegetables, and all the potatoes you can eat—then it would be difficult to grow fat.

It would also be difficult to remain overweight, assuming the quantities to be moderate. The New American Diet and Cuisine described in this book is in itself a *permanent* weight-loss program, even though that is not its primary objective. Energy is produced in our cells through a complex interaction of carbohydrates, proteins, fats, vitamins, minerals, and enzymes; complex carbohydrates are the category of food which contain the best balance of all those essential elements; therefore they should be the principal food for everybody, overweight or not.

Vegetarians are generally thinner than meat-eaters. In a study of 200 people reported by the American Dietetic Association, vegetarians averaged twenty pounds less than meat-eaters, who averaged almost fifteen pounds overweight (*Journal of The American Dietetic Association*, March, 1973). This does not mean that the cure for obesity is pure vegetarianism. With an understanding of Chapters 8 and 9, you realize that pure vegetarianism may be wrong for your metabolic type (it may, of course, also be right). What it certainly does mean is more grains and vegetables in general, thus going in a vegetarian direction if not into a pure form.

I have seen many people who were overweight but not obese normalize their weight without trying, by switching to a diet dominated by whole grains and fresh vegetables, augmented by other foods such as beans, dairy products, meat, nuts, and seeds. Such a dietary approach is the most healthful road to weight reduction. And it will last for the rest of your life.

MODERATION

One commonly hears people on a weight-reducing diet complain that they are "starving to death." They're talking about how hungry they feel but often they're about half right in describing their condition—starving, though not to the point of death. Starving, as in fasting, for a brief period can be healthy, but generally speaking starving is unhealthy. All of our experience and observation confirms that good health depends on good nutrition. Poor health is an unncessarily high price to pay for slenderness. Losing weight too fast also puts undue stress on the heart. So, in most cases "crash" programs are inadvisable.

The *Harvard Medical School Health Letter*, December 1980, said this about crash diets:

A bad idea. Crash diets, especially when they are low in carbohydrate, produce rapid fluid loss in the first week or so. (This fluid loss has nothing to do with how much liquid is drunk; it is a change

BLOCKING THE STARCH BLOCKERS

A year of your life will not go by without at least one company stepping forward to proclaim, "You can outwit nature with our new Magic Bullet." Wizards of the laboratory will invent clever ways to short-circuit natural processes and you can be sure that they will thereby create imbalances. It may be years before the side effects of the imbalances appear, by which time the wizards will be playing entirely new games with your body—if you allow it.

The best way to judge their claims is to ask, "How does it work?" It will always be some kind of easy answer, but if it works by playing tricks with your metabolic processes, it is not a magic bullet: it's a time bomb. I asked Dr. Jimmy Scott, director of *A Center for Nutrition and Natural Healing*, in San Francisco, about this season's easy-answer Magic Bullet. He said:

Starch blockers are being pushed as the magical new way to lose weight. They are a substance extracted from raw beans which interferes with an enzyme in the pancreas called alpha-amylase. Its function is to break down complex carbohydrates into simple sugars that the body can utilize. If you interfere with the action of this enzyme the complex carbohydrates don't get broken down, the food is not digested, and those calories, therefore, don't count. The typical tablet or capsule will interfere with about 100 grams of complex carbohydrates, which is about 400 calories.

The effectiveness of the process is not so much in question, as are the *side effects*. Complex carbohydrates, such as whole grains and potatoes, are among the most nutritious foods available. Starch blockers may deprive the body of the vitamins, minerals, protein, etc. contained in them, which can lead to nutritional deficiencies and severe problems.

Also, research studies have shown that animals do not grow as fast even *after* they've quit taking the starch blocker, indicating that there may be permanent, unrecognized, effects.

Because starch blockers interfere with the digestive process, particles of food get into areas of the intestines where they're not supposed to be. The body attempts to reject these particles, creating an allergic reaction and leading to the production of mucous and other protective substances. People who take starch blockers frequently, especially over a long period of time, will, I believe, produce food allergies in themselves.

There may be additional side effects as well. Because starch blockers interfere with one function of the pancreas, they may also affect other functions, such as blood sugar control or other enzymes. These possibilities have not been researched.

In summation, I am quite convinced that people who take starch blockers will produce effects in themselves that they will undoubtedly wish they hadn't.

A month or so after the above was written, the FDA banned starch blockers, agreeing with Dr. Scott that their safety is unproven. I approve of their action but must observe that the FDA only seems able to move so swiftly in our interests when there are no big corporate power brokers lobbying for a product. The giants of industry had no large stake in starch blockers, so for once the public did not serve as industry's laboratory rats.

in the body's ability to hold fluid.) Many dieters, fooled by the scales, think their fat is "melting off." It isn't. Fat is coming off, slowly, but it is easily regained when the diet is abandoned. And most crash diets, because they are so extreme, are soon abandoned. Also, not only fat but protein can be lost during an extreme diet (or a fast) and when weight is regained it is regained first as fat. So, indeed, the crash dieter may wind up with more fat than he or she started with.

Losing a pound a day is too fast; a half pound is fast enough. If you were 100 pounds overweight, it would be better to lose it in a year than in six months, to avoid straining your heart and kidneys. This moderate approach is accomplished naturally by changing to the New American Diet.

12   Vitamins & Minerals

The question usually goes something like this: "If you eat a good diet—no junk, nothing but organically grown natural foods—doesn't that cover your nutritional needs?" Probably not, though it may. It depends on who you are and how you live. It may if you have an efficient metabolism, choose the foods right for your type, in the right amounts; if you live in the country where the air and water are clean, free from noise pollution and the other stresses of fast-paced, competitive metropolitan life; if you exercise a lot, spend a lot of time outdoors, live by the sun and your intuition instead of the clock. But those qualifications apply to only the tiniest percentage of us. Most of us, because of the way we have chosen to live (not necessarily wrong choices), are subjected to unnatural stress. This stress, both external and internal pollution, is at least to some degree natural to contemporary life. But our bodies—developed over hundreds or thousands of centuries without industry and technology—react to modern physiological, psychological, or environmental stress as to a foreign invader. Most of us need help to resist the invasion of the various pollutants.

Other reasons for taking vitamins and minerals trace directly to the land. Virgin soil broken to the plow by our forefathers had 5 percent and more humus (organic matter). Once humus falls below 2.5 percent, the tendency is for minerals to leach out. Most of our farmland now averages between .5 and 1.5 percent humus. Deficiencies of vital trace elements such as cobalt, zinc, and selenium have become widespread.

Six inches of virgin topsoil with 5 percent humus could hold six inches of rain in an hour and produce wheat with 18 percent protein. Our depleted soil with 1.5 percent humus can hold only a half inch of rain and produces wheat of 11 percent protein. The impoverished soil still produces crops when the artificial fertilizers are poured on. But the complete nutrition they should contain is not in them because *it is not in the soil.* To keep up the yields, each year more and more fertilizer must be poured on, the real soil fertility is further degraded, and the nutritional value of the crops that feed us is further impoverished.

Even further impoverishment occurs due to the widespread use of hybrid seeds, bred not to increase the nutritional value of food crops but to produce ever more quantity from each and every acre—yet another example of the quantity-over-quality choice encouraged by our culture. Compared to old-fashioned open-pollinated seeds, hybrid seeds consistently fail to take up minerals, both major and minor, from the soil. "Compared to some 4,000 samples of corn tested in ten midwest states in a single year, Steinbronn's [an organic farmer] open-pollinated corn [non-hybrid seed] contained 75 percent more crude protein, 875 percent more copper, 345 percent more iron, and 205 percent more manganese. The same trend has also been seen in the content of calcium, sodium, magnesium, and zinc." (*An Acres U.S.A. Primer*, Walters and Fenzau.)

People who grew up before World War II wonder why food does not taste as good as it used to. One reason is that being older, their taste buds are duller. Another reason is that the food is not as good nutritionally and the lack of flavor betrays the fact. Food that is as nourishing as nature intended is a dream that will not come true until we employ organic methods to rebuild our farmland on a wholesale scale (see Epilog).

Almost all of us need nutritional help. One of the best forms of help, or insurance, is a good vitamin/mineral supplement. The question, then, is what does "good" mean when applied to vitamin/mineral supplements? I would like to be able to simply say, "Good means natural" and move on to the next subject. But it is not possible to be so simple.

NATURAL VS. SYNTHETIC: A BOGUS ISSUE?

Chemists commonly make two statements about natural as compared to synthetic vitamins. One is that "chemically they are the same;" the other is that "there is no difference." The first statement is correct; natural and synthetic are chemical look-alikes. But the second statement is incorrect: there is a difference between natural and synthetic vitamins.

The chemist feels obliged to deny a difference between natural and synthetic vitamins because there is no precise definition of what that difference is. Offered shreds of evidence, he dismisses them as "anecdotal," which they are. But for me they simply confirm what hardly requires confirmation, because I consider a significant difference between natural and synthetic to be self-evident.

Perhaps the clearest method of discerning this difference is by chromatography. Chromatograms, long used in urine analysis, were first used to display biological differences in foods and soils by Dr. Ehrenfried Pfeiffer in 1953. In this method of analysis the material to be analyzed is liquified and the solution is absorbed by a strip of filter paper. The solution leaves a profile on the paper which, enlarged and photographed, is called a chromatogram. Every chromatogram I have seen comparing natural with synthetic vitamins has shown distinct differences of color and pattern. Although the chemical analyses are the same, *something* is different about them.

The differences between natural and synthetic chromatograms may be at least partially explainable by the difference in polarization. Polarization is the state in which rays of light exhibit different properties in different directions. The natural vitamin may be *dextrorotary*, meaning that its molecules rotate light rays clockwise. The synthetic vitamin may be *levorotary*, rotating light rays counterclockwise. When Dr. Roger Williams was learning to synthesize pantothenic acid, he discovered that he could produce an exact chemical duplicate of the natural form, but it was "useless" until he learned to make it dextrorotary like the natural form.

Chromatograms can provide clues about biological activity. Biological activity measures the degree to which a substance exhibits lifelike qualities, and the assumption is that the higher the biological activity, the more compatible the substance is with live organisms. Synthetic vitamin E, according to research cited by J.R. Carlson Laboratories, was found to have only about 21 percent of natural E's biological activity. Jeffrey Bland, Ph.D., has found that synthetic E inhibits the anti-oxidant properties of natural E, one of the major reasons for taking E in the first place. (Technical information on vitamin E is available from Carlson Laboratories, 15 College Dr., Arlington Heights, IL 60004; ask for their publication *Your Questions About Vitamin E.*)

When a vitamin is made in nature, it is a by-product of a complex life process. Intricately involved with that isolated chemical structure we call a vitamin, are all sorts of enzymes, amino acids, hormones, starches, minerals and, yes, things as yet undiscovered. Processes of metabolism, transmutation, respiration and photosynthesis are involved, as are blood and lymph or sap. The laboratory and the factory are incapable of simulating the natural complexities; no attempt is made to do so. The synthetic imitation of the natural vitamin is manufactured by combining the chemical constituents; the chemistry is the same but the biochemistry is not. The chromatogram is telling us that there is a difference between made-by-nature and made-by-man—mysterious perhaps, but nonetheless real.

"Chemical analysis might appear the same," says pharmacist Earl Mindell in his *Vitamin Bible* (Rawson/Wade, Pub.), "But there's more to natural vitamins because there's more to those substances in nature." Mindell moves from the mysterious to the substantive: acceptability. "According to Dr. Theron G. Randolph, a leading allergist, 'synthetically derived substances may cause a reaction in a chemically susceptible person while the same material of natural origin may be tolerated—even though the two substances have identical chemical structures.' "

Confronted by this difference, people have often asked, "Do synthetic vitamins work as well as natural?" Knowing my bias for things natural, some people have been surprised by my answer: "Sometimes synthetic vitamins do work as well as natural." Sometimes. From simple observation I know of no way to predict when a natural vitamin will work better than its synthetic counterpart. It seems that either will work but sometimes the natural form works better.

How can a natural vitamin work better when the synthetic is ten times as potent? The answer is that the natural form might be twenty times as biologically active. "Potency" only measures how much of a substance is present. There is not—but should be—a measurement called *usable* potency. It is certainly useful to know that there are 100 milligrams of a substance in a formula. It would be at least as useful to know that only 60 milligrams are usable, and 40 percent biologically inert.

I believe that in general the human body prefers natural substances because their biochemical nature is more compatible with the biochemical—not chemical—nature of life. But that very life has enormous transformative powers, capable of imbuing synthetic substances with the life force they lack. Whether or not you utilize a synthetic substance with low biological activity has much to do, I think, with need. The greater your need for a vitamin, the more motivated your body is to transform the synthetic substance into the stuff of life.

The Five Kinds Of Vitamins

My idealized application of the theory is: Natural vitamins for everyday use; synthetic vitamins to augment natural when high therapeutic potencies are the objective. That is an "idealized" application because truly natural vitamins are hard to find. And when you do find them, you may consider them to be prohibitively expensive. For example, I priced one of these rarities at $32 for a month's supply, while a compromise competitor emphasizing the word "natural" in its marketing was $7.75 for a month's supply. To understand what I mean by "compromise," it is necessary to read between the lines of labels. To do that you need to know that there is more to the story than just natural or synthetic. There are actually five kinds of vitamins. They are:

Food concentrates
Natural extractions

Crystalline vitamins
Fortified vitamins
Synthetic vitamins.

Food concentrates. Nutrient-dense foods with only moisture and fiber removed. A good example of this sort of supplement is the $32-a-month product mentioned above, Sonné's "Greenlife." This is made from cereal grasses organically grown in composted soil and cut at the first jointing stage of growth (about four inches), when the vitamin content is at its peak. Expensive to make, it is at the same time quite low in potency. The maker, Earl Irons says,

> Nature never concentrates its elements in high potency. Even at the first joint stage of growth of grass, where concentration of vitamins is at its height and is probably as high as one can find in nature, the potency is minute compared to many synthetic and crystalline vitamins in use today. People forget that one thousand times a *fragment* away from its supporting synergists can be toxic and cause the reverse of what was expected of it.

Advocates for this kind of supplementation, who include some doctors and nutritionists, say that results exceed those of high-potency vitamins because of the extremely high biological activity and the multiple synergists, and that there is far less need to be concerned about possible negative reactions. I think there is a strong case for this kind of supplementation if you can afford it.
Food concentrates commonly found in vitamin-mineral formulas are:

alfalfa	dessicated liver
kelp, dulse, other sea vegetables	pollen
powdered herbs	rose hips powder
yeast	acerola cherry powder
bone meal	

Some "natural" vitamins are really synthetic vitamins with traces of a few of these concentrates mixed in, the label saying something like ". . . in a natural base containing . . ." After learning about the other four kinds of vitamins, you will know how to spot the ersatz and identify it accurately.

Natural extractions. A further concentration of a food concentrate, usually accomplished with solvents and distillation. Examples of this are vitamins A and D extracted from the livers of fish, and vitamin E extracted from wheat germ or soybeans.

Crystalline vitamins. This is a narrow category, referring to the purified forms of naturally extracted vitamins B12 and E. The common way of obtaining B12 is a fermentation process accomplished with yeast-like bacteria. The natural extraction form is *cobalamin concentrate*, which is accompanied with associated factors. The cystalline form is *cyno-cobalamin*, which has no associated factors. Natural extraction forms of vitamin E: *d-alpha tocopherol* (about 30 percent vitamin E, 70 percent associated factors) and *d-alpha tocopherol acetate* (about 60 percent E, 40 percent associated factors). The crystalline form is *d-alpha tocopherol succinate* (no associated factors).

Fortified vitamins. In this class are vitamin C and B vitamins other than B12. There are two ways of fortifying the B vitamins. One is to simply mix yeast, which is naturally low in potency, with synthetic B vitamins. There is no change in molecular structure and the label usually says "fortified yeast" or lists yeast together with the name of the synthetic form: "yeast, thiamine; yeast, riboflavin."

The other way to fortify B vitamins is to add the synthetics to the yeast culture while it is growing. The yeast cells incorporate some of the synthetic vitamins into their molecular structure. This marriage of natural and synthetic is a transformative process creating a higher potency natural vitamin. There is no standardized labeling language for this process, but it is accurate to call this type "fortified primary-grown yeast."

In the following hypothetical examples, the left-hand column shows the potencies before fortification, the middle column after fortification. The right-hand column shows B vitamins that are just a mix of yeast and synthetic; the tip-off on that one is the higher potencies and the arithmetical exactness.

ONE TABLET PER DAY SUPPLIES

	Primary-Grown Yeast	Fortified Primary-Grown Yeast	Fortified Yeast
B1	3 mg	10 mg	50 mg
B2	6 mg	15 mg	50 mg
B6	19 mcg	45 mcg	50 mg
Niacin	1 mg	6 mg	50 mg
Folic Acid	2 mcg	7.5 mcg	400 mcg

Where vitamin C fortification is concerned, there is no opportunity to take advantage of a marriage between natural and synthetic as in fortified primary-grown yeast because no such process has been invented. Vitamin C fortification is always merely a matter of mixing ascorbic acid with natural substances such as rose hips, acerola, and the white inner rind of citrus (bioflavinoids). The expectation here is that the natural associated factors will have enough biological activity to make the synthetic ascorbic acid more effective.

Therapeutic requirements for vitamin C are in thousands of milligrams. Such a potency can be achieved with a couple of ascorbic acid tablets; the same potency of natural vitamin C would be a tablet as big as your fist. Therefore synthetic vitamin C is the most frequently used, with some fortification becoming increasingly popular. In vitamin C fortification, the addition of naturally synergistic substances does not boost the actual amount of C. What is being attempted is to encourage the ascorbic acid to mimic natural vitamin C, which is never found in nature isolated as pure ascorbic acid. It is in a complex with associated food factors, a complex like vitamin B, but a simpler one. Dr. Albert Szent-Gyorgyi, the distinguished biochemist who received a Nobel Prize in 1937 for isolating and identifying ascorbic acid, recognized more than forty years ago that ascorbic acid is only a fraction of the C complex. But that fact has been obscured because ascorbic acid has proven therapeutic value by itself.

Consumers should not be misled by some of the vitamin C labels that are worded to imply that they are solely natural C, seemingly all rose hips or acerola. Invariably the small print says "ascorbic acid"—your tip-off that the tablets are synthetic vitamin C fortified with something natural. Manufacturers should be required to disclose how much natural ingredients we are paying for.

Ascorbic acid is extremely cheap, rose hips and acerola are in scant supply and expensive; without disclosure we have no way of evaluating competing products.

Synthetic vitamins. This refers to all vitamins that are molecular copies of natural vitamins. Various raw materials are the basis for synthesizing: coal tar, wood pulp, corn syrup, mined minerals, food manufacturing waste products, as examples. But there is no meaningful distinction that can be made according to whether the raw materials were a petroleum product or a food product. By the time synthesizing is complete, all resemblance to the raw materials is long gone. Synthetic vitamins are "pure" in the sense that there is nothing but the vitamin, no associated factors. (It should be noted that while most associated factors are synergistic, a few are inhibitors. On balance, however, the scale is heavily weighted in favor of the positive effects of associated factors.)

Personally, I take food concentrates, natural extractions, crystalline and fortified vitamins. Currently I am using eighteen different bottles, spending about $55 a month on vitamins and minerals. These figures vary as my needs and experiments change. I wouldn't expect you to match me, just as I make no attempt to match people who have forty bottles going and spend $200 a month. We all have different priorities, budgets, and, as with food, different needs based on differing metabolisms. The best service this book can render is to provide some of the information that will enable you to make informed choices. With the terminology now defined, the following table will help you determine what labels are really telling you according to the source identified for the vitamin. If no source is given, that almost certainly means the vitamin is synthetic.

VITAMIN SOURCE GUIDE

Vitamin	*Label source identified as*	*It is a*
A (Retinol)	fish liver oil	natural extraction
A	acetate; palmitate; lemon grass; carrot oil	synthetic

If the source of a B vitamin is *yeast, bran,* or *rice bran,* it is a *food concentrate.* If the source is *fortified* or *high potency yeast,* it is a *fortified vitamin.* •

B1 (Thiamine)	thiamine hydrochloride; thiamine mononitrate	synthetic
B2 (Riboflavin)	riboflavin	synthetic
Niacin (B3)	niacinamide; nicotinic acid	synthetic
Pantothenic Acid (B5)	calcium pantothenate	synthetic
B6 (Pyridoxine)	pyridoxine hydrochloride	synthetic
B12	cobalamin concentrate	natural extraction
B12	cyanocobalamin	crystalline
PABA (Para-amino-benzoic acid)	para-amino-benzoic acid	synthetic
Folic Acid (Folacin, vitamin M)	pteroglutamic acid	synthetic
Inositol	soybeans; corn	natural extraction
Choline	soybeans	natural extraction
Choline	choline bitartrate, chloride, or citrate	synthetic
Biotin	d-biotin	synthetic

VITAMIN SOURCE GUIDE (*cont.*)

Vitamin	Label source identified as	It is a
Pangamic Acid	apricot kernels	food concentrate
C (vitamin C complex)	acerola; rose hips	food concentrate
C (ascorbic acid)	ascorbic acid or fortified ascorbic acid; calcium ascorbate; sodium ascorbate (ascorbates are non-acidic)	synthetic
D	fish liver oil	natural extraction
D	irradiated or activated ergosterol; calciferol; ergocalciferol	synthetic
E	wheat germ oil; soybean oil; mixed tocopherols; d-alpha tocopherol; d-alpha tocopheryl acetate	natural extraction
E	d-alpha tocopheryl succinate	crystalline
E	all tocopherols or tocopheryls with prefix *dl*	synthetic
F	vegetable oils; essential fatty acids	natural extraction
K	alfalfa; chlorophyll; phylloquinone; fish meal; yeast	food concentrate
K	menadione	synthetic
P (Bioflavinoids, Rutin, Hesperidin)	citrus; green peppers; buckwheat	food concentrate

*See page 137 for the distinction between the two kinds of fortified B vitamins.

MINERALS

Of the two classes of nutrients, vitamins and minerals, vitamins have been discussed and written about more frequently and are thus more prominent in the public eye, for no particularly good reason. In fact, it may very well be that mineral deficiencies are more widespread than those of vitamins, due to the ubiquitous mismanagement of our farmland. Minerals, as *ions* or *electrolytes*, provide the spark that triggers enzymatic reactions. Magnesium, as just one of countless possible examples, triggers the breakdown of glucose for conversion into energy within cells. But whether or not minerals are more important than vitamins is not the point: they are certainly no *less* important.

Unlike vitamins, man does not make minerals. But we can combine them in various ways, imitating nature. Having a positive electrical charge, minerals are almost never found in the pure, or ionized, form, known as cations. Instead, they seek to combine with negatively charged anions, forming mineral salts. When people talk about minerals, it is usually mineral salts they are talking about. And it is these salts that we know how to split apart and recombine in various ways.

Whether combined in nature or by man, there are two kinds of mineral salts: organic and inorganic. Neither kind is more natural than the other. Organic minerals are salts formed with organic acids (called organic because of their chemical structure). Examples are the salts known as oxalates, gluconates, ascorbates, phytates, lactates, citrates, fumarates. Typically, these organic mineral salts are found in plant and animal tissues.

Inorganic mineral salts are typically found in the ground or dissolved in water. Examples are carbonates, sulphates, oxides, chlorides, phosphates, nitrates.

There are two semi-popular myths concerning mineral salts.

Myth 1: It makes a difference whether the mineral salt is combined in the environment—naturally—or in the laboratory—synthetically. The synthetic mineral salt, says the myth, is inferior. The fact is that the sorts of differences existing between natural and synthetic vitamins do not apply to mineral salts. The synthetic versions, being free of contaminants, may even be better.

Myth 2: Organic minerals are more assimilable than inorganic. The fact is that there is no difference in assimilability. In the words of Len Mervyn, Ph.D. biochemist and author of *Minerals and Your Health* (Keats Publishing, Inc.), organic minerals as supplements are "just as inefficient" as organic. (See also Bates, G.W. et al, *American Journal of Clinical Nutrition*, 25:983, 1972).

Mervyn calls mineral salts inefficient because only 1–6 percent of them are assimilated (see Taher Fouad, Ph.D., in *Journal of Applied Nutrition*, vol. 28, no. 1). This is true whether the mineral salts are organic or inorganic, found in the earth, water, plants, or put together by man.

Lack of assimilation of mineral salts is due to two main factors:

1. After being ionized into cations and anions in the stomach, roughly 80 percent of the mineral ions recombine into insoluble salts which cannot pass through the intestinal walls.
2. The other 20 percent of the mineral, as ions with positive electrical charges, adheres to the intestinal wall, which has a negative electrical charge, sticking like metal filings to a magnet.

Little or no mineral in the ionized form is allowed through the walls of intestinal cells unless it is first neutralized. This can be accomplished to some extent if amino acids from dietary protein are also present in the intestine. Certain amino acids have the complementary negative structure to form a neutralizing circle around the mineral ion. This structure, which is as if a pebble were buried in a ball of clay, is called a *chelate* (kee-late).

Once allowed through the wall into the intestinal cell, most chelates are separated and recombined into new chelates. The second chelate gets the mineral back out of the intestinal cell and into the bloodstream. A third chelate carries the mineral through the wall of the cell that needs it.

As well as being made within, mineral chelates come preformed in natural foods. Typical examples of natural chelates are iron in meat, magnesium in chlorophyll, calcium in milk, iodine in kelp, chromium and selenium in certain strains of nutritional yeast. *The Complete Book of Minerals for Health* (Rodale Press) recommends the following as "super-mineral" foods (super not just because they contain minerals, but because much of the mineral content is in chelates): liver, yogurt, buttermilk, fish, blackstrap molasses, and nutritional yeast.

Amino Acid Chelates

The greater assimilability of chelates lies in their being in a form ready to pass through the intestinal wall. Being ready, the processes of digestion, following inherent body wisdom, don't separate the amino acids from the minerals. Using radioactive tracer minerals, it has been possible to learn that the course of manmade, or amino acid, chelates closely imitates those occurring naturally in foods. The following table illustrates the great differences in assimilability between amino acid chelates and mineral salts:

Increase of Assimilation of Minerals as Amino Acid Chelates Compared to

copper carbonate	copper sulphate	copper oxide
580%	410%	300%
iron carbonate	iron sulphate	iron oxide
360%	380%	490%

(Adapted from *Minerals and Your Health*, Table 23.)

Amino acid chelates are usually made by combining the mineral with hydrolized (dissolved in water) vegetable protein (often soy). They may be our most effective attempt to imitate nature in nutrition. Apparently we are even able to duplicate nature's most efficient chelates, known as *aspartates* and *orotates*, which do not have to change into other chelates to reach target cells. The amino acid aspartic acid has been shown to carry minerals as far as the inner lining of the cell wall. The amino acid orotic acid transports minerals right to the core of the cell.

A final reason for getting minerals either as natural or amino acid chelates is to avoid the side effects sometimes associated with mineral salts. Iron sulphate, for example, has been observed to cause constipation, backache, even intestinal bleeding.

Ascorbates

Another mineral form capable of transporting minerals to target cells is in combination with ascorbic acid. Ascorbic acid/mineral combinations—ascorbates—are, in fact, the form in which most ascorbic acid reaches cells. Ascorbic acid combines in the bloodstream with minerals (and amino acids), forming compounds such as calcium, magnesium, or chromium ascorbate. It was this observation which has led to the synthesized process, imitating nature in the manner of amino acid chelates.

Since the acid portion of the ascorbate compound is neutralized by the mineral, ascorbates are gaining favor as a non-acidifying way of taking vitamin C. Calcium ascorbate and sodium ascorbate are the common forms. For most people, calcium ascorbate is probably better since calcium is a widespread nutritional deficiency whereas sodium is often consumed in excess. It is also usually the best form of large dosages (1,000 mg or more) for those with parasympathetic metabolisms, since they don't tolerate ascorbic acid very well.

EXCIPIENTS

Apart from the nutrient ingredients in vitamin-mineral formulas, there are almost always other ingredients, the general name for which is *excipients*. The functions of excipients in gelatin capsules, which are filled as if they were tiny jars, are primarily as fillers, disintegrators, and drying agents. Tablets, on the other hand, are formed by pressing ingredients into a mold, requiring binders and lubricants; without them the nutrients could not be delivered in one piece.

Listed below are the major categories of excipients in descending order according to the amounts used in most tableting. There is an informal sort of consensus among manufacturers of natural vitamins and minerals as to what qualifies as natural excipients. The examples I have listed are the most commonly used of these "generally recognized as natural" excipients. Some of these are the equivalent of food concentrates in being absolutely natural: arrowroot, calcium, and magnesium carbonate, dicalcium phosphate, silica, talc (sometimes contaminated with asbestos, a carcinogen, and therefore avoided by some manufacturers), whey, yeast. Others are a step or two away from genuine naturalness, the excipient equivalents of natural extractions (acacia gum) and crystalline vitamins (carotene).

Fillers (dilutents). The further you go down the scale of naturalness from food concentrate to synthetic, the more fillers are needed to bulk out the product. This is not just to give the appearance of value received, but to provide enough material for practical compression in the machinery. *Ex.*: arrowroot, calcium and magnesium carbonate, dicalcium phosphate, whey, yeast.

Binders (granulators). As the words suggest, this class of excipient acts to hold all the ingredients together. *Ex.*: arrowroot, acacia gum, algin, sodium alginate, cellulose, ethyl and methyl cellulose, silica gel, lecithin.

Lubricants prevent the tablets from sticking in the machinery as they get punched out. *Ex.*: calcium and magnesium stearate, silica, talc.

Disintegrators prevent tablets from dispersing too quickly after ingestion. *Ex.*: gum arabic, algin, sodium alginate, ethyl and methyl cellulose.

Coatings are used to protect the nutrients from moisture, to mask unpleasant odors and flavors, and to provide a smooth surface for ease of swallowing. *Ex.*: food glaze, zein (a protein derived from corn), Brazil wax (derived from palm trees).

Other excipients are colors, flavors, and sweeteners. In general, high-quality vitamins and minerals are not colored, flavored, or sweetened. There is the occasional worthwhile exception to that generalization, but it certainly would not contain artificial color or flavor, or sugar. Food supplements made to look and taste like candy are not really food supplements, they are profiteering gimmickry.

Excipients are "other ingredients" that perform a manufacturing function. Another way they sometimes appear on labels is as a "base." Often you will see entirely synthetic vitamins, or synthetic vitamins mixed with fish liver oil, being hawked as natural. Somewhere on the label you will read the statement, "in a natural base containing . . ." then going on to list some food concentrates such as alfalfa, yeast, rose hips, and kelp. This base, which gives you wisps and puffs of natural substances, is usually a marketing ploy designed to get a premium price for cheap synthetics or offer fire-sale prices on "natural" vitamins and minerals. A careful reading of the label should enable you to see through such hoaxes.

TIMED RELEASE VITAMINS

Whereas fat-soluble vitamins (A, D, E, F) are stored in the body, water-soluble vitamins (B and C) are not. The idea behind timed release (also called sustained, or delayed release) is that coating the water-soluble vitamins so they don't all dissolve at once will allow them to be utilized later instead of being eliminated unused. This can be of particular interest to people who are unwilling or unable to take vitamins with every meal. But it is really a good idea?

That depends on how it's done. Sometimes it's done with porous types of vinyls, plastics, waxes, shellacs, and indigestible protein. Not only are such substances questionable, but not everybody has the digestive power to separate them from the vitamins. On the other hand, everybody's digestive tract has moisture and body heat with which to soften water-soluble, heat-sensitive coatings.

The problem for consumers is that we usually can't tell from labeling information whether or not the coating is water-soluble or requires copious secretions of hydrochloric acid. It should yield to the weakest flow of digestive juices under the least favorable of circumstances, but if the label is not informative enough, all we have to go on is our degree of trust in the manufacturer or some nutritional advisor. I'm taking a timed-release vitamin C which makes the following statement:

. . . accurately provides a constant supply of the vitamin C complex over a period of 8 hours, using a new all-natural, sustained release mechanism. Patent pending. This natural product contains no sugar, starch, salt, preservatives, artificial color or flavoring, and no wheat, yeast or soy derivatives. FULL DISCLOSURE. Tableted with cellulose, magnesium stearate, natural food glaze.

What they call full disclosure does not really explain to lay people what they've done and I don't agree with their use of the word natural. But the product, from the local natural foods store, discloses more and sounds more natural than products I've perused in the local drugstore. Since I have a gut feeling that the manufacturer is conscientiously trying to put out good products with minimal compromises, I'm taking the product. We have to make our decisions along such lines until timed release becomes standardized and *completely* disclosed.

SHOPPING FOR VITAMINS

A question frequently asked of me is, "Why are vitamins in a health or natural foods store better than something like 'One-A-Day'?" "One-A-Day" brand was mentioned so often that I decided to do a comparison between that and a multiple called "Natural Source" manufactured by Gides, Inc.

"NATURAL SOURCE" VS. "ONE-A-DAY"
(Based on a day's dosage)

	Natural Source	One-A-Day
Vitamin A	10,000 Units	10,000 Units
Vitamin D	400 Units	400 Units
Vitamin E	100 Units	15 Units
Vitamin C	150 mg.	60 mg.
Vitamin B1	10 mg.	1.5 mg.
Vitamin B2	10 mg.	1.7 mg.

	Natural Source	*One-A-Day*
Vitamin B6	2.5 mg.	2 mg.
Vitamin B12	100 mcg.	6 mcg.
Niacin	50 mg.	20 mg.
Pantothenic Acid	10 mg.	10 mg.
Folic Acid	.025 mg.	4 mg.
Choline	12 mg.	—
Inositol	12 mg.	—
Biotin	7 mcg.	—
PABA	.04 mg.	—
RNA	60 mg.	—
Calcium	390 mg.	100 mg.
Phosphorous	190 mg.	100 mg.
Iron	30 mg.	18 mg.
Iodine	100 mcg.	150 mcg.
Copper	.08 mg.	2 mg.
Potassium	55 mg.	—
Zinc	.22 mg.	15 mg.
Magnesium	9 mg.	100 mg.
Lecithin	200 mg.	—
Protein	1500 mg.	—
Dulse	100 mg.	—
Rutin	20 mg.	—
Hesperidin	50 mg.	—
Bioflavinoids	50 mg.	—
Digestants (4)	63 mg.	—
Alfalfa Concentrate	30 mg.	—
Liver Concentrate	30 mg.	—
Cost per day	24.6¢	7.7¢

When a salesperson offers you a cheap insurance policy, the sensible thing to do is find out what kind of coverage the cheap policy offers. Is it really cheap compared to a more expensive policy? Or do you get what you pay for? The difference in number of ingredients and potencies show an overall superiority of "Natural Source" over "One-A-Day." "One-A-Day" is entirely synthetic. "Natural Source" is a combination of food concentrates, natural extractions, and fortified vitamins. So I think the greater degree of naturalness of "Natural Source" and similar brands is worth paying a premium for.

"Natural Source" is not a one-tablet-a-day approach; rather, you take two with every meal. This is far preferable for purposes of assimilation and utilization, particularly where water-soluble vitamins B and C are concerned, as they do not remain long in the body. "One-A-Day" is a poor form of insurance.

Here is what to look for in your search for a good vitamin/mineral supplement:

—Number of ingredients
—Potency of ingredients
—Naturalness of nutrients and excipients
—Asimilability (once a day or with every meal?)
—Purity (freedom from sugar, shellac, artificial colors, and preservatives)

Regarding purity, "One-A-Day" did well compared to a competitor named "Theragran," manufactured by Squibb. "Theragran" contained the following ingredients, either potentially harmful or unrelated to nutrition: *sugar, povidone, shellac, mannitol, BHA, BHT, sodium benzoate, methyl paraben, polyparaben, sorbic acid, sodium bisulfite, F D & C Red numbers 40 and 3, Yellow number 6 and Blue number 1, white wax, carnauba wax.* You'd be better advised to take nothing. These are the kinds of things to look for; you can't assume purity because the word "vitamin" is on the bottle. (See Appendix Three for more on vitamins and minerals.)

SUPPLEMENTATION AND METABOLIC INDIVIDUALITY

Recall Tests 2 and 3 on page 96. The reason they indicate your metabolic category is that the same vitamins (and minerals) have different effects on people according to metabolic individuality. The parasympathetic reaction to Test 2 results from excessive stimulation of the parasympathetic's already rapid blood-sugar oxidation rate. There is no sympathetic reaction because of a comparatively slower oxidation rate.

Whereas Test 2 indicates metabolic category due to differences in oxidation rates, Test 3 indicates metabolic category due to differences in acid-alkaline balance (explained in Chapter 9). The sympathetic normally functions with a relatively acid body chemistry, where they feel "comfortable"; the parasympathetic is comfortable in a more alkaline state. An acidifying influence keeps the parasympathetic from getting too alkaline, but eight grams of ascorbic acid is far too much, causing the negative effects of this acidifying test.

In general, sympathetics should seek alkalinizing influences for their balancing effect, and avoid making their already acidic body more acid. Vitamin C is an exception to that general rule because of the tendency of sympathetics to detoxify slowly at the cell level and vitamin C's action of "burning" toxins. The elevated feeling sympathetics experience from megadoses of vitamin C explains why some people are so zealous in recommending it.

Test 3 illustrates why we hear of "high vitamin C people." If parasympathetics are to dose heavily with C and escape the negative side effects peculiar to them, they have to take the non-acid forms, sodium or calcium ascorbate. A balanced metabolizer will probably not experience negative effects from two or three grams of ascorbic acid but would be advised to use the non-acid forms for heavier megadoses.

Many times I have had the experience of conferring with people about their experiments with dietary supplements who understood and agreed with the excellent case for using them but were disappointed. "I really thought they would do me a lot of good. My wife takes this formula and ever since she began taking it, she's been a new woman. But for me they're a disaster. I thought I needed vitamins, but I guess I don't."

He does—the right kinds for his metabolic individuality. Supplementation has failed for him because he was unaware of the second factor of nutritional supplementation. The first is widely understood and accepted: to offset excessive stressors and the nutritional deficiencies endemic to the American food supply. Aimed at boosting the strength of metabolism, this aspect is the metabolic *efficiency* factor.

The second factor is metabolic *balance*. Our disappointed experimenter did not know that not only food, but the nutrients taken to supplement food, affect how well he functions. The effect is through links in a chain, from acid-alkaline balance, to stimulation of the autonomic nervous system, to hormone production. He would not have been disappointed if his supplementation had promoted the equilibrium of his metabolism.

The more nutrients incorporated into a supplementation program, the more critical the balance factor becomes. If you are only taking two multi-vitamin-mineral tablets with each meal, there is probably not enough material there to have a noticeable effect on body chemistry. I say "probably", however, because some people are more sensitive than others. Once again, it is a question of who you are. The kind of something-of-everything vitamin-mineral formula analyzed earlier in this chapter is most suitable to balanced metabolizers, who, according to Dr. Kelley's estimate, comprise roughly half of the population.

Sympathetics comprise perhaps 20 percent of the population and generally do best on an all-vegetarian type of formula, which has the most alkalinizing effect on body chemistry. Parasympathetics, comprising the other approximately 30 percent, should not only favor non-acid forms of vitamin C, but avoid the copious B vitamin intake that is so often recommended as if it were ideal for everybody. They would generally do best avoiding formulas with vitamins B1, B2, and B6 because, as Dr. Kelley pointed out to me, these stimulate a blood sugar oxidation rate which is already high in parasympathetic metabolizers. The B1, B2, and B6 in a natural foods diet is generally enough for parasympathetics, who can benefit otherwise by taking A, D, E, B12, and minerals separately.

Dr. Kelley is the nutritional scientist who has made what is probably the most thorough study of metabolic individuality, his computerized data having come from more than 30,000 people. A consequence of his work is a complete line of supplements designed with both the efficiency and balance factors of metabolic individuality built in. They are made by Ultra Life, of Palatine, Illinois. This company is alone on this particular nutritional frontier, but in time they will be emulated by all their competitors. We will look back amused at the archaic notion that one supplement program, any more than one diet, could be ideal for everybody. (See Appendix Seven for additional information on health foods and acid-alkaline balance.)

13   A Folk Medicine Sampler

FOLK REMEDIES FOR COMMON PROBLEMS

People for whom medical self-care is a part of life are fond of quoting Hippocrates, the father of western medicine, who told his students that their food should be their medicine. That advice is unheeded by contemporary physicians but remains the foundation of modern folk medicine.

"Folk medicine" in the context of this chapter means those items available over-the-counter and in the woods and fields, which might be of therapeutic value, even though their primary use is either as food, beverage, or nutritional supplement. It also refers to materials that are self-administered, not depending on application from a therapist, professional or amateur.

My own entry into the world of natural foods was through the folk-medicine door. Many people go through life feeling the way I felt in those days, assuming that they are feeling the only way they can. Once in a while you feel really good; most of the time you're just sort of getting by; now and then you get sick—that's "normal." Or is it?

I wasn't a case for a doctor; I was a case for self-help. If I wanted to be healthy, it was up to me to do something about it. I looked in the yellow pages to locate the nearest health food store, went and bought the first of hundreds of books I've owned on this subject: *Let's Eat Right to Keep Fit,* by Adelle Davis, recommended by the proprietor of the store, Thom Hamilton—a good friend even as I write this nineteen years later.

During my first year of eating naturally and taking natural supplements I lost weight, gained vigor, and stopped catching colds and losing hair. Fervor was kindled. I decided to open a natural foods store. Thom encouraged me and gave me beginner's lessons in shopkeeping.

Over the years, Thom's reputation as a nutritional consultant has spread. People came to his store from hundreds of miles away and call him from more distant places. His consulting is primarily an amalgamation of vitamin and mineral therapy and therapeutic foods and herbs. Extremely well read on nutrition, Thom considers *Folk Medicine* by Dr. Jarvis, the reknowned Vermont country doctor, to be the single greatest influence on him.

The following material combines Thom's experiences and mine with those of customers and friends. We have all done the same thing: read or heard about a remedy and tried it. Remedies become "folk remedies" when they have succeeded often enough to be passed along by word of mouth—they have, indeed, worked for a lot of folks. But, as Thom points out, there's no such thing as a 100 percent effective remedy, no matter where it comes from. If a remedy doesn't work, try something else or see your doctor or some other qualified person.

Colds

You are probably not susceptible to cold germs unless you are out of acid-alkaline balance. Normally, your stomach pH is acid. People with colds (in fact, most sicknesses) test alkaline in the stomach. This is not to say that acid-alkaline imbalance is the primary cause of colds, any more than germs are. Germs and acid-alkaline imbalance are both secondary factors. The primary cause is that somehow you have weakened your body's defenses. You may have created excess toxic material by making persistently wrong food choices. Or you may have failed to nourish your body well enough to support the efficient elimination of toxins. These are two common ways to prepare the ground for a cold and either way, your organs of elimination do not keep up with your internal toxicity level.

When organs of elimination—kidneys, bowels, lungs, skin—suffer from toxin overload, the thyroid gland becomes a fail-safe mechanism. It flushes out toxins via secretions of the mucus membranes of the nose and throat. Accompanying the runny nose and throat discomfort may be a headache and general malaise. You say you feel like you are coming down with a cold, and indeed you may be—your straining mucus membranes are ripe for the action of cold germs.

Perhaps you take aspirin for the headache. But this only worsens the cold. In one experiment, volunteers who took aspirin had up to 36 percent more live cold viruses than volunteers who took placebos (see *Journal of the American Medical Association*, March 24, 1975). Dr. Edith Stanley and associates at the University of Illinois School of Medicine, who conducted the experiment, suggest that aspirin suppresses the body's natural defense mechanisms.

There is, however, an easy, harmless way to intervene in the progress of the cold. You can restore the acid environment of your stomach, and this often stops the progress of a cold dead in its tracks.

Step one in restoring your stomach acidity is to eliminate alkaline-forming foods that do not have a cleansing effect on the system: salt, spices, coffee, tea, and alcohol. (Also eliminate mucus-forming foods: pasteurized dairy products and refined carbohydrates.)

Step two is to take some apple cider vinegar. Usually, a tablespoon of apple cider vinegar in a glass of water, repeated three or four times a day, erases colds before they really get started. Occasionally, a cold is not to be denied but taking vinegar during its course keeps it mild and short-lived.

If the soured water tastes too objectionable, it can be sweetened with a little honey. Dissolve the honey in a little warm water, then add to the tap-temperature water and vinegar. It is acceptable even to most children in this form. An alternative to apple cider vinegar is hydrochloric acid (HCL) tablets, a couple of them with a glass of water instead of the vinegar.

What about vitamin C-rich citrus fruits to fight colds? Fruit containing citric acid alkalinizes body chemistry because the body nullifies the citric acid, reducing it to carbon dioxide and water. Even though the fruit also contains ascorbic acid, the net effect is alkaline. You actually recover more quickly from a cold without citrus juices.

Vitamin C is more effective as a cold preventive than a cold cure. Apple cider vinegar has a bigger wallop against a cold at the onset of symptoms. But if you want to try for a double-barreled approach, take vitamin C tablets with your vinegar water. Taken hourly in high dosages of 2,000–5,000 mg (2–5 grams), vitamin C can have an antibiotic-like effect. But it can also have a depressive effect and/or cause diarrhea in people with a parasympathetic metabolism (see Chapter 8).

Besides acid-alkaline imbalance, two other contributors to cold susceptibility are overeating and lack of sleep. Statistics show that colds increase following holidays, especially Christmas and New Year's. Recovery from colds is therefore speeded by light eating or fasting and extra sleep. Expectorants—substances that encourage the discharge of mucus—are helpful. These include chicken soup and other hot drinks, fluids in general, garlic, ginger, horseradish, mustard, and hot peppers.

Diarrhea

Again, it's apple cider vinegar (or HCL tablets) to the rescue. In most cases, one tablespoon of vinegar in a glass of water will suffice to stop excessive elimination. If not, repeat several times until symptoms abate. (When traveling, particularly to southern hemisphere countries, take a bottle of HCL tablets along.) If diarrhea doesn't clear up in a couple of days, keep taking it for a few more days, accompanied by some dietary modifications. Eliminate all alcohol, sweeteners, salt, spices, meat, and large doses of vitamin C. Eat apples, apricots, bananas, berries, garlic, raw vegetables, rice, millet, and cultured milk products. Drink plenty of fluids, particularly the raw juices of carrot, apple, celery, and beet. Take vitamins A and B complex and comfrey-pepsin capsules. Should the symptoms persist beyond three days of the cider vinegar/dietary approach, a strong medicine such as paregoric, which must be prescribed by a doctor, will probably be necessary.

Two other remedies are offered by Alan H. Nittler, M.D., in his book A New Breed of Doctor (Pyramid House):

Another remedy is to use simmered skim milk (skim milk just brought to a boil); take one glassful four times daily. Eat it like soup; use a spoon so that you drink it slowly.

Barley water can be used as an alternative: boil 5 cupfuls of water, then add 1 cupful of barley grain. Simmer twenty minutes. Strain off fluid and drink. Repeat this four times daily.

For diarrhea in babies, pat a little vinegar on the soles of their feet, where the pores are four times larger than elsewhere, allowing for rapid osmosis. (The skin on other areas of the body will also work, although not as quickly.) Only mildly acidic, vinegar won't bother most babies' skin, but watch for extreme redness. One or two applications should stop the diarrhea within a few hours. But keep in mind that your baby—or anyone else—has diarrhea because something is irritating the intestinal tract, which is therefore trying to eliminate the irritant. So try to isolate the factor that is irritating your baby's bowel.

Two foods that act to check diarrhea in babies are applesauce and carob powder. A teaspoon of carob powder can be stirred into applesauce or some other pureed food. But don't overdo the carob powder or you'll cause the opposite problem—constipation. If the baby is old enough, she can chew on a carob pod, a less concentrated form which most babies find to be a tasty substitute for teething rings (another is a piece of orris root).

Flatulence

The same apple cider vinegar remedy as for diarrhea. It will even work on your gas-emitting dog. Rub it on his belly where the hair is thinnest and in a half hour the emissions should abate.

Acid Indigestion

You guessed it, apple cider vinegar again. Heartburn, an accompaniment to this complaint, has an acid taste, so you head for the drugstore antacid compounds. They neutralize the acidity, alleviating the heartburn, but they don't do anything to improve your digestion. You've probably eaten too much, too richly, or an incompatible mixture of foods, perhaps all three. The antacid will actually slow down the process of digestion, causing intestinal problems as faultily digested food moves from your stomach to your bowel. You *need* acid for proper digestion; the walls of your stomach secrete hydrochloric acid copiously—if you're lucky (see also *Ulcers*).

Acid indigestion is much more a problem of older people because there is a general tendency for the hydrochloric acid secretion of our stomachs to slow down as we grow older. The first steps against acid indigestion are to eat less, reduce fatty foods, and simplify your meals. If acid indigestion persists, take a hydrochloric acid tablet or a good multi-digestant tablet (which will contain HCL combined with digestive enzymes) with every meal; you almost certainly need to supplement your stomach's production of hydrochloric acid.

Ulcers

There are two common kinds of ulcers of the digestive tract: stomach ulcers and intestinal ulcers. Both kinds can respond to natural remedies, stomach ulcers usually more quickly.

A common misconception about ulcers is that stomach acid "burns a hole" in the lining of the stomach or intestine. The idea is, the stomach produces too much hydrochloric acid and that causes ulcers. I offer an opposing viewpoint: that too *little* hydrochloric acid is one of the factors, not too much. The stomach and intestinal walls are totally compatible with acidity. It is alkalinity—protein putrifying instead of digesting—due to lack of HCL, that is irritating to the digestive tract. That's why people with ulcers have commonly been sufferers of acid indigestion and heartburn, taking frequent doses of antacid compounds, thereby preparing the way for ulcers. I'm not saying antacids are *the* cause of ulcers—the causes are complex—but they are frequently a contributing factor. In the future I think people will look back at the use of antacid compounds somewhat as we view the use of leeches by our ancestors—a bizarrely counterproductive practice.

In *A New Breed of Doctor*, Dr. Nittler has this to say about antacids and their relationship to ulcers:

Antacids work on a temporary basis, only until the next time. In the meanwhile, the antacids grossly upset the normal acid-alkaline balance in the whole system, not only the stomach. Of course, the acidity of the stomach is immediately neutralized or even made alkaline by ingestion of antacids. This means that your stomach protein digestion processes immediately stop. Acidity in the lower intestines is necessary for proper absorption but is disturbed by antacid therapy. Even the normal pH of the blood is adversely affected by the hyperalkaline intestinal contents which are being absorbed.

So you see, taking antacids is not without eventual harmful consequences.

In reality, most, but not all, causes of heartburn are due not to too much acid, as TV commercials would have you believe, but to *lack* of stomach acid. The symptoms of too much and too little acid are identical. There is very simple test: drink a solution of apple cider or wine vinegar (2 tp. in a glassful of water) when you have heartburn. If you get almost immediate relief, your need is for more acid and not for antacids. If the vinegar intake aggravates the heartburn, your need is for the antacid, which can then be taken with no added risk to your stomach.

Oddly enough, where an ulcer or pre-ulcerous state exists, initially the basic need may have been for more acid. Lack of it may have caused the glands in the stomach wall to overwork and eventually resulted in a breakdown of the stomach lining . . .

Here is a program for ulcers combining the best natural remedies:

1. Quit coffee and alcohol (and curtail their use after the ulcer is gone, if you're wise).
2. Drink either okra powder or slippery elm powder with a little water before eating. This will provide a mucilaginous coating to offer some protection to the ulcerated tissue, a coating which also has nutritional value. The over-the-counter drugs sold for this purpose are actually *too* effective, coating the intestinal walls so well that they are no longer able to properly pass nutrients through to the bloodstream. You need all the nutrients you can get to heal tissue, no matter where that tissue is; vitamins A and C are particularly important for healing, as well as calcium, zinc, and protein. (But take your vitamin C only with meals if you have an ulcer).
3. There are two drinks that have been proven marvelously effective for ulcers. One is raw cabbage juice (which requires a juicer)—three glasses a day. If it tastes too weird, make it half and half with carrot juice—much more palatable and almost as effective.

The other drink is made with aloe vera, a cactus with thick leaves filled with a gelatinous substance. Many natural foods stores sell aloe vera leaves; some even sell whole plants in pots. They're great to have around as a terrifically effective first-aid treatment for burns, including sunburn, and skin abrasions. For ulcers, cut off a hunk of leaf that will give you the equivalent of several tablespoons of gel, peel it and blend it with water or apple juice, three times a day. The cabbage juice and the aloe vera drinks have both been known to heal ulcers within ten days.

4. Rub some apple cider vinegar on your skin. Soles of feet are the best place, but anyplace will do. The skin will absorb the mallic acid in the vinegar, balancing the pH of the entire body in a way that is nonirritating to the ulcer, improving your digestion and assimilation. This should be done at least twice a day.

Milk is highly touted as a food easy on ulcers but, being hard to digest, really is not. Cultured milk products such as yogurt, kefir, and buttermilk, in which the protein is partly broken down, are a far better choice.

Constipation

Peristalsis is the progressive wave of contraction and relaxation of a tubular muscular system by which the contents are pushed through the system. The digestive tract, or alimentary canal, is such a system. In a greatly simplified way, you imitate peristalsis when you squeeze toothpaste from its tube. Lack of strong peristalsis by the intestinal muscles is a primary cause of constipation. The eating of refined foods is, in turn, a primary cause of weak peristalsis. Refined foods are at fault on two counts: first, because they lack the B vitamins that feed the nerves that stimulate the intestinal muscles; second, they lack the fiber which, by offering resistance to the intestinal muscles, promotes good muscle tone. This is why people on "primitive" diets don't suffer the digestive ills of people on "civilized" diets.

There is much more to fiber than its role in conditioning the intestinal muscles. It is also *hydroscopic*, meaning that it attracts and absorbs moisture. In the intestine, the fiber draws moisture through the intestinal walls by osmosis, maintaining the optimum moisture content for proper movement. Augmenting this function is the cellulose content of fiber, giving it a broomlike, cleansing action. With inadequate fiber, the intestines tend to clog, and waste material that should be eliminated becomes impacted.

Dissections of cadavers of people who lived on refined carbohydrates often reveal colons nearly closed by impacted waste matter, some of it decades old, almost as hard as cement. This is like having a cesspool built into your belly. Toxic emanations from the putrifying mess travel through your intestinal walls, polluting your bloodstream. Constipation is usually considered a minor problem, but it is not minor—no one who suffers from chronic constipation ever feels really well, except perhaps for brief spells.

Constipation, resulting from reliance on refined carbohydrates (as well as the lack of exercise characteristic of sedentary living), has never been thoroughly investigated for a role I believe is causative for many *seemingly* unrelated conditions. The dumping of toxins into the bloodstream from clogged colons is certainly a primary cause of headaches, halitosis, acne, and boils. I'm sure it plays a role in more serious conditions. (It's hard to convince somebody who suffers from constant headaches that the condition isn't serious.) Constipation is also a precursor of the digestive tract ailments we will look at next.

I have been asked how people can know whether or not they are constipated. That sounds like the height of ignorance unless you realize that what the question really asks is: What is normal? what should I expect regarding elimination? If you eat every day, your bowels should evacuate every day. After at least six months on the New American Diet, coupled with at least a half hour of vigorous exercise four times a week, most people will begin to approach good health and often have more than one bowel movement per day.

The most counterproductive measure against chronic constipation is the regular ingestion of laxatives. They work by irritating the intestinal walls to produce artificial peristalsis. Over time, the disused intestinal nerves become inoperative, accustomed to the regular arrival of the irritant. And the user has become addicted to laxatives.

Laxatives can be replaced by bran. Up to three tablespoons of bran per day can be taken, but that amount should be reached gradually, starting with a couple of teaspoons. Unlike laxatives, bran will not work suddenly, but may take a couple of weeks to help establish regularity, during which time it may also cause some intestinal gas. Bran is hydroscopic and therefore becomes soft in the alimentary canal, acting like a soft broom.

Similar in effect to bran are flax seeds and psyllium seeds. Up to a tablespoon of the seeds per day can be taken, but that amount also should be reached gradually, starting with a teaspoon. The seeds work best when soaked overnight in water. They are mucilaginous, absorbing a great deal of water and becoming jelly-like. In that form they can be drunk in juice or added to any number of foods.

Vitamin A should accompany the B complex to assure good intestinal health. Vitamin A is important because of its role in maintaining a healthy mucus membrane lining all the cavities and passages within the body. (A note here to anyone who might read or be told that it should be your aim to eliminate mucus from your body, as in the "mucusless diet healing system" championed by Arnold Ehret: You should *not* eliminate mucus, it is essential for lubrication, and your body won't allow it anyway. You should eliminate excess mucus, by eliminating excess dairy products, reducing fats, consuming more fresh produce, and switching from refined to unrefined carbohydrates.)

Bran, flax, and psyllium seeds, though replacements for laxatives and preventives of constipation, are not cures. They can, in fact, be dangerous, causing blockage if they are consumed before the constipation is relieved. One might consider consuming *nothing but fluids* until constipation is relieved.

A tablespoon of molasses in a cup of warm water twice in a day is a reasonably effective stimulant to a reluctant colon for about half of those who try it. If that fails, a quart of warm salt water (two teaspoons salt to a quart of water) drunk first thing in the morning is also quite effective. You can also stimulate your colon from the outside by massaging: start with your hand flat against the lower right side of your abdomen; press in, then up and across your abdomen just below your navel, then down the left side. You'll feel it; what you've done is follow the natural course of your colon—ascending colon, transverse colon, descending colon—encouraging the peristaltic action to move things along.

Spastic Colon, Colitis, Diverticulitus

These are grouped together because they are a direct degenerative line, one leading to the next, generally preceded by chronic constipation. They, in turn, are frequently the precursors of colon cancer, one of the most common forms of cancer.

A spastic colon is one which works in spasms—stopping, starting, stopping again—instead of steadily and smoothly. Colitis is inflammation of the colon, caused by the irritation of improper functioning. If colitis is prolonged, diverticulitis can result, the wall of the colon bulging out to form pockets in which fecal matter is trapped. There is no quick fix for these conditions, but the health of the intestines can be restored by eliminating their causes. How long this will take depends on the individual and on how far degeneration has proceeded. It is reasonable to expect recovery from spastic colon in six weeks; colitis may take a few months; diverticulitis, depending on how bad it is, may take a year, even longer.

If your body has degenerated as far as having spastic colon, you should receive the signal being sent: change your way of living. Don't look for a natural, "healthy" medicine to replace those from the pharmacy, don't expect to drink a medicine or pop a pill that will make you better. You can only make the symptoms go away—maybe—and lull yourself into allowing further degeneration.

People suffering from spastic colon often notice they're at their worst after soaking in an alkalinizing soapy bath. They also often get relief from splashing vinegar directly on their skin. Yes, we're back to apple cider vinegar again, but this time it won't knock the condition out, as it often does for colds, acid indigestion, or flatulence. But faulty acid-alkaline balance seems to be a related factor here. A program to reverse the degeneration of the colon and restore it to health should include:

—Plenty of whole grains (except wheat) and fresh produce, raw and cooked, in your diet.
—The addition of bran, or flax or psyllium seeds (see *Constipation*).
—Elimination of wheat (except sprouted), citrus, and dairy (milk and hard cheese but not yogurt, kefir, and cottage cheese).
—Eating cultured milk products such as yogurt and kefir, and taking acidophilus for the beneficial bacteria in them, which aid in the promotion of healthy intestinal flora.
—Supplementing your diet with vitamins A, B, C, and HCL tablets, or a multi-digestant including HCL.
—Washing your body with something that has a neutral or slightly acid pH.
—Massaging your colon, and spending at least five minutes a day in *the shoulder stand*. The shoulder stand is a yoga posture in which you lie on your back, then raise your legs

and trunk to the vertical, supporting yourself by bracing your hands against your back. This provides an invigorating stimulation of the colon by reversing its position against the pull of gravity.

—Engaging in regular, vigorous exercise.

A Few Words About Wheat: You have seen wheat incriminated twice in this chapter. Why am I suddenly slamming the staff of life? I'm not: wheat is a good food for most healthy people. But there seem to be some properties connected with its protein—gluten—that make it hard to handle. Wheat and milk are two of the most common "allergy foods." The process of sprouting changes the properties of the wheat protein (as culturing changes the properties of milk protein), making it easier to digest. The establishment of a high level of general health usually eliminates digestive problems with wheat.

Hemorrhoids

If we are to believe the TV commercials, one out of three people know about hemorrhoids, or piles, from personal experience. As usual, faulty living is the cause. A hemorrhoid is the dilation of one of the veins around the anus, which bulges out painfully. They are generally prevented by right diet, proper elimination, and good condition of the circulatory system.

Hemorrhoids can often be cleared up by taking 25 mg of vitamin B6 after each meal. This should be accompanied by the other B vitamins, vitamin A (30,000 IU), vitamin E (600 IU), vitamin C (1,000 mg), bioflavinoids, calcium, and magnesium. Although relief may occur after one day, it could take up to six weeks for a complete return to normalcy.

People report that the following substances applied externally have provided relief: vitamin E; wheat germ oil; olive oil; lemon juice; grated raw potatoes or macerated comfrey leaves applied as a poultice: a raw, peeled garlic clove, oiled and inserted in the anus; propolis salve; castor oil.

Hemorrhoids are often associated with chronic constipation resulting from the strain associated with poor intestinal condition. Therefore bran is an extremely important supplement for hemorrhoids as well as constipation because it promotes good intestinal condition. Remember, however, that bran added to a lot of fat and refined carbohydrates doesn't magically produce a good diet. And good as it is as a supplement, too much bran can cause nutritional imbalances—as with everything else, there can be too much of a good thing. The aim should be, again, to improve the overall quality of the diet with whole grains and fresh produce. According to Dr. Nittler, the cure of hemorrhoids is "directly related to improved liver function."

Hepatitis

"Hepa" refers to liver, "itis" means infection of—literally, infection of the liver. Hepatitis has become a more common disease in recent years because of sexual promiscuity and increased drug use: two common ways people are exposed are venereally and by dirty hypodermic syringes. It can be a devastating disease but doesn't need to be; the liver is the only organ that regenerates itself, even when as much as 90 percent is removed surgically.

Vitamins A and C are always important in clearing infection and so they are helpful for hepatitis. The liver also likes the B complex vitamins, which should be part of recovery from hepatitis. Foods that are good for the liver include liver (make it calves' liver for freedom from pesticide and antibiotic residues, or liver from an animal raised organically), nutritional yeast, beet juice, yogurt and acidophilus, wheat germ, raw fruits and vegetables.

Avoid alcohol, coffee, chocolate, sugar, and fat—all antagonistic to the liver. Remember that the liver is the main organ of detoxification so you want to keep your diet *fanatically* pure and natural when the liver is in trouble. Search out sources of organically grown food—a sick liver deserves nothing less. Drink spring water with verified purity.

With plenty of the right foods—particularly liver and beet juice—and vitamins A, B, and C, none of the wrong foods, and plenty of rest, recovery from hepatitis should be rapid and complete.

Kidney Stones

People who have had them usually say they have never experienced such vicious pain as that from kidney stones. There generally isn't any pain until the stones get into the duct leading to the bladder. There it cuts the delicate tissue and big ones sometimes block the urinary tract. At that point people usually go to the hospital, assenting to an operation— anything to get rid of the excruciating pain.

Circumstantial evidence leads me to believe that perhaps 75 percent of surgical removals of kidney stones could be avoided. When the urinary tract is blocked, the insertion of a catheter is necessary to relieve the pressure. In most cases, the next step ought to be the drinking of chamomile tea, lots of it. Make it by the quart and drink it hot and cold, all day long, in lieu of water and every other beverage. Chamomile is a variety of low-growing meadow plant; a pleasant-tasting tea is made from its tiny flowers. It is a strong diuretic, but more important in this case is that it has the ability to quickly dissolve many types of kidney stones.

Bear in mind that there are varying chemical components among kidney stones, so chamomile, like anything else, is not 100 percent effective. But it is *highly* effective. I have heard of people getting relief from kidney stones within hours by the copious drinking of chamomile tea. Other herbs that have been effective for dissolving stones are shave-grass, cornsilk, buchu, uva ursi. Fresh parsley juice (mix it with carrot, or some other juice—parsley is strong tasting) and cranberry juice can also be useful to dissolve kidney stones.

To avoid bouncing any stones from the kidney into the duct, don't do any strenuous exercise during the period in which you are drinking copiously to dissolve kidney stones. Most sufferers have multiple stones, analogous to a handful of gravel; the degree of pain from passing stones relates to the size of those pieces of gravel. It would also be prudent to avoid spinach, rhubarb, chard, almonds, and cashews, in case your stones are of the oxalate variety. While the urine is flowing and the pain is tolerable, you can safely pursue your effort to dissolve your stones. How long it will take depends on the type of stone, their number and size. It is advisable to follow this course under a doctor's supervision; if it is going to work, you should experience dramatic improvement within two weeks. There may be painful interludes while dissolving is taking place, as stones exit the kidneys.

Once kidney stones are gone, whether it be by dissolution or surgery, change your diet to keep more from forming—if you were eating (and drinking) right, you wouldn't have gotten them. Kidney stones, unknown in primitive people eating their traditional natural diets, have been shown to be connected to the consumption of excessive meat (*Journal of Chronic Diseases*, Vol. 32, No. 6, 1979) and excessive sugar (*British Journal of Urology*, Vol. 50, No. 7, 1978).

Magnesium and vitamin B6 have been shown to be preventives of kidney stones (*Journal of*

Urology, October, 1974). Foods rich in both of those nutrients include dried legumes (soy, lima, and kidney beans, peanuts), wheat germ, and blackstrap molasses. Also, vitamins A, E and F are all important to the health of your kidneys.

Enlarged Prostate And Impotency

Impotency has multiple causes but is often related to an enlarged prostate, and is, in fact, often a warning signal that the prostate gland is enlarging. Another early sign is a dull ache deep in the lower abdomen, close to the rectum. The prostate partially surrounds the urethra, the tube from the bladder to the penis, in a crescent shape. The dull ache is due to the pressure the enlarging gland applies on the tube, which may also result in a noticeably slow urine flow. As the swelling of the prostate advances, the pain becomes sharper, urination problems become obvious, impotency can become complete.

To reduce the swelling you should have a mixture of vegetable oils, for example safflower, corn, and sesame, but any three will do, to supply all seven essential fatty acids. Break and squeeze the oily contents of a couple of capsules of vitamin A (10,000 units) and a couple of vitamin E (400 units) into a couple of tablespoons of the mixed oils. Draw the mixture into a baby rectal syringe or an ear syringe and squirt it into the rectum just before going to bed. By osmosis, the lipotropic factors will work their way through the intestinal wall, and make contact with the prostate. This treatment has been known to alleviate the swelling after an application, but several might be necessary.

Take vitamins A and E regularly to keep the problem from recurring. The mineral zinc is also vital to the health of the prostate. Pumpkin seeds are an excellent source of zinc, sunflower seeds a good one. They are literally "prostate food" because they combine zinc with vitamins E and F; men who eat a handful of pumpkin seeds or sunflower seeds daily almost never suffer from prostate problems. Other good food sources of zinc are nutritional yeast, liver, seafood, soybeans, and mushrooms. Sugar and alcohol are major enemies to the prostate, as they are to every other part of the body.

The Complete Book of Natural Medicines (Carroll, Summit Books) reports that in Sweden bee pollen has become a popular folk medicine for prostate problems: "Pollen is known to include the hormone testosterone plus traces of other important male hormones. It acts as a catalyzing agent on the prostate, stimulating it into self-healing." The recommended amount is two teaspoonfuls per day.

Where impotency is not related to an enlarged prostate, ginseng can have a truly amazing regenerative effect. American, Chinese, and Korean varieties of ginseng are all considered effective. The most effective form is the whole root. It's bitter, but you don't eat much at a time; just slice off a sliver and chew it thoroughly. You might spend fifteen dollars on a good ginseng root but you should take a month to eat a big one. I've heard from men that ginseng restored them from what seemed to be total impotency. Vitamin E has also helped, since it enhances circulation and erection depends on an increased blood flow to the penis.

Bleeding Gums

Pyorrhea—where the gums at the roots of the teeth become infected, pus forms, and the teeth loosen—is almost always preceded by bleeding gums, gingivitis being the milder stage. The condition is created gradually and people commonly ignore the bleeding gums, considering it a mere annoyance. Dentists and dental hygienists rightly tell us that improper cleaning is a major cause and encourage us to floss every day—excellent advice. But they rarely tell us we shouldn't drink citrus juices every day.

It's not that you should never eat another orange or let a sip of orange juice pass your lips. The problem is quantity, the daily drinking, year after year. Citrus juices contain a great deal of citric acid (which is not the same as ascorbic acid, vitamin C). Citric acid is a solvent of calcium. So in persistent drinking of citrus juices you are subjecting your teeth to a bath that, bit by bit, day by day, dissolves calcium from your teeth. Perhaps calcium metabolism replaces some of the eroded calcium, but not all of it; gradually the substance of the teeth suffers citric acid erosion, and space between teeth and gums is created. Tartar forms on the teeth where the gum tissue becomes loosened, and gums bleed when the tartar irritates the gum tissue.

People are usually into their forties or fifties before the erosion is advanced enough to become a severe problem. But bleeding gums should serve as a signal to wean yourself from the orange juice habit. (Coffee, milk and orange juice, liquids that are consumed together at millions of American breakfasts every day, constitute a terribly incompatible mixture.)

Refined carbohydrates in general and white sugar in particular (as most of us have heard to the point of boredom) are enemies of the teeth and gums. What should also be appreciated is that *all* concentrated sweets, including honey and molasses, are bad for your teeth; white sugar is simply the worst of the lot.

Tissue health, in the mouth or anywhere else, requires adequate vitamins A, C, D, and calcium. Where do you get your C if you curtail citrus consumption? From all kinds of raw fruits and vegetables and from tablets.

Headaches

People often notice that headaches accompany constipation; clear up the constipation and the headache disappears. There are also times when constipation is not present but elimination is nevertheless poor; this condition can also be accompanied by headache. So the measures used against constipation (see page 152) are often also effective against headaches.

Headaches also seem to be related often to mineral deficiencies. Many people report that once they regularly began taking a good vitamin-mineral supplement, their headache problems largely disappeared. Other factors involved in headache are eye strain, anxiety, close proximity to fluorescent lights, bad posture, and misaligned neck vertabrae (see your chiropractor). All these factors put stress on the nervous system and many medical experts believe that almost all headaches are caused by some form of nervous tension.

Mark Bricklin, editor of *Prevention* magazine, writes in *The Natural Healing Cookbook* (Rodale Press) that certain foodstuffs and additives are associated with headaches. Among them are coffee, monosodium glutamate (MSG), sodium nitrate and nitrite (in most hot dogs, bacon, ham, sausage, and salami), alcohol, wheat, oranges, chocolate, and sugar.

Dr. Jarvis's headache remedy is three tablespoonfuls of apple cider vinegar with three teaspoonfuls of honey mixed in water and drunk at the onset of a headache. His explanation of the efficacy of this remedy is that restoration of stomach acidity corrects the poor digestion of protein and calcium responsible for headaches.

You might wonder why apple cider vinegar emerges here as a sort of "champion" folk remedy. Does it indicate that we are supposed to have an acid body chemistry? No, there is no single optimum pH. Skin is slightly acid, saliva is slightly alkaline, the stomach is acid, the small intestine is alkaline, the large intestine is acid, blood is alkaline, cells are alkaline, urine is acid. But all are, of course, interconnected; so a change of pH somewhere affects the pH everywhere.

As noted previously, many common ailments have as one characteristic (it is not necessarily a cause) an acid/alkaline imbalance. Apple cider vinegar is made acid by the presence of mallic acid, which can be viewed as a chemical cousin to the hydrochloric acid created by our bodies. Taken into the stomach or applied to the skin, apple cider vinegar will acidify imbalanced organs, returning them to nearer optimum if they have become too alkaline. Such changes, in turn, can have an optimizing effect on the associated organs, glands, and systems.

All of the above folk medicine remedies have worked frequently for a broad cross-section of people. Nobody will get rich from the money you spend on them; it all represents inexpensive self-help. The remedies also might not work; but your doctor's remedies don't always work either and since nutritional therapy is nonpoisonous, there are no significant or irreversible side effects.

IATROGENIC DISEASES

Iatrogenic, or drug induced, diseases are currently responsible for one out of five deaths. The doctors aren't really to blame; drugs are all they've been taught in medical school. Doctors and patients alike have been snowed under by an enormous medical monopoly and we have come to rely on doctors and drugs to help us with all sorts of conditions we may be able to treat more effectively ourselves without drugs.

The side effects of drugs are often more subtle than pathological. For example, the administration of antibiotics for colds kills more than harmful bacteria. It also kills beneficial bacteria of the small intestine, which participate in digestion, assimilation, and the production of B vitamins. The antibiotic actually does nothing to cure colds; what it really does is leave you in worse condition than if you had not taken it, suffering from indigestion, flatulence, and vitamin deficiencies. If you eat the right foods (particularly cultured milk products) and avoid the wrong ones (particularly refined carbohydrates), you will gradually restore healthy intestinal flora. But that may take weeks, even months.

Mention of colds brings us back to the point of departure regarding remedies, and to another point. Remember that the aim of the remedy was to intervene in the cold process by affecting stomach acidity, which in turn would affect the other levels of acid-alkaline balance. Remember also that acid-alkaline imbalance was not the primary cause of the cold. *Folk medicine is just as much a form of symptomatic medicine as drug therapy.* The reason folk medicine is to be preferred—when it works—over drug therapy is not that it is healthy; it is just less unhealthy.

It has often seemed to me that people successfully using folk remedies get an undeserved feeling of security: "I'm all right, Jack—I've got my bottle of apple cider vinegar." But it is no less medicine than penicillin just because it is vinegar. We need medicine of any kind only because somewhere in the course of daily life we've been making some mistakes. We don't get sick unless we have lessons to learn about how to live right.

A major factor behind the attraction of folk medicine and other forms of medical self-care is that contemporary medical education properly equips doctors to deal with only contagious diseases and trauma, which account for about 30 percent of what ails us. In many cases (cancer is an exception), doctors are also excellent diagnosticians. We frequently need professional diagnostic help when we're in serious trouble. But, since we're largely responsible for our own ill health, we can often treat ourselves more effectively than someone else can. Thom consistently exhorts people to tune into their own body wisdom and so do I. So also do most practitioners of holistic medicine, whose greatest contribution to our health is helping us to learn how to take care of ourselves.

SELF-HELP AND DEGENERATIVE DISEASES

The ailments discussed above are all nonpathological. Nonetheless, they are no less degenerative conditions than "killer" diseases such as cancer, heart disease, and diabetes. Pathology tells us that degeneration is "a process by which tissue deteriorates, loses functional activity . . ." We see, then, that what degenerate are the general processes by which cells are created and maintained and energy is produced. In degenerative disease, we lose physiological and biochemical efficiency—metabolism degenerates.

Once the nature of degeneration is clearly seen, the contribution of faulty nutrition should be obvious. A friend of mine is a foreman on a large cattle ranch. He says, "The cattlemen around here are real clear that if their cows don't get the proper nutrients, they get sick. It blows my mind that they refuse to see that what's true for cattle is true for people."

Killer diseases seldom arrive suddenly to someone who never showed any signs of ill health. It is usually a downward evolving spiral from the simple to the more complex. For example, in my book *Metabolic Ecology: A Way to Win the Cancer War* (Wedgestone Press), Dr. Kelley lists the true early warning signs of cancer:

—Gas on the stomach or bowel.
—Sudden weakness of the eyes.
—Tired feeling most of the time.
—Muscle weakness and cramps—first in the back, then in the chest.
—Extreme mental depression.
—Sudden change in hair texture and color.
—Development of various hernias (only in slow-growing tumors).
—Confusion—difficulty in making even simple decisions.

I am not avoiding the subject of self-help in relationship to killer diseases because it won't help. It will. But your responsibilities are heavier, the procedures more complex, the consequences more fearsome—far beyond the scope of a chapter in a natural foods book, no matter how complete.

The point to be made regarding folk medicine and degenerative diseases is that the simple diseases are often the precursors of the more complex ones. They can serve as a warning signal that you are beginning to slip down the metabolic spiral. How often do you need the folk remedies? Are you on an unceasing search for ways to alleviate physical complaints? Be forewarned and be grateful that you have time to help yourself.

You can spin quite far down the metabolic spiral and still reverse the direction and climb back up. Down to a certain point, what degenerates can regenerate. But the sooner you begin, the easier the return journey. Once you evolve up the metabolic spiral far enough, folk remedies become almost as irrelevant as drugs. But as in cattle, so in people: optimum health is impossible without a sound nutritional foundation.

14 New and Future Natural Foods

SOY FOODS

Can a lowly bean change the appearance of American menus? Soybeans have a chance of doing so. Soybeans produce more abundantly and can be grown more widely than any other bean crop. Rotated with corn, they form the backbone of our great midwestern cropping system. Many of them are fed to chickens, cattle, and hogs.

Soybean by-products are widely used, though not so widely recognized: most protein powders use soy as a major ingredient; lecithin, a natural soy derivative, is the most ubiquitous food emulsifier; texturized vegetable protein (TVP), is widely used as a hamburger extender.

Soybean futures are a major play on the commodity exchanges and soybeans are a major export crop. Most of our soybean exports go to the Orient; it is how they are used there that is of most interest to us in our search for nutritious, low-cost, natural foods. Centuries of Oriental tradition have clearly established the value of soy foods, allowing their rapid incorporation into the New American Cuisine.

Tofu

Soybean curd originated in China before the birth of Christ. Also called "soybean cheese," TOH-foo is the pronunciation. It is made by boiling soybeans, mashing the boiled beans through a sieve to yield a kind of "milk," adding a coagulant to the milk, then pressing the water from the curdled milk. The resultant tofu is kept fresh by storing in water or by vacuum packing. It looks like natural, uncolored cheese but it is not as dense as most cheese. It is also much blander in taste. This blandness, a liability if tofu is eaten plain, is also a virtue: the absence of a powerful flavor makes it versatile.

Tofu is already well on its way to becoming a popular food. Rich in protein and minerals, low in fat, its uses are almost unlimited. It can be sliced, seasoned and fried like meat, cubed and stir-fried with vegetables, added uncooked to salads, blended into dips and dressings, and used as a cheese replacement in everything from pizza to cheesecake. In Japan it is made fresh daily in more than 38,000 small local shops, versions of which are popping up in U.S. cities. This natural food cottage industry is being promoted by William Shurtleff and Akira Aoyagi, who have also co-authored the definitive book on the subject, *The Book of Tofu* (Ballantine Books), which is full of the lore and methodology of tofu production, as well as its use. (See Chapter 20 for tofu recipes.)

The best quality tofu is made from organically grown soybeans, coagulated by *nigari*, also called "bitterns" in English. Nigari is a natural coagulant, primarily calcium and magnesium salts, derived from sea water. This quality of tofu is sold widely in natural foods stores. Ordinary tofu made with nonorganically grown soybeans, generally coagulated with calcium sulphate, is still a quite acceptable natural food, found in Oriental specialty food stores and many supermarkets.

Tempeh

This is a staple food of Indonesia, pronounced TEMpey. Where Japan has its tofu shops, Indonesia has its tempeh shops. Tempeh is made from soybeans that have been hulled and split. After they have been cooked, they undergo a process similar to yogurt-making, in that microorganisms are introduced to transform the original food by fermentation into something quite different. In the case of tempeh, microscopic spores are left to multiply on cooked soybeans spread on trays at about 1½ inch thickness.

The spores spread quickly, forming a thin fuzz over the beans, transforming them into a firm cake. When fried like meat, tempeh has a succulent flavor, somewhat like a cross between chicken and mushrooms. It is a high-protein, low-fat food, phenomenally high in vitamin B12, which is of great interest to vegetarians. (A four-ounce serving of tempeh supplies 10 percent of the RDAs for iron and calcium, 15 percent for vitamin B2, 25 percent for vitamin A, 30 percent for protein and 39 percent for vitamin B12.)

The promotion of tempeh is several years behind that of tofu but its potential is just as great. Since it isn't as bland, it is not as versatile as tofu; but its texture and taste make it an extremely attractive meat substitute. A tempeh burger on a whole wheat bun with alfalfa sprouts, tomato and mayonnaise would be the healthiest fast food in America, and a delicious one. Tempeh also has the advantage of being a whole food—there is neither pulp nor whey to discard, as in tofu—without the tendency to create flatulence typical of unfermented beans.

Tempeh-tofu comparisons are almost unavoidable because the two foods have so much in common. I use them both, but use tempeh much more often. It is extremely easy to incorporate into all kinds of dishes, since, like tofu, it is made from soybeans already cooked, rendering it ready to eat as is or just warmed through. Tempeh can be treated as a filet, cubed or diced for mixed vegetable dishes, salads, soups, and sauces, and makes fine sandwiches—for all these purposes, tempeh can be used instead of tofu, giving an entirely different flavor and texture.

Shurtleff and Aoyagi are the champions of all soy foods, having also co-authored *The Book of Tempeh*, Autumn Press. Joining this effort is The Farm, Summertown, Tennessee 38483, from whom split soybeans and tempeh culture are available by mail. Using a culture sold in many natural foods stores, tempeh is simpler to make at home than tofu. With the directions supplied in the culture package, tempeh can also be made from other kinds of beans, and grain-bean mixtures.

Miso

Another Japanese soy food, pronounced MEEso. It is made with wheat, with barley, sometimes rice, sometimes without added grain; each type has a slightly different flavor. Miso is a fermented food, made by adding an enzymatic culture to the cooked soybeans or soybean/grain mix. Salt and water are the only other ingredients of natural miso. After twelve or more months of aging, the protein is pre-digested, vitamin B12 is increased and the miso has become a thick, dark, salty, pungent paste. (Mass-produced "white" miso is made with white rice, aged no more than three months, is light colored and complete with chemical preservatives. It cannot be considered a natural food.)

Miso, with its high salt content, is used mainly as an ingredient of sauces, spreads, and dips and as a base for meaty-tasting soups. It is an excellent replacement for bouillon cubes, most of which are made with hydrogenated vegetable fat. Our friends Shurtleff and Aoyagi have written the definitive book for this one too: *The Book of Miso,* Ballantine Books.

Soy Sauce

Soy sauce has long been popular in the U.S. in its mass-produced, chemically preserved form. With the increased interest in natural foods here, the traditional versions from Japan have begun to become popular. There are two versions of Japanese soy sauce, one called *shoyu,* the other *tamari.* A mistake was made when the importation of natural soy sauce from Japan began in the mid-sixties. Shoyu was mistaken for tamari; the misnomer wasn't recognized for years and only recently have the importers begun to try to correct it.

Shoyu is made from soybeans and wheat, tamari from soybeans only. Shoyu is thinner and lighter in flavor, a versatile seasoning; tamari is noticeably thicker and stronger tasting, suitable to thin into broth or use as a dip. About 95 percent of the soy sauce consumed in Japan is shoyu and about 95 percent of the imported "tamari" has really been shoyu, mistakenly identified. Tamari can be as much as twice as expensive as shoyu. Neither of the words shoyu or tamari necessarily means *natural.* Natural shoyu and tamari are identified as having been aged for 18 months or more and having no chemical preservative added. When either type of soy sauce is used in cooking, salt should be eliminated or greatly curtailed, since soy sauce has approximately 440 mg of sodium per teaspoon.

Soy Milk

Making soymilk is the simplest part of making tofu and can be done quite easily at home. According to Shurtleff and Aoyagi, when soymilk is made with the same percentage of water as cows' milk it has 51 percent more protein, 12 percent less calories, and 24 percent less fat. It also has 82 percent less calcium, 93 percent less sodium, and fifteen times more iron. However, these comparative values can be considered valid only in judging the relative food value of the two kinds of milk when you compare soymilk with *pasteurized* cows' milk. If certified raw milk were the norm, there would be far fewer people in need of a cows' milk substitute and soymilk would be left to stand on its own considerable merits.

Most canned soymilk is made with poor quality vegetable oils and has other synthetic additives; the word "soymilk" on the can may well describe a product that bears only a slight resemblance to what you could make at home. The best alternative is fresh soymilk, made at home or bought in a natural foods store. Next best is to make your own from the natural soy milk powder also sold in natural foods stores.

Other Soy Products

The two newest soyfoods which are the most likely candidates to find places in the American market are *yuba,* made from the skins formed on hot soybean milk, layered and pressed into slabs or cakes, eaten as a meat substitute, and *sufu,* which is tofu inoculated, fermented, pickled in rice wine and brine, and eaten as a condiment.

In the continuation of their promotion of and research in soyfoods, Shurtleff and Aoyagi have founded The Soyfoods Center in Lafayette, California, and helped to establish the trade organization, Soycrafters Association, with offices in Colrain, Massachusetts. At the time of writing, Soycrafters says there are now 154 tofu factories and 32 tempeh factories in America, with $52 million annually in retail sales. There are also 13 soy delicatessens specializing in such ready-to-eat soyfoods as tofu and tempeh burgers, soymilk shakes, tofu and tempeh salads, tofu yogurt and cheesecakes.

America has always led the world in adopting and adapting the foods of foreign cultures. Soy foods have truly tremendous potential for becoming a popular addition to our national, natural cuisine. As we feed fewer soybeans to our hogs and eat more of them ourselves, we will become sounder both nutritionally and ecologically.

VEGETABLE GELS AND THICKENERS

Two "vegetarian gelatins" are fairly widely used in food manufacturing. Most Americans have had them without realizing they are sea vegetables.

Irish moss, also known as *carrageen*, can be bought in bulk in natural foods stores and boiled down to form a clear gel for puddings, jelly, or "jello" desserts. High in protein, vitamin A, and iodine.

Agar-agar in flakes or bar form is ready to dissolve in hot water or juice to make desserts and aspics. Use 1½ tablespoons per quart of liquid. The Japanese dessert made from agar-agar is called *kanten*.

Arrowroot is a fine powder without the chalkiness of cornstarch or the graininess of flour. Use 1½ teaspoons to replace 1 tablespoon of either cornstarch or flour.

Kudzu is a vine that grows prolifically in the South. The root is processed into powdery chunks. To thicken sauces, dissolve 2 tablespoons in ¼ cup cold water, pour through strainer into sauce ingredients. The Japanese name is *kuzu*.

FUTURE FOODS FROM THE SEA

Sea Vegetables

People have eaten sea vegetables for thousands of years. Yet today farming of the sea is called the only agricultural frontier left on the planet. One visionary in this field has envisioned forty billion people being fed by farms covering half the ocean's surface by the year 2100. The scenario would seem particularly farfetched if you had never knowingly eaten a sea vegetable, and it will still be many a year before we see them piled like lettuce and parsley in our markets. But the door has been opened by natural foods companies importing dried sea vegetables from Japan. Here are the most popular varieties:

Arame, which supplies vitamins A, B1, and B2.
Hijiki, especially high in calcium, also supplying vitamins A, B1, B12, and iron.
Wakame, high in iron, calcium, and magnesium, also supplying vitamins A, B1, and B2.

The three above varieties have similar uses: in soups, stews, and bean dishes, in salads, and steamed or sauteed, either alone or with land vegetables. A popular macrobiotic dish, for example, is sauteed carrots, onions, and hijiki, flavored with a little garlic and soy sauce.

In soups and stews, simply add a handful as is, or crumbled or torn. Before adding to salads or sautéing, hydrate them in a dish with a small amount of water, soaking for twenty to thirty minutes.

Kombu comes in many forms, but the most common here is *dashi kombu*, sold in thick wide sheets which are added to soups, stews, and beans to enhance flavor and improve digestibility—called "the natural MSG."

Nori is cultivated in Japan, gathered wild in Ireland, where it is called *sloke*, and in Scotland, where it is called *laver*. The Japanese version is cooked and processed into thin, deep purple sheets used to wrap rice balls and sushi. (Sushi is a mixture of cooked vinegared rice and any one of a wide assortment of seafoods or pickled vegetables.) The sheets torn into pieces can be used as a seasoning in salads and vegetable dishes. Nori is extremely high in protein (35 percent), and high in vitamin A.

Dulse, harvested in Nova Scotia, is known in New England as a cocktail snack. High in protein, vitamin A, also supplying B6, B12, C, and E, dulse has the same uses as arame, hijiki, and wakame.

Sea vegetables (or "seaweed" or "marine algae") absorb nutrients through their entire surface from the sea water they float in. Since they average 39 percent salt, other forms of salt can be eliminated or curtailed wherever sea vegetables are used. They are all high in protein and, since sea water is a solution of all the minerals vital to human health, they are all excellent mineral sources. Since sea water can also be a solution of industrial pollutants, anyone wishing to experiment with their own hand-gathered sea vegetables should harvest them far from industrial sites or the emptying rivers that may have picked up factory discharges.

Protein From The Sea

What high-protein, low-fat sea creature is plentiful off both our east and west coasts, is approximately 75 percent delicate tasting flesh, is eaten widely in Mediterranean and Oriental countries, and strikes most Americans as too ugly to eat? The answer: squid. Once squid is cleaned and cooked, it is as good-looking as any other firm, white meat, with flavor to match. To get a hint of its potential as a versatile protein source, try *calamari* in an Italian restaurant.

Another neglected species is the mussel, a mollusk related to the clam and the oyster, and more popular than either around the Mediterranean. Mussels can be found off all our coasts, but their great potential lies in their prolific ways in captivity. In *Future Food*, Barbara Ford calls Spain's mussel farms "the most successful form of aquaculture in the world," yielding up to 250 tons per acre. That would not matter if they were not good eating; but they are. More tender than the clam, firmer than the oyster, the mussel has a milder, more delicate flavor than either of its cousins. They even look good—orange meat in a blue-black shell. In restaurants you can discover them in French *bouillabaisse* and Spanish *paella*.

Blue-Green Algae

Like most "new" and "future" foods, the use of blue-green algae as food is new only to us; its future lies in its past. Algae has been used for centuries by Africans and Chinese and was a major food of the Aztecs. Grown in fresh water, there are four principal types: *chlorella*, *anabaena*, *aphanizomenon flos-aquae*, and *spirulina*. They are all good protein sources, each having different concentrations of nutrients.

The algaes are so nutritious that they are exploitable as "miracle" foods. Not many years ago chlorella received a big promotional push. At the time of writing, we are being blitzed by superlatives about spirulina. Probably by the time you read these words the spirulina fever will have abated as consumers realize that much of the furor has been caused by those who profit from its sale.

Spirulina is approximately 65 percent complete protein and is the most potent natural source of vitamin B12 known. It is a good source of vitamins A and B1 and iron, and a fair source of vitamins B2 and E, selenium, zinc, and chlorophyll.

While its virtues are impressive, so much is being claimed for it that we need to be able to see it in perspective. Spirulina has no vitamins B6, C, or D; no carbohydrate, fat and fiber. As Dori Smith points out in *Spirulina: Facts Behind the Fad* ("Whole Life Times", Sept/Oct 81), spirulina's deficiencies invalidate the claims for its being a whole, complete food. It will take its place with the other blue-green algaes—all bland, extremely fine green powders, most useful as food supplements in tablets or capsules or added to basic staples to boost their nutritional potencies in protein, B vitamins, and minerals.

OTHER FUTURE FOODS

Another Germ

So widely known is wheat germ that for millions of Americans it is the first thing that comes to mind when they hear the words "health foods." A younger cousin is now bidding for recognition—

ANOTHER PERSPECTIVE ON PROTEIN

One of many ways of looking at protein is to focus on its biological value (BV). The BV of protein is measured by feeding the food in question and measuring the amount of nitrogen excreted unassimilated in the feces. The amount of nitrogen excreted is subtracted from 100 percent, the amount consumed as protein; since the difference is assimilated, it is said to have "biological value," a reasonable assumption.

Protein Source	% Assimilated, or BV
Egg	96
Milk	83
Meat (an average)	80
Potato	78
Soybeans	75
Spirulina	72
Rice	70
Corn Germ	70
Black Beans	65
Garbanzo Beans	65
Chlorella	54
Lentils	45

corn germ. Corn germ is a complete protein rich in lysine, making it a good complement to whole grains. Compared to wheat germ, corn germ has 33 percent more vitamin E, 20 percent more iron, eight times more zinc, and twice as much fiber. It is just behind liver as a natural source of iron and is a good source of potassium, magnesium, and copper. It has all the uses of wheat germ—in baking, sprinkled on cereals, soups, salads—and one more: being a bit bigger and crunchier than wheat germ, it makes a delicious snack eaten right out of your hand.

Another Bran

Just as widely known as wheat germ, perhaps even more so, is wheat bran. In fact, when the word "bran" is uttered, it is almost universally taken to refer to the bran of wheat. But oats are bidding to change that, with Quaker Oats, which has plenty of oat bran to sell, behind the move. You will be able to choose your type of bran according to the consistency and function you prefer to emphasize.

Oat bran is much finer, with a smoother texture than wheat bran. Functionally, the big difference is that the fiber of oat bran is water-soluble, whereas wheat bran fiber is insoluble. The water-soluble oat bran fiber has been found to reduce blood levels of LDL cholesterol, the type associated with fatty deposits. The active agent in the fiber is oat gum, which gives cooked rolled oats its characteristic stickiness. The cholesterol-reducing effect is entirely absent in wheat bran, which, on the other hand, is more effective as a stimulant of the bowel than oat bran. Oat bran substituted for wheat bran in baking recipes will yield quite different results—more dense, moist, and silky in texture.

Amaranth

An Aztec grain that faded into obscurity, amaranth is a future food largely because of the efforts of Robert Rodale, editor of *Organic Gardening* and *Prevention* magazines, and founder of the Organic Gardening and Farming Research Center. In the mid-seventies, Rodale and his organization, with many of their readers growing seed that had been sent to them free, began a massive development program. They have already bred varities that stoutly resist drought, produce 1500 pounds of grain per acre, and can be harvested by combine, as well as grown in home gardens.

The Rodale test kitchens have found that amaranth has good baking properties when mixed with whole-wheat flour. It is also rich in lysine, combining with wheat and other grains into complete protein. It also has a future as a snack—it pops.

Rodale's organization is not making a business out of amaranth; instead of patenting the varieties it is developing, it is giving the seeds to researchers and seed companies. This selfless promotion is electrifying the grapevine and the use of grain amaranth is already spreading quickly.

Halophytes

Three-quarters of the earth is covered with salt water which is useless as irrigation water and billions of acres of land is desert, useless for agriculture. Except, that is, for growing edible plants in sand watered by salt water. Those are halophytes. Most plants block salt from entering, and the salt accumulates around their roots, eventually killing them. Halophytes allow the salt in and then get rid of it. Halophytes for our tables are further in the future than the other foods discussed in this chapter, but researchers are working hard to make it happen. Among the more promising varieties are *pickleweed, saltbush,* and *Palmer's grass,* which produces salty leaves and stems yet whose grain-like seed accumulates no salt.

PART TWO: The New American Cuisine

15 Making the New American Cuisine Work

There are two goals intertwined throughout this book: (1) Raising the quality of your diet, and (2) Lowering the cost of your diet. Eating better for less is achieved by observing the following principles:

a. Make low-cost, natural staples the center of your cuisine.
b. Avoid high-priced junk foods.
c. Reduce or eliminate high-priced protein foods.
d. Take on more food processing responsibilities.

I have found that points *a*, *b*, and *c* are much easier for most people to accept than *d*. They object, "But there's so little time . . . We're both working full time and by the time the kids' needs are taken care of, the shopping's done, our social obligations are met and we've taken a little time to relax, there just isn't time for a lot of food preparation." That kind of statement could describe millions of contemporary American families.

A CUISINE FOR EVERYBODY

I've experienced the time squeeze. I know what it feels like; still, I maintain that *everybody* has enough time to adopt the New American Cuisine. I say so because there are levels of involvement that break down neatly and practically into three clearly identifiable phases. At all phases the primary purpose of improving dietary quality is met. In Phase One, the greatest qualitative improvements are made. Here all the dietary goals are met and significant money is saved—both at the expense of little extra time. Phase One will be as deep as many will want or be able to go, and it is enough. In terms of Phase One, you can't afford *not* to get involved, even if your time is heavily pressured. As Harvard professor Mark Hegsted said in *Dietary Goals*, "The question to be asked, therefore, is not why we should change our diet, but why not?"

In saying that Phase One is accessible to everybody, I am including single people. Books of this type usually ignore singles; yet in metropolitan areas, they compromise 45 percent of the marketplace. As a divorcee, I am at the Phase One level; when I was married and had three children, we were at the Phase Two level. Most aspects of Phase Two are practical for singles as well as families—it is simply a matter of how you choose to use your time. A fundamental underlying the New American Cuisine is that *the more food processing and preparation you take into your own hands, the higher the quality of your diet and the less you spend on food.*

173

INVESTMENT/SAVINGS IN THE NEW AMERICAN CUISINE
Family of Four

	Investment		Savings	
Cuisine	Additional Time	Budget Reduction	Annual Budget	Reduced by
Your Old Cuisine			$3,120	
——compared to——				
New American, Phase One	15%	15%	$2,652	$468
New American, Phase Two	25%	30%	$2,184	$936
New American, Phase Three	50%	45%	$1,715	$1,405

Note: In every case where I have decided to use dollar amounts to illustrate a point, I have done so reluctantly. This is being written in 1981; you may read it in 1984, by which time the dollar amounts may be wishful thinking. However, no matter what happens to our economy, the relativity of the dollars as expressed by the percentages will hold true. A 15–25 percent time investment in your own food processing as an economic "can't lose" situation is a reliable constant. *Guidelines for Food Purchasing in the United States* (Nick Mottern) points out that "achieving a diet in line with the recommendations of the Dietary Goals alone may enable the consumer to save 12 to 16 percent in total food costs."

The base figure of $3,120 is the USDA estimate for food for a family of four in 1980. The figures for the three phases were obtained by making shopping lists for similar weekly menus done according to the methods of the three phases, as described in Appendix Four. Sets of figures were taken for four hypothetical weeks, taken as an average, then extended to represent a year.

Two general factors distinguish the three phases: as you move from one phase to the next, more special equipment and more time are required. Seeing food processing in phases adds clarity to the generality that the more foods you process yourself, the less you spend on food. And it enables you to make connections to quality and time and make decisions regarding commitment with a maximum of consciousness, a minimum of guesswork. A cautionary note: don't let the grouping into phases hamper your freedom. They are not etched in marble. In a real sense, there are no phases of the New American Cuisine; we are into it according to our needs, tastes, and circumstances. That understood, let's see what phases actually mean.

THE THREE PHASES OF THE NEW AMERICAN CUISINE AT A GLANCE

Activity	Special Equipment	Additional Time Commitment
Phase One Cooking from scratch with grains, vegetables, vegetable proteins and animal proteins	None	Moderate
Making your own snack foods from wholesome ingredients	None	Minimal

THE THREE PHASES OF THE NEW AMERICAN CUISINE AT A GLANCE (*cont.*)

Activity	Special Equipment	Additional Time Commitment
Making your own baby foods from wholesome ingredients	Blender	Minimal

(Additional time commitment = 15%
Budgetary savings = 15%)

Phase Two Growing sprouts and herbs	Glass jar or specially made sprouter; planting containers and dirt	Minimal
Making mixes	None	Minimal
Making yogurt	Glass jars, incubating system	Minimal
Baking bread	Loaf pans	Major
Making pies, cookies, cakes, confections and ice cream	Pie pans, cookie sheets, cake pans, ice cream maker	Moderate

(Additional time commitment = 25%
Budgetary savings = 30%)

Phase Three Juicing	Electric juicer	Moderate
Grinding flour and meal	Manual or electric flour mill or multi-attachment food processor	Major
Canning and pickling	Canning jars, lids, cooling racks, pressure cooker for vegetables	Major
Freezing	Freezer, containers, wrapping materials for meats	Major
Drying	Dehydrator (solar is best) or racks and covering material for sun drying	Major

(Additional Time Commitment = 50%
Budgetary Savings = 45%)

There are general considerations to be discussed regarding all the above activities. But before you get to them you have to spend some time in the marketplace, so let's look at that first.

IN THE MARKETPLACE

What Not To Buy

One principle to keep in mind is that *the more the hand of man is involved, the lower the quality and the higher the price.* In order to achieve our double objective of raising the quality of our food while lowering its cost, we should avoid as much as possible foods that depend heavily on complex processing and artificial ingredients (which themselves depend heavily on complex synthesizing processes). Examples are:

—sugared and artificially colored and flavored "fruit" drinks
—heat-and-eat frozen dinners, entrees and desserts
—meat, egg and dairy substitutes (including margarines)
—infant formulas and most baby foods
—most luncheon meats (hot dogs, bologna, etc.) and sandwich spreads
—dessert mixes and most salad dressings and syrups

For most Americans, adhering to the above list will leave many holes in the menu plan; but it will become clear in the following pages how to fill those holes.

The Package Is Not The Product

As technologically advanced as food processing has become, food packaging has kept pace, perhaps even outstripped it. Since the end of World War II, the weight of food packaging has increased over 100 percent, energy use for food packaging has more than tripled and the cost of food packaging to the consumer has increased over 400 percent. Packaging accounts for approximately 14 percent of the food dollar, up from 5 percent in 1958. An estimate produced for the Environmental Protection Agency concluded that 5 percent of our industrial energy goes into packaging our food.

There is a line of progression from processing to packaging; usually, the more complex the processing, the more expensive the packaging needed to present the product in marketable form. From there the line progresses further: since the manufacturer has a big investment in processing and packaging, he is obliged to invest heavily in advertising and promotion. According to *Guidelines,* "more promotional money is devoted to food than any other category of consumer products." And, grim news for our children and nutritionally innocent adults, almost five times as much money was spent advertising highly processed foods than slightly processed foods. Saturday morning TV ads for sugar coated bleeps abound; you'll wait in vain to see one for oatmeal.

The manufacturer does not invest money merely to have it returned, he invests money to *make* money. So the advertising of food products that cost manufacturers over three billion dollars in 1980 may well have cost us, the consumers, four billion dollars when the manufacturers' return on investment is calculated. The innovative package, admirable from a technological viewpoint, generally translates into high profit margins. For economy, then, as well as your health, *avoid packaged food as much as is practically possible.*

What To Buy

The New American Cuisine is as natural as possible, requiring three purchasing principles:

—Buy as many whole, or unrefined, foods as possible
—Buy as much as possible in bulk (unpackaged)
—Buy as much fresh food produced locally as possible

As we have seen, the principal foods of the New American Cuisine are whole grains in all their various forms (such as brown rice and millet and such whole grain products as rolled oats, whole grain pastas, breads, and crackers). All natural foods stores, many health food stores, and a rapidly increasing number of supermarkets sell whole grains (and beans) in bulk. The whole grains are augmented by beans and seeds, fresh produce, dairy products, fish, and lean meat—the classical ingredients of every traditional cuisine the world has ever known and which technology can only replace at incalculable health and financial costs. Having left the slickly packaged, highly advertised foods loaded with refined and artificial ingredients to gather dust on the shelves, we have instead a shopping basket full of natural foods to take home.

The New American Cuisine enables you to

—climb high on the ladder of food quality, while
—stepping several rungs down the ladder of food cost

and whole grains are what make that possible. Grains are the most balanced type of food in terms of the ratio of calories to overall nutritional value. They yield the widest possible variey of tastes and textures (whole grains can be sweet, salty, buttery, spicy, mushy, firm, crisp, crunchy, wet, dry, hot or cold, depending on how you prepare them). Furthermore, grain production is the most energy-efficient use of agricultural land, making whole grains the cheapest type of food.

The New American Cuisine can be a radical adventure in tastes and textures, taking you far and wide in foreign territory; or it can be an extremely conservative adaptation of what you already know and like. The middle ground between those extremes is where most of us will find ourselves, each niche at least a little different and each engaged in a lifelong process of change.

IN YOUR HOME

The Larder

The larder is a support system for your kitchen, providing a supply of staples that you use regularly and replenish according to price and storage considerations. Quite simply, what the larder means in pragmatic terms is that whatever staples you purchase in bulk, you must arrange to store properly at home. The objective is to keep the food away from heat and light, which encourage insect infestation and vitamin loss.

The larder requires, then, containers; what kind, how big, how many, containers depends on what level of food processing you undertake: it can be anything from a few coffee cans with plastic

THE GALLERY OF GRAINS

Whole grains explain the term "complex carbohydrates" perfectly. They are complex because the whole seed package with its three major departments is intact. The departments are Protection, Nourishment, and Life.

Protection is accomplished by the bran layer, or skin, which contains fiber, minerals, and protein.

Nourishment is provided by the endosperm, which has granules of carbohydrate, enclosed by protein and mineral combinations, to sustain the seedling until it grows leaves for manufacturing its own food.

Life springs from the embryo, or germ, which is a rich source of valuable protein, minerals, and vitamins, particularly E.

The seeds of cereal grasses have an almost perfectly balanced combination of nutritional elements interrelated in the complexity of those three departments. The discovery of grains as human food led to the development of agriculture and every civilization until modern times utilized whole grain as a foundational food.

Recently our science has discovered that the abandonment of these complex principal foods leads to degenerative diseases virtually unknown to people on "primitive" diets. We are now returning to them, with the major difference that our ancestors were limited to one or two grains. Blessed with modern transportation and storage, we know no such limitation; we enjoy the unparalled opportunity to explore and enjoy the particular virtues of all the main members of the gallery of grains: barley, corn, oats, millet, oats, rice, rye, and wheat.

The grains range from eight to eighteen percent in protein and are generally good sources of such major nutrients as B vitamins, calcium, and potassium. Using the gallery in its entirety also brings a wide range of trace minerals, such as zinc, copper, selenium, to your table. Broad use of grains is demonstrated throughout this book (see particularly Chapters 17, 18, 24, 28, 31). Let us note here, however, that novice shoppers for natural foods are sometimes fooled by products that don't really belong in the gallery. The most notable:

Converted rice. Conversion means steaming before removing the bran. Eighty percent of the B vitamins of the bran are retained by the endosperm, but fiber is sacrificed. Since it keeps well, it is a good compromise when fresh brown rice, which does not keep well, is unavailable.

Degerminated corn meal. This one sometimes appears on the ingredients list of "natural" products, but whole corn meal has 25 percent more niacin, more than twice as much vitamin A, and more than four times as much calcium and magnesium.

Pearl barley. This is virtually the only kind you can find, but it is by no means whole. Unpearled (also variously called "blue", "gray", or "brown") barley has 25 percent more protein and potassium, almost twice as much calcium, and three times as much iron. Ask for it; demand will eventually create a supply.

lids to twenty gallon crocks and thirty-five gallon garbage cans. If you're going to take a deep plunge, you'll have jars, bottles, crocks, cans, and canisters lining shelves and cupboards, containing grains, beans, seeds, nuts, dried fruits, flours and meals, cereals, nut butters, vegetable oils, honey, syrups, herbs, and spices. At either extreme or anywhere between, the larder is the core of the New American Cuisine.

Equipment

An integral corollary to the larder is the equipment needed to process the staples it contains. Referring to the old days again for a moment, much of the processing now accomplished by assembly lines was done in the home—baking, preserving, pickling, canning, drying, grinding. Then the industrial revolution reached the kitchen and the efficiencies of mass production made it cheaper to relinquish such tasks to mechanization. However, the economics of the eighties is a tighter affair and it is no longer cost-efficient (not to mention quality-effective) to delegate food processing tasks to the factories. For most of us it will still be desirable to take advantage of mechanization. The difference is that within the New American Cuisine only *minimum* processing is acceptable—no refined foods or artificial additives. Using myself as an example again, though I do my own cooking, other processes such as baking and making sprouts, yogurt, and tofu are done for me by small-scale mass producers.

The equipment required for Phase One, aside from containers, is probably in your kitchen already; if all you have is a knife, cutting board, and pot, you're ready to begin. Phase Two, in which you do such things as bake your own bread, make your own yogurt and grow your own sprouts, may require that you pick up a few minor things like additional pans, jars, and bowls. In short, you can get deeply into the New American Cuisine without spending much, if anything, to equip yourself for it.

In Phase Three—the greatest time commitment—an economic irony arises, a variation on the old cliche, "It takes money to make money": it takes money to *save* money (of course, merely another way of *making* money). If you're going to be making your own fruit and vegetable juices, grinding your own flour and hamburger, you'll need machines to do it. Nevertheless, a family of four can more than pay for Phase Three equipment with a year's savings on food costs (see table on page 174). We will examine the subjects of larders and kitchen equipment in more detail as we explore the three phases in the following chapters. Before doing so, however, let's examine what happens at the fringes of the New American Cuisine, for even there practical and significant consequences can be experienced by adhering to some of the fundamentals discussed to this point.

OUR COSTLY FAVORITES

A recent study by the Department of Agriculture comparing the costs of various convenience foods with their home-prepared counterparts found that out of 25 meat dishes tested, 21 were more expensive per serving when purchased ready-made. Many of the cost differentials were dramatic . . .

GOALS

There is another trend just as popular as convenience foods these days: 45 percent of our meals are being eaten in fast food restaurants. The three most popular meals eaten in these places are hamburger, fried chicken and pizza. It is possible to duplicate these meals at home, so I undertook to compare two ways of doing that, resulting in a three-way comparison:

(1) Fast food: I chose McDonald's, Kentucky Fried Chicken and Shakey's Pizza.
(2) Convenience food: purchased at Safeway, heated up at home.
(3) Natural food: purchased at Sunburst Farmer's Market, prepared "from scratch" at home.

SUMMARY

Homemade Burger Meal
Saving vs. Convenience version: 8%
Saving vs. Fast Food version: 27%

Homemade Fried Chicken Meal
Saving vs. Convenience version   33%
Saving vs. Fast Food version   57%

Homemade Pizza Meal
Saving vs. Convenience version   40%
Saving vs. Fast Food version   69%

When all meal costs were averaged, natural homemade versions saved 27 percent against convenience versions and 51 percent against fast food versions. (See Appendix Four for details.)

The burger meal carries the least economic incentive to prepare it from scratch with natural ingredients and is the cheapest meal. But nutritionally, the burger meal is the poorest of the three—notoriously so in the fast food version—impoverished regarding vitamins and minerals, loaded with fat, sugar, empty calories, and synthetic additives. A meal of Big Mac, fries, shake, and pie obtains 45% of its 1,400 calories from fat and has the equivalent of 16 teaspoons of sugar.

Convenience Reevaluated

There are weighty liabilities connected with what we commonly understand to be convenience. Convenience may be largely illusory. Just how much time is being saved through the use of highly-processed food? The answer, furnished by Tibor Scitovsky, professor emeritus of economics at Stanford University, is a minuscule 1.4 minutes per day "less than is needed by the gourmet French who would not touch a pre-mixed, bottled salad dressing with a ten-foot pole . . ." (*The Joyless Economy*, Oxford University Press).

If convenience foods save a mere three percent in time, why bother? In *Guidelines*, Mottern moves from the "convenience" illusion to a more important point, observing that it is our responsibility to see that nutrition is not sacrificed in the name of convenience:

Reliance on staple foods is the only means, given current manufacturing and labeling practices, by which the consumer can adequately control consumption of fat, sugar, salt and food additives. . . . The most absolute control over the diet comes through the preparation of meals from scratch.

Finally, there is the need to nourish our souls, no less important because there is no objective measurement for this intangible; it can, in certain circumstances, be the most important factor of all. Mottern quotes an editorial from the *Washington Star*, in praise of Mary Goodwin, public health nutritionist for Montgomery County, Maryland, who said, "If you eat enough pre-cooked, frozen, reheated foil-and-plastic packed lunches out of machines, part of you will starve to death."

Soul starvation, caused by reliance on convenience foods, has two aspects. Mechanized, assembly line food production is absolutely impersonal—the food is not prepared tenderly, respectfully, for *you*. Rather, it is prepared without thought or feeling for *anybody*. In fact, it is likely to be prepared with a negative attitude because there is no chance that a worker's extra effort—just repetitive, mechanical motion—will make the food better.

Soul starvation is also caused by missing out on what Mottern identifies as "the benefits from investing more time in the selection and preparation of food." Paradoxically, whereas we think we need to save time to prevent exhaustion, we could in fact rejuvenate ourselves by becoming personally involved in our own sustenance: "New ways of doing these tasks, such as advance preparation and freezing of foods and involvement of all family members in food purchasing and preparation, can provide at once more homemade convenience and *more pleasure* [my italics]." It is the difference between passive disassociation and active participation: we feel better about life when we are creatively involved in our personal destinies.

16 Saving Money, Finding Time

Some of the basic ways to save money have very limited appeal—relatively few people can, for example, raise livestock or forage for wild food. The major fundamentals of saving money, however, are options available to almost everyone.

THE MAJOR FUNDAMENTALS

Bulk Buying

Many natural foods stores sell complex carbohydrate staples in bulk from crocks, barrels, and bins. This enables the stores to buy *and* sell in the most economical fashion. When I began buying and selling grains, beans, nuts, and seeds in bulk, I was able to lower my retail prices by at least 20 percent, often even more. Yesterday, to see if what was true fifteen years ago still holds true, I checked the prices of some packaged items in a nearby supermarket with the same items sold in bulk by a nearby natural foods co-op:

Item	Packaged/lb.	Bulk/lb.
Lentils	$ .70	$ .61
Green split peas	.42	.34
Kidney beans	.72	.69
Blackeyed peas	.71	.57
Pinto beans	.59	.52
Red beans	.73	.69
Baby limas	.83	.82
Great Northern beans	.69	.57
Brown rice	.64	.56

The average cost of the above nine items is 11 percent less when purchased in bulk, but that is just part of the story. Natural foods stores sell hundreds of bulk items, including pasta, cereals, snacks, dried fruits, vegetable oils, herbs, and spices. The bulk herbs and spices average less than half the price of their counterparts in the little glass jars sold by the supermarket. In response to the inflationary squeeze, bulk merchandising is being taken to the nth degree, encompassing items such as powdered and liquid soap, shampoo, honey and maple syrup, tofu, and even natural dog food.

Indirect savings result from the fact that a bulk food handling system is energy efficient. Unless we own stock in a company, their advertising and promotion is money out of our pockets. Beyond that, packaging uses expensive energy sources—petroleum by-products, paper, and electricity.

Home Food Storage

Home food storage is based on buying bulk staples and creating a *larder*. In the old days, every home had a larder, defined in the dictionary as "a room or place where food is stored." When it was a separate room it was called the pantry. Our modern larders can be separate rooms, corners of garages, shelves in broom closets, basements, kitchen cabinets. In essence they are small-scale replicas of the bulk sections in the natural food stores.

The larger the quantity of purchase, the lower the price per pound. Bulk brown rice bought from a bin, barrel or crock at 59 cents a pound can usually be had for 54 cents a pound bought in an unopened 25 pound bag. If that's a six-month supply for your family and brown rice inflates to 64 cents four months from now, for the last two months you are eating brown rice at 10 cents under current market price. Until your larder runs out, you are actually *beating inflation.*

Larders run a gamut of sizes. My own larder, since I'm a bachelor, is a small one—a dozen or so glass and plastic jars, a few metal canisters, none of them with more than a few pounds of any staple. I can't save money the way a family can unless I participate with people in some sort of group buying scheme (which is becoming more and more common). The other end of the larder spectrum really looks like a miniature grocery store, with thirty gallon garbage cans for storage, or even custom-built bins. The larger the family, the more sense that sort of arrangement makes.

About containers: Glass, ceramic, or metal are best because there is the least interaction between the container and the food. You may have heard that plastic does not contaminate food, but there is uncontested propaganda from plastic manufacturers behind that commonplace belief. Try this test: Leave the supposedly stable plastic container closed for a few days, then open it and sniff. Is there an odor? If so, it is a signal of an unstable plastic and that container should not be used for storing food. If not, chances are better that it is a relatively stable form of plastic, though passing the odor test does not guarantee stability. Plastic should always be the last choice, since it is really impossible for you to know how volatile and toxic the polymers and resins of the plastic might be. It should be "virgin food grade polyethylene," complying with FDA standards.

Paper, cellophane, and plastic bags suffice for home food storage only for small amounts for a short time. Never store flour or meal or other forms of broken grains, beans, seeds, or nuts, in paper; paper absorbs oil from the food and moisture from the air, virtually guaranteeing rapid deterioration of quality.

THE FOUR ABSOLUTES OF PROPER STORAGE

COOLNESS prevents	(1) insect infestation
	(2) mold growth
	(3) rancidity
DRYNESS prevents	(1) mold growth
	(2) insect infestation
DARKNESS prevents	vitamin loss
AIR LIMITATION limits	oxidation

Kitchen Self-Reliance

Kitchen self-reliance is based on becoming your own food processor. Why pay corporations to do what you can do better and cheaper? Cook "from scratch," making multiple uses of staples such as whole grains, whole grain pasta, dry beans, meat, eggs, dairy products, and seasonal produce, stressing a wide variety of stews, casseroles, and other kinds of one-pot meals.

Zucchini can be 39 cents a pound on the produce shelf and $2.39 a pound with cheese sauce in a zipper pouch in an artfully designed carton in the frozen food department. Obviously, not everyone has the time or inclination to go into home food processing in a big way. But everyone can get into it enough to improve quality tremendously and save a bit in the process. It is the sort of activity that allows you to choose your level.

Kitchen self-reliance constitutes a major change for most modern Americans, involving a great deal of practical "how to" detail. The subsequent chapters will deal with those details in depth, step by step.

Choosing Food By Region And Season

For health reasons it is important to buy seasonally and regionally. We are meant to live harmoniously within our environment. This is particularly critical regarding fruits and vegetables. A sure way to get your body out of synchronicity is, for example, to eat a diet of tropical fruits while living in northern latitudes or a diet of summer fruits in winter. A moment's reflection will tell us that such practices don't make sense. There is harmony between you in your local environment and the food growing there. The further from home the food gets, the thinner the biochemical connection between you and your food (though contemporary science has no way of measuring or quantifying this phenomenon—in fact, hasn't yet undertaken to investigate it). For the sake of our internal biochemical balance we need to be attuned to regional production and seasonal maturation.

The monetary correlation to these principles is that local, seasonal fruits and vegetables are the least expensive. A few weeks ago, in early May, for 60 cents I bought one small, organically grown peach which came from the desert some 600 miles away. I'm not rich; it was a treat, harbinger of peaches to come. I'll eat my next peach when they're in season around here at three large ones for 60 cents. If I really want to spend a lot of money on food, I can buy things like nectarines from Chile at $1.99 a pound in January (when they're in season in Chile) or kiwi fruit from New Zealand at $4.99 a pound. But I'm much more interested in resonating with my Northern California environment with Northern California fruits and vegetables, properly mature in due season.

Regional choices. The closer to home the food is grown, the better. Food grown locally is fresher and cheaper than that which comes from outside your region. It has the least amount of transportation, storage, and handling costs built into the price you pay. (This applies primarily to perishable foods; grains and beans are transported without refrigeration, in bulk, at a relatively low expenditure of energy.)

Seasonal changes. Follow the law of supply and demand, avoid out-of-season selections (scarce, costly); choose what's in season (abundant, inexpensive). Your diet should change with the seasons. A winter diet, for example, makes extensive use of grains, beans, winter vegetables, home-canned fruits and vegetables, pickles, kraut and sprouts. Eating seasonally also correlates to eating fresher, at the peak of nutrition and flavor.

THE MINOR FUNDAMENTALS

Gardening

The tangible rewards in terms of money can be enormous, sometimes reducing the cost of fresh produce by more than 90 percent. Also quite tangible are the superiority of taste and nutritional value. (Taste reflects nutritional value, another fact contemporary science has yet to investigate.) In a few days, greens can lose almost all of their vitamins C and B1. Beyond that, and much more important to some people, are the less tangible rewards of gardening—fresh air, sunshine, exercise, getting grounded in Mother Earth.

Livestock

Chickens and ducks provide both eggs and meat; turkeys and rabbits don't need much space and can be fed so economically as to provide low-cost protein.

Foraging

Wild foods free for the picking abound in most areas if you know what to look for. But don't pick even the most luscious food by the roadside. It will be impregnated with lead and other heavy metal residues from exhaust fumes, which no amount of washing can eliminate. Foraging by veterans is always done according to an honor system: your obligation is to forage lightly, always leaving enough for other humans and wildlife, and for reseeding and regeneration.

Bartering

Goods can be exchanged for goods and goods can be exchanged for services. You may not have anything to exchange with someone who owns a surplus but you probably can *do* something, trade services for goods.

Buying Clubs

These are becoming more and more popular as inflation marches on. They can save a lot, whether times are inflationary or not, particularly on the bulk staples. Most wholesalers can't or won't deal with buying clubs, but most retailers will. The easier the buying club makes it for the retailer, the more attractive it is to him. The retailer can't miss if he gets paid half in advance, the

---

STARTING A BUYING CLUB

Buying clubs or co-ops always start the same way: one person takes the initiative to get things started. That person may do nothing more than say a few words about it to a friend, but whatever is done, nothing has happened until that person has generated the initial energy.

The person who is going to initiate the buying club needs to look at the various existing networks already touching their life: relatives, friends, neighbors, fellow club members, brothers and sisters at their church or temple. One such existing network, or a combination of them, is the best framework from which to spin off this new form of collective action.

The element that makes a buying club or co-op work is purchasing power. The more members you have, the more power. Generally, you probably don't have enough power until your group represents at least six families.

The buying clubs that depend largely on one person to do most of the work inevitably fall apart—of course, it isn't fair. The labor that needs to be divided falls mainly into these divisions: Who researches the possible sources and the discounts offered for what quantities? Who accumulates and consolidates the orders into one? Who handles the money? Who is in charge of distribution, including breaking the collective order into individual orders and letting everybody know it's pick-up time?

No, it isn't easy. But it can be fun and if it's done well, can save members roughly 15 percent. Are you the initiator?

---

other half when the club picks up the merchandise, which should be done immediately—preferably from the back of the delivery truck as far as some retailers are concerned. The faster a retailer gets paid and rid of the merchandise, the better discount a buying club can expect—up to 15 percent for a smooth, swift transaction.

Other Values

I have tried to make it clear that the savings on natural food diets over devitalized and adulterated foods do not come without cost: the cost is time. A common reaction to that is, "Great—time is the thing I have least of." And that's a real and serious problem. I recommend to such people that they take some of the little time available to them—maybe sitting quietly for a while before falling asleep—and think about living the kind of life that doesn't leave you time to do the things that could benefit you the most. Breathe deeply and slowly, let your body relax, gradually, part by part, completely . . . Let your thoughts drift around the mental images of the way you live . . . Maybe there's nothing you can do about it . . . But maybe . . . or maybe later . . . Taking that bit of time to meditate about the quality of your life might become a regular thing because it feels so good to truly relax and experience yourself deeply. And one thing leads to another, as the saying goes.

FINDING THE TIME

"But the problem is, I don't have more time available. Where would it come from?" There are two possible answers to this question, neither of them as simple as they sound, both requiring changes. The first answer is directed to housewives and househusbands who do not have other employment: The extra time can come only from establishing new priorities and reorganizing your time around them. Changes will have to be made. Will it be worth it? Only you can know; a six-month trial is a reasonable experiment.

The second answer is directed to women and men who are employed outside the home: There is probably only a little time available from reorganization, particularly if both jobs are full time. You will need help. The only help available will be from within the family. In most cases this means a change from kitchen as one-woman-show to one in which men and children are involved.

Children who are not accustomed to kitchen responsibilities would rather not be bothered, particularly the older children. In the past, perhaps, they haven't been allowed to help in the kitchen. Given the chance, it can become a routine part of their lives and there will be no point in struggling against it. As they begin to understand more about food and nutrition and learn new skills, they may even find themselves enjoying their involvement. You could start like this:

HUSBAND: He could be responsible for most of the shopping.
WIFE: She could do most of the cooking.
CHILDREN: They could help put groceries away, assist in cooking, and be in charge of cleaning up.

One evening each week, while you are eating, you could discuss the dinner plan for the following week.

After a couple of months, once you are satisfied that the children have absorbed enough to shift for themselves, you could install "free day,"—perhaps Sunday. It means that no one cooks and everybody is free to fix whatever they want for themselves (assuming the children are old enough). If the only raw materials available are natural, even if the kids come up with ideas that strike you as weird, the result is always wholesome. And they will have a good time learning.

This plan worked for my family until my wife began to work full time. The children were into the kitchen routines; no problem with them. But if my wife was not going to spend an inordinate amount of time maintaining our version of Phase Two of the New American Cuisine, she would need more help from me. What was my problem? Well, it wasn't machismo: I have seen enough men in kitchens around the world to know that food preparation isn't "women's work." My problem was just getting over the idea that when we got home from work, I would head for the living room and my wife would head for the kitchen. I had to surrender a mythic privilege connected somehow to the fact of being a man. Like so many unconscious attitudes, it had its roots in another era and another lifestyle. What could be the logical grounds for protest—that being a member of the weaker sex, I needed more rest than my wife?

We dropped the division of labor that had been fair while she had been a housewife, because it wasn't fair any more. Instead of me shopping, which took less time, and her cooking, which took much more, we divided shopping and cooking more or less equally. There was no need to change the children's involvement; I was the only one who needed to change.

Making The Kitchen A Family Room

The kitchen is not a family room in the full sense of the word as long as members of the family do not connect the privileges of its use with the responsibilities of its operation. Of course we can't expect much help from our four-year-olds. But children old enough to be learning to read, write, and do arithmetic, play pianos, hit baseballs, and ride horses, are old enough to begin learning kitchen skills. A man who hasn't mastered basic kitchen skills has missed an important aspect of being well-educated and would be a better father for making sure his children don't suffer the same fate. The adults in the family don't have to be geniuses at teaching to pass on the fundamentals of meal planning. Just by being involved in the process, children absorb the procedures and appreciate the decisions that bring the elements of a meal together. Cooking is always some combination of

—washing
—peeling
—cutting
—chopping
—mixing
—stirring
—seasoning
—tasting
—timing,

all basically simple tasks that are learned by doing them. To be sure, some of us have a "flair" or natural aptitude for cooking—such people turn out dishes the rest of us would never dream of, seemingly with little extra thought or effort. The rest of us—if we can dress ourselves, drive a car, read a book—can turn out wholesome, tasty meals. Great cooks are geniuses; good cooks are all the rest of us.

Beyond knowing that we can all do it, or be a part of it, and should know our way around the kitchen simply as a basic element of knowing how to take care of ourselves, is one more aspect, this one with a special radiance. The process of getting food on the table can be much more than the mere mechanics of nourishing bodies. The very soul of the family can be nourished when the kitchen is truly a family room. The more a family does together, the more together a family is. Mundane matters are elevated by cooperation and sharing. Good food is best when impregnated with good vibrations.

It's natural for young children to be eager to be involved in what the adults are doing, and to be fascinated by the growing, processing, and preparation of food; it is unfair and unwise to deprive them of the opportunity. Children from a convenience food cuisine take food for granted and know little more about it than what TV would lead them to believe. Indeed, without some homework on this subject, they are unlikely to develop the discernment they will need to avoid being duped by ads for junk and foodless foods. Furthermore, time in the kitchen is far more creative and practical than time spent glued to TV sets. Finally, when children have had a hand in the preparation of their food, they invariably have more enthusiasm for it at the table.

Young children can help in gardens, rinse sprouts, move things about, sort, stir, taste, wipe, throw things in the garbage. Older children can learn to take full responsibility for all sorts of more complicated activities, such as making yogurt, cheese, and granola. All ages enjoy helping in the making of bread, pies, cakes, cookies, and ice cream. Being involved with both father and mother in the kitchen illustrates for children that such activities are as masculine as they are feminine. Mastering the plainly pragmatic tasks of food processing and preparation sparks their natural curiosity in a way that spills over into other areas of their lives, gives them a sense of fulfillment and confidence, and prepares them to render service to others in a way that will be honored and appreciated.

PHASE ONE: *Simple Steps toward Eating Better for Less*

17 Breakfasts

The three basic ways of serving whole grains for breakfast will not surprise anybody: cold cereals, hot cereals, and flour made into bread, muffins, pancakes, and waffles.

COLD CEREALS

Ready-Made Cold Cereals

Some really atrocious "foods" appear on supermarket shelves as cold cereals, sugar sometimes comprising more than 50 percent of the product, along with artificial colors, flavors, and preservatives. But a few supermarket cold cereals are decent food; you can discover them by ignoring the deluge of TV advertising and reading labels. The name of a grain should be listed first; unless it is preceded by the word "whole," the grain is refined. The cereal should be free of sugar, artificial colors, flavors, and preservatives. Beware of granolas that list "brown sugar" as the first ingredient—that means the sugar content is approximately 25 percent.

As a rule, I avoid mentioning products by name because I have no control over their quality, and what I observe to be good today could be totally denatured and adulterated tomorrow. But I am making an exception here, in order to illustrate what I am talking about. I went to the local supermarket yesterday and went down the cereal aisle reading the labels. I found three varieties that met the criteria of being whole food, free of sugar, artificial color, flavor, and preservatives: Uncle Sam Cereal, Shredded Wheat, and Nutri-Grain.

Nutri-Grain is particularly interesting because it is a fifty-million-dollar new product investment by Kellogg, testifying to their belief that the interest in natural foods is here to stay and showing us how much control consumers ultimately have over the marketplace. It is also interesting because it is a reminder of the origins of the company. Mr. Kellogg started making cereals about a century ago, after he had been a patient at a sanitorium, in response to the need for whole grain cereals to help patients restore their health.

The innovative little natural foods manufacturers of today may well be the Kelloggs of the twenty-first century; it will be interesting to see what kind of products they make when they become giants. A small company named Erewhon may already have provided the answer. Erewhon has entered the ready-to-eat cold cereal market with Crispy Brown Rice Cereal. They illustrate how a dedicated concentration on quality can produce superior products. Erewhon has gone Kellogg a couple of steps better, using organically grown brown rice, and preservative-free packaging.

Making Your Own Granola

Granola is often assumed to be synonymous with good-quality natural food. But too often, in the hands of the big league manufacturers, it would be better left to gather dust on the supermarket shelf. To judge, compare their ingredients to the following recipe.

4 c. rolled oats	¾ c. almond, slivered
¾ c. sunflower seeds	1 T. cinnamon
¾ c. coconut, shredded	⅔ c. molasses, honey, (half and half mixture
½ c. sesame seeds	of both), or maple syrup
½ c. wheat germ	
⅓ c. sesame oil	

Other kinds of flaked grains, seeds, nuts and spices (coriander, allspice) can be substituted or added. Or add a dash of orange oil to the vegetable oil for a unique flavor. The granola can be oven- or pan-roasted. Buy bulk ingredients and make a week's supply if you store it unrefrigerated, or up to a month's supply if you store it refrigerated.

Oven: Mix dry ingredients. Mix sweetener with oil. Combine wet and dry ingredients. Spread over cookie sheet. Bake at 325° for 30–40 minutes, stirring often for even roasting.

Pan: Combine ingredients in a heavy skillet. If your skillet isn't big enough, make batches. Cover and roast over medium heat, stirring often for even roasting and to prevent burning, about 10 minutes.

When cool: Mix in ¾ c. raisins or currants. Yield: 6–8 servings, or 9 cups after raisins or currants are added. (Adapted from *The Sunburst Farm Family Cookbook.*)

If a recipe such as the one above, containing less than 8 percent sweetener, were commercially produced, the ingredients would be listed in the following order: rolled oats, almonds, sunflower seeds, coconut, sesame seeds, wheat germ, sesame oil, honey, molasses, cinnamon. There is no salt because none is necessary.

Muesli. From *Sunburst Farm Family Cookbook* comes this adaptation of an energy-packed cereal idea from Switzerland.

1 c. rolled oats	1½ c. milk or water
⅔ c. dried apricots, chopped	⅛ t. nutmeg
¼ c. dried apples, chopped	1½ t. vanilla
⅛ c. sesame seeds	½ c. almonds
¾ t. cinnamon	½ c. sunflower seeds
¼ t. salt	

Soak oats, dried fruit and spices in milk or water overnight. Next morning add nuts and seeds. Other dried fruits, nuts, and seeds can be substituted or added. Served uncooked. (Grains should be cooked for digestibility but steaming is part of the process of making rolled oats, so the oats in the muesli really are cooked; all other muesli ingredients are fully digestible uncooked.) Yield: 5 cups.

Instant muesli. The quick or instant variety of oatmeal is a thinly flaked version of rolled oats, easily chewable without prior soaking. So an instant version of muesli can be mixed as follows:

2 c. quick oats	½ c. almonds
½ c. toasted wheat germ	½ c. sunflower seeds
½ c. dried apricots, chopped	¼ t. salt
½ c. raisins	½ t. cinnamon

Serve with milk or yogurt, sweetened with honey, molasses, or maple syrup if desired. Use fresh fruit according to availability and preference. A hot version can be made simply by serving with boiled milk. Yield: 4½ cups.

HOT CEREALS

Good Ready-Made Cereals

The most widely recognized hot whole grain cereal in America is oatmeal, available everywhere groceries are sold. In natural food stores, oatmeal is usually sold in bulk, identified as "rolled oats." In this form, they are not as quick as the packaged variety but still don't take long—as little as 10 minutes, depending on the texture you prefer. The ratio is 2 to 1 water to oats. Bring water to boil, add oats, turn down and simmer until done.

While in the supermarket reading cold cereal labels, I moved along into the adjacent hot cereal section. There I found, along with the oatmeal, a couple of natural hot cereals: Roman Meal and Wheatena. Looking at hot cereals is an even more vivid testimony to the folly of food refining: the less the whole-grain simplicity is interfered with by the manufacturer, the better the cereal—"leave well enough alone," as the cliché has it.

Making Your Own

Porridge. Porridge or mush can be made from cornmeal, cracked wheat and store-bought mixtures of cracked grains, such as seven grain cereal. It can be most economical to buy your own bulk ingredients and mix them at home. Something like this would be excellent:

1 c. cracked wheat	½ c. sesame seeds
1 c. steel cut oats	½ c. flax seeds
1 c. cornmeal	½ c. toasted wheat germ
½ c. soy grits	

Whatever the mix, the method for porridge is to add the grain to boiling water (4 to 1 water to grain) which has up to ¼ t. of salt per cup of grain (optional). When mixture boils, stir, cover, and simmer over low heat for 20 minutes or a little more. A double boiler is ideal for porridge, particularly if milk is substituted for water as the cooking liquid. Porridge can be eaten sweet or seasoned, topped with poached eggs or grated cheese. Wheat germ can be cooked or held out to sprinkle on after cooking.

Nothing dictates that breakfast must be a sweet meal. Many people have found they enjoy seasoned grains for breakfast as much as or more than sweetened. Bulgur (a type of cracked wheat) and buckwheat groats are good for this purpose. A half cup of uncooked grain per person makes a generous serving. Sauté grain in a bit of vegetable oil with a small amount of chopped onion. Stir on medium flame until grain is browned, giving off a toasted odor. In a separate pot have boiled water ready, two to one water/grain ratio. Pour hot water (or soup stock, or broth) into pan with toasted grain. Add a teaspoon of soy sauce for each cup of grain. Any herb whose flavor pleases you (basil, oregano, cumin) can be added. Cover and simmer until water is absorbed (approximately 15 minutes for buckwheat groats, 30 for bulgur). Millet can be cooked by this method too, about the same time required as for bulgur. Eggs can be poached on top of the grains during the last five minutes, cheese melted on top, and hot sauce added.

Pre-preparation. Any whole grain can be ready instantly for breakfast with a minimum of preparation the night before. Try whatever variations you can think of on the following method: in a pint-sized wide mouth thermos, put six tablespoons of whole grain wheat and one each of

THE MOST POWERFUL BREAKFAST OF ALL?

The basis for this one is soaking a mixture of raw grains and seeds overnight. Ordinarily, grains need cooking to make them digestible. But soaking activates enzymes which split the protein and carbohydrate from the minerals. The result is grain that is much more nutritionally potent than cooked grain, since no enzymes or vitamins have been destroyed. Soaking is the key—cooked grains are nutritionally superior to raw grains that have not been soaked.

The variations on this theme are almost endless. A general approach: take a tablespoon of each of five kinds of grain and three kinds of seeds and grind them to a medium-coarse consistency in your blender or coffee/seed grinder. Add enough water to double the volume and stir thoroughly. Soak overnight. You can add fresh or dried fruit, honey or molasses, yogurt or cream, nuts, wheat or corn germ, or add flavor extracts to the soaking water.

I'm suggesting the base of eight tablespoons as a serving for one. But you may not be able to eat it all—it's very filling. How powerful a breakfast is it? I find it to be more than just a breakfast. I think of it as a sort of Super Brunch, powering me for eight or ten hours, right through lunch, with perhaps a mid-afternoon apple.

---

sunflower seeds and raisins; then fill with boiling water, stir briefly and close. In the morning all you need do is empty the thermos into a bowl, drizzle in a little honey (or molasses, or maple syrup), sprinkle on a bit of wheat germ (or bran, or both) and eat. Done this way, the grain is chewy. Using the same general approach, an all-night electric cooker can be used, yielding a very soft cereal. Wheat or rye flakes can also be prepared this way.

Cereal creams. Another alternative for grains is to make them into "creams" with the aid of a coffee grinder (some blenders can handle the task). Dry roast grain (seeds can be added: sunflower, sesame, chia, flax, pumpkin) in a pan—stirring frequently, almost steadily toward the end—until grains are toasted. Grind like coffee. The finer the grind the smoother the cream, and the quicker it cooks. Have water boiling, three parts to one of grain; a pinch of salt per cup of grain is optional. Stir grain into water. After mixture boils, reduce flame to low, cover, and simmer, stirring occasionally until creamy consistency is achieved. It will take ten minutes or more, depending on the consistency you like. The cereal creams can be sweetened and buttered, and milk, fruit, and nuts can be added. Or they can be cooked in broth or stock, seasoned as above. If the cereal creams are cooked in a double boiler, a little more time is required, but less stirring. (A suggestion: 3 parts brown rice, 2 parts sesame seeds, 1 part millet.)

Polenta is an Italian version of corn meal cooked as a dinner grain to a very firm consistency. Leftover for breakfast, polenta can be sliced, eaten cold or heated up, spread with butter and honey, peanut butter, jam, or both. Polenta can be reheated by slicing, then frying, steaming, or warming in the oven. It can also be served for breakfast with leftover vegetables.

Indian Pudding is a corn meal dessert that is also a highly adaptable leftover for breakfast:

2 c. cornmeal	3 well-beaten eggs
4 c. milk	4 T. butter (or ½ stick, or ¼ c. oil)
¾ c. molasses or honey (or mixture of both)	1 t. cinnamon
1 t. salt	½ t. ginger

Soak cornmeal in milk for a few hours (or cook for 25 minutes over low heat, uncovered). Combine with other ingredients in a casserole dish. Place dish in a larger baking pan with hot water in it. Bake at 300° for one and one-half hours (faster cooking or higher temperatures tend to make the pudding rubbery). Yield: 6–8 servings. (Adapted from *The Sunburst Farm Family Cookbook.*)

Innumerable variations. Wheat and rye are available in flake form, similar to rolled oats. They are cooked the same way as rolled oats, with the same ratio of water to grain, but need about twice as much time.

Brown rice and millet can be cooked by the same method as for dinner but accompanied differently. Or they can be given a more porridge-like consistency by cooking with more water. For example, to be dry and fluffy for dinner, brown rice requires a ratio of two parts water to one part rice, three to one for millet. To be wetter and mushier for breakfast, the ratios would be 2½–3 to one and 3½–4 to one. Then serve with milk, cream, butter, yogurt, wheat germ, various nuts and seeds, fresh and dried fruit, honey or maple syrup. The dried fruit can also be cooked with the grain.

Leftover grains from dinner are highly adaptable to breakfast purposes. A cup of leftover millet or brown rice can be heated in a half cup of milk, sweetened with honey, and spiked with cinnamon.

PANCAKES AND BAKED GOODS

Bread For Breakfast

Good quality whole grain bread can be the substance of a highly satisfying breakfast. It is frequently said that breakfast is the most important meal of the day. But how important breakfast is depends on the individual; some people can hardly look at food in the morning. For others, there are occasional mornings like that. The point here—and it holds everywhere—is *don't force yourself (or anyone else) to eat when there is no appetite*, in the morning or any other time. Just as you should rest when tired, you should eat when hungry. Heed the signals your body sends. You can't store up rest; too much of it can induce lassitude. Likewise, food your body isn't asking for can be a liability. There are people for whom, or times at which, a piece of whole grain toast and a hot beverage comprise an adequate breakfast.

But that is not meant to imply that a bread-based breakfast is necessarily a lightweight meal. Try spreading whole wheat toast with peanut butter and topping it with sliced banana—a couple of pieces of that make a substantial morning meal. Considering all the spreads made of nuts, seeds and fruits, there are dozens of breakfast possibilities, not all of them sweet, just based on spreading things on bread.

Bread And Eggs

There are many breakfast combinations in which whole grain bread and eggs are of equal importance— poached eggs on toast, for example. Then the ever-popular French toast:

Sweet Version	*Un-sweet Version*
2 eggs	2 eggs
¼ c. milk	¼ c. milk
¼ t. cinnamon	¼ t. basil
⅛ t. vanilla	⅛ t. soy sauce

Beat thoroughly, soak whole grain bread in mixture, fry over low to medium heat in oil or butter. Serve sweet version with honey, molasses, or maple syrup. A tasty and less-expensive-than-maple-syrup topping can be made by mixing honey and molasses half and half. Top unsweet version with sauted onions and carrots or any heated leftover vegetables. Yield: 4 pieces.

Muffins, Pancakes, Etc.

BASIC MUFFINS

2 c. whole wheat flour	½ t. salt
3 t. baking powder	½ c. butter
2 eggs, beaten	½ c. honey
¾ c. milk	

Mix dry ingredients. Cream butter and honey, then add eggs and milk. Combine wet and dry ingredients. Take care not to overmix the batter, in order not to activate the baking powder too soon. Pour ⅔ full into oiled muffin tins. Bake at 400° for 20–30 minutes. You can dress, shower or shave while muffins are baking. Yield: 24 muffins. (From *The Sunburst Farm Family Cookbook.*)

Variations: add 1 c. blueberries; or 1 c. chopped dates, ½ c. walnuts; or 1½ c. mashed bananas.

PAN BREAD

1¾ c. cornmeal	½ t. salt
1½ c. whole wheat flour	⅓ c. oil
3 eggs	½ c. molasses or honey
2 t. baking powder	2 c. water

Beat eggs. Add and mix liquid ingredients. Add and mix dry ingredients. Pour mixture ¼-inch thick into a hot skillet, lightly coated with oil. Cover and cook over medium heat about 30 minutes, turning after 15 minutes. Serve plain or buttered. Good with fruit preserves accompanied by yogurt. (Adapted from *The Sunburst Farm Family Cookbook.*)

BASIC PANCAKES

2 c. whole wheat flour	2 t. oil
1 t. salt	2 eggs
2 t. baking powder	½ c. honey
1¾ c. milk	

Let the ingredients sit until they are at room temperature, then add liquid to dry ingredients. Cook on a griddle or pan with evenly distributed heat until bubbles appear, then flip. Yield: 18–20 cakes. (From *The Sunburst Farm Family Cookbook.*)

Basic pancakes can become *buckwheat* cakes by substituting one cup of buckwheat flour for one of the cups of whole wheat flour. *Buttermilk* can be substituted for milk. The pancakes can be made fluffier by separating the egges, beating the whites stiff, then folding them into the mixture after all the other ingredients are mixed.

WALNUT COFFEE CAKE

(Consider substituting herb tea for the coffee)

2½ c. whole wheat pastry flour   1⅓ c. honey
1 T. baking powder   3 eggs, beaten
1 t. salt   1 t. vanilla
⅓ c. butter   ¾ c. milk

   Mix together flour, baking powder, salt. Cream butter and honey, then add eggs, vanilla, and milk. Combine and pour into an oiled 9″ × 12″ baking pan dusted with flour.

TOPPING

¼ c. melted butter   2 T. whole wheat pastry flour
¾ c. honey   2 t. cinnamon
1 c. chopped walnuts

   Mix well, making sure flour doesn't lump, pour on top of batter. Bake at 350° for 1 hour. You can lay a cup of sliced apples or pineapple on top for variation.

POTATOES

   In the New American Cuisine, whole grains are more important than potatoes, based on the number of them and the number of uses that can be made of them. But that is not to say that potatoes are unimportant; on the contrary, potatoes *are* an important staple food. How much whole grain you eat compared to potato is primarily a matter of personal preference. In the New American Cuisine, potatoes are cooked and eaten with the skins, for it's that wholeness that makes the potato a complex carbohydrate.

Home Fries And Hash Browns

   For home fries, it is best to use leftover boiled or baked potatoes; then slice, fry in a little oil with onion, garlic, peppers, herbs, according to taste.

   Hash browns essentially follow the same method, but in this case you are working with diced potatoes instead of sliced. If you don't have leftover potatoes, hash browns are the best option, with red potatoes the fastest cookers. Dice the raw potato into small pieces, then fry in a small amount of oil in a covered skillet over medium high heat. Stir and toss until all potato pieces have a thin film of hot oil. Add a small amount of water, stir and cover and reduce heat to medium. Cook 10 to 15 minutes, depending on the amount of potatoes. Remove cover, add a little more water, raise heat a little, toss and turn until brown.

   Any breakfast of which potatoes are a part is a meal meant to stay with you—a workingman's meal, an athlete's meal, or a brunch that will last till dinner time. Any of the usual accompaniments— eggs, meat, whole grain toast, beans—fit right into the New American Cuisine.

   For french-fried, baked, and mashed potatoes, see the following chapter.

18   Lunch and Dinner

LUNCH

Whole Grain Sandwiches

We exceed all the world's nations in the variety of our sandwiches and it is in sandwiches that we have a major opportunity to consume whole grain. The sandwich is an American institution and nobody will be surprised that the New American sandwich is made with whole grain bread. What surprises some is that sandwiches needn't lose their character because the top and bottom become whole food. Is it, then, simply a matter of "whatever" on whole wheat? Almost, but not quite.

Remember that we are aiming to reduce the amount of fat, salt, and chemical additives that we eat. In those regards, cold cuts or lunch meats are a major culprit. Most lunch meats are quite high in both fat and salt; I've seen breakdowns that revealed well over 50 percent fat content. Bologna, for example, is usually approximately 75 percent fat, made with scrap meat that would otherwise be dog food.

Then there is sodium nitrate and its breakdown form sodium nitrite. Both are common food additives used to color cold cuts pink or red and to prevent botulism. If it weren't for nitrite, cold cuts would come mostly in shades of tan and gray. That might take some getting used to but it wouldn't matter otherwise. Botulism, on the other hand, can be a deadly matter. But so, also, are nitrosamines: they are potent carcinogens formed by nitrite. And, quoting Dr. Jacobson in *Eater's Digest*, "Nitrite is one of the most toxic chemicals in our food supply." Added to its cancer-causing potential, "Dozens of persons have died from nitrite poisoning and countless others have been incapacitated. Nitrite toxicity is due to its ability to disable hemoglobin, the molecule in red blood cells that transports life-giving oxygen."

There are two alternatives to nitrite consumption. The first is to avoid all foods that contain sodium nitrate and sodium nitrite. That would include not only cold cuts but most frankfurters, sausages, hams, smoked meats and fish, and many baby foods.

The second alternative rests with the meat packers. They could produce cured meat products that are whatever color is natural and are then frozen to prevent growth of the spores that cause botulism. At this time, frozen sausage, hot dogs, and lunch meats are beginning to appear in small quantities, particularly in natural foods stores. Unless they are nitrate/nitrite free, as those frozen versions are, I strongly urge that cold cuts be eliminated from your sandwich repertory.

Other than the nitrate/nitrite category, there are really no holds barred in New American sandwiches. A few of the possibilities:

201

—sliced cold meat

—meat loaf

—chicken, turkey, egg, fish, as salads

—cheese, avocado, tomato, cucumber, sprouts, combos

—cream cheese with olives or dried fruit

—peanut or other butters made of nuts or seeds

Sandwich Idea 1. Dice celery, pepper and olives, mix with peanut butter for a spread.

Sandwich Idea 2. Spreads.

FISH SPREAD

1 c. leftover fish, flaked	¼ c. chives, chopped fine
1 carrot, grated fine	1 t. dill seeds, crushed
1 onion, grated fine	mayonnaise or favorite salad dressing

Blend all ingredients together, adding only enough dressing to moisten the spread. Makes about 1½ cups. (Adapted from *The Natural Foods Cookbook.*)

Varying the vegetables and seasonings, you can improvise spreads using mashed beans, mashed avocado, cream and cottage cheeses. Diced cold meats and fish can be incorporated into any of the spreadables.

GARBANZO SPREAD

3 c. garbanzo beans, cooked and mashed or blended	2 T. oil
juice of 1 lemon	½ bunch parsley, chopped fine
salt to taste	1 t. basil
⅔ c. toasted sesame seeds, ground (optional)	½ t. oregano
½ onion, chopped	dash cumin
	dash garlic powder

Sauté onion in oil until soft. Add herbs and parsley at the last minute, sautéing just long enough to soften parsley. Mix all the ingredients together thoroughly with a fork. Yield: 4½ cups (with sesame seeds included). (Adapted from *Laurel's Kitchen.*)

Sandwich Idea 3. "Melts."

AVOCADO MELT

2 ripe avocadoes	¼ t. garlic powder
2 T. mayonnaise	2 t. hot sauce (optional)
juice of 1 lemon	

Mash avocadoes with a fork, add other ingredients, and blend thoroughly. Spoon avocado spread onto bread, spreading to desired thickness. Cover with sliced cheese (swiss, cheddar, jack), place under broiler until cheese melts. Generally, one medium avocado makes two sandwiches.

"Melt" sandwiches can be made with tuna or any other spread.

Sandwich Idea 4. Summer salad: Sliced cucumber, sliced tomato, watercress, lettuce, sprouts, mayonnaise—a good way to pack fresh vegetables in your lunchbox.

Sandwich Idea 5. Smorgasbord: Cream cheese, diced dill pickle, sunflower seeds, slices of avocado, raw mushroom, tomato, sprouts. Toast bread, mix cream cheese, pickle, and sunflower seeds, spread on toast. Layer on mushroom, avocado, and tomato. Top with sprouts. Serve open-faced.

Virtually endless varieties of sandwiches can be made open-faced, eaten with knife and fork. Then you don't have to be concerned about what might ooze out of the other side of the sandwich as you bite down on it.

The Improvised Lunch

Lunch is a good time for creative meals, a good framework for whole grains. Let's say there is some leftover oatmeal or seven-grain cereal from breakfast and some leftover casserole or steamed vegetables from dinner. Out of these we can generate a hearty soup with crackers for lunch.

Adapted from *Sunburst Farm Family Cookbook,* soup and crackers from leftovers:

To make that extra cereal into crackers, all you need do is add enough flour to make a stiff, pliable dough that you can roll out. Season with salt or whatever your taste buds suggest—sesame, sunflower, or caraway seeds. Roll out and score, then bake at 375° for 15–20 minutes . . . Cool a little, then cut.

Yesterday's Soup: You can take many casseroles or leftovers and recreate them into other very appetizing dishes—like soup. I have added scalloped potatoes, quiche, etc., to cream sauce for a quick, delicious soup . . . Also, if you have leftover steamed vegetables, add them to a clear broth or tomato or cream broth.

The same thing can be done with leftover beans or diced leftover meat or fish.

Another leftover idea with many possibilities could be called "Comprehensive Salad" because it can combine so many types of food. Let's say you have some leftover brown rice or millet and some leftover pinto beans. Combine one-third each of the grain, beans and raw vegetables (diced carrot, celery, and green pepper or any combination you fancy). If the beans are on the soupy side, just season to taste. If the beans are drier, add a bit of your favorite salad dressing. The food types can be expanded by a yogurt dressing, the addition of nuts or seeds, diced leftover poultry. "Comprehensive Salad" is an idea you can really improvise on.

DINNER

Cooking Whole Grains

Here's a review of liquid ratios, cooking times, and yields per cup of dry grains:

Grain	Liquid/Grain	Time	Yield, Cups
Barley	3:1	60 min.	3
Buckwheat	2:1	20 min.	2½
Bulgur	2:1	20 min.	2½
Cornmeal	4:1	60 min.	4
Millet	3:1	25–30 min.	3
Oats, rolled	2:1	10–30 min.	2
Oats, steel cut (Scotch oats)	3:1	90 min.	2½
Brown rice	2½:1 (long grain)	45 min.	2½
	2:1 (short grain)	50 min.	2
Rye	3:1	90 min.	2½
Wheat	3:1	90 min.	2½

The general dos and don'ts of grain cooking are:

—Bring water to boil
—Stir in grain.
—Bring to boil again.
—Add small amount of salt to taste (optional).
—Turn down heat to very low, cover tightly, cook until tender.
—Remove cover seldom or not at all.
—Don't stir grain unless it begins to burn, meaning water is absorbed but grain is not yet tender, the result of cooking at too high a temperature. In such a case, add hot or boiling water, stir, cover, and cook over very low heat until tender.

Fluffy Brown Rice

Some people complain that brown rice is too sticky. Long grain brown rice is less sticky than either short or medium grain brown rice, which are the choices where a slightly nuttier flavor and chewier consistency are desired. In addition, there are four different cooking methods that yield a fluffier brown rice.

Method 1. Before boiling, lightly pan roast the rice in a skillet, stirring constantly to avoid scorching. Then cook as usual.

Method 2. The same as above with the addition of a small amount of vegetable oil, just enough to coat the grains lightly. A little goes a long way, about a tablespoon for two cups of rice. Heat the oil to thin it before adding the rice.

Method 3. The same as Method 2, except this time you stir in a beaten egg thoroughly while the rice and oil are heating together. One egg is enough for two cups of rice.

Method 4. Boil until rice absorbs all the water, then transfer to a steamer or colander and steam for another fifteen to twenty minutes until tender, keeping the rice out of contact with the steaming water.

Each of these methods yields rice of a slightly different consistency. Try them all and see what you like. All four methods can be used for other whole grains.

Dinner Grain Recipes

MILLET CHEESE

Cook millet as usual. When it is done, turn off heat and add diced or grated cheddar or any other cheese, stirring in about ⅓ cup per 2 cups of cooked millet. Cover and let sit a few minutes; the cheese will melt and blend with the grain. The smaller the pieces, the better the cheese will blend. Season to taste at the table with soy sauce. Serve with salad, cooked vegetables, beans, meat.

VEGETABLE BULGUR (OR BUCKWHEAT OR MILLET)

2 c. bulgur, buckwheat, or millet   4 c. vegetable broth (6 c. for millet)

1 med. onion, chopped   3 T. soy sauce

Sauté bulgur or buckwheat or millet in a large skillet with oil and chopped onion. Cook until grains are browned and give off a toasted smell (a little wisp of smoke is another signal). Add mixture of broth (don't forget that millet requires more liquid) and soy sauce which has been brought to boil separately. Cover and simmer 20–30 minutes (bulgur and buckwheat toward the 20 side, millet toward the 30). Yield: 4–6 servings. (Adapted from *Sunburst Farm Family Cookbook*.)

REFRIED RICE (OR ANY GRAIN)

2 c. cooked brown rice or any cooked grain   3 eggs, beaten

   (*cold* for best results)   1 c. mushrooms, sliced

¾ c. onions, chopped   ½ t. garlic powder or fresh garlic, minced

1 T. soy sauce

Put a small amount of oil in a large frying pan over medium heat. When oil is hot, add onions and garlic and cook 3 minutes, adding mushrooms after about 1 minute. Add rice and soy sauce and fry a few more minutes, stirring frequently. Move rice to one side of pan. Pour in half of eggs and scramble, then mix thoroughly with rice. Add rest of eggs, mixing thoroughly. Fry until mixture is dry. Season to taste at table. Serve with stir-fried or sautéed or steamed vegetables and salad. Yield: 4–6 servings.

Also, any cooked grain makes a good base for a casserole, to which you can add fresh vegetables, cooked beans or meat, cheese or yogurt, nuts and seeds, various sauces, your favorite herbs. The possibilities are limited only by your imagination. For example,

CHICKEN RICE CASSEROLE

2 c. cooked brown rice	1 c. buttermilk
1½ c. chopped mixed vegetables	2 T. soy sauce
¾ c. diced cooked chicken	¼ t. garlic powder

Combine rice, vegetables and chicken in casserole dish. Mix buttermilk, soy sauce, and garlic powder and pour over casserole. Cover and bake at 350° for 30 minutes. Yield: 4–6 servings.

Almond Rice Casserole is a variation that can be made simply by substituting sliced almonds for the chicken.

LENTIL KASHA

1 c. buckwheat	1 onion, chopped
1 c. lentils, soaked	3 T. parsley, minced
2 plus c. soup stock or broth	1 t. rosemary

Cover lentils, onions, parsley, and rosemary with stock or broth, bring to boil, reduce heat, cover, and simmer for 10 minutes. Then add buckwheat and 2 cups stock or broth, bring to boil again, stir, reduce heat, cover, and simmer another 20 minutes. Season to taste at table (salt, cayenne pepper, soy sauce, hot sauce, parmesan cheese). Serve with salad. Yield: 4–5 servings.

SOY BURGERS

2 T. oil	⅓ c. whole wheat flour
2 T. chopped green onions	2 eggs, beaten
1 c. cooked soy pulp, or coarsely chopped cooked soybeans	1 t. salt
	2 t. soy sauce
1 c. cooked brown rice	½ t. basil
½ c. grated cheese	

Sauté onions in oil and mix into remaining ingredients. Shape into patties and cook on a griddle or in a skillet. You can also bake patties in a 350° oven for 20 minutes. To keep them from sticking, sprinkle griddle or baking dish with seasame seeds. Yield: 8 soyburgers. (From *Laurel's Kitchen.*)

Other cooked grains and beans can be substituted for the brown rice and soybeans. Cooked ground beef or turkey can be substituted for the beans. Or substitute other beans to make Navy

Burgers or Pinto Burgers. Served on a whole wheat bun or whole wheat toast with mustard and mayonnaise, lettuce, tomato, and alfalfa sprouts, this type of burger is a complete, low-cost meal.

WHEAT BALLS

1 c. cooked bulgur

½ c. peanut butter, or other nut or seed butter

½ c. whole wheat bread crumbs

½ t. salt.

¼ c. cottage cheese or grated Swiss cheese

1 t. soy sauce

Preheat oven to 350°. Combine all ingredients and form into 1½-inch balls. Bake on greased cookie sheet for 10 minutes on each side. Makes 15–18 balls. These can be eaten plain, with any number of sauces, or served with tomato sauce on whole grain pasta.

POTATOES

French fries. Potatoes baked in the skins are no mystery to anyone. And even if you've never done it, it's easy enough to imagine how to make French fries with the skins on. I don't recommend making French fries often by the conventional deep-fry method because of the large amount of oil the potatoes absorb. They can, however, be cooked with much less oil by baking them in the oven: slice potatoes as usual for French fries, spread on oiled cookie sheet, brush lightly with oil. Bake at 375° for 20 minutes, turn with spatula, brush again lightly with oil, finish baking for approximately 15 minutes.

Potatoes boiled, potatoes mashed. Equally unmysterious is the potato boiled in the skin. It is when we come to mashed potatoes that people often balk: "If you mash potatoes with the skins on, you get these big sort of papery hunks." But there's a simple way around that: dice the potatoes into small pieces before you mash them. Then the skin blends quite well into the whole mass.

PASTA AND SAUCES

Pasta, literally *paste* made of flour and water, refers to all forms of spaghetti, macaroni, and noodles.

In the New American Cuisine, whole grain pasta is used in all pasta dishes that ordinarily use white pasta. I have found that most people quickly learn to like whole grains but that many have a problem with whole grain pasta. "It's too sticky," they say. But that is not because whole wheat pasta is inherently sticky, it's because some natural foods manufacturers have been in too big a hurry to get whole wheat pasta on the market and have used the wrong kind of wheat. When you make whole wheat pasta from bread wheat you get sticky pasta. It has a gluey consistency that tends to make the individual strands glob together, in turn making it impossible to get each strand coated with sauce. The right kind of wheat for making pasta is *durum* wheat: it is always used in white pasta and should always be used for whole grain pasta too. Not only does whole grain pasta made from durum wheat have a consistency comparable to white pasta, it has, like other whole grain products, more flavor and nutrition. You cannot assume that whole grain pasta is made from durum wheat; in fact, it probably isn't unless it says so. The wording should be something like "whole durum wheat" or "whole wheat flour made from durum wheat."*

Pasta variations, such as those made with a percentage of powdered eggs, artichoke or spinach powder, are also available made with whole durum wheat. If the whole durum pasta is not available, excess stickiness can be removed by running hot tap water over the cooked pasta for a minute, shaking vigorously, then returning it to the covered pot and stove for a couple of minutes of reheating before serving. A couple of tablespoons of oil in the cooking water also helps prevent pasta from sticking, and it is important to use enough water—about four quarts per pound of pasta.

To ensure that you will turn out pasta that will please, let's review the steps:

1. Bring water to a rolling boil. Adding oil and salt are optional (it takes only a half teaspoon of salt in four quarts of water to bring out the flavor of the pasta).
2. With pot uncovered, cook pasta at a rolling boil.
3. After several minutes of boiling, begin cooling little samples and tasting. It is cooked when the pastiness in the center is gone but the pasta is still firm; this is the stage the Italians call *al dente*, meaning it is tender but still resistant to the bite.
4. Drain in a colander, shake off excess water, add sauce while still hot and damp; if sauce is not added at this stage, pasta will begin to stick.

One more place where stickiness rears its pasty head is in leftover cooked pasta that has not been coated with sauce. This can be remedied by reheating it in the steamer ordinarily used for steaming vegetables. Steam just long enough to make the pasta piping hot and the strands or pieces should come unstuck, ready to be sauced and served.

All your favorite pasta dishes—spaghetti and tomato sauce, macaroni and cheese, lasagne, stroganoff—can be readily and deliciously turned out with whole grain pasta. My favorite form of pasta is called *soba*, a thin Japanese spaghetti made of buckwheat flour and whole durum wheat flour, but I do improvisations with all types of pasta.

Sauces

As many types of pasta as there are, however, variety really begins with the sauces: whether you are cooking for one or a dozen, you can make sauces almost endlessly without repeating yourself.

Most sauces have three components: the *base*, which is the medium for cooking the other ingredients; *primary ingredients*, which give the sauce its substance; *secondary ingredients*, whose nuances tip the flavor one way or another. The general procedure for most sauces is to heat the base

*The desirability of durum wheat for dried, store-bought pasta does not hold true for homemade pasta, which has an entirely different texture and consistency (see Chapter 28).

first, then add the secondary ingredients so that they can impart their flavors to the base, then add the primary ingredients, simmering everything until the three aspects have united into a flavorful oneness.

The bases	Primary Ingredients	Secondary Ingredients
Vegetable oils (olive and sesame)	Ground beef	onions
	Ground turkey	garlic
Dairy products (butter, clarified butter or ghee, sour cream, buttermilk, yogurt, kefir, cream cheese)	Leftover diced meats	parsley
	Diced vegetables of all kinds	basil
	Chopped nuts	oregano
	Shellfish	rosemary
Bouillon (meat, vegetable, or fish stock reduced or thickened by simmering in an uncovered pan)*	Diced cooked fish	basil
	Tomatoes	thyme
	Mushrooms	curry powder
	Diced tofu	cumin
Nut butters (thinned with water or bouillon)	Diced tempeh	cilantro
	Chopped chicken liver	soy sauce
	Soft and medium cheeses (cream to cheddar)	mint
		cinnamon
		nutmeg
		sunflower and sesame seeds
		hard cheeses (Romano, Parmesan)
		mustard

*As in the *nouvelle cuisine* of France, thickening is done by reduction rather than by addition of cornstarch or flour (except for *bechamel* sauce, best made with whole wheat pastry flour). Vegetable stock has a tendency to be quite bland; this can be remedied by the addition of a little soy sauce—enough to make it the color of meat bouillon (which isn't much) imparts a rich flavor.

Chapter 19 has some sauce recipes for vegetables. These sauces are also adaptable to pasta. Furthermore, any sauce made for pasta is also adaptable for use on whole grains. Sauces make *all* forms of whole grains more interesting, just as salad dressings make eating salad more interesting. There are many similarities between sauce making and the creation of salad dressings—for that matter, leftover cooked grains and pasta can become salad ingredients.

Improvisational Cooking

When a jazz musician improvises, his solo is constructed from a vocabulary of musical phrases he has practiced over and over, each time combining them in slightly different ways, giving them new twists and turns to suit mood and moment. Making sauces is your greatest opportunity for improvisational cooking, and the columns above provide the food phrases for improvising in your kitchen. Like the jazz musician, the wider your vocabulary, the greater are the possibilities for your solos. Also like jazz, not all sessions achieve the same level. There is risk involved, leaving room for great flights and flops. But the better acquainted you become with your vocabulary, the fewer flops, and when you're using first class ingredients, even flops are edible.

19 Vegetables

If whole grains are king of the New American Cuisine, vegetables are the queen. Where grains provide the solid stability in the royal couple, vegetables provide the glamor, the excitement. The king, at the center of the circle of the royal family, reaches first to the queen, who provides complementary qualities of texture, flavor, and color—the guises of nutrition. For in the vegetables we match with grains, we invariably find additional and complementary vitamins, minerals, complex carbohydrates, protein, and enzymes.

Enzymes are the orphan of nutritional science. The written material on the other nutritional categories dwarfs that of enzymes, yet they are no less important. Indeed, from one standpoint, they are most important: it is enzymes that distinguish live cells from dead. Biochemists regard enzymes, largely destroyed by heat, as the basic unit of life. As many as one thousand enzymes may be found in a single liver cell. They are a great mystery—catalysts that promote countless biochemical changes within our bodies. And one of these processes of change takes place in the stomach, where the enzymes of raw vegetables greatly facilitate digestion. For this reason, the New American Cuisine places particular emphasis on raw vegetables, borrowing from the great European cuisines, where salads receive their deserved prominence. French meals often have two courses that feature raw vegetables: salad, and the type of hors d'oeuvres literally translated as "crudities," crude indicating that nothing much other than washing and cutting has been done. Similarly, the Italian antipasto has, for example, sticks of celery, carrots, radishes, olives, flowerettes of cauliflower and broccoli. Many other traditional cuisines have found over many generations that digestion is facilitated by including raw vegetables, particularly when they open the meal.

Digestive enzymes are not the only important reason for emphasizing raw vegetables. Vitamins (themselves a type of enzyme) are sensitive to both heat and water, particularly B and C vitamins. Depending on cooking time, temperature, and the amount of water used, losses of up to 90 percent of these vitamins are possible and more than 40 percent are common. And, since the cellular structure of vegetables is delicate, amino acids are also susceptible to cooking temperatures. This means that raw vegetables make a far more valuable contribution to our protein requirements than is possible for cooked vegetables. While the *percentage* of protein is often low in vegetables, the *quality* of protein, its biological value, is often high: the 6 percent protein of raw kale, the 3 percent of mustard and turnip greens, the 2 percent of avocadoes—a fruit used like a vegetable—the 1 percent of lettuce, are all complete proteins *while uncooked* (see Chapter 2).

Extolling the virtues of uncooked vegetables does not translate into relegating cooked vegetables to the garbage can. Other nutrients are more securely locked into the cellular structure and are actually made more available by cooking. Cooking also destroys harmful compounds such as the oxalic acid in asparagus and the cabbage family, which is a primary constituent of one variety of kidney stone. What the New American Cuisine seeks to do in this regard is cook in such ways (sautéing, stir-frying, steaming) that the maximum amount of fragile nutrients will be preserved. Cooked and raw vegetables are both important and we need to be masters of both.

ABOUT SALADS

Perhaps your childhood impression of salads, like mine, was iceberg lettuce and tomato, coleslaw once in a while, maybe once in a great while a mixture of grated carrots and raisins. Nothing to get excited about at best, at worst something to avoid. I would have been unable to believe that someday I would be promoting a cuisine in which salads are anything from a welcome and stimulating side dish to a fully satisfying meal.

There are highly important nutritional reasons other than enzymes for eating raw vegetables every day. They are a good source of fiber, and an excellent source of minerals, as well as vitamins altered or destroyed by cooking. Raw vegetables eaten at the beginning of a meal often stimulate appetite and always stimulate the flow of digestive enzymes, promoting the digestion of the cooked foods that follow. Salad eaten after cooked food cleans the palate, leaving it fresh.

I like to talk about "building" salads because that word emphasizes that saladmaking can be a creative process limited only by your imagination, using virtually everything you can sprout, grow, or buy and eat cold. Let's consider the engineering of salad building:

The foundation of most salads—*usually* but not always—is salad greens. Start with any one of them or, better yet, a mixture: romaine, red leaf, green leaf, butter leaf, and head lettuces, watercress, endive. Alfalfa sprouts add color, texture and nutrition. Another delicious, highly nutritious foundation is raw spinach, either with lettuce or by itself. This tender, leafy green is a good source of vitamins A and C and adds a unique, slightly bold flavor. Try it with fresh sliced mushroom, sunflower seeds, herb dressing, and tangy feta cheese.

Upon this foundation, you can build with a nearly endless variety of vegetables: carrots, celery, fresh corn, bell peppers, cucumbers, fresh raw peas, string beans, squash, jicama, broccoli, cauliflower, and radishes. Be daring, experiment: combine these and other raw vegetables to make a different salad every night.

Nuts and seeds, raw or toasted, top a salad deliciously, as does virtually any cheese, crumbled, grated, or cubed, sliced hard boiled eggs, avocado strips, olives, artichoke hearts, cooked chicken or turkey, marinated fish, or croutons toasted in garlic butter. And you can sprinkle on nutritional yeast or add it to your salad dressing, imparting a unique flavor, and adding B vitamins and protein.

The following recipe illustrates how one dish can be both the center of a meal and a salad simultaneously.

BULGUR SALAD (TABOULI)

1 c. bulgur wheat	¼ t. mint or thyme
2½ c. water	½ c. bean sprouts, lightly sautéed
1 t. salt	1 c. parsley
2 green onions	¼ c. olive or sesame oil
1 stalk celery, diced	2 T. lemon juice

Add bulgur to boiling, salted water. Reduce heat and simmer, covered, for 30 minutes. Remove cover and cool to lukewarm. Mix with green onions, celery, parsley, and sprouts; place in refrigerator to chill.

Mix oil, lemon juice, mint, or thyme, pour over bulgur, toss and serve.

Try sprinkling with sunflower seeds, substituting other cooked grains, serving on a bed of watercress or alfalfa sprouts.

(Adapted from *The Sunburst Farm Family Cookbook*.)

Salad Dressings

We are dressed when our bodies are covered; we are well dressed when the covering complements our natural characteristics. It is the same for a salad: dressed when covered, but well-dressed when all the ingredients of the salad have slipped into something that enhances the flavor of all it envelops. We use flavored vegetable oils because they can so easily be encouraged to flow over a jungle of leaves, imparting a whiff of garlic, a sniff of lemon, a breath of mustard, a hint of mint, a trace of tarragon. Our slippery, shiny dressing brightens the appearance of everything it dresses and makes the flavors seem more piquant, giving zest, tang, zip.

Oil-based dressings. Before considering how to flavor the oil, there is the question of what kind of oil. I recommend olive or sesame oil and refer you to Chapter 6 for complete information on vegetable oils.

Flavoring the oil is usually accomplished through combinations of liquid, solid and semi-solid ingredients. Natural liquids good for the purpose are apple cider or wine vinegar, lemon juice, and soy sauce. Solid ingredients include garlic, dozens of herbs—both dry and fresh—and hard cheeses such as Parmesan and Romano. Semi-solid ingredients include such preparations as mustard, tomato sauce or catsup, and mayonnaise.

FRENCH-STYLE PIQUANT DRESSING

1 c. olive oil

¼ c. apple cider vinegar

2 cloves garlic

1 t. French-style mustard

½ t. soy sauce

Mix all ingredients in a bottle or jar suitable for shaking vigorously. Peel and split the garlic cloves before adding them, or squeeze in a garlic press.

Variations: Other kinds of oils and vinegars can be substituted. The ratio of oil to vinegar can be altered from four to one to three to one for a more sour taste, to five to one for less sour. Herbs such as dill, tarragon, parsley, rosemary, and thyme can be added. Tomato sauce or mayonnaise can be substituted for mustard and soy sauce. As in other recipes, what's good is what you like.

A trick. Oil-based dressings require a lot of shaking because oil floats on other liquid ingredients. You can get the liquids to blend by using a capful of liquid lecithin, a natural emulsifier widely used by food manufacturers whenever oil needs to be blended with water-based liquids.

Other dressing bases. I use other foods as a base for salad dressings more often than I use oil.

Yogurt is a tasty and versatile base for salad dressings. Buttermilk and kefir are also excellent and can be used to thin yogurt that is too thick. The principle here is the same as in oil-based dressings: flavor the yogurt with things you like. One of the simplest dressings I make is simply to mash some blue cheese and mix it with yogurt (the kind I use is thin and runny) and a shake of garlic powder. Another simple one is buttermilk or kefir flavored with garlic and dill and just a touch of soy sauce.

Tahini and other nut and seed butters (see page 232). Tahini's consistency makes it an ideal base for salad dressings. It can be substituted for oil, yielding a creamier version of an oil-based recipe. Thicker butter (peanut, cashew) can be thinned with tahini or oil to a pleasing consistency, and flavored to please your palate. Sesame seeds and sunflower seeds can be whirled into a creamy consistency with a little oil in your blender, then flavored with celery seeds or fennel and lemon juice. Hummus also makes a tasty salad dressing; it can be thinned with water, yogurt, buttermilk, kefir, or tomato juice.

Avocado. Mashed avocadoes can be thinned to a creamy green dressing with most of the things above—oil and vinegar or lemon juice; yogurt, kefir, or buttermilk; tahini.

CALIFORNIA GREEN DRESSING

1 large, ripe avocado

½ c. buttermilk (or kefir or yogurt)

¼ t. garlic powder

⅛ t. cayenne pepper

⅛ t. salt

Put all ingredients in a blender or mash and mix by hand.

Mayonnaise. If for no other reason, mayonnaise is worth mentioning because it is the base for the ever-popular *Thousand Island Dressing:*

THOUSAND ISLAND DRESSING

1 c. mayonnaise

¼ c. tomato sauce (or catsup)

1 t. honey

Mix until smooth.

1 t. garlic powder

½ t. basil

½ t. oregano

Unrefined vegetable oils don't work in making your own mayonnaise; the natural constituents which give the unrefined oils their color and flavor make them too heavy to hold the other mayonnaise ingredients in the emulsion. Even though you can't improve on the quality of commercial mayonnaise with unrefined oil, you can improve the quality noticeably with fresh eggs. Commercial mayonnaise is generally made from the lowest quality eggs, often frozen in bulk without their shells. And even though you pay far more for eggs than manufacturers do, you'll make your own better-tasting mayonnaise for less money with only a small expenditure of time.

MAYONNAISE

1 c. safflower oil (or soy or sunflower)

2 egg yolks

2 T. lemon juice

1½ T. apple cider vinegar

¼ t. salt

¼ t. mustard powder

Add egg yolks to blender, blend until thick, then add vinegar and blend a little longer while getting ready to pour in the oil. Pour the oil in very slowly in a thin trickle, then add lemon juice, salt, and mustard powder, blending until thick and smooth.

Since I don't like to use refined oils, I make a mayonnaise substitute which is also good for people who wish to avoid eggs. Since its base is tahini, I call it *Sesanaise:*

SESANAISE

1 c. tahini

¼ c. lemon juice

1 T. honey

¼ t. mustard powder

¼ t. salt

⅛ to ¼ c. water

Put ⅛ cup of water and everything but tahini in your blender, then gradually blend in the tahini with machine running. If it's too thick, add additional water gradually until desired consistency is achieved. Mixed with yogurt, kefir, or buttermilk, sesanaise makes an excellent salad dressing.

Remember:
—When using fresh herbs, one teaspoon equals a quarter teaspoon of dried herbs (see Appendix Six for herbs and their uses).
—Before dressing a salad, make sure it's dry, either by spinning or towelling it, since dressings don't adhere well to wet leaves.

—When tossing a salad, the minimum is better than the maximum—you don't want to beat the juices out of the vegetables.

COOKING VEGETABLES

Cookware

There are five types of cookware I recommend: enamel, iron, stainless steel, pyrex or glass, and clay or porcelain. When hot water or steam interacts with food, certain mild acids form. Aluminum is quite unstable in the presence of these food acids, interacting with them and forming aluminum salts. Little is known about the amount of aluminum salts we are exposed to by cooking in aluminum or about their cumulative effects; but it is known that aluminum salts are toxic. They have a slightly bitter taste, especially detectable if you compare vegetables sautéed in aluminum to vegetables sautéed in iron. A British study concluded that we should avoid aluminum cookware; its use may cause indigestion, heartburn, flatulence, constipation, and headaches.

Copper is a vital nutrient in minute quantities, but, as is often the case, too much is not better, it is toxic. Therefore, copper cookware is not advisable if the cooking surface itself is copper. But both copper and aluminum are excellent heat conductors; so when the copper or aluminum is bonded to a layer of ceramic or stainless steel, they become nontoxic and give first-rate results. For many, the problem with such cookware is its cost. Some of the "miracle" non-stick surfaces are less expensive but they may not be as safe as claimed, either: how often have we seen yesterday's miracle proven today's disaster?

Cast iron is the greatest bargain in kitchen equipment available in the contemporary marketplace. It can be had for 20 and even 10 percent of the cost of other safe types of cookware, and is one of the best conductors of heat. But doesn't iron interact with food in the same way aluminum does? Yes, but iron salts are not toxic. In fact, cooking in iron is an additional way we can absorb an important nutrient into our bodies.

Iron cookware needs seasoning before use. To season it, rub the inner surface with vegetable oil and heat it on a low flame for an hour; after the pan has cooled, wipe off the excess oil with a paper towel. The finish is spoiled by scouring pads or abrasive powders; wash in hot, soapy water, rinse in hot water, turn upside down for quick drying or heat until water evaporates to prevent rusting. Cast iron cookware has another drawback besides the special handling requirements: it is heavy. But weighed against its great cooking efficiency, durability, and low cost, its advantages are heavily on the plus side.

A simple way to make any kind of pot or pan stick-proof is to spread a film of liquid lecithin over the cooking surface before using it, repeating after each use. Liquid lecithin can be bought inexpensively in most health and natural foods stores. It is an extremely thick oily substance derived from soybeans and has excellent nutritional properties (more on lecithin in Appendix Seven). Lecithin is sold for cooking purposes under brand names vaguely like "no stickum food on pan" at much higher prices than a can of plain old lecithin.

After your iron, steel, enamel, or clay cookware, the most important item you can have is a steamer, which should also be stainless steel rather than aluminum. Boiling vegetables is an outrage: the result is soggy, waterlogged pulp that has lost most of its flavor and nutritional value to the water. Not even in soup-making should vegetables be boiled: they should be *simmered.* A vegetable steamer is an inexpensive piece of equipment—definitely one of the very best nutritional investments you can make. (See Chapter 35 for more on cookware.)

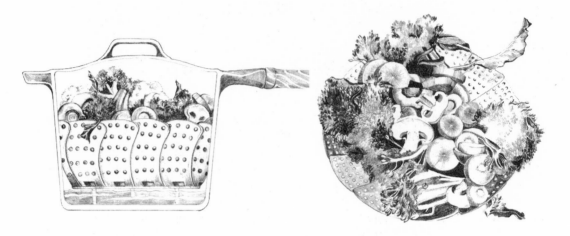

Steaming

Be sure the water level stays below the bottom of the steamer. The vegetables should remain untouched by the water. But don't put in so little water that it will all be steamed off before the vegetables are tender—you will get scorched vegetables, perhaps even ruin a pot. The water left when the vegetables are done can be saved for stock. The pot should be tightly covered and once the water is boiling, the heat reduced to low. The vegetables can be lightly sprinkled with salt and herbs beforehand, as taste dictates.

Steaming is ideal for almost all vegetables, including broccoli, cauliflower, carrots, beets, greens, green beans, lima beans, summer and winter squash, potatoes, and corn on the cob. Steaming is quick, even for the hard vegetables if they are cut up small. Serve with butter or soy sauce, sprinkle with toasted sesame or sunflower seeds, or top with a sauce.

WHEN TO BOIL VEGETABLES

Although boiling vegetables is nutritional homicide, there is a case for *parboiling.* Let's say you want to serve green beans to guests and you want them crisp but tender, without that raw taste, and as bright green as possible. Bring water to the boil, throw in your prepared beans, and after the water returns to the boil, cook for about a minute. Drain in a colander or strainer. If you want to stop the tenderization at that point, rinse in cold water. Otherwise, they will tenderize a little more as they cool. This method accentuates the color: not only will they look greener than when cooked by any other method, they will even look greener than when they were uncooked. Parboiled vegetables are especially delicious marinated in olive oil, garlic, and a chopped fresh herb such as basil.

Vegetable Sauces

CREAM SAUCE

½ lb. butter
1 c. flour
(barley or whole wheat)

1 qt. milk
(or cream or half-and-half)
salt

Melt butter over medium heat; slowly add flour, stirring constantly with a whisk to remove all lumps. Add milk (or half-and-half or cream depending on desired richness) and stir until well blended. Salt to taste and remove from heat. As sauce cools it will thicken; if storing, you will probably have to thin with milk or water when you reheat it. This will make over one quart of cream sauce; if you want one cup of sauce, make one quarter of the recipe; 2 T. butter, 2–4 T. flour (more flour makes thicker sauce) and 1 cup of milk. (Adapted from *The Sunburst Farm Family Cookbook.*)

Variations: add curry powder and soy sauce or mustard powder; instead of flour, use sesame seed meal; use soup stock and/or soy sauce to thin for use as gravy; use as a base for cream soup.

CURRY SAUCE

5 cooking apples sliced thin
5 onions, sliced in half moons
2 T. butter
½ T. salt

2½ T. whole wheat pastry flour
3½ T. curry powder
1 T. ginger
¾ t. nutmeg

Sauté apples and onions slowly in butter until onions are transparent. Lightly blenderize the mixture, adding the spices and flour, and return to pan. Cook to desired thickness. (From "The Farmer and the Fisherman.") Yield: 3 cups.

SWEET 'N' SOUR SAUCE

2 c. unsweetened pineapple juice
¼ c. apple cider vinegar
¼ c. honey
1 T. soy sauce
1 T. arrowroot powder

1 t. ginger, ground
1 lg. tomato, cut in half-moons
⅓ pineapple, cut in chunks (1 c.)
1 lg. green bell pepper, sliced

Put juice and vinegar in a large sauce pan and heat. Add honey, soy sauce, and ginger. Remove some liquid, add arrowroot, blend with whisk to a smooth paste, then add back to sauce. After sauce thickens, add tomato, pineapple, and pepper. Cook 1 minute, remove from heat, check for taste. If too sour, add a little more pineapple juice and honey; if too sweet, add a little more vinegar. Yield: 5 cups. (Adapted from *The Sunburst Farm Family Cookbook.*)

Sautéing And Stir-frying

These two methods have much in common, the first done in a covered saucepan, the second in a wok. Start with a little oil. If you like onions, garlic, and herbs, add them first and cook briefly over a high flame. Then, for sautéing, add chopped vegetables, stir to cover them with a film of oil, add a few tablespoons of water, cover tightly, and turn heat to low. Stir occasionally, adding a little water if needed, cooking to desired tenderness. Adding water prevents scorching but cooking leafy greens and watery vegetables such as summer squash this way usually requires no added water, especially if they have recently been washed and have droplets of water still clinging. Whatever water is added should steam off. Soy sauce can be drizzled in at any stage; the longer it is in, the more is absorbed, and the darker the vegetables will look.

Stir-frying differs in that it is done in the funnel-shaped Chinese wok over high heat. The unique shape concentrates the oil in the bottom of the wok, and less is needed than with sautéing. But heat is also concentrated and the food must be stirred frequently to prevent burning.

Stir-frying and sautéing can be interchanged in recipes. Both preserve much of the flavor and nutritional value and are suitable for a wide variety of vegetables, including broccoli, cauliflower, carrots, greens, onions, celery, peppers, green beans, lima beans, eggplant, summer squash, cabbage, and bean sprouts. Stagger their cooking according to their hardness. For example, carrots need a few minutes headstart over summer squash. It is not a good idea to reduce the cooking time requirements by cutting the vegetables into very small pieces because that reduces the flavor and nutritional value; leave the vegetables in "bite-size" pieces.

Cooked by these waterless methods, vegetables are so flavorful that people who have said, "I don't like vegetables," have changed their minds to "I never knew vegetables could taste so good."

Variations: Add bite-sized chunks of tofu or tempeh; almonds; various seeds; chunks of cooked meat, or fish, or very thinly sliced raw meat, or ground meat. A one-pot meal can be achieved by mixing in a cooked grain toward the end, stirring until thoroughly heated, serving with a salad or sticks of raw vegetable.

Sautéing or stir-frying are excellent methods for precooking vegetables intended for quiche and casseroles. (How to feed any strong-tasting vegetable like spinach to someone who ordinarily won't eat it: sauté it and hide it away in a cheese quiche.)

QUICHE

4 c. vegetable (greens, broccoli, cauliflower, summer squash, or a mixture)	½ t. salt
	1 t. thyme
1 med. onion, sliced	1 t. cumin
3 cloves garlic, minced	1 t. basil
6 beaten eggs	1 t. garlic, minced
½ c. milk	or powder
2 c. grated cheese (Swiss, cheddar, jack)	

Lightly sauté garlic, onions and other vegetable. Meanwhile, mix eggs, milk, and cheese, then add seasonings. Mix in sautéed vegetables and pour into oiled casserole dish. Bake at 350° for ½ hour, or until firm in center. Yield: 6–8 servings. (Adapted from *The Sunburst Farm Family Cookbook.*)

VEGETABLE BURRITOS

1 c. zucchini, diced	½ c. grated cheese
½ c. broccoli, diced	½ c. tomatoes, chopped
½ c. mushrooms, sliced	dash salt
¼ c. onions, chopped	dash cayenne pepper
8 corn tortillas	

Heat only enough oil to cover bottom of skillet. Add onions, stir and cover, cook one minute. Add broccoli, stir and cover, cook one minute. Add zucchini, stir and cover, cook one minute. Add mushrooms, stir and cover, reduce heat and cook 5 minutes. Add tomatoes and spices. In another skillet or on a grill, heat dampened tortillas (dampening softens them) in a little butter, turn, sprinkle with cheese. When cheese is melted, top with sautéed vegetables and serve. Yield: 8 burritos. (Adapted from *The Sunburst Farm Family Cookbook*).

WINTER VEGETABLE STIR FRY

1 c. carrots, sliced	½ c. almonds
1 c. onions, chopped	¼ c. sunflower seeds
1 c. broccoli, sliced	2 T. soy sauce
1 c. cabbage, chopped	½ t. basil
2 cloves garlic, minced	¼ t. cumin

Heat two tablespoons of oil in wok, add carrots, onions, garlic, and herbs, stir thoroughly, cover, and cook 5 minutes. Stir a couple of times, add a couple of tablespoons of water if mixture looks too dry or begins to brown. Add broccoli and almonds, stir thoroughly, cover, cook 2 minutes. Add cabbage, sunflower seeds, and soy sauce, stir thoroughly, cover, cook 3 minutes with a couple of good stirs. Serve with any whole grain.

Vegetables can be substituted freely according to season and preference. Example variations: substitute summer squash or peppers for broccoli. Substitute brussel sprouts cut lengthwise in half for chopped cabbage. Add corn kernels shaved from the cob, mushrooms, or bean sprouts.

EGG FOO YUNG

⅓ c. onion, chopped	1 t. salt
⅓ c. celery, chopped	1 t. kelp
½ c. bean sprouts	8–10 eggs

Heat two tablespoons of oil in wok, fry onion and celery until tender. In last minute of frying, add bean sprouts. Remove from heat. Beat eggs, adding salt and kelp. Add vegetables to eggs. Pour spoonfuls of mixture onto hot oiled frying pan or grill. Lightly brown on both sides like pancakes. Top with any sauce of your liking, serve with any whole grain. Yield: 4–5 servings. (Adapted from *The Sunburst Farm Family Cookbook.*)

Baking Vegetables

This is one of the simplest methods of cooking vegetables, but is not suited to all of them. It works best with root vegetables, winter squash, and vegetables that you can stuff, like green peppers.

Baked vegetable ideas. Wash and dry vegetables, place on a baking sheet or in a baking pan. Lightly oil potatoes, carrots, and onions, and bake together. Winter squash may be cooked whole, then served cut in half with the seeds scooped out. Or cut raw squash in half, scoop out seeds, and place on a baking dish, with ¼ to ½ inch of water in the bottom of the dish to keep it from drying out. Put a dab of plain butter in the center of each half, or butter with honey and cinnamon. Stuffed winter squash makes a great entree in which you can vary the stuffing from week to week while they are in season. Carrots can also be baked with a honey-butter glaze, if you like them sweet.

Cooking In Milk

I thank the authors of *Laurel's Kitchen* for calling my attention to this method. If you or people you are cooking for object to the strong flavors of such vegetables as brussel sprouts, cabbage, spinach, kale, or turnips, this one is an answer. The explanation is that strong flavors are imparted by acids which are neutralized by milk's alkalinity, turning the bitter flavors sweet.

The real surprise is that the milk too is sweet and flavorful. Not at all strong, it's a real asset for cream soups or sauces. Use reconstituted powdered milk for this. If you mix it only half strength, it will still do its job but won't be as likely to scorch (the one hazard in this method).

Here, too, heavy pans are helpful. Preheat the milk just to scalding, then add the vegetables, put the lid on, and simmer, stirring frequently with a wooden spoon. If you stir them often, you won't need to worry about completely immersing them.

A Few More Vegetable Ideas

PLOUGHMAN'S SHARE

This recipe needs no proportions; it all depends on your family's hunger.
First have ready:

baked potatoes

steamed broccoli, cut lengthwise into
small sections

steamed cauliflower, cut into small flowerettes

steamed onions, sliced in half-moons

Toss all the above except the baked potatoes with soy sauce and herbs of your choice.
Also have ready:

sliced cheese of your choice
(cheddar is nice)

chopped green onions

sliced mushrooms

Rub pan with butter, cut baked potato in half lengthwise, surround and cover with all the above vegetables and cover with cheese. Bake until cheese melts; serve as is or with sour cream topping. (Adapted from "The Farmer and the Fisherman" restaurant.)

STROGANOFF

4 c. vegetables, chopped
(according to season or preference)

1 lg. onion, chopped

1 c. mushrooms, sliced

2 t. basil

1 t. nutmeg

1 T. worcestershire sauce

1½ c. sour cream

Sauté vegetables according to their requirements (described previously). Add salt and pepper to taste, then add worcestershire sauce. Finally, add sour cream. Heat but don't boil. Serve over whole wheat noodles. Yield: 4–6 servings. (Adapted from *The Sunburst Farm Family Cookbook.*)

EGGPLANT PARMIGIANA

1 lg. eggplant, sliced
2 eggs, slightly beaten
1½ t. salt
¼ t. pepper
2 T. oregano, crushed

1 c. cornmeal
1 c. mozzarella cheese, grated
1 c. tomato sauce
½ c. mushrooms, sliced

Slice eggplant, sprinkle slices lightly with salt, put on paper towel for about 15 minutes to drain water from eggplant, removing bitterness. This is a good practice for any eggplant recipe.

Beat eggs, salt, and pepper in a bowl. Put cornmeal in another bowl. Dip drained eggplant slices in eggs, then in cornmeal. Heat ¼ inch oil in heavy skillet until almost smoking. You want the oil hot enough to sear the egg/cornmeal to the eggplant, preventing it from absorbing too much oil. Lay eggplant slices in a baking pan, layer with tomato sauce, oregano, mushrooms and cheese, as many layers as it takes, ending with cheese. Bake at 375° until cheese melts. Serve with whole grain pasta or any whole grain. Yield: 4–6 servings, depending on size of eggplant. (Adapted from the *Sunburst Farm Family Cookbook.*)

While most of us were growing up, we were served vegetables that were "done" after they'd been boiled to oblivion, into some sort of bland mush. But that isn't what "does" a vegetable. We need to re-educate ourselves. Vegetables have far more flavor and food value when they are cooked within these general parameters: tender but still firm. This can be accomplished by all the methods outlined above—steaming, sautéing, stir-frying, baking, and milk-cooking. The recipes are enough to provide strong hints of the myriad choices open within the realm of fresh vegetables. Whatever vegetables, whatever method, of course "just right" is best, but undercooked is better than overcooked. Remember that vegetables in a hot pot or pan keep cooking after removal from the burner.

Observe that none of these recipes require complex skills. Anybody can carry them to completion the first time. Of course, with practice comes dexterity, but not even dexterity is essential to cooking a good meal. *Anyone* can cook.

20 Beans, Nuts, Seeds

The New American Cuisine relies heavily on the plant kingdom for protein in order to achieve its twin goals of raising dietary quality while lowering its cost. Therefore, in the chart below, you depend primarily on the low and medium priced foods, using the expensive ones sparingly. Exactly how you do that is a matter of discovery and experimentation for you, greatly dependent on taste preferences and local availability. Other factors important in how your protein needs are met are: how foods are combined, whether they are cooked or raw (see Chapter 2), and your individual nutritional needs (see Chapters 8 and 9).

PROTEIN COST COMPARISONS

low priced	*medium priced*	*high priced*
non-instant non-fat dry milk	hamburger	pork, lamb, steak
cottage cheese	hard cheese	some fresh fish
buttermilk	poultry	shell fish (fresh and canned)
eggs	millet, cornmeal	pumpkin seeds
all kinds of legumes	canned fish	chia seeds
most whole grains (whole	some fresh fish	all kinds of nuts
wheat flour, oatmeal,	nutritional yeast	
brown rice, pasta)	peanut butter	
some fresh fish	peanuts	
wheat germ	sunflower seeds	
tofu	sesame seeds	
	flax seeds	
	tempeh	

Note: The above categories are based on price per pound, reflecting average supply/demand circumstances. They can change up or down according to shortages or surpluses. In 1980, for example, the heat wave destroyed 60 percent of the peanut crop, driving them into the high-priced bracket.

BEANS

I am using the word "beans" loosely, covering all dried legumes, including peas and lentils, but not including fresh beans, which are treated like fresh vegetables. At a third, or even less than, the price of meat, beans play an important role in the New American Cuisine, whether the vegetarian or omnivarian version. But, many protest, for the intestinal tract their role can be villainous— uncomfortable within, sulphurously antisocial without. Even if they're a tenth the price of meat, are they worth it? For me personally, the answer would be *no*, except that I have learned how to deflate beans before they inflate me.

Beans produce intestinal gas, or flatulence, due to two forms of starch (*stachyose* and *raffinose*) that are difficult to digest. They do not pass through the intestinal walls and instead of being converted to blood sugar they are attacked by intestinal bacteria, which split them into carbon dioxide and hydrogen, the two main constituents of intestinal gas. There are several ways to attack those stubborn starches *before* you eat beans, relieving your intestine of the burden and your family and friends of the gas.

Cooking Beans

The first attack on the stubborn bean starches is made by the simple act of soaking, a common practice most people have employed every time they have cooked beans because they take forever to cook if they're not presoaked for at least eight hours. Where the stubborn starches are concerned, presoaking helps just a little, making a dent in their armor. It's in the cooking, however, that the job is really done. (Two tips about soaking: Use plenty of water, so the beans will absorb the maximum possible amount. Also, when soaking soybeans, refrigerate them to prevent fermentation.)

For cooking, beans generally require 3 parts water to 1 part soaked beans (soybeans and garbanzos take 4 to 1). Water, plus heat, plus time, cooks beans but still has little effect on the stubborn starches. *The secret lies in changing the properties of the cooking water,* and the single most effective agent of change is apple cider vinegar. Apple cider vinegar added to the cooking water tames beans and a surprisingly large amount of vinegar can be employed without making the beans taste vinegary. The vinegary taste boils off and my guess is that the acid of the vinegar, plus heat, plus time is what actually breaks down the stubborn starches.

This method is extremely helpful for all kinds of beans. However, its helpfulness varies somewhat according to the type of bean and the person. I have found it to completely tame pinto beans and black beans, be reasonably effective for kidneys and limas, with navy beans falling somewhere in between. But it is important to employ the cider vinegar only in the latter stages of the battle. If it is added from the beginning of the cooking, it tends to toughen the beans and lengthen the cooking time.

To a lesser degree, there are herbs and vegetables that in mysterious ways render beans more digestible when added to the cooking water, also in the latter stages. Some herbs that enhance the digestibility of beans are:

Primary	*Secondary*
tumeric	thyme
cumin	marjoram
coriander	oregano
rosemary	basil
sage	bay leaf
parsley	pepper (cayenne and black)
garlic	cilantro (Chinese parsley)
savory	onion
	chili pepper

The vinegar method of cooking beans. Let's say I want to cook pinto beans, utilizing the magical apple cider vinegar. A cup of dry beans will yield over three cups of cooked beans, enough for a couple of meals and some to freeze for a later week. So I soak a cup of beans in plenty of water overnight, knowing they'll more than double in volume by morning.

In the morning I add four cups of water and nothing else, not even salt, cover, bring to boil, then reduce to simmer temperature. From this point I know they'll take two hours to cook.

The key maneuver: When the last half hour arrives, I take the bean pot off the burner, remove a quarter cup of liquid and replace it with apple cider vinegar, stir and set the pot aside. If I want the beans a little soupier, I just add the vinegar without drawing any liquid off. Then in a couple of tablespoons of sesame oil, I sauté a chopped onion and a couple of minced cloves of garlic. After a few minutes I add 2 tablespoons of chopped parsley and a half teaspoon each of tumeric, cumin, coriander, rosemary, and sage, sautéing until the herbs are brown. Then I add the sautéed mix, a quarter-teaspoon of cayenne pepper and a couple of bay leaves, cover and bring to the boil again, then simmer for another half hour.

I don't add my half teaspoon of salt until the beans are cooked because salt tends to lengthen the cooking time. Beans should always be well cooked, meaning they shouldn't offer resistance to the pressure of your teeth or, judged another way, if you press a cooked bean between your thumb and forefinger, it should squash easily. These beans will be deliciously savory and shouldn't produce an intestinal tremor. I can do a lot of things with them—beans, rice and vegetables for dinner; with hot sauce for Mexican-style meals; with eggs and whole wheat toast for breakfast; with leftover vegetables and pasta for a quick minestrone-type soup; as a casserole ingredient. No matter what type of bean, the same general method applies, varying the added herbs and vegetables—cilantro one time, chili pepper another, oregano-marjoram-thyme another. The variations depend on purpose and preference.

Warning: Stones can be similar to beans in size and color. I once cracked a tooth in a restaurant eating a bean burrito. A sensible precaution is to spread your beans out on a newspaper or paper towel before soaking to check for stones—much cheaper and less painful than having a porcelain crown made for a cracked tooth.

Shortcut: What if you decide around midday that you want beans cooked for that evening? The quick-soak method: Pour 3¼ cups water to 1 cup of dry beans in a pot, bring to boil for two minutes, remove from heat, cover and let sit for two hours. Then cook by the vinegar method.

Some cookbooks recommend boiling beans for a half hour, then pouring off the water and starting over with fresh water. This does reduce their gassiness but it also greatly reduces their flavor and nutritional value. It will help a little to pour off excess soaking water and very little flavor and food value will be lost by doing so.

Beans benefit from slow cooking, as they develop flavor over time. If you turn up the temperature to hurry them, beans are liable to split, making them watery and mushy. A final point about beans and gas: the proliferation of the intestinal bacteria responsible for breaking down stachyose and raffinose is promoted by eating beans frequently, one more example of the great adaptability of the human body.

A Glossary Of Beans

Adzuki beans: small, dark red, highly flavorful, probably the easiest bean to digest; best quality generally imported from Japan, domestic usually appear lighter and duller in color.

Black beans: also called black turtle soup beans, most often used for thick soup in Cuban, South American, Mediterranean, Chinese, and Japanese cuisines; claimed by some to be the most flavorful of all beans.

Black-eyed peas: also called black-eyed beans or cow peas, they really are beans, not peas. They are small, oval, off-white with a black spot.

Fava beans: also called broad beans or horse beans, fava beans look like oversized limas, with a similar taste. They were the only known bean in Europe before the discovery of the Americas. Widely used in South America, where they are also ground into flour and roasted as a snack.

Garbanzo beans: also called chick peas, appear frequently in Middle Eastern and Mediterranean cuisines, often in salads, the main ingredient of *hummus* (see page 227 for recipe.)

Great Northern beans: also called large whites, often boiled, then baked, also used in soups, stews, and casseroles.

Kidney beans: red, kidney-shaped, quite flavorful and versatile, often used in chili and salads.

Lentils: the most common type is called green but is actually as brown as it is green; the other type is called red and is red. We are most familiar with them as soup but in India they are eaten at almost every meal as *dal*—lentils cooked with onions, garlic, and spices, then pureed. They also make a good stew cooked with potatoes and vegetables, are good in *pilaf,* cooked with rice or bulgur and dried fruits. Excellent sprouters, in which form they are a vegetarian source of vitamin B12.

Lima beans: come both small and large, which has nothing to do with quality. Flavorful, good alone or in casseroles.

Mung beans: green, the smallest of all beans, excellent sprouters and though they are seldom cooked, tasty when they are.

Navy beans: also called small whites or pea beans, often used for baked beans.

Peas, split: can also be bought whole, in both green and yellow varieties, used interchangeably for each other, though most people seem to agree that the green variety has a more distinctive flavor.

Pink beans and red beans: similar, but reds are generally considered to have a slightly stronger flavor, both can be used interchangeably in Mexican dishes.

Pinto beans: beige, speckled, same species as kidneys but more delicate flavor, turn brown when cooked, widely used in Mexican cuisine.

Soybeans: a major agricultural commodity and export, fed to hogs and cattle in the U.S., in the Orient made into a wide variety of foods now gaining popularity here (tofu, tempeh, shoyu).

Things To Do With Beans

—All beans can be eaten alone.

—They can be used whole in soups, stews, and casseroles.

—They can be pureed to form the base for soups.

—Cold, they can be added to salads.

—Mashed or pureed, they can be incorporated into bread doughs, nut loaves, and sandwich spreads.

—They can be sprouted. Sprouting also helps considerably with the gas problem because the starches are partially converted to sugar. For cooking, sprout beans just to the stage where the white tip of the sprout pokes through. For eating raw, allow the sprouts to grow out to about one quarter inch. (See Chapter 26 for complete sprouting information).

—The following fast-cooking beans can be cooked in the same pot with grains:

adzukis
lentils
small limas
mung beans
split peas

COOKING BEANS

Bean	Water to Beans Ratio	Cooking Time*	Yield, in cups per cup of dry beans
Adzuki	3:1	45 mins–1 hr	2
Black beans	4:1	1½–2 hrs.	2
Blackeyed peas (cow peas)	3:1	1½–2 hrs.	2
Fava (broad) beans	2:1	1½ hrs.	1½
Garbanzo beans (chickpeas)	4:1	3–4 hrs.	2
Great Northern beans (white beans)	3½:1	1½–2 hrs.	2
Kidney beans	3:1	1½–2 hrs.	2
Lentils	3:1	¾ hour (no soaking necessary)	2¼
Lima beans, small	2:1	1 hour	1¼
Lima beans, large	2:1	1½ hour	1¼
Marrow beans	4:1	2–3 hours	2
Mung beans	3:1	1 hour	2
Navy beans (small whites)	3:1	1½–2 hrs	2
Peas, split (both green & yellow)	3:1	1 hour (no soaking necessary)	2¼
Pink beans	3:1	3–4 hours	2
Pinto beans	3:1	1½–2 hours	2
Red beans	3:1	3–4 hours	2
Soybeans	4:1	3–4 hours	2

*Soaking time assumes pre-soaking from 4 to 8 hours, or the quick soak method.

One way to make an inexpensive dish even cheaper is to combine meat and beans, as in beef and bean stew. Any kind of bean would do, but let's say I were in the mood for kidney beans. Stew meat usually comes in big chunks; to serve four, I would reduce a half pound to small pieces, brown them in hot oil. Then add them to a cup of beans when the bean water comes to a boil, proceeding otherwise according to the vinegar method. I could juice the whole thing up by adding a cup of tomatoes or expand it all the way to a one-pot complete meal by adding some potatoes, carrots, and celery.

GARBANZO SPREAD (HUMMUS)

2 c. cooked garbanzos (chickpeas)
½ c. tahini
juice of one lemon
½ t. garlic powder
¼ t. salt

Mash garbanzo beans, then thoroughly mix in the other ingredients. Or add all ingredients and puree in blender. A Middle Eastern specialty.

HEARTY PEA SOUP

1 onion, diced	2 t. salt
2 T. oil	dash pepper
1 bay leaf	½ t. basil
1 t. celery seed	½ t. thyme
1 c. green split peas	1 carrot, chopped
¼ c. barley	3 stalks celery, diced
½ c. lima beans	½ c. parsley, chopped
10 c. water	1 potato, diced

Sauté onion in oil until soft, along with bay leaf and celery seed. Stir in peas, barley, and limas. Add 10 cups cold water and bring to a boil. Cook on low heat, covered, for about 1 hour and 20 minutes.

Add salt, pepper, vegetables and herbs. Turn heat down as low as possible, and simmer another 30 to 45 minutes. Thin with additional water or stock if necessary. Makes about 8 to 9 cups. (From *Laurel's Kitchen.*)

LENTIL-NUT LOAF

2 c. lentils	1 c. chopped almonds
2 sm. onions, chopped	6 eggs, beaten
4 cloves garlic, minced	2 t. salt
6 celery stalks, chopped	1 T. basil
1 c. whole wheat bread crumbs	2 t. thyme
⅔ c. rolled oats	
1 c. chopped walnuts	

Sauté onions, garlic, and celery in a little oil until tender. Mix with cooked lentils. Add seasonings and other ingredients. Mix well and put into two oiled loaf pans and bake at 375° for an hour or more. Serve plain or with tomato or hot sauce. (Adapted from *The Sunburst Farm Family Cookbook.*)

Variations:
—add 1 c. chopped tomatoes and 1½ c. cheese.
—add 2 c. chopped, hard boiled eggs. Serve with hot gravy.

We have seen the major ways of using beans, employing pintos, kidneys, garbanzos, lentils, and green split peas. Various types of beans are widely interchangeable, including red beans, navy beans, black beans, blackeyed peas, and soybeans.

Pressure Cooking

The family that eats a lot of beans can save a lot of cooking time with a pressure cooker. Cook at fifteen pounds pressure as follows for presoaked beans:

lentils and split peas	10 minutes
soybeans	20 minutes
garbanzos	25 minutes
all other kinds	15 minutes

If the beans are not presoaked, add 5 minutes to the above times; if you use vinegar, add a minute.

Pressure cooking should only be of interest when time is short. The excessive pressure tends to make things mushy and there is a detectable loss of flavor. And, since flavor and nutrition are inseparable, that loss affects more than just our taste buds. We can be sure that the intense pressure is a kind of overkill, destroying more nutritional value than ordinary cooking methods.

COOKING WITH SOYBEANS

Just as soybeans are the one bean that should be refrigerated while being soaked, they are the only bean that foams when boiling. After bringing soybeans to the boil, let them boil a few minutes, skim off the foam, then reduce heat and simmer as you do other beans. The tendency to ferment if soaked at too warm a temperature and the characteristic foaming are both unique to soybeans. There is another unique aspect to soybeans: many people assume they aren't fit for human consumption. Perhaps that is because they are so widely fed to livestock in this country and exported to other countries (where people eat them).

Soybeans deserve wider attention because of their extremely high protein rating, the highest among common beans. Their protein percentage is even higher than meat. When complemented by whole grains, the bean/grain protein is not just higher than beef, it is the highest of all bean/grain combinations. "But," people complain after they learn about the soaking/cooking idiosyncrasies of soybeans, "They don't taste as good as other kinds of beans." Some describe the flavor as "soapy." With the usual disclaimer that taste is subjective, I admit I agree about the lack of truly good flavor in soybeans; therefore I offer three partial remedies:

1. Season them highly or use them in combination with more flavorful foods, as in stews and soups.
2. Combine them with a more flavorful bean, i.e., soy/pinto, soy/kidney.
3. Mash or puree them for use in soyburgers, spreads, and dressings.

Tofu

There is one more remedy to the soybean flavor problem—tofu. Alternate names for tofu are "bean curd" and "soy cheese." But whatever it's called, its versatility, low cost, high protein, and low calorie content make it an excellent food. Since cooking is part of the tofu-making process, it needs only heating for most of its applications; in some recipes it is unheated.

Tofu usually comes packed in water; in this form you can keep it in your refrigerator for about five days. Shrink-wrapped and vacuum-sealed packaging for tofu is becoming more common because it gives the shopkeeper and the consumer more shelf life. You can keep it several weeks in your refrigerator in this form. But if you unwrap it and don't use it all, it then has the same shelf life as water-packed tofu. Rinse the tofu under cold running water daily, no matter how it's been packaged. (To make it even cheaper, many natural foods stores sell tofu in bulk, out of a refrigerated, five-gallon bucket from which you transfer, with tongs, blocks of tofu to plastic bags.)

Tofu has a low calorie/protein ratio. The calorie/protein ration is roughly 35 percent higher for hamburger and roughly 45 percent higher for cheddar cheese—one reason why tofu is rapidly becoming a popular food.

Tofu Idea 1. Every combination of sautéed, stir-fried, or steamed vegetables you can think of can include tofu. Tofu comes in blocks approximately 5 ½ inches long, 2 ¾ inches wide, and an inch thick, weighing about 10 ounces. Make cubes by slicing lengthwise, making two half-inch-thick pieces, then slice across the length and width from top to bottom. Add tofu cubes to the vegetables as if it were a quick-cooking vegetable. This will give the cubes enough time to heat through thoroughly and absorb some of the mixture of flavors from the vegetables. Don't cook tofu a long time—about 15 minutes should be your limit—as it will begin to break down, losing its firm texture.

Tofu Idea 2. Tofu "Fillet." Slice the block lengthwise to reduce its thickness in half; lay on paper towel for several minutes, turn to other side for another few minutes. Place fillets in dish or shallow bowl, dribble a little soy sauce on them, flip, and repeat. Fillets are now sitting in a little pool of soy sauce; leave them there for about 15 minutes. The tofu won't absorb all the soy sauce; what's left over can be retrieved and reused. If desired, sprinkle tops of fillets with herbs (rosemary, sage, garlic, green onions, sesame seeds). Have a little oil heated in a hot skillet; fry the fillets a couple of minutes on each side.

The baked version constitutes a good conservation of energy when the oven is going for some other reason. Follow the same preparation procedure, then put fillets in the oven on an oiled cookie sheet for fifteen minutes.

Tofu Idea 3:

ENCHILADAS

1 package of 12 corn tortillas
2 c. enchilada sauce

In a pan, heat enchilada sauce. If tortillas are stiff, they can be steamed briefly to soften them. Dip into sauce, then fill with the following:

1 onion, chopped	½ t. salt
2 garlic cloves, minced	½ t. garlic powder
1 c. mushrooms, sliced	½ block tofu, cubed
2 bunches fresh spinach, chopped	½ c. grated cheese

Heat skillet with ⅛ cup of oil. Add garlic cloves and onions; sauté until onions are transparent. Add mushrooms, tofu and seasonings; cook one minute. Remove from heat and stir in spinach. Fill each tortilla with grated cheese and vegetable filling. Roll and put into baking pan. Cover with remaining sauce and sprinkle with cheese. Bake approximately 25 minutes. (Adapted from *The Sunburst Farm Family Cookbook.*)

Tofu Uses Go On and On

Whirled briefly in a blender, tofu can be reduced to a consistency resembling that of cottage cheese. Then it can be used interchangeably with cottage cheese in, for example, a cottage cheese salad or a cheesecake. Tofu is basically bland but does have a flavor and this flavor is different from cottage cheese; so substituting it for cottage cheese takes some experimentation with seasonings and sweeteners. Blended to a mushy consistency, tofu is also useful for all sorts of sandwich spread improvisations.

For sandwiches it can also simply be sliced as for fillet, playing the role of cheese now, combined with things like mustard and mayonnaise, lettuce, tomato and sprouts, and nut butters. Or a leftover fried or baked tofu fillet can be used the same way. A grilled cheese version can be made with either a plain slice or a fillet.

Back to the blender: Tofu can be combined with liquids—such as oil, vinegar, lemon juice, buttermilk, soy sauce—and other seasonings—such as garlic, cumin, basil, dill—to make dressings and sauces. Nut and seed butters and meals can be incorporated for these uses too. Again, experimentation and improvisation are the key words; tofu is particularly adaptable to both.

NUTS AND SEEDS

NUTS	SEEDS
almonds	sunflower
cashews	sesame
walnuts, English	pumpkin
walnuts, black	squash
filberts (hazelnuts)	chia
pecans	flax
brazil nuts	poppy
coconut	psyllium
peanuts	

Peanuts are not nuts; they are a bean, a member of the legume family. And, technically, brazil nuts are seeds, and almonds are fruit. But we *call* them nuts and we think of them that way and use them that way. Most of the uses for nuts and seeds are in the uncooked, or raw, form. They do not need cooking to make them either edible or palatable and are nutritionally far superior in the raw form. Cooked, their significance in the New American Cuisine is mainly in the minor role of providing flavor and texture variations.

Nuts and seeds perform the same function as grains: they are responsible for the reproduction of the species. They are nutritionally potent because they embody the life principle and the nutrients to support the generation of life. But they don't contain the perfect balance of nutrients characteristic of grain, being higher in both protein and fat (unsaturated). The higher fat content also means they do not keep as well as grains, since the fat is subject to rancidity.

Nuts and seeds keep for about a year in their shells and are roughly half the price of shelled nuts and seeds. Shelling, however, is very time consuming, best accomplished with the many hands of a group operation. Generally speaking, allow twice as many nuts and seeds in the shell as any recipe calls for in shelled form.

Provide good storage conditions for shelled nuts and seeds: cool, dry, dark. Expect them to stay fresh in good storage conditions for about four months.

Roasting Nuts And Seeds

Nuts and seeds are twice as nourishing in the raw form as roasted, because heat denatures the protein and fat. Once denatured, the fat is much more subject to rancidity; this leads to free radical formation, believed damaging to the circulatory system (see Chapter 6). Commercial processors, knowingly or unknowingly, can disguise rancidity by roasting and flavoring. Since stability and food value are decreased by roasting, but the calories remain the same, it is wise to exercise restraint toward roasted nuts and seeds, a bit of a challenge since roasting makes them tastier and crunchier.

The healthiest method of roasting is dry roasting at home in small batches. This can be done either on a cookie sheet in the oven while baking something else, or in a skillet over a burner with a lot of stirring. They are "done" when they taste the way you like them. If you want them salty, you'll have to add a little oil toward the end, stir to get them all covered by a thin film of hot oil, then sprinkle in the salt, stirring until the salt is clinging to the oiled nuts.

An increasingly popular alternative to roasted and salted nuts and seeds are *tamari roasted* ("tamari" is a type of soy sauce). For tamari roasting, no oil is needed; simply drizzle soy sauce onto the hot nuts and seeds and stir to coat them lightly, roasting until they have become dry again. Pan roasting is the only practical method here; you'll squander soy sauce trying to do them in the oven.

Nut And Seed Butters

Peanut butter is one of the all-time American favorites to the tune of 500 million pounds a year. However, few of us realize the full extent of peanut butter's versatility. In sandwiches, for example, it goes with much more than jelly: it accompanies hard cheeses such as cheddar and crisp vegetables such as cucumber in surprisingly delicious ways. One of my favorite breakfasts is whole wheat toast with peanut butter and banana. Peanut butter can be thinned with stock for a creamy soup, thinned with buttermilk for a salad dressing. Peanut butter cookies are so easy to make that young children can manage them with only a little help and supervision.

Since peanut butter is such a popular American food, let's consider when it is wholesome and when it isn't. The federal standards allow a concoction that is only 70 percent peanuts to be called "peanut butter." That's what most of the popular brands are. What is the other 30 percent? Usually hydrogenated fat and refined sugar (dextrose). That kind of "peanut butter" is not wholesome food. Real peanut butter has one ingredient: peanuts. Many natural foods stores have fresh roasted peanuts and grinders. You dump in your peanuts and the next minute know forever that the best peanut butter is *fresh* and *100 percent peanuts.* And combined with whole wheat, rye, or corn, peanut butter on bread yields complete protein.

PEANUT BUTTER COOKIES

½ c. butter
¾ c. honey

4 T. whole wheat
pastry flour

Cream together and set aside.

2 eggs
1½ c. peanut butter
1 t. vanilla

1½ c. whole wheat pastry flour
½ t. salt
1 t. baking powder

Mix together and add to wet ingredients. Use small scoop and press out on an oiled cookie sheet. Bake at 375° for 12 minutes. Makes about 24 cookies. (Adapted from *The Sunburst Farm Family Cookbook.*)

PEANUT-CHEDDAR SPREAD

Combine equal amounts of peanut butter with grated cheddar cheese. Use as a sandwich spread, dip, stuffing for celery stalks, topping for baked potatoes. It can be glamorized with the addition of a little chopped olive.

PEANUT BUTTER FROSTING

¼ c. peanut butter
2 T. oil

⅓ c. honey
¼ c. warm milk

Combine in blender until smooth. Will frost two 8-inch layers. (From *The Natural Food Cookbook.*)

PEANUT BUTTER SAUCE

½ c. peanut butter
1 onion, grated
1 clove garlic, crushed
2½ T. skim milk powder
(or 3½ T. instant)

¼ t. honey
2–4 T. lemon juice
4 T. soy sauce

Blend all ingredients and add hot water until the mixture has the consistency of heavy cream. If you wish a very smooth sauce, blend the mixture in a blender with hot water.

Serve over hot or cold tofu . . . or with cooked grains and vegetables. Makes about 2 cups. ¼ c. = 2 g usable protein; 5 to 6% of daily protein allowance. (From *Diet for a Small Planet.*)

PEANUT BUTTER BARS

2 c. peanut butter	1 c. dried skim milk
1 c. granola	½ c. honey
1 c. toasted wheat germ	¼ t. vanilla

Mix wet and dry ingredients separately, then combine. Press by hand or rolling pin into desired thickness. (The consistency should be stiff, not crumbly; since peanut butter textures vary, you may need to add more peanut butter if the mixture is too crumbly or more milk powder if it's too runny). Cut to desired lengths and widths, which can be sprinkled with or rolled in shredded coconut, sunflower seeds, or chopped nuts. Keep wrapped and refrigerated until the day of use.

Making Butters

Other butters can be used interchangeably with peanut butter. The types of nuts and seeds most suitable for buttermaking are almonds and cashews, sunflower and sesame. All the various butters can be made at home in your blender by reducing them to a meal consistency, then adding a little oil and continuing to blend until the desired butter consistency is achieved. Be careful with the oil. Add it in small amounts, at a very thin trickle—it doesn't really take much. It may not seem to be working, then suddenly you've got too much oil; it's too runny. Be patient. Sesame oil is most compatible with all kinds of nuts and seeds, as an alternative to using almond oil for almond butter, sunflower oil for sunflower butter, and so forth.

Almond butter: can be made with either raw or roasted almonds; both versions are delicious.

Cashew butter: the same thing can be said for cashew as almond butter, except that there really is no such thing as *raw* cashews: they are always steamed in Mozambique or Brazil or India before we ever see them. Otherwise they aren't edible.

Sunflower butter: can also be made from either raw or roasted stock, though most people find the roasted version tastier.

Sesame butter: made from brown (unhulled) sesame seeds, but don't try to do it with raw ones—extremely bitter. Pan roast the seeds in a dry skillet over a medium flame, stirring constantly, until there is a whisp of smoke and/or a distinct "toasted" aroma; the seeds will, of course, look much browner.

The hulls of sesame seeds are of no nutritional significance, so white sesame seeds are just as useful as brown ones. Creamed white sesame seeds are known as *tahini*, a Middle Eastern specialty.

Nut and seed butters can be kept unrefrigerated for a week or so. Beyond that, it is much safer to store them in the refrigerator to prevent rancidity. This is particularly true if you have used a refined oil in the making. Unrefined sesame oil is best because of its superior stability and agreeable flavor.

Gorp And Other Mixes

Some people who don't care for raw nuts and seeds by themselves do like them when mixed with dried fruit. Fruit and nut mixes, trail mixes, "gorp"—these are all quite familiar names and little guidance is needed to put together your own. The advantages of making your own mixes are that you can make them cheaper by buying ingredients in bulk and you can control the ingredients (which is also an important aspect of controlling cost) to suit your preferences. Also, you can be sure the nuts aren't rancid, often a problem with pre-packaged mixes.

Lowering the cost. For good economic reasons, a lot of people steer clear of nuts, seeds and dried fruits—they are expensive foods. Peanuts and sunflower seeds are exceptions in any year in which the harvest is decent. Sesame seeds are generally an exception, too, but they aren't useful in mixes—they are so small that most of them don't get crushed by normal chewing and pass through the gastrointestinal tract undigested. Here are two easy ways to lower the cost of otherwise expensive mixes:

(1) Use a lot of peanuts and sunflower seeds.
(2) Reduce the volume of the mix by one quarter to one half with granola. (See page 194.)

A tip for those who don't like sticky finger food. Before mixing the sticky raisins, currants, or dates with the nuts and seeds, mix either wheat germ, bran, or milk powder with the fruit, using just enough to coat.

Nut And Seed Snacks

Unlike grains and beans, which must be soaked, cooked, or sprouted in order to be digestible, nuts and seeds are more digestible uncooked. Roasting nuts and seeds reduces the food value of the protein and the fat by altering their biological structures, and destroys some of the vitamin and enzyme content. For these reasons it is best to determine experimentally whether raw nuts and seeds are palatable to you and to whatever extent possible, eat them unroasted.

A Nuts And Seeds Miscellany

Nuts and seeds can be reduced to meal consistency in a blender or coffee grinder. Nut and seed meals can be used in the following ways:

—In all kinds of baking recipes, to vary the flavor and texture, increase the protein content: substitute for 10–20 percent of the flour (more than that would lead to excessive heaviness).

—To sprinkle on many kinds of foods—salads, cooked vegetables and grains, casseroles. Let your taste buds be your guide.

—As a base for dressings that can be used for salads and on anything else you think might be enhanced by it.

GROUND SEED DRESSING

1 c. sunflower seed meal	1 t. ground basil
1 c. sesame seed meal	¼ t. tarragon
1¼ c. oil	1 t. thyme
½ c. lemon juice	¼ t. celery seed
1 t. oregano	2 T. soy sauce

Mix in blender or shake in jar. Yield: 1 quart. (Adapted from *The Sunburst Farm Family Cookbook.*)

One of the best uses for sesame seed meal is as a Japanese seasoning called *gomasio*, or "sesame salt." Different people prefer different degrees of saltiness. A popular ratio is about 8 parts sesame meal to 1 of salt (at the Zen Center in San Francisco they make it 14 to 1). Stir the sesame meal fairly constantly in a dry skillet over medium heat. When meal is thoroughly toasted, remove from skillet, put salt in skillet, stir until thoroughly hot. Then return the toasted sesame meal. Stir together until thoroughly heated and mixed together. Remove from skillet to cool, store in covered container, use as seasoned salt—it has a delicious way of stretching the saltiness of salt.

Variations on the sesame salt theme can be made with celery and caraway seed meals, kelp powder, parsley flakes, cayenne pepper, and other herbs that come in powder and flake form. There is a wide opportunity for experimentation here—what's best is what tastes best.

Seed sleepers. There are two of them: flax seed and chia seeds. Flax seed is the only seed that is truly inexpensive and it has some very interesting properties. Like all seeds, it is an excellent source of protein. It is also mucilaginous, meaning that when it comes into contact with liquid, it becomes soft and jelly-like. Therefore, flax is highly useful as an intestinal cleanser and as a regulator of the bowel. The two most common ways of using it are to soak it overnight in water and drink it in juice in the morning and to add the meal to breakfast cereals.

Chia seed comes from a desert bush found in the Southwest and Mexico. Folklore calls it "Indian running food" and tells us that Apache Indians took to the warpath for weeks at a time with only a small sack of chia seeds for food, exhibiting endurance that astonished their enemies. Whatever may have been the case, some contemporary reporters have touted chia seeds as an "energy food," saying they have noticed an energizing effect about an hour after eating them. They are tiny, round, black seeds with the same mucilaginous properties as flax.

Nuts and seeds as garnishes. The simplest way to use nuts and seeds to complement other foods is just as they are, in their whole form, raw or roasted, as a garnish. Simply sprinkle them wherever you like—in your soup, on your salad, steak, cereal, vegetables. Whatever suits your palate is where they fit and wherever they're added they add flavor, texture, and food value.

21   The Animal Proteins

Animal protein plays a secondary role to vegetable protein in the New American Cuisine because

1. Nutritionally, plant foods contain twice as many vitamins and minerals as animal foods.
2. Economically, animal foods are more expensive than plant foods.
3. Ecologically, plant foods make more efficient use of agricultural and energy resources.

Nevertheless, we have an abundance of animal protein; many of us can afford at least a moderate amount and enjoy eating it. Furthermore, there are significant numbers of us who *should* eat at least *some* animal protein for health reasons (for a detailed discussion, see Chapters 8 and 9), and whether we need it or not, some of us simply want it and there's the end to that.

Very little animal protein is needed to complete whole grain protein. In *Diet for a Small Planet*, Lappé says:

> High amino acid ratings (especially lysine) give even small portions of meat and poultry the ability to complement plant foods. . . . only 3½ ounces of meat contribute from 30 to 61 percent of your daily protein allowance. These figures make it very clear that the enormous quantities of meat we now consume are hardly needed! In Eastern cuisine small amounts of meat supplement staple vegetable dishes. This dietary tradition, although perhaps determined by the limited availability of meat, more correctly reflects the body's actual needs.

A drawing or photograph of a typical meal from the old American cuisine usually shows a large portion of meat flanked by an assortment of complementary dishes; meat, in whatever form, is understood to be the centerpiece of the meal. The picture of a typical meal from the New American Cuisine may or may not have meat. But if it does, meat is not the centerpiece. Instead, it is an ingredient that complements whole grains (or some other complex carbohydrate) and vegetables. For some it assumes the role of a condiment.

Whether or not meat is a side dish or a condiment is not the point. The real point is to have a flexible attitude towards the use of meat, rather than being locked into the old pattern. The new pattern provides a procession of meals in which meat can be entirely absent one time, a side dish another, a condiment another, and even sometimes the centerpiece as in days of yore.

An additional dimension of flexibility is possible when the menu offers meat as a side dish. Those with a strong yen for meat can take relatively more while those with a stronger attraction to the vegetables follow their predilections. The same meal is a distinctly different experience depending on the needs of different metabolic types.

MEAT

You may remember from Chapter 15 that one of the major fundamentals to making the New American Cuisine work is to reduce or eliminate high-priced protein foods. (See also the chart on page 28.) The focus in the following material, therefore, is on inexpensive cuts of beef, although the same principles can be applied to the more expensive beef, lamb, and pork. (See Chapter 24, under *Buying Meat*, for additional material on this subject.)

Tenderizing

Nobody every complains about lack of flavor in cheap cuts of beef: "The problem is, I can't chew it." It's lean, cheap, flavorful, and too tough to eat. So the problem really is how to make tough meat chewable. First let's see how to handle tough steak—flank steak, for example.

To begin with, of course, your butcher can tenderize it with some pounding; but usually that is just a good first step. You can also do the pounding at home if you're buying your meat in a supermarket. *Avoid commercial meat tenderizing preparations*—too much salt, too many chemicals. The best tenderizer is papain, an enzyme found in papaya. Slices of fresh papaya or pure powdered papain tenderize effectively but both are expensive.

In Oriental cooking, tough meat is sometimes tamed by slicing into strips across or against the grain to break up the tough fibers. One popular example of this is sukiyaki, perfected by the Japanese.

SUKIYAKI

1 lb. flank steak, thinly cut on the slant across the grain (or beef tenderloin or sirloin steak sliced as thin as possible)	1 5-oz. can bamboo shoots, drained
	1 c. green onions, cut in diagonal slices ½ in. wide
3 T. oil	1 c. celery, cut in diagonal slices, 1 inch wide
1 c. soy sauce	1. c. fresh mushrooms, thinly sliced
1 T. honey	5 c. torn fresh spinach leaves, or shredded Chinese cabbage
½ c. stock	
1 5-oz. can water chestnuts, drained and thinly sliced	1½ c. fresh bean sprouts

Partially freeze beef beforehand to make slicing easier. Before cooking, arrange sliced meat and vegetables in separate piles on a large platter or tray. Using a large skillet, heat oil to medium high temperature, add beef strips and cook quickly, turning them over and over, until browned. Combine soy sauce, honey, and beef stock, pour over sautéed beef. Cook until soy mixture bubbles. Push meat aside.

Add onions, then celery, then mushrooms. Stir-fry each vegetable one or two minutes and push aside before adding next vegetable. Add spinach or cabbage, then water chestnuts, bamboo shoots, then bean sprouts, stir-frying each one just until heated through. Mix all together and serve immediately with brown rice. Yield: 6 servings. (Adapted from the *Rodale Cookbook.*)

The principle illustrated by the sukiyaki recipe—slicing meat in thin strips across the grain, and sautéeing or stir-frying in either a wok or skillet—is a generalized adaptation of a widely used Chinese method. Start with the meat as in the sukiyaki recipe and proceed as with sautéed or stir-fried vegetables (pages 217 through 219). Almost all vegetables are suitable.

Seasoning the meat and vegetables can be an adventure: A couple of tablespoons of vinegar and of honey or molasses with some raisins or currants and pineapple chunks gives you sweet and sour vegetable beef; curry powder imparts a hint of India; chili powder suggests Mexico; fine herbs are reminiscent of Mediterranean cuisines; cumin hints of the Middle East; sour cream or yogurt will give a stroganoff effect.

All such variations go with whole grains, whole grain pasta, or potatoes to provide complete meals. The basic theme we are varying is:

a. fresh vegetables, not overcooked, in little or no water, with
b. whole grains, whole grain products, or potatoes, and
c. small amounts of inexpensive meat.

The other good way to defeat tough meat is to marinate it.

ALL PURPOSE MARINADE

½ c. oil (if using this marinade for lamb or pork, reduce oil)
½ c. wine vinegar
¼ c. soy sauce
2 T. lemon juice

1 clove garlic, peeled
1 T. pepper
½ t. each thyme, parsley, marjoram, basil, rosemary

SWEET 'N' SOUR MARINADE

½ c. oil
⅓ c. lemon juice
⅓ c. orange juice
½ c. soy sauce
⅓ c. molasses

4 cloves garlic
a piece of fresh ginger
1 chopped pineapple
1 t. cloves

You can cook in the marinade (braising) and, though delicious, this is expensive, because it adds the expense of the marinade ingredients to the cost of the meat. Marinate at least overnight in refrigerator, turning a few times to treat all sides. Cook the meat by broiling or pan frying. The longer you marinate, the more tender; four days is ideal for a truly tough customer. The marinade may be stored in the refrigerator for reuse.

You might want to marinate even the expensive cuts of steak when using grass-fed beef, since it is generally tougher and leaner than grain-fed. Marinated meat is also delicious sliced thin and used Chinese style, described above.

Types Of Meat

Hamburger. Brown and season, add to soups, casseroles, beans, sautéed and stir-fried vegetables, and sauces, in much the same way as you would add another vegetable. You use enough to get the flavor and texture but the meat is not at all a *dominant* ingredient. Where a recipe calls for a pound of ground beef, for example, you would use a third or even a quarter of a pound. Where that doesn't yield quite the meaty flavor you're looking for, a couple of tablespoons of soy sauce can do wonders. Try that for giving vegetable stock a meat broth flavor, too.

Stew beef. This is usually chuck cut into chunks. You can save money if you buy chuck steak, trim fat and bones, and cut into cubes yourself. Stew is only one way of using stew beef. Cut the chunks into smaller pieces, brown in hot oil; add onion, garlic, herbs, salt and enough water or stock to cover, then bring to a boil; reduce heat, cover tightly and simmer until tender, periodically adding any needed extra liquid. Use this basic meat and gravy as an ingredient in soups, casseroles, beans, or to cover cooked grains and vegetables. Again, as with the hamburger, we are looking at beef as one of many more-or-less equal ingredients rather than the dominant one.

Roasts. Now, what to do with a tough roast, such as a chuck roast? Besides pot-roasting, there is the slow-roast method promulgated by Adelle Davis (*Let's Cook It Right*).

The slow-roast method requires approximately three times as much time as ordinary roasting, plus one hour for sterilization. Sterilization is necessary because without it bacteria would proliferate at the low oven temperatures of slow-roasting. To sterilize, place roast in oven on rack in open pan for one hour at 300°. Remove from oven, brush with oil, sprinkle surface with salt, pepper, garlic powder, rosemary, and sage. Return to oven for approximately one and a half hours per pound at 160°.

A meat thermometer takes a lot of guesswork out of roasting. Insert meat thermometer into the thickest part of the roast, making sure it isn't touching bone. Roast meat to 140° for rare, 155° for medium, 175° for well-done. Slow cooking allows the fiber responsible for toughness to break down; even a chuck roast should be tender and juicy when roasted this way.

Slow-roasting is not as wasteful of energy as it sounds because the oven temperature is kept so low. But it is not energy-efficient either, and so should be used infrequently. Alternatives for tough roasts involve not using them as roasts at all, as in reducing them to small chunks, thin slices, and ground meat.

The leftover roast. To some palates, the roast that was delicious fresh from the oven or pot is unappealing left over. To such, it is usually at least somewhat more acceptable between slices of bread accompanied by mustard, mayonnaise, lettuce, and tomato. Beyond sandwiches, here are a couple of different ways to handle the leftover roast:

MEAT IN FRESH VEGETABLE SAUCE

Sauté a chopped onion in oil until it turns golden brown. Add some chopped green pepper and cook for a minute or so. Next, add a few diced tomatoes, salt and pepper, and cook over moderate heat until the tomatoes become soft and release their juice. This will take about 10 minutes. Now you can add the leftover meat, in slices or thin strips, and heat through.

When you add the green pepper, consider the other possibilities in your vegetable bin. Try adding some sliced mushrooms, leftover zucchini squash, green peas, or anything else that touches your fancy along with the peppers. (From *The Supermarket Handbook*.)

The above recipe is really an outline for the method of making leftover roast one of the most versatile items in your repertory. Cooked meat can take the place of fresh meat in any vegetable/beef idea you might try. The three main differences between using a fresh meat such as flank steak and, say, cooked pot roast are (1) fresh meat will give a stronger beef flavor to the mixture; (2) in the fresh meat version, the vegetables will have more influence on the flavor of the meat; and (3) in the leftover version the meat can be added much later since it only needs heating.

Following this general approach, any vegetarian recipe can become an omnivarian one. You can achieve different effects according to how you use your knife—slices or chunks. You can even run cold cooked meat through a food mill and use the ground meat as a garnish, much the same as you would sprinkle sunflower seeds into a vegetable dish to vary the texture and flavor.

Another leftover roast idea:

SHEPHERD'S PIE

Mince the meat and mix with onions, celery, and carrots, add gravy, then bake with a topping of mashed potatoes at 325° until the potatoes are nicely browned on top, about 40 minutes.

POULTRY

Although you need to stick with the inexpensive cuts of beef to stay in the medium-priced protein category, turkey and chicken are consistently medium-priced, sometimes even lower. Chicken completes plant protein as effectively as beef and, according to *Diet for a Small Planet*, the ability of turkey to complement plant protein surpasses all other meats. One ounce of turkey with four ounces of bulgur wheat is the protein equivalent of five ounces of beef.

Ground turkey can be used by itself, mixed with ground beef and/or ground organ meats, and used in place of straight ground beef for meat loaf, meatballs, burgers, sauces, or almost any recipe calling for ground beef. I use it to make spaghetti sauce, with a bit of soy sauce to boost the flavor. Add uncooked rolled oats and eggs if the ground turkey needs something to hold it together in loaf form or meat balls.

A Bit Of Butchering

When you plan to cook chicken pieces, you can save, on the average, 30% by buying a whole chicken and cutting it up yourself. All you need is a very sharp knife and a cutting board to preserve your blade; here are the steps:

1. Rinse, drain, disjoint. Pull on legs and wings as you cut through the joints.
2. Cut from end of breastbone to backbone along ends of ribs. Separate breast and back. Break backbone, cut back in half.
3. Cut breast straight down between wishbone and point of breast. Leave meat on wishbone.
4. Remove breast meat from center bone by carving down the bone on one side of breast. Repeat on other side of breastbone.
5. Cut legs into drumsticks and thighs. Saw drumsticks off short, if desired.

As with all forms of meat, it will be easier to cut up chicken if it is first thoroughly chilled. It may take a little longer the first time or two, but with a little practice, cutting up a chicken is a ten minute job, quite a profitable tradeoff of time for money.

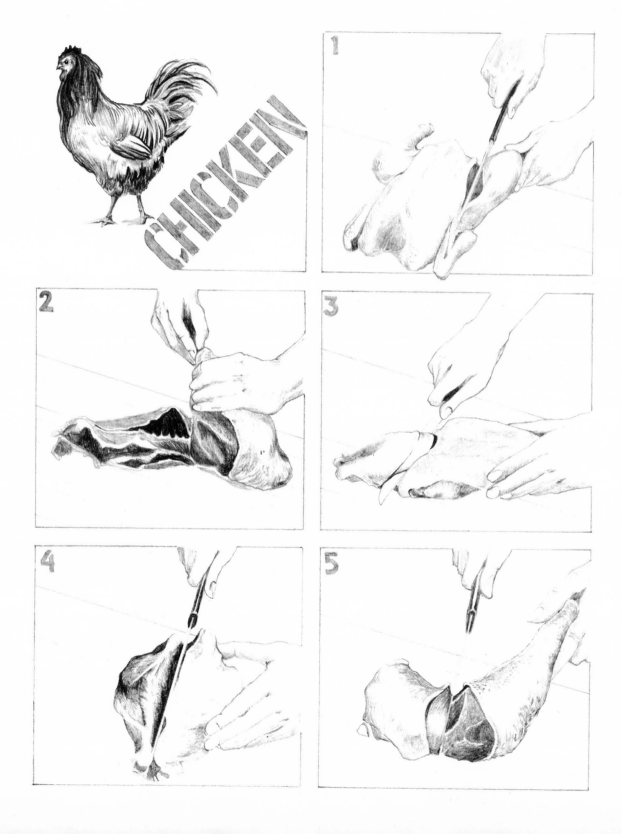

The Bird In The Oven

It is fairly common for people to observe that when a bird is roasted with a stuffing, the meat tends to dry out. The stuffing, on the other hand, is quite moist, having absorbed most of the meat juices. Consequently, some of us enjoy the stuffing more than the meat. You can prevent the drying out to a large degree by roasting in a covered pan. Clay pots yield a particularly moist chicken, as will a crockpot. But neither is big enough for most turkeys. Some turkeys are even so big that the cover of a roasting pan will sit on top of the bird without closing, like a hat. Covering the bird with foil and basting every forty-five minutes both help keep the bird moist. To get the skin crisp, leave bird uncovered and turn the oven temperature up to over 500° for the final five or ten minutes.

If you want the meat as moist as possible, you have to surrender the traditional stuffing recipes, all of which are absorbent. Instead, stuff the cavity with moisture-*producing* substances. Let's say you have a medium-sized turkey: coarsely chop a bunch of parsley, a couple of leeks, an onion, a few stalks of celery with their leaves, a couple of apples, and an orange with peel, and pack the cavity with the mixture of fruits and vegetables. When roasting is completed, remove and discard the mixture from the cavity.

You can still have "stuffing" by baking it separately in a pan, withdrawing some of the meat juices to spread over the top of the stuffing while it bakes, if you want the meaty taste. To adapt a traditional stuffing recipe, use whole grains in the form of whole wheat bread, cooked rice, bulgur, millet, rolled oats, or mixtures of them.

Poultry can be turned into a low-fat meat by skinning it before you cook it, since most of the fat is attached to the skin and the meat picks up most of its fat content by seepage during cooking. The fat is responsible for moisture and flavor, however, so a flavorful broth for basting should be provided to prevent the meat from being dry and tasteless.

Both chicken and turkey can be used as a minor ingredient in the same wide variety of dishes as beef or any other kind of meat. A roasted turkey of average size for a family of four always leaves ample meat to be used in various ways during subsequent days. With chicken, however, you may want to process a bigger, older bird directly to produce slices and chunks for use in combination with whole grains and vegetables. Here's a good way to do that:

SIMMERED CHICKEN

1 3-lb. roasting chicken, whole or cut in half or quarters (3 breasts may be used if all white meat is desired)	3 sprigs parsley
	1½ t. salt
	¼ t. paprika
5 c. cold water	4 whole allspice
1 stalk celery with leaves	4 whole peppercorns
1 med. onion, peeled and quartered	

Wash chicken; place in six-quart pot and add 5 cups cold water. Add remaining ingredients. Slowly bring to a boil, skimming foam from surface. Reduce heat, cover and simmer one hour or until chicken is tender.

Remove from heat. Lift out chicken, cool, and remove meat from bones. Cut into pieces of desired size.

Strain broth. Cool and refrigerate. When cold, skim off fat. . . . Freeze stock if not planning to use in a few days.

Yield: Approximately 2½ cups diced chicken. (From *The Rodale Cookbook.*)

Reversing A Trend

A well-established trend in natural foods has been the transformation of meat-containing recipes into vegetarian versions. Since the New American Cuisine is, however, omnivarian as well as vegetarian, you can just as easily take a vegetarian recipe the other way. In fact, reversing the trend is generally even easier because in most cases it is simply a matter of adding a little meat. This is a handy technique because many of the best whole foods recipes are vegetarian ones. Here is an example of a transformed vegetarian recipe using the cooked chicken from the recipe above:

[CHICKEN] CHOP SUEY

1 recipe for Chinese Sauce, doubled (see below)
2 c. broccoli, chopped small
3 c. mushrooms, sliced
1 c. chicken, cooked and sliced into thin strips

4 c. bean sprouts
1 c. carrots, grated
1 c. jicama or water chestnuts

Prepare Chinese sauce and when sautéing onions and celery, add the broccoli and carrots. When thickening is added, also add mushrooms, bean sprouts and chicken. Turn off and cover. It's ready to serve with brown rice or whole wheat noodles. It is important to serve immediately so your vegetables remain crisp.

Variations: substitute or add other vegetables; try some chopped walnuts or almonds on top, with chives or green onions; try some different Chinese and Japanese vegetables, such as Chinese cabbage, lotus root, bamboo shoots, or bok choy.

CHINESE SAUCE

¼ c. butter or corn oil
1 c. onion, chopped
2 cloves garlic, chopped
1 t. salt
⅛ t. pepper
1 c. celery, finely chopped

¾ c. water
⅓ c. cold water
2 t. soy sauce
2 T. arrowroot
1 t. honey

Melt butter or heat corn oil in a large skillet. Add onions, garlic, celery, salt, and pepper. Sauté for a minute, then add ¾ c. water. Cover and cook 4 minutes. Mix cold water, soy sauce, arrowroot, and honey. Make sure there are no lumps. Add to the above mixture and cook just to boiling point. Serve over whole grains, whole-grain pasta, leftover vegetables and/or meat, or combine with above recipe for [Chicken] Chop Suey.

(Adapted from *The Sunburst Farm Family Cookbook.*)

FISH

The popularity of fish in America has grown tremendously during the last twenty years. As I traveled America in the late fifties and early sixties, fish on restaurant menus was not commonplace; now it is, even in inland cities, which receive it under ice by air freight. We are becoming more appreciative of the wide variety of tastes and textures in seafood, more sophisticated regarding its many uses. Fish has

1. an even higher quality protein than meat;
2. much less fat than meat, and fish fat is unsaturated;
3. more vitamins and minerals than meat.

But tragically, and much to our collective shame, our oceans and particularly our inland and coastal waterways are polluted. Therefore I cannot endorse the uninhibited use of what *should* be an excellent type of food. Here are some important generalities to consider before deciding how fish fits into your diet.

1. The bigger the river or lake, the more likely it is to be polluted. Pollutants are concentrated in fish.
2. The bigger the fish, the more pollutants are likely to be concentrated in it. Therefore, a big fish, like a catfish, from big rivers like the Ohio, Missouri, or Mississippi, should be considered unfit for human consumption. The cleanest fish, on the other hand, are small ocean fish (cod, snapper, flounder, sole, bass, haddock, mackerel, perch, herring, sardines) and freshwater fish from remote lakes and cold swift streams.
3. Shellfish (shrimp, crab, crayfish) are bottom or "garbage" feeders, thus should be considered the most unclean of all—definitely a *high risk* food—until we collectively stop all the polluters from contaminating our inland and coastal waters.

Freshness

Fish must be *fresh.* Look for these signs of freshness:

—clear, bright eyes, protruding rather than sunken;
—bright red or pink, not dark-colored, gills and intestinal cavity;
—flesh that springs back when pressed;
—shiny skin and mild odor.

A sleazy commercial practice is to freeze fish when it doesn't sell fresh. To avoid this, look for the term "individually quick frozen" (I.Q.F.)—it was intended to be sold frozen and therefore was frozen right after being pulled from the water, sometimes right on the fishing boat itself. Truly fresh fish is best and fresh frozen is the only alternative that should be considered. (For more on buying fish, see Chapter 24.)

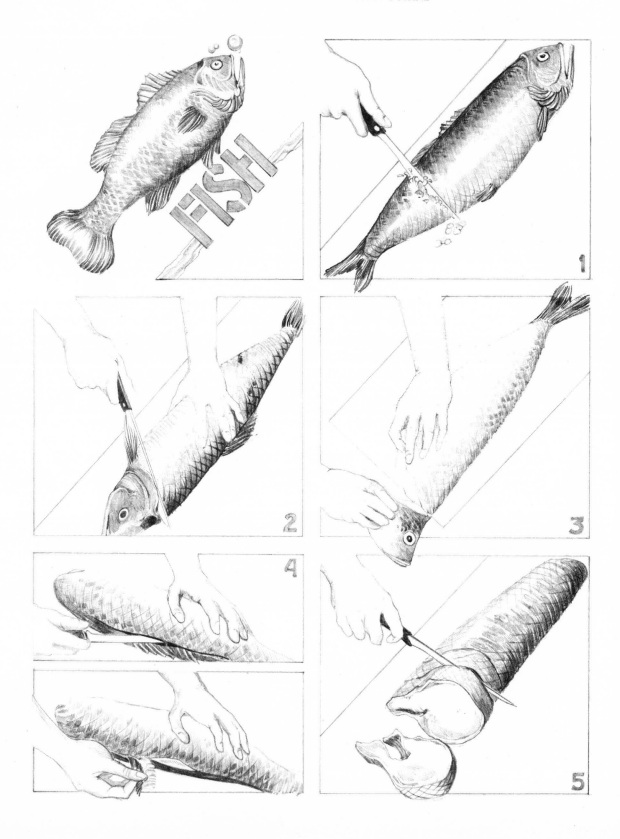

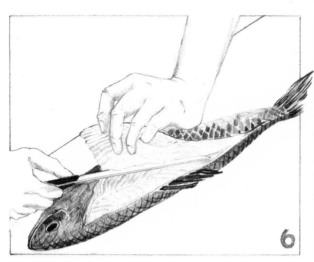 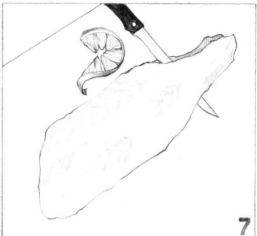

Cooking Fish

Generally speaking, Americans know much more about cooking meat than fish. We all know you can fry (sauté) fish; but what else can you do with it? You can bake fish, boil or steam or poach it, broil it, make sticks, balls and patties with fish, make soup or salad with it, and yes, even eat fish raw!

Buying a whole fish can often save even more than buying a whole chicken, sometimes as much as 50 percent. Here are the steps to clean and dress a whole fish:

1. Wash fish, remove scales by scraping from tail to head with the dull edge of your knife or a fish scaler.
2. Remove the entrails after cutting the entire length of the belly from vent to head; remove head by cutting up to collarbone, then breaking the collarbone over the edge of the table or cutting board.
3. Remove the dorsal or large back fin by cutting the flesh along each side and pulling the fin out. Never trim the fins off with shears or knife—the bones at the base of the fin will be left behind in the meat.
4. Wash fish thoroughly in cold running water. The fish is now dressed, or pan dressed, depending on its size.
5. For steaks, cut across the whole fish in sections ¾ of an inch thick.
6. To fillet: cut down the back of the fish from tail to head. Then cut down to the backbone just above the collarbone. Turn the knife flat and cut the flesh along the backbone to the tail, allowing the knife to run over the ribs. Lift off the entire side of the fish in one piece, freeing the fillet at the tail. Turn the fish over and repeat on the reverse side.
7. Skinning the fillet (optional): Lay fillet flat on the cutting board, skin down. Hold the tail end with your fingers, and cut through the flesh to the skin. Flatten the knife on the skin and cut the flesh away from the skin by running the knife forward while holding the free end of the skin firmly between your fingers.

Steps 1 through 5 will take only a little longer than cutting up a chicken. If you fillet the fish and skin the fillets, it will take considerably longer; but considering the large savings, processing your own fish is another highly advantageous tradeoff of time for money.

Different Approaches To Soup

Soup stock or broth can be made by boiling fish heads, tails and fins in water with some greens, a quartered onion, a bay leaf, and a little salt. Simmer about 45 minutes and strain. The clear broth can be consumed as is, or used to poach in. Add vegetables and chunks of fish, grains and/or potatoes for thickness.

In soups, clams, oysters, and mussels can be all handled the same way. Boil until the shells open, remove meat from shells, and return to broth. Add vegetables and potatoes, season to taste, boil until tender. Using clams, we call it "chowder" (add milk to broth for Boston or New England style, tomatoes to broth for Manhattan style); using oysters it is "stew." Mussels are usually an ingredient of *bouillabaisse*, a French seafood stew, made many different ways. The general approach is to use a fish broth for preparing such shellfish as mussels and scallops, then add seasoning (saffron especially), and a couple of kinds of fish and vegetables. Aside from the astronomically expensive saffron (it only takes a pinch, however), traditional bouillabaisse seasonings are fennel and thyme.

Boiling Or Steaming

Boiling is for stews. The big difference between making fish stews and meat stews is that fish cooks so much quicker than meat. Whereas in a meat stew you cook the meat for a long time before adding the vegetables, in a fish stew you start the vegetables before the fish. Start with fish broth if you have it. The cooking order is grains and root vegetables first, fish and tender vegetables next, leafy vegetables last.

Steaming is the preferred method when a special sauce is separately prepared to go over the fish (as opposed to actually cooking the fish *in* the sauce). Proceed as in steaming vegetables, which can also be steamed concurrently with the fish. Allow 10 to 15 minutes, depending on kind of fish and thickness of cut.

POACHED FISH

You can use fish or vegetable stock, any sauce of your choice, or water. Not much liquid is needed, just a shallow pool in a skillet. Bring to a boil, add fillets, steaks or chunks, cover and reduce to simmer; cook 5–10 minutes, or until tender, according to thickness of cut.

FISH STICKS, ETC.

2 c. cooked fish	1 or 2 eggs, beaten
2. c. cooked grain or mashed potatoes	salt, pepper, onion powder, garlic powder,
½ c. whole wheat flour	parsley, herbs
½ c. whole wheat bread crumbs	

Flake the fish. Mix with grain or potatoes and whole wheat flour. Add 1 beaten egg if using potatoes, 2 if using grain. Season to taste, mix thoroughly, adding just enough water to make mixture pliable (it should be as dry as possible, just wet enough to not be considered crumbly).

222

Shape as desired, dip in bread crumbs, sauté in a small amount of oil over medium heat 5 minutes each side or until thoroughly brown.

BAKED FISH IN HERB-BUTTER SAUCE

1½–2 lbs. fish fillets or steaks
½ c. butter
3 T. soy sauce
1 t. garlic
½ t. basil
1 t. oregano
¼ t. thyme
½ t. rosemary
¼ t. tarragon
¼ c. mushrooms, sliced
¼ c. green onions, chopped
1 lemon, sliced

Lay fillets in baking pan. In a small pan, melt butter, add soy sauce, garlic and herbs. Pour over fillets and bake at 375° for 8 minutes. Remove and put mushrooms, green onions, and lemon slices on top of fish. Baste until mushrooms and green onions are well-coated. Return to oven and bake 5 minutes. (Adapted from *The Sunburst Farm Family Cookbook*.)

BROILED FILLETS OR STEAKS

2 lbs. fillets or steaks
½ c. onion, chopped
1 recipe Barbecue Sauce (see below)

Prepare Barbecue Sauce. Lay fish on a cookie sheet, put onions on top and cover with sauce. Put under broiler and cook about 3–5 minutes on each side. Cooking time depends on thickness of fish, up to 15 minutes for thicker pieces. It is best to have a thicker piece—¾ to 1½ inches. Broil 3–5 inches from heat.

BARBECUE SAUCE

½ c. ketchup
¼ c. molasses
¼ c. apple cider vinegar
¼ t. mustard
½ t. garlic powder
1 T. soy sauce

Mix ingredients and pour over food before cooking or steep food in sauce. (Adapted from *The Sunburst Farm Family Cookbook*.)

SEAFOOD SALAD

2 c. fish cut in 1-inch squares
¼ c. celery, chopped fine
½ t. basil
¼ c. green onion, chopped
¼ c. mayonnaise
½ t. kelp
1 t. soy sauce
½ t. dry mustard

Poach fish, allow to cool, then add celery, green onions, mayonnaise, and seasonings.

This is good in pocket sandwiches (pita bread), stuffed in tomatoes or avocadoes. (Adapted from *The Sunburst Farm Family Cookbook*.)

Eating Raw Fish

This is one of those, "you won't believe how good it is until you've tried it" ideas—the usual reply to, "Yuck, how could anyone eat *raw fish*?!" The Japanese do (sashimi) and the Chileans do (seviche) and after overcoming my prejudice, I do, too—and find it delicious. It should be the fillet of large deep water fish, such as marlin, swordfish or albacore tuna (the Japanese prize the best and freshest tuna for sashimi), as fresh as possible (and not unless it *is* fresh). Skin and cut fillet into strips about ¼- inch thick.

Marinate seviche in the refrigerator for several hours. The marinade must contain either lime juice, lemon juice or vinegar—lime juice is by far the best.

A good seviche marinade formula is three parts lime juice to one part olive oil with some minced onion and garlic and chopped tarragon and parsley. Make enough to completely cover the fish. Serve on a bed of lettuce. Try mixing it with chopped, fresh tomatoes, green onion, and cilantro.

The Japanese dip sashimi, which is not marinated, into a mixture of soy sauce and horseradish, and accent it with shredded raw vegetables. Although raw fish is not likely to be inexpensive, it is usually eaten in small quantities.

Fish is every bit as versatile as meat. In fact, many of the ideas previously presented for meat and poultry can be adapted to fish. The main things to remember when combining it with grains, beans and vegetables is that you want it filleted (boneless) for these uses and that it will need very little cooking time.

22   Snacks and Beverages

SNACKING

A few nights ago I went to a movie that started at 7:30 p.m. It's safe to assume that almost everybody in the theater had already eaten dinner, as I had. And yet, almost everyone was snacking: big cups of pop, buckets of popcorn, candy bars, ice cream. Why? It couldn't have had much to do with hunger. I think we've programmed ourselves to associate visual treats with taste treats. You look around and see hundreds of people staring at a screen and stuffing their faces and it's hard to escape the conclusion that we're just reacting automatically: *movie = snack*.

Now TV sets have turned all our homes into theaters. Does the same *movie = snack* button work in our homes, at least to some degree? Certainly television commercials go to innovative, clever, expensive lengths to persuade us to snack; we will, they would have us believe, be missing a great experience if we don't. Advertising persuasion and habit have to be significant reasons why we are a nation of snackers.

I only partially subscribe to the you-are-what-you-eat school of thought. You are also what you think and feel, what you have inherited in your genes and absorbed from your social and natural environments. Furthermore, we are also subject to *super*natural influences we know almost nothing about. In spite of all that, the food we eat exerts a profound influence on who we are because it is so fundamental to our health, which in turn influences everything from our energy level, to the clarity of our thinking, to the longevity of our lives.

Am I leading up to a declaration of war on the practice of snacking? No. There are two valid reasons for snacking: hunger and pleasure. But when we snack, we should snack on food, not foodless food. Most especially, we should see that our children are nourished by their snacks. Sometimes our children seem absolutely ravenous to us because their bodies send signals for needed nutrients that are much stronger than the signals adults ordinarily experience. The tragedy is that most American snack stuff does more harm than good. But we can do something about it. First let's see what the government says about snacking (from *Food* published by the FDA):

Different snacks for different people:
Who you are and *what* you do has a lot to do with choosing snacks that are right for you.
Start with small children. Often they just can't consume the amount of food in regular meals that will add up to their daily nutritional needs. A slice of cheese, a wheat cracker, or a banana eaten at mid-morning or mid-afternoon could help supply the added energy to keep them from pooping out.
And teenagers—you *know* how much they eat! Growing, active bodies need extra helpings of foods which provide protein, vitamins, and minerals as well as added energy. A nice big slice of pizza with cheese, meat, and vegetable toppings is a sure way to satisfy a huge appetite.

Senior citizens can benefit from snacking too. Problems with chewing or digestion sometimes interfere with regular eating habits. Snacks, which can be eaten anytime, let them choose their own personal eating schedule.

Good Snackers THINK AHEAD:

When you're hungry, you're likely to grab the first munchies in sight. The trick is to have the right snacking foods handy. You can't go wrong stocking up with foods like fresh fruits, juices, yogurt, milk, cheese, nuts, whole grain bread and crackers.

Fruit For Snacks

It is extremely important to this discussion to remember that snack foods are the worst offenders against anyone trying to hold a lid on food expenditures. Apart from ingredients which are either questionable or unquestionably harmful, snack foods have *exorbitant* price tags relative to nutritional value. At home, you can change that dramatically.

Fruit for snacking is the closest thing I will have to an easy answer in this whole book. It adds yet another virtue if you follow the season in your fruit purchases; fruit in season is usually inexpensive. Through the autumn and winter the inexpensive fruits are limited mainly to apples, pears, citrus and bananas; but that's not exactly deprivation. Then in the summer things get exciting—cherries, apricots, peaches, nectarines, plums, grapes, melons, berries, even more, depending on locale.

Buying fresh fruit in season is important for reasons beyond simplicity and economy, though they are reasons enough. Our own biological rhythm follows the seasons. We are drawn to the sweetness and juiciness when the weather is hot. We are energized by the naturally occurring sugars, cleansed by the enzyme-laden juices. As with raw vegetables, the greatest nutritional virtues of fresh fruits are enzymes. Their other nutritional virtues are that, in general, they are good sources of vitamin C and fiber. It is the combination of vitamin C, fiber, and enzymes that is responsible for fresh fruit's reputation as a cleansing food. But the cleansing action of fresh fruit is largely destroyed by cooking: of the four major nutrients of fruit—fruit sugar, enzymes, vitamin C, and fiber—enzymes and vitamin C are destroyed by heat. To benefit fully from fresh fruit, eat it raw.

An interesting way to eat raw fruit is in fruit salad. Fruit salads are limited only by what's available and the range of your imagination. It is best, however, to apply your imagination with restraint—the most successful fruit salads tend towards simplicity. As Karen MacNeil points out in *The Book of Whole Foods*, when a great number of fruits are mixed together, individual fruits lose their distinct and dominant characteristics. To allow them to retain their personalities, she recommends using three fruits with similar characteristics: bananas, pears, and grapes (all sweet and soft); oranges, grapefruit, and pineapples (all acidic, watery, and fibrous); nectarines, plums, and cherries (all fleshy, juicy, sweet/sour).

Fruit In Combination

Here is one way to look at food:

A) *Complex carbohydrates:* grains, beans, vegetables.
B) *Concentrated protein and fat:* meat, fish, fowl, dairy products, nuts, seeds, salad, and cooking oils.
C) *Concentrated sugars:* fruits, sweeteners.

Most of the A and B foods require from two to five hours to digest and combine more or less well, depending on the person. But most C foods spend no more than fifteen minutes in the stomach. The problem comes when C foods are combined with A or B foods. Instead of being quickly released into the small intestine, the C foods become trapped with the foods that require more digestion time. If there is too much sugar mixed with complex carbohydrates, concentrated protein and fat; fermentation is the result. One can often taste fermentation in the unpleasant belching after a too-complicated meal. Fermentation is a major cause of belching, halitosis, and flatulence.

Turning Desserts Into Snacks

Rather than eat dessert right after dinner, wait an hour or two. While watching TV or taking a break from reading or homework, have dessert. In this way, dessert becomes a snack. This is really intelligent eating—you digest and assimilate the food better because you have less quantity and simpler combinations of food in your stomach at one sitting.

Delicious and healthful jello can be made using fruit juice and honey with gelatin, then adding fresh fruit to the mixture as it begins to jell.

You can mix fruit with yogurt. Even though yogurt is a dairy product, its protein is largely predigested and so usually does not lead to digestive fermentation.

You can stew fruit with honey to make compotes and you can bake apples.

You can puree fruit in your blender to freeze with yogurt and honey or to make "freezer" ice cream or sherbet.

You can make "smoothies" in your blender with fruit and fruit juice. The smoothie mixture can be frozen; when partially frozen, sticks can be inserted for popsicles.

In addition to fruit, try egg custard, rice pudding, milk puddings, etc.

Simple Dessert Snacks

GELATIN-APPLE SALAD

1 pkg. unflavored gelatin
1 c. hot water
1 c. apple juice

1 c. grated apple
½ c. seedless grapes

Dissolve gelatin in hot water; add apple. Put in refrigerator until gelatin begins to set. Add grated apple and grapes. Return to refrigerator until gelatin has molded. (From *The Sunburst Farm Family Cookbook.*)

BAKED APPLES

6 apples	2 T. butter
¼ c. raisins	2 t. cinnamon
¼ c. walnuts	1 t. nutmeg
¼ c. honey	½ t. coriander

Core apples and place in a baking dish. In a small pan, melt butter, honey, and spices. Fill each apple with raisins and walnuts. Pour sauce over. Bake at 350° for 40 minutes or until done. Baste a few times during baking. (Adapted from *The Sunburst Farm Family Cookbook*.)

For another snack-dessert recipe, see BAKED CUSTARD, page 269.

Dried Fruit

Dried fruit adds variety to our winter months. If you compare the price of dried fruit with fresh, there are two things to consider: (1) we are paying processors and middlemen who have no hand in bringing us fresh fruits (see Chapter 34 on drying your own fruit); (2) since most of the moisture has been removed, dried fruit is much more concentrated, so it is *worth* more.

To lessen the cost of using dried fruit, hydrate it—that is, soak it in water to flesh it out. This reduces the cost by "stretching" the dried fruit. In mixtures of dried fruit and nuts, keep the cost down by keeping the proportions of high-priced nuts down and the proportions of peanuts, soynuts, and sunflower seeds (medium-priced) up. (Use raw or dry roasted peanuts and soynuts to avoid unnecessary oil and salt.)

NATURAL READYMADES

Natural foods and health food stores, supermarkets, and even drugstores, increasingly offer an ever-widening assortment of natural snacks. But please remember that the word "natural" is being used these days to hawk everything from beer to shampoo. The word "natural" on the label doesn't guarantee anything, not even naturalness, when you go beyond the obvious things like dried fruits, nuts, and seeds. To deal sensibly with confectionery items you have to be a label reader.

Remember that ingredients are listed in quantity order. If the first ingredient is a sweetener such as brown sugar or corn syrup or if three of the first five ingredients are three different sweeteners, what you have in your hand isn't very natural. The first ingredient should be a *food*—nuts, seeds, dried fruit, peanut butter, milk powder. As you move down the ingredient list, you don't want to see sugar, corn syrup, or even brown sugar.

Carob is a highly desirable ingredient in natural confections. Carob is often referred to as a chocolate substitute and is used as such. But it would be fairer to think of it as a food in its own right, a substitute for nothing, really a much healthier choice of food than chocolate. Chocolate is processed with harsh alkalis and contains *theobromine*, both toxic to the liver. It's also so bitter as to be inedible without being heavily sweetened. Carob contains 50 percent natural sugars and needs little if any sweetener to make it palatable. In contrast to the heavy flavor of chocolate, carob is delicate. It is also a nutritious food, having significant quantities of vitamin B and minerals. It is actually the seed pod from the tree of the same name, also known as "St. John's Bread." The only processing it needs is drying, roasting, and grinding. Carob is not second-rate chocolate; it is first-rate food—look for it in natural confections.

When you're looking at the various readymade cookie and pastry items you might buy for snacking, the same rules apply. Where flour is concerned, *unbleached* is a red flag: the fact that white flour is unbleached doesn't mean it isn't white. The lack of *bright* whiteness because of the lack of bleach means next to nothing; 99 percent of the damage is done by refining the wheat into white flour, 1 percent by bleaching. The label should read "whole wheat pastry flour."

ICE CREAM

Natural ingredient ice cream presents a quantity problem. Ice cream is an extremely high-fat, high-sugar food, no matter what the sweetener. As such, it should be eaten in moderation. If you are sedentary or overweight it would be best to eat ice cream rarely; if you have heart or circulatory problems, it would be best to never eat it at all.

The bigger problem with ice cream is determining the quality of 98 percent of what is offered. It's one of those food products that usually doesn't have an ingredient list because it falls into the group covered by FDA "Standards of Identity." You could obtain a copy of the standards for ice cream from Washington and still not know what's in an unlabeled ice cream because the standards only tell you what's *allowed*. The only way you could know which of over a hundred allowable ingredients is in the ice cream in question is to ask the manufacturer and hope he answers truthfully and completely.

Ice cream can be a veritable frozen soup of chemicals. Some ice cream hardly melts. That's due to dozens of allowable thickening and stabilizing agents. Did you assume that ice cream was "rich" because it had a lot of cream in it? Don't be too sure. It probably had the minimum of cream and the maximum of one of a dozen chemical emulsifiers. Expensive ice cream doesn't necessarily reflect high cream content either; it often merely reflects the use of an expensive emulsifier and an elegant package. There are also ten different chemicals ". . . used ostensibly to maintain the uniformity of ice cream from batch to batch; their presence may reflect the use of slightly soured milk or cream" (*Eater's Digest*). The bright green, pink, or whatever color? If it's artificial, they're not required to tell you so.

The manufacturer of an ice cream with no ingredient listing doesn't want to scare you away from his product with all those long, unpronounceable names. You might suspect that some of those five-syllable tongue twisters might twist more than your tongue; after all, some of them are used for making plastic, shoes, and paint thinner. You might not want to take a chance on stuff like that. The first rule of food manufacturing is, what you don't know won't hurt you.

The answer to such irresponsibility and arrogance may not be to give up ice cream but it certainly should be to give up frozen chemical soup. And don't be fooled by phrases like "made with real cream." What else is in it? If they won't tell you what they propose to feed you, let the stuff sit until hell freezes over. Looking for ice cream that's fit to eat should lead you to one that lists ingredients.

like this:	*not like this:*
fresh cream	milk fat
fresh milk	nonfat milk
honey or maple syrup	sugar
whole fresh eggs	corn syrup
natural flavoring	whey
	guar gum
	sodium carboxymethylcellulose
	Polysorbate 80
	carageenin
	artificial flavors

A quart of left-hand column ice cream will usually weigh at least two pounds; a quart of right-hand column ice cream will generally weigh no more than one pound, two ounces. The difference? Air—up to 50 percent air is legal, therefore normal. If a pint of ice cream weighs only nine ounces net, a quart weighs eighteen, a half gallon thirty-six, or a gallon seventy-two ounces, you are buying half air. A natural-ingredient ice cream, perhaps weighing twice as much, may not really be more expensive and will have the advantage of being real food. (For making your own ice cream, see Chapter 29.)

BEVERAGES

Sweet And Bubblies

We love drinks that are sweet and bubbly, even though we usually go for a drink of water to *really* quench our thirst soon after drinking a soft drink, and even though we know the soft-drink companies are drowning us in sugar, artificial sweeteners, artificial flavors, and colors. There are natural alternatives to conventional soft drinks, available in natural and health food stores or supermarket health food sections, distinguished by honey and fructose as sweeteners and the absence of artificial ingredients. You may decide they're too expensive to fit into your budget, but at least they prove that a soft drink doesn't have to be artificial to be refreshing.

Where sweet and bubbly drinks are concerned, it can be simple to make your own. Start with carbonated water and add pure fruit concentrate to taste. Next add honey syrup—honey warmed in a pan and diluted with enough water to make a syrup consistency—to taste. Homemade soft drinks are as simple as that. You can make syrup out of fresh juices such as orange, lemon, lime, or combinations of them, mixing juice with honey syrup. You can get a "cream" soda effect making a syrup of honey, molasses (not too much), and vanilla. Homemade soft drinks can be much more fun than readymade because you can make flavors that are commercially unheard of: Blueberry? Raspberry? Orange/apple?

You can carbonate fruit juice with a carbonation machine but the only ones I've seen have been imported from Europe. It seems to me that one would need an intense love affair with carbonated drinks to justify their cost.

If you don't demand the carbonation of your sweet and bubbly drink be really fierce, an even simpler alternative to soda pop is to mix fruit juice and carbonated water more or less half and half. To my taste, some fruit juices are too sweet to be drinkable. Diluting them with carbonated water transforms them into something I can enjoy. A sweet tooth is like anything else you have acquired: you can lose it. And the less you indulge it, the sooner the loss will occur.

Fruit Juices

The best alternatives to soft drinks are fruit juices. In recent years the demand for fruit juices has expanded greatly but the supply has not, and the cost of glass has soared, and so fruit juices that once were inexpensive no longer are. However, ounce for ounce, canned pineapple and grape juices are still cheaper than most pop. Bottled apple juice, in the same price range as pop, is the most popular juice sold in natural and health food stores. The level of quality is higher when the juice is pressed from organically grown apples.

A question I have often encountered is whether apple juice and cider are the same thing. No. Apple cider is fresh, unpasteurized apple juice, capable of becoming hard, or alcoholic, and, if left a little longer, of turning into vinegar. Pasteurization defines it as apple juice, guaranteeing that it will not turn into hard cider or vinegar and will keep up to a year in the bottle. All canned and bottled fruit juices are pasteurized, but need refrigeration after opening to prevent them from souring.

Unfiltered fruit juices are nutritionally superior to those which have been clarified. The pulp left in unfiltered fruit juices contains minerals, fiber, and *pectin*. Pectin, familiar as a jelling agent in jellies, is a carbohydrate that is beneficial to the intestines. Clarification is usually achieved by adding diatomaceous earth and special enzymes that act to coagulate the pulp, then filtering the mass from the juice. The clarity of this thin juice is achieved at the expense of both food value and flavor.

Much unfiltered apple juice is sold blended with other fruits such as papaya, mango, guava, and various berries. These other juices are generally from puree, concentrate, or nectar. Puree undergoes the least processing, being strained and frozen fresh or pasteurized and canned. Driving off the water from juice yields concentrates. Nectar is made by thinning and sweetening puree. The absence of sugar, preservatives, artificial colorings, and flavorings distinguishes a natural nectar from most of those found on supermarket shelves. The high cost of these thick liquids account for the high price of apple-and-other-juice blends. The alternatives are to stick with less expensive pure juice, use the blends sparingly, or do your own juicing (see Chapter 30).

Orange Juice

One hundred years ago most Americans had never even heard of orange juice. But oranges are prolific, colorful, sweet, ship and store well. Of such things are industries made and within the last fifty years entrepreneurial ingenuity has made orange juice an American institution. During that time gum disease has increased tremendously and there is a virtually unnoticed connection to our new citrus institution.

Pyorrhea—where the gums at the roots of the teeth become infected, pus forms, and the teeth loosen—is almost always preceded by bleeding gums, gingivitis being the milder stage. The condition is created gradually and people commonly ignore the bleeding gums, considering it a mere annoyance. Dentists and dental hygenists rightly tell us that improper cleaning is a major cause and encourage us to floss every day—excellent advice. But they rarely tell us we shouldn't drink orange juice every day.

I know coming out against orange juice will seem almost as bad as being against motherhood and apple pie. But I like orange juice too and it's not that you should never eat another orange or let a sip of orange juice pass your lips. The problem is quantity, the daily drinking, year after year.

Citrus juices contain a great deal of citric acid (which is not the same as ascorbic acid, vitamin C). Citric acid is a solvent for the mineral calcium. So in persistent drinking of citrus juices you are subjecting your teeth to an acid bath that bit by bit, day by day, dissolves calcium from your teeth. Perhaps calcium metabolism replaces some of the eroded calcium, but not all of it. Gradually the substance of the teeth suffers critic acid erosion, and space between teeth and gums is created. Gums bleed because tartar forms on the teeth where the gum tissue becomes loosened from its contact with the teeth, the tartar irritating the gum tissue.

People are usually into their forties or fifties before the erosion is advanced enough to become a severe problem. But bleeding gums should serve as a signal to wean yourself from the orange juice habit. (Coffee, milk and orange juice, liquids that are consumed together at millions of American breakfasts every day, constitute a terribly incompatible mixture.) Many people receive a much earlier signal—citrus is one of the most common of all food allergies.

Herbs For Bargains

Any herb tea you like as a hot beverage can be drunk as a cold one. A box of twenty-four tea bags might well cost more than a six-pack of pop but it will make the equivalent of four six-packs. If you buy the herbs in bulk pack you can reduce their cost by as much as half. If you buy bulk herbs unpackaged in natural foods stores, you can reduce their cost by half again. Make a quart or half-gallon at a time. Mint is almost universally popular, so let's say you want a quart of cold peppermint or spearmint tea. Bring the water to a boil, remove from heat, dump in a heaping tablespoon of mint, stir, cover, and let steep for five minutes. Strain through a fine-mesh strainer, sweeten, and refrigerate. Drink it as is or serve it with ice and a slice of lemon, lime or orange. If you drink it iced, you may want the tea made stronger—a little more herb, steeped a little longer. Use approximately one teaspoon of herb per cup of water.

If you want to have more than a quart of cold tea on hand, the most practical method is to make your quart extremely concentrated and dilute it with water and ice. This not only makes sensible use of refrigerator space but allows for easy alteration of the strength of the beverage to accommodate individual preferences. (See Chapter 23 for more on herb teas.)

Hot Drinks

Whereas the New American Cuisine would eliminate commercial soft drinks entirely, it would greatly *reduce* the consumption of coffee. The main fault with American coffee drinking lies with the *amount*. I've talked with many people for whom eight cups of coffee per day is normal. Normal and unwise: bad for the liver, bad for the heart, bad for the nervous system. "Oh, but I don't notice a thing," they'll say. "I sleep like a baby." Yes, so do cigarette smokers and alcoholics. "But coffee's no drug." No? Then let's see you give it up.

Honest, copious coffee drinkers admit they have a habit; they're addicted. The drug in coffee is caffeine. According to recent evidence published by Harvard University, coffee drinkers suffer at least twice the incidence of pancreatic cancer as non-coffee drinkers, the rate directly proportional to the amount of coffee consumed. But it doesn't correlate with caffeine consumption—tea drinkers don't suffer any more pancreatic cancer than any other group. It may correlate with the heavy use of pesticides on coffee plantations, since most pesticides are soluble in oil and coffee has a high oil content. It may also be connected to rancid oil, since most coffee is not used freshly ground. Since the oil in coffee beans is highly volatile, rancidity is virtually guaranteed within a couple of days after grinding. Vacuum packing prevents rancidity but once the can is opened, freezing the grounds is the only way to prevent it.

Caffeine may not be the culprit in pancreatic cancer, but an article in *The New England Journal of Medicine* (July 1973) named caffeine as being responsible for 60 percent more heart attacks at a consumption level of one to five cups of coffee per day and a 120 percent increase when consumption exceeds five cups per day. Robert Picker, M.D., Director of the Center for Holistic and Nutritional Medicine, Berkeley, California, listed some other effects of caffeine in his article "The Caffeine Rush" (*Lifestyles* magazine, November, 1981), including:

Constantly elevated cholesterol, blood fats, and blood pressure cause accelerated hardening of the arteries, leading to heart attacks and strokes.

Headaches are common if a caffeine addict is without this stimulation for a few hours.

Increased incidence of heart rhythm irregularities is reported.

Increased acid secretion from the stomach, causing indigestion and ulcers.

Pregnancy: data continues to accumulate demonstrating increased rate of miscarriages, premature births, and birth defects among women coffee drinkers. Warnings for pregnant women are now appearing in supermarkets.

Fibrocystic Breast Disease is aggravated and perhaps caused by coffee.

Psychological effects: excess caffeine consumption can cause insomnia, anxiety, and panic attacks, depression, and aggravation of schizophrenic psychosis. . . .

Dr. Picker explains the caffeine mechanism like this:

The body reacts to caffeine as it does to an emergency stress situation: the adrenal gland secretes increased adrenalin, blood pressure and heart rate go up, as do fats and sugar in the blood. Putting the body under this continual stress is like beating a tired horse. It may run faster for a little while, but the ultimate breakdown will come that much sooner. . . . Constant adrenal stress eventually leads to adrenal exhaustion. . . . As the effects wear off, blood sugar drops, often leading to hypoglycemia, and leading to a feeling of fatigue. This often leads to compulsive drinking of caffeinated beverages in an attempt to avoid this let-down. This creates a physical addiction and the constant stress of arousal-stimulation.

Copious coffee drinking is really suicidal, albeit a slow form of suicide; prudence dictates a cup of coffee a day, with two being the sensible maximum, and none being most sensible of all. Caffeine withdrawal symptoms can last as long as ten days but can be alleviated by frequent doses of vitamin C and natural B complex.

Warning: It seems quite possible that the pancreatic cancer associated with coffee is related to the chemicals used to instantize coffee or from interaction of those chemicals with the pesticide residues and rancid oils. If you're going to drink coffee, I suggest you avoid the instant type.

Decaffeinated coffee can also be dangerous. Until quite recently, trichlorethylene was a solvent frequently used to decaffeinate coffee. Then it was banned because it has been proved a carcinogen. But how many tons of it were consumed in the decades before it was banned? Anybody drinking decaffeinated coffee for health reasons would have been doing their health less harm by drinking

CAFFEINE FOR YOUR KIDS

When my friends and I were growing up, we weren't allowed to drink coffee or tea. Our parents didn't know all there was to know about caffeine, but they knew enough to know that it would be even worse for growing people than for the fully grown. But keeping caffeine out of your kids is much tougher than it was when I was growing up in the forties and early fifties because the number of brands of soft drinks has proliferated so greatly and the consumption of them has become so enormous (37 gallons per year for each American). So popular are they now that, abomination of abominations, they have even become a common breakfast beverage for our young. Look at the caffeine doses per bottle of the following brands, according to *Consumer Reports*:

Soft Drink	Milligrams of Caffeine
Diet Mr. Pibb	52
Mountain Dew	52
Mello Yello	51
Tab	44
Sunkist Orange	42
Shasta Cola	42
Dr. Pepper	38
Diet Dr. Pepper	37
Pepsi	37
Royal Crown Cola	36
Diet Rite Cola	34
Diet Pepsi	34
Coca Cola	34
Mr. Pibb	33
For comparison, the average cup of	
Coffee, brewed	100
Coffee, instant	53
Tea, brewed	45

The combination of caffeine and sugar in soft drinks is particularly deadly because they are both addictive. People breaking caffeine and sugar habits suffer withdrawal symptoms, not as strongly as alcohol and drug addicts, but far too strongly nevertheless, especially when we are talking about children. Once the child is weaned from the caffeine and sugar habits, it is usually like having birthed a new child at the age of eight, ten, or twelve—hyperactive and psychotic behavior drops away, as does the frequency of many physical illnesses (see also pages 43 ff., *The Sugar Story*).

natural, fresh-ground coffee. How long will it be before the petroleum-based solvents still being used for decaffeinating are banned?

Even unhealthful food is usually better in its natural form. If something is decaffeinated, or "de" anything else, we need to ask, what is it "de-ed" *with*? An uncommon method of decaffeinating coffee uses steam; if you're going to drink decaffeinated coffee, you should know whether steam or a chemical solvent is used. If it's a chemical solvent, expect to be told that it isn't harmful, of course.

Grain Coffee

Grain "coffee" or "cereal beverage" is widely available in powdered form that dissolves quickly like instant coffee. But if you're looking for a really inexpensive hot beverage, make your own grain coffee. Use rye, wheat, or soy grits for this purpose; a mixture of two-thirds rye or wheat grits and one-third soy grits is good. Dry roast them in a skillet, stirring constantly so they don't burn, until they are dark brown (coffee colored). Boil the roasted grits, two teaspoons per cup of water, for about ten minutes. Add a bit of chicory root for a more bitter flavor. Strain and serve.

Perhaps a better option than replacing coffee with hot drinks that resemble coffee is to replace it with things that don't resemble it at all. That brings us back to herbs. There are dozens of possibilities. Herbs can be drunk for pleasure, as well as for their medicinal effects. Experiment, find out what you like, notice the subtle effects of various herbs. They are almost without exception less expensive than coffee and almost none have caffeine (matté, also called "Brazilian coffee," is an exception). Lack of caffeine, however, does not mean herbs are innocuous; the pharmacopoeia of modern medicine is replete with herbs and herbal extracts. Refer to the recommended reading list for books on herbal medicine.

ALCOHOL: PROS AND CONS

Both wine and beer can be healthy in moderation. Dan Georgakas points out in *The Methuselah Factors* that studies of long-lived peoples show that two drinks a day is healthier than not drinking at all and studies at Yale University agreed, showing that two drinks a day provided optimum health and performance with the levels plunging sharply when the two-drink mark is passed.

To understand the delicate balance between "good" and "bad" drinking, it helps to have a rudimentary understanding of alcohol metabolism. It has a twofold effect: first, it stimulates the liver to release blood sugar, which can give the drinker that almost instant lift. Secondly, alcohol itself is broken down in the liver to produce an energy-rich acetate compound, explaining why the quick lift is not followed by an immediate letdown. This double effect is particularly rewarding to anyone whose nutritional reserves are low.

The paradox of alcohol is that its overuse leads to the very exhaustion of nutritional reserves it seems to alleviate: every bit of alcohol drunk creates nutritional metabolic demands for vitamins, minerals, and enzymes. The alcoholic finds himself in a nutritional bind in that he is simultaneously starving himself and anesthetizing his ability to recognize his needs.

Anyone who chooses wrong foods for his metabolic type may consistently feel "down" and be especially susceptible to the elevating effects of alcohol. Ironically, the more undernourished you are, the more alcohol you can tolerate. To the poorly nourished, inefficient metabolism, alcohol can easily become a physically and psychologically dangerous drug; the addict "can really hold his liquor." To the well-nourished, efficient metabolism, a drink or two may be pleasant, but more is literally sickening, producing headache, sweating, perhaps nausea, maybe even vomiting. The well-nourished person can't hold his liquor; moreover, he doesn't want to.

Beer

The word "natural" often appears in the marketing of beer. The problem has been that we have had no full disclosure law for alcoholic beverages. That is supposed to change as of January, 1983, unless the Treasury Department bows to industry pressure to rescind the regulation. Assuming the regulation holds, the brewers will have to tell us *everything* in that "natural" beer, not just the ingredients they want us to know about. Decision time: change the formula or change the advertising?*

"Additive-Free Beer" in *East West Journal*, August, 1981, was written by Charlie Papazain, president of the American Homebrewers Association, for seekers of the real thing. While water, malted barley, hops, and yeast are the four traditional ingredients of natural beer, Papazain says the Department of Agriculture has been allowing *fifty-two* other ingredients. These legally hidden additives have allowed brewers to get away with wording such as "Natural beer made only from water, malted barley, hops, and yeast" on their labels. Papazain's list of additive-free brewers:

Brewery	*Country of Origin*
Anchor Brewing Company	U.S.
Bamberg	Luxembourg
Boulder Brewing Company	U.S.
Cardinal	Switzerland
Cooper & Sons, Ltd.	Australia
Diekirch	Luxembourg
Guiness-Harp Corp.	Ireland
Hacker-Pschorr	Germany
Hofbrau Bavaria	Germany
Kiekirch	Luxembourg
Kulmbacher Monkshof	Germany
Lederer-Brau	Germany
Lowenbrau (import)	Germany
Lowenbrau, Zurich	Switzerland
New Albion Brewery	U.S.
Pilsner Urquell	Czechoslovakia
River City Brewing Company	U.S.
Sierra Nevada Brewing Company	U.S.
Spaten	Germany
William S. Newman Company	U.S.
Wurzberger	Germany

*The above was written in 1982. This footnote is being written in January, 1983, at which time I am displeased to report that the Treasury Department did bow to industry pressure. The regulation has been rescinded. When will consumers ever be able to find out what has been added to beer and wine? Never, if the makers continue to have their way.

Any German beer made in compliance with the "Bavarian Purity Decree" is pure, but in any case we are not looking at a list of widely distributed beers. Nor are they cheap, averaging about ninety cents a bottle. You can, however, match their purity for about fifteen cents a bottle by making your own. The American Homebrewers Association publishes *Zymurgy*, a magazine devoted to the art of brewing. For subscription information, write the American Homebrewers Association, Box 287, Boulder, CO 80306. For information about the fifty-two additives in beer, enclose a stamped, self-addressed envelope and fifty cents.

(For wine, see pp. 120.)

23 Babies and Children

BREAST MILK

Human breast milk is the perfect food for human infants. Or is it? It's a question nobody should have to ask. If they did, it should be answerable by one word: yes. Unfortunately, wallowing in the contemporary flood of industrial chemicals, the one word answer might also be no. Or maybe. Or it depends . . . Parents trying to decide how best to feed their babies are faced with a dilemma.

It has long been known that insecticide residues such as DDT have been found concentrated in breast milk. More recently, breast milk has also been found to be contaminated by PCBs. PCBs (polychlorinated biphenyls) are chlorinated hydrocarbons of the same family as DDT, chlordane, and dieldrin, but are even more toxic and much slower to break down than the insecticides. And the purity of breast milk is not only dependent on the purity of the environment but on choices the mother makes on a daily basis. Nicotine from cigarettes, medical drugs, social drugs, alcohol, caffeine, and theobromine from chocolate all migrate from the bloodstream into the milk, posing a threat to the baby's chances of normal development.

Marcella Mosher and Greg Moyer, in *PCBs and Breast Milk* (*Nutrition Action*, November 1980) answer the dilemma with an affirmation of breast-feeding:

> Despite these ominous signs, [Dr. James Allen, a leading researcher in this area] does not suggest women return to bottle-feeding their babies: "The values of breast-feeding outweigh the deleterious effects . . . I would advise my wife to breast-feed unless we lived in an area of high exposure to PCBs."

Contact regional offices of the EPA or state health departments for information on PCB testing. Mosher and Moyer go on to write about the benefits of breast milk:

> During the 1970's scientists undertook new studies to better understand the attributes of breast milk. They discovered that mother's milk contains:
>
> —a thyroid hormone which babies cannot produce for themselves;
> —adequate amounts of iron and zinc, long thought to be deficient in breast milk;
> —antibodies and white blood cells to fend off disease.

For the mother, nursing immediately after birth acts as an anti-hemorrhaging agent while the uterus contracts. Nor is any drug, such as DES (a carcinogen), necessary to relieve the discomfort of breasts temporarily engorged with milk.

Of all the benefits claimed for breast-feeding, the ones least susceptible to measurement are the psychological and emotional. Through skin contact and sensory stimulation, a woman who enjoys nursing may be passing on a real sense of security and attachment to her baby . . .

264

Eggs are often recommended for Baby because breast milk is low in iron. But we should know by now that it is always a mistake to attempt to correct nature's "mistakes." Research in the 1970s revealed that iron and zinc, previously thought deficient in breast milk, are actually there in sufficient quantities. (*Nutrition Action*, Center for Science in the Public Interest, November, 1980.) The milk of every species is *the* perfect food for the infant of that species.

WHAT'S IN BABY'S BOTTLE

The principal baby food of the New American Cuisine remains breast milk—for at least three months and up to a year (or even more, depending on mother and baby). But what of the mother who must return to work after three months, or for some other reason can't nurse or must quit nursing early?

As we all know, the most common substitute for breast milk is cow's milk. Unfortunately, it is also one of the most common allergy foods. The milk of a cow is designed for a bovine infant that weighs 80 pounds and will grow up to weigh 1,000 pounds, eating grass all day, digesting it in five stomachs. Nevertheless, some humans handle it well; others handle raw milk well, but not pasteurized. Raw milk is the best form (see Chapter 5 for a detailed explanation), but some babies don't tolerate *any* form of cow's milk and you should recognize the signals.

Common symptoms of allergic reaction to milk are: colic, constipation, excess mucus, frequent colds, diarrhea. When any or all of these symptoms are present to any significant degree, there are three alternatives. The first is to boil the milk first; this sometimes improves the digestibility enough to make cow's milk a tolerable food for babies. The other alternatives to consider are:

Goat's Milk

The fat content and the size of the fat globule itself in goat's milk is similar to breast milk. The fat content of cow's milk is four to five times higher and the fat globule itself is huge in comparison to goat's milk. Digestion time in the human stomach is twenty minutes for goat's milk, two hours for cow's milk. Goat's milk would be the ideal replacement for breast milk if it were more available.

Soy Milk

Many commercial infant formulas have a soy base. They also contain sugar, salt, and a host of synthetic ingredients. You can do better yourself, using fresh soy milk, or making your own from full fat soy powder, both available in most natural and health food stores. But even the best soy milk is a highly processed food. The protein is denatured, calcium and iron are deficient. It should not be relied on as a principal food capable of supplying complete, balanced infant nutrition.

Fruit Juice

There's nothing wrong with a few ounces of fruit juice a day but fruit juice is not a healthy alternative to breast, cow, or goat milk. It doesn't have enough protein, enough calcium and other minerals, and it does have too much sugar. In hot weather, when Baby needs extra fluids, give her fresh fruit juices diluted with water that has been boiled and cooled (see below). Don't give it to her refrigerator-cold, just cool, without ice. Orange and grapefruit juice tend to cause colic and diaper rash and the citric acid dissolves dental enamel.

Herb Teas

Herb teas slightly sweetened with a few drops of blackstrap molasses are usually pleasing to Baby. But one should read about the medicinal effects of herbs before employing them widely as a baby beverage (see Appendix Six). Their medicinal effects are mild but Baby is extremely small and could be very sensitive. Try alfalfa, red clover blossoms, red raspberry leaves, peppermint, spearmint, wild cherry bark, dandelion, wintergreen, hyssop, fennel, chickweed, sarsaparilla, chicory, rose hips, juniper berries, sage.

Water

Since so much of your baby's diet is liquified food, water is not as critical for it as for people who subsist primarily on solid food. Nevertheless, it is a part of the diet and should be of high quality too (see Chapter 3 for a discussion of water quality). Even the cleanest water sometimes has bacteria that can upset Baby's intestines, so in the early months it is best to boil all Baby's water before using. This practice can be dropped after she is nine months old.

Without realizing what they're doing, many mothers use bottles as pacifiers. This often means Baby is overfed. Beyond that, the practice of using pacifiers is questionable. A better name for pacifiers would be "silencers"—she can't cry if she's busy sucking. But babies don't cry because they need pacification or because they're cantankerous. They do get angry; anger is accompanied by crying, but we need to find out what produces the discomfort that precedes the anger. Beyond the wet diaper, diaper rash, constipation, gas, and other physical discomforts, are the needs to be held, talked to, sung to, amused, and the chance to amuse themselves in interesting ways. It's really grossly unnatural for babies to be sucking on something all the time and, ironically, it's a case of shut Baby up now and pay the orthodontist later to straighten her teeth with braces.

FIRST FOODS

Riddle: What's another name for canned fruits and vegetables, grown with pesticides and herbicides, cooked, watered down, sweetened and salted, thickened and preserved, put into cute little expensive jars and promoted as one of the bedrocks of American civilization?
Answer: Babies, of all people, deserve something better.

Until recently, the question, "What should I feed my baby?" was rarely asked. There was no such question because we assumed the answer was *commercially prepared baby foods*. As Vikki and David Goldbeck say in *The Supermarket Handbook*, "Advertising has created the feeling that unless you feed your child prepared baby foods you may not be satisfying his/her nutritional needs." They go on to say, "Look at the facts more critically, however, and you'll find the processed, highly adulterated and overpriced baby foods are the most reprehensible aspect of the American food scene."

What escaped our notice under the tinseled cloud of advertising propaganda is that commercially prepared baby foods are not Baby's life blood but simply one more form of *convenience food*. And convenience foods for your baby suffer the same weaknesses as convenience food for you: the quality is low, the price is high.

Quality: Notice that the first ingredient listed on most jars of baby food is water. The vegetables and fruits are almost always accompanied by salt and sugar. Then come preservatives and, in meat, nitrates and nitrites. There often are thickeners and such other forms of sugar as dextrins, corn syrup, and glucose.

Price: One little jar of baby food is not a big investment until you analyze what you get for your money in terms of the net food content. According to *The Supermarket Handbook*, one-third of the price of most baby foods is the jar.

Since you can't feed the jar to your baby and shouldn't feed her/him what's inside the jar either, you are expecting that I will promote preparing your own baby foods. Yes, you can do *much* better yourself for *much* less money. Convenience is always relative: you can have a quick meal but it is always related to some prior investment in preparation. The same is true for your baby; but it's so simple to make your own baby foods that even the most time-pressed mother—one who goes back to work when the baby is three months old and has other children to consider—can find the time to do it. Time-pressed fathers can as easily do it, even if they see themselves as being unskilled at kitchen tasks.

Let's hypothesize a case where you buy no commercially prepared baby foods at all, depending entirely on your own homemade baby foods. To be ready for this, the only special equipment you will need is a blender, already in use in most kitchens.

Fruits

Fruits in general are the easiest foods for babies to digest, though allergies to citrus and berries are quite common in infants (uncommon in older children).

Ripe bananas are a favorite first or early food—no blender necessary. Just mash with a fork, add a little boiled milk or water to thin it.

Ripe avocado, mixed from one-third to one-half with banana, is digestible and extremely nourishing for babies.

Other fruits can be fed to babies uncooked when they are thoroughly ripe, pureed in the blender with enough apple juice to achieve the right consistency. Do not add sweetener.

Summer fruits can be canned (see Chapter 32) for use in winter, and probably will need no additional liquid to puree.

Another favorite early food is applesauce. To make it, simply peel, core, and quarter apples, put them in a pot with a little water (just enough to prevent burning on the bottom) and slowly simmer until mushy, then whiz them into sauce in the blender.

Vegetables

For most vegetables, steam them as you would for the rest of the family. Then puree them in the blender or grinder, using a bit of the water from beneath the steamer. Do not add salt.

For green leafy vegetables (chard, kale, cabbage, spinach), broccoli, and cauliflower, bring a small amount of milk to scalding, add fresh vegetable and simmer until tender. Puree in the blender with a bit of the milk, if needed for consistency. This milk method neutralizes the oxalic acid of these vegetables, making them more palatable and digestible for your baby. Do not add salt.

Mashed potatoes are good for babies too. Cook in jackets, peel, mash with boiled milk to desired thinness. Do not add salt.

A Few Words About Sugar and Salt

The common objection to my advice not to use sugar and salt when preparing baby foods is, "But she won't eat it—it won't taste good without sugar and salt." That's not true. Perhaps it won't taste good to you; but what you must realize is that *the taste for sugar and salt is an acquired taste.* Furthermore, your children are almost certain to acquire that taste, but the later in life they acquire it, the better off they will be. There is no single food important enough to your baby that you need to induce her to eat it by adding sugar and salt. Let your baby eat what she likes, refuse what she doesn't. Your role should be to discover what your baby will accept. She has not developed ego and will. Your baby is not being stubborn when she refuses food; rather, she is responding to the intuition that works well for her because there has been no overlay of learned information, behavior, and habit. You, on the other hand, have acquired information about sugar and salt which she is many years away from appreciating. So it is up to you not to hook your baby on them, especially when she is so tiny.

Honey

An unidentified ingredient of raw honey causes a reaction called "honey botulism" in infants. This is a misnomer since botulism is caused by spoiled food. But the severe gastric distress is real and raw honey should not be fed to babies until they are more than a year old, and then only in tiny amounts. Remember that honey, though a natural food, is still a concentrated sweet, causes tooth decay and, when used in large amounts, creates the same kind of addiction as sugar.

Grains And Beans

It is unlikely that your baby will have the ability to digest grains before she is six months old or beans before she is a year old. Although these are staple foods in the New American Cuisine for adults and children, they are not staples in a proper diet for infants.

After six months, oatmeal and brown rice and millet as cereals can be introduced. Rolled oats can be pulverized in the blender before cooking to render a smooth cereal, or use quick-cooking oats. Brown rice and millet can be reduced to a meal in the blender, then cooked with four parts water to one of meal, or cooked millet and brown rice can be blended with boiled milk or water for a smooth cereal.

These whole-grain cereals can be served to Baby in combination with vegetables but it is best not to combine them with fruits, to avoid digestive upsets. After your baby is two years old and her enzyme systems are completely active and stomach acid is at full strength, she will be able to eat grain in combination with small amounts of fruit.

Wheat is a common baby allergy. It is best to wait until your baby is at least nine months old to introduce wheat in the forms of smooth cereal, crackers, and bread.

After twelve months, your baby should be able to eat small quantities of beans in combination with grains and vegetables, *but not with fruit.* (See page 253). The blender is not necessary. Simply cook the beans as for the rest of the family (without any of the more exotic styles of seasoning) and mash with a fork. Depending on how well the baby is chewing, they may not need mashing at all. If you have doubt, check her feces for whole beans. Beans cooked by ordinary methods may be too difficult for Baby's intestines; try the vinegar method described on pages 224–225.

Dairy Products

Cow's milk (also see Chapter 5) is another common infant allergy. There are, however, two types of dairy solids that are easy to digest.

Yogurt, because the protein is predigested and because of the presence of lactic acid and beneficial bacteria, is an excellent infant food. The sour lactic acid taste, disagreeable to many adults, is acceptable to many babies. Avoid commercial fruited yogurts, which have sugar and other ingredients that don't belong in babies. Yogurt can be mixed with mashed banana, pureed fruit, vegetables, meat, and soft boiled egg yolk. Yogurt can be fed to most babies at the age of three months.

Cottage cheese is digestible enough for most babies but not so early as yogurt. It is best to wait until about six months to introduce it. Avoid cottage cheese that has calcium sulphate, salt, and stabilizers added. Calcium sulphate is also known as gypsum, used for plaster of paris and fertilizer, and babies have no attachment for the sort of gummy product many adults have come to accept as normal. Watch for allergic reactions. Serve with mashed banana, avocado, pureed fruits, and vegetables.

Eggs

Eggs are another food that commonly cause allergic reactions. That seems to be largely confined to *whole* eggs fed before the age of six months; however, some babies just can't tolerate them until they are much older. Before six months, soft boil or poach egg, spoon feed the yolk plain or stir into pureed foods. After six months, your baby can be tried on homemade custard sweetened with honey, and whole egg soft boiled or poached. When the baby is chewing fairly well, hard boiled egg can be crumbled into other foods.

BAKED CUSTARD

½ c. powdered milk	3 whole eggs
⅛ t. salt	½ c. fresh milk, plus 1½ c. fresh milk
⅓ c. honey	1 t. vanilla

Mix everything but 1½ c. milk until smooth, then add the rest of the fresh milk and mix thoroughly. Pour into shallow baking dish. Place dish in pan of water (important—prevents scorched milk). Bake at 300° for 40 minutes. Plenty for the rest of the family (sprinkle with cinnamon or nutmeg for them). (Adapted from *The Sunburst Farm Family Cookbook*.)

Meat, Chicken, And Fish

These foods usually don't cause allergies. On the other hand, they are dense and digest slowly, so it is best not to introduce them before six months. It is an error to assume they are necessary to Baby's health; as a rule, they are less necessary than the other foods we have discussed. They may become more necessary after the age of two, depending on the child's metabolic type (see Chapter 8). If Baby shows little enthusiasm for these foods, or refuses them, don't push it.

Preparation: Thinly shave lean meat, place in pyrex cup which in turn is placed in water to simmer until meat turns brown.

Bake, broil, or stew chicken, remove from bone.

Bake, broil, steam, or poach fish, then flake it. (Watch for small bones.)

Blend them to puree, adding broth to thin. They can also be pureed with vegetables or grains or served in combination with them.

Many babies like liver. But remember that the liver is the main organ of detoxification; hormones and antibiotics added to animal feed and insecticide residues left on the grain will be *concentrated* in the liver. For the long-term safety of your child, feed it only the liver of range-fed (grass-fed) or organically fed cattle. (See Chapter 24.)

Soups And Stews

No soup or stew you can buy for babies is as good as the one you make yourself for the rest of your family. Blend it for your baby to puree consistency, or feed the broth only, until she is able to chew.

TEETHING FOODS

One reason your baby puts a lot of things in her mouth is to find out if they're good to eat. Another reason is because it feels good to press things against those tender gums that have just been broken by teeth or soon will be. You might be surprised at the variety of foods Baby will chew on if they're offered. (We are talking about a baby able to sit up by herself and able to push solid foods back in her mouth with her tongue.) Here are some suggestions:

Carrot sticks or any crisp, raw vegetable that can be cut into long strips; celery stalks; carob pods; orris root; quartered raw fruit such as apples, pears, peaches, and nectarines; whole-grain toast or dry bread, whole grain crackers without salt; after about nine months, wedges of hard cheese or cheese melted on whole-grain bread or crackers.

By nine months, your baby will probably be doing well with milk and grain puddings and be able to join in on the family's weekend breakfast treats like French toast and pancakes. Remember when pouring on the syrup that your baby is only one-tenth your size. Also starting about now she can be offered many other things the rest of the family is eating, using the blender only as necessary—the baby should be encouraged to use her teeth. Babies should not be offered highly seasoned dishes and will usually refuse most if not all strong flavors.

ALLERGIES

I have mentioned five types of food that commonly cause allergic reactions in infants: milk, wheat, citrus, whole eggs, and berries. This is not meant to suggest that a reaction to these in infancy predicts a permanent allergy. Infants are far more sensitive than older children, who are, in turn, far more sensitive than adults. Furthermore, I doubt that there really is any such thing as a permanent allergy. People I've talked to about their long histories of food allergies have generally agreed that this year's list is different from the list of a few years ago and that list was different from the ones of years before that.

A problem for Baby is often a parent's rigid conviction that there is some food that is absolutely essential: "She must drink milk to build strong bones and teeth." Or, "He must drink orange juice or he won't get enough vitamin C." Nonsense—there is no such thing as a *must* food, not even breast milk. She may be quite willing to drink cow's milk but if it makes her colicky and turns her into a mucus factory, she is better off without it. There is plenty of calcium elsewhere in nature.

Something to remember when preparing baby food (and food for older children too): taste buds are like mountains rising from the plain of your tongue. Those mountains are tallest—that is, they have the most exposed surface, and are therefore the most sensitive—when you are a baby. As time goes on, your taste buds literally get worn down—that is, your sense of taste gradually becomes less acute as you grow older. That's why you like foods now that you hated when you were a kid; the taste was so strong for your high-mountain taste buds that it was overpowering, unpleasant. Hardly anything tastes the same to your baby as it does to you.

All the food additives that are either unproven or proven unsafe, as well as all the chemicals that inadvertently find their way into our food supply, are a threat to the future health of your children. Those little people have so much growing to do that their assimilation rate is wonderfully efficient. We need to be deeply concerned about what the blood, bones, and organs of these people are made of. When I was growing up, children rarely died of cancer; now it is comparatively common.

If you can find certified organically grown foods, buy them for your baby. If you can't find them, wash all produce thoroughly with mild, uncolored, unperfumed soap with a little bleach and rinse thoroughly. But don't soak produce, as it leaches out water-soluble vitamins and minerals.

Remember that Baby's digestive system can be sensitive to slight chemical and biological changes that occur in leftover foods, changes you would not perceive and that wouldn't upset you. If you make things in quantity for Baby, let them cool in the refrigerator, then freeze them. With soups and stews, you can freeze them in ice cube trays, then store the cubes in plastic bags, giving you baby-sized portions to thaw and serve.

BEYOND BABYHOOD

Infants will normally adjust easily to the New American Cuisine, usually needing just a few weeks. Older children, however, can be a radically different story. They've become attached to certain things totally without regard for their nutritional worth, and can be extremely rebellious about new food. The most problematical ages are roughly three through twelve. Teenagers, however, are much less likely to pull hunger strikes; the change to natural foods can even seem quite attractive to them if they perceive themselves to be eating like the movie stars and professional athletes eat.

One strategy is to change gradually without grand pronouncements and a lot of fanfare. Any hoopla will probably just serve to alert the little people to the necessity to raise their defenses. The gradual approach is in general easier for several reasons: people who are not used to a lot of fiber and B vitamins need time for their intestines to adjust; gradual change is psychologically less traumatic than sudden and complete change; you probably can't afford to throw away everything in your cupboard and wouldn't want to be that wasteful if you could afford it.

Beyond that is the matter of choice. The first is yours, wherein you do not give your children the chance to choose anything but natural foods. When you have made it abundantly clear that natural foods are the only kind that are being served in your home, your kids will be eating natural foods in preference to going hungry. The rough period of resistance may seem to be lasting forever, but usually within a few weeks, or sooner, it will blow over. They may even *enjoy* this lack of choice, not only because they will come to enjoy natural foods, but because children enjoy constraints. It's a serious mistake to think children desire complete freedom. What they really desire is guidance and a clear understanding of what the limits are: freedom, yes—but within constraints. You needn't feel sorry for them because they are being "deprived" of junk food treats in the home. You can assume they will make wrong choices of their own outside the home away from your supervision.

I once helped a lady with kids ten and twelve years old switch them over to natural foods. They were as deeply rooted in the old American cuisine as most other kids and for a few weeks there were some wrinkled noses and balkiness. But their mother and I just let it slide; we weren't offering any alternatives to natural foods. They soon recognized that what they were being offered tasted good and, as they heard explanations over the weeks, it made sense to them. Problems disappeared and fun took their place: Mexican, Italian, Chinese meals, teaming up on group projects like homemade pizza and making ice cream.

This brings us to the other kind of choice—theirs. Your children should be given some latitude in food selection for the following reasons:

1. The child is probably a different metabolic type than you (see Chapter 8.)
2. Your child's taste buds are more acute than yours, so what tastes good to you might well taste quite unpleasant to the child.
3. Children have different nutritional needs than adults.
4. Your child's intuition regarding food choices is probably less atrophied, therefore more reliable than yours.

I'm not suggesting you prepare fourteen different dishes for every meal. But if your daughter wants only a taste of squash and wants to fill up on brown rice, let her; and if your son wants just a token portion of salad but seconds on flounder, let him have it (or if there is no more flounder, let him get the peanut butter jar and load up a couple of slices of whole wheat bread).

Where you are headed with the New American Cuisine is to a home where pure, nutritious, delicious food is the only kind available. In such a home even the snacks and desserts are wholesome. But what do you do when Johnny wrinkles his nose with disgust because the casserole has spinach in it and Mary does the same because it has cheese in it?

"You can't tell me you don't like something you haven't even tasted. Taste it."

They taste it. They don't like it.

"Okay, you don't have to eat it. But there's nothing else to eat except salad and bread and cheese; you'll have to make a meal out of that."

That doesn't sound like a very good meal to them.

"Well, that's all there is. Maybe you want just a small portion of casserole to help you fill up? It's up to you—salad, bread, cheese, casserole."

Mary will have a small portion of casserole. Johnny isn't hungry.

Is he really not hungry? Or just stubborn? Or actually incapable of eating what's available? In any case, he'll undoubtedly wade into breakfast with a vengeance.

With children, it's impossible to escape situations that will try your patience. But far too many of us remember far too many grim scenes around the dinner tables of our childhoods, made tortuous by battles over food we *hated*. We don't need to perpetuate that sort of misery. Freedom of choice within limitations is not simple and easy but it is worth striving for because it is conducive to emotional peace and meeting nutritional needs that almost always differ radically from person to person.

All the recommended nutrient doses refer, as usual, to some mythical "average" child, not your child. But you can be sure that your children have a much greater need for "nutrient dense" food than you, meaning that junk food is even more harmful to them than it is to you. How do you prevent them from trashing out on chips, candies, pop, and pastry? By not having anything but wholesome food to snack on: fresh fruit, vegetable sticks, yogurt, raw milk cheese, nuts, dried fruit, whole grain crackers, fruit juice, as examples. Pretzels for Daddy but not for Junior is a double standard and it won't work; the best preaching is done by example.

Your best efforts will be no guarantee that your children have seen the last of junk foods. You can't supervise what they're offered at friends' houses or what they buy with their own money when you're not around. But your best efforts can produce the long-term result of a child who has lost interest in junk foods or buys wholesome versions of ordinary junk foods.

For lunch at school, you can send your children with a lunch box packed with wholesome food. You can also work for the improvement of the school lunch program. This has been done successfully in Santa Cruz, California; Hazen, South Dakota; South Bend, Indiana; Sudbury, Massachusetts; and Montreal, Canada—examples cited by *Nutrition Action*, September, 1981 (published by Center for Science in the Public Interest, 1755 S St., NW, Washington, DC 20009). In those communities children are doing such things as learning to grow vegetables and to choose fresh vegetables from the cafeteria salad bar, and to bake whole grain bread as well as eat sandwiches made with it.

There is no special New American Cuisine for children because the same cuisine that is best for you packs the best nutritional wallop of vitamins and minerals for your children. But for the same reasons that I recommend a natural vitamin/mineral supplement for adults (see Chapter 12), I recommend one for children (in half doses until they're around twelve years old).

Adjusting to a new way of eating can be a problem for everyone in the family, due to intestinal gas. This occurs because the intestinal bacteria requires time to adjust to the unaccustomed amounts of fiber and B vitamins that come with the new way of eating. Time is the best remedy; most children, and most adults, adjust within three or four weeks.

24   What to Buy

BUYING BREAD

It is the winter of 1979/80, shortly after the Winter Olympics at Lake Placid. Claus W. Sellier is being interviewed by Kevin Starr, a columnist for The San Francisco Examiner, *in the Carnelian Room atop the Bank of America Building in San Francisco. Mr. Sellier is vice president of the restaurant division of ARA Services, Inc., a giant national food service company. He has just returned from the Winter Olympics at Lake Placid, having been in charge of feeding the athletes—in the realest possible terms, catering to a wide variety of national tastes. Mr. Sellier has just commented that the Chinese delegation was extremely easy to get along with. By contrast, the Russians were extremely difficult. He now says:*

> One thing I can't disagree with the Russians about, however, is American white bread. The Russians refused to eat it. They said it tasted like putty. The chief commissar of the Russian team, a man called Valerie who spoke impeccable American-style English despite the fact—so he claimed— that he has never been in the United States, came in personally to complain to me about American-style white bread. Actually, he was doing us a favor. No nation in the world, it turned out, would touch it either . . . [*San Francisco Examiner*, March 17, 1980.]

John Hess, a syndicated columnist, in his article, "Bread and Factories" in *Saturday Review*, February 2, 1980, delivered a scathing and accurate description of the process and the product:

> The new factory loaf was "improved" to its present condition of wrapped, sliced styrofoam, dosed with fungicide to prevent mold and with polysorbates to keep it from drying . . .
>
> The most advanced bakeries now resemble oil refineries. Flour, water, a score of additives, and huge amounts of yeast, sugar, and water are mixed into a broth that ferments for an hour. More flour is then added, and the dough is extruded into pans, allowed to rise for an hour, then moved through a tunnel oven. The loaves emerge after 18 minutes, to be cooled, sliced and wrapped. They call this bread.
>
> A century of complaint about the impoverishment of the staff of life has led the industry to "enrich" it by adding a few of the nutrients it has removed—only a few—and none of the rich array of earthy flavor and body that our forebears loved.
>
> Clinicians recently discovered what the ancients well knew, that roughage was an important element of diet. ITT Continental Baking Company met this need with a loaf that promised added fiber. The government has insisted that the company identify the ingredient more plainly. It is sawdust. We have come to that.

In these days "purified and enriched" chicken manure is cattle feed, sawdust is people feed— anything goes if we let them get away with it. It would be a better world than it is if food manufacturers were dedicated to producing the purest, most nourishing food possible. But can anyone harbor the illusion that food manufacturers see their business that way? Any food company executive worth his $70,000 per year and stock option plan would think you were crazy for suggesting that your health and well-being are the essence of his business. From the limited viewpoint of the bottom line, the price/earnings ratio and the price of the stock on the market, he is right. From where he sits, the bottom-line viewpoint isn't the least bit limited; it's the only way to see things.

But when we look at it, we see them pushing sliced white putty at us. Logjam. What do we do? What do they do? What we do is take the profit out of sliced white putty by not buying it. What they do then is bake good bread for us because that's all we're willing to buy. Granted, the doing will take more time than the telling. But the speed of producer response to consumer pressures in the marketplace can be quite fast. The first requirement is to be clear about what we want.

Nonbread: What A Good Loaf Of Bread Isn't

First and foremost, a good loaf of bread is not white. Not ever. I enjoy the taste of crusty French sourdough bread and in France they even make it with unbleached white flour. But that's still not the staff of life; it's white, okay for a treat but not strong enough to lean on.

Yesterday I stopped at a supermarket to see what the label of a loaf of nonbread would say. I could be blind and tell nonbread in a flash just by feeling a loaf. The mushy, flabby feel of the thing was actually a bit repulsive to me. The thought of people eating that gutless pap day after day chilled my spine with dismay. I know it's not the worst crime being perpetrated on suffering humanity; there are people whose death from starvation could be prevented by such "food." But this is America, a land that could be blessed with the best at no cost to hungry people elsewhere. We suffer an appalling rate of degenerative disease, overfed but undernourished, because of food like that. The label on the limp, flaccid package read:

Enriched bleached flour, water, high fructose corn syrup, vegetable shortening, yeast, calcium sulphate, dough conditioners (may contain one or more of the following: sodium stearoyle/2 lactylate ethoxylated mono and diglycerides, monocalcium phosphate, succinylated monoglycerides, calcium carbonate, polysorbate 60, calcium peroxide, dicalcium phosphate, potassium bromate and potassium iodate), mono and diglycerides, yeast nutrients (diamonium phosphate and/or ammonium chloride or ammonium sulphate).

That's nonbread; the only ingredients on that list you would find in a good loaf of bread are water and yeast.

This package had a surprise statement right after the last listed ingredient: *"No artificial preservatives added."* It was written as if it were part of the ingredient statement but it had quotation marks around it. "No preservatives" is becoming a buzz statement like "natural" has become a buzz word Were they hedging their buzz statement because most of the dough conditioners function to "inhibit staleness," making them quasi-preservatives? Better for sales to have the buzz qualified with quotes than not to have it at all? Whatever, you can't turn nonbread into bread just by leaving out a bit of preservative.

The same company has another loaf they call "Premium Wheat Bread." It has exactly the same ingredients with one exception: after the enriched bleached flour is some whole wheat flour (ingredients are listed in quantity order). Freckled putty. Another sack of pap.

There are a couple of ingredients that make it easy for bakers to fake whole wheat bread. They can call it "whole wheat" as long as whole wheat flour is one of the ingredients. So the fake will start out something like this: *enriched wheat flour* (that's just white flour, remember), *water, corn syrup, whole wheat flour*—so there really is a mere token of whole wheat. But, you observe, it's so dark. That's because further down the ingredient list you'll see *molasses* or *caramel* (burnt sugar), often both. They're both almost black and it doesn't take much to impart that good, wholesome color that's becoming so popular these days as more and more people start looking for wholesomeness.

According to John Hess in "Bread and Factories," the following flour additives and processing chemicals are allowed by the Code of Federal Regulations without needing to be listed: *oxides of nitrogen, chlorine, nitrosyl chloride, chlorine dioxide, benzoyl peroxide, acetone peroxide, azodicarbonamide, plaster of paris.* Nonbread can be even less bread than labels reveal. There are a bunch of other nonbread ingredients, with preservatives a major category, but why beat a dead horse?

Friends who would like to see a successful campaign against nonbread say, "The trouble is, that's what Americans are used to." The implication is that since we're unaccustomed to real bread, we don't like it when we try it.

That's true. I've often heard complaints like, "It's so heavy," "It's so coarse," "It's so hard to chew." Those *are* characteristics of real bread—relative to nonbread, that is. But when you become used to the real thing, you don't compare it to the ersatz any more. You compare one loaf of real bread against another; there's much variety among them all.

Real Bread

As with the loaf of mush experience I related earlier, your first hint of a good loaf of bread comes from feeling it. It is solid, firm to the touch, and resists pressure.

It is dense; the same volume compared to nonbread will weigh about 50 percent more.

The color is definitely brown (unless we are talking about corn bread or tortillas). The first ingredient is a whole grain, always identified by the word "whole"; there is no refined flour, unbleached or otherwise. Whatever secondary grains, seeds, nuts, or beans are added will also be whole, natural foods.

The ingredients of our loaf of good basic bread might read like this: *organically grown,* * *fresh stone-ground whole wheat flour; yeast; malt syrup and honey; unrefined corn oil; spring water; salt.*

This is by no means meant to indicate that those ingredients are definitive of a good loaf of bread. Other grains, other sweeteners, other shortenings can make good bread too. Some people who are allergic to wheat find that they are not allergic to sprouted wheat. Sprouted grains also result in some remarkable nutritional transformations (see Chapter 26). Seeds, beans, vegetables, herbs, fruits, spices, nuts, dry milk, protein powder—these are all ingredients that can find a home in a loaf of good bread.

Organically Grown

Most states still do not recognize the relevance of organic farming to human and agricultural health (Oregon, California, Michigan, and Massachusetts are exceptions). In the absence of a definition by the state that informs the consumer what the term means, it is only fair that the manufacturer using organically grown wheat in his bread define the term right on the label. The asterisk in the hypothetical label above would be explained something like this: **Grown on composted soil without artificial fertilizers, pesticides, or herbicides.*

Food that is certifiably organically grown is not yet widely available, though it is hundreds of times more so than when I entered the natural foods business in 1965. The rule of thumb in buying is always to buy the best quality available. If other factors such as freshness are equal, organically grown food generally is the best quality. It is most important in the categories of grains and vegetables, since those are the foods of greatest importance. Buy it if you can find it; otherwise, be patient. Rapidly spreading consumer awareness is creating a market for organically grown food, but it takes three years or longer for farmers to convert to organic production. (See Epilog.)

BUYING GRAINS, BEANS, NUTS, AND SEEDS

Grains are the simplest type of food to buy. They are relatively imperishable, usually with 12 percent or less moisture content. They are naturally endowed with long-term keeping qualities. Wheat still capable of germination has been unearthed from Egyptian tombs several thousand years old. Look for plump kernels, uniform in size and color, free of chaff and unhusked grains. Whole grains that are used frequently (brown rice, rolled oats, whole wheat pasta) are the best candidates for full sack or box purchasing (even cheaper than buying from bulk bins). Store as cool, dry, and dark as possible, cellar to room temperature range, at the least in a cupboard away from the stove.

Three forms of whole grain in the "frequently used" category for many people require special precaution: Brown rice, rolled oats, and whole wheat pasta, are all subject to rancidity within one to three months after milling. For this reason, the Lundberg brothers, growers of organic brown rice in California, store their rice unmilled, then mill and ship within three days of receiving an order. They advise storage of brown rice at under 40°F for any bulk quantities that will not be used within one month, which is also advisable for rolled oats and whole wheat pasta.

Beans are also easy to buy. Premium quality is defined as large and uniform in size and color. Smaller and irregular beans should be priced lower but are just as nutritious; the color of such beans should still be uniform. There should be no more than 2 percent of beans split in half, or with pitted surfaces, or split seams (called "fish eyes"), or with broken skins. The skin of the bean protects the nutrients from oxidation and beans with the sorts of irregularities mentioned will not sprout. Instead, they will start to rot after soaking, becoming moldy. Wrinkled skins indicate the bean was dried too fast or too much, neither of which lessens the nutritional value. Store whole beans as you do whole grains.

Nuts and seeds are generally available both shelled and unshelled. In the unshelled form, nuts and seeds keep fairly well, though not as well as grains and beans. Nuts and seeds have a relatively high oil content and are subject to rancidity. Therefore, in their shelled form, nuts and seeds should be bought frequently in small quantities, unless it is possible to store them in glass or ceramic in the refrigerator. Beware of shelled sunflower seeds tinged with patches of yellow or tan, which indicate that the oil has turned rancid; shelled sunflower seeds should be a uniform gray color.

BUYING PRODUCE

Some Generalities

The best quality produce comes fresh from the garden, organically grown. You-pick-'em and roadside stands can be excellent sources for freshness and low prices. Freshness is associated with

WINTER

SPRING

SUMMER

FALL

good flavor and good flavor is associated with high nutritional value. The characteristics that blend to communicate good taste to us through our taste buds are *nutrients*—vitamins, enzymes, minerals. This elementary body wisdom works for almost everybody. So for freshness, as well as price, buy locally and in season. Most produce is available out of season from Mexico, California, and Florida, but emphasize what is in season—winter vegetables in winter, summer vegetables in summer, for health and economy.

Organic produce should be rinsed before eating. Wash nonorganic produce in water with soap and a little bleach added, scrub lightly to remove wax and spray residues, then rinse in plain water. Wax is most common on apples, cucumbers, and peppers; insecticides are common on just about everything except cherries and watermelon.

Fresh fruit and vegetable grades are U.S. Fancy, U.S. No. 1, and U.S. No. 2, with No. 1 the common marketing grade. The grades refer only to appearance and have no relationship to nutritional value. Bargains at produce stands often result from the smaller and irregular sizes of No. 2 grade. If they are fresh and ripe, have aroma, flavor, and juiciness, No. 2 grades can be even better quality than No. 1.

"The bigger, the better" is a false way of measuring quality. In America, we have been miseducated to buy according to cosmetic standards: big, no blemishes. The commercial objective has been to popularize the varieties that look, ship, and store the best. Consequently, we often have pulpy, tasteless, good-looking fruit, and tasty varieties nobody will buy because they don't look "right." Many of us have never even seen our best varieties of fruits and vegetables. A poor shipper like a Granny Smith apple has five times as much Vitamin C as a Golden Delicious. As we return to more regional choices, we will not only squander less energy, we will eat tastier fruits and vegetables because shipping and storage considerations will no longer dictate the varieties farmers grow.

Unless otherwise indicated, store vegetables refrigerated in the crisper or wrapped in plastic.

Year-Round Vegetables

Cabbage: green, red, Savoy (crinkly leaves), should be heavy, dense heads, crisp leaves. Avoid limp, yellow, split heads. Store up to ten days.

Carrots: are fresh if the greens are fresh. Greens are good for soup stock or pot herbs. With topped carrots, look for deep orange color and firmness. Avoid them when they are limp, dark, or slimy. Store up to two weeks.

Celery: should be bright green with firm stalks, fresh leaves, ribs not enlarged. A seed stalk in the center indicates it is old but this is generally unavoidable in late spring. Avoid limp stalks and yellowed leaves. Store up to one week.

Garlic: same storage rules as onions.

Onions: yellow (Spanish), red (Bermuda), white, should be hard and dry with papery outer skin. Avoid moist (decayed) and sprouted necks. Do not refrigerate—too damp—onions must be kept dry. Properly stored—cool, dry, dark—onions will keep for months.

Potatoes: white, red rose, russets, should be hard, no soft spots, no tinges of green, no sprouts. (Sprouts on potatoes are toxic.) Same storage rules as onions.

Sprouts: include alfalfa, mung bean, soybean, other kinds of beans, fenugreek, and other kinds of seeds. Should be crisp and moist without being slimy. Avoid browning and the extremes of either wetness or dryness. Store up to one week.

Winter squash: acorn, butternut, Hubbard and other hardshelled varieties can be kept through winter and into spring. Avoid signs of shriveling, soft areas, decay spots, cracks. Pumpkin is not the only squash that makes good pie—try Hubbard, butternut, or banana squash. Store in a cool, dry place; darkness is not particularly important.

Seasonal Vegetables

Year-round vegetables are relatively stable in terms of quality and price. Seasonal vegetables, when available out of season, rarely have good flavor and usually are expensive. The seasons indicated are their peaks; that is, when quality and price are most favorable to the consumer.

Asparagus: *February through June.* The harbinger of spring; we eat the shoots of this beautiful fern-like member of the lily family. Avoid limp, discolored stems; for best flavor avoid thick, white, woody stems. Store up to three days.

Beans, green: *May through September.* Should be crisp, make a *snap* sound when broken (therefore sometimes called "snap beans"), have strong green color. Avoid limp or spotted pods, beans with overdeveloped, hard seeds, pods that are bulbous, hard, or stringy. Store up to one week.

Beets: *June through October.* They are at their best when their greens are in good condition; then slice beets and chop greens and steam or sauté them together. Otherwise, look for small to medium size (big ones tend to be woody), hard, no cracks or signs of decay. Avoid soft flesh. Store up to two weeks.

Broccoli: *October through May* (much shorter season in northern latitudes), a winter vegetable. Look for dark or purplish green heads (these are immature flowers) with firm stalks. Thin stalks are edible as is; for thick stalks, pare off the outer layers, slice the inner part and cook with the heads. Avoid heads with open buds or yellowing and wilted leaves. Store up to five days.

Brussels sprouts: *September through February,* a winter vegetable. Should be compact and dense, completely green. Avoid loose, light, soft, and yellowed heads. Store up to five days.

Cauliflower: *September through March* (shorter season in northern latitudes), a winter vegetable. As with broccoli, look for compact, tightly clustered flower heads, white or creamy white, green leaves. Avoid yellow leaves, browned or spotted heads, opened buds. Store up to one week.

Corn: *June through September.* Twenty minutes after picking, the sugar begins converting to starch—corn on the cob should be fresh if you want it to be sweet. Fresh from a garden or roadside stand it is tender enough to be eaten raw, as succulent as fruit. Most stores "window" the corn so that you can see the kernels, which should yield a milky substance when punctured by your thumbnail. Husks should be green, silk should be moist. Turn ear in palm of your hand to feel that it is well-filled with kernels, no flat or empty places. Avoid excessive worm damage, yellowed husks, dry, brown silk.

Cucumbers: *June through September.* Deep green with no more than a streak of yellow. Overly large ones will have pithy flesh, big, hard seeds. Also avoid withered ends, which indicate toughness and bitterness. Store up to one week.

Eggplant: *August through September.* Of the two popular varieties, the Japanese is smaller. The large variety is more convenient for making eggplant parmesan; otherwise they are interchangeable. Color ranges from maroon to deep purple, skin should be smooth, fruit should be firm. Avoid softness and wrinkled skin—they indicate bitterness. Store up to two days.

Greens, including white and red Swiss chard, spinach, collard, kale, mustard, beet and turnip greens: *June through October* (except kale, a winter vegetable). Young greens are more tender; look for dark green colored leaves that are crisp, no limpness or wilting. Avoid yellowed leaves. Store up to one week.

Lettuce, including iceberg, Boston, bibb, greenleaf, red, and romaine: *June through October.* Iceberg and romaine are the best keepers but iceberg is the least nutritious of all lettuce varieties, indicated by its lack of greenness. The other varieties are extremely perishable. Leaves should be firm, crisp and green. Avoid wilting, soft spots, decay at stem area, yellow leaves, brown leaf fringes. A heavy cluster of leaves in the center signifies that the plant is starting its reproductive cycle, liable to be bitter. Store up to one week.

Mushrooms: *November through April,* not really a winter vegetable, but a cellar-grown fungus. Caps should be dry, not slimy, and close around the stems. Color should be nearly white, with either a tan or pink cast. Avoid brown spots and black gills. Store up to three days.

Onions, green: *May through August.* Should have white bulbs, firm, green tops. Avoid browned bulbs, wilted and yellow tops. Store up to five days.

Parsnips: *October through April,* a winter vegetable. Should be firm, tan colored, no soft spots. Select small to medium-sized roots; big ones are too tough. Avoid flabby roots. Store up to two weeks.

Peppers, bell: *June through October.* Also known as "sweet" peppers because they are not hot. The green ones are immature (but quite edible and nutritious), the red ones are ripe, much sweeter, and much more nutritious. A half cup of green peppers has 6 percent and 160 percent of the RDAs for vitamins A and C; a half cup of red peppers has 67 percent and 250 percent. They should be crisp and firm, richly colored. Avoid shriveling and soft spots. The same qualities apply to chili and jalapeno peppers. Store up to one week.

Squash, summer, including zucchini, crookneck (yellow), scallop: *June through September.* As opposed to winter varieties, summer squash is thin-skinned and highly perishable. Should be firm, not too large (unless you want to stuff and bake them, for which the large ones are ideal). Avoid limp, shriveled, or spotty ones. Store up to five days.

Sweet potatoes and yams: *October through April,* winter vegetables. Sweet potatoes are rounder, thinner-skinned, lighter in color; yams are more tubular, thicker-skinned, darker, and even sweeter. They should be hard, without blemishes. Do not refrigerate. Store like potatoes, up to three months.

Tomatoes: *June through October.* "Night and day" difference between vine-ripened tomatoes and those picked green or slightly red. Unripe tomatoes should not be refrigerated, as temperatures below 55° stop the ripening process. To ripen immature fruit, place in bowl or paper bag (not plastic; the tomato must be able to breathe to ripen). *Never place any fruit or vegetable in direct sunlight to ripen it; this will burn or dehydrate it, rather than ripen it.* Avoid tomatoes that are very soft, spotted or have transparent areas on the skin. Refrigerate ripe tomatoes unwrapped up to three days.

Year-Round Fruits

Apples: A year-round fruit because some varieties keep well in cold storage. By the time the supply of winter apples is exhausted, early summer varieties are arriving. The cold-storage technique eliminates oxygen from the atmosphere, thereby interrupting the ripening process. At home, in the presence of oxygen, ripening continues, faster at room temperature, slower in the refrigerator, where crispness is more effectively maintained. There are so many varieties of apples that generalities are difficult. The most popular varieties—Rome, Winesap, Pippins, Macintosh, Red and Golden Delicious—have become so because they store well and don't bruise easily. Other uniquely flavored varieties appear locally and briefly and are eminently worthwhile. Apples should be chosen for crispness and clear skins without wrinkles or brown spots.

HOW HOT ARE HOT PEPPERS?

The degree of hotness in peppers is due to the presence of *capsaicin,* found in the membrane to which the seeds are attached, and so potent that it can be detected at one part per million.

THE PEPPER HEAT SCALE

Bell	mild & sweet
Pimentos	mild & sweet
Anaheim	mild to mildly hot
Ancho	mild to mildly hot
Pasillo	mild to mildly hot
Yellow Wax	mild to hot
Hungarian Wax	mild to hot
Chile Tepin	very hot
Jalapeno	very hot
Fresno	mildly hot to very hot
Serrano	very, very hot

Source: The consumer's Coop of Berkeley, CA.

Avocados: are year-round because different varieties mature at different times and the unripe fruit (avocados ripen properly only off the tree) ships well enough to appear in all areas of the country. Hard fruit will ripen properly at home when left out at room temperature. Fruit is ready to eat when it yields slightly to thumb pressure. Refrigerate only after ripe. Avoid fruit that is mushy or has soft spots.

Bananas: The only popular fruit that does not grow commercially anywhere in the U.S. (Hawaiian bananas are not exported to the mainland.) If fruit is extremely green and hard, it may not ripen properly at home. Buy light green or green mixed with yellow for home ripening. When skin is all yellow, lightly spotted with brown, it is ripe. Refrigerate only after ripe and then for no more than a few days. Fruit that is fully ripe can be peeled and frozen for use in baked desserts.

Seasonal Fruits

Apricots: *June and July,* the most delicate of stone fruits. Look for red blush and yellow/orange skin, absence of green. Fruit is soft when ripe but avoid mushiness, brown spots, wrinkles.

Berries: Blackberries, *July through September;* **Blueberries,** *June through August;* **Raspberries,** *July and August;* **Strawberries,** *May through August.* All berries are highly perishable, should be bought firm, used quickly, though they will hold decently under refrigeration for a few days. Avoid mushy fruit oozing juice; fruit on bottom will almost always be moldy. Can be frozen raw and after thawing be *almost* as good as fresh.

Cherries: *May and June,* the first fruit of the season, with the shortest season. In the approximately eight-week season, unripe cherries and high prices prevail during the first week, overripe cherries and high prices during the last week. Cherries are the best of all stone fruits in terms of keeping under refrigeration.

Other stone fruits, including nectarines, peaches, and plums, with their many varieties, are continually available from *June through September.* Look for high-toned, well-colored fruit, firm but not rock hard. Avoid discoloration or excessive softness.

Citrus, including grapefruit, lemons, limes, oranges, tangerines and tangelos: with the many types and varieties, citrus of some kind is always available, despite seasonality. Oranges are, of course, by far the most popular citrus fruit, the two main varieties being Navels and Valencias. Navels, with thick, easy-to-peel skin are the "eating oranges," available December through May. Valencias, available the rest of the year, are the "juicing oranges." Unlike other fruits, decay in citrus affects the whole fruit and cannot be effectively cut out. Good citrus has firm skin and is heavy for its size.

Melons, including cantaloupe, Crenshaw, honeydew, Persian, watermelon, are hot-month fruits. Melons should be heavy for their size, yield a fragrance where the stem has parted from the vine. Melons do not ripen off the vine, and keep better under refrigeration, though it isn't necessary. Thumping a watermelon is a way of determining whether or not it is heavy for its size—that is, *juicy;* a juicy watermelon gives off a deep, soggy reverberation relative to one that is drier.

Pears, *August through March:* come in two classes, summer and winter. Summer pears, headed by Bartletts, ripen from the outside toward the core. They should be gold skinned, yield to gentle pressure when ripe. Winter pears, such as Anjou, Bosc, and Comice, ripen from the core toward the skin. They should yield to gentle pressure at the neck. In both classes, forego fruit that is excessively soft.

Pineapples, *March through June:* should be large and heavy, have green leaves, a gold or orange/red cast to the skin. A ripe pineapple is fragrant; ripening will not progress at home. Avoid soft spots, refrigerate if it will not be used soon, don't attempt to hold for more than a few days.

In general, fruit should not be refrigerated unless it is ripe; then refrigerate for up to three days to prevent it from becoming overripe.

BUYING MEAT

Pity the poor steer standing around in the typical feedlot. He came from the range where he roamed in the fresh air and ate the prairie grasses. Now he wallows in his own manure and urine, with nowhere to roam, getting sprayed with insecticides and fed with antibiotics. He eats grain now, along with whatever else will get him fat fast at the lowest possible cost—like specially processed chicken feathers, purified chicken manure. When he's finally as fat as he is filthy, he gets slaughtered.

Fat is the objective of the feedlot and the problem for you. The fat represents more than just cholesterol and concentrated calories: it represents concentrations of antibiotic, insecticide, and hormone residues fed intentionally to cattle. Furthermore, it represents concentrations of agricultural and industrial pollutants unintentionally delivered to cattle in their feed and water: mercury, lead, pesticide residues, PCBs. The U.S. General Accounting Office was pointing at nearly 150 such contaminants when they blasted the FDA, the USDA, and the EPA in 1979 for the dangerous levels of chemical residues allowed in our meat.

There are two ways around such generally unhealthy meat. Both of them are even more difficult than finding organically grown grains and vegetables. First there is "naturally fed" beef, meaning that the animals have been fed only organically grown hay and grain without hormones or antibiotics. Naturally fed beef is in extremely limited supply, necessarily expensive, and generally only available in natural foods stores.

The most logical alternative is not widely available either: grass-fed beef, logical because it simply skips the feedlot, and therefore most of the fat, and considerable expense. Grass-fed beef is simply a return to pre-World War II beef, before we had so-called grain "surpluses". Grass-fed beef is also the beef of the future, because it is healthier and is the only form of beef that makes ecological sense.

Beefalo is a hybrid animal—three-eighths buffalo, five-eighths beef. It is a muscular animal, naturally low in fat, and is marketed as strictly range-fed. Beefalo prices range from comparable to beef, down to 20 percent less, depending on where you live.

If you are unable to find naturally fed beef or range-fed beef or beefalo, the best you can do is to buy the leanest beef available. The leaner cuts are also the less expensive cuts, which are, in turn, the cuts most suitable to the meat-as-minor-ingredient approach.

Beef Grading

Top grade: *"Prime,"* very fatty (28 percent), from the obese steer. Marbling of fat in muscles of *Prime* is strictly for flavor and tenderness. Steers fattened for about 120 days.
Second grade: *"Choice,"* a very fat steer (25 percent), usually fattened for ninety days in the feedlot. *Choice* is usually the beef producer's goal, generally your supermarket meat. This is fat-marbled also and what consumers have been trained to want.

Third grade: *"Good"* (22 percent fat). This is a better buy. It's tender enough and tasty enough, but not overfed, and is less likely to contain hormones. If your supermarket is not selling *Prime* or *Choice*, it is selling *Good* grade. *Good* is leaner beef, can be inconsistent in tenderness and flavor, but is still better for you.

Beyond grades: Look for ungraded beef, advertised as *lean*, meaning less than 22 percent fat. It may have had a very short stay at the feedlot, or it may have come directly from the range: grass- or range-fed beef cannot be sold graded. It contains about 18 percent fat.

Other Meats

Liver: Liver is highly nutritious, the best bargain, but can be the most dangerous meat available. All the impurities of our environment gather in the liver, because it is the primary detoxification organ. The growth hormones and medicines administered to the animal also end up here. I do not recommend buying beef liver unless it is from certified naturally fed beef, or grass-fed beef. Then it is your best nutritional buy, the richest storehouse of vitamins and minerals found anywhere in nature.

Bargain burger: Some of the other organs, such as kidney and heart, are the cheapest of all cuts of beef. They can be ground and mixed with regular hamburger, from one-third to one-half, substantially reducing the cost of hamburgers. Heart, with its lack of "organ" taste, is particularly good for this purpose.

Lamb: Lamb from New Zealand comes from a relatively clean environment. It comes frozen year-round, though it is called spring lamb. It is generally a good buy, but since it is a frozen item, look for sales on it, then stock up your freezer. Lamb is usually tender, and is generally not fed hormones. USDA grades are Prime, Choice, Good, and Utility or Cull. Grading of lamb is optional, paid for by the packer, who can also use names of his own choice that don't coincide with USDA grade names. Lamb quality varies less than beef because the animals are young. The meat should be lean, pink, firm, and fine-textured. Do not judge quality by the color of the external fat, which varies according to feed, age, and breed.

Veal: Generally veal is expensive, but if you watch for specials, you can occasionally get a good deal on veal. Avoid "pre-prepared" breaded veal cutlets: they are expensive, made with white flour and artificial ingredients. If you are sensitive to the unusual cruelty issue, you will want to avoid veal: veal calves are generally penned tightly in the dark so they cannot move and will see nothing that makes them want to move. Weak muscles give you the utmost whiteness and tenderness.

Pork: Pork is usually not sold by grade because the USDA grades are intended only to indicate the potential amount of trimmed meat a carcass will yield. Pork, like lamb, varies less in quality than beef. Look for a pinkish gray color and relatively little fat; avoid meat that is soft and watery. Ham is the leanest cut but is usually loaded with salt for preservation, sodium nitrite for coloring, and sugar for flavoring; fresh ham has none of those, and is therefore the best choice.

Poultry Grades And Classes

Grades are intended to indicate quality, classes to indicate the age (tenderness) of the bird.

Grade A birds are fully fleshed, well-finished, and attractive in appearance.

Grade B birds are less than fully fleshed and below the highest standards of finish and appearance, though they can be as fresh as Grade A birds.

Young birds are most suitable for roasting, broiling, barbecuing, or frying. Old birds are most suitable for boiling, stews, and soups. The old birds are usually identified by the words "stewing," "mature," or "old."

Chicken: "Naturally fed" means the same in poultry as it does in beef and is at least as important. Most of the cheap chicken in today's marketplace is the result of stimulating birds to kill size in eight weeks with hormones and arsenic compounds and keeping them from dying with antibiotics such as penicillin, streptomycin, tetracycline, sulfonamides, and nitrofurans. That's why people born before World War II say, "Chicken doesn't taste like chicken any more." Name-brand producers will usually respond to consumer requests for information about their methods. If they won't, they don't deserve your patronage.

Look for reputable brands on specials. Avoid specials on brands you don't know. You can freeze fresh chicken at home, so stock up at a sale. Roasting and baking chickens are larger than fryers, but you should not pay more per pound for a larger bird. Unfortunately, you usually do pay more. There are no particular bargains as far as parts go; legs and thighs are more likely to be on sale than breasts. When buying a whole chicken, you can always use the backs and necks to make stock for soups (chicken, vegetable, and rice or barley) gravies, sauces, etc. Parts you don't use for dinner can be frozen and later cooked up into soup.

Chicken liver is generally inexpensive, can be frozen, and is less strong tasting and less membranous than beef liver. However, because the same toxicological problems occur for chicken liver as for beef, look for reputable, nonchemically raised brands when buying livers.

According to Jennifer Cross, writing in *The San Francisco Bay Guardian*, USDA studies not released to the public at the time of writing "show that 28% of the sausage and 36% of the broilers leaving the plant may contain salmonella. They also show that over a 12 year period (1967–79) this contamination level has *not improved*; in the case of broilers, it has gone up by 22%." Cross cites these three factors as primary causes for the appallingly high salmonella rates: (1) poor policing by state and federal agencies; (2) lax enforcement of sanitary standards; (3) overdependence on antibiotics in "animal factories."

However, a 1978 report by the U.S. Advisory Committee on salmonella, an ad hoc group of experts, stated that salmonella could be *reduced* (experts agree that the bacteria cannot be *eradicated*) by a simultaneous, four-pronged campaign to (1) produce salmonella-free feed, (2) develop clean breeding stock, (3) improve sanitation (particularly in poultry raising and processing) and (4) educate the public.

A 1975 Gallup survey found the public widely ignorant regarding the salmonella problem.

Turkey: Turkey is low priced, high protein food. Look for grade A fresh turkey; go with a reputable name in your area. Avoid "butterballs"; they are injected with cheap oil. Almost all turkeys, even "fresh" ones, have been lightly frozen. It's best to deal with a butcher you know who will get you the freshest whole bird. Fresh turkeys are a lot juicier than frozen ones.

Turkey parts such as breasts and legs are becoming more available and are usually a good buy. Ground turkey is very low in fat and is excellent to add to ground beef, or to eat by itself. Make into a meat loaf or patties, mix in oats, bulgur or wheat germ, and add your favorite green herbs, onions, garlic, etc.

Turkey ham, turkey hot dogs, and turkey lunch meats are all low in fat, but have the regular dose of nitrates and nitrites. At this writing, brands without additives are rare. Read the label before buying.

Processed meats: Cheeks and jowls, lymph nodes and salivary glands, stomachs and spleens—these are often the stuff of processed meats, as well as additives like sodium nitrite, sodium erythorbate, sodium acid pyrophosphate, and plenty of salt. The FDA allows manufacturers to use 30 percent fat and 10 percent water in hot dogs and bologna. Not too bad, you say? There's a catch. There's no limit to the amount of fat that may be attached to the 70 percent meat. So hot dogs and baloney are likely to be 75 percent fat. Here's what the FDA allows in *pure* fat with no meat attached:

Meat Product	Fat
Knockwurst	30%
Frankfurter	30%
Bologna	30%
Breakfast sausage	50%
Smoked pork sausage	50%
Luncheon meat	no limit

If you have ever thought of such products as being cheap, think again. In view of the amount of fat you pay for, the quality of the ingredients, the amounts and kinds of additives, there is no worse use of your money than this category of food.

FISH

Most ocean fresh fish is dipped in preservatives right on the boat, so it's better to buy fillets than steaks with the skins on, or fillet your own fish at home (see Chapter 21). Try not to hold fish in your refrigerator for more than a day. If buying frozen fish, buy only I.Q.F. (individually quick frozen). It is dipped in water and put in freezers 40° below zero so that it freezes fast. I.Q.F. fish was meant to be fresh frozen, and therefore wasn't already going bad, then frozen in an attempt to salvage it. Old fish will taste very strong and disagreeable. Try your best to buy fish *really fresh* (see page 245 on how to identify it).

The best place to buy fresh fish is a fisherman's retail outlet, not a supermarket. A large fish market is okay, but not as good as the fisherman's retail outlet, because it goes through a middleman and so takes longer to get to you. The supermarket also buys from a middleman, a wholesaler who bought it from the fisherman, so it's already a few days old when you see it. It's best to buy fresh fish as close to the fisherman as possible. Some inland cities have fish markets that get fish on ice, air freight from the coasts. Otherwise, I.Q.F. is the best bet.

Fish is sometimes expensive when compared with the other "meats," but it is high in protein and low in fat. However, strong public support for water pollution control measures is absolutely essential if the cleanliness of this food is to match its excellent nutritional qualities.

GENERICS

Unbranded products such as paper towels, toilet paper, and soap powder are a good way to save money. But, with a few possible exceptions, generic food is *not* a good way to save money. Most generic foods are canned, and canned food is the poorest quality. Considering the salt and sugar in them and the flavor and nutrition not in them, canned foods give you an extremely poor return on your investment. Some generics don't even identify ingredients or the address of who to ask. It's not smart to buy such mystery products, no matter how low the price. But the crux of the matter is that it is self-defeating to save money at the expense of quality, when it is possible to save while *raising* quality.

PHASE TWO: *Going Further*

24 Natural Convenience Foods

There is no question about the convenience of mixes, which need only a few additions and manipulations to produce a finished dish. Although we pay the food processors dearly so they can package attractively and advertise widely, we feel that it's worth it for convenience's sake. Many of us just don't have the time or the energy to start from scratch every time we want to make muffins, pancakes, soup, or sauce. Let me assure you, I appreciate the importance of convenience. Without it, many of us would have little or no chance to rest, relax, enjoy familial and social relationships, or in some cases even get anything done that needs doing.

No, I don't propose you surrender convenience, even though the price of it is usually high and the quality is usually low. I have a far more attractive proposition: I propose that you create your own convenience, save up to 50 percent and more, and improve quality immeasurably while doing it. It is not hard work; for most people the hardest part is reorganizing their time. Once this is done, however, there is a ratio that is enormously favorable to you—it actually takes relatively little time *now* in the making of your own mixes to save a lot of time *later*. (If it didn't, it wouldn't be truly convenient.)

HOW TO MAKE YOUR OWN MIXES

For pancakes, quickbreads, and cakes, the mixes will include flours, leavening, salt, and spices. For seasoning main dishes, salad dressings, and sauces, the mixes will be composed of herbs and spices. The basic way to proceed is just pick out your favorite recipes, look at the dry ingredients needed, and multiply them. The amounts will depend on the size of the containers you use and how fresh you want your mixes to be. Then label the container, stating how many cups, tablespoons, and teaspoons of the mixture are required to make up one complete recipe. Include on the container the name of the recipe and where it is located, or simply write out the recipe on a label on the back of the container. Then you are ready to use the mix.

For example, take a favorite pancake recipe from one of your cookbooks. Here is a basic recipe:

2 c. whole wheat pastry flour	2½ c. milk
1 t. salt	2 t. oil
2 t. baking powder	2 eggs
1 t. cinnamon	½ c. honey

291

You make pancakes two or three times a week, and would like to fill a gallon container with pancake mix. Looking at your dry ingredients, you estimate that you can fit 7 times the recipe in a container of this size. The largest amount of one ingredient you have is flour, and you can figure on fitting 16 cups in a gallon container. Since you have other dry ingredients, you would estimate 7 times the recipe instead of 8 times to make room for the salt, baking powder, and cinnamon. Go ahead and multiply each of the dry ingredients by 7.

In a large bowl or tub, mix together thoroughly: 14 c. pastry flour, 2 T. plus 1 t. salt, 4 T. plus 2 t. (or to round it off, 5 T.) of baking powder, and 2 T. plus 1 t. of cinnamon. Put the mix in a gallon container and label it. Go back to the original recipe and add up the cups, tablespoons, and teaspoons of dry ingredients. In this case, use 2 c. plus 1 T. plus 1 t. of dry mix for one recipe of pancakes. You could label the container that way, or elaborate: use 2 c. plus 1 T. plus 1 t. of dry mix with 2½ c. of milk, 2 t. oil, 2 eggs, and ½ c. honey.

Using the basic pancake recipe as the basis for your mix, a repertory of variations listed on your container could prepare you to make such things as carrot cake, spice cake, raisin-nut cake.

For another example, take your favorite muffin recipe:

2 c. whole wheat flour	¾ c. milk
2 t. baking powder	½ c. butter
½ t. salt	½ c. honey
4 eggs, beaten	1 c. blueberries

To fill a gallon container, you estimate that you can fit 7 times the recipe in it, again because flour is the largest quantity in the recipe and 16 cups fit into a gallon. So multiply each dry ingredient by 7. In a large bowl or tub, mix thoroughly 14 c. whole wheat flour, 4 T. plus 2 t. (or round off to 5 T.) of baking powder, and 1 T. plus ½ t. salt. Put this mixture in a gallon container and label, "Blueberry muffin mix. Use 2 c. plus 2½ t. of dry mix with 4 eggs, ¾ c. milk, ½ c. butter, ½ c. honey and 1 c. blueberries." Or, you could label the front of the container "Muffin Mix" and put the recipes and directions for a few muffin favorites on the back of the container.

With a repertory of variations, the muffin recipe above could prepare you for a variety of quickbreads and muffins using additional ingredients like mashed bananas, cheese, and herbs. Whether they are quickbreads or muffins is largely determined by the shape you choose.

Obviously, we are not able to duplicate our old "instant" ways; but with a couple of large containers, you can be ready to get quickly into a nice variety of low-cost, wholesome recipes. With stone ground whole wheat flour as the main ingredient you can come reasonably close to having your own homemade all-purpose bread mix; with whole wheat pastry flour as the main ingredient, you can do likewise for cake mix. Compared to the add-water-and-stir types, your homemade mixes don't represent the "nth degree" of convenience—what they accomplish is to eliminate a few steps in preparation in order to make the quality and cost improvements a reasonable time investment.

Remember that the price you pay for convenience is almost always quality. this is true when you make your own mixes too, because flour quality deteriorates rapidly after grinding. To maintain reasonable quality, make mixes in small batches with the freshest possible ingredients, and don't make more than you will use in a few weeks. If you have refrigerator space, store mixes there; otherwise, follow the general rules of good storage: cool, dark, and dry.

Spice mixes for main dishes, salad dressings and sauces will take up much less space, for example, Herb Dressing:

⅔ c. oil	1 t. oregano
⅓ c. apple cider vinegar	1 t. rosemary
½ t. garlic powder	1 t. thyme
1 t. salt	

Let's say your objective is to have a pint jar of the dry ingredients ready-mixed. There are 96 teaspoons in a pint. So divide 4½ teaspoons, the total amount of dry ingredients, into 96, giving you approximately 21. Converting each 3 teaspoon to its equivalent 1 tablespoon, you mix together 3 T. plus 1½ t. garlic powder, 7 T. salt, 7 T. oregano, 7 T. rosemary and 7 T. thyme. Put in a pint jar and label, "Herb Dressing, Use 4½ t. dry mix with ⅔ c. oil and ⅓ c. apple cider vinegar."

Make up a dry mix for spaghetti sauce if you serve it often. Suppose this is your recipe:

¼ c. olive oil	1 t. salt
2 cloves garlic	½ t. garlic powder
1 onion	2 t. oregano
1 10. oz can whole tomatoes	1 t. basil
1 10 oz. can tomato paste	1 t. thyme
1 12 oz. can tomato sauce	1 t. marjoram
1 T. honey	

Your dry ingredients for one recipe amount to 6½ t. or 2 T. plus ½ t. Again using a pint jar, since two tablespoons equals 1 ounce, you estimate one recipe to be 1 ounce plus, so you multiply the recipe 15 times. Mix well 15 t. or 5 T. sea salt, 2½ T. garlic powder, 10 T. oregano, 5 T. basil, 5 T. thyme and 5 T. marjoram. Put in a pint jar and label, "Use 2 T. plus ½ t. dry mix with"—then list the rest of the ingredients for one recipe.

It makes sense to grind and mix your own spices for chili and curry powders if you use them frequently. Here are formulas:

CHILI POWDER

4 T. chili pepper, dried and powdered	1 t. oregano
1 t. cumin	½ t. cloves
1 t. allspice	½ t. coriander
1 t. garlic powder	

CURRY POWDER

½ c. cumin	1 T. cayenne pepper
½ c. turmeric	1 T. cardamom
3 T. ginger root powder	1 t. black pepper
1 T. coriander	¾ t. mustard powder

When you are using your own spice mixes, be sure to shake them really well before using. Salt has a larger particle size than powdered garlic. If you are using leaf herbs as well as powdered herbs, the leaf ones will tend to sit on top while the smaller powdered particles fall to the bottom. Also, don't worry if you have trouble with fractions estimating how many times to multiply the recipe. It is probably better to underestimate, then you can always add more of each ingredient if you want to fill the container to the top.

THE SCALE OF EXPANDING VOLUMES

60 drops	=	1 teaspoon	(⅙ ounce)
3 teaspoons	=	1 tablespoon	(½ ounce)
2 tablespoons	=	⅛ cup	(1 ounce)
4 tablespoons	=	¼ cup	(2 ounces)
5 tablespoons plus 1 teaspoon	=	⅓ cup	(2⅔ ounces)
¼ cup plus 2 tablespoons	=	⅜ cup	(3 ounces)
8 tablespoons	=	½ cup	(4 ounces)
½ cup plus 2 tablespoons	=	⅝ cup	(5 ounces)
⅝ cup plus 2 teaspoons	=	⅔ cup	(5⅓ ounces)
12 tablespoons	=	¾ cup	(6 ounces)
¾ cup plus 2 tablespoons	=	⅞ cup	(7 ounces)
16 tablespoons	=	1 cup (½ pint)	(8 ounces)
2 cups	=	1 pint	(16 ounces)
4 cups	=	1 quart	(32 ounces)
8 cups	=	½ gallon	(64 ounces)
16 cups	=	1 gallon	(128 ounces)

SOUPS

You can totally eliminate dry soup mixes and canned soups. There are three basic constituents to all soups:

    the seasonings
    the solids
    the liquid

Let's see how you make it convenient for yourself to put together your own wholesome, economical soups.

The Seasonings

Using the principles above, you can have an all-purpose soup seasoning on hand. Here are some basic ingredients: salt, pepper, onion powder, garlic powder, ground celery seed, dried parsley flakes, powdered bay leaf.

The Solids

Obviously the quickest way to have solid ingredients ready for soup is to have grains, vegetables, beans, beef, poultry, or fish left over from previous meals. Small quantities of them can be accumulated in a large container in your freezer; when the container you have reserved for soup makings is full, make soup. A variation on this theme is to specifically plan on cooking extra grain or potatoes to put away for soup. These can be mixed with sautéed carrots, onions, and celery, scraps of meat from the carcass of a roasted chicken, to become soup.

The Liquid

This is as good a place as any for a short dissertation on *the stock pot*. Stock pots are a core feature of most traditional cuisines. There are three excellent reasons for having an active stock pot in your kitchen: (1) you save minerals nutritionally essential to your health; (2) you save the flavors that are inextricably bound to the nutrients; (3) you save money by having what is, in a way, a constant supply of "free" soup base.

The stock pot can include any vegetable parts you don't serve: wilted leaves, tough stems, tops, peelings and overall limp vegetables. If your family is large and dinner preparations yield a good amount of vegetable scraps, you can put on a stock pot to simmer while you enjoy dinner with your family. Let it cook until dinner clean-up is about done. When the meal is done, add any leftover cooked vegetables and jucies. If your family is smaller and vegetable scraps are fewer, you can save them in an airtight container in the refrigerator until you have enough of them to warrant cooking up a stock pot.

Once the vegetable parts are well-cooked, strain and save the broth, throwing away the vegetables, as the nutrition that was in them is now in the broth. You have just salvaged nutrition and a flavorful broth from vegetables that would otherwise have ended up in the garbage. This broth can be served as is as a hot drink, be used as a base for soup, or as a flavorful addition to cream soups, sauces, and gravies.

A good ratio of water to vegetables for cooking the stock is 2 to 1. Generally an hour to an hour and a half will be enough cooking time. If you want the broth to be more concentrated, cook the pot longer, uncovered, to allow more of the liquid to evaporate. Yo can simmer meat, chicken, and fish scraps and bones in the same manner to extract a nutritious broth. Use a greater amount of water per scraps since this stock pot will need to cook for 2 or 3 hours for chicken and fish, and up to 5 hours for meat; hence more of the liquid will evaporate. When the broth has been strained and chilled in the refrigerator, you can easily skim off the fat that has risen to the top. Then use the broth in the many ways you would use the vegetable broth described above.

The flavor of a vegetable broth will vary greatly according to the types of vegetable parts you use. Carrots, sweet potatoes, and various types of winter squash will give a sweet broth. Members of the brasicaceous family—broccoli, cauliflower, Brussels sprouts and turnips—will overpower a broth unless used sparingly. Leafy greens, lettuces, celery, onions, garlic, green beans, eggplant, and summer squash trimmings will yield a pleasant tasting broth. Potatoes will thicken the broth. Onion skins will give it a good, golden color. Beets will turn it dark pink.

You can add pizazz to the broth with your favorite herbs while the stock pot simmers. The types of herbs you use will also alter the flavor of the broth, and greatly enrich it. (See Appendix Six.)

If you are going to make soup from the stock pot broth, here are a few good additions: soy sauce or miso will add a richness of flavor to the broth. Brewer's yeast will add protein and a meaty flavor. Be sure to add the brewer's yeast without boiling, just before serving, so your family gets the full benefit of the B vitamins it contains. Water from cooking beans, grains, and steaming vegetables is another nutritional and flavorful addition to soups.

Home Food Systems suggests making vegetable chips and instant soups from dried vegetables. For chips, slice thin and add garlic powder and cayenne pepper, or your preferred powdered herb seasoning, before drying. For soups, powder the dried vegetables in your blender, mix with miso for instant miso-vegetable soup, or with powdered milk for instant cream soups. (For other natural convenience foods see *Snacks*, Chapter 22, and *TV Dinners*, Chapter 33.)

26 Indoor Gardens

An indoor garden can be as simple as a jar of sprouts on the counter, or as elaborate as an entire garden under lights, depending on your time and inclination. You will probably choose to have your indoor garden in the kitchen but it can be in the bathroom, garage, or anywhere else convenient for you. I've even had an indoor garden on the back seat of my car while driving coast to coast. In that case, it was the simplest form of indoor garden—no dirt, just a couple of jars with alfalfa sprouts and mung bean sprouts.

SPROUTS

Were this book being written even a few years ago, I would expect the question, "Who eats sprouts?" But not any more: sprouts have become a popular food, deservedly so. In the process of germinating, the seeds create a phenomenal increase in the water soluble vitamins C and B complex. The protein content is also increased by sprouting, as amino acids are produced at the expense of carbohydrates and fats.

Enzymes help create vitamins in growing plants. When a vegetable is picked, those same enzymes begin to break down the vitamins in the vegetable and continue to do so until you eat it. Vitamin C especially is destroyed in this manner. This is an important reason why fresher vegetables give you more nutrition and better flavor. Sprouts, however, continue to grow and produce vitamins until the moment you begin to eat or cook them. Beans are easier to digest if they are sprouted first, as enzymes break down starches in the sprouting process.

There are mysteries surrounding the sprouting process. For example, it is not known how vitamins are so dramatically increased, sometimes tenfold. An even greater mystery is transmutation. Some vitamins are found in sprouts that are not present in the unsprouted seeds. Most mysterious of all is the occasional presence in sprouts of *minerals* which in the unsprouted seeds, exist in smaller quantities, in changed ratios with other minerals, or not at all. It is apparent from analyzing some sprouted seeds that calcium has been transmuted into magnesium, something that most respected biochemists deem impossible. Sprouting unlocks the tremendous energies that are stored in seeds for reproduction and whether or not transmutation is in scientific disrepute, you and I can be satisfied to benefit from those forces and let them remain mysterious.

Sprouting Made Simple

Use only seeds that have been intended for direct human consumption; almost all seeds intended for planting have been chemically treated, sometimes with compounds containing mercury, lead, or

SOAKING

SPROUTING

arsenic. Most seeds will increase in volume six to eight times when they sprout. Start with three to four tablespoons of dry seeds or a cup of grain or beans in a quart jar, preferably wide mouth. Fill jar with warm water to soak seeds and place in a warm, dark area overnight. The following day, drain and rinse seeds, perhaps saving the water to nourish your house plants, or to use in soups or baking. Cover the top of the jar with nylon netting or cheesecloth, secure with a rubber band, and tilt the jar enough so that the excess water will drain out. Sprouts do not need to be left in darkness, as some believe, but can grow in daylight. You can either leave the jar in the sink to drain, or tilt it to drain into a tray or baking pan. If the sprouts are left sitting in water, they will mold. From here, you need only rinse the sprouts twice a day, in the morning and in the evening. Be sure they have good ventilation. The exact time for your sprouts to mature cannot be given, as their rate of growth depends on external conditions, which vary from place to place. You may put sprouts in direct sunlight for the final day to develop the chlorophyll in them. One of the truly delightful aspects of sprouting is that it is simple enough for young children to learn. They almost invariably enjoy being involved with it, even taking responsibility for the whole project.

You can sprout and enjoy alfalfa seeds, mung beans, sunflower seeds, wheat, rye, barley, millet, oats, soybeans, garbanzos, whole peas, lentils, pintos, kidney beans, and navy beans. Use sprouts in sandwiches and salads, with cooked vegetables, in casseroles, egg foo yung, quiches, various types of vegetable burgers and loaves, in numerous Oriental meat, chicken, or fish entrees, vegetable pancakes, and soups. Grain and sunflower seed sprouts are great additions to breads and stuffings.

Where cost is concerned, *Inflation Fighters* points out that:

Growing sprouts is very economical. Just one pound of dried seeds or beans produces about 8 pounds of sprouts. A pound will serve 8 people for 2¢–8¢ per serving, depending on the variety and price of the seeds. Alfalfa seeds are in the more expensive range, but 1 pound of alfalfa seeds gives you 10 gallons of sprouts!

Sprouts are so nutritious, simple and refreshing that they have a way of inspiring devotion. I'm not the only one who has taken sprouts on the road—*Inflation Fighters* gives the following advice on sprouting while traveling:

Take sprouts camping and traveling. You'll never be strapped for fresh vegetables either under a tent fly or in any fast-food restaurant. Spice up a budget hamburger or fishburger with a generous handful of fenugreek, alfalfa, or radish sprouts. Stir crunch into a camper's stew with mung beans.

The simplest sprouter is a *sandwich size zip lock bag.* Put 1 tablespoon of seeds in water; let soak overnight. In the morning drain well, and puncture bag in several places. Tie bag to knapsack, or place under canoe seat or in trunk of car. You can also put it inside a plastic container, the top perforated with holes, in your handbag. At noon and in the evening rinse and drain again. Keep several bags going and you can feast on sprouts every night. . . .

AMOUNTS OF SEEDS AND SPROUTING TIMES

Seed or bean	Amount per quart of water	Time for sprouting
Alfalfa seeds	3 T.	3–4 days
Mung beans	¾ c.	2–3 days
Lentils	¾ c.	3 days
Sunflower seeds*	1 c.	2 days
Garbanzos	1 c.	3 days
Wheat*	1 c.	3 days
Barley*	1 c.	3 days
Soybeans*	1 c.	3 days
Peas	¾ c.	3–4 days
Oats*	1 c.	2–3 days

*Good ingredients for sprouted breads (recipe page 318).

Most natural and health food stores sell various special pieces of equipment designed to make sprouting easier and/or more efficient. Store personnel should be able to help you decide whether such equipment is worth the investment. The range is between a couple of dollars for some special lids for recycled jars, to twenty dollars or more for dome-shaped, multi-level, plastic constructions complete with built-in drains (see below). Back at the other end of the equipment spectrum, you can use a colander or sieve, for sprouting. With or without the special equipment, you can do your own sprouting at less than half the cost of store-bought sprouts and grow sprouts that are generally not commercially available, such as lentils, and sunflower seeds.

Sprouters

There have been many attempts to manufacture "ideal" sprouters. An ideal sprouter would have perfect moisture and temperature control, produce abundantly and quickly, and be easy to operate and clean. Nobody has attained perfection yet, but the sprouters listed below all work well. Most natural foods stores carry at least some of them. Prices are for comparison purposes only (at the time of writing, a Mason jar costs about fifty cents).

Sprouter	Design	Price
Beals's Famous Sprouter Box 323 Ft. Washington, PA 19034	Covered clay bowl which sits in ½ inch of water	$9.50
Redwood Sprouter 2506 Southland Dr. Austin, TX 78704	Rectangular redwood and plastic box	$12.50 (sm) $17.00 (lg)
Seedsmith Kienholz Products, Inc. 4400 Loch Alpine West Ann Arbor, MI 48103	Round plastic trays stacked three high	$12.50
Sprout Garden Vitality Farms, Inc. Box 7049 Fruitvale Station Oakland, CA 94601	Plastic wide mouth jar with mesh snap-on lid	$5.00
Sprout-Ease Tube Sprouter Bima Industries, Inc. P.O. Box 88007 Tukwila Branch Seattle, WA 98188	Mason jar shape made of plastic with threaded mesh lids for both ends	$8.00
Kiva Sproutfarm Kit Great Northern Distr. Co. 325 W. Pierpont Ave. Salt Lake City, UT 84101	Plastic tube with capillary action cap and cheesecloth wick, on wood stand	$9.00
***Sprout Kit** Sprouts Are Good 226 Hamilton Ave. Palo Alto, CA 94301	Quart Mason jar with stainless steel screen, booklet of instructions and recipes and a supply of seeds	$5.00

*This company sells stainless steel screens for wide mouth canning jars (83¢), a ½ gal. Mason jar Sprout House ($6.50), seed packs for sprouting and other related supplies.

GROWING HERBS INDOORS

If you can successfully grow house plants, you can also grow herbs. The main requirement is a sunny window. The herbs will be more flavorful if the window is opened when the weather permits to allow them direct exposure to sunlight and fresh air (even city air). Plant your window box densely to produce a blanket of growing plants. One or more types can be planted in the same window box. Try rosemary, sweet basil, marjoram, sage, winter savory, tarragon, thyme, chives, chervil, lemon balm, parsley, mint. Check with your local nursery to find out if there are other herbs that grow successfully indoors in your area. The same organic fertilizers sold for houseplants will rejuvenate your herb soil, as will powdered kelp. Wheat and rye can be planted in this fashion, the grass clipped with scissors and chopped for salads, cooking or juicing.

Herbs grown outdoors are generally more flavorful than those grown indoors, but indoor herbs are still far more flavorful than the dried, store-bought herbs in the little jars. No matter how much you

enjoy your fresh herbs, however, you will probably not use them as quickly as they become ready. To dry them, tie in bunches and hang upside down. They should not be dried in direct sunlight, and may be hung inside of paper bags, but not touching the bags, to keep out dust. Hang in a cool place: drying will take a little longer in cool areas but the herbs won't mold. When dry, remove the leaves from the stems and store in airtight containers, preferably lightproof, in a cool place. (See Chapter 34, *Drying Food.*)

When cooking with fresh herbs, use 1 tablespoon of fresh chopped herbs for ½ teaspoon of crushed dried herbs, or for ⅓ teaspoon powdered herbs. To bring out the flavor of dried herbs, first sauté in butter or oil, or let them soak in some of the liquid you will be using in your recipe, such as water, milk, soup stock, lemon juice, or oil.

For salad dressings, put a few sprigs of fresh herbs in your apple cider vinegar or wine vinegar; this will impart subtle aromas and flavors to the salad dressings made with the vinegar. Alternatively, you can put fresh herbs into the mixed dressing, finely minced or in sprigs.

Oriental cuisines use a lot of ginger, an herb both stimulating to the palate and a tonic for the whole body. As *Inflation Fighters* points out, you can grow your own ginger plant. Put a healthy knob of fresh ginger in a large pot of good soil. Keep it moist, not wet, and in a sunny place. Within a few months, you will not only have a beautiful plant, but the root will have multiplied enough to be harvested. By replanting one knob, you can keep recycling the plant.

If you have an outdoor garden from which to transplant them, you can grow lettuce, tomatoes, peppers, and even strawberries in your windowsill. Fertilize them liberally with fish emulsion and/or seaweed to keep them from going dormant. Pollinate them by blowing hard into the blossoms.

The nighttime temperature for herbs and vegetables should not fall below 55°F. If the nighttime outdoor temperature is likely to be less than fifty-five and you don't have double panes of glass, pull the plants about a foot back from the window panes or drop curtains between plants and glass. Your sunny (south facing) window should have about six hours of direct sunlight a day. Growth can be accelerated and sunlight augmented by suspended fluorescent lights about six inches above the tops of the plants.

27 *Making Dairy Products*

MAKING YOGURT

The New American Cuisine eliminates all food processes that detract from the nutritional potential of real food. It also eliminates all food processes that produce synthetic food—unreal food. The food processes that are left fall into two categories: those that alter the form of food to make it more palatable (alteration), and those that transform food by natural processes into entirely different food substances (transformation). In alteration processes—making bread, for example—you do more work. In transformation processes, nature does most of the work; you just set up the necessary working conditions. The previous two chapters have given us examples of both kinds of processes: sprouting is transformation, making mixes is alteration. To make yogurt, we return to transformation. (Refer to Chapter 5 for a discussion of the nutritional properties of yogurt.)

As with almost everything this book discusses, there are both quality and cost considerations relevant to yogurt making. Where cost is concerned, yogurt as a protein source is expensive: with roughly the same protein content as milk (3.5 percent), store-bought yogurt costs three to four times as much as milk. But making your own yogurt reduces the cost by 50 to 80 percent. It can cost very little more than milk, depending on how you make it, how you buy your milk, whether or not you flavor it and, if you do, what you flavor it with. Reduced to the same price range as milk, and considering all its nutritional advantages over milk, homemade yogurt is appropriate for even the lowest food budgets.

The problem with most commercially made yogurts is that they are made by the "flash" method, taking about three hours, and often use gelatin, various gums and other thickeners and stabilizers. Your homemade yogurt may take seven or eight hours, time for the full development of the health-giving yogurt microorganisms. Properly developed in the ideal temperature range, homemade yogurt will have a custard-like consistency; if you consider it too runny, you can thicken it by adding powdered milk. You also eliminate the sugar and the artificial colorings and flavorings found in commercially flavored yogurts by making your own.

Yogurt is rapidly becoming a popular food on the basis of its being healthful and low in calories:

One cup of	has this many calories
low fat yogurt	124
regular yogurt	152
commercially flavored yogurt	263
ice cream	294

The figures were obtained from "Exploring the Yogurt Mystique" by Dr. Mort Walker, *Consumer's Digest*, March/April, 1979.

Commercially flavored yogurt has almost as many calories as ice cream because most yogurt is flavored with heavily sweetened fruit preserves. After a few trials, many people discover that yogurt doesn't really need flavoring and sweetening, perhaps a bit of honey at most, because homemade yogurt is usually less tart than the commercial versions.

Yogurt making is an extremely simple process requiring a minimum of special equipment. A dairy thermometer is indispensable, at least for a beginner. Otherwise, you probably already have everything you will need. Here is a basic recipe:

> 1 qt. milk (whole milk will make creamier yogurt; skim milk will be a little lower in calories)
> ½ c. fresh nonfat dry milk powder
> Yogurt culture, or 2 T. plain yogurt as the culturing agent. (If the yogurt you use for a starter fails to work, it probably means the yogurt was weakly cultured. Use the yogurt failure in cooking and try another brand next time. The success or failure of a commercial yogurt as a starter for homemade yogurt is one good test of the commercial yogurt's quality.)

The milk powder will thicken the yogurt, though too much milk powder will make the texture chalky. I prefer it with no milk powder at all. If you add more culture, it will thicken the yogurt up to a point, then won't make it any thicker. Too much culture makes yogurt extra tart; too little makes it lumpy. If you add a little honey, it will help the culture bacteria to multiply, which is necessary for the transformation of milk into yogurt. But the essential ingredient is a good culture. Here are the steps:

1. Heat milk to scalding (170°F. kills the bacteria that interfere with the yogurt process). Remember: milk tends to scorch if heated too quickly, even if you are stirring frequently. So take a little extra time and heat milk at low to medium temperature.
2. Cool the milk down to 120°. Whisk the milk powder in a separate bowl with some of the heated milk, or use a blender to mix it. Then stir this in with the rest of the milk.

3. The milk should then be cooled to 115°F., which is the ideal temperature at which to add the culture. At this temperature, you can put your finger in the milk and it feels very hot, but not too hot to keep your finger in it. Add the culture to the rest of the heated milk and stir in thoroughly.

4. Pour the milk into a really clean container that you will use to incubate the yogurt. Maintain a constant temperature between 115° and 100°F., 107° being nearly ideal. Here are some suggestions for incubating:
    a) Use a thermos
    b) Use a glass jar which you can cover with a fiberfill or down sleeping bag
    c) Place the jar on top of a heating pad set low
    d) Put in a gas oven heated by the pilot light or an electric oven set at warm
    e) In an ice chest filled with warm water at 115°F. With methods b) through e) you can make larger quantities of yogurt, say 6 to 8 quarts
    f) Set a glass jar outside in the summer sun in an area sheltered from the wind

5. To test for readiness, put a chopstick in the center of the yogurt. If it stands by itself, it's ready. If you incubate the yogurt too long, it will become too tart.

Refrigerate the yogurt until it is chilled.

Incubators

For small-scale yogurt making, there are commercial yogurt makers that depend on electrical elements to maintain a constant temperature and those that depend on insulation alone. In my own experience, the nonelectrical type produces a better tasting product. I theorize that the difference is due to the fact that in the insulation method the temperature gradually drops. We actually have a range of temperatures of perhaps fifteen degrees, and different microbiological activities occur at different temperatures. This range of activities corresponding to the range of temperatures cannot occur in a machine that maintains a constant temperature.

The best yogurt I have made was in a yogurt-making device manufactured by a friend of mine in Denver, Mary Moody. Mary's device is also the simplest I have seen—it can't properly be called a machine at all—depending solely on the right size, shape, amount, and kind of insulation. Called the "Manfood Yogurt Maker," it requires no external energy, as it is simply an insulated canister that controls the temperature of the milk perfectly. The nonelectrical, insulation type of yogurt incubator is a more precise way of accomplishing what can also be done by simply wrapping the jars in a blanket or quilt. The electrical type of yogurt maker is a more precise way of accomplishing what can also be done with the heat of an oven pilot light or the heat of a small light bulb in a closed box.

Starters

For centuries in the Middle East and Eastern Europe it has been common to pass strains of yogurt from one generation to the next. I once helped to keep a yogurt culture thriving over a couple of years. It was started from store-bought yogurt made by Mountain High in Colorado and was terminated because we chose not to bother transporting it when we moved from Colorado to California. That yogurt strain could have journeyed with us, but most yogurt cultures will not remain viable as long as that one.

Most commercial yogurt cultures are made of equal quantities of freeze-dried bacteria known as *S. thermophilus and L. bulgaricus*. During succeeding batches of yogurt, various alterations of composition can, and with most cultures, usually do, occur: one type of bacteria begins to dominate the other; airborne bacteria (harmless) join the yogurt and begin to multiply; the acidity level changes. The taste and consistency of your yogurt will begin changing. At that point, you may wonder if you are doing something wrong. Probably not, but it's time to buy another envelope of starter and begin a new series of batches. On the average, this will be after about eight weeks if you are making yogurt every week. However, how soon you will want to renew your culture also depends on such factors as the kind of milk you use, the temperatures you employ, what taste and consistency you prefer, and the nature of the culture itself.

Using Homemade Yogurt

Yogurt can be served plain, or with fresh fruit, honey, molasses, preserves, ground seeds, dried fruit. Add it to smoothies. Substitute it for sour cream. Use yogurt as a base for low-calorie salad dressing.

Salad dressing. Yogurt made at home can be inexpensive enough to reduce the cost of salad dressing usually made from a mayonnaise base, and to reduce the calories of the mayonnaise itself. How much yogurt you use depends on its consistency, what consistency of dressing is acceptable, and your taste preference. The yogurt can be either the major or minor ingredient. There is a range between ¼ cup mayonnaise–1 cup yogurt, to 1 cup mayonnaise–¼ cup yogurt. Here's a way to make Russian Dressing:

1½ c. mixed yogurt and mayonnaise	¼ t. powdered dill
½ c. tomato sauce	¼ t. powdered tarragon
1 T. minced parsley	

Mix all ingredients together, chill, and serve. (For more on salad dressings, see Chapter 19.)

Spaghetti sauce. As an ardent fan of both whole grain pasta and yogurt, I often make pasta sauce with yogurt, using ingredients like mushrooms, onions, garlic, ground turkey, tuna fish, herbs that strike my fancy. If you follow my lead with improvisations of your own, add the yogurt after everything else is done and bring the whole mixture up to serving temperature, but not to boiling. If you boil yogurt, it curdles—nothing wrong with that, it just looks weird. You can prevent the curdling by adding one teaspoon of oat bran, cornstarch, or potato flour per cup of yogurt before adding yogurt to the recipe.

Yogurt cream cheese. Here's a recipe for yogurt cream cheese:

1. Suspend one quart yogurt in cheesecloth over a bowl.
2. Let it drip for 12 to 24 hours. The longer it hangs, the drier it will be.
3. Take the yogurt cream cheese out of the bag and use as you would regular cream cheese, as a spread, a dip, etc. Do not use this cream cheese to cook with. Since it is yogurt-based, it will tend to separate when cooked. You can make raw cheesecake from it. Whole milk yogurt, of course, will make creamier cheese than low fat.

PIIMA AND VIILIA—YOGURT'S EXCEPTIONAL COUSINS

The first step in making yogurt is to scald or boil the milk—the rule because the culture will not produce yogurt unless you do. But piima (pronounced *peema*), the Finnish yogurt-like clabbered milk made with a culture containing four strains of bacteria (unlike yogurt, which ordinarily contains two), is different.
Piima is exceptional for two reasons:

1) It can be made from raw milk, 72°F. being the ideal temperature for this culture;
2) it is self-regenerative, lasting indefinitely if handled according to directions.

Piima is an old culture developed in Scandinavia, still common in Finland, where it was observed that when cows grazed on the wild herb motherwort, their milk tended to curdle without special encouragement into a yogurt-like consistency. From this "spontaneous yogurt," piima culture was extracted and has been passed down for generations. It will work with any kind of milk, including soy milk (when it is fresh, not made from soy powder), but is best when made from high quality raw milk. The custard-like quality of piima breaks down when it is shaken, so piima is not suitable for commercial production. The culture is available from natural foods stores, or from Piima, Box 2116, La Mesa, CA 92041, for $2.75.

Viilia (pronounced *vee* lee ya) is another raw milk culture from Finland, found to contain two strains of bacteria and one form of yeast responsible for its culturing action. Other differences between viilia and piima are that the latter is sold in powder form and is a recent emigrant from Finland, whereas viilia has been in the Finnish community of Ft. Bragg, California, for over eighty years, and the culture is sold in liquid form. Despite the differences, however, they are made similarly and are quite similar in taste and consistency. Viilia is available from Gem Cultures, 30301 Sherwood Rd., Ft. Bragg, CA 95437, for $3.50.

Baking. Yogurt can be substituted for milk in baking and pancakes with the addition of a half teaspoon of baking soda per cup of yogurt. Use equal amounts of yogurt for milk. If your yogurt is thick, you may have to add a little water to get the batter consistency right. No baking soda is needed when substituting yogurt for buttermilk.

Toppings and frostings. For toppings, thicken yogurt with nonfat dry milk powder, sweeten with honey, flavor and spice to taste. For frostings, follow the topping procedure but make it thicker; chopped fruit and/or nuts can also be added.

Drinks. Mix yogurt half and half (more or less, according to taste) with fresh fruit or vegetable juices. At mealtimes, these are cooling soups; between meals, they are energizing refreshers.

MAKING KEFIR

Whereas yogurt is a solid made from a liquid culture, kefir is a liquid made from a solid culture. The starter for kefir is known as kefir "grains"—tiny pellets composed of various strains of yeast, bacteria, and milk protein. Kefir grains can be found in natural foods stores and, unlike yogurt cultures, do not weaken and need to be replaced. The kefir grains settle to the bottom and can be saved and used in your next batch. Kefir started from the liquid of a previous batch without including the grains will deposit its own grains. If you keep saving and re-using your kefir grains, you will find your supply increasing. Kefir grains can be considered seeds, making this a unique food—*the only animal product that reproduces itself through its own self-generated seed.* If you are unable to find them locally, kefir grains can be bought by mail from RAJ Biological Laboratory, 35 Park Ave., Blue Point, NY 11715.

You can easily turn your homemade kefir into sweetened and flavored kefir with pureed fruit, fruit syrups, honey, molasses, maple syrup, carob syrup, vanilla, and almond extract. These additions should be stirred in *after* the kefir is made. Kefir is on a par with yogurt nutritionally and you may find it an excellent alternative. It is often described as a mild-flavored liquid yogurt. This is an accurate description of the kefirs sold commercially, which are made from a culture. There is nothing wrong with these products, but they will not reproduce themselves from grains in the manner of your authentic homemade kefir (which will also develop a slight effervessence and a little alcohol—about 2 percent).

Another major difference between yogurt and kefir is that kefir does not have to be incubated. The first step in kefir making is the same as for yogurt—scalding milk. From that point, kefir is much simpler: you let the milk cool to room temperature, add the kefir grains or three tablespoons of liquid kefir, cover, and let sit at room temperature for approximately twenty-four hours. You know it's ready when it has thickened to the consistency of thick buttermilk. Your first batch may be a little runnier than you'd like, but subsequent batches should turn out thicker. As in yogurt, nonfat dry milk powder can be added to the milk before heating to yield a thicker product; add up to one quarter cup per quart of milk.

MAKING BUTTERMILK, SOUR CREAM, AND COTTAGE CHEESE

The natural way to make these is to make them simultaneously, starting with raw milk. The general procedure is to skim off the cream, then make cultured buttermilk from the skim milk, and then make cottage cheese from the buttermilk. It could break down as follows, assuming you start with a gallon of milk: you would get around six ounces of sour cream; taking two quarts of buttermilk for cottage cheese would yield a pint of cottage cheese, three pints of whey (the whey will have water soluble vitamins and minerals in it, and can be used for drinking, baking, making soups and sauces); and you would have one and three quarters quarts of buttermilk for drinking. (If you were more interested in cottage cheese, using a third quart of buttermilk for that purpose would give you another half pint of cottage cheese; if you weren't interested in sour cream, your cottage cheese and buttermilk would be full fat instead of low fat.) You need:

—a shallow ladle for skimming off the cream;
—a small bowl for the sour cream;
—a gallon crock or bowl (or two of half that size);
—some cheesecloth;
—a quarter cup of souring agent. The souring agent can be yogurt, buttermilk, or kefir; if you have none of those, lemon juice or vinegar will also work.

1. Let the milk stand at room temperature for about four hours to allow the cream to rise to the top.
2. Skim off cream, put in small bowl, stir in half of souring agent, cover bowl with cheesecloth.
3. Stir the rest of the souring agent into the skim milk, cover with cheesecloth.

Note: You are covering with cheesecloth in order to allow a necessary air flow over the cream and milk while keeping foreign matter out.

4. Allow eighteen to twenty-four hours for the souring in a warm place.
5. Remove cheesecloth covers, put solid covers on sour cream and drinking buttermilk, and refrigerate.

Note: Your sour cream and buttermilk will not have the uniform smoothness of their commercial counterparts, but store-bought will not come close to your sparkling homemade flavor.

6. Cottage cheese: The lumpiness of your buttermilk is the beginning of the separation into curds and whey. Now encourage this process by heating the buttermilk to between 105° and 115° for about half an hour, stirring occasionally.
7. Pour the curds and whey into a strainer or colander lined with cheesecloth set in your crock or bowl or some other container to catch the whey. Let the curds drain until they are dry enough to suit you. Your cottage cheese is now ready to eat and/or refrigerate. A quarter teaspoon of salt per pint of cottage cheese can be stirred in at this point as an optional ingredient.

(Commercial cottage cheese usually contains salt and often other additives as well; but high quality brands will have no other ingredients than these: milk, cream, salt, culture. Anything else indicates that the manufacturer is taking shortcuts, lowering quality in the effort to lower cost.)

MAKING BUTTER

In the procedure outlined above, making butter is an alternative to making sour cream. Some natural foods stores sell small butter churns. A glass jar is an alternative to a churn, but it takes about forty-five minutes of shaking. I've been asked if you can use a blender. The answer is no, they spin too fast.

Start with chilled cream. When churned or shaken, the cream creates a large lump; pour the contents of the churn or jar through a strainer. The liquid is *churned* buttermilk, contrasted with the *cultured* buttermilk made above. Press the lump of butter into the desired shape with the flat edge of a knife and refrigerate.

28 Baking Bread, Making Pasta

. . . good bread can be ludicrously simple. If you use mainly wheat flour, if· you do not make the dough too wet, if you mix it thoroughly, and if you make sure it is cooked through, then anything goes. It is just a question of doodling intelligently . . .   (Colin Tudge in *Future Food*)

BAKING BREAD

Experienced bakers like to talk about the "art" of making bread and about the mysteries of the process. Bakers with a mystical bent have been overheard talking about the alchemy of baking. It can be artful, and there are subtle aspects hidden from even the most skilled baker. But don't let the "art" of baking intimidate you. Tudge is right: if you can make a stew, casserole, spaghetti sauce, or omelette, you can bake a loaf of bread. Let's look at the basics of intelligent doodling with flour and water.

The Flour

There are two terms that modify the words whole wheat to indicate superior quality; the first is *100 percent stoneground.* It is important to specify 100 percent because it is legal to remove 30 percent of the bran and germ and still call the flour "whole wheat."

Stoneground is meaningful because it produces superior quality flour. Making flour with steel roller mills and hammer mills are the fast ways of doing it—not so much grinding it as splintering and crushing it. True *grinding* is achieved between stones. There are both gross and subtle differences between steel-crushed and stoneground flour. On the gross level, stoneground flour comes out both cooler and coarser, resulting in higher food and fiber values. "But," people ask, "if the flour is going into the oven anyway, what difference does it make? The vitamins that you save by cool grinding are going to be destroyed by baking." That brings us to the subtle differences. I realize that taste is subjective but there is a definite consensus among people who have worked with both, that stoneground flour tastes better. I agree; words like "fuller" and "nuttier" come to mind.

Trying to assess what is responsible for the fuller, nuttier flavor moves us into the realm of theory. My theory is that there is an interplay of forces between the bread ingredients that can't be described by vitamins and other chemical terminology. What our taste buds are discerning is more akin to alchemy. That is to say, I don't really know what's happening but *something* is, the theory being that the better the chemical qualities of the flour, the better the alchemy in the oven, the better the bread tastes.

311

The other meaningful term that can modify whole wheat is *organically grown*, meaningful, that is, if it really is organically grown. A good natural foods store using the word organic really means it and has taken care to apply the term only to proven sources. That's an incalculable advantage found in the independently owned, specialized natural foods store: the owners/managers/employees are usually personally dedicated and knowledgeable because their personal integrity is on the line. ("Organically grown" is the subject of the Epilog; Chapter 31 has more on flour.)

Another advantage to dealing with a good natural foods store is that you can find out how fresh the flour is. After the wheat is ground, each day more vitamins and enzymes oxidize, so the fresher the flour, the better. I used to grind the flour in my stores; when people baked with fresh flour for the first time they would always be amazed at how much better their bread tasted.

The Four Optional Ingredients

Although flour and water are all that are necessary to make bread, for a more traditional American style bread there are four basic optional ingredients: leavening, sweetener, shortening, and salt. Leavening modifies the bread by lightening the texture and consistency. The usual leavening agent is *yeast*, a type of one-celled plant (a type of fungus, actually) that produces bubbles of carbon dioxide which rise, expanding the dough as they push up through the heavy, spongy mass. The yeast cells feed on sugar and can live on the naturally occurring sugars of grain, but usually a little extra *sweetener* is added to make them more active, to mask the yeasty flavor and to act as a natural preservative. *Shortening* is always some form of fat, giving the bread a softer texture. *Salt* performs the same function in bread as in most other foods, being a flavor enhancer and natural preservative. As you go down the list of optional ingredients from yeast and sweetener to shortening to salt, they become more and more optional.

The Sponge Method

Coarsely ground flour allows you the most benefit from the bran fiber and gives the bread a stronger texture. However, the gluten takes longer to develop with coarse flour, so it is best to use the sponge method. In this method, the ingredients are combined in stages, rather than all at once.

The sponge allows the yeast cells to multiply in the absence of salt and shortening, which inhibit yeast somewhat; the gluten also develops, which reduces your kneading requirements.

SPONGE METHOD WHOLE WHEAT BREAD

2 T. yeast	¼ c. oil
2 c. lukewarm water	½ c. milk powder
¼ c. molasses	2 t. salt
¼ c. honey	7 c. whole wheat flour

Step 1: Dissolve yeast in lukewarm water, add honey and molasses and enough flour (about 2 cups) to form the sponge. Cover and let sit in a warm place for 45 minutes to an hour.

Step 2: Fold in the rest of the ingredients and just enough flour so that the dough hangs together and pulls away from the sides of the bowl. Let sit another half-hour, covered, in a warm place.

Step 3: Fold in remaining flour and knead, knead, knead. Divide in half and place in two

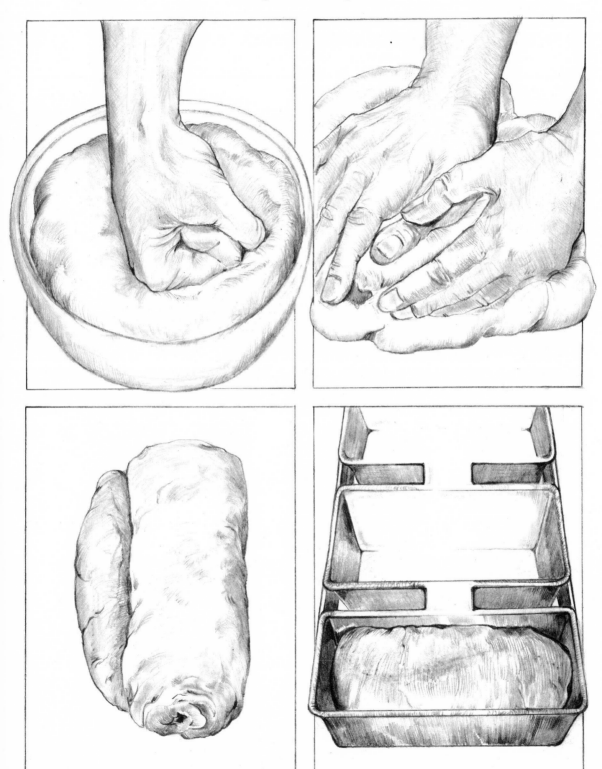

oiled bread pans (4½″ × 8½″ for a 2 pound loaf. The dough should occupy half to two-thirds of the pan). Cover and let rise again until double in bulk.

Step 4: Bake in preheated oven (350°) about 1 hour or until done. When done, it will shrink from the sides of the pan, and sound hollow when tapped. Color will be golden brown.

I chose the word "fold" rather than "mix" in Steps 2 and 3 because you want to keep the dough in one piece as much as possible: As *The Tassajara Bread Book* points out, "Each cut and tear will lessen the elasticity and strength of the dough."

Kneading mixes the dough, gives it a smooth texture, and develops the rising power. Flour the board or table you use for kneading, and flour or oil your hands. Start by folding the dough, towards you, in half. Then push it down and away from you with the heels of your hands. Turn the dough a quarter turn, fold in half as before, and rock forward pushing with the heel of your hands again. As you push, you rock your whole body forward; you will develop a rhythm as you go. Continue to flour the board till the dough no longer sticks to it. Kneading will take 10 minutes or more, depending on your enjoyment of it and your perseverance.

Variations: The recipe above is basic and could be the foundation for many variations: you can add such nutritional supplements as soy flour, wheat germ, bran, and nutritional yeast; eggs and cheese; fruit, nuts, and seeds; herbs and spices, vegetables such as onions, carrots, and zucchini; other whole grain flours and meals. Interesting tastes and textures can be achieved by substituting other whole grains for wheat, from 10 percent to 50 percent. Corn meal and millet meal will make your bread crunchier; rye flour, brown rice flour, buckwheat flour and barley flour will make it more dense and moist; rolled oats will make it chewier, and each grain adds its own distinctive taste.

Pita Bread

Pita bread is also called both "pocket" and "Bible" bread. Here are the instructions, from *Sunburst:*

Prepare recipe for whole wheat bread. After the first rise, punch down, knead, and return to bowl. Let rise again. Roll out into pieces about ¼ inch thick, about 6-8 inches in diameter. Put them on a cookie sheet sprinkled with cornmeal to prevent sticking. Bake at 400° for 10 minutes or until they have "poofed up." Remove and cool.

(In case you're not familiar with pita bread, which is Armenian in origin, when the rounds are cut across the diameter, the half rounds form two pockets, especially good for sloppy sandwich ingredients that can't be contained by sliced bread.)

About Yeast

Many natural foods stores carry two kinds of baking yeast: fresh yeast, compressed into cakes, and dry yeast, in granule form. (Nutritional yeast is an entirely different creature; see Appendix Seven.) When a recipe says, "a tablespoon of yeast," it is usually talking about fresh yeast. Otherwise it will say, "a tablespoon of yeast granules" or "active dry yeast." Both kinds are equally active but the dry granules are in the dormant state until moisture is introduced. If you want to substitute one form of yeast for another, remember that one tablespoon of active dry yeast granules represents twice the rising power of one of fresh yeast.

Sunburst, under "Bread Baking Hints from Our Bakery," has the following hints about yeast:

Be sure yeast is fresh; that is, has been kept airtight and cool—not necessarily in refrigerator. Yeast shouldn't be much over a month old.

All ingredients should be at room temperature or warmer. 75° is a good temperature. Water or milk should be at 90° or so; too cold and the yeast goes to sleep.

Remember that dough works best when used fresh. Once you have mixed and kneaded the bread, it should be watched carefully and let rise until only double in bulk, then put in loaf pans and let rise less than double—then bake! Too much rising and bread will be dry and possibly taste yeasty or like alcohol vapor . . .

Unyeasted Breads

Beginning and novice bakers are usually surprised to discover how much whole grain baking can be accomplished without yeast. One type is *quickbread*, which often uses baking powder and/or eggs to produce a degree of lightness. They are quick because all you do is combine the wet ingredients with the dry, which are premixed separately, lightly mixing them together. Take care not to overmix if leavening is an ingredient or you will activate it prematurely. Baking soda, which can cause stomach inflammation, is not recommended for quick breads. In the following recipe *air*, beaten into the egg yolks, is the leavening agent. An all-time American favorite quickbread, adapted from *Sunburst*:

CORN BREAD

3 c. cornmeal (whole, not degerminated)	¼ c. oil
2 c. milk	¼ c. honey or molasses
3 eggs, separated	1 t. salt

Beat egg yolks and combine with all ingredients except egg whites, mixing to remove all lumps. Beat egg whites until stiff and fold into batter. Bake in oiled pan for about an hour at 375°, the exact time depending on the coarseness of the cornmeal.

Most commercial baking powders are high in sodium. Some are made with aluminum compounds and leave a bitter aftertaste. Health and natural foods stores carry brands that are low in sodium, made with cream of tartar, and relatively free of bitterness.

Homemade baking powder. To make your own aluminum-free baking powder, combine ½ c. of baking soda with one cup of cream of tartar and one cup of arrowroot powder. For aluminum-free *low sodium* packing powder, substitute potassium bicarbonate for baking soda.

Unleavened Bread

Made without yeast, baking powder/soda, or eggs, this is "peasant" fare—dense, coarse, chewy, ideal if you want something to sink your teeth into and give your jaw muscles a workout. Any mixture of flours and meals will work, with wheat giving the most rise. Use two parts flour to one of hot water, making a pliable, elastic dough. Salt to taste, add a tablespoon of oil per two cups of flour if you want the texture a little softer. *Tassajara Bread Book* gives these tips concerning unleavened bread:

—"When kneading is first begun, the dough will tear rather than stretch. Keep working with it until it is smooth and elastic (about 300 kneads). Resting now and then is permitted.

—"When loaves are in the pans, make a wedge-shaped slit the length of each loaf with a knife." This allows the loaf to expand without bursting.

—"Brush the tops of the loaves with warm water or oil to keep moist. Cover with damp towel and let sit in a warm place for 8 to 12 hours . . ." This is called "proofing." Proofing can be extended up to 24 hours—the added time should produce lighter texture.

—"Bake until . . . dark brown." Approximate time and temperature for a large loaf are one hour at 350°.

Kneading and proofing produce a surprisingly light unleavened bread, particularly when the dough is two-thirds or more wheat. Loaves are not the only way to shape unleavened bread: chapattis and tortillas show us another way.

We don't usually think of them this way, but *crackers* are just another form of bread. If you weigh a box, you'll realize they are an expensive form of bread. Homemade, they are no more expensive than regular bread and they are easy to do. Adapted from *Sunburst*, these sesame crackers are also unleavened bread:

SESAME CRACKERS

½ c. water	1½ c. whole wheat flour
4 T. oil	½ c. soy flour
2 T. milk	½ c. sesame seeds
½ t. salt	

Mix all ingredients and make a stiff, pliable dough. Roll out—the thinner the better. Lay on an oiled and floured cookie sheet, sprinkle with salt and sesame seeds. With a fork, prick the crackers and mark into squares. Bake at 350° for 20 minutes, cut them after they have cooled a bit.

Phytates

Leavening breaks down phytates, formed by phytic acid in the bran of wheat, which binds the calcium, iron, and zinc in the bran, preventing absorption. Since the phytates only involve the minerals of the bran, and not minerals from any other sources, unleavened bread should not lead to mineral deficiencies unless it is a major part of the diet. Other ways to break the phytic acid bond are soaking, sprouting, and souring.

Natural Sourdough

Many books on baking give instructions for making sourdough starter with commercial yeast. But authentic sourdough starter is made with just two ingredients: flour and water. Combine equal amounts of flour and water, cover with a light cloth, and leave in a warm place for two to five days. The flour and water are a medium in which airborne yeasts can multiply; it is ready for use when it is bubbly, frothy, and sour. It will take more time to develop in cold climates. As you use it, replace the used portion with more half water/half flour, letting it redevelop the bubbly, frothy, sour effect. Unless you use it a couple of times a week, it will become too acidic. To prevent that, freeze between uses; thaw and warm to room temperature before using.

SOURDOUGH BREAD

8 c. whole wheat flour	½ c. sesame oil
2 c. sourdough starter	1 T. salt
2 c. warm water	

Thoroughly mix four cups of the flour, the starter, and the water, and let it rest in a warm place overnight, or for twelve hours.

Add the remaining flour, oil, and salt to your sponge and knead for 10 minutes. Let the dough rise until doubled, then punch down. Divide dough in half, place in two oiled pans, let rise again. Bake at 400° for 20 minutes, reduce heat to 350° and bake an additional hour.

THE SIMPLEST BREAD OF ALL

Sprouted wheat bread, adapted from *Sunburst*: The idea here is to make a dough-like mash from sprouted wheat. Sprouted wheat is the only ingredient unless you also want a bit of salt.

Fill a gallon jar half full of wheat berries (kernels). Soak overnight in water. Drain, rinse, and drain again. Put the jar of berries in a dark place, around 80° if possible, for 3 days, rinsing 3 times a day.

After 3 days, put sprouts through a food mill. Add salt to taste, shape into loaves or rounds about 6 inches in diameter and 1 inch high. Put in oiled pans or on oiled cookie sheet and bake at 250° until dry and dark brown.

Sprouted rye or triticale can be made the same way; corn takes five days to sprout. Sprouted wheat is amazingly sweet and people usually allergic to wheat often don't react to it after it's been sprouted.

The short course above illustrates the fundamentals of New American baking and gives you enough material to get a handle on the essential techniques. Now let's say you're not ready to buy *Sunburst Farms Family Cookbook* or *Laurel's Kitchen* or *The Tassajara Bread Book*—you love your stained, dog-eared *Joy of Cooking* (by the way, the latest edition has been made far more natural than older editions). It's been the textbook with which you learned to cook, the encyclopedia of culinary wisdom. Okay, your old faithful cookbook is still useful. The difference will be that your old bread was white, your new one will be brown. So it's time to talk about how that difference will come about.

SUBSTITUTION

Where your old recipe reads	*substitute*	*or*
flour	100% stoneground whole wheat flour	other whole grain flours
sugar	honey	malt syrup, molasses, date sugar
shortening or lard	butter	unrefined vegetable oil

Whole Wheat For White Flour

Wheat is the most widely used grain for baking because it contains a high percentage of gluten, a protein which traps air in the dough, giving it its rising power. Most recipes call for all-purpose white flour. In substituting whole wheat flour, there are two choices. For bread, rolls, biscuits and crackers, look for the words "100% stoneground whole wheat flour." For cakes, pastries, pancakes, and waffles, look for the words "100% stoneground whole wheat pastry flour." Regular, or bread, whole wheat flour is made from hard, high protein wheat. Whole wheat pastry flour is made from soft wheat, lower in protein, producing a lighter texture. Hard wheat is sometimes called "red," as it is darker in color than pastry wheat, which, in contrast, is sometimes called "white." But don't be confused by the words soft and white. Whole wheat pastry flour is still whole, and the color is still brown.

For 1 cup of white flour substitute ¾ cup of whole wheat flour or ⅞ cup of whole wheat pastry flour.

Honey For White Sugar

Use ¾ cup honey to replace 1 cup sugar. At the same time, decrease the amount of liquid in the recipe, up to ¼ cup for each ¾ cup of honey used. The more delicate the flavor of the recipe, the lighter the honey should be. (Darkness in honey indicates mineral content and stronger flavor.) Clover, mesquite, thistle, and fireweed are examples of light honeys.

As well as minerals, honey contains enzymes and small amounts of vitamins. These, however, are largely destroyed by cooking temperatures. So, the use of honey instead of sugar is much more important in uncooked foods. In cooking with honey, you will want to ask yourself, (1) do you like the results? and (2) are the results worth the cost?

Where the cost of honey seems prohibitive, it can be lessened by mixing it half and half with molasses or malt syrup. But this alternative is limited to those recipes where the molasses or malt flavor is compatible.

Another alternative is date sugar, which is simply dehydrated and granulated dates. Using date sugar one-for-one gives generally excellent results. Its primary disadvantage is that it is expensive.

Unrefined Vegetable Oils For Shortening or Lard

If the recipe calls for shortening or lard in its solid form, substitute ⅞ cup vegetable oil for 1 cup—that is, 1 cup minus two tablespoons. If the recipe calls for liquified shortening or lard, substitute an equal amount of vegetable oil.

MAKING BULGUR

Bulgur differs from cracked wheat in that it is cooked before it is cracked. Store-bought bulgur is not an expensive food but you can make it even less expensive by making your own. You may find quality an even greater incentive for making your own bulgur: I have never seen commercially made bulgur from organically grown wheat, but you will find organically grown wheat berries in most natural food stores.

To make bulgur, cook the whole-wheat berries for an hour, two parts liquid to one of wheat. The liquid can be plain water, as it is when bulgur is made commercially, or stock, or water seasoned any way you like.

Next drain off any liquid that has not been absorbed by the wheat, spread the berries on a cookie sheet, or some other suitable tray, and put them in the oven at 225°F. Toast the berries until they are completely dry, approximately one hour, stirring them around a few times.

The final steps are simply to let the wheat cool, then crack it in your blender or your grinder. If you're doing it in a blender, watch it closely so that you don't grind it too finely.

Butter makes more crumbly cookies and flakier pie crust than vegetable oil. (For more on substitution see Chapter 29.)

A note about time: don't forget that the times of most recipes are quoted for sea-level elevations and that higher elevations require more time. A working rule of thumb is to allow 5 minutes for every 2,500 feet above sea level, so that if you are 10,000 feet up in the Rockies, you'd allow about 20 extra minutes. You should watch each recipe closely the first time and make a note of how it acts; all kinds of recipes will not follow the same strict time pattern.

MAKING PASTA

Making pasta is much like making unleavened bread. The big difference is that this form of unleavened bread is boiled instead of baked. The pasta-as-another-form-of-unleavened-bread similitude seems a little farfetched to most of us because the only kind of pasta we've seen or eaten is the kind that has been dried and packaged. But the connection becomes clear when you make your own pasta. And even if you're not a pasta lover like me, I think you'll like your own homemade pasta better than store-bought.

You don't need a $200 machine to make your own pasta. It can all be done by hand, and most people are surprised to discover what a simple production it is. You gain time with a machine and there are shapes you can't get easily by hand. Very long and very thin spaghetti and spaghettini would be so laborious to produce by hand that they could hardly be worth the trouble. But you can make fairly long and fairly thin noodles, short noodles, wide noodles, lasagne noodles, and pasta pouches for ravioli, all by hand. You can, in fact, invent shapes you've never seen in a package.

Basic Pasta

Use 2 cups of whole wheat flour to 1 cup of hot water. Use whole wheat bread flour of the best possible quality. You do not need durum wheat, as used in commercial, dried pasta. Durum is used because it is lower in gluten than regular wheat. It therefore dries better and is not sticky after boiling. Home-made pasta is an entirely different experience: it is soft and absorbent, sponging up sauce readily. By contrast, commercial pasta absorbs much less sauce, tending more towards floating in it. The difference between them is like the difference between a bagel (commercial pasta) and a doughnut (home-made pasta).

A quarter teaspoon of salt is optional. This will serve four people where the pasta is a side dish; if it is to be the main dish, double the recipe.

Egg Pasta

1 beaten egg substitutes for a half cup of hot water. So, as an example, where egg pasta is to be the main dish for four people, you would have four cups of flour, two eggs, and one cup of hot water.

Variations

—You can steam any vegetable long enough to tenderize it, puree it in your blender, use the puree in place of the water, with or without eggs.

—You can substitute 50 percent of the whole wheat flour (not more, as the wheat acts as the glue for your mixture), creating different flavors and textures with different flours and meals. Possibilities include rye flour, corn flour, soy flour, sesame seed meal, sunflower seed meal; your wheat substitutes should not be coarse or the pasta will be crumbly.

—You can add an herb such as fennel for some special flavor, even add spices and/or honey for dessert noodles.

The method: save out enough of the flour to dust your hands and your board or table. Have the hot water ready in something easy to pour from. The hot water is always the last ingredient to go into your mixing bowl. Add it gradually, working the mixture with your hands or a wooden spoon until you have a dough that pulls away easily from the sides of the bowl. If you are using vegetable puree, have some hot water ready in case you need to moisten the dough further.

Next knead the dough until it becomes smooth and elastic. This will require only a few minutes if your dough is all wheat, up to a couple of extra minutes depending on how much of another ingredient has been substituted for wheat.

Next divide your dough into two or four or more pieces, depending on the size of your recipe, for rolling out on a floured surface. (If you can't get it as thin as you would like by hand, then you need a machine. It doesn't have to be an expensive electric one; there are manually operated machines for 25 percent of the cost of electric ones.) Before rolling, shape your dough into a rectangle, so the ends and edges will be reasonably regular once the dough is pressed out.

You can make little squares, fill them, and press the edges together for ravioli. You can dust a clean bottle, wrap the dough around it, cut strips and slide them off, making pasta rings. Using your imagination can make a hand operation more fun than a machine-assisted one, and there is no way to have pasta for less money.

Remember when you cook fresh pasta that it cooks quicker than dried pasta: equal thicknesses take roughly half as long, so keep your eye on it. It should be *al dente*, the Italian term that means tender, firm, without any trace of glueyness in the center. You can dry your own pasta on a rack, although of course it will take longer to cook. You can freeze pasta in floured trays, layering it between floured sheets of waxed paper, dropping the frozen pasta directly into boiling water. Of course, that too will take longer to cook.

Freezing the pasta as dough takes less space in your freezer. Allow a couple of hours for it to thaw. You can keep pasta dough in your refrigerator tightly wrapped so that it won't absorb moisture and odors and grow mold. But try to use it within a week—the fresher it is, the better it tastes. If you could find organically grown wheat, grind it yourself, make and eat your pasta the same day you ground the flour, you would be at the very top rung of pasta quality. But even if practical considerations leave you a rung or two down the ladder, you are in for a great treat when you eat your first batch of homemade fresh pasta.

Pasta Tools

Gourmet and department stores are the best sources for tools to save labor in pasta making. A pasta crimper, about $2, cuts noodles and cuts and seals ravioli. About $7 buys a rolling pin with scooped-out squares for making ravioli and about $8 buys a ravioli maker that is shaped like a shallow ice cube tray. For $20 you can buy a small machine that cranks out curly noodles and for about $40 you can buy a rolling pin with variably spaced discs to make noodles of different widths (the Matfer French Rolling Cutter). About $40 also buys an Atlas pasta machine, which efficiently cranks out noodles from extremely thin to lasagna width. Adding a couple of hundred dollars to the price of an Atlas will get you an electric pasta machine like the Bialetti, which can do a few additional tricks and do everything faster.

People are often sorely tempted to move from the inexpensive hand tools up the scale to the fancy electric machines as homemade pasta insidiously worms its delicious way into their lives. But electricity does not make better pasta and it is still easy enough with only a measuring cup, mixing bowl, wooden spoon, rolling pin, something to roll on, and a sharp knife.

29 Desserts From Scratch

You embrace most of Phase Two of the New American Cuisine when you decide to take on responsibility for making most or all your own desserts. In Chapter 22 we touched on ideas for simple desserts. Generally speaking, those desserts were not only simpler than the ones described in this chapter, but healthier: keep in mind when doing your meal planning that desserts such as those in this chapter are the source for a great deal of fat and sugar. We improve the nutritional quality by substituting whole foods for refined flour and sugar, but we can't change the fact that some form of shortening and some form of sweetening are the bricks and mortar of which these desserts are built. If you're like me, knowing what you know won't change your yen for goodies. Elimination may or may not be necessary; moderation certainly is. Moderation is an extremely general word. For me it might mean once a week, for you it might mean once a month—it depends on things like time, budget, lifestyle, health, body weight, doctor's orders, your goals, your self-image.

Desserts are a good metaphor for the fundamental attitudes behind this entire book. I can make a broad statement like, "If you make your own desserts out of natural ingredients, they'll be better for you and cost less than what you buy at the supermarket." I can suggest things to do that will demonstrate principles you can apply to a broad range of shifting circumstances. But I can't tell you what desserts to eat, how often, how much. I'm not the only one who can't tell you those things; nobody else can either, nor can any other book. This book is intended to encourage and inform your process of discovering what's right for you.

SUMMARY OF BAKING WITH NATURAL INGREDIENTS

More On Substitution

Baking powder: When you use baking powder in lieu of yeast or sourdough starter for leavening, to avoid excessive bitterness don't add more than one tablespoon for each cup of flour. When replacing baking soda with baking powder, use 1 T. baking powder for 2 t. baking soda. Use low sodium, aluminum-free baking powder. (Aluminum salts are toxic. For aluminum-free baking powder formulas, see Chapter 28.)

Eggs as leavening: Eggs are a leavening in quick breads and cakes. They can be used solely as the leavening (though it takes quite a few), or used in conjunction with baking powder, which you can then cut down in amount. Eggs should be at room temperature (as should all of your ingredients), carefully separated, and the whites well-beaten till fluffy. They are folded in after all of the other ingredients have been mixed together to incorporate air bubbles into the quickbread or cake to make it light.

Substituting arrowroot for flour or cornstarch to thicken sauces, puddings, and pie fillings: Since arrowroot is a source of protein, nutritionally it is a better food to use, though it can be somewhat temperamental. In sauces, it cannot be reheated, and it should be served soon after preparation, i.e. within 10 to 15 minutes. When substituting in baking, use 1½ teaspoons arrowroot for 1 tablespoon of white flour or 2 teaspoons arrowroot for 1 tablespoon cornstarch.

A substitute for whipped cream: From *Inflation Fighters*: "Instead of cream, beat a sliced, ripe banana and 1 egg white with electric mixer until banana dissolves and mixture is stiff. About 5 minutes . . ."

Substituting honey for sugar: When you make quickbreads or cakes with honey, they are going to be heavier and more moist than those made with sugar. Whole wheat and other whole grain pastries will be heavier than white flour pastries. The secret of using honey in baked goods is to whip the honey and egg yolks really well to incorporate tiny air bubbles.

There are certain things that you cannot make with honey. Only sugar will give you a chewy brownie, a chewy or a crunchy cookie. Honey makes each of these items cakey instead.

When making icings with honey and butter, and to some extent with honey and cream cheese or ricotta cheese, you will need to add nonfat dry milk powder or carob powder in order to make the icing stiff. Arrowroot will thicken honey-fruit sauces, honey puddings, and pie fillings. To some extent sugar has a natural thickening effect because it crystallizes when cool. Whipping cream can be sweetened with honey as easily as with sugar and will still be stiff. Ice cream will also work as well with honey as with sugar.

Changing white to brown: Below are three recipes from *The Joy of Cooking* which illustrate how you substitute natural ingredients for refined ingredients. Some of the amounts have been rounded off for ease of application. For specific step-by-step directions, read *Joy*.

JOY OF COOKING	SUBSTITUTES
Gingerbread	
½ c. butter	
½ c. sugar	⅓ c. molasses
1 egg	
2½ c. sifted all purpose flour	2 c., 2 T. whole wheat pastry flour
1½ t. baking soda	2½ to 3 T. baking powder (low sodium, no aluminum)
1 t. each cinnamon powder and ginger	
½ t. salt	
½ c light molasses	
½ c. honey	
1 c. hot water	
Jelly Roll	
¾ c. sugar	½ c. plus 1 T. honey
4 egg yolks	
1 t. vanilla	
¾ c. cake flour	⅔ c. whole wheat pastry flour
¾ t. double acting baking powder	

½ t. salt
4 egg whites
Spread with ½ c. jelly or tart jam or   *Spread with honey jam or honey*
   cream or custard filling

Caramel Custard Cornstarch Pudding
3 c. milk   3¼ c. milk (instead of 4 c. milk because of the liquid of
1 c. cold milk   the ¾ c. honey/molasses mix subbed for the sugar)
1 c. sugar   ⅜ c. honey plus ⅜ c. molasses (for caramel flavoring)
4 T. cornstarch   3 T. arrowroot
2 well beaten eggs
1 t. vanilla

ICE CREAM

Good ice cream requires obtaining an additional piece of equipment for your kitchen: an ice cream freezer, preferably a hand cranked one instead of an electric one because they burn calories instead of electricity and toughen arm muscles. You can't come close to the price and quality of homemade ice cream no matter what you buy in a store. The price of ice cream freezers varies widely—anywhere from $20 to $100. Manual freezers are harder to find but tend to be a little cheaper and often better made. Another, somewhat sly, advantage of a manual machine is that you will eat ice cream less often if you have to work for it.

Here is a basic recipe for churned ice cream:

    1 gallon whole milk (or ½ gallon whole milk plus ½ gallon half and half, or replace up to one
       quarter of either with cream)
    2 c. honey
    1 T. vanilla extract
    1 t. salt
    2 eggs, beaten (optional)

Even better to use than vanilla extract is a fresh vanilla bean: simmer it in a small amount of water to extract all of its flavor, add the honey to this water, then mix with milk. If the milk is very cold and you don't use warm vanilla water to melt the honey, it will help to slightly heat up the honey so it thoroughly mixes in. Or beat the eggs, if you use them, and add them to the honey to liquify it. The eggs are not crucial to churned ice cream, though they will make it taste richer. (Eggs act as an emulsifier in nonchurned ice cream, so are essential to its success.)

Once you have mixed up the basic ingredients, it is good to let the natural flavorings of fruit you are using sit in the milk mixture for a few hours, or even overnight. This way the flavoring will strongly permeate the milk before you churn it.

Pour the milk (or mixture with half and half or cream) into the center container of the ice cream freezer, insert the dasher, cover securely with the lid, and place the container inside the bucket.

Then pack layers of ice and rock salt around the container, inside the bucket. Let it sit for a few minutes to chill the container, then start to crank. Cranking at a moderate to slow speed is your best course—the ice cream will come out creamier that way. It may take up to 20 minutes to complete the process, so have the family take turns doing the cranking. Once you are done, remove the center container with the ice cream in it, remove the dasher and replace the lid, and put it in the freezer until ready to serve. Don't let it melt before serving and refreeze or it will form crystals.

Frozen Yogurt

You need your ice cream freezer for this too. You can't simply freeze yogurt in a tray in your freezer; that will give you a mixture of mush and ice crystals. You make frozen yogurt at home the same way you make ice cream. Use the basic ice cream recipe, substituting thoroughly cold yogurt for milk. If you are going to sweeten and flavor the yogurt, do so before chilling. For fruit-flavored yogurt, puree the fruit in the blender, add the yogurt to mix them thoroughly, chill, and proceed as for ice cream.

Although thickening yogurt with powdered milk is normally unnecessary, you should do so if your intention is to turn it into frozen yogurt. You might want to divide your yogurt-making into two batches, one for eating, the other for frozen yogurt.

Not all of the live yogurt culture survives freezing, but most of it does when the yogurt is served right from the tub of the ice cream freezer. This means that it is a genuinely healthy alternative to ice cream. I have heard people say about ice cream, "I'm addicted," meanwhile being afflicted with guilt over all the fat they're consuming. For such people buying an ice cream freezer and using it about three-quarters of the time for frozen yogurt instead of ice cream can provide relief.

PIES, CAKES, COOKIES, AND CANDIES

Pies

The two most popular types of pie crust are *flaky* and *cracker* crusts. Flaky crusts take longer to make, but the dough can be refrigerated for a few days and it will keep well; or it can be frozen for months. Here is a good flaky pie crust recipe:

FLAKY PIE CRUST

2 c. whole wheat pastry flour (sift if you like   ½ t. salt
   it lighter)   4 T. cold water
¾ c. butter (or ¾ cup less 1½ T. vegetable
   oil if flakiness isn't important)
Yield: two 9-inch pie crusts.

A pastry cutter is a big help here. Otherwise use two knives crossing and cutting away from each other. Mix salt and flour. Then add the butter, mixing with the pastry cutter until the dough is in ½ inch chunks. You want to do this in as few strokes as possible so that you don't work up the

gluten in the flour. If you do, the dough will rise somewhat and be cakey instead of flaky. When the butter and flour are thoroughly mixed, add the water, as cold as possible. The cold will keep the dough from being sticky and keep the butter solid when you roll out the dough.

Divide the dough evenly into two balls, if you are making a top and bottom crust, and roll out one at a time, from the center outward in all directions to form a circle. Use a sleeve on your rolling pin, or roll out the crusts inside a large plastic bag. Otherwise, you will have to flour the countertop and rolling pin, as a result adding more flour to the dough. The dough should be rolled out very thin, and should be larger than the bottom diameter of the pie pan by 4 inches or more. If using a plastic bag, place the pie pan on top of the crust and flip them over together. Otherwise, roll the crust over the rolling pin and unroll it into the pie pan.

If the filling for the pie is very wet, brush the bottom crust with egg white or melted butter or vegetable oil to keep it from getting soggy. If you cover the filling with a second crust, poke holes or slashes or make a design in it to let steam escape. Or cut strips of dough and make a latticework design on top. Flaky crust is ideal for fresh fruit pies, deep dish pies, custard or pudding-filled pies, squash (butternut or banana squash generally make tastier pies than pumpkins) or mincemeat pies, walnut or pecan pies, as well as unsweetened vegetable or chicken pot pies, and quiche.

Cracker crusts take less time and are best suited for lemon meringue or key lime pies, cream, custard or pudding-filled pies, cream cheesecakes, ricotta or cottage cheesecakes, and yogurt-filled pies. Here is a basic graham cracker crust recipe:

CRACKER CRUST

1⅓ c. crushed graham crackers (without preservatives)
⅓ c. melted butter

Crush the dry crackers by putting them in a blender, just a few at a time, or place in a plastic bag and crush with a rolling pin. Add melted butter to crackers and mix. Press the crust evenly into the bottom of your pie pan. For best results, precook this crust for 10 minutes at 350° before adding the filling. For variety, add chopped nuts, wheat germ, or shredded coconut to the graham cracker crumbs. Or substitute crushed granola crumbs or ground nuts for crackers.

Cakes

BASIC HONEY CAKE

⅔ c. butter	2 t. vanilla
1¼ c. milk	2½ c. whole wheat pastry flour
1 c. honey	1 T. baking powder
4 eggs, separated	½ t. salt

All ingredients should be at room temperature. First, soften the butter with a spoon or fork. Do not melt it—this would prevent the air needed for rising from being incorporated into the butter and sweetener. Then cream the butter with the honey, mixing together till they are light and creamy in texture.

Next beat in one egg yolk at a time, and finally add the vanilla. If these ingredients are mixed well in this order, your batter will be free of lumps, thoroughly mixed and light.

In another bowl, mix the dry ingredients. Then alternate, adding the dry ingredients and the milk into the original wet ingredient mixture. This should be done quickly with few strokes.

The final step is to whip the egg whites and fold them into the cake batter. You can whip them by hand, and be ready for a workout, or do it with an electric mixer. Whip till the whites form soft peaks, but aren't too dry. Then gradually fold the egg whites into the cake batter by lifting the batter from the bottom of the bowl and covering the whites, then slicing across and down to the bottom, turning the bowl as you go. Do this in as few strokes as possible, but mix thoroughly. Pour the batter into two 8-inch pans you have lightly oiled and floured, pop into a preheated oven, and cook for about 25 minutes at 375°. Check to see if the cakes are done by inserting a toothpick or thin knife—if it comes out clean, the cake is done. It should also have shrunk somewhat from the sides of the pan.

The same technique and steps should be followed if you substitute vegetable oil for butter. Vegetable oil will yield a denser cake.

Variations: The simplest variations on Basic Honey Cake are to substitute other extracts for vanilla or add a quarter cup of orange or lemon peel or experiment with various spices. The same general procedure, cooking time and temperature, with wider variations, gives you an even wider cake repertory.

CARROT CAKE, with changes from BASIC HONEY CAKE

Butter: increase to 1½ c. *Vanilla:* increase to 1 T.
Milk: reduce to ½ c. *Flour:* increase to 3 c.
Honey: no change *Baking powder:* no change
Eggs: reduce to 3 *Salt:* no change

Additional ingredients: 1 T. cinnamon; 1 t. nutmeg; 1 c. diced fresh pineapple or canned, unsweetened and drained; 1½ c. shredded carrots.
Additional instructions: use three pans.

RAISIN CAKE, COCONUT CAKE, BANANA CAKE, WALNUT CAKE, can each be made by substituting for the carrots in the recipe above—variations on a variation.

APPLESAUCE CAKE

Butter: increase to 1 c.   *Vanilla*: eliminate
Milk: change to buttermilk, increase to 2 c.   *Flour*: increase to 3½ c.
Honey: increase to 1½ c.   *Baking powder*: no change
Eggs: reduce to 3   *Salt*: no change

Additional ingredients: 2 t. cinnamon, 1 t. nutmeg, ½ t. cloves, ½ t. allspice; 1¼ c. raisins or currants; 1 c. chopped walnuts; ¾ c. applesauce.
Additional instructions: mix the applesauce with the buttermilk; use three pans.

Cookies

The two basic types of cookies are drop cookies and rolled cookies. The doughs are different: drop cookie dough is more liquid; rolled cookie dough is stiffened by refrigeration, therefore easy to roll out and cut into shapes.

As with cakes, you start by creaming the butter/oil with the sweetener, then beating in the eggs. The dry ingredients may be premixed and added to the wet ingredients, a part at a time, or beaten in separately, depending on the recipe. Much of the success of cookie baking lies in the handling. A heavy baking sheet with low sides will bake cookies evenly, without burning them on the bottom. You may need to turn the sheet during the course of baking. When the cookies are done, they should be removed from the sheet immediately so they don't keep cooking, as they are usually quite thin. Cookies should then be cooled in a single layer so they don't stick to each other.

BUTTER COOKIES

Cream together 1½ c. butter, ¾ c. honey, and 4 T. whole wheat pastry flour.
Add 3 beaten eggs, 2 t. vanilla, and ½ t. lemon rind.
Slowly mix in 2¾ c. whole wheat pastry flour. Chill mixture for 2 hours or more. Roll out ½ inch thick and cut into desired shapes.
Mix 2 eggs and 2 t. water. Spread egg mixture over each cookie. Optional: sprinkle with cinnamon or finely chopped nuts.
Bake until slightly brown at 375°. Yield: about 36 cookies.

ALMOND COOKIES

Cream together 1 c. butter and ¾ c. honey.
Add 1¾ c. whole wheat flour; 1¾ c. almonds, toasted, then ground; 2 t. almond extract; 2 t. lemon rind; ¼ t. salt.
Drop by tablespoonfuls on an oiled cookie sheet and press to ½ inch thickness.

Dip an almond in honey and press it into the center of each cookie, then bake at 400° for 10 to 15 minutes. Yield: about 24 cookies.

Bars And Squares

These treats are generally mixed in the same manner as cookies but, not being made one by one, they are faster. Start with the butter/oil and cream in the sweetener. Add beaten eggs and vanilla if called for. Then gradually add the premixed dry ingredients to the wet ingredients. If the bars are to be filled, the procedure will vary somewhat. The dough is mixed separately from the filling, and placed on the bottom of the pan. The filling is then spread on top and covered with another layer of dough. Probably the most important single factor in baking bars and squares, as well as brownies, is the size of the pan. If the pan is too small, the batter will be too high in the pan and will result in cakey bars. If the pan is too large so the batter is spread thinly, it will result in a hard, dry bar. To produce a chewy bar, be sure to use the size pan called for in the recipe you are following.

DATE OR FIG BARS (FROM THE SUNBURST BAKERY)

Combine ¼ c. sesame oil and ½ c. honey. Mix in the following:

¾ c. whole wheat pastry flour	½ t. baking powder
1 c. rolled oats	¼ t. salt
2 T. soy flour	2 t. orange rind
Filling:	
To 1 c. hot water, add:	1 t. lemon rind
2 c. chopped dates or figs	1 t. orange rind
1 T. fresh lemon juice	

Press half of crust mixture into a baking pan. Spread on the fillings. Cover with the rest of the crust. Bake at 375° for ½ hour. Cool and cut into squares.

Candies

If you are going to make a candy in the traditional manner, cooking it till it reaches a certain stage of hardness, I suggest you use a butter and honey or molasses base (a 1 to 3 ratio) and, for accuracy, buy a candy thermometer. This mixture can then be made into butterscotch, used as the base for peanut brittle, poured over popcorn with or without peanuts to make cracker jacks, or used as a coating for candied apples. In each case, you want to cook the mixture till it reaches the soft ball stage, between 234° and 242° when using a candy thermometer. You can test it by dropping some syrup from a spoon into cold water—if it forms balls that will hold their shape unless flattened between the fingers, it is cooked enough. If you cook it any longer it will turn dark and taste somewhat burned. Be sure that the pot you are using has a heavy bottom and is at least three or four times larger than the volume of the candy, so that it doesn't boil over as it cooks.

At Sunburst the children are steered away from traditional candies toward candies made from ground nuts, peanut butter, granola, wheat germ, coconut, raisins, dates, and ground sunflower and sesame seeds which are sweetened with honey, and stiffened up if needed with milk powder. These candies do not have to be cooked, are quick to prepare, and nutritious. Here are a couple of recipes:

CAROB CRUNCHIES

½ c. peanut butter   1 c. carob powder
½ c. granola   ¼ c. honey
2–4 T. honey   milk

Mix peanut butter, granola, and honey. Shape into domes or balls. For topping, blend carob powder and honey, add enough warm milk to make a thick liquid. Dip the balls in carob, allow to dry.

DRIED FRUIT AND NUT BALLS

You can use any dried fruits or nuts of your choice. You just run them through a grinder and roll into balls. The fruit makes a sticky paste which holds the balls together. You can roll them in toasted wheat germ, coconut or carob powder. Here is one example:

¾ c. dates   ⅛ c. sesame seeds
¼ c. raisins   ¼ c. toasted wheat germ
¼ c. almonds   ⅛ c. carob powder or milk powder
¼ c. sunflower seeds   coconut

Grind nuts and seeds. You can either grind fruit or chop fine and combine. If your mixture isn't sticky enough, add a little honey. Form balls and roll in coconut. *Variations:* Try using bee pollen, mint leaves, or chia seeds.

PHASE THREE: *Moving toward Self-Sufficiency*

30 *Juicing*

Arriving at the topic of juicing marks off the territory we can regard as "serious" food processing. The following at-a-glance review of the logical division of the food processing tasks makes it easy to see how you can cross the lines between them to suit yourself.

THE NEW AMERICAN CUISINE

Phase One	*Phase Two*	*Phase Three*
Buying natural food staples	Growing sprouts	Juicing
Cooking from scratch	Making mixes	Grinding flour
Making your own snacks	Making yogurt	Canning and pickling
Making your own baby foods	Baking bread	Drying
	Making your own desserts from scratch	Freezing

Experience, observation, and logic lie behind the division into phases, but they are also somewhat arbitrary. It is easy enough to imagine people performing some of the tasks described as Phase Two activities and not others, while also undertaking some Phase Three activities and not others. Whatever is right for you is right. But one thing about Phase Two and Phase Three food-processing activities is almost certain: a family wherein both husband and wife have full-time jobs would be unable to do them all. They could do all the Phase Two tasks or some combination of Two and Three tasks but somewhere in there is a hazy area that obscures a boundary line. You are the only one who knows when you've crossed over the line—"That's it, that's enough time spent on food processing, any more just wouldn't be worth it."

Couples with a househusband or housewife at home, on the other hand, could make the homemaking vocation much more profitable—for budget, health, and soul—by taking on the full range of processing responsibilities. For retired people there is the unique advantage of being able to expand the value of a fixed income.

The differences between Phase Two and Three activities lie in the areas of necessary commitment and of complexity. Nevertheless, there might well be a selection of Phase Two and Three activities that fit your circumstances. I suggest you look them all over to judge which activities best suit your circumstances. It would probably be best for most people to ease into deeper levels of commitment to food processing over a period of many months, perhaps even years. Finally, if your worst fears are realized and the whole thing is a grim ordeal instead of a rewarding experience, forget it. But don't let your doubts prevent you from trying; the chances are good that you'll be pleasantly surprised.

THE JUICES

Many converts to the New American Cuisine have much more trouble finding satisfactory beverages than they do foods. Formerly they drank a lot of coffee and soft drinks; changing to herb teas and pasteurized fruit juices provides only a partial substitute. Many then venture into a new category of beverages: raw fruit and vegetable juices.

Whereas the differences between pasteurized and raw milk are subtle to the palate, in juices the differences are radical. The usual reaction to tasting the raw counterpart to a bottled juice is an amazed, "No comparison!" When juices are pasteurized for bottling, most of the vitamins and enzymes are destroyed. By contrast, raw juices are a potent source of those vital elements. The tremendous vitality of these juices is one of the characteristics that make this beverage category so unique.

Vegetable Juices

Another unique characteristic is the very fact of drinking vegetable juices. Everyone is familiar with tomato juice and mixed vegetable juice in a tomato base. Not a lot happening there—the raw juice world must be dominated by fruit juice. No, raw juices are dominated by vegetables. In particular, carrot juice. I've talked to a lot of people who wrinkled their noses in disgust at the mention of carrot juice. That's because they tasted canned carrot juice once. Ugh. I agree. But fresh, raw carrot juice . . . ambrosia . . . its sweet flavor is as bright as its orange color.

There is no food that everybody likes, but carrot juice comes close. It comes to the rescue of almost any vegetable juice that has an overpowering flavor. Cabbage juice, the juices of greens, celery juice, parsley juice, are all powerfully nourishing but, on their own, taste too strong for most people, including me. Mixed with 50 to 80 percent carrot juice, they fall into a range between acceptable and delicious. A popular vegetable mix is carrot/celery/parsley, with about 7 oz. of carrot, 2 oz. of celery, 1 oz. of parsley. Another is two-thirds carrot, one-third cabbage. The carrot/cabbage mix is said to be a startlingly effective remedy for stomach ulcers (see Recommended Reading List for books on raw juice therapy). Vegetable juices are known as "the builders," fruit juices as "the cleansers." Contrary to popular opinion, they can be mixed as well. A popular mix is carrot/apple/celery, in about equal proportions.

Wheatgrass Juice

When wheat and other cereal grasses are about four to six inches high they reach the "first jointing" stage, meaning that the stem is throwing its first branch. At this point the grass is at its peak of vitamin and chlorophyll content. When juiced, this grass makes a deep green, intensely sweet (sickeningly so, to many people), powerfully nutritious drink.

The grass is usually grown in a small garden patch, or in a windowsill box, or in artificially lighted trays. Too overpowering for most people to drink straight, it is usually mixed with other juices: for example, one or two ounces of wheatgrass juice with six to eight ounces of carrot juice.

Aficionados of wheatgrass juice often prefer to make it by hand, getting a better quality of juice and a better extraction rate. The Chop-Rite or Alfa (see *The Juicers*) are suitable for this purpose.

The great nutritional virtue of raw juices is that the vitamins, minerals, and enzymes are quickly assimilated into the blood stream, providing nourishment at the cellular level within fifteen minutes. The disadvantage is that the fiber is discarded, meaning that juices are not a substitute for whole foods. They are, however, the most nourishing of all ways to take fluids into your body. The following table identifies the nutritional "all-stars" of raw fruit and vegetable juices. Because other fruits and vegetables are not on the list does not mean they are not good for juicing. However, as in everything, some are better than others.

BEST RAW JUICES FOR MAJOR NUTRIENTS

Nutrient	Fruit Juice	Vegetable Juice
vit. A	apricot	carrot greens (lettuce, turnip, kale, escarole, endive) watercress parsley
vit. B		carrot cabbage celery broccoli dandelion okra
vit. C	citrus pineapple cranberry strawberry peach melon	carrot cabbage parsley green pepper tomato watercress

Nutrient	Fruit Juice	Vegetable Juice
vit. E		spinach
		watercress
		lettuce
		celery
calcium	citrus	carrot
	rhubarb	cabbage
	cranberry	green pepper
	peach	cucumber
		radish
		celery
		cauliflower
		greens
iron	blackberry	carrot
	strawberry	spinach
	cherry	beet
	grape	cabbage
	pear	okra
	plum	greens
potassium	blueberry	carrot
	coconut	celery
	pineapple	greens
	grape	cabbage
		parsley
		mint
		green pepper
magnesium	citrus	greens
	plum	
	peach	
	apple	
	pear	
	grape	
	cherry	

Juicing is a Phase Three operation because it takes time to prepare the vegetables for juicing. Root vegetables should be scrubbed with a brush, other things have to be peeled, cut up, or quartered. Also the electrical machines for extracting juice are a major investment and need to be cleaned after every use.

THE JUICERS*

Although most juice extractors are electric, there are two exceptions: The *Chop-Rite Health Fountain*, Box 294, Pottstown, PA 19464, $60; The *Alfa*, Basic Living Products, 2990 Seventh St., Berkeley, CA 94710, $50. Their configurations are similar to those of a meat grinder, making pulp

*This discussion does not include citrus juicers because they do not juice other fruits or vegetables and because so much is generally known about them.

and pressing the juice out as the pulp is squeezed out of the machine. Both work well but take approximately five times as long as their electrical counterparts.

I have made a lot of juice, both personally and professionally, owned several juicers, and used a lot of others. Experience has taught me that there are basically three categories of electric juice extractors: the "lightweight" type suited to making a glass or two of juice, not suited for more than five minutes of continual use; the "mediumweight" type, more stable on the countertop, capable of making a quart of more without overheating; and the "heavyweight" type that can keep on truckin', right through a twenty-five pound bag of carrots if need be. I will use the code LW, MW, and HW to indicate which is which.

In electric juicers, most makes are the centrifuge type. Centrifuge juicers all have a grinding plate spinning rapidly in a basket when the material to be juiced is pushed into the machine. The grinding plate pulps the material, which is thrown against the sides of the basket, centrifugal force then throwing the juice out through the holes of the basket as the pulp spins. Some centrifuges have automatic pulp ejectors; those that don't have to be stopped periodically for cleaning if you are making a lot of juice. Pulp ejectors, on the other hand, tend to be noisy and sacrifice juicing efficiency for convenience.

The Centrifuges

Acme Juicerator. This machine is generally considered the king of the centrifuges. Solid, well-built, it does not eject pulp, but has a ten-year guarantee, the longest of any juicer made. $150 in plastic, $190 in stainless steel. Acme, Tenth & Lowther Streets, Lemoyne, PA 17043. MW

Braun Multipress MP 50. A well-built machine but only moderately efficient, does not eject pulp. One-year guarantee, $80. LW

Healthmaster. One of the oldest juicer manufacturers, this company makes three all-metal pulp-ejecting machines: The Healthmaster, for home use at $219, MW; the Juicemaster, for commercial use at $850. The Super Juicemaster, between $1,850 and $2,260, depending on size of motor. One-year guarantees. Valmont Corporation, 13421 Grass Valley Drive, Grass Valley, CA 95945.

Phoenix. Ejects pulp, five-year guarantee, $120. Phoenix Housewares, New York, NY. LW

Invento Electric Vegetable Juicer. Karen MacNeil says it "does a decent job on all but the most difficult vegetables like parsley," $70. LW

Krups Biomaster. Drawbacks to this machine are that it has an aluminum basket (aluminum is unstable in the presence of food acids, forms toxic salts), overheats easily, does not eject pulp. One-year guarantee, $80. Robert Krups North America, Allendale Industrial Park, Allendale, NJ 07632. LW

Miracle CE 11. *Advantages:* good volume of juice, ejects pulp. *Disadvantages:* pulpy juice, does not grind carrots well, hard to clean, juice leaks. "Limited" one-year guarantee, $100. LW

Miracle XM 10. *Advantages:* has a blender attachment, makes good quality juice, ejects pulp. *Disadvantages:* low volume of juice, hard to clean. One-year guarantee, $130. LW

Miracle Ultra-matic. *Advantages:* powerful motor, ejects pulp. *Disadvantages:* low volume of juice, inconvenient blade removal system. Five-year guarantee on blade, one-year on the other parts, $300. Miracle Exclusives, 3 Elm St., Locust, NY 11560. MW

Oster Automatic. *Advantages:* high volume of juice, quiet, ejects pulp. *Disadvantages:* pulpy juice, hard to clean. "Limited" one-year guarantee, $86. Oster Manufacturing Co., 5055 N. Lydell Ave., Milwaukee, WI 53217. LW

*Rated by the staff of Rodale Press, in their book *Home Food Systems.*

Other Types of Juicers

Vita-Mix. Not a true juice extractor, this machine makes what the manufacturer calls "total" juice. This is a multi-purpose machine which makes pulp of the vegetable or fruit, then water or ice is added to produce a drinkable liquid. A separate, hand-operated hydraulic press is available for extracting juice from pulp. The Vita-Mix also grinds flour, kneads dough, makes soup and ice cream. $375. Vita-Mix Corporation, 8615 Usher Road, Cleveland, OH 44138.

Champion. This machine makes juice as the material hits a rotating set of blades, which also force the pulp towards a spout, squeezing out the juice. Not as much oxygen gets mixed into the juice under this system, so it tends to keep better than centrifuged juice. Also has an attachment for grinding grains, making peanut butter. Five-year guarantee, $205 ($90 for attachment). Plastaket Mfg. Co., 6220 E. Highway 12, Lodi, CA 95240. In my opinion, the Champion is well-named; it is my personal choice for anyone of modest means. It gets a good extraction rate, good quality juice, ejects pulp so you don't have to stop for cleaning, and is a real workhorse. HW

Norwalk 240. This is the Rolls Royce of juicers. It is an electrified, countertop variation on the old cider press theme: in the two-step operation, first you pulp, or "triturate," the material, then you press the juice out hydraulically. The Norwalk extracts far more juice with a much higher mineral content than other juicers. It also incorporates much less oxygen in the juicing, giving its juice much better keeping qualities. It can also grind flour and cereals, make peanut butter, salads, and baby foods. Two-year guarantee, $795. Norwalk Manufacturing Co., P.O. Box 4769, Thousand Oaks, CA 91359. HW!

K & K. This company describes its machine as "an inexpensive Norwalk." The shredder and press are separate units, the shredder being electrical, the press mechanical. They claim an average 25 percent greater extraction rate than centrifuges. One-year guarantee, $525 . D & E Knuth Engineering Co., 3901 S. First St., Rogers, AR 72756. HW

Talking with people who have bought and used various juicers, it seems that most of the inexpensive machines prove to be unsatisfactory if used for more than the occasional glass of juice. The typical pattern is to buy a juicer for under $100, use it long enough to develop a love of fresh juices, retire the cheap juicer and buy an Acme, Healthmaster, Champion, or Norwalk. From personal experience, I rate these four tops in terms of strength and durability.

Cider Presses

There was hardly a pioneer family without at least one apple tree and a cider press, replaced by "progress" with the six-pack of pop. Now real progress replaces cider presses with electric juice extractors. But there are still the occasional families with an apple tree or two, or access to local unsprayed apples at a good price or even free. In such circumstances, consider getting a bunch of people together with bushels of apples, an old-fashioned hand-operated hydraulic cider press, and a day free for making cider.

This is more a barnyard operation than one for the kitchen: a cider press is approximately the size of a barrel. The cider can be drunk fresh, fermented into hard cider, and frozen in plastic jugs. The press is available from Garden Way, Charlotte, VT 05445, (802) 425-2121. $219 assembled or $189 as a kit.

Other possible sources for cider presses are:

Cumberland General Store, Route 3, Crossville, TN 38555.
Day Equipment Corp., 1402 E. Monroe, Goshen, IN 46526
Good Nature Products Inc., P.O. Box 233, East Aurora, NY 14052
Happy Valley Ranch, P.O. Box 9153, Yakima, WA 98909
(Source: *Home Food Systems*, Rodale Press.)

31   Becoming a Miller

Grinding your own flour is perhaps the ultimate in kitchen self-sufficiency. There is no better example of the twin functions of improving quality and saving money. If your store-bought loaf of bread costs you a dollar, you can produce a similar loaf at home for fifty cents. Grinding your own flour can reduce the cost of that loaf to a range between thirty and forty-five cents, depending on how you buy your wheat. If you buy your wheat in small quantities, particularly if you buy it packaged, the savings are slight. A household of one, two, or three wouldn't have much choice other than to buy relatively small quantities, and would be grinding primarily for reasons of quality. Larger households, however, have the opportunity to reduce the cost of bread substantially. *Inflation Fighter* estimates the average saving by grinding to be 17 percent.

Let's say you're a family of four aiming to reduce your Phase Two food budget from $2,184 annually to $1,715. Let's also say your family is consuming five pound-and-a-half loaves of bread a week. By producing your bread for thirty cents a loaf instead of fifty, you save $52 a year—more than 10 percent of your budget reduction is accomplished simply by grinding your own bread flour.

However, you won't accomplish this great a savings unless you buy right. Buying right in this case means buying wheat by the 50-pound sack. I've seen everything from a single sack to a ton split by a group, each family taking five to ten sacks. I've heard of Mormon churches ordering a whole truckload of 40,000 pounds to be split among the members of the congregation. The hypothetical family of four referred to earlier would need about eight sacks to last a year. The purchasing possibilities range from buying direct from the farm, to your local buying club or co-op, to your local natural foods store.

Inflation is another strong reason for the kind of bulk purchases I have just suggested. Food prices have been escalating even faster than the general inflation rate. In a year in which there is a 12 percent inflation rate, your inflation hedge represented by large food investments might be worth 15 percent or even more.

STORAGE

If you buy grain a sack at a time and use it quickly, storage is simple: just put the sack in the coolest, dryest, darkest spot you have, the bottom of the sack off the floor, perhaps on an overturned crate, and scoop your grain from the sack as you need it. But when you get into multiple sack buying you need to get a bit more sophisticated about storage. *Cool*, *dry*, and *dark* remain the constants no matter what the quantity. In bulk storage, however, you need to take extra precautions. There are two things you are protecting yourself against: what can get in and what's already in.

What can get in are rodents and insects. Store in something impervious to their assaults—metal or heavy-duty plastic pails, or crocks with lids. What most people don't realize is that the impervious container is only half of the solution because the other half of the problem is that insects are potentially in the grain before you put it in the container. Their potentiality is in the form of eggs, a microscopic few of which are in every sack of grain, deposited on the farm or in the grain elevator.

You have already eaten hundreds of such microscopic eggs without knowing it, no matter what kind of diet you've been on. Eggs from critters such as the Indian meal moth are an unavoidable fact of nature. The eggs are destroyed by cooking; the trick is to keep them from hatching in storage. You've seen a tiny white larva squirming in your grain or a little gray moth fluttering around your kitchen? Too late. Of themselves they can't do much damage. But the moth will lay more eggs, the larva will turn into a moth who will lay more eggs, the eggs will hatch into more larvae . . . it all happens rather quickly and a lot of larvae eat a lot of grain and make a big mess while they're at it.

The simplest way to keep eggs from hatching is to keep the grain cool, 50° F. or less. For that you need a cellar, a long, cold winter, or a walk-in refrigerator. Being unsure of your ability to keep your grain cool enough long enough leaves you with two effective home storage techniques.

The DE method: (The following description is borrowed from Phil Levy's Talking Food Pamphlet, *Storing Grain*.)

> Diatomaceous earth (DE) is a fine white powder made from the remains of prehistoric algae, known as diatoms, mined in deep quarries in Nevada, California and Utah. This powder is mixed directly into the storage container with the grain and churned by hand. The ratio for pantry storage is about one ounce, or two Tb., per five-pound jar. For large-scale home storage the ratio is about 1 lb. DE per 100 lbs. grain.
>
> DE is composed of silica and several trace minerals, and is edible. Be sure not to breathe the dust, however, since it can cause irritation of the lungs. DE works, simply enough, by scratching the waxy film which covers the worm, causing immediate dehydration and death. Don't get squeamish about this, because the grain can be washed off before cooking to get rid of the dried-out bugs (and the diatomaceous earth). By eliminating the bug problem in one jar, you are preventing bug-madness from proliferating throughout your pantry.

The dry ice method: This method works by depriving the container of oxygen, thus depriving the eggs of oxygen, without which they will not hatch. Spread a two-inch layer of dry ice on the bottom of your container, spread a few sheets of newspaper over the dry ice and fill the container with grain on top of the ice/paper. It's important to choose a container with a very snug fitting lid, which you lay loosely on top while the dry ice is evaporating. The rising carbon dioxide of the evaporating dry ice pushes the oxygen from the container; when the evaporation is finished, you press the lid down tightly, perhaps adding a bit of weight on the lid if you think it's necessary to form a tight seal.

How long the ice takes to complete evaporation depends on how much you've used in how big a container with how much grain; you'll be guessing until you've gained some experience or followed the exact specifications of someone who already has the experience. Let's say you had fifty pounds of grain in a thirty-five gallon plastic garbage can with two inches of dry ice on the bottom. I would push the lid down tight after about six hours; if during the next few hours I noticed bulges, indicating that the ice hadn't finished and pressure was building, I would crack the seal to let the excess escape, then reseal it. Use only a container with an extremely snug-fitting lid or the carbon dioxide will seep out.

Poor storage techniques can eliminate some of the savings of bulk buying and create conditions that can only be remedied by time-consuming hand cleaning. It's unlikely you can afford to throw away buggy or moldy grain; hand cleaning is the only remedy. Some people combine the DE and dry ice methods so as to thoroughly protect their investment. If you have a place cool enough to make those methods unnecessary, remember that dryness is also critical. (In Chapter 16 we saw that the four absolutes of proper storage of *all* bulk foods are coolness, dryness, darkness, and air limitation.)

HOW TO CHOOSE WHEAT

Even though grains are milled for other purposes, it is with baking in mind that you will be doing most of your grinding. And in baking, wheat flour is king. The quality of your flour is determined by the quality of your wheat and the quality of your grinding. With a focus on your budget, it can be tempting to buy the cheapest wheat available; but as is so often true with products from the bargain basement, the results can be disappointing. It is easy to deceive yourself because bad flour and good flour look the same. But poor quality wheat berries can only make bad flour and the best you can expect from bad flour is mediocre bread.

The best wheat is organically grown, but you may not be forunate enough to have access to organically grown wheat. Failing that, perhaps you can find wheat with enough pride of accomplishment behind it to have been tested for protein content. The protein content of hard red wheat can vary between 11 percent and 17 percent, occasionally a bit higher and lower. Higher protein wheat tends to produce a higher loaf of bread (springier dough with better rising characteristics).

Protein content is not as critical with soft wheat (which is used for pastry flour) as it is in hard wheat, though the same factors influence the protein content of both hard and soft wheat. Those factors are:

Soil fertility: The richer the soil, particularly in humus, the higher the protein. (The dictionary defines humus as "the dark organic material in soils, produced by the decomposition of vegetable or animal matter and essential to the fertility of the earth." Most of us understand this on an intuitive level even if we know nothing about agriculture; we see black earth being turned up behind a plow and we say, "The soil looks rich.")

Soil moisture: Dry land wheat (not irrigated) is generally higher in protein than irrigated. Irrigation increases yields but tends to reduce quality. There is an optimum rainfall (or irrigation) level for the best combination of yield and quality. If rainfall is on the light side, yield goes down but quality goes up. But the rainfall can be too far over on the light side: no crop.

Spring or winter wheat? In the northern plains of our wheat belt, winter comes early, is severe and long. Wheat is planted in the spring, matures in about 95 days and is harvested in time to beat the first killing frost. This is spring wheat.

Winter wheat is grown in the southern reaches of our wheat belt because winter comes later, and is not as long nor as severe. There is time to plant in the fall, time for the wheat to germinate and establish itself before frost halts growing activity. After the spring thaw, the wheat, already started in the fall, is on its way before the spring wheat is even in the ground further north. Winter wheat is harvested in very late spring or early summer, depending on the weather, hopefully ahead of the summer hailstorms that can mow down everything in their paths.

Spring wheat generally tends to be higher in protein than winter wheat, perhaps because it grows so much faster. Winter wheat, however, establishes a more extensive root system and can produce wheat with a higher mineral content, if the minerals are in the soil in the first place (another critical factor in soil fertility). It's possible to see a comparison like this between spring and winter wheat:

	Spring	*Winter*
Moisture content:	10%	10%
Protein content:	16%	14%
Weight per bushel:	62 lbs.	66 lbs.

The difference in weight is attributable to the higher mineral content of the winter wheat. The higher protein spring wheat will give a higher rising, airier bread. The higher mineral winter wheat will give a denser, more flavorful bread *if* the minerals are there. You can't assume that a lower protein wheat has a higher mineral content; it does for sure if it is 10 percent or less moisture and 64 pounds or more per bushel.

There are positive things to say about both spring and winter wheat; one type is not clearly better than the other. Whatever the type, whatever the protein and mineral contents, there are other things to look for. Hard (red) wheat should be a uniformly deep, reddish brown. Soft wheat (sometimes called "white" wheat because it is lighter in color) should also be strongly and uniformly colored. There should be few or no undersized kernels and few or none with the husks still attached. (The husks, unlike the bran layers, are inedible.) There should also be little or no chaff visible as you let a few handfuls of grain—often called wheat "berries"—run through your hands.

OTHER GRAINS

Although wheat is king, the other grains are all princes (read queens and princesses if you prefer); each one has unique and valuable nutritional properties (see Chapter 8) and each adds special character to a loaf of bread. The most popular way to use the other grains is combined with wheat; the less wheat the denser the bread. Even seven, nine, and fourteen grain breads are usually more than 50 percent wheat because Americans are unaccustomed to dense bread. But bread without wheat is not only possible, it is even easier to make because you don't bother with risings—the other grains either don't rise or rise very little. Bread made without wheat and without yeast can be extremely nutritious and flavorful and extremely *heavy*, as, for example, the dark German rye bread made without yeast, usually sold as a gourmet food in the U.S.

Rye can be used as either flour (fine grind) or meal (coarse grind). It does not have enough gluten to warrant trying for wheat-like results, producing a dense, moist, heavy loaf from a sticky dough. "Small amounts (10–15%) add smoothness and workability to doughs with a high proportion of granular ingredients, e.g. corn-rye, rye-oatmeal" (*Tassajara Bread Book*).

Triticale (triti-*cay*-lee) is a new grain bred from a triple cross of two different types of wheat and rye. It is higher in protein than most wheat, has enough gluten to be treated as wheat, yielding a loaf that is neither as airy as wheat nor as dense as rye.

Corn, aside from corn bread, can be used as an addition to whole wheat flour (up to 25 percent, flour or meal), yielding a loaf that is more compact while being more crumbly, more coarse, more sweet.

Millet can be used as either flour or meal, with textural effects similar to corn, without the sweetness.

Brown rice flour added to whole wheat flour (up to 25 percent) will make a loaf which is denser, smoother, and moister.

Oat flour will have similar effects as brown rice flour with a slightly more pronounced sweetness. *Rolled oats* added to whole wheat flour instead of oat flour will yield a lighter, chewier loaf.

Buckwheat flour added to wheat flour will add heaviness and that familiar flavor we know from buckwheat pancakes.

Barley flour will be a whole grain only if you can find unhulled barley (as opposed to *pearled*), sometimes called "blue" or "gray" barley. The pearling process removes more than 30 percent of the grain. This flour when added to whole wheat will give the loaf a moist, cake-like quality.

Oat flour and brown rice flour are the best choices for wheat-free cookies and pastry. A generous addition of bran—which is usually not the part of wheat responsible for wheat allergy—alleviates the heaviness of these flours with a sort of feathering effect.

GRINDING

Loose settings on grinders yield cracked grain; partially tightening the setting yields meal; tightening all the way yields flour, with, of course, a range of textures depending on how tightly you set your stones or plates. For most baking, coarse flour works fine—in fact, produces a more interesting texture than fine flour—and the looser setting doesn't generate as much heat, and produces flour quicker. Some people not only prefer the rough texture of bread made from coarse flour but add cracked wheat to the flour to produce an even coarser texture. If you experiment along these lines, you'll probably want to steam cracked wheat of really big particle size before mixing it with the other ingredients or it will be a bit like having gravel in your bread.

People who have baked with flour fresh from the mill often use words like "erratic," "unruly," "volatile," to describe it, meaning that absolutely fresh flour tends toward unpredictability. They have learned from experience that flour that has aged for a day at room temperature is more predictable. What has happened during the day of aging is that some of the enzymes that might otherwise have interfered with yeast activity have oxidized, taming the flour enough to give consistent results. Further aging, however, does not improve flour. In fact, it does the opposite: each day after grinding, flour loses from 10 to 20 percent of its oxidizable enzymes and vitamins per day, depending on storage conditions. The choice between absolutely fresh flour and one-day aged flour is a choice between optimum food value and optimum baking conditions. Whether you bake on grinding day or the next, do your baking for the week all on one day for the most efficient use of time. When contemplating whether or not you want to get involved in this project, remember you can do other things while bread is rising and again while it is baking; in this regard it doesn't really take as much time as it seems to.

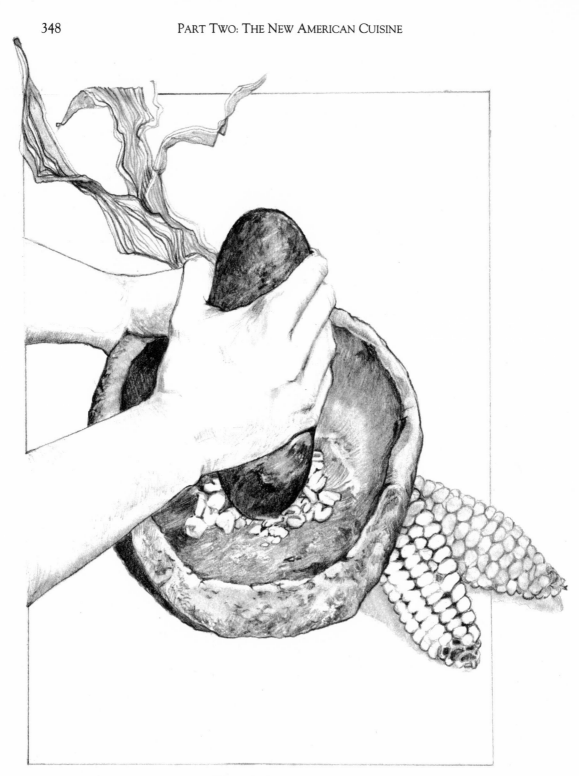

THE FIRST MILL

The Machines

Mechanically speaking, there are two ways to grind grain at home—with blades or with plates made of metal or stone. Small quantities—up to a cup—can be sliced into flour or meal in a blender or coffee mill. I know of no way blades will do the job without the aid of electricity. The only blade system I know capable of handling larger quantities is the Vita-Mix Total Juicer, sold in health and natural food stores. The blades of this machine are hammerlike and chop rather than slice; this is a multi-purpose machine that performs many of the same functions as a food processor. Some food processors, discussed in Chapter 35, also are capable of slicing grains into meal or flour with their blades; more about the Vita-Mix in Chapter 31.

Improved quality and lower cost are achieved with the above machines, but the best quality flour is produced by plates that crush the grain. This is true grinding as opposed to the slicing action of blades; when the plates are made of stone, it is, of course, stone grinding. By observation I know that grinding yields better flour, because the oils of the germ are mashed into the endosperm and bran flakes and there is less exposure to oxygen. Why stone grinding yields the best quality flour of all is, I think, because it is usually accomplished at lower temperatures and without the establishment of the electromagnetic field formed between metal plates, which slightly alters the electromagnetic properties of the grain.

The choices in grinding are to do it by hand, to adapt a hand-operated mill to pedals so you can use leg power, or to use electricity. To go electric requires roughly three or four times the investment. There are more electric mills on the market than manual ones, as you would expect in our motorized society. My personal experience with electric mills has been with a commercial type manufactured in North Wilkesboro, North Carolina, by Meadows Mill Company. In each of two stores I had mill rooms with three mills, one with twenty-inch (diameter) stones and two with eight-inch stones. The big mills were strictly for grinding wheat, the small mills were for all the other grains. Meadows promotes their eight-inch as a home mill, but I don't think it really is unless you have a huge family or home is a commune. If so, however, there is no better machine, with old fashioned workmanship made to outlive you; the eight-inch can do 100 pounds of whole wheat flour an hour all day, every day. The Meadows is a serious machine and delivered to your door, with motor (it can also be bought without motor), will run you about $500 (roughly $350 without motor).

No matter how you do your grinding, when you plunge your hand into flour as it comes directly from the machine, it should be warm, not hot. If it isn't even warm, so much the better; but if it's hot, consult the manufacturer's directions and adjust the machine accordingly.

The milling temperature should not exceed 180°F, the level at which six essential amino acids are destroyed—sometimes referred to as "denaturing" the protein. Denaturing begins at around 140°F. It is true that once the dough is in the oven, it will reach much higher temperatures. But cool-milled flour is another aspect of that alchemy I mentioned in Chapter 28. Experienced whole grain bakers agree that cool-milled flour makes a better loaf of bread (and they also agree that it is a mystery why).

Warning: Flour dust can explode. In ordinary household conditions it won't. But if you had a Meadows and were doing really large volumes of flour, you would probably want to set the mill up in a closet or some other confined space because of the large amount of flour dust and noise. Striking a match in an unventilated closet where the dust had been accumulating for a half hour could easily trigger an explosion. Don't be afraid of the motors, though—the manufacturers of electric mills know the danger and supply motors that do not throw an exposed spark.

In my mill rooms I had negative ion generators. The negative ions made the flour dust particles heavy, they quickly dropped to the floor, and the air was relatively dust free. But ventilation is the simplest method of keeping dust from filling the air to the danger level. A small mill in a kitchen doing ten or twenty pounds of flour is not a dangerous situation.

What you don't use on baking day, refrigerate in some sort of closed container, not a paper bag if you can help it—the bag will absorb oil from the flour, the flour will absorb moisture and food odors. If possible, take refrigerated flour out a couple of hours before baking, letting it warm up to room temperature, which will make it more workable.

Mills

(The 1981 prices are included to show the cost relationships between mills. Write for current prices.)

HAND MILLS

Name & Manufacturer	Grinding Surface	Production Rate-lbs/hr.	Cost
Atlas In-Tec Equipment Co. Box 123 D.V. Station Dayton, OH 45406	Steel	12*	$225
Bell #2 Grist Mill C.S. Bell Co. P.O. Box 291 Tiffin, OH 44883	Steel	6*	$ 50
Corona King Convertible R & R Mill Co. 45 W. First North Smithfield, UT 84335	Steel/Stone convertible	4*	$ 45

Name & Manufacturer	Grinding Surface	Production Rate-lbs/hr.	Cost
Country Living Grain Mill B & J Industries, Inc. 514 State Ave. Marysville, WA 98270	Stone (convertible to electricity)	10 (21)	$250
Diamant Domestic Mill In-Tec Equipment Co. Box 123 D.V. Station Dayton, OH 45406	Steel/Stone convertible	12*	$280
Great Northern "6B" Stone Hand Mill 325 W. Pierpont Ave. Salt Lake City, UT 84101	Stone (convertible to pedal or electricity)	4	$ 70
Hi Life Tempco Products, Inc. 564 W. 800 South Bountiful, UT 84010	Stone	4*	$ 50
"OB" Stone Mill Nelson & Sons, Inc. Box 1296 Salt Lake City, UT 84110	Steel/Stone convertible	4	$ 50
Retsel Little Arc Retsel Corporation P.O. Box 291 McCammon, ID 83250	Stone	3*	$ 48
Samap Miracle Exclusives 16 W. 40th St. New York, NY 10018	Stone	4*	$100

TOP VIEW

ELECTRIC MILLS

Name & Manufacturer	Grinding Surface	Production Rate-lbs/hr.	Cost
All Grain All Grain Distribution Co. 3333 S. 900 East Salt Lake City, UT 84106	Stone	8*	$180
Excalibur Excalibur Flour Mills 5711 Florin-Perkins Rd. Sacramento, CA 95828	Stone	16*	$190 (kit) $260 (assembled)
Garden Way Garden Way Catalog Ferry Rd. Charlotte, VT 05445	Stone	18*	$170 (kit)
Golden Grain Grinder Kuest Enterprises Box 110 Filer, ID 83328	Stone	77*	$270
Granzow Granzow Grain Mill Co. 2516 E. Jackson Phoenix, AZ 85034	Stone	15*	$280
Great Northern Electric Stone Mill Great Northern Distr. Co. 325 W. Pierpont Ave. Salt Lake City, UT 84101	Stone (convertible to hand or pedal operation)	65	$300
The Lee Mill Lee Engineering Co. 2023 W. Wisconsin Ave. Milwaukee, WI 53201	Stone	9*	$150
Marathon Uni Mill The Grover Co. 2111 S. Industrial Park Ave. Tempe, AZ 85282	Stone	40*	$310
Miller Box Model 1 Magic Valley Industries Inc. Box 10 Filer, ID 83328	Stone	19*	$200
Retsel Mill Master Retsel Corp. Box 47 McCammon, ID 83250	Stone (convertible to hand operation)	20*	$280

* Rating obtained from Home Food Systems, Rodale Press; others obtained from the manufacturers.

     The production rates were calculated for fine flour and would all increase somewhat at coarser settings. (More benefit is derived from the fiber of whole grains when the flour is coarse.) Production rate and price are only two factors to weigh in choosing a mill. Write to the manufacturers for their product literature and compare all the specifications. How big are the motors, the hoppers on top, the bins underneath? What temperature is the flour when it exits the stones?

32 Small-Scale Canning and Pickling

Too many cooks may spoil the broth but the more canners the merrier. Canning is a process that is ideally suited to group participation. "Canning bees" are an American tradition that can be revived with family, friends, or fellow church or club members, as participants. According to a USDA survey, there are over 250 community canning centers in the U.S., providing equipment and technical assistance as a public service to home food processors. The same survey also discovered that 33 percent of all American households canned fruits and vegetables, whether or not they had gardens. With a little resourceful investigation, you can find a lot of help near at hand.

Canned food may have no place at all in your scheme, but if it does, you can do it much better and far cheaper yourself. You can place an accent on *cheaper* if you keep your canning/pickling operation on a small scale because you won't need to buy any expensive special equipment. By "small scale" I mean that you don't buy lugs and crates of everything just because the prices are right and you don't plant three times more of everything than you can use fresh. I mean something more like this for a family of four:

36 pints assorted fruit preserves, jelly, syrup
24 quarts tomatoes
12 pints apricots
12 pints peaches
 6 pints cherries
12 quarts dill pickles
12 pints sauerkraut
 6 pints relish
24 pints corn
24 pints green beans
12 pints black eyed peas

A list like the above is worth about $195 at my neighborhood supermarket in the autumn of 1981. If you were canning your own garden produce, you could do it for under $40. If you were buying the produce, you could do it for under $100. In either case, you could assure yourself of top quality, leave out most or all of the salt and sweetening, and add herbs and spices no commercial canner would use because they process for that mythical average consumer.

[*A note to experienced canners*: Most of this chapter is a quick course in small-scale home canning for those who never have done it before, which you don't need. However, there are some points in the material that are especially important to a natural approach to canning and may be different from what you have been doing. I have marked them with the symbol # to make it easy for you to pick them out. The recipes may also give you some new ideas.]

CANNING IN GENERAL

Equipment

For the tomatoes, fruit, pickles, kraut, and relish, you need a water-bath canner, which is relatively inexpensive in almost any hardware store. All it is, really, is a big pot with a tight-fitting lid and a rack that raises the jars off the bottom and keeps them from touching each other or falling over in the pot. You might already own a big pot suitable as a water-bath canner. When the jars are on the rack in the pot there should be two to four inches of space between the tops of the jars and the top of the pot to allow for brisk boiling.

With tomatoes, fruits and pickles, the boiling-water bath suffices to preserve them; but for most vegetables you need a steam-pressure canner. Vegetables are low in acid, and therefore need the higher temperature produced by a pressure cooker to keep them from spoiling. There are big pressure cookers made especially for canning but they are much too big an investment for the small-scale canning I'm talking about. If you already own a pressure cooker, it will hold pint jars and do the same job as the oversized pressure cooker.

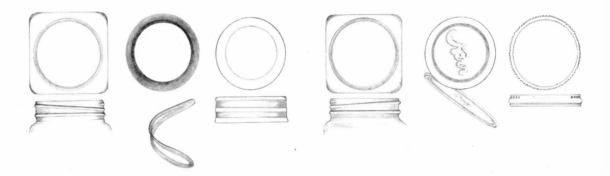

In small-scale canning you can in glass jars, not metal cans, because cans require a special sealing machine (expensive) and you can use your glass jars over and over as well as using them for other purposes. So you need glass jars—widemouth are recommended—and lids. There are two types of lids: the metal screw band with flat metal lid or the porcelain-lined lid with rubber ring. Use whichever closure system you prefer. Neither the metal lids nor the rubber rings should be reused for canning.

You'll need a rack or towel to put the hot jars on for cooling—placing them on a cool, solid surface can cause them to crack—but the rack can be taken from your oven or refrigerator. The only other thing you will need is some labels to date the jars. (If you've done it right and keep the jars in a cool, dark place, you can count on them being good for at least a year.)

Procedures

The raw materials should be the best possible quality; they determine the quality of the finished product. Use organically grown fruits and vegetables if possible. Choose fresh, firm fruit and young tender vegetables without bruises. If there are any small bruises or soft spots with discolored flesh, cut them out because they will otherwise almost certainly spoil the entire contents of the jar. Your canning produce should be as fresh and firm as possible.

Remember that the objective of canning is to destroy organisms that cause spoilage—molds, yeasts, bacteria, and enzymes. So you must employ the highest standards of cleanliness in preparation and handling. Prepare the jars by washing them in hot, soapy water, then rinse them well to remove all traces of soap. The manufacturer of the lids should provide instructions for preparing them, but if in doubt follow the same procedure as for the jars. Wash the produce thoroughly, finishing under running water. Don't let produce soak; vitamins and minerals, which also translate into flavor, will leach out.

Cold pack or hot? In canning instructions, directions are usually given for processing two ways: (1) pouring boiling water over raw produce after the jar is packed—"cold pack"; (2) cooking the produce first, then pouring it into the jars—"hot pack." But once the jars are in the water bath or pressure cooker, the contents are being cooked. Therefore it is primarily a matter of whether you want to cook in two phases or one. In cold pack, your jars will stay in the canner longer. So, although there is a clear savings in labor, there is no significant energy saving. It is generally believed that unsweetened fruit must be hot packed. But according to the USDA pamphlet on canning, this isn't so: "You may can fruit without sweetening—in its own juice, in extracted juice, or in water. Sugar [or honey] is not needed to prevent spoilage; processing is the same for unsweetened fruit as for sweetened." Cold packing is called "raw" packing in some literature.

Light colored produce can brown slightly. If you want to prevent discoloration, you can make an anti-browning solution by adding the juice of a lemon, ⅛ tsp. crystalline vitamin C, or 400 mg. of vitamin C tablets ground into powder, to a pint of water. Dip the produce into the solution before packing it into the jars. The produce can also be canned in the solution.

Most raw fruits and vegetables should be packed tightly in the jar but a few—corn, peas and other legumes—should be packed loosely, because they expand. There should be enough liquid to fill the spaces between the pieces of produce and to cover it, leaving about a half inch of space between the top of the liquid and the closure. Before putting the closure in place, run a sterilized knife around the inside of the jar in the liquid to release any trapped air bubbles.

Prepare and pack only enough food to fill the number of jars that will fit into your canner and can only one type of food at a time, unless their processing times happen to be the same. Produce—whole, halved, chopped, unpeeled or pared—should go into jars that have been washed and rinsed just before canning. Eliminate any jars with imperfect rims. Wipe the rim with a clean cloth that has been submerged in boiling water, then wrung out. Fill one jar at a time and cover.

Metal screwbands and flat lids should be tightened firmly by hand. You need not be afraid you will screw it so tightly by hand that air won't escape during processing. Don't retighten it after processing. Leave it alone, or you will probably break a successful seal.

Porcelain-lined caps with rubber rings should be tightened firmly, then backed off a quarter inch. Upon taking the jar from the canner, tighten the cap back firmly to complete the seal. If some liquid escaped in processing, just seal the jar as is.

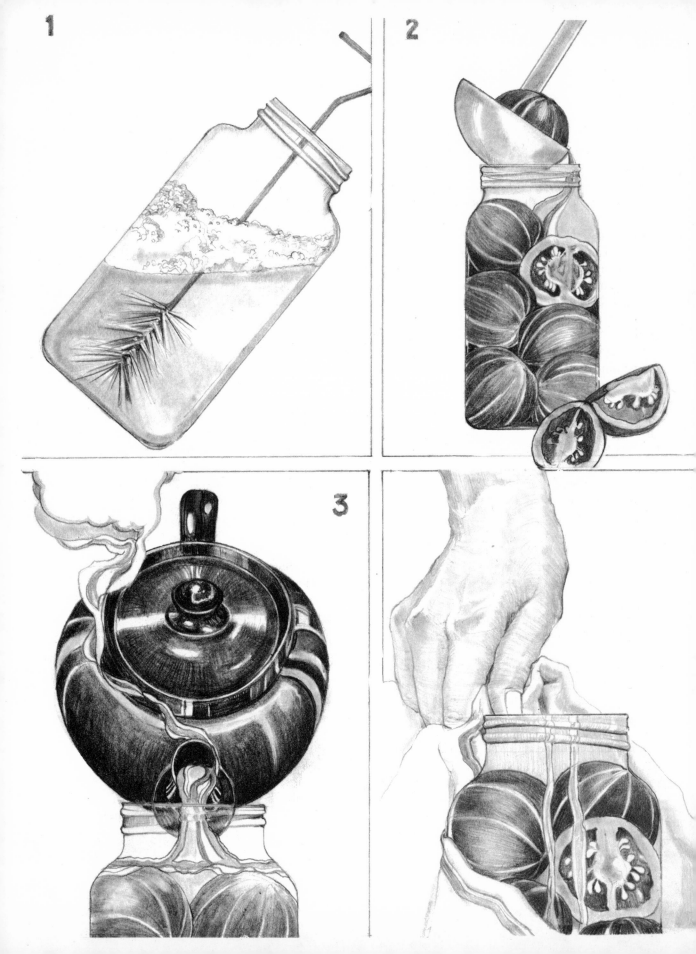

Cool jars right side up, on a rack or towel, allowing air space between the jars. Hot jars take a long time to cool. Let them sit uncovered at room temperature for a day; only then can you test the seals successfully. The successful seal of a flat lid will leave the lid concave or, if pushed down, it will stay down. If the lid pops back up, it didn't seal. To test the porcelain/rubber ring closure for a successful seal, tilt and rotate each jar in your hands; a leaky jar did not seal. Jars that didn't seal can go into your refrigerator for near-future use or the contents can be repacked, starting over again with a freshly sterilized jar. In the latter case, be sure to check the rim for defects, and use a new lid or rubber ring.

The cooler, dryer (to prevent rusting of the lids), and darker, the better your canned food will keep. Freezing, however, does not improve the keeping qualities of canned food, and may, in fact, make it less palatable.

WATER-BATH CANNING OF TOMATOES, FRUITS AND PICKLED VEGETABLES

Preparation

\#   It shouldn't be necessary to add any water to tomatoes. Pressing them down into the jars should squeeze out enough juice to cover them. But a note of warning regarding tomatoes: new hybrid varieties are often less acidic as well as less flavorful. The USDA has identified four varieties that are not acidic enough to can safely by the water-bath method: Ace, Cal Ace, Garden State, and 55 VF. If you are in doubt, can tomatoes under pressure. Also, tomato sauces can have their acidity reduced by the addition of vegetables and herbs where vinegar is not an ingredient (as it is in catsup). So Italian style tomato sauce and Mexican style salsa are also good candidates for pressure canning. The alternative is to can the older varieties plain and make the sauce from them as needed.

\#   Juicy fruits can also be pressed into the jar to squeeze out enough juice to cover. Or boiling water, juice, or syrup can be poured over the fruit. Here are three strengths of syrup in terms of sweetness:

Light syrup: 4 cups water or juice to 1 cup light honey

Medium syrup: 4 cups water or juice to 1 ½ cups light honey

Heavy syrup: 4 cups water or juice to 2 cups light honey

Use light-colored honey to keep the honey flavor from being too dominant. Stir the honey into hot water or juice until thoroughly dissolved. Molasses, sorghum, and malt syrup taste too strong for most people, though theoretically they could be used instead of honey.

If you want your tomatoes or other fruit peeled, dip them into boiling water for a half minute, then quickly into cold water long enough to cool them, after which the skins will come off easily. Fruits with stones can then be halved and pitted. Unpeeled, whole fruit cans perfectly well but doesn't utilize the jar space as well. Whole fruit canned in syrup with spices and/or a couple of shots of liqueur added to the syrup can be a real gourmet treat.

In pickling, the necessary acidity is provided by vinegar. Cucumbers are the most frequently pickled vegetable, though you can pickle onions, peppers, green tomatoes, green beans, sweet corn, cabbage, carrots, zucchini, and watermelon rind. The vegetables are first soaked in a salt and water brine for twelve to twenty-four hours. This process draws out extra moisture so that the finished product will be crisp; alum, lime, or calcium chloride to crisp the food are unnecessary. Next the vegetables are packed in clean jars, and a boiling vinegar/water solution is poured over them. I suggest that you use cider vinegar instead of distilled white vinegar, even though it will make your food appear a little darker. You can substitute honey for sugar in those recipes calling for a sweetener. Just don't decrease the amount of vinegar—if the solution is too tart for your taste, add more honey.

Canning

Water-bath canning may sound complicated, and the first time you try it, it will take you some time. But after a while, you will develop your own rhythm and it will go more quickly. Have all of your utensils at hand. You will need a pot with a cover for the boiling water bath. Pots for syrup or food cooking should be enamel or stainless steel, but *not* aluminum or iron because they will discolor the food. Have on hand clean towels and pot holders. You can use a wooden spoon to lift empty jars out of the sterilizing water. Removing full jars from the boiling water bath requires a jar lifter that works well, to keep you from burning your hands or dropping the completed jars.

If you are cold packing fruit or pickled vegetables, be sure you pack them in clean jars. Pack one jar at a time, and add boiling syrup or vinegar/water to the cold food, leaving the proper headroom. When you place these jars in the water bath, the water should be very hot but not boiling, as it will likely crack the jars. As a precaution, you can run the filled jar with lid on under hot tap water before submerging in the hot water of the water bath. Once the jars are in place, turn up the heat to achieve a rolling boil, and cover.

Hot pack jars may be lowered into a water bath that is already boiling. Jars should be placed on a rack inside the pot so as not to touch each other or the bottom of the pot directly. To insure that the food content of the jars reaches the temperature required to kill any bacteria inside, keep the jars in water at a rolling boil for the specified time in your recipe or directions for timing purposes, beginning once the water is at a rolling boil. The water must cover the tops of the jars by two or more inches when boiling to achieve the proper seal and to sterilize the contents.

When the jars have completed their bath, pick them up carefully with the jar lifter and place on a table or shelf to cool. The jars will seal themselves as they cool. You cannot tell if a seal was successful until twelve hours later when the jar is completely cooled down. (see page 358) When the jars have cooled down completely, label each one with the date, adding any notes about particular things you did with the contents to help you later in perfecting your recipes.

WATER-BATH CANNING TIMES IN MINUTES

Product	Cold Pack		Hot Pack	
	Pts.	Qts.	Pts.	Qts.
Tomatoes	35	45	10	10
Tomato juice	—	—	10	10
Applesauce	—	—	10	10
Apricots	25	30	20	25
Berries (not strawberries)	10	15	10	15
Cherries	20	25	10	15

Product	Cold Pack		Hot Pack	
	Pts.	Qts.	Pts.	Qts.
Fruit juices	—	—	5	5
Fruit purees	—	—	10	10
Nectarines	25	30	20	25
Peaches	25	30	20	25
Pears	25	30	20	25
Plums	25	30	20	25
Pickles, fresh pack, dill	20	20	—	—
Sauerkraut	—	—	15	20

Note: The above times are for sea level; higher altitudes should be adjusted.

WATER-BATH CANNING ALTITUDE ADJUSTMENT

	Increase of minutes when time is	
Altitude in feet	*20 minutes or less*	*More than 20 minutes*
1,000	1	2
2,000	2	4
3,000	3	6
4,000	4	8
5,000	5	10
6,000	6	12
7,000	7	14
8,000	8	16
9,000	9	18
10,000	10	20

Always count time when the rolling boil has begun and the cover has been placed on the pot.

Making tomato juice: Wash, remove stem ends, cut into pieces. Simmer until mushy, stirring often. Press through strainer. Either add no salt or up to ½ tsp. per quart of juice. Reheat at once, just to the boil, and can.

Making fruit juices: Wash, remove pits, crush fruit. Heat to simmering, strain through clean, white cloth bag. Either add no honey or up to ⅛ cup per quart of juice. Reheat at once to simmering and can.

Making fruit purees: The process is the same as for making fruit juices except that the fruit is put through a strainer or food mill instead of a cloth bag so that the pulp is retained.

FRESH-PACK DILL PICKLES

Cucumbers, 3 to 5 inches long	17–18 lbs.
5% brine (1½ cup salt in 2 gallons water)	2 gallons
Vinegar, apple cider	1½ qts.
Salt	½ c.

Water	2¼ qts.
Whole mixed pickling spice	2 T.
Whole mustard seed	2 T./qt. jar
Garlic	2 cloves/qt. jar
Dill, fresh or dried, or	3 heads/qt. jar
Dill seed	1 T./qt. jar

Wash cucumbers thoroughly, scrub with vegetable brush, rinse thoroughly and drain. Cover with 5% brine overnight, drain the next day.

Combine vinegar, salt, water, and pickling spice (tied in a clean, white cloth), heat to boiling. Pack cucumbers into jars, adding mustard seed, dill and garlic, then cover with the boiling liquid to within half inch of top. Affix lids and process in water-bath for 20 minutes. Yield: 7 quarts.

SAUERKRAUT

| Cabbage | About 10 lbs. |
| Salt | ¼ c. |

Pickling: Remove leaves in poor condition, wash, core, and drain cabbage, then shred it. Sprinkle the salt on the shredded cabbage, let it stand for a few minutes to wilt slightly; this allows packing without excessive breaking or bruising of the cabbage.

Pack the salted cabbage firmly and evenly into a clean one gallon crock, jar, or enamel pot; whatever the container, it should have straight sides. Using a wooden spoon or your hands, press down firmly until juice comes to the surface. Fill to within 2 inches of the top.

Cover the cabbage with something heavy that fits snugly against the sides of the container. A water-filled plastic bag works well; it should be heavyweight plastic intended for use with food. Store at room temperature (68° to 72°F) for 3 weeks, allowing cabbage to pickle.

Processing: Heat kraut to simmering but do not boil. Pack hot kraut into clean jars, cover with hot juice to within ½ inch of top. Process in water-bath for 15 minutes (20 minutes for quarts). Yield: 6 pints.

GREEN TOMATO RELISH

9 or 10 lbs. green tomatoes	½ t. black pepper
1 lg. onion, sliced	⅛ t. cayenne pepper
1 clove garlic, chopped	½ t. cinnamon
1 bell pepper (red or green), chopped	½ t. ginger
½ c. vinegar	½ t. cloves
¼ c. honey	½ t. celery seed
1 t. salt	½ t. lemon rind, grated
1 T. mustard powder	

Cook all ingredients together in a large pot for about 45 minutes. Pack into jars with ½ inch headroom, process in water-bath for 25 minutes. Yield: 6 pints. (Adapted from *The Sunburst Farm Family Cookbook.*)

CATSUP

Cook and strain about 10 lbs. of tomatoes down to about 5 quarts of puree. Add:

2 c. cider vinegar   ½ t. cumin
1 c. water   ½ t. pepper
2 t. salt   ½ t. mustard powder
2 t. oregano   ½ t. nutmeg
¼ t. garlic powder

Mix well, bring to boil, reduce to simmer for about an hour or until thick. Process in water bath for 20 minutes.

PRESSURE CANNING

Since we are talking about small-scale canning in an ordinary pressure cooker, we will be talking about pint jars only, as quart jars are too tall.

Put two inches of water in the bottom of the pressure cooker. Set jars on rack without touching so steam can flow around each jar. Close cooker securely, so that no steam escapes except through vent. Let steam escape ten or more minutes to drive out all the air, then close petcock or set weighted gauge in place. Let pressure rise ten pounds. From this moment start counting processing time, keeping pressure constant by controlling the heat. Ten pounds pressure is for altitudes up to 1000 feet; adjust pressure according to altitude as follows:

1,001	-	2,000 feet	11 lbs.
2,001	-	4,000 feet	12 lbs.
4,001	-	6,000 feet	13 lbs.
6,001	-	8,000 feet	14 lbs.
8,001	-	10,000 feet	15 lbs.

Remove pressure cooker from heat as soon as processing time is up. Let it stand at room temperature until pressure is zero. Don't try to rush cooling under the cold water tap. After pressure reaches zero, remove jars for cooling and proceed as in water-bath canning.

PROCESSING TIMES IN MINUTES FOR SOME COMMON VEGETABLES

Vegetable	Cold Pack	Hot Pack
Asparagus	45	45
Beans, green	40	40
Beans, lima	60	60
Beans, steamed and peeled	—	50
Carrots	45	45
Corn, whole kernel	75	75
Mushrooms, sauteed or steamed	—	50
Okra, parboiled	—	45
Peas, fresh black-eyed	55	55
Peas, fresh green	60	60
Potatoes, new, whole, steamed	—	50
Spinach, other greens, steamed until wilted	—	90
Squash, summer	45	45
Squash, winter, cubed and steamed	—	75

APPROXIMATE FRESH POUNDS PER PINT JAR CANNED

Asparagus	2	Okra	¾
Beans, green	1	Peas, black-eyed	2
Beans, lima (in pods)	2	Peas, green	2
Beets, without tops	1½	Potatoes, new	1½
Carrots, without tops	1½	Spinach and other greens	2
Corn, in husks	2½	Squash, summer	1¾
		Squash, winter	1½

Note: Salt is not necessary for preservation of canned vegetables; it is added for flavor only.

SWEET SPREADS

There are five types of sweet spreads:

(1) *Jam:* the sweetened puree of fruit cooked with a thickening agent.
(2) *Preserves:* like jam, but the fruit is whole instead of puree.
(3) *Conserves:* a type of preserve with chopped nuts added.
(4) *Jelly:* the sweetened *juice* of fruit cooked with a thickening agent (unlike jam or preserves, no pulp).
(5) *Fruit Butter:* the sweetened puree of fruit cooked *without* a thickening agent.

\#   When you buy most commercial jams, jellies, preserves, and conserves, only 45 percent of the product is fruit—the legal minimum. Approximately half of the product is sugar. It will also have pectin which contains a preservative not required to be listed on the label. You can improve greatly on this situation by making your own with honey and agar agar, a pure, flavorless gelatin derived from seaweed.

STRAWBERRY PRESERVES

1 qt. strawberries	1 stick agar agar
1½ c. honey	½ lemon, juiced

Wash and stem strawberries. Cook slowly in a heavy pot until warm and juicy throughout. Prepare the agar agar by flaking, then soaking for 15 minutes. Add it to jam after honey and lemon juice have been mixed in. Simmer until thick. (Adapted from *The Sunburst Farm Family Cookbook.*)

The same method is used for preserves of all other berries and for conserves of all sorts. Jams follow the same procedure, with the fruit pureed in a food mill or mashed by hand (producing a chunkier jam). Jellies, since the juice is thinner than the fruit, take proportionately more time to cook down to a jelling consistency. Agar agar may be hard to find in supermarkets, but can be found in most health and natural foods stores. *Pectin*, a dense, sticky starch usually derived from apples, can be used in place of agar agar. The problem is finding it without the preservative. Even natural foods stores have trouble finding it for their shelves.

\# Fruit butters are a healthier alternative to jam, jellies, and preserves because they contain only half the amount of sweetener. They have the additional attraction of eliminating the search for agar agar or preservative-free pectin.

APPLE BUTTER

Cover 5 lbs. apples, sliced and cored, with apple juice and bring to a boil. Simmer until mushy, about 20 minutes. Remove from heat and push through a sieve, puree in a food mill or blender. Add:

2 c. honey	1 t. nutmeg (optional)
1 t. cinnamon	1 t. cloves

Stir in and return to boil, then lower heat to simmer for 2½ hours or more, stirring often, until very thick—until it sheets from a spoon. (Adapted from *The Sunburst Farm Family Cookbook.*)

The same procedure can be followed with other fresh fruits and dried fruits that have been soaked overnight. There is too much variation between various dried fruits to be able to generalize about how much weight they gain from soaking. Other fruit juices can be substituted for apple but are usually more expensive. Substituting water works, yielding a blander product which might be acceptable nevertheless. Fruit butter with fruit juice can also be made without honey for those who wish to avoid sweeteners altogether. In that case, you need to cook longer and stir more often. The addition of a few tablespoons of lemon juice will bring out the fruit flavor and improve the color a bit.

None of the sweet spreads need to be processed in a water-bath. The acidity of the fruit, the long

---

FRESH ALTERNATIVES TO CANNED SPREADS

—Use slices of raw fruit or chopped dried fruit instead of sweet spreads.

—Many fresh fruits can be mashed, dried fruit soaked, and both blended to a preserve or jam-like consistency. These are good as is or with a bit of honey, a dash of lemon juice. Here's an alternative from *The Supermarket Handbook*:

Make a simple jam by cooking diced fruits with honey until thickened and store the rich pulp in the refrigerator to use just like jam. This recipe for homemade Blueberry Jam will give you the idea. Try it with other fruits if you like.

---

cooking, and the high percentage of sweetener suffice for preservation. Sterilize the jars in boiling water, and put the hot product in the hot jars and seal. They can be sealed with hot paraffin as an alternative to metal lids. The exception to this method is unsweetened fruit butter, which should be processed in a water bath for ten minutes.

BLUEBERRY JAM

1½ c. blueberries   ¼ c. honey
1 T. lemon juice

Combine all ingredients in a saucepan. Bring to a boil and let boil for 20 minutes. Stir occasionally to prevent scorching. Pour into clean (sterilized) jar and chill. It will thicken on cooling. *Yield*: about 1 cup.

QUESTIONS ABOUT CANNING

Some questions and answers adapted from the USDA's *Home Canning of Fruits and Vegetables*:

Q. *Is it safe to process foods in the oven?*
A. No, oven canning is dangerous. Jars may explode. The temperature of food in jars during oven processing does not get high enough to insure destruction of spoilage bacteria.

Q. *Why is open-kettle canning not recommended?*
A. In open-kettle canning, food is cooked in an ordinary kettle, then packed into hot jars and sealed without processing. For vegetables, the temperatures are not high enough to destroy all the spoilage organisms and spoilage bacteria may get in when the food is transferred from kettle to jar.

Q. *Must glass jars and lids be sterilized by boiling before canning?*
A. No, not with boiling water-bath or pressure canning. The containers as well as the food are sterilized during processing. But be sure jars and lids are clean.

Q. *Why is liquid sometimes lost from jars during processing?*
A. Packing jars too full, fluctuating pressure or lowering pressure too suddenly.

Q. *Should liquid lost during processing be replaced?*
A. No, never open a jar and refill with liquid—this would let in bacteria and you would need to process again. Loss of liquid does not cause food to spoil, though food above the liquid may darken.

Q. *Is it safe to use home canned food if the liquid is cloudy?*
A. Cloudy liquid may be a sign of spoilage. But it may be caused by the minerals in hard water, or by starch from overripe vegetables. If liquid is cloudy, boil the food. Do not taste or otherwise use any food that foams or has an off odor during heating.

Q. *Why does canned fruit sometimes float in jars?*
A. Fruit may float because pack is too loose, or syrup is too heavy, or because some air remains in tissues of the fruit after heating and processing.

Q. *What makes canned food change color?*
A. (1) Darkening of foods at the tops of jars may be caused by oxidation due to air in the jars or by too little heating or processing to destroy enzymes. Overprocessing may cause discoloration of foods throughout the containers.

(2) Pink and blue colors sometimes seen in canned pears, apples and peaches are caused by chemical changes in pigments.

(3) Iron or copper from cooking utensils or in the water of some localities may cause brown, black and gray colors in some foods.

(4) When canned corn turns brown, the discoloring may be due to the variety of corn, its natural sugar content, to overprocessing or to iron or copper pots.

(5) The packing liquid may dissolve pigments from the food.

Q. *Is it safe to eat discolored canned foods?*
A. The color changes noted above do not mean the food is unsafe. However, spoilage may also cause color changes. Any canned food that has an unusual color should be examined carefully before eating.

Q. *Why do the undersides of metal lids sometimes discolor?*
A. Natural compounds in some foods corrode the metal and make a brown or black deposit on the underside of the lid. This deposit is harmless.

Q. *Can fruits and vegetables be canned without heating if aspirin is used?*
A. No. Aspirin cannot prevent spoilage. Adequate heat treatment is the only safe procedure.

Q. *Does ascorbic acid help keep fruits and vegetables from darkening?*
A. Yes. The addition of ¼ t. of crystalline ascorbic acid (synthetic vitamin C) to a quart of fruit or vegetable before processing retards oxidation, one cause of darkening. [One teaspoon of crystalline vitamin C weighs about 3 grams (3000 milligrams); so ¼ t. is the equivalent of about 750 milligrams if you use crushed tablets.]

SPOILAGE

Canned food that has spoiled may cause serious illness. Look at each jar carefully before opening; look for these signs of spoilage before, during and immediately after opening:

—Discoloration
—Cloudy liquid
—Bulging lids
—Leaky seals
—Bubbles in liquid
—Spurting liquid when jar is opened
—Off odors
—Mold
—Sliminess
—Foaming

Vegetables are trickier than fruits. According to the USDA

It's possible for canned vegetables to contain the poison causing botulism—a deadly food poisoning—without showing signs of spoilage. To avoid any risk of botulism, it is essential that the pressure canner be in perfect order and that every canning recommendation be followed exactly.

Bring home canned vegetables to a rolling boil; then cover and boil for at least 10 minutes. Boil spinach and corn 20 minutes. If the food looks spoiled, foams, or has an off odor during heating, destroy it.

Burn spoiled vegetables, or dispose of the food so that it will not be eaten by humans or animals.

When you consider the extra cooking required to safeguard yourself against botulism, you have to ask yourself whether canned vegetables are worth the trouble. Firm vegetables such as corn, peas, beans, and peppers, withstand the cooking best.

I cleared away my ambivalence about canning and recommend this general approach:

—Maintain the emphasis on fresh vegetables with the assorted varieties of winter squash, root vegetables, the cabbage family, and various kinds of sprouts to see you through the winter.

—For nutritional reasons, make minimal use of canned vegetables. Frozen vegetables are a more nutritious way to add variety to your winter meals.

—Use home-canned fruits, pickles, and preserves to add zest to your winter meals and enjoy the warm memories of companionship you enjoyed while doing the canning.

33   Freezing

I have not used the term "small scale" to describe this chapter because there may be some good reasons for freezing to be on a relatively larger scale than canning in your home. You may have a big garden or the opportunity to buy in season at prices too good to resist. But whatever the scale, in my experience questions about the nutritional quality of frozen foods come up frequently. Compared to canning, freezing yields better quality because it does not require as much cooking, or, in the case of fruit, no cooking. Frozen fruit can even be nutritionally superior to fresh where "fresh" is not really fresh. The major losses in vegetables occur in the blanching before freezing, where heat-fragile and water-soluble vitamins B and C are partially lost. During freezing there is some breakdown of vitamins A and E in grains and vegetables.

The nutritional losses in frozen food do not mean the food is ruined. Frozen meat, fish, poultry, and fruit compare reasonably well to fresh. Vegetables and grains do not fare quite so well in the freezer, but the deterioration is slow. As a corollary to the maxim that fresh is best, the closer to fresh, the better. More nutrients are preserved when cooking frozen food if it is not allowed to thaw, but goes right to the stove from the freezer.

Another frequently asked question has become common during the recent years of increasing energy consciousness: Which uses more energy: canning or freezing? I've read and heard three different answers, the obvious contradictory ones and the third one: it depends.

The "it depends" answer says that if you keep frozen food for more than about nine months, the energy consumption of running the freezer catches up with the energy consumption of all the cooking involved in canning, and past that point freezing becomes more expensive than canning. But, since frozen food is generally much better in taste and texture and more nutritious when consumed within six months of freezing, it should demand less energy at its best. If you are trying to preserve food for a year and have the choice of methods, there is a case for freezing the first six months' supply and canning the second.

What if you don't already own a freezer? Is it worth the investment? This time it depends on how big your family is and how much the freezer costs. A big family, second-hand freezer in good working condition? It could pay for itself within a year. Small family, new freezer? It will take perhaps three years to pay for itself unless you live on frozen food, which you shouldn't. In other words, if you're already into freezing food, there's no reason not to continue. But if you're not, the question you need to answer is, "Can I satisfy my needs adequately twelve months of the year eating the seasonably available fresh foods?" Two people living next door to one another might well answer that question differently.

You need to ask yourself other kinds of questions each of us would answer differently: What would

I put in a freezer? How much of those things would I use? How much would that save me? Is that saving worth the time it would take?

Where time and labor are concerned, freezing is relatively simple and quick, especially when compared to canning. One way to answer your questions about buying a freezer is to rent space in a freezer locker for a year or two. This would give you the opportunities to figure out a pattern of use, find out from experience how much freezer space you require, learn how to wrap foods properly and label them with dates that will enable you to rotate your stock properly. These are all important lessons for learning to utilize a freezer efficiently.

An alternative is to buy and share a big freezer with other families. One editor for this book, Lindy Hough, as part of her family of four, shared a freezer with three other families while living in Vermont. It worked well on the practical level and she enjoyed the interdependence. A big freezer is also more economical to operate: when you go from a five cubic foot freezer to a fifteen foot, increasing your capacity by 200 percent, your cost of electricity goes up less than 50 percent. If you happen to have a freezer too big for your needs, sharing it would bring the cost of operation down—the fuller a freezer, the more efficient.

If you are fully engaged in the Phase Three level of the New American Cuisine for economic reasons, it is unlikely that you would choose freezing for preservation of food that would keep well in your cellar—potatoes, for example. But even for such a person, some frozen parboiled potatoes might be a consideration for one reason: convenience. Unquestionably, when mealtime arrives, especially when it arrives in conjunction with a scrambled schedule, frozen food can be wonderfully convenient as an alternative to scrambled eggs. Allied to convenience is the consideration that a freezer leaves you ready for the unexpected.

WHAT TO FREEZE AND HOW TO FREEZE IT

What To Freeze

There are few things that cannot be frozen. Some vegetables, such as salad greens, radishes and raw tomatoes, turn to goop. But virtually all other vegetables are freezable, though they require blanching, unlike fruit, which is the simplest category of food to freeze. Meat, fish, and poultry freeze reasonably well, as do most cooked foods. But no matter what you are freezing, *speed is of the essence.* Your aim should be to freeze *fresh* food as quickly as possible. Though you can freeze almost everything, remember that it is almost never as good frozen as fresh. So if you can buy a lug of fruit on the verge of going bad for next to nothing, pass it up. If you can get the lug in better condition for a good price but won't have the time to get it frozen soon, pass it up.

The same USDA study cited in the previous chapter revealed that 45 percent of American households froze some fruits and vegetables, regardless of whether or not they had gardens. Much of the information that follows, which is intended for those who have had little or no experience with freezing, will be unnecessary to readers with a lot of experience. I suggest you check the material on pages 372–380, which may be new to you.

Containers For Freezing

The primary purpose of packaging is to keep food from drying out and to preserve food value, flavor, color, and texture.

All containers should be easy to seal and waterproof so they will not leak. Packaging materials should be durable and should not become so brittle at low temperatures that they crack.

To retain highest quality in frozen food, packaging materials should be moisture-vapor-proof, to prevent evaporation. Glass, metal, and rigid plastic are examples of moisture-vapor-proof packaging materials. Many of the packaging materials on the market for frozen food are not moisture-vapor-*proof*, but are sufficiently moisture-vapor-*resistant* to retain satisfactory quality of fruits and vegetables during storage. Most bags, wrapping materials, and waxed cartons made especially for freezing are moisture-vapor-resistant. Ordinary waxed papers, and paper cartons from cottage cheese, ice cream, and milk are not sufficiently moisture-vapor-resistant to be suitable for packaging foods for freezing.

Rigid containers: Rigid containers made of glass, tin, plastic or heavily waxed cardboard are suitable for all packs and especially good for liquid packs. Glass canning jars may be used for freezing most fruits and vegetables, except those packed in water.

Nonrigid containers: Bags and sheets of moisture-vapor-resistant cellophane, heavy aluminum foil, pliofilm, polyethylene or laminated papers and duplex bags consisting of various combinations of paper, metal foil, glassine, cellophane, and latex rubber are suitable for dry-packed vegetables and fruits. Bags also can be used for liquid packs.

Bags and sheets are used with or without outer cardboard cartons to protect against tearing. Bags without a protective carton are difficult to stack. The sheets may be used for wrapping such foods as corn-on-the-cob or asparagus. Some of the sheets may be heat-sealed to make a bag of the size you need. Sheets that are heat-sealed on both sides may be used as outer wraps for paperboard cartons.

Size: Select a size that will hold only enough of a fruit or vegetable for one meal for your family.

Shape: Rigid containers that are flat on both top and bottom stack well in a freezer. Round containers and those with flared sides or raised bottoms waste freezer space. Nonrigid containers that bulge waste freezer space.

Food can be removed easily, before it is thawed, from containers with sides that are straight from bottom to top or that flare out. Food must be at least partially thawed before it can be removed from containers with openings narrower than the body of the container.

Bags, sheets, and folding paperboard cartons take up little room when not in use. Rigid containers with flared sides will stack one inside the other and save space in your cupboard when not in use. Those with straight sides or narrow top openings cannot be nested.

Sealing: Care in sealing is as important as using the right container. Rigid containers usually are sealed either by pressing on or screwing on the lid. Some rigid cardboard cartons need to have freezer tape or special wax applied after sealing to make them airtight and leakproof. Glass jars must be sealed with a lid containing composition rubber or with a lid and a rubber ring.

Most bags used for packaging can be heat-sealed or sealed by twisting and folding back the top of the bag and securing with a string, a good quality rubber or plastic band, or other sealing device available on the market. Some duplex bags are sealed by folding over a metal strip attached to the top of the bag.

Special sealing irons for heat-sealing bags or sheets for freezing are available on the market, or a household iron may be used. To heat-seal polyethylene or pliofilm bags or sheets used as overwraps, first place a piece of paper or heat-resistant material made especially for the purpose over the edges to be sealed. Then press with a warm iron. Regulate heat of the iron carefully—too much heat melts or crinkles the materials and prevents sealing.

Reuse: Tin cans (with slip-top closures), glass, rigid plastic, and aluminum containers can be reused indefinitely. It is difficult to reuse aluminum foil boxes, because edges of lids and containers are folded over in sealing. Tin cans that require a sealer must be reflanged with a special attachment to the sealer before they are reused. A tin can or lid that is dented should not be used if it cannot be sealed.

Reuse of rigid cardboard cartons, unless plastic-lined, is not generally advisable because cleaning is difficult. Folding paperboard cartons used to protect an inner bag can be reused.

Cost: When you compare prices of the containers that are available in your locality, consider whether they will be reusable or not. If containers are reusable, a higher initial cost may be a savings in the long run.

Care of packaging materials: Protect packaging materials from dust and insects. Keep bags and rolls of wrapping materials that may become brittle, such as cellophane, in a place that is cool but not too dry.

Freezing accessories: Check on other items that help make packaging easier. Some containers are easier to fill if you use a stand and funnel. With some sealing irons, a small wooden block or box makes sealing of bags easier and quicker.

Packing

Pack food and syrup cold into containers. Having materials cold speeds up freezing and helps retain natural color, flavor, and texture of food.

Pack foods tightly to cut down on amount of air in the package.

When food is packed in bags, press air out of unfilled part of bag. Press firmly to prevent air from getting back in. Seal immediately, allowing the head space recommended for the product.

Allow ample head space. With only a few exceptions, allowance for head space is needed between packed food and closure because food expands as it freezes. A guide to the amount of head space to allow is given in the table below:

HEAD SPACE TO ALLOW BETWEEN PACKED FOOD AND CLOSURE

Type of Pack	Container With Wide Top Opening[1]		Container With Narrow Top Opening[2]	
	Pt.	Qt.	Pt.	Qt.
Liquid pack (fruit packed in juice, honey, syrup or water; crushed or puree; juice)	½ in.	1 in.	¾ in.[3]	1½ in.
Dry pack[4] (fruit or vegetable packed without added sugar or liquid)	½ in.	½ in.	½ in.	½ in.

[1]This is head space for tall containers—either straight or slightly flared.
[2]Glass canning jars may be used for freezing most fruits and vegetables except those packed in water.
[3]Head space for juice should be 1½ inches.
[4]Vegetables that pack loosely, such as broccoli and asparagus, require no head space.

Keep sealing edges free from moisture or food so that a good closure can be made. Seal carefully. Label packages plainly. Include name of food, date it was packed, and type of pack if food is packed in more than one form. Gummed labels, colored tape, crayons, pens, and stamps are made especially for labelling frozen food packages.

Loading The Freezer

Freeze fruits and vegetables soon after they are packed. Put them in the freezer a few packages at a time as you have them ready, or keep packages in the refrigerator until all you are doing at one time are ready. Then transfer them to the home freezer or carry them in an insulated box or bag to the locker plant. Freeze at 0° or below.

Put no more unfrozen food into a home freezer than will freeze within 24 hours. Usually this will be about two or three pounds of food to each cubic foot of freezer capacity. Overloading slows down the rate of freezing, and foods that freeze slowly may lose quality or spoil. For quickest freezing, place packages against freezing plates or coils and leave a little space between packages so air can circulate freely.

After freezing, packages may be stored close together. Store them at 0°F or below. At higher temperatures foods lose quality much faster.

Most fruits and vegetables maintain high quality for eight to twelve months at 0°F or below; citrus fruits and citrus juices, for four to six months. Unsweetened fruits lose quality faster than those packed in honey or syrup. Longer storage will not make foods unfit for use, but may impair quality.

It's a good idea to post a list of frozen foods near the freezer and keep it up to date. List foods as you put them in the freezer, check foods off the list as you remove them.

FREEZING FRUITS

Most fruits can be frozen satisfactorily, but the quality of the frozen product will vary with the kind of fruit, stage of maturity, and type of pack.

Generally, flavor is well-retained by freezing. Texture may be somewhat softer than that of fresh fruit. Some fruits require special treatment when packed, to make them more pleasing in color, texture, or flavor after thawing. Most fruits are best frozen soon after harvesting. Some, such as peaches and pears, may need to be held a short time to ripen.

Before Packing

All fruits need to be washed in cold water. Wash a small quantity at a time to save undue handling, which may bruise delicate fruits such as berries. Using a strainer, lift washed fruits out of the water and drain thoroughly. Don't let the fruit stand in the water—it may lose food value and flavor that way or get waterlogged.

In general, fruit is prepared for freezing in about the same way as for serving. Large fruits generally are better cut into pieces or crushed before freezing. Many fruits can be frozen successfully in several forms. Good parts of less perfect fruit are suitable for crushed or pureed packs.

Trim, pit, and slice fruit; if the peel is edible, leave it on to save time and nutritional value. It is best to prepare enough fruit for only a few containers at one time, especially those fruits that darken rapidly. Two or three quarts is a good quantity to work with.

If directions call for fruit to be crushed, suit the method of crushing to the fruit. For soft fruits, a wire potato masher, pastry fork, or slotted spoon may be used; if fruits are firm they may be crushed more easily with a food chopper. For making purees, a colander, food press, or strainer is useful.

Use equipment of earthenware, enamel ware, glass, nickel, stainless steel, or good quality tinware. Do not use galvanized wire in direct contact with fruit or fruit juices because the acid in fruit dissolves zinc, which is an important mineral but harmful in that form. Metallic off-flavors may result from the use of iron utensils, chipped enamel ware, tinware that is not well-tinned, or aluminum. Fruit acids dissolve aluminum and the resulting aluminum salts are toxic.

Methods Of Freezing Fruit

Most of the existing literature on freezing fruits calls for the extensive use of sugar. The New American Cuisine substitutes honey (½ cup honey for 1 cup sugar), using one of the lighter colored honeys. There are seven methods of freezing fruit:

1. Honey syrup pack
2. Honey pack
3. Juice pack
4. Unsweetened
5. Crushed fruit
6. Fruit puree
7. Juice

Any fruit can be packed without sweetening but most have better flavor, texture, and color if packed in honey or honey syrup. Gooseberries, cranberries, rhubarb, and figs are exceptions which turn out as well unsweetened as with honey. Honey syrup is best for fruit intended for dessert as is, honey pack is best for fruit intended for cooking because it has less liquid.

Honey syrup pack: Mild tasting and sweet fruits require a light syrup, very sour fruits a heavy one. If the fruit you are freezing is not on the table on page 374 and you are unsure, use a medium syrup.

HONEY SYRUPS

Strength	Honey	Water
Light	1½ cups	4 cups
Medium	2½ cups	4 cups
Heavy	3½ cups	4 cups

Use a light-colored honey. Dissolve it in warm, not hot, water; then let it cool before adding to fruit. Be sure to cover all the fruit with syrup, otherwise the top pieces will brown off. To keep them under the syrup, put a small piece of crumpled water-resistant wrapping material such as parchment, foil, or waxed paper on top so that closing the lid pushes the fruit down.

Honey pack: Cut fruit into bowl, drizzle honey over it. Mix gently (a large wooden spoon is best) until juice is drawn out and honey is dissolved. There should be enough liquid to cover the fruit when packed in containers; if not, add a little water. Keep fruit under liquid as above. If you are freezing fruit not on the chart below, get a feel for the right amount of honey from other items on the chart and play it by ear.

Juice and unsweetened packs: The juice pack can be a way of freezing fruit without added sweetener. Apple juice can be substituted for the juice of the particular variety of fruit you are freezing. The two other alternatives for an unsweetened pack are to treat it the same way as in honey packing without using honey or to simply pack it in water.

Crushed and pureed fruit: The difference between these two is that crushed is chunky, most likely just mashed by hand, whereas puree is smooth, pressed through a sieve or made with food mill or blender. They also can be packed with or without honey. If you are making a sweetened crushed or pureed fruit that doesn't appear on the chart, get a feel for the right amount from the chart and just go ahead and wing it from there.

Juice: This method is for fruits such as grapes and berries which can't be juiced effectively in some juices or for all fruits if you don't have a juicer. Crush fruit and heat just enough to loosen juice—don't boil, no higher temperature than 160° F. Strain through a jelly bag or clean, white cloth to remove juice. Add honey to taste or freeze unsweetened.

HONEY AND YIELD QUANTITIES FOR FROZEN FRUITS

Fruit	Syrup Pack Type of syrup	Yield	Honey Pack Honey per quart	Yield	Crush/Puree Honey per quart	Yield
Apples (44 lbs/box)	light	20 qts.	¼ c.	18 qts.	½ c.	16 qts.
Apricots (22 lbs/lug)	light	36 qts.	¼ c.	33 qts	½ c.	30 qts.
Berries (all except raspberries and strawberries, 24 qts/flat)	medium	18 qts.	⅓ c.	17 qts.	⅔ c.	16 qts.
Cherries (56 lbs/box), sweet	light	22 qts.	¼ c.	20 qts.	½ c.	18 qts.
sour	heavy	22 qts.	½ c.	20 qts.	1 c.	18 qts.
Cranberries (25 lbs/box)	heavy	25 qts.	½ c.	22 qts.	1 c.	19 qts.
Melons (1 doz. weighing 28 lbs)	light	11 qts.	¼ c.	10 qts.	—	—
Peaches (20 lbs/lug)	light	24 qts.	¼ c.	20 qts.	½ c.	16 qts.
Pears (46 lbs/box)	light	25 qts.	¼ c.	23 qts.	½ c.	20 qts.
Pineapple (5 lbs.)	light	2 qts.	¼ c.	1¾ qts.	½ c.	1½ qts.
Plums and prunes (20 lbs/lug)	medium	28 qts.	⅓ c.	24 qts.	⅔ c.	19 qts.
Raspberries (24 pts/flat)	light	12 qts.	¼ c.	11 qts.	½ c.	10 qts.
Rhubarb (15 lbs)	heavy	11 qts.	½ c.	10 qts.	1 c.	8 qts.
Strawberries (24 qts/flat)	medium	19 qts.	⅓ c.	18 qts.	⅔ c.	17 qts.

Note: Yields are approximate, will vary according to size, ripeness and variety of fruit. Yields for juice and water packs will be about the same as syrup pack.

Preventing Darkening of Fruit

Light-colored fruit darkens as the natural vitamin C is oxidized, and browning occurs after most of the C is gone. The best preventative measures are to freeze only fully ripe fruit because its C content is fully developed and to minimize in every way you can think of the fruit's exposure to air. You can also add vitamin C in the form of crystalline or powdered ascorbic acid or crushed vitamin C tablets. Use about a quarter teaspoon (750 milligrams) per quart. You may want to offset the sourness of ascorbic acid with a bit of extra honey.

(My brother and sister purists may wonder why I'm recommending synthetic vitamin C. I'm not recommending it; there's no other choice. Even the so-called "natural" vitamin C tablets are, except in *extremely* rare cases, largely synthetic. See Chapter 12).

FREEZING VEGETABLES

Fresh, tender vegetables right from the garden are best for freezing. The fresher the vegetables when frozen, the more satisfactory will be your product.

First Steps

Washing is the first step in the preparation of vegetables for freezing. Wash vegetables thoroughly in cold water. Lift them out of the water as grit settles to the bottom of the pan.

Sort vegetables according to size for heating and packing unless they are to be cut into pieces of uniform size.

Peel if necessary, trim and cut into pieces convenient for packing and cooking.

Heating Before Packing

An important step in preparing vegetables for freezing is heating or "blanching" before packing. Practically every vegetable, except green pepper, maintains better quality in frozen storage if heated before packing.

The reason for heating vegetables before freezing is that it slows or stops the action of enzymes. Up until the time vegetables are ready to pick, enzymes help them grow and mature. After that they cause loss of flavor and color. If vegetables are not heated enough, the enzymes continue to be active during frozen storage. Then the vegetables may develop off-flavors, discolor or toughen so that they may be unappetizing in a few weeks. (These are the same enzymes which are vital nutrients when the vegetables are eaten uncooked.)

Heating also wilts or softens vegetables and makes them easier to pack. Heating time varies with the vegetable and size of pieces.

Boiling water: For home freezing, the most satisfactory way to heat practically all vegetables is in boiling water. Use a blancher, which has a blanching basket and cover. Or fit a wire basket into a large kettle and add the cover.

For each pound of prepared vegetables use at least one gallon of boiling water in the blancher or kettle. Put vegetables in blanching basket or wire basket and lower into the boiling water. A wire cover for the basket can be used to keep the vegetables down in the boiling water.

Put lid on blancher or kettle and start counting time immediately. Keep heat high for time given in the table for vegetable you are freezing. Heat one minute longer than the time specified if you live 5,000 feet or more above sea level.

Steam: For broccoli, pumpkin, sweet potatoes, and winter squash both steaming and boiling are satisfactory methods.

To steam, use a kettle with a tight lid and a rack that holds a steaming basket at least three inches above the bottom of the kettle. Put an inch or two of water in the kettle and bring the water to a boil.

Put vegetables in the basket in a single layer so that steam reaches all parts quickly. Cover the kettle and keep heat high. Start counting steaming time as soon as the lid is on. Follow same times as for blanching (see table).

Other ways to heat: Pumpkin, sweet potatoes, and winter squash may be heated in pressure cooker or in the oven before freezing. Mushrooms may be heated in oil in a frying pan. Tomatoes for juice may be simmered.

Cooling

After vegetables are heated they should be cooled quickly and thoroughly to stop the cooking.

To cool vegetables heated in boiling water or steam, plunge the basket of vegetables immediately into a large quantity of cold water—60° F or below. Change water frequently or use cold running water or iced water. If ice is used, you'll need about one pound of ice for each pound of vegetable. It will take about as long to cool the food as it does to heat it. When the vegetable is cool, remove it from the water and drain thoroughly.

To cool vegetables heated in an oven, pressure cooker, or frying pan, set pan of food in water and change water to speed cooling.

Dry Vs. Brine Pack

Either dry or brine pack may be used for most vegetables to be frozen. However, the dry pack is recommended, because preparation for freezing and serving is easier.

YIELD AND TIMES TABLE FOR FROZEN VEGETABLES

Vegetable	Yield (qts.)	Blanching Times in Minutes/ According to Vegetable Size		
		Small	Medium	Large
Asparagus (1 crate 12-2 lb. bunches)	8–11	2	3	4
Beans, lima (1 bushel, 32 lbs.)	6–8	2	3	4
Beans, green (1 bushel, 30 lbs.)	15–23	—	3	—
Beet greens (15 lbs)	5–8	—	2	—
Beets, topless (1 bushel, 52 lbs.)	17–22	25	35	45
Broccoli (1 crate, 25 lbs.)	12	—	3	—

Vegetable	Yield (qts.)	Blanching Times in Minutes/ According to Vegetable Size		
		Small	Medium	Large
Brussels sprouts (4 qts.)	3	2	3	4
			(diced or sliced)	
Carrots, topless (1 bushel, 50 lbs.)	16–20	—	5	—
			(floweretts)	
Cauliflower (4 medium heads)	3	—	3	—
Chard (1 bushel, 12 lbs.)	4–6	—	2	—
Collards (1 bushel, 12 lbs.)	4–6	—	3	—
Corn, in husks (1 bushel, 35 lbs.)	7–9	7	9	11
Kale (1 bushel, 18 lbs.)	6–9	—	2	—
Mustard greens (1 bushel, 12 lbs.)	4–6	—	2	—
Peas, in pods (1 bushel, 30 lbs.)	6–8	—	1½	—
Peppers (4 lbs.)	3	may be frozen without blanching		
Pumpkin, winter squash (6 lbs.)	2	boil or steam until tender		
Spinach (1 bushel, 18 lbs.)	6–9	—	2	—
			(sliced)	
Squash, summer (1 bushel, 40 lbs.)	16–20	—	2	—
Sweet potatoes, yams (4 lbs.)	3	any method of cooking until tender		

Note: Yields are approximate, varying according to size, ripeness and variety

FREEZING MEAT, FISH, AND POULTRY

Freezing is an excellent method of preserving meat and fish. It can be done simply and effectively at home if

—meat and fish are carefully selected, prepared, and packaged; and

—home freezing equipment freezes quickly at 0° F or lower and maintains these temperatures for storage of frozen products.

Too high or constantly changing storage temperatures cause even properly packaged and frozen foods to lose quality and food value.

Freeze only high-qaulity fresh meat and fish. Freezing cannot improve quality; chances are the quality will actually deteriorate at least a little.

Keep all food to be frozen—and anything that touches it—clean. Freezing does not sterilize foods; the extreme cold simply slows down changes that affect quality or cause spoilage in food.

If you are not going to freeze it right after getting it home, thoroughly chill meat and fish. The ideal temperature range for aging is 33–38°F. (According to the editors of *Organic Gardening and Farming* magazine in the Rodale Press book *Stocking Up*, the tenderization advantage is lost after holding meat frozen for more than one month. They also say that pork, veal, and fish should not be aged at all, lamb for not more than three days, lean beef for not more than five days.)

Prepare and package in quantities to be cooked at one time.

Freeze quickly at 0° F or lower. Turn the temperature control to the coldest position to speed up freezing and help prevent warming of stored frozen food. To freeze a maximum load and reduce it to storage temperature, wait twenty-four hours before returning the control to storage position; for a half load or less, eight to twelve hours is sufficient.

Place the unfrozen packages against a refrigerated surface. Arrange them so that they do not touch any packages of frozen food stored in the freezer. If necessary, use a board or heavy cardboard, such as corrugated carton material, between the frozen and unfrozen packages to prevent them from coming into contact with each other. Store at 0°F or lower.

Limit storage time. See the table below for maximum storage times recommended for meats and fish in moisture-vapor-proof or moisture-vapor-resistant wrappings.

Usually it is best to freeze meat, fish, and poultry in meal-size packages; this eliminates the maximum amount of waste portions, makes for efficient space utilization, and is more convenient at meal time.

Wrap meat, fish, and poultry in moisture-resistant coverings to make the package airtight and prevent drying. Put two layers of waxed paper between individual pieces so they can be easily separated. Pull paper tight to drive out air, make package smooth to pack together snugly. Tape seams and ends with freezer tape.

RECOMMENDED MAXIMUM STORAGE PERIODS

		Months
Beef	Ground	4
	Steaks and roasts	12
	Stew	4
Lamb	Ground	4
	Chops and Roasts	9
	Stew	4
Pork	Chops	4
	Roasts	8
Veal	Cutlets, Chops & Roasts	9
	Ground	4
Organ Meats		4
Fish		9
Poultry		7

Note: Cooked and cured meat, poultry and fish lose quality quickly and should be used within a month.

Thawing Meats, Poultry And Fish

Most frozen meats and fish may be cooked either with or without previous thawing. But extra cooking time must be allowed for meats not thawed first—just how much will depend on the size and shape of the cut.

Large frozen roasts may take as much as one-and-a-half times as long to cook as unfrozen cuts of the same weight and shape. Small roasts and thin cuts, such as steaks and chops, require less time.

Frozen fish fillets and steaks may be cooked as if they were in the unfrozen form if additional cooking time is allowed. When fish are to be breaded and fried, or stuffed, it is more convenient to thaw them first to make handling easier.

Thaw frozen meats and fish in the refrigerator in their original wrappings.

THAWING TIMES

Product		Hours in Refrigerator
Meats	Ground	8
	Steaks, chops	12
	Small roasts	4 per lb.
	Large roasts	6 per lb.
Fish	Whole	36
	Steaks, fillets	4
Poultry	Smal	24
	Medium	36
	Large	48
	Pieces	4

Note: Thawing times are approximate; if thawing is not complete, increase cooking time.

TV DINNERS

Much of the lowest quality, most expensive food is eaten in the form of TV dinners. Admittedly, they are convenient. But why put up with the quality and cost disadvantages when you can do it so much better and cheaper yourself? Almost everybody has a refrigerator and most refrigerators have at least a small freezer compartment, and that plus a stove are all you need to become a manufacturer of good, cheap TV dinners.

Every time you make pots of beans, stews, and large casseroles, you can become a TV dinner manufacturer. Pasta dishes like lasagne and ravioli are quite freezable, as are most kinds of desserts. Make it the rule rather than the exception to cook more than you need of all kinds of grains and vegetables, and freeze the extra for next week or next month.

Let's say you've made double portions of fish fillet, brown rice, and sautéed mixed vegetables. Spread out a piece of foil, lay the extra portions on it, fold over the edges to make a rectangular package, and freeze. You can reheat your TV dinner in the oven or toaster oven, or, if there are just one or two of you, in a steaming basket in a covered pot with a little bit of boiling water.

MISCELLANEA

An alternative method of dry-freezing fruits and vegetables: freeze them spread out on a tray, then put them in bags or some other container of your choice. In this way, they will not stick together and you can remove small amounts.

In Case Of Emergency

If power is interrupted or the freezer fails to refrigerate properly, do not open the cabinet unnecessarily. Food in a loaded cabinet usually will stay frozen for two days, even in summer. In a cabinet with less than half a load, food may not stay frozen more than a day.

Dry ice to prevent thawing: If the power is not to be restored within one or two days, or if the freezer may not be back to normal operation in that time, use dry ice to keep the temperature below freezing and to prevent deterioration or spoilage of frozen food.

Twenty-five pounds of dry ice in a ten-cubic-foot cabinet should hold the temperature below freezing for two to three days in a cabinet with less than half a load and three to four days in a loaded cabinet, if dry ice is obtained quickly following interruption of power. Move any food stored in a freezing compartment of a freezer to the storage compartment. Place dry ice on boards or heavy cardboard on top of packages.

Open freezer only when necessary. Don't handle dry ice with bare hands; it can cause burns. When using dry ice, room should be ventilated. If you can't get dry ice, try to locate a locker plant and move food there in insulated boxes or wrapped in newspaper or blankets.

Refreezing: Occasionally, frozen foods are partially or completely thawed before you discover that the freezer is not operating. What is important is the temperature at which thawed foods have been held, and the length of time they were held after thawing.

You may safely refreeze frozen foods that have thawed if they still contain ice crystals or if they are still cold—about 40° F—and have been held no longer than one or two days at refrigerator temperature after thawing. In general, if a food is safe to eat, it is safe to refreeze.

Even partial thawing and refreezing reduces the quality of fruits and vegetables. Foods that have been frozen and thawed require the same care as foods that have never been frozen. Use refrozen foods as soon as possible to save as much of their eating quality as you can.

Refreezing meat, fish, and poultry is not recommended except when held for a short time; cook, freeze what can't be eaten, use within thirty days.

The best way to thaw all types of frozen food is in the refrigerator. By freezing the food, you have temporarily stopped spoilage from occurring, but once it has thawed, the process of deterioration goes on. You did not kill the organisms that cause spoilage as you do when you can foods. Frozen foods should be used immediately after thawing, especially prepared foods containing gravies, sauces, or stuffings. This also applies to blanched foods, which quickly lose nutrition, flavor, and texture as they defrost. In fact, frozen vegetables should be cooked without thawing whenever possible, preferably by steaming or sautéing, or adding them directly to stews and soups. Just remember that frozen vegetables cook in about half the time that fresh ones do.

In Brief

Frozen foods retain more of their original flavor, texture, and nutrients than do canned foods. And freezing is a quicker way of preserving foods than either canning or drying. But the storage life of frozen foods is much shorter than that of canned foods or dried foods.

34 Drying Food

Dry food was perhaps the first processed food, preceding even cooked food. Discovering raisins on the vine where grapes had been harvested earlier perhaps gave prehistoric people the idea of dry grapes for winter. Raisins may in fact be the oldest dried fruit; they are certainly the most ubiquitous in our niche of history. However, to some extent, every type of food has been dried; we've all seen dried vegetables, dried meat, dried fish, dried herbs and spices.

The enzymes and microorganisms responsible for spoilage all require warmth, air, and moisture. Drying is effective when you reduce the moisture content to about 20 percent in fruit, 10 percent in vegetables, and store the dried produce in a cool, dry, dark atmosphere. Fruit keeps at the higher moisture content because of its acidity. In general, drying is a much better method of preservation for fruit than for vegetables (beans excepted).

Except for carrots, onions and cabbage, which have a storage life of about six months, dried food has a storage life that can be measured in years. But the older the food, the lower the quality. It is sometimes assumed that dried food has nearly the nutritional quality of fresh, but it doesn't. In general it falls somewhere in between freezing (the least nutrient loss) and canning (the most). It can have the advantage over the other two methods of requiring the least amount of labor, special equipment, and energy, depending on which of the following drying methods you use. In all methods there must be enough heat to dispel moisture and ventilation to disperse it.

METHODS OF DRYING

Sun

The best conditions are temperature over 90° F and humidity less than 60 percent. There is a race in sun drying between souring or molding, and drying; if the temperature is too low or the humidity too high, the results of the race are highly uncertain. The other requirements for sun drying are clean trays on which to spread the produce and cheesecloth to cover it (without touching), keeping insects off. Avoid spreading food on metal screens, which may be made of alloys containing toxic metals. An old window screen can provide a good frame, the metal screening replaced by nylon mesh or something similar. Turn produce daily; if there is any danger of rain and more than 20°F difference between day and night temperatures, put the produce in a sheltered area at night. Allow three to four days, depending on type of produce and other variables (see below).

Oven

If your oven temperature can be maintained at 140° F, it is suitable for drying.

—Trays should be at least ½ inches narrower than the inside of the oven to allow air circulation. Allow at least 2½ inches between trays and 3 inches of empty space above the top tray.

—Produce should be in a single layer on the trays. Different kinds of produce can be mixed, but don't mix onions or other pungent types of vegetables with fruit, unless you like onion-flavored apricots.

—Preheat oven to 160° F, load trays, put thermometer at the back of the top tray, load oven, propping door open at least 4 inches.

—Place a fan outside the oven so that the draft is directed into it and across it. Occasionally change the position of the fan to vary the air circulation pattern.

—Maintain oven temperature at 140° F, which takes less heat as the produce dries, so keep your eye on it.

Dehydrators

There are three types of dehydrators: (1) solar; (2) natural draft with electric or gas heating; (3) forced draft (fan) with electric or gas heating. Solar dryers are so effective and safe that they really make the other types obsolete. They can rather easily be home-built at substantial savings. I would only recommend using the other types if you already own one or can somehow get one for nothing or nearly nothing. If you're going to build a dryer, build solar. Any place in the U.S. has enough summer sun to make it effective. Plans for solar dryers are available from the following sources:

The Lightning Tree
P.O. Box 1837
Sante Fe, NM 87501

This company publishes the book *Homegrown Sundwellings* by Peter van Dresser, $5.95, including plans for solar homes and greenhouses as well as dryers.

Brace Research Institute
MacDonald College of McGill University
Ste. Anne de Bellevue
Quebec, Canada H9X ICO

$3.00 covers mailing charges and plans for the Brace Hot Box. Ask for their publications list, which includes plans for solar stills, cookers, and water heaters.

Solar Survival
Box 275
Harrisville, NH 03450

Plans and instructions for a barrel dryer, $10.75 postpaid.

Rodale Press
Plans Dept.
33 E. Minor St.
Emmaus, PA 18049

Solar Growing Frame, $14.95, shows how the frame can be easily modified to make an excellent dryer.

An inexpensive dryer than can be used in the sun or in your oven is the Sun Pantry Dryer, $25.95, Ambit Enterprises, P.O. Box 1302, Paramount, CA 90723.

—With solar and other natural draft dehydrators, alternately place the trays with front and then back edges almost against the front and rear panels to create an even flow of air over the trays.

—As with oven drying, preheat dehydrators to 160° F if possible. When the oven or dehydrator is opened for loading, the temperature will drop. This is desirable—it is best to start produce at about 120° F so the outside doesn't harden too quickly. Then the temperature should be brought up to 140°F.

—For uniform drying in solar and other natural draft dehydrators, rotate the trays at least once during drying and turn the produce on the trays if it looks necessary.

Packaging and Storage

To prevent insect infestation, dried produce should be packaged as soon as it is dry enough. A good system is plastic bags inside of crocks, cannisters, jars, or coffee cans. Such containers should then be held in the cool, dry, dark place that is favorable for all of your stored food.

Remember that the process of drying is useless to ripen fruit or vegetables, even if it is solar drying. Drying makes no qualitative improvements—in fact, as in all food processing, the opposite is the case. So select produce for drying that is at the peak of maturity; the best produce to dry is the produce just right to eat.

DRYING FRUIT

Most instructions for drying fruit include instructions for sulfuring and blanching. Both of these procedures are unnecessary, as is dipping fruit in boiling lye, another procedure you might see recommended. It's hard to imagine anything more dangerous in your home than boiling lye; give it a wide berth. Sulfuring is done by leaving the fruit for hours in a box with burning sulfur. The primary reason for doing it is cosmetic—sulfured fruit doesn't darken much while drying. But bright dried fruit is no advantage unless you're trying to sell it in a supermarket where that's the norm. The sulfur also imparts a sour taste; people tasing unsulfured dried fruit for the first time are usually surprised by its sweetness. Finally, there is reason to suspect that sulfured fruit supplies more sulfur than we need; it is quite common that a vital nutrient becomes a toxin when oversupplied. Sulfuring does prevent the loss of some vitamin A and C, while destroying B vitamins—a zero net advantage.

Blanched dried fruit is moister than unblanched. But blanching means that you dry a cooked fruit instead of a raw fruit, so unblanched dried fruit is superior to blanched in flavor and nutrition. Furthermore, it's really okay for dried fruit to be dry. People complain, "But it's so *tough.*" It is, but the chewing is good exercise and as you soften the fruit with your chewing, saliva, and body warmth, wonderful flavors you can't experience with sulfured, blanched fruit explode on your tastebuds. If you want to use the fruit for baking or soften it for any other reason, soak it in water until it's soft enough to suit you (see instructions for rehydration below).

Drying fruit for the New American Cuisine, then, is the essence of simplicity: (1) preparation; (2) drying; (3) packaging; (4) storage. Here are preparation suggestions and drying times for some common fruits; in all cases, cool before testing for proper dryness. Dried fruit is ready when moisture

is no longer evident but there is still some pliability, before brittleness sets in. After allowing it to cool, cut across to expose a cross-section: no moisture should appear but the texture should still be leathery.

Apples. Core and cut in rings or halve and cut in slices. Peeling is unnecessary. 3–4 days in the sun, 2–4 hours in oven, 6–12 hours in dehydrator.

Apricots. Halve and pit for most uses but for a special treat dry some small ones whole and unpitted. 2–3 days in the sun, 8–12 hours in oven, 24–36 hours in dehydrator (increase times for whole).

Figs. Dry whole. In coastal areas, pick when ripe; inland, leave on tree until two-thirds dry. 2–5 days in sun, 2–7 hours in oven, 6–20 hours in dehydrator. Flesh should be sticky without being wet.

Grapes. 3–5 days in sun, 4–7 hours in oven, 12–20 hours in dehydrator. Flesh should be just like the raisins you've been eating all your life.

Nectarines and Peaches. Halve and pit, 3–5 days in sun, 12–16 hours in oven, 36–48 hours in dehydrator.

Plums. Rinse in hot tap water to remove spores that can cause mold, dry whole. 4–5 days in sun, 12–16 hours in oven, 36–48 hours in dehydrator.

DRYING VEGETABLES

We saw in canning that vegetables, lacking the acidity of fruits, need extra processing. So it is with drying vegetables if they are to be kept six months or longer. Blanching before drying inactivates the enzymes that cause gradual deterioration during storage. There are two methods of blanching—steaming or boiling. However, I will refer only to steaming since it requires no extraordinary equipment and boiling leaches so much more of the flavor and nutrition out of the vegetables. Steaming requires only a kettle with a tight fitting lid and a steaming basket, colander, or sieve that will fit in the kettle. Put the vegetables in loosely, not over two-and-a-half inches deep, with not more than a couple of inches of water, and steam until vegetables are wilted or limp. In a word, properly blanched vegetables are cooked. Here are preparation suggestions, steam blanching times, if necessary, and drying times for some common vegetables, assuming in all cases thorough washing first:

Beans, green. Leave whole or cut in short pieces. Steam 2–2½ minutes; 8 hours in sun, 3–6 hours in oven, 8–14 hours in dehydrator.

Beets. Steam until tender, peel if outer layer is discolored, cut in strips or slices, no further steaming required. 8–10 hours in sun, 3–5 hours in oven, 10–12 hours in dehydrator.

Broccoli. Cut as for serving with stems either quartered lengthwise or cut across in slices. Steam 3–3½ minutes; 8–10 hours in sun, 3–5 hours in oven, 10–12 hours in dehydrator.

Cabbage. Remove outer leaves, quarter, core, cut into strips about ⅛ inch thick. Steam 2½–3 minutes; 6–7 hours in sun, 1–3 hours in oven, 10–12 hours in dehydrator.

Carrots. Cut off tops and tips, cut in slices or strips. Steam 3–3½ minutes; 8 hours in sun, 3½–5 hours in oven, 10–12 hours in dehydrator.

Cauliflower. Prepare as for table use, steam 4–5 minutes; 8–11 hours in sun, 4–6 hours in oven, 12–15 hours in dehydrator.

Celery. Cut in slices or strips, steam 2 minutes; 8 hours in sun, 3–4 hours in oven, 10–12 hours in dehydrator.

Corn, cut. Steam on cob 2–2½ minutes, cut from cob. 6 hours in sun, 2–3 hours in oven, 6–10 hours in dehydrator.

Horseradish. Remove small rootlets and stubs, peel or scrape and grate. Steam 3½ minutes; 7–10 hours in sun, 3–4 hours in oven, 4–10 hours in dehydrator.

Mushrooms. Discard tough, woody stalks, cut tender stalks into short sections. No steaming; 6–8 hours in sun, 3–5 hours in oven, 8–10 hours in dehydrator.

Onions. Remove "paper" skin, tops and tips, slice ⅛–¼ inch thick. No steaming; 8–11 hours in sun, 3–6 in oven, 10–18 hours in dehydrator.

Parsley. Separate clusters and discard thick, tough stems. No steaming; 6–8 hours in sun, 2–4 hours in oven, 1–2 hours in dehydrator.

Peas. Shell, steam 3 minutes, 6–8 hours in sun, 3 hours in oven, 6–10 hours in dehydrator.

Peppers and pimentos. Stem, core, and remove "partitions." No steaming; 6–8 hours in sun, 2–5 hours in oven, 8–12 hours in dehydrator.

You know vegetables are dry enough when they become brittle and tough, rattle when stirred. Dried vegetables, which lose a lot of flavor in comparison to fresh, are best in soups, stews, sauces, casseroles, omelettes, and stuffings rather than served alone. (See p. 295 for instant soups.)

Rehydration

Depending on how they are being used, dried vegetables may need to be rehydrated. If there is ample liquid in the recipe, cooking will accomplish rehydration. If not, soak them for ½ to 2 hours. Fruits take longer, anywhere from 2 to 8 hours. Soak one cup of fruit or vegetable in 1½ cups warm water until desired consistency is achieved.

DRYING HERBS

Many who are into the third phase of the New American Cuisine will have gardens, an opportunity to reduce the cost and improve the quality of your herbs, as well as your fruits and vegetables. (See Chapter 36.) Our discussion of drying herbs will break the subject down according to which part of the plant is being dried.

Leaves. Examples are basil, chervil, lemon balm, marjoram, mint, oregano, parsley, rosemary, sage, savory, thyme. Don't wash clean leaves, as it removes some of the aromatic oils. Wash only when truly dusty or dirty, then quickly shake off water droplets and hang in the sun to evaporate the rest. For drying, tie them in bunches, wrap the bunches with brown paper bags with many holes punched for ventilation, fastening the bags to the bunches at the top with wire ties, string, or rubber bands. Hang the bunches indoors in a warm, dry, well-ventilated space. Drying will take from a few days to a few weeks, depending on conditions. The leaves are dry enough when they crumble when rubbed between the palms of your hands. The leaves can then be removed from the stems.

Seeds. Anise, caraway, coriander, cumin, dill, and fennel, are examples. After the seed pods are dry and change color, follow the same procedure as with leaves, but don't punch ventilation holes in the bottom of the bag. The pods will shatter, and the bags will catch the seeds as they drop.

Flowers. How the flowers are to be used determines how you dry them. If only the petals are to be used (rose petals, for example), separate the petals from the rest of the flower and spread them on trays; they will dry quickly in the sun. If the whole flower is to be used (chamomile, for example), use the same drying procedure as for leaves.

Roots. Examples are angelica, burdock, comfrey, ginger, ginseng, sassafras. Scrub thoroughly to remove dirt, cut thick roots lengthwise in strips or across in slices; thin roots can be dried whole. Dry like fruit or vegetable, 8–10 hours in sun, 3–4 hours in oven, 10–12 hours in dehydrator.

For packaging and storage of dried herbs, follow the same general procedure as for dried fruits and vegetables. Premix your own herb mixes as whole leaves and seeds, saving the grinding for just before they are to be used—this saves the full potency of the aromatic oils for your cooking.

SOME UNUSUAL DRIED FOODS

(Instructions are adapted from the USDA booklet *Drying Foods at Home*.)

Fruit Jerky

Also known as fruit leather or rolled fruit, fruit jerky can easily be made of most fruits—grapefruit, lemons, persimmons, and rhubarb being exceptions because of their extreme acidity.

Preparation:
1. Select ripe or overripe fruit.
2. Remove stones or pits from fruit. Seeds of berries or grapes need not be removed. Peel or not, depending upon individual preference.
3. Cut fruit into chunks and place it in a food chopper or mechanical blender.
4. To yellow or light-colored fruit, add 1 T. of lemon or lime juice for each quart of fruit.
5. Chop, grind, or blend until a thick puree is formed.
6. Add 1 T. honey per quart to orange and pineapple pulp. Additional sweetening is not needed for other fruits.
7. Line a cookie sheet or similar flat tray with cling-wrap plastic or waxed paper. Make sure that the cookie sheet or tray has an edge to prevent spillage of the puree.
8. Pour the puree onto the sheet or tray about ¼ inch deep. Distribute evenly by tilting the tray; do not use a spatula or knife. When all spaces are covered, the right amount of puree has been applied.

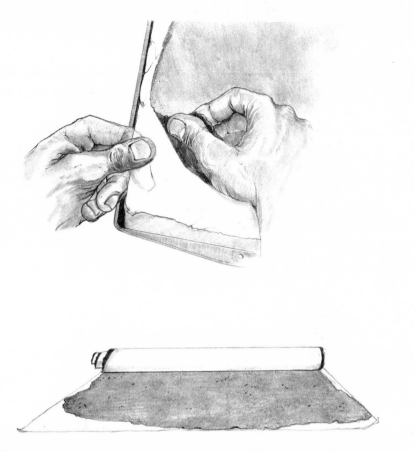

Sun drying: This will take from two to three days depending upon temperature and humidity. Test frequently for dryness.

If the weather is hot (above 85° F) and dry (less than 60 percent relative humidity), the trays can be placed in direct sunlight or behind a pane of glass or plexiglass to concentrate the heat. Cover or bring inside at night if the nighttime temperatures vary more than 20° F from daytime temperatures or if fog or humidity is common at night.

Oven drying: Set oven at lowest setting (140° F). Place the sheets or trays in the oven and leave the oven door cracked open—2 to 6 inches, depending on the oven door. The fruit leather will be dried in 4 to 5 hours.

Dehydrator drying: Place sheets or trays in the dehydrator. Set temperature control at 140° F. Dry for 4 to 5 hours and test for dryness.

Testing for dryness: Properly dried fruit leather will be sticky to the touch, but will peel easily from the cling-wrap plastic or waxed paper. Lift the edge, which will adhere tightly to the surface, and peel it back about an inch. If it peels readily, it is properly dried.

Storage: After loosening the edge and peeling it back about an inch, roll the cling-wrap plastic or waxed paper and the dried leather in one piece in a loose roll.

The dried fruit roll can be stored for years in the freezer, for months in the refrigerator, and for many weeks at room temperature (70° F or less).

Beef Jerky

Preparation:

1. Slice 5 pounds uncooked lean beef (flank steak or similar cut) into strips ¼ to ½ inch thick, 1 to 1½ inches wide, and 4 to 12 inches long. Cut with grain of meat; remove the fat.
2. Lay out in a single layer on a smooth clean surface (use cutting board, counter, bread board, or cookie sheet; wash wooden surfaces immediately after use.)
3. Sprinkle strips liberally with salt on both sides; heavy salting repels flies; excess salt can be brushed off after the meat is dry. Add pepper to taste and garlic salt or powder if desired.
4. Place strips, layer on layer, in a large wooden bowl or crock and place a plate with a weight on top.
5. Let stand for 6 to 12 hours.
6. Remove strips and blot dry with clean paper toweling. Other flavors: instead of the garlic treatment, you may brush or marinate the strips before drying in such mixtures as teriyaki sauce, sweet and sour sauce, soy sauce, hot chili sauce, or Worcestershire sauce—or combinations of these according to your choice.

Oven drying: Remove racks from oven and stretch meat strips across the racks. Allow the edges of the meat strips to touch, but not overlap. Leave enough space free on the racks for air to circulate in the oven.

Set the temperature at 140° F and let strips dry for about 11 hours. Check early in the drying process for excess drip. This drip can be caught on aluminum foil on a rack placed near the bottom of the oven. Lower the temperature of the oven until it feels warm, but does not cook the meat.

Keeping the oven door ajar will faciliate drying, as will the use of an electric fan placed in front of the open oven door.

Dehydrator drying: Follow instructions as you would for fruit or vegetables.

Air or sun drying: An open barbecue with a grill suspended over the charcoal container, or a comparable arrangement, may be used for this method.

Line the bottom of the barbecue with aluminum foil to reflect the sun. Stretch strips of meat over the grill. Place in the sun and allow the meat to dry for 4 to 6 days, depending upon the temperature, your storage method, and how long you intend to store it. If the nights are cool, place the barbecue under cover (for example, in the garage) at night to reduce condensation of moisture on the meat. If the barbecue has a cover, you may use it. The strips of meat can also be strung on wire, fishing line, or strong, thin string. Insert a small button between each strip to prevent touching.

Place in a sunny area and dry for several days. Jerky is properly dry when it is chewy and leathery. If brittle, it is too dry.

Storage: Finished jerky can be stored at room temperature in airtight containers, if the jerky is dry enough. More moist jerky can be placed in plastic bags and frozen. If there is too much moisture, it will become moldy. If fat is excessive, it will turn rancid more rapidly.

Salmon Jerky

Slice salmon fillets into thin strips. Salt fish in a dish or enameled pan using 2 T. salt per pound. Place in refrigerator for 12 hours. Remove from the refrigerator and place strips on a rack in the oven to dry. Set the oven to 140° F and allow to dehydrate for 3 to 5 hours.

The salmon strips may also be dried in the sun or on the barbecue (see beef jerky recipe) for about 3 days. The meat should be brought in at night to prevent moisture condensation.

35 Machinery & Miscellany

Some cooks, myself included, would rather perform most kitchen chores by hand. I like having as much control over the product as possible, and whisks, old-fashioned egg beaters, spoons, hand grinders and such, allow me to do that. Then, too, not only are most hand tools cheaper than electric ones, there are few moving parts to wear out, no trips to my service repair center, never a fear of power failure, lower electric bills and a lesser imposition on the environment. Few appliances clutter my kitchen countertops and overload my electric and psychic circuits.
(Sally Freeman, one of the authors of *The Kitchen Almanac*, compiled by Stone Soup Co.)

Sentiments like that are often accompanied by such semi-mystical statements as, "The choice is between mechanical vibrations and human vibrations." "Machines have no love in them, but I do." "That machine can never make food taste as good as my hands can." There is real, though nebulous, truth behind such statements; in our mechanized world a mystique has built an altar for things made by hand. Yet, in spite of appreciating such soft realities, the hard reality is that most of us don't have the time and few of us the willingness to be purists.

But still, [continues Sally Freeman], I am not such a purist as all that. Certain tasks are done far more quickly and easily in a machine: whipping egg whites to a stiff foam, for example, or mixing cookie dough, or blending a cup or two of homemade mayonnaise. And at those times when my cookery forges full speed ahead, I find my electric blender and my mixer of incomparable assistance.

I have friends, though, who are dedicated to a lifestyle of grow-your-own, do-it-yourself and make-it-from-scratch, who perpetually have a big pot of something bubbling on the back of the stove, and seat ten or more to lunch and dinner as a matter of course. They swear by the electric churn that turns the family cow's cream to butter, and the electric ice cream maker that produces incomparable desserts from cream and home-grown berries, the blender that grates their homemade cheese, the Kitchenaid mixer that provides the daily offering of breads and cookies, and the Cuisinart processor that grinds several pounds of home-grown steer meat at a time or chops bushels of fruit and vegetables in canning season.

Freeman has ranged over the kinds of individualized decisions that determine how you will accomplish the mechanics of food processing: What will you do by hand? With manually operated machines? With electrical machines?

Mail-order houses such as Garden Way and Cumberland General Store sell such manually operated esoterica as peelers and pitters to go along with more conventional fare like food mills and steamers. Most of these don't represent big financial decisions, although the bill will climb if you get gadget happy. It usually doesn't become thought-provoking until you consider enlisting the aid of electrical motors. Although you can do them manually, most people will opt for electrified milling and juicing—perhaps $500. Other big investments for Phase Three are not necessary. But

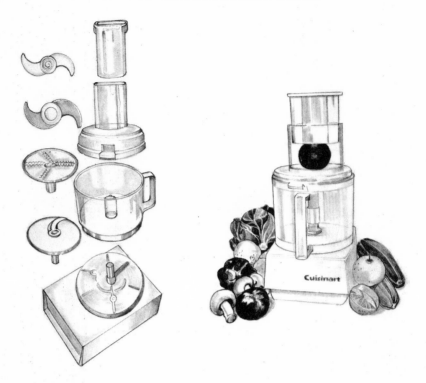

they are certainly possible. As a Phase One bachelor, I have no need to electrify my kitchen further. But when I imagine myself back in Phase Two and Three activities, as I have been in years past, the idea of having a food processor intrigues me.

FOOD PROCESSORS

Separately, you can buy an electric blender, a mixer, and a meat grinder and still not be able to do as many things as you can with a food processor. Food processors are such an advancement in the craft of home food processing that they might decide whether or not a family takes on Phase Three processing responsibilities. Since their popularization, many more families than before have been able to disengage themselves from industrialized food.

In *A Mostly French Food Processor Cookbook*, authors Rossant and Herman call food processors a rare example of a "necessary luxury" they never knew they needed until they had one. They call it "a skilled apprentice and sauce maker" that inspires them to cook well, to prepare dishes they would not otherwise undertake, and to do elaborate dishes more often. One of the most common remarks about the New American Cuisine is, "The only trouble is, I have to spend so much time chopping vegetables now." A food processor can chop, puree, julienne (shred) and slice vegetables; grate cheeses and bread crumbs; blend sauces and spreads; grind meats and fish; knead bread and pastry doughs; and, in many cases, beat and fold eggs and cream.

Food processors not only offer spectacular versatility, their cost is generally less than the combined costs of all the separate machines they supplant. Still, the best food processors are not cheap—in 1981, between $240 and $400. (As a means of comparison for a 1985 reader, three different makes of 14-speed blenders ranged between $45 and $55 in 1981.) So, if you have a family of four, are attracted by the qualitative improvements and the more than $1,400 savings made possible by entering Phase Three, but would do it only *if* you could enlist the aid of a food processor *and* wonder how quickly such a large investment could pay for itself, start saving your pennies or dust off your credit card—a food processor can pay for itself in a few months. Let's take a conservative hypothetical case where you only stand to save $1,000 in a year and go for a $300 food processor—you're still $700 ahead after the first year has ended.

Since neither I nor collaborators at Sunburst have experience with a wide variety of food processors, I undertook to do what I would do if I were getting ready to buy one. I scanned food processor cookbooks looking for those that rate different machines, and of those that do, looked for a couple that inspired confidence. I settled on the previously mentioned *Mostly French . . .* and *Food Processor Cookbook*, by the editors of *Consumer Guide*, to help me form my overview of the food processor scene. My first lesson was that there are two basic themes in food processor construction: one is the multi-attachment theme, emphasizing near perfect results; the other is the one-bowl theme, emphasizing convenience.

I next found that I could group them into inexpensive, moderate, and expensive categories, and that all the inexpensive machines are the one-bowl type. At about that point I made the perfection versus convenience decision, deciding I would go for perfection. Even if I were interested in one-bowl food processors, from the comments made about them it struck me that the inexpensive ones are more like expensive toys than serious machines, another one of those gadgets that wind up gathering dust on some remote and dark shelf.

When I was finished reading about all the food processors, I had a list of five possibilities: the multi-attachment Bosch, Kenwood, and Kitchen Aid; the Waring because the authors of *Mostly French . . .* say it has revolutionized one-bowl type machines; and the Sunbeam Food Preparation Center because it attempts to combine the two approaches. My preference would be the Kitchen Aid because I've heard raves about it from people I respect and because it is made by Hobart, manufacturers of fine restaurant equipment which I owned and truly appreciated when I was in the restaurant business.

No matter what machines might be on your list after reading about them, Julia Child advises that you not buy a food processor until you have tried it. Good advice. At the least, you should see it thoroughly demonstrated. To judge any machine, make yourself aware of all the manufacturer's claims about what it can do, then see just how well it does them. If you do that with at least three competitive machines, you can usually invest your money with confidence.

To Buy Or Not To Buy

This will help you decide whether or not to buy a food processor or any other machine. Give it the "Save" Test: Does it

—Save nutrients?
—Save time?
—Save money?
—Save energy?
—Save effort?
—Save flavor?

Of course the more yesses you get, the better the proposition looks. Food processors don't save money or energy, but the more people you're cooking for, the more time and effort they save. For me in my present life style, my knives, cutting boards and blender are enough—no food processor. But for you a food processor might bring a new dimension of joy and adventure into your kitchen.

COOKING EQUIPMENT

Ovens

Microwave ovens remind me of food additives in that they represent another gigantic experiment that millions of us have been led into by commercial interests. There is strong disagreement among researchers about the dangers of microwave emissions. Do they cook your innards without your being able to feel it, causing vision impairment, cataracts, hair loss, fatigue, headaches, loss of memory, thyroid enlargement, loss of sex drive, sterility, decreased lactation in nursing mothers?

Once again we are victims of a system that works backwards. Microwave ovens never should have been allowed in the marketplace until they were proven safe. They are a good candidate for another of those "Oh my God, what have we done?" reactions after everybody already has one. Our experts can't agree. We shouldn't allow ourselves to be guinea pigs for the sake of convenience, even if the investment were less than $300, which most microwaves are not.

Russian scientists have found that

chronic exposure to low levels of microwave emissions may result in many biological changes, including a decreased rate of heart muscle contraction; low blood pressure; changes in the blood's composition; increased activity and enlargement of the thyroid gland; hormone imbalance; alteration in the central nervous system, brain wave patterns, and behavior; and a wide range of nonspecific ailments. [*How Safe is Food In Your Kitchen?*, Beatrice Trum Hunter, Scribner's.]

It seems that the disagreement among researchers is mainly between those who have done the research and those who have not. Says Hunter:

In general, American scientists have viewed the USSR reports skeptically and have conducted few experiments. The few American scientists who have investigated the effects of chronic human exposure to low levels of microwave radiation tend to give credence to the Soviet findings.

If you are willing and able to spend that kind of money, consider a convection oven. They can do things microwaves can't, like crisping and browning. On the "Save" Test, they save everything but money. And they are safe. Convection ovens save energy and time compared to conventional ovens by circulating the heat within the oven; there is no hazardous radiation.

Toaster ovens are another safe innovation and have the advantage of being inexpensive. Operationally, they are versatile and save an enormous amount of energy, using about 80 percent less than conventional ovens and about 50 percent less than microwaves. In my low-energy kitchen, the toaster oven and the electric skillet, which uses less than half the energy of a burner on my electric stove, are the most frequently used appliances. (Wherever I live next, I hope there is a gas stove—I far prefer cooking with gas.)

Cookware

How convenient it would be if there were one kind of cookware to answer the needs of all kinds of cooking. But of course there is no such thing; each type has its pros and cons. Here is a brief review of them:

Aluminum. *Pros:* An excellent heat conductor, lightweight, usually moderately priced. *Con:* Apparently, little aluminum is absorbed from the human digestive tract. Nonetheless, reactions to aluminum sensitivity are said to be headaches, indigestion, and blood pressure irregularities.

According to Beatrice Trum Hunter in *How Safe is Food in Your Kitchen?* the dangers of aluminum toxicity depend on the possible negative indirect effects of excessive aluminum. Aluminum can bind calcium and phosphorous, causing deficiencies of those minerals:

> Aluminum compounds that may deplete the body of phosphorus and calcium are used extensively in consumer goods (deodorants), over-the-counter drugs (antacids), baking ingredients (aluminum baking powders), many food additives (anticaking agents, dispersing agents, binding agents, emulsifying agents, defoaming agents, and certain food colors), metal cans (containing soft drinks and beer), and toiletries (toothpaste), in addition to pots and pans. Also to be considered are the millions of pounds of aluminum powder added to municipal water supplies to speed the precipitation of sediments.

> It should be apparent that any examination of the health effects, if any, resulting from the use of aluminum cookware, needs to be explored in relationship to *all* sources of environmental exposure to aluminum.

Anodized aluminum. The aluminum is placed in an electrolytic solution and subjected to a high-density electrical current, which changes its molecular structure. The anodized aluminum is changed to a dark gray color, which looks like a coating but is not. Anodized aluminum is highly praised by professional and gourmet cooks. Like regular aluminum, it is an excellent conductor of heat, but unlike regular aluminum, it does not react with food acids. The anodizing process also seals the pores of the aluminum and greatly increases its hardness, making it easy to clean. There don't seem to be any serious functional disadvantages to this material—a good choice for those who can afford it.

Copper. *Pros:* It is beautiful and an excellent conductor of heat. *Con:* Copper is a vital nutrient in minute, or trace, quantities, but, as is often the case, too much is not better, it is poisonous. There are records of copper poisoning going back over two hundred years. Do not cook with it if the copper will contact the food. Copper (or aluminum) clad with stainless steel gives first-rate results, but is expensive.

Stainless steel. *Pros:* Easy maintenance and little interaction with food. *Cons:* It is a poor conductor of heat. To cook really well, stainless steel should be heavy gauge, sandwiched or clad with copper, aluminum, or high-quality ceramic, any of which makes it expensive.

Enamel. *Pros:* Impervious to food, easy to clean. *Cons:* It can crack or chip, after which it should no longer be used for cooking. Any additional chip which might find its way into the food could slice up the stomach and intestines.

Good quality enamelware is much less likely to chip than the cheap versions. Beatrice Trum Hunter calls inexpensive enamelware "foolish economy," pointing out that its softness is due to the use of antimony oxide, which in some circumstances can be quite poisonous. High-quality enamelware, made with tin oxide, can give excellent results providing it is handled carefully.

Porcelain-clad metal. *Pros:* This one is almost all positive, being one of the very finest types of cookware. Non-stick, easily cleaned porcelain is bonded to iron, aluminum, or steel. The effect is like having a cooking utensil that is metal on the outside, glass on the inside—a superb combination. *Cons:* It can be quite heavy and expensive. Buy this type when you can afford the best money can buy.

Glass. *Pros:* No chemical interaction with the food and it's nice to be able to see it while it's cooking. *Cons:* Poor conductor of heat, easy to break, will crack from sudden temperature changes.

Clay. Also called "earthenware," it is most important to know what kind of clay it is. Is it glazed? Then beware. Glazes usually contain lead or cadmium and both are hazardous. You need a manufacturer's guarantee that the glaze is stable in the presence of food acids and will not leach lead or cadmium into the food. Even with such a guarantee, you had better be sure you trust it.

Unglazed clay poses no hazards and is particularly good for long, slow, moist cooking. It needs diligent scouring to limit food residues accumulating in the pores of the clay, and careful handling to avoid breakage.

Non-stick finishes. *Pro:* Convenience. *Con:* German manufacturers are required to label them "Dangerous When Overheated." The best of the newest breeds are probably safe enough if used properly under ordinary conditions. But why not stick with a type of cookware that is never dangerous under any conditions?

If it's nonstickiness you're after, there is a safe and simple way. Spread a film of liquid lecithin over the cooking surface before using it, repeating before each use. Liquid lecithin can be bought inexpensively in most health and natural food stores. It is an extremely thick, oily substance derived from soybeans and has excellent nutritional properties (see Appendix Seven). Liquid lecithin is sold for cooking purposes in spray cans at much higher prices than a can of plain old lecithin.

Iron. *Pros:* Cast iron is the greatest bargain in kitchen equipment available in the contemporary marketplace. It can be had for 20 and even 10 percent of the cost of other safe types of cookware. It is one of the best conductors of heat, giving gourmet-quality results. The iron interacts with food acids, creating iron salts, but instead of being toxic, they are beneficial—nutritious cookware.

Cons: It is heavy and requires special care to prevent rusting. Ironware needs seasoning before use. To season it, pour in enough oil to cover the bottom and smear some up on the sides. Then heat it on a low flame for an hour, pour off the oil, and after the pan has cooled, wipe off the excess. The finish is spoiled by scouring pads or abrasive powders; wash in hot, soapy water, rinse in hot water, turn upside down for quick drying, or heat until water evaporates, to prevent rusting. When the special handling requirements of ironware are weighed against its great cooking efficiency, durability, and low cost, its advantages are heavily on the plus side.

Warning. Some manufacturers think we are so ignorant and lazy that we will not buy ironware unless we don't have to take care of it. So they are coating it with plastic. This ruins the classic beauty of ironware and substitutes the migration of plastic into our food instead of iron—a decidedly unhealthy tradeoff. One manufacturer of uncoated ironware is Lodge Manufacturing Company of South Pittsburg, Tennessee. There may be others, and the manufacturers coating the ironware might yield to consumer pressure to stop ruining a good thing.

Crockpots

Slow-roasting is just one way you can cook while doing other things like going to work or to sleep or for a hike. Electric crockpots are an excellent device for this purpose. Pot roasts, stews, soups, beans, casseroles, breakfast cereals, and puddings can be all cooked in a crockpot while your attention is turned to other matters.

Your crockpot comes with directions and usually a small recipe book. There are also full-sized books devoted to crockpot cookery; any recipe can be adapted to the New American Cuisine by substituting whole foods for refined ones.

To adapt recipes designed for conventional equipment, reduce the amount of water or stock by roughly one-third—you'll need to do some experimenting to learn this aspect of your crockpot. Set on "low," your crockpot dish will need about four times as long to cook as the top-of-the-stove version of the recipe.

Equipment tip: The "low" setting on crockpots is only a little over 200°, not high enough to kill all bacteria. So it is best to buy the type that starts off at "high" (about 300°) and then automatically turns down to "low." Crockpots conserve both food value and energy, using little more energy than a light bulb by keeping the food contained in a small, well-insulated space.

36   Beyond the Phases

The completeness of this book lies in its revelation of the interrelationship of natural foods' quality, cost, and nutritional value. When people work through the omnivarian-vegetarian, Phases One-Two-Three, kinds of decisions, they discover what is right for them. The New American Diet and Cuisine are American in the sense that we all fit somewhere within them. The book is complete in the corresponding sense of being a book for everyone.

This book began to germinate when I saw how food-processing tasks can logically be classified according to time, effort, and cost of equipment. But it was never intended to be a complete book of food processing. For many, it will be complete enough; for others, it will be a food processing primer. For books that can guide you past the territory I have chosen here, see the Recommended Reading List (Appendix Eight).

Two things I have not covered are butchering and the making of the soyfoods tofu and tempeh. As to butchering, my reasoning was that I am describing a way of eating in which meat is a minor ingredient. In most cases there will not be enough incentive for buying a carcass or even a side and taking on butchering responsibilities. I can imagine, however, that there are readers who will disagree due to necessity or preference. To them I admit that butchering can save as much as 60 percent and for them it clearly would be a Phase Three activity.

Making tofu and tempeh are activities I would have included in Phase Three were I writing this book about five years from now. I think the day is coming when they will have become so widely familiar and appreciated that there will be a great deal of interest in making them at home. Some, I know, will argue, That day is already here! I would be glad to be wrong—I am particularly enthusiastic about tempeh. The books on making soyfoods are listed in the Recommended Reading List.

THE BACKYARD LEVEL

Another decision I made was to confine myself to indoor activities. Certainly great qualitative improvements can be made and much money saved by gardening and with backyard fish tanks and livestock. There is the strongest connection between those backyard activities and what goes on in the kitchen. But in the backyard you are talking about food production, not processing. Sunburst and I discussed whether I should do a chapter on gardening. They are farmers and gardeners and I have been and love both farms and gardens. I decided we should draw the line at the back door but the idea of a gardening chapter died hard. Dick Roth, one of my main Sunburst collaborators, said,

"You've got to say *something* about gardening." It's true that if you have a yard without a vegetable garden in it, you're missing some great opportunities.

When the USDA questioned gardeners about their motivations for doing it, 66 percent said to improve quality, 50 percent said to save money. Tending a well-planned garden in the 350–400 square foot range could easily save a family $40 in 1981. To make that applicable to the expected ravages of future inflation, I have translated that figure to percentages in the following table.

THE GARDENING EFFECT ON NEW AMERICAN CUISINE BUDGETS

Phase	Savings Without Gardening	Saving With Gardening
One	15%	24%
Two	30%	41%
Three	45%	60%

Several years ago the Rodale Press *Organic Gardening and Farming* magazine polled 20 gardeners and found they were enjoying a 30%–70% range of savings with gardening. The National Garden Bureau pegged the savings even higher. So if my figures are wrong, they are on the conservative side.

Even more people are interested in the quality improvements resulting from gardening—impossible to quantify, though nonetheless real. Tasting organically grown produce fresh from the garden brings delicious, albeit subjective, proof to the table that home-grown is better than store-bought. Other benefits, while even more subjective, may be even more valuable: the healthy influences of fresh air, sunshine, and exercise; the semi-mystical energy exchanges between the earth, plants, and human beings. Gardening brings peace to the soul and serenity to the spirit.

Gardening can have a positive effect on your food budget and marvelous effects on your health and general well-being. Anyone who is a candidate for the twin goals of lowering food costs while raising its quality is a good candidate for raising some of their own food. There are many fine books, booklets, and magazines to assist home gardeners who would grow their own natural food, listed in the Recommended Reading List.

THE HOMESTEADER

A full three-phase involvement in the New American Cuisine can be accomplished by two or more people working together in their spare time, or with the vocational commitment of househusbanding or housewifing. Yet most people find that identifying themselves as a houseperson falls short of being inspiring. Instead try, I'm a homesteader. What's a homesteader? A homesteader's business is producing, processing, and preparing natural foods. It's a vocation with advantages few other lines of work can offer. You get to work indoors and out, physically and mentally. You get to use your abilities to plan and to be creative. You control your own working conditions, don't have to commute, set your own hours, and nobody is looking over your shoulder. You are a craftsperson utilizing a blend of antiquity and modernity to produce the very best quality. You have no boss, no stress, and no taxes.

The new terminology doesn't change anything, it offers a fresh perspective. Clearly, homesteading is one of the best vocational choices a person can make. And like being a potter, weaver, or baker, being a homesteader has no gender—noble work for woman or man.

INTERCONNECTIONS

With the headline "Proper diet saves lives, land, oil . . . ," *Science News*, January 17, 1981, reported on a meeting of the American Association for the Advancement of Science. The course of the meeting drew a line that crisscrossed over our land and our society and the rest of the world until an all-encompassing net had been drawn. It began by tracing how the old American diet was engineered.

World War II required of our nation a productivity level that erased every vestige of the Great Depression. Once the war had ended, that productivity level was perceived as the preventive medicine against the return of hard times. From our farms, millions upon millions of pounds of wheat, corn, and soybeans in excess of what we could consume poured into every available storage facility. The huge surpluses were bought by the government in support of farm prices and our USDA had an enormous, expensive storage problem on its hands. The problem was solved because the USDA realized that animals could eat the grains and beans, and then people could eat the animals. Feedlots proliferated and a massive promotional campaign succeeded in doubling our beef consumption.

The meeting next reviewed the health benefits that can result from eating more fruits, vegetables, and whole grains, and less fat, sugar, salt, and other refined foods. Obesity, animal fat, and lack of fiber were cited as the three major dietary causes of cancer. It was estimated that the recommended dietary changes could reduce the incidence of cancer by 50 percent and coronary heart disease by 88 percent.

The connection was then made between diet and land and water use. To support the old American diet, dominated by animal protein, earns us the dubious distinction of using more water for food production than any other country in the world. Our ways of land and water use, pointed out George Borgstrom of Michigan State University, lead to soil degradation, desertification, ground water depletion, and water pollution.

J.B. Penn of the USDA linked diet with personal, corporate, and national economics. Meat protein costs five to six times as much as vegetable protein, adding approximately $4,000 to the average household's annual budget (including the cost of increased medical care). Reduced meat consumption therefore releases personal spending into other sectors of the economy. Further economic connections: lower demand for foreign oil, reduction of our international trade deficit, strengthening of the value of the U.S. dollar.

David Pimentel of Cornell University extended the line into the energy sector, where a "healthier diet," one in which the consumption of animal products is reduced by 50 percent, would save up to thirty gallons of oil per person per year. Such a diet, he said, could provide 67 grams of protein per person per day while saving half of our energy, mineral, and land resources and one third of our water resources. Pimentel had two major energy-saving suggestions. Because beef protein is twice as expensive to produce as chicken protein, he advocates more chicken and less beef. And because we feed ten times as more grain to livestock than we eat ourselves, he advocates grass feeding for livestock.

With these suggestions, recognized by this gathering of prestigious scientists, Pimentel closed the net over the whole planet. These measures could release 135 million tons of grain for feeding people. And, as *Science News* pointed out in their coverage of the meeting, "90% of our grains and legumes and 50% of our fish catch is fed to livestock, while 800 million people are going hungry . . ."

Lessons learned about interconnectedness through studying ecology apply equally to your emotional and social environments. There is no question, from either logical or scientific viewpoints, that the quality of your diet is directly connected to the quality of your health. In turn, the quality of your health is just as intimately connected to the quality of your experiences. And on to you and your social environment: feeling well improves your relationship with other people. If the majority of a society is ill, we can have nothing less than a sick society, as, indeed, it sometimes seems we have.

And in the broadest sense, we are firmly enmeshed in the web of interconnections. You are more important to the health of this planet than one of your own cells is to your personal health: there are 100 trillion cells in your body, only four billion people inhabiting the planet. Cell, blood, bone, muscle, organs, limbs and body; you, city or town, state, country, continent, hemisphere, and planet: how well the whole works always depends on how well the parts work. In the last two decades we have come to call it ecology, but for eons it has simply been the nature of things. It is enough to know that to eat according to the principles laid down in this book is good for you; it is more than enough to know that it is somehow, intriguingly and mysteriously, good for everyone.

Epilog Organically Grown: *Big Words or Buzz Words?*

One weekend day in the spring of 1954, when I was a senior in high school in White Plains, New York, I was on my way to a golf course on the outskirts of town for a day of caddying. As I walked to the bus stop, I projected ahead to the time I would spend sitting in the caddy shack or in the yard in front of it. The older, more experienced caddies would be called out first for their "loops" (a loop being a full 18-hole round of golf). The kids and the older guys with bad hangovers (the caddy master recognized them easily) would have time to kill, an hour or two. There were three main activities among waiting caddies: there was talk, there were penny ante card games, and then there were always a few readers.

I stopped in a cigar store to check out the magazine rack. Nothing that interesting. There was a revolving rack of paperback books, more money than I had planned to spend, but I spun it anyway. A cover and a title jumped out at me: a bucolic farm scene, *Pleasant Valley* by Louis Bromfield. The two previous summers I had worked on a Vermont dairy farm, loved it, and now that it was spring, the farm was beckoning again. I could pay the 75 cents for the book and would still have bus fare to the golf course. I bought it, perhaps the most influential purchase of my life.

Louis Bromfield wrote a lot of popular books during the thirties, forties, and fifties, wrote films, made a lot of money, had rich and famous friends, but none of that made any impression on me. The only books of his I ever read were *Pleasant Valley* and *Malabar Farm*, a sequel. Those two books told of Bromfield's experience with several adjacent farms he bought in a small Ohio valley. They had been farmed until they were farmed out, the soil exhausted by imprudent management, then abandoned. The book told of Bromfield's inspiring success in reviving the farms—combined into one called "Malabar Farm"—and in helping the entire ecosystem of the valley to flourish by employing organic farming methods. The valley had been dead, another sad example of the legacy of exploitation; it was brought back to life by recognizing that nature has rights we cannot violate if we expect her to support us. By employing organic farming, the valley once again became a pleasant place.

Until then, I hadn't even known there was such a thing as organic farming. But oh my, how my idealistic nature was fired that day by Louis Bromfield. The caddymaster called me to go out for a loop; later, I told him, I had to finish my book. I decided that morning I would go to agricultural school in the fall to learn more about organic farming. I wanted to join this force, to have a hand in the salvation of our farmland. It was a just cause, worthy of idealistic fervor looking for an attachment.

You had to be extremely naive to expect an organic education at an "ag" school in 1954 and the situation has not changed a great deal since then. My youthful ideals frustrated, my attendance at agricultural school was short-lived. But I have often told people that I'm on a very long, circuitous path back to the farm. What farm and when, I have no idea, but I have no need to know. What I do know, however, is that the cause that seemed so urgent twenty-nine years ago is much more so now.

Most people know that vast areas of Africa and Asia are desert. These areas were once fertile land, supporting the ancient empires of Mesopotamia, Babylon, Egypt, Persia, Greece, and Rome, all of which died while playing their roles in creating the Arabian and Sahara deserts. Most people don't know that we're rapidly on the way to turning vast areas of the U.S. into desert too. The desert we are bidding to create could include all the land west of the Mississippi, minus the mountains and the Pacific coast strip.

To understand the process known as desertification, it is instructive to know how the ancients did it. For hundreds, in some cases more than a thousand years, they irrigated with the waters of such great rivers as the Euphrates and the Tigris. Dissolved salts in the water, a constituent of all river water, slowly accumulated in the soil. While they were doing so, the ancient farmers were also using more humus—organic matter—than they were replacing. The time came—perhaps in five hundred years, perhaps in a thousand, depending on the original fertility of the soil—when the accumulated salts, poisonous to food crops, and the exhausted supply of humus combined to become barren farm land. Agriculture moved elsewhere. The wind blew and what little organic matter may have been left dried up and left with the wind as dust. It was desertification: the process of transforming grassland or prairie, its topsoil rich in humus, into sand, land that has no humus, only minerals. Without the transpiration of moisture from grassland to the atmosphere, the air, like the soil, dried out, ensuring that the grassland would never reestablish itself: the desert is permanent.

Modern chemical agriculture is so much more efficient at loading the soil with salts and burning up the humus in the topsoil that we are producing our desert in an astonishingly short period of time. We could, at our current rate, complete the process in around 200 years. Considering how deep the virgin topsoil was in many places, our effectiveness is amazing. Iowa, blessed with more deep, black sod than any other prairie state, has already lost two-thirds of it. Further west, where there wasn't as much to start with, there are places where it has all washed or been blown away.

I remember thinking when I was a kid reading John Steinbeck's *Grapes of Wrath* that his descriptions of the Dust Bowl pictured conditions that were no longer with us. Then I spent time with friends living on the high plains of the Texas Panhandle and traveled through western Oklahoma and southeastern Colorado. Every spring, after the snow melts and before the crops take hold, the Dust Bowl lives again. If there is no snow, the winter air is full of dust too. Driving in a dust storm in western Oklahoma in the winter of 1976, I had to pull off the road at midday because visibility went down to zero; I never knew daytime could be so dark. When the air is full of topsoil, you don't know where the sun is, but you do know you are surrounded by a monstrous tragedy.

Organic agriculture is called "organic" because it has as its major aim the preservation of humus in the topsoil, and in the most favorable conditions, even increasing the humus content. The difference between the sands of the desert and the black sod of the prairie is humus. It is humus that spells the difference between dead soil and that which is teeming with life, between soil that supports life and that which cannot. Humus makes topsoil a complex, living organism, full of bacterial, microbial, and crawling forms of life. Humus is spongy, holding water; humus is what we are talking about when we call moist, dark soil "rich." Rain falling on such rich soil is absorbed by the capillaries of the humus, remaining where it belongs, the excess draining down through the subsoil into the underground water system. The organic content of such topsoil is perhaps 5 percent.

But most American topsoil these days is 2 percent or less organic matter. Such ground is hard, and when the rain arrives in quantity, little of it can be soaked up. It rolls off the fields in brown sheets, gouges, gullies, fills ditches with silt, muddies all our rivers. Water erosion is the twin of wind erosion, the other precursor of desert. With chemical fertilizers to hasten the burning up of humus, wind and water erosion can erase a foot of topsoil in 100 years; aided by a few prolonged droughts it can happen even faster.

A system of agriculture that does not treat humus as a treasure—which contemporary chemical agriculture does not—loses its topsoil. In the truest sense of the word, that system is a loser, farming itself out of business. But I am writing a message of hope here; organic agriculture is winning support in our farming community. And it is doing so as both a literal and figurative grassroots movement. There is virtually no support from land-grant agricultural colleges who are supported by the corporations who profit from the sale of agricultural chemicals.

The vigor of the move towards organic farming was signaled clearly in 1980 by the United States Department of Agriculture in its *Report and Recommendations on Organic Farming*. In the words of Bob Bergland, Secretary of Agriculture, the report was published because "Energy shortages, food safety and environmental concerns have all contributed to the demand for more comprehensive information on organic farming technology." In the words of Dr. Anson Bertrand, USDA Director of Science and Education, "One of the major challenges to agriculture in this decade will be to develop farming systems that can produce the necessary quantity and quality of food fiber without adversely affecting our soil resources and the environment."

THE USDA REPORT AND RECOMMENDATIONS ON ORGANIC FARMING

The following extract is from *The USDA Report and Recommendations on Organic Farming:*

In April 1979, Dr. Anson Bertrand . . . designated a team of scientists to conduct a study of organic farming in the United States and Europe . . .

It has been most apparent in conducting this study that there is increasing concern about the adverse effects of our U.S. agricultural production system, particularly in regard to the intensive and continuous production of cash grains and the extensive and sometimes excessive use of agricultural chemicals. Among the concerns most often expressed are the following:
1) Sharply increasing costs and uncertain availability of energy and chemical fertilizer, and the heavy reliance on these inputs.
2) Steady decline in soil productivity and tilth from excessive soil erosion and loss of soil organic matter.
3) Degradation of the environment from erosion and sedimentation and from pollution of natural waters by agricultural chemicals.
4) Hazards to human and animal health and to food safety from heavy use of pesticides.
5) Demise of the family farm and localized marketing systems.
Consequently, many feel that a shift to some degree from conventional (that is, chemical-intensive) toward organic farming would alleviate some of these adverse effects, and in the long term would ensure a more stable, sustainable and profitable agricultural system.

Organic farming is a production system which avoids . . . the use of synthetically compounded fertilizers, pesticides, growth regulators, and livestock feed additives. To the maximum extent feasible, organic farming systems rely upon crop rotations, crop residues, animal manures, legumes, green manures, off-farm organic wastes, mechanical cultivation, mineral-bearing rocks, and aspects of biological pest control to maintain soil productivity and tilth, to supply plant nutrients, and to control insects, weeds and other pests.

The concept of the soil as a living system which must be "fed" in a way that does not restrict the activities of beneficial organisms necessary for recycling nutrients and producing humus is central to this definition.

Organic farming operations are not limited by scale. This study found that while there are many small-scale (10 to 50 acres) organic farmers in the northeastern region, there are a significant number of large-scale (more than 100 acres and even up to 1,500 acres) organic farms in the West and Midwest. In most cases, the team found that these farms, both large and small, were productive, efficient and well managed. Usually the farms had acquired a number of years of chemical farming experience before shifting to organic methods.

Motivations for shifting from chemical to organic farming include concern for protecting soil, human and animal health from the potential hazards of pesticides; the desire for lower production inputs; concern for the environment and protection of soil resources.

Contrary to popular belief, most organic farmers have not regressed to agriculture as it was practiced in the 1930's. While they attempt to avoid or restrict the use of chemical fertilizers and pesticides, organic farmers still use modern farm machinery, recommended crop varieties, certified seed, sound methods of organic waste management, and recommended soil and water conservation practices.

The study revealed that organic farms on the average are somewhat more labor intensive but use less energy than conventional farms.

In conclusion, the study team found that many of the current methods of soil and crop management practiced by organic farmers are also those which have been cited as best management practices . . . for controlling soil erosion, minimizing water pollution and conserving energy. These include sod-based rotations, cover crops, green manure crops, conservation tillage, strip cropping, contouring, and grassed waterways. Moreover, many organic farmers have developed unique and innovative methods of organic recycling and pest control in their crop production sequences . . .

The growing interest in organic agriculture reflects an ideology shared by many urban and rural people, that is, that a stable and sustainable agriculture can be attained only through the development of technologies that are less demanding of non-renewable resources, less exploitive of our soils, and at the same time environmentally and socially acceptable . . .

Organic Agriculture: Some Basic Tenets

Despite the range of agricultural practices followed by organic farmers, most of them are guided by certain basic beliefs which may be called the "organic ethic." Some of the principal tenets of this ethic are summarized below . . .

Nature is Capital—Energy-intensive modes of conventional agriculture place man on a collision course with nature. Present trends and practices signal difficult times ahead. More concern over finite nutrient resources is needed. Organic farming focuses on recycled nutrients.

Soil is the Source of Life—Soil quality and balance (that is, soil with proper levels of organic matter, bacterial and biological activity, trace elements, and other nutrients) are essential to the long-term future of agriculture. Human and animal health are directly related to the health of the soil.

Feed the Soil, Not the Plant—Healthy plants, animals and humans result from balanced, biologically active soil.

Diversify Production Systems—Overspecialization (monoculture) is biologically and environmentally unstable.

Independence—Organic farming contributes to personal and community independence by reducing dependence on energy-intensive agricultural production and distribution systems.

Antimaterialism—Finite resources and Nature's limitations must be recognized.

In summary, organic farmers seek to establish ecologically harmonious, resource-efficient, and nutritionally sound agricultural methods.

Can a Farmer Make a Living Farming Organically?

Short term studies of organic and conventional crop production by the Center for the Biology of Natural Systems at Washington University in St. Louis, Missouri, over a 5 year period, 1974–78, showed that on selected farms in the Corn Belt, major yield differences appeared to occur in corn and wheat production . . . "Organic farmers had corn yields that averaged only about 9% below those of their conventional neighbors. Under highly favorable growing conditions . . . the conventional farmers did considerably better. But under drought, which was a serious problem . . . during the mid–1970s, organic farmers seemed to do as well as, if not better than, their conventional counterparts." Soybean and oats yields over the 5 year period averaged slightly higher on organic farms . . .

USDA cites two independent studies:

. . . in a study of fourteen selected organic crop/livestock farms in the Midwest compared with similar conventional farms, [the researchers] found that, on the average, net returns per cropland acre were about equal for the two groups . . .

In a study of 15 organic crop/livestock farms with conventional farms in the western Corn Belt (five states involved), [the researchers] found that in most cases the net return from organic farms exceeded the net return from those using conventional methods . . .

In the USDA case studies, most of the farmers with established organic systems reported that crop yields on a per-acre basis were comparable to those obtained on nearby chemical-intensive farms . . .

Even where the yields are lower, the net return to the organic farmer is as good or better because of his greater energy efficiency.

On a crop-by-crop basis, [the researchers] concluded that the organic farmers received more output per energy input than conventional farmers. They found that organic farmers were 300% more energy efficient in producing corn and 16% more energy efficient in growing soybeans.

A study of New York wheat growers found that the energy consumption per bushel of organic wheat was "15% less than the energy consumed in conventional production."

IS ORGANICALLY GROWN FOOD BETTER FOR ME?

Inferences for the superior healthfulness of organically grown food can be drawn from the experiences of farmers, since they routinely monitor the health of their livestock.

. . . A number of farmers reported that with previous chemical-intensive programs they had often incurred a higher rate of birth mortality, decreased reproductive efficiency, and increased respiratory ailments among their livestock, resulting in lower production and higher veterinary costs . . .

Many organic farmers believe that organically produced foods are more healthful than similar products from conventional farms. Such superior healthfulness could presumably arise from greater amounts or better proportions of beneficial nutrients in the food, for example, more or better quality of protein, more nutritionally important trace elements, more important vitamins, or more of some other known or unknown but nutritionally important constituent. The organic food would thus have better "nutritional quality." Superior healthfulness could also arise from a lower content in the food—or a complete absence from it—of health-harmful residues of pesticides, antibiotics, hormones, or accidental contaminants or pollutants. If the detrimental health effects of such extraneous chemicals in the conventional food were real, the organic food might then have superior "health safety."

Some organic farmers also believe that not only foods but also forages and feeds from their farms have superior nutritional quality and health safety and that this is, at least in part, the cause of the superior health which they believe to be seen in animals on their farms.

ORGANIC VS. INORGANIC FOODS

Variations in Mineral Content in Vegetables. (*Firman E. Baer Report, Rutgers University*)

	Percentage of dry weight		Millequivalents per 100 grams dry weight				Trace Elements parts per million dry matter				
	Total Ash or Mineral Matter	Phosphorus	Calcium	Magnesium	Potassium	Sodium	Boron	Manganese	Iron	Copper	Cobalt
SNAP BEANS											
Organic	10.45	0.36	40.5	60.0	99.7	8.6	73	60	227	69	0.26
Inorganic	4.04	0.22	15.5	14.8	29.1	0.0	10	2	10	3	0.00
CABBAGE											
Organic	10.38	0.38	60.0	43.6	148.3	20.4	42	13	94	48	0.15
Inorganic	6.12	0.18	17.5	15.6	53.7	0.8	7	2	20	0.4	0.00
LETTUCE											
Organic	24.48	0.43	71.0	49.3	176.5	12.2	37	169	516	60	0.19
Inorganic	7.01	0.22	16.0	13.1	53.7	0.0	6	1	9	3	0.00
TOMATOES											
Organic	14.20	0.35	23.0	59.2	148.3	6.5	36	68	1938	53	0.63
Inorganic	6.07	0.16	4.5	4.5	58.8	0.0	5	1	1	0	0.00
SPINACH											
Organic	28.56	0.52	96.0	203.9	257.0	69.5	88	117	1584	32	0.25
Inorganic	12.38	0.27	47.5	46.9	84.6	0.8	12	1	19	0.5	0.20

The absence of pesticide residues as a "health safety factor" can hardly be denied by even the most vociferous champion of agricultural poisons. This can be seen as the negative benefit of organically grown food. The positive benefit—that organically grown food is nutritionally superior—is, however, disputed even by many proponents of organically grown food on the basis of insufficient evidence. But it might not be so controversial if the work of the Soil Association in England with its Haughley Experiment were more widely known.

The achievements of the Haughley Experiment are chronicled in a little known book called *The Living Soil* (Universe Books, N.Y.) by Lady Eve Balfour, co-founder of The Soil Association.

The field of interest, which gave rise to the Experiment, is that of *health*: health of the soil; of the crop; of the animal, and thus, by implication, of man.

It was planned to be a piece of fundamental research to explore the ecological interplay between these different links in the food chain, and their bearing on the health of each. It could be described as a search for conditions attendant upon biological wholeness. The founders started with the assumption that apparently separate links in the nutrition cycle were functionally interrelated, interdependent, and inseparable.

They put it thus: Nutrition is a basic biological function and requirement. It consists of a flow of materials and energy between organism and environment. This flow is a cycle: it passes through the interconnected forms of life—from the minute soil organisms to the plants, thence to animals and man, and back to the soil. This cycle must be studied as a whole, and these forms of life as part of it, and through successive generations, if we are to learn more about nutrition and health in each stage of the cycle.

The founders decided to study this biological cycle in operation, under three different systems of land use, on a farm scale . . .

The site chosen for the experiment was two adjoining farms in the parish of Haughley, near Stowmarket in Suffolk, that were already being farmed as one holding.

The area, comprising 216 acres, was divided into three units to be run as three self-contained small farms. The divisions were carefully chosen so that such slight variation in soil type, aspect, etc., as existed should be represented in all three. The fairness of the split was subsequently confirmed by a soil survey undertaken by the Rothamsted Agricultural Experimental Station.

Two of the three sections, each having a working acreage of approximately 75 acres, were destined to be the stock-bearing sections, each to carry its own self-contained herds and flocks of *not less than three species of farm livestock*. The third section of only 32 working acres was to be a stockless section.

All three were to be established with seed, and two with foundation animals, of common origin and thereafter each was to grow and breed its own requirements.

One stock-bearing section was to be called the Organic section, the fields of which were to receive only the crop residues and animal manure produced on the section.

The fields of the second stock-bearing section were likewise to receive the crop residues and manure produced on it, but also to have standard supplementary applications of chemical fertilizers. Because it received both, it was to be called the Mixed Section.

The fields of the Stockless section . . . would receive the crop residues it produced, together with chemical fertilizers, but no animal manure . . .

In a wilderness area, where no human exploitation exists, it is well known to naturalists that, assuming the area to be big enough, nature establishes a biological balance. With the result that although the many species of plants and animals comprising such an environment subsist by "preying" on each other, almost never does any species become extinct, nor does it build up to pest proportions, so that the whole ecological system of soil, plants, insects, birds and animals . . . continues to function and prosper.

The planners asked themselves—to what extent can nature and man, working together in harmony, establish a similar biological balance among the living organisms involved in an agricultural food chain, which by its very nature must be subject to a large degree of human interference.

We are accustomed to thinking of ecology as a new study area; the Haughley Experiment was conceived in 1939. However, it was interrupted by World War II and was not fully in place until 1952. Intended to be thirty years in duration, it was terminated in 1969 because of internecine squabbling within the association. But eighteen years was long enough to compile some compelling data. As the table below indicates, trace elements in the Organic section were generally higher than in the other two.

AVERAGE TRACE ELEMENTS ON SECTIONS
(all as ppm)

	Stockless	Mixed	Organic
Magnesium	24.0	26.0	24.0
Manganese	48.0	50.0	51.0
Molybdenum	.78	.69	.88
Copper	2.49	2.53	2.69
Nickel	.79	.74	.77
Cobalt	.77	.79	.90
Iron	145.0	161.0	174.0
Zinc	1.18	1.24	1.26
Boron	.065	.066	.072

About protein:

Although the bulk yield of the organic cereals is usually less than that from the other sections, the trend seems to be for protein content to be highest from the Organic section . . . The protein from the cereals of the stockbearing sections is usually higher than that from the Stockless section.

When the greater yields of the Mixed section were considered holistically, it was found that (1) "the value of the extra tonnage obtained by the addition of fertilizers to the Mixed section barely covered the cost of the fertilizers . . ." and (2) "when the crops were used as animal food no benefit resulted from the extra tonnage, rather the reverse." Along those lines, figures for total milk production for a seven-year period favored the organic by 7 percent.

In spite of [a] greater food intake on the Mixed section, milk production from 1956, when second generation animals were coming into the herds, has been consistently higher from the Organic section herd, whether measured as total milk produced, or production per cow, or production per acre. At the same time the cows on the Organic section have carried better condition, more "bloom", and have shown quite clearly a greater contentment and placidity. This more-milk-for-less-food experience has been one of the Experiment's most interesting farm findings . . .

The comparative health of the livestock of the two sections has naturally been watched with great interest. For the first few generations there was little or nothing to choose between them, both being high, but during the last year or two, indications of loss of stamina have made their appearance in the Mixed stock.

Dr. R. F. Milton, Director of Research for the Soil Association during the ten-year period referred to above, wrote:

In concluding our comments on the period we must come back to one major fact emerging: in both health records and quantity of milk, the Organic herd appears to be superior to the Mixed herd, in spite of the substantially greater quantity of food available to, and consumed by, the latter.

I am well aware that no cows will read this book and that the evidence is not conclusive. Nevertheless, the evidence is substantial and indicates, since we are subject to the same natural law as cows, that not only might we achieve greater health by eating organically grown food, but that we might do so eating less of it. 68 percent of the time, Organic milk tested higher in vitamin C than Mixed, which tested higher only 21 percent of the time, 11 percent being equal.

The Haughley Experiment also pointed out the ecological folly of judging farm performance solely on the basis of yield per acre:

> We have to report that the greatest bulk yield of cereals came from the two sections which are given fertilizer [don't forget that this differs from the USDA findings] . . . If, however, we consider the cost of the chemical fertilizer added to the Mixed section, then the yield differences did not seem to justify the additions, particularly as . . . we have shown that with intensive fertilizer application on a mixed farm only about one-fifth of the chemical applied is recovered in the crop. The rest either finds itself in bound form unavailable to the plant or is leached into the deeper layers to pollute brooks, streams, lakes and rivers.

Time has done nothing to dim my conviction that organic farming represents salvation for American agriculture. When you look at soil substrata, you see crumbling rock. It is a hard, dense, mineral world, with only the barest traces of life. As you move upwards, you begin to encounter more and more life the closer to the surface you get—*if* there is humus in the topsoil. A system of agriculture that does not nurture humus thereby writes its own obituary and the civilization that must be nourished by that agriculture will die with it.

And what about the health of that civilization during its dying days? When a farmer fertilizes with synthetic chemicals, he uses three chemical salts—nitrogen (N), phosphorus (P), and potassium (K). NPK farming has been in vogue for the past forty years because it was discovered that those three major minerals were all that is needed to stimulate growth. The myopia of this method consists in part in the fact that there are thirty other minerals—"trace" minerals—essential for health in plants (and animals and man). The fact that they are needed in smaller quantities makes them no less vital.

Modern agriculture wages an enormous, poisonous battle against a relentless attack of plant pests and diseases. They have become a monstrous problem since the advent of chemical fertilizers. Our crops suffer because natural law always conspires to destroy the unhealthy, sending disease and pestilence to eliminate that which is unworthy of survival. A plant which has been artificially stimulated by NPK may look normal; but it is not—not healthy, capable of promoting health.

Lady Eve Balfour explains it thus:

> The work which has been, and is still being, done on trace minerals and proteins, which has revealed the extremely complex nature of the latter, has resulted in the disappearance of another previously firmly held dogma, namely, that a high protein content in fodder . . . is a measure of its value as a foodstuff. It is now known that what matters is the *quality* of the protein, and that depends (according to present knowledge) on the range of amino acids composing it. Plant protein may, or may not, contain certain amino acids which are essential to animal nutrition. Whether they do or not depends largely on the soil conditions in which the plant is grown, for the enzyme systems which control cell metabolism are dependent on trace minerals, and the availability of these to the plant is dependent on soil micro-organisms [living in humus].

Even a slight deficiency in one of a given range of trace minerals has been shown, in recent research, to result, not only in the absence in the plant protein of such amino acids as tryptophane and lysine (two of the musts for animal health) but can also lead to the plants being attacked by aphids, while neighboring plants, not suffering from any deficiency, remain free from attack.

This throws new light on the often reported pest resistance of compost-grown crops. I have myself seen two lettuce crops divided only by a foot-wide strip of grass, one belonging to an orthodox holding, the other belonging to an organic holding. The first was nearly destroyed by aphids, despite dustings; on the other I failed to find a single insect.

It now seems reasonably well established that on this interplay between soil micro-organisms and the trace elements may depend, not only the health and disease resistance of plants, but the range of amino acids contained in their protein. Also that on this quality of plant protein depends the health and disease resistance of the animal (and probably the human being) who consumes it. Hence, since soil micro-organisms play such an important part in this chain reaction, the biological importance of humus . . . becomes plain for all to see.

Perhaps you are wondering why, after addressing *everybody* throughout this book, I end up addressing the farmers. But I'm not; I'm still addressing everybody, even though only 2 percent of us live on the land. *All* of us live *from* the land; we all need to understand the important fundamentals about the farming that sustains us. It may be true that a little bit of knowledge is dangerous but in this case it's not dangerous to you. It is dangerous to the manufacturers of artificial fertilizers, pesticides, herbicides, the manufacturers of drugs, the entire corporate complex that treats disease instead of preventing it, that champions agricultural chemicals because profits from them fill the corporate coffers. Already the power of their influence in Washington and their grip on the universities are weakening because people are waking up.

The quality of our air, water, and topsoil ought to be universally recognized as the resources of most concern to us. We can't drive without oil or construct without wood, but we don't live at all without air, water, and food. We urbanites are accustomed to taking our food supply for granted; we can no longer afford to do so.

Farmers are custodians of a primary natural resource. They have a title to their land but all it means is that they have paid for the privilege of living on and caring for *your* land. Private property rights are real and deserve our respect. But in the ultimate sense, private property is a myth; the land belongs to everybody. How the farmer-custodians care for your land is within your power to decide. The mechanism is the marketplace. The marketplace exists to satisfy your demands as a consumer. Don't underestimate your power as a consumer: in a dozen years I watched a billion dollar industry—the natural foods industry—appear from nowhere due to the consumer power of less than 10 percent of the population. You *are* the marketplace and the demands of the marketplace determine what the farmers grow and *how* they grow it—*if* you speak. The marketplace will be filled with organically grown food if you demand it. Speak and you will be heard, ask for organically grown food and you will get it. And the farmer who sets about fulfilling your demand will be glad he responded because you will have set him on the road to solving problems only organic agriculture can solve.

The USDA has finally accorded organic agriculture some of the recognition that has long been due it as a solution to many of our contemporary agricultural/ecological problems. In the relatively near future, I expect its role as a remedy for many of our health problems will also be recognized. It will be widely recognized that our health depends not only on us choosing the right food, but on our farmers growing that food properly—organically. The relationships are there, it remains only to trace, tabulate, and verify them. The division between ecological and human health, between soil, plant, animal, and human health are artificial and the scientific community will soon erase them. But you don't have to wait for that; you have intuition and common sense to guide you. We are faced with grave problems, but don't look elsewhere—you are the solution. Answering the question about what factors will widen the scope of organic farming in the future, the USDA says, "increased public support for research and education programs, which address organic farming problems and concerns, and increased demand for organically grown food."

SWITZERLAND: A MODEL FOR CHANGE

On December 20, 1982, National Public Radio's news program *All Things Considered* aired a report by Daniel Zwerdling on Megro, Switzerland's largest supermarket chain. What he found in that little democracy illustrates what will happen in this big one when an informed public awakens a sense of responsibility in some of our corporate leadership. It also reflects the kinds of problems encountered at all levels when we force monoliths to change direction. The transcript of Zwerdling's report is printed with the permission of National Public Radio (NPR).

Transcription Of News Broadcast By Daniel Zwerdling

Announcer

One of the most expensive problems squeezing farmers today is the growing dependence on petrochemical fertilizers and pesticides. Overuse of chemicals is causing ecological and financial problems. Many researchers criticize the government for not doing much to change it but now somebody is trying to get farmers to back off chemicals. It's not the environmentalists, it's not government, it's Swiss big business. NPR's Daniel Zwerdling visited Switzerland and has a report.

Zwerdling

Fantasize for a moment that you're in your local supermarket, part of the biggest supermarket chain in the country. You push your cart down the isle and produce counters stretch before you, lush with lettuce and leeks and carrots and cauliflowers, but there's something different about these vegetables that you've never seen before. They're wrapped with a special label with a symbol that stands for health. And a nearby poster proclaims why. "We grow our vegetables and fruits with less artificial fertilizer and less pesticides," the poster proclaims, "and that means better soils, better energy use and less pollution, so we can protect our clients."

The chance of seeing this sort of thing in your local Safeway or A&P seems farfetched, but here in Switzerland it's happening today. The multibillion dollar Megro supermarket chain has been teaching the nation's farmers to kick the chemical habit. Now, most of these vegetables are not yet organic. They're still grown with pesticides and synthetic fertilizers, but much less than on conventional farms. And store manager Max Earsman says that's important to the Swiss.

Earsman   In effect I grow vegetables in my own garden at home with absolutely no chemicals at all. According to the latest opinion polls, living healthfully and protecting the environment—that is the very high priority for us.

Zwerdling   Megro officials told me that to understand our farming experiment, you have to understand Megro.

Megro Executive The aim of Megro is not just to make money. It's more than that.

Zwerdling   Hans Peter Berchy runs the special farming program and he says that the key is that Megro is not just a normal corporation, it's a cooperative. Consumers who shop here own equal shares in the company and vote on major policies. And this democratic history has helped give the corporation a sense of social mission. On the other hand the co-op is enormously powerful. The sales last year topped 3½ billion dollars and the supermarket chain buys and sells one quarter of all the food grown in Switzerland. So when the environmental movement took off in the early 70's, Berchy says Megro executives decided they should do something about it.

Berchy   So because of Megro's position in the Swiss market, it's practically the duty for Megro to do everything possible to help produce the best product that can be made in Switzerland.

Zwerdling   And Megro decided the only way to sell food grown with less chemicals was to go right to the source, and teach farmers how to grow it. Here's how the program works. If you're a farmer and you want to take part, Megro farm advisers will give you all the help you want, free. And Megro buyers will give you favored treatment. They'll buy your crops before they'll buy someone else's, but in return you, the farmer, have to promise to grow your crops the Megro way. To see how the program works I drove into the countryside one morning with Alex Fertur. Fertur is one of Megro's 13 full-time farm advisers.

Fertur   The farmers haven't been trained too well by schools. So we have to train them a second time. It takes a lot more intelligence; it's more difficult to farm biologically instead of chemically.

Zwerdling   On this foggy morning we visited the farm of Reinhard Geesy, just down the road from the village church in Muudica. Geesy grows 24 acres of vegetables, a good size farm by Swiss standards. If you'd come to him 10 years ago, Geesy says, he'd have told you he was using more fertilizer and more pesticides than ever, and profiting less. One year he lost a whole field of radishes because a chemical still in the soil from a previous crop turned them into gnarled stumps. And Geesy was using lots of synthetic fertilizer to grow the biggest possible yields, but too much fertilizer weakened the vegetables and they would rot in the warehouse.

Geesy

When I went to agricultural school they taught how much fertilizer to use—more rather than less. But afterwards when we joined the Megro program, we realized we can do with much less fertilizer then we were taught.

Zwerdling

In fact, since he joined the Megro program, Geesy says, he's cut back on synthetic fertilizers by 50 percent. His adviser, Alex Fertur, has taught him to make organic compost.

Geesy

And we use much less pesticides now. We used to look at a list of recommended pesticides and just spray even when there were no pests. We never really knew what we were using, or how poisonous it was. And the consumers didn't know either.

Zwerdling

But now Geesy releases special wasps and spiders and other natural predators over his crops, and he sprays pesticides only when he absolutely has to. The Megro methods demand more labor than chemicals do, Geesy says, and that costs more money. But on the other hand, Geesy has cut back on fertilizers and pesticides and that *saves* money. In addition, he says, the Megro methods have helped him grow better quality crops so he can sell them for a better price. Net result: Reinhardt Geesy is making as much profit as ever, maybe even more. But Reinhardt Geesy can't just sit back and relax, not yet. The Megro computers are keeping track of his progress—how healthy his soil is, how bad his bug problems are, how much pesticide winds up in his crop. And the computers keep setting new goals for him to achieve, and that, Geesy says, is perhaps his main complaint.

Geesy

The biggest problem today is to produce up to the quality that Megro demands. The demands for quality keep getting more strict.

Zwerdling

The Megro corporation has signed up more than one thousand farmers in the program now. They're growing more than 25 percent of all the fruits and vegetables the supermarkets sell. The special food is all wrapped under a special label and sold alongside the conventional produce at exactly the same price. Some of the goals of the Megro program seem to challenge the basic assumptions of modern agriculture. Official policy in Switzerland and in the United States proclaims that big is beautiful. The bigger the farmer's yields, the better the farm, but according to Hans Peter Berchy of Megro, that policy is wrong. By straining to produce every possible bushel, Berchy says, the typical modern farmer is ruining his soil and hurting the quality of his food.

Berchy

We warn him from the danger to grow too far.

Zwerdling

So in other words, don't push for too high a yield.

Berchy   That's correct, because too high yields also mean very often that you change the equilibrium in your soil. It will ask for even more chemicals and you will end up in a bottleneck.

Zwerdling   As a result of views like that one, the Megro program is drawing criticism, ironically from inside Megro's own management. And here's why: If Megro implies that the food grown with less chemicals is better, some executives say, then that implies that the rest of the food sold in Megro is inferior—not such smart advertising, they say. So top Megro executives have decided not to advertise the special food too vigorously. So while Megro persuades more farmers to grow food the Megro way, many shoppers in the supermarkets don't even know what it's all about.

Zwerdling   Do you know what the Megro "S" label means?

Store customer I don't.

Zwerdling   The Megro "S" vegetables are grown with less chemicals.

Store customer Ah—no, I didn't know it.

Zwerdling   Some of these labels have Megro "S" on them. Do you know what the differences are between those labels?

Another customer No I never see that, and I look never on the label.

Zwerdling   There's another criticism against the Megro program, this one from environmentalists. They say that Megro isn't getting farmers off chemicals fast enough. But Hans Peter Berchy says if Megro pushes farmers too far, too fast, it will only alienate them. But even as he says that, Megro is already launching a dramatic experiment. For the next five years Megro advisers will work with six conventional farms to see if they can go completely organic. Maybe they'll succeed or maybe the farmers will become only 80 percent organic. But Berchy says it doesn't really matter. The Megro supermarket chain just wants to see how far modern farmers can go kicking the chemical habit and still make a decent profit. For National Public Radio, I'm Daniel Zwerdling.

GETTING INVOLVED IN THE FUTURE OF FOOD

Our agricultural system is sick because it is addicted to chemicals like a junkie hooked on heroin. The junkie cannot begin to think of feeding himself properly and his life inexorably wastes away. Likewise, the junkie syndrome in agriculture is creating a wasteland. We would have to write

"The End" to our food producing system right now if we didn't know that every front has a back.

The back of the ecological disaster of chemical farming is the opportunity to correct our errors and create an agriculture that is sustainable and sustaining because it is in harmony with natural law.

The back of powerlessness is the ultimately irresistible force we embody through our choices in the marketplace and the alliances we form. Remember that we were ignorant of the problem until somebody told us about it. Through knowing, we were liberated from the prison of being part of the problem into the freedom of being part of the solution. You can activate the second part of the equation by supporting some or all of the following organizations and/or others you can learn about through them.

Robert Rodale is the chief executive officer of Rodale Press (founded by his father, J.I. Rodale), mentioned frequently in the pages of this book. In 1980 he started the Cornucopia Project, a nonprofit educational and research organization, to study our food system in all its aspects. Cornucopia finds the American food system traveling rapidly and directly towards a collision with disaster. The findings are published in its 189 page report, *Empty Breadbasket?*, available for $4.00. The subtitle of the report is our clue that it reaches beyond the dissemination of bad news: *The Coming Challenge to America's Food Supply and What We Can Do About It.*

With a free quarterly newsletter, Cornucopia addresses, among many others, these questions:

—Do you know where the nearest farm is and what food you could get from it?
—How much food could your community produce?
—Do you know how much soil is lost in the production of your food?
—What is the energy cost of your food?
—Who is in control of our food system?
—Do you know how government food policy affects you?
—Does what you choose to eat make a difference?
—Could you plan to make yourself more self-reliant?
—How much self-reliance in food is possible for the average person?
—Where is the U.S. food system going?
—Where *could* the food system be headed?

A letter from Cornucopia informs us that consideration of such questions

is intended to function in two ways. One is to provide specific information to consumers who want to protect themselves against rising food costs and work for constructive changes in the food system, whether on an individual or group basis.

The second function . . . is to generate information that might be useful to government agencies, planners, farmers, and companies that serve the food industry.

To receive the newsletter and a packet of information, write:
The Cornucopia Project
33 East Minor St.
Emmaus, PA 18049

One of the most critical problems facing our country is the loss of prime agricultural land: one million acres of this irreplaceable treasure succumb to urban sprawl each year. The time to prevent more of our farmlands from disappearing is now, not only for the sake of our future food supply but for the sake of a livable environment. Write:

American Farmland Trust
1717 Massachusetts Ave., N.W.
Washington, D.C. 20036

The Price–Pottenger Nutrition Foundation, America's preeminent, nonprofit nutrition education organization, has undertaken the EARTH Project, described in their quarterly journal as follows:

Price–Pottenger Nutrition Foundation shares responsibility for the preventive health care needs of America. Since nutritional values evolve first and foremost from the fertility of the soil, PPNF will seek to establish:

(1) Prototype working organic farms;
(2) Educational programs teaching the skills and knowledge of organic agriculture and ecological lifestyles;
(3) A research laboratory;
(4) Library facilities for scientific and lay people;
(5) A mobile soil and tissue testing facility.

These interlocking efforts will collectively be known as the EARTH Project (the acronym reflects the project's purpose: *Earth's Agricultural Return To Health*).

PPNF will seek to coordinate the EARTH Project with other organizations working towards the same goals. Therefore, PPNF will offer the inter-organizational services of being the linking mechanism in the network. This communication service will be known as EARTH-Line.

Write:

Price–Pottenger Nutrition Foundation
P.O. Box 2614
La Mesa, CA 92041

The Nutrition Education Center is devoted to nutrition based on natural foods and organic gardening. NEC conducts workshops, furnishes taped lectures, and publishes a newsletter.

Nutrition Education Center
P.O. Box 303
Oyster Bay, NY 11771

The International Federation of Organic Movements coordinates research done worldwide by organic farming and gardening organizations. IFOM also initiates, promotes, and publishes the results of research, as well as organizing symposia and conferences.

International Federation of Organic Movements
Postfach, CH 4104
Oberwill/BL
Switzerland

The Soil Association has continued its promotion of the organic way of life, stating

Organic husbandry is the best means of building up soil fertility to produce better crops of high nutritional value leading to better health.

The Soil Association is concerned with health—of man, of animals, of plants, and therefore especially with the health and fertility of the top few inches of the soil on which all life depends.

TSA advises farmers, conducts conferences, lectures, and exhibitions throughout England, and publishes a magazine.

> The Soil Association
> Walnut Tree Manor
> Haughley, Stowmarket
> Suffolk, IP14 3RS, U.K.

The three farms of the Haughley experiment formerly owned and operated by the Soil Association are still being operated as organic, mixed, and chemical farms by the Pye Research Centre (same address as TSA). PRC is highly respected for its scrupulously scientific approach to organic farming research.

Similar to the EARTH Project, the Coolidge Center for the Advancement of Agriculture

was established in 1978 to explore alternative agricultural strategies for small farmers. In pursuit of that goal, the Coolidge Center conducts a broad interdisciplinary investigation of cropping systems, appropriate mechanization, animal husbandry, protected cultivation, long term maintenance of soil fertility, and environmentally sound pest control.

The Center is located in Topsfield, Massachusetts on a 60 acre farm bordering the Ipswich River. Encircling the farmhouse, machinery sheds, and livestock housing are 35 acres of open land including a four acre experimental orchard. Twelve acres of field crops and vegetables, plus hay fields, pastures and trial grounds. The Center maintains an office, a conference room, and an extensive library of pertinent books and agricultural research data from worldwide sources. Visitors are welcome to use the library facilities and tour the farm by appointment. The Coolidge Center is a part of the River Road Charitable Corporation.

The Coolidge Center publishes a quarterly newsletter. Write:

> The Coolidge Center
> Riverhill Farm
> Topsfield, MA 01983

There are two notable organizations dedicated to the analysis of global food issue. Lester Brown, author of *Building a Sustainable Society* (Norton), is president of:

> Worldwatch
> 1776 Massachusetts Ave., N.W.
> Washington, D.C. 20036

Frances Moore Lappé, author of *Diet for a Small Planet* and *Food First: Beyond the Myth of Scarcity* is the founder and director of:

> Institute for Food and Development Policy
> 2588 Mission St.
> San Francisco, CA 94110

Michael Jacobson, a doctor of biochemistry, is head of Center for Science in the Public Interest.

CSPI is a nonprofit, tax-exempt organization that seeks to provide the public with reliable, interesting, understandable information about food, the food industry, and the government regulation of food. CSPI tackles food-related problems at the national and local levels. Nationally, CSPI watchdogs federal agencies that oversee food safety, trade, and nutrition. CSPI catalyzes action at the local level by working with citizen groups around the country. The project also publishes how-to manuals on improving school lunches, vended foods, and community food policies.

CSPI membership ($10) includes twelve issues of the magazine "Nutrition Action."
  CSPI
  1755 S St., N.W.
  Washington, D.C. 20009

The concept of the Earthsteward has emerged from a growing awareness of the intimate and total connection of all beings. This connectedness transcends all established lines of race, nationality, belief and even species. In this time of planetary crisis, an energy form is being tapped, which, if developed and released in a loving, compassionate manner, can utilize this time of crisis as a doorway to a new, more holistic existence. This energy form is our own human consciousness, elevated to the level at which we become clear about our real reasons for being here on this planet. When we, as Earthstewards, begin to accept responsibility for our part in the unfolding drama of the evolution of consciousness, then this transformation of our own personal lives affects all other life on our planet, and planetary transformation is possible. This is the essence of the Earthstewards Network: taking personal responsibility for one's part in it all. Earthstewards are people everywhere, connected by a network of communication and consciousness, who know the power of their thoughts and actions and are directing them in the service of their brothers and sisters and of their planet.

Earthstewards have committed themselves to the spreading of consciousness, based upon the Sevenfold Path of Peace:

—When we are at peace within our own hearts we shall be at peace with everyone and with our Mother the Earth.
—When we recognize that our planet itself is a living organism co-evolving with humankind we shall become worthy of stewardship.
—When we see ourselves as stewards of our planet and not as owners and masters of it there shall be lasting satisfaction from our labors.
—When we accept the concept of Right Livelihood as the basic right of all we shall have respect for one another.
—When we respect the sacredness of all life we shall be truly free.
—When we free ourselves from our attachment to our ego-personalities we shall be able to experience our Oneness.
—When we experience our Oneness—our total connectedness with all beings—we shall be at peace within our own hearts.

As an Earthsteward, you will receive materials from many sources and be part of a network which will assist you in turning the thrust of humanity toward more holistic, loving, sharing relationships with each other and with all life forms, including our planet itself.

Write:
  Holyearth
  Box 873
  Monte Rio, CA 95462

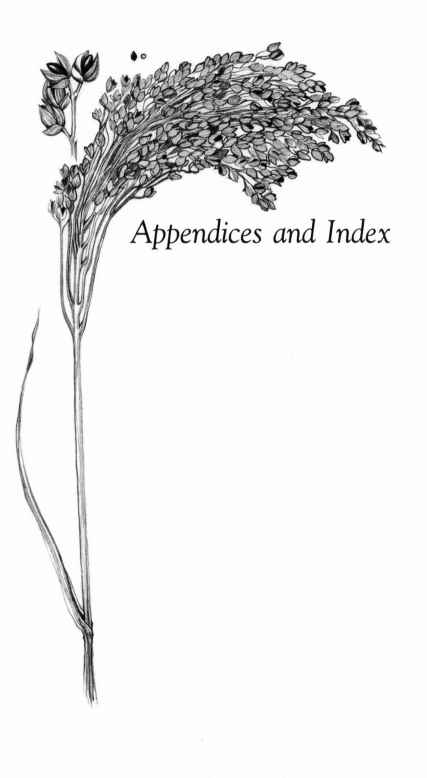

Appendices and Index

Appendix One   Where to Find Pure American Spring Waters

Arizona
Arizona Sparkling Bottled Water
Phoenix
*Crystal Bottled Waters Co.
Phoenix

Arkansas
Mountain Valley Water
Hot Springs

California
A Santé Mineral Waters, Inc.
Santa Rosa

Arrowhead Puritas Water Co.
Los Angeles

Artesian Water Co.
San Francisco

Calistoga Mineral Water Co.
Calistoga

Crystal Geyser Mineral Water Co.
Calistoga

Deep Rock Water Co.
Los Angeles

Eureka Water Supply Co.
Eureka

Feather River Spring Water
Sacramento

Forest Lake Spring Water Co.
Lake County

Mountain Spring Water Co.
Santa Barbara

Mountain Springs Water Co.
San Francisco

Napa Valley Springs Mineral Water Co.
Calistoga

Ramona Bottling, Inc.
(also Sequoia Springs Natural Pure Mineral
   Water)
Ramona

Silver Springs Water
San Diego

*Sparkletts Drinking Water Corp.
Los Angeles

Vichy Springs Water Co.
Ukiah

Colorado
Manitou Mineral Water
Manitou Springs

Florida
Good Hope Water Co.
Jacksonville

Zephyrhills Bottled Water
Zephyrhills

Illinois
Hinckley & Schmdit Natural Spring Water
Chicago

Purity Bottling Co.
Elk Grove Village

Louisiana
Kentwood Spring Water
New Orleans

Maine
Poland Water
South Poland

Massachusetts
Belmont Springs Water Co.
Belmont

Sand Springs, Inc.
Williamstown

Minnesota
Glenwood-Inglewood Spring Water
Minneapolis

Montana
Big Springs Bottled Water
Lewistown

New Mexico
Springsweet Deep Well Water
Albuquerque

New York
Deer Park 100% Spring Water
New York

*Great Bear Spring Water Co.
New York

Saratoga Springs
(also Saratoga Vichy Water, Quevic, Eau
    Minerale Saratoga)
Saratoga

Pennsylvania
Cloister Pure-Spring Water Co.
Ephrata

Valley Forge Springs
Noistown

Wissahickon Spring Water Co.
Philadelphia

Texas
*Ozarka Water Co.
(also Caddo Valley Ozark Mountain Spring
    Water)
San Antonio

Utah
Mount Olympus Waters, Inc.
Salt Lake City

Rocky Minerals Brand
Marysvale

Virginia
Seawright Springs
Mount Sydney

West Virginia
Tyler Mountain Water Co.
Charlestown

Wisconsin
Chippewa Springs Corp.
Chippewa Falls

Wyoming
Rock Crest Water Co.
Cheyenne

Canada
Montclair Natural Mineral Water Co.
Chambly, Quebec

Sparkling Spring Water, Ltd.
Valley, Nova Scotia

St. Justin Mineral Water
St. Justin, Quebec

Sources: *Oasis,* Arthur Von Wiesenberger, Capra Press, Santa Barbara and Napa Valley Springs Mineral Water Company of Calistoga, California.

*The waters of these companies have their mineral contents modified by the bottlers; therefore, according to the standards of the Council of Natural Waters, they are "processed" rather than natural waters, while still being pure spring waters.

Appendix Two   A Look at Food Additives

Additive	Defect
Artificial Colors	Twelve previously used artificial colors have been banned since 1950. There are nine synthetic colors currently permitted by the FDA, four of which are considered unsafe by the World Health Organization. There are seven natural colors, at least one of which is unsafe. The greatest use for artificial colors is in junk foods. There is evidence that artificial colors contribute to hyperactivity in children. In general, high quality food is not artificially colored. Conclusion: *avoid artificial colors*.
Artificial Flavors	There are approximately 1,500 artificial flavors. Most are "probably" not toxic, but evidence gives cause for suspicion that artificial flavors contribute to hyperactivity in children. The greatest use for artificial flavors is in junk foods, because the real thing has been left out. In general, high quality food is not artificially flavored. Conclusion: *avoid artificial flavors*.

Additive	Use	Defect
Brominated Vegetable Oil (BVO)	Emulsifier, clouding agent in soft drinks.	On the FDA "suspect list."
Butylated Hydroxanisole (BHA)	Antioxidant in chewing gum, candies, ice cream, potato chips, many other foods.	Can cause allergy, affect liver and kidney function. Being studied by the FDA.
Butylated Hydroxytoluene (BHT)	Same uses as BHA.	Same defects as BHA but apparently more toxic. Banned in England; further study recommended by the FDA.
Caffeine	Flavoring in colas and root beers.	Powerful stimulant to central nervous system, heart and respiratory system. Could be damaging to children.

Additive	*Use*	*Defect*
Corn Syrup* Corn Syrup Solids*	Sweetener in candy, toppings, syrups, snack food, imitation dairy products.	Empty calories, no nutritional value, promotes obesity and dental disease.
Dextrose (Glucose, grape or corn sugar)*	Sweetener, coloring agent in bread, caramel, soft drinks, candy.	Empty calories, no nutritional value, promotes obesity and dental disease.
Hydrogenated Vegetable Oil*	The primary ingredient in margarine and vegetable shortening.	Artificially saturated fat, chemically resembles plastic.
Invert Sugar*	Sweetener in soft drinks, syrups, candy	Empty calories, no nutritional value, promotes obesity and dental disease.
Monosodium Glutamate (MSG)	Flavor enhancer in a wide variety of foods.	Can cause "Chinese Restaurant Syndrome" (numbness, burning, chest discomfort, headache). May have mutagenic, teratogenic and reproductive effects.
Phosphates	*Phosphoric Acid* acidifies and flavors colas. *Sodium Aluminum Phosphate* is a leavening agent. *Ammonium Phosphate* is a yeast food. *Sodium Acid Pyrophosphate* prevents color changes.	Phosphorus is one mineral found in abundance in most diets. Phosphates are not toxic but can lead to calcium imbalance.
Propyl Gallate	Antioxidant in vegetable oil, meat products, ice cream, candy, chewing gum, gelatin desserts	Commonly used in conjunction with BHA and BHT for its synergistic effects with them; this synergistic effect in humans is inadequately understood.
Quinine	Flavoring in tonic and quinine water, Bitter Lemon.	Can cause nausea, vomiting, disturbances in vision, ringing in ears.
Saccharin	Synthetic sweetener in "diet" products	Carcinogenic. Subject to proposed FDA ban in 1977, the beginning of another DES-type saga.
Salt (Sodium Chloride)*	Flavoring, preservative.	Not toxic but present in excessive amounts in processed foods. Associated with edema and hypertension.
Sodium Nitrite (Sodium Nitrate)	Preservative, coloring, flavoring in a wide variety of meat products.	Nitrate breaks down into nitrite; nitrite can lead to formation of nitrosamines, potent carcinogens.

Additive	Use	Defect
Sugar (Sucrose)*	Sweetener	Empty calories, no nutritional value, promotes obesity and dental disease. Suspected causative factor in diabetes.
Sulfur Dioxide	Preservative and bleach in fruits and vegetables, wine, corn syrup, beverages soups, condiments.	Destroys vitamins A and B1; further study recommended by the FDA

*Discussed in detail in Chapter 4.

The above list contains only the most commonly found defective additives; there are hundreds more. For a comprehensive review see A Consumer's Dictionary of Food Additives, Ruth Winter; Crown Publishers.

The FDA has deemed the following common additives to be in need of further study:

QUESTIONABLE ADDITIVES

Calcium Propionate
Calcium Stearoyl Lactylate
Diglycerides
Ferrous Gluconate
Furcelleran
EDTA

Gum Arabic
Locust Bean Gum
Mannitol
Modified Food Starch
Polysorbate 60
Sorbitol

The following common additives are apparently safe, based on sufficient test data:

SAFE ADDITIVES

Alginate*
Alpha Tocopherol*
Ascorbic Acid*
Beta Carotene*
Carageenan*
Casein*
Citric Acid*
Ethyl Vanillan
Fumaric Acid
Gelatin*
Glycerin (Glycerol)

Ghati Gum*
Guar Gum*
Karaya Gum*
Hydrolyzed Vegetable Protein*
Lactic Acid*
Lactose*
Lecithin*
Monoglycerides
Polysorbate 80
Potassium Sorbate
Sodium Benzoate

SAFE ADDITIVES

Sodium Carboxymethylcellulose	Sorbic Acid*
(CMC)	Sorbitan Monostearate
Sodium Proprionate	Starch*
Sodium Stearoyl Lactylate	Vanillin

*Keep in mind that in speaking of "safe" additives, I refer to the FDA's satisfaction with data submitted to them by food processors, in itself a questionable procedure. The responsibility for testing should be in the hands of a disinterested, independent agency, not those who propose to capitalize on the use of the additives. How confident would we be of medical doctors who obtained their licenses by testing themselves, then informing the licensing board that they were satisfied with the results? To most natural food purists, only those additives starred would qualify as safe, at least a third would be eliminated. Purist or not, the bottom line under additives is that *not much needs to be added to good food.* The motivation for additives is most often commercial, not nutritional, an effort to make the ersatz look and taste like something real.

Appendix Three   Vitamin and Mineral Profiles

VITAMINS

The dictionary defines vitamins as a group of organic substances essential in small quantities for normal metabolism and health, found in natural foodstuffs. If there were a fire burning in your body, the logs would be complex carbohydrate, protein, and fat, the kindling would be enzymes, and the match would be vitamins. All the right elements for a fire can be there, but without a match nothing happens. Vitamins are sometimes referred to as "co-enzymes" because they join with enzymes to make transformation possible.

Vitamins A, D, E, F, and K are dissolved in fat, meaning they can be stored within our fatty tissue for future use. All the other vitamins are soluble in water. This means we cannot store what we don't use; they must be constantly replenished.

RDAs (Recommended Daily Allowances) are averages, required by the FDA to be stated on the labels of vitamins. But, as has been emphasized in the body of this book, there really is no such thing as an average person; therefore, RDAs are of little practical value. Due to the genetic construction and physiological condition of the individual, people differ biochemically. Variations from one person to another or within one person from one time to another can be twentyfold or more. Because of genetic factors, an individual might destroy certain vitamins rapidly. Because of their physiological state—due to stress, for example—people can have a temporary need for extra-large quantities of particular vitamins. Compared to the RDA, your needs might be huge—a not uncommon situation. I have included RDAs in the information that follows so that you can be aware of the official FDA opinion.

More to the point in most cases are the quantities described as "therapeutic dosage." The quantity ranges listed as therapeutic are also much more reasonable for ordinary maintenance purposes than RDAs. As to vitamin therapy, the same factors of individual differences mentioned above are at play when vitamins are used for cures. The upper limit of the therapeutic dosages are ordinarily well within safety; the quantities listed as toxic are truly dangerous.

Vitamin A

"The anti-infection vitamin." Oil soluble, stored in the liver, normally very little is excreted.

Body parts nourished: eyes, skin, bone, hair, teeth, soft tissue, adrenals.

Body functions aided: growth, maintenance, and repair of body tissue (therefore resistance to infections); secretion of gastric juices for protein digestion; visual purple production (for night vision); building of bones, teeth, and blood; production of glucose.

427

Deficiency symptoms: retarded growth; allergies; horny skin lesions; fatigue; night blindness and other visual defects; loss of smell; rough, dry skin; dryness of mucus membrane; soft tooth enamel; susceptibility to infections.

Therapeutic uses: acne, alcoholism, allergies, arthritis, asthma, athlete's foot, bronchitis, colds, cystitis, diabetes, eczema, heart disease, hepatitis, migraine headache, psoriasis, sinusitis, stress, tooth and gum disorders.

Therapeutic dosage: 10,000–25,000 I.U./day.

RDA:
Children, 3500 I.U./day
Adults, 5000 I.U./day
Pregnancy, 6000 I.U./day
Nursing, 8000 I.U./day

Protects: mucus membranes and lungs against smog.

Toxic level: more than 50,000 I.U./day.

Synergies: B complex, C, D, E, F, calcium, phosphorus, zinc, protein mobilizes A from storage in liver.

Destroyed by: alcohol, coffee, cortisone, mineral oil, excessive iron, insufficient vitamin D; partially destroyed by cooking.

Natural food sources: liver, eggs, dairy products, colored fruits and vegetables.

Natural vitamin sources: fish liver oils.

B Complex

Water soluble, some individually produced in the human small intestine, stored in various organs in small amounts, the rest excreted in urine and feces.

The various B vitamins are highly synergistic, so, unless there is a specific therapeutic use involved, should be taken as the whole B complex as found in nutritional yeast or desiccated liver. When using an isolated B vitamin for therapy, it is advisable to supplement with the entire B complex, otherwise imbalances are likely to occur.

When starting B complex supplementation, flatulence may occur. Therefore begin with small doses and increase gradually. For example, start with a quarter teaspoon of yeast for several days, then every few days increase by a quarter teaspoon until two tablespoons per day is reached.

Brewer's yeast is one type of nutritional yeast, a by-product of beermaking. Other types of yeast are called "primary"—that is, they are not by-products but grown specifically for food purposes. "Torula" yeasts are grown on wood pulp. Other mediums, such as molasses, are also used for the production of primary grown food yeasts.

Body parts nourished: eyes, gastrointestinal tract, hair, liver, mouth, nerves, skin.

Body functions aided: energy production, metabolism of carbohydrates, fats and proteins, maintenance of gastrointestinal tract.

Deficiency symptoms: acne, anemia, constipation, high cholesterol, digestive disturbances, fatigue, dry, dull, falling hair, insomnia, dry, rough skin.

Therapeutic uses: alcoholic psychosis, allergies, anemia, baldness, barbiturate overdose, cystitis, heart abnormalities, hypoglycemia, hypersensitive children, Meniere's syndrome, menstrual difficulties, migraine headaches, obesity, postoperative nausea, stress.

Therapeutic dosage: two or more tablespoons per day in the form of yeast or the equivalent in tablets. To maintain proper calcium/phosphorous ratio, augment each tablespoon of yeast with four tablespoons of spray-dried skim milk, unless the yeast label indicates "calcium balanced."

No RDA.

Protects: against toxic residues in food and counteracts toxic drugs.

No toxicity.

Synergies: C, E, calcium, phosphorus.

Antagonists: alcohol, birth control pills, coffee, infections, sleeping pills, stress, sugar, sulpha drugs.

Natural food sources: whole grains, liver.

Natural vitamin sources: nutritional yeast, desiccated liver.

Vitamin B1 (Thiamine): The "anti-beriberi" and the "morale" vitamin. Water soluble, small amounts stored in heart, liver, kidney and brain, production in small intestine increased by dietary fiber, one milligram per day destroyed in body tissue.

Body parts nourished: brain, ears, eyes, hair, heart, liver, kidneys, nervous system.

Body functions aided: growth, nerve activity, energy production, learning capacity, appetite, blood building, carbohydrate metabolism, hydrochloric acid production (protein digestion), muscle tone, maintenance of intestines, stomach and heart.

Deficiency symptoms: numbness of hands and feet, pain and noise sensitivity, pains around heart and slow heart beat, shortness of breath, inflammation of spinal nerves marked by paralysis, pain, wasting of muscles, appetite loss, digestive disturbances, fatigue, irritability, nervousness, edema.

Therapeutic uses: alcoholism, anemia, congestive heart failure, constipation, diarrhea, diabetes, indigestion, nausea, mental illness, alleviation of pain, rapid heart rate, stress.

Therapeutic dosage: 2–10 mg/day.

Protects: against the effects of lead.

RDA:
Children, .6–1.1 mg/day
Adult female, 1 mg/day
Adult male, 1.4 mg/day
Increased requirements for pregnancy and lactation, depending on the individual.

No toxicity.

Synergies: B complex, C, E, manganese, sulphur.

Antagonists: alcohol, coffee, fever, raw clams, excessive sugar, stress, tobacco, cooking heat, and water.

Natural food sources: whole grains, most vegetables, nuts, legumes, eggs, organ meats, fish, pork, molasses, nutritional yeast.

Natural vitamin sources: yeast, rice bran.

Vitamin B2 (Riboflavin): Water soluble, small amount stored in skeletal muscles, 57 percent of intake excreted in 24 hours.

Body parts nourished: blood, liver, lymph nodes, muscles, nerves, skin.

Body functions aided: antibody formation, production of hydrochloric acid (digestion), production of bile acids (protein and fat utilization), maintenance of sodium/potassium balance (nerves), production of red blood cells and neural hormones.

Deficiency symptoms: acne, anemia, arthritis, convulsions in babies, dermatitis, depression, dizziness, hair loss, learning disabilities, nervous disorders (depression, irritability), weakness.

Therapeutic uses: atherosclerosis, baldness, cystitis, facial oiliness, hypoglycemia, mental retardation, muscular disorders, nervous disorders, nausea in pregnancy, obesity, postoperative nausea, stress, sun sensitivity.

Therapeutic dosage: 4–50 mg.

RDA:
Children, .5–1.2 mg/day
Adults, 2 mg/day
Pregnancy and lactation, 2.5 mg/day

No toxicity.

Synergies: B complex, C, magnesium, potassium, linoleic acid, sodium.

Antagonists: alcohol, birth control pills, coffee, 40 percent lost in cooking, radiation, tobacco.

Natural food sources: whole grains, cantaloupe, cabbage, green leafy vegetables, prunes, milk, meat, organ meats, fish, eggs, peas, wheat germ, molasses, nutritional yeast.

Natural vitamin sources: yeast, bran.

Vitamin B12 (Cobalamin): Water soluble; small amount stored in the liver; limited sources available to vegetarians; "intrinsic factor," a protein-related enzyme, must be present for good absorption; 34 percent of ingested dose appears in feces.

Body parts nourished: blood, kidneys, muscle, nerves, skin, bone.

Body functions aided: appetite; blood cell formation; cell longevity; healthy nervous system; metabolism of carbohydrate, fat, and protein; maintenance of healthy skin and mucus membrane; bone marrow; gastrointestinal tract; normal growth.

Deficiency symptoms: degeneration of spinal cord, disturbed carbohydrate metabolism, general weakness, nervousness, pernicious anemia, walking and speaking difficulties.

Therapeutic uses: alcoholism, allergies, anemia, arthritis, bronchial asthma, bursitis, epilepsy, fatigue, hypoglycemia, insomnia, obesity, shingles, stress.

Therapeutic dosage: 5–50 mcg.

RDA:
Children, 2–5 mcg/day
Adults, 5–6 mcg/day
Pregnancy and lactation, 8 mcg/day

No toxicity.

Synergies: A, B, complex, C, E, potassium, sodium.

Antagonists: alcohol, coffee, laxatives, tobacco, intestinal parasites and intestinal diseases, partially destroyed by cooking.

Natural food sources: organ meats, meat, fish, eggs, dairy products, tempeh.

Natural vitamin sources: yeast, rice, bran (fermentation concentrate).

Biotin: Water soluble, stored in liver, readily produced by intestinal flora, member of the B complex.

Body parts nourished: bone marrow, hair, muscles, liver kidneys, sex glands in males, skin.

Body functions aided: maintenance of skin, hair, oil-secreting glands, nerves, bone marrow, male sex glands, cell growth, fatty acid production, metabolism of carbohydrate, fat, protein, utilization of B complex vitamins.

Deficiency symptoms: depression, dry skin, fatigue, grayish skin color, insomnia, muscular pain, poor appetite, boils.

Therapeutic uses: baldness, dermatitis, eczema, leg cramps.

Therapeutic dosage: 300–500 mcg/day.

RDA: 150–300 mcg/day.

No toxicity.

Synergies: B complex, C, sulphur.

Antagonists: alcohol, avidin (raw egg white), coffee, antibiotics, sulfa drugs, partially destroyed by cooking.

Natural food sources: whole grains, legumes, eggs, organ meats, sardines, nutritional yeast.

Natural vitamin sources: yeast.

Choline: Water soluble, a basic constituent of lecithin, also combines with other ingredients in the liver to produce lecithin; a member of the B complex.

Body parts nourished: eyes, hair, heart, circulatory system, kidneys, liver, thymus gland.

Body functions aided: lecithin formation, liver and gall bladder regulation, fat and cholesterol dissolution, nerve transmission, strengthening of capillary walls.

Deficiency symptoms: atherosclerosis, ateriosclerosis, bleeding stomach ulcers, growth problems, heart trouble, high blood pressure, impaired liver and kidney function, intolerance to fats.

Therapeutic uses: alcoholism, atherosclerosis, arteriosclerosis, baldness, high cholesterol, constipation, dizziness, ear noises, hardening of the arteries, headaches, heart trouble, high blood pressure, hypoglycemia, insomnia.

Therapeutic dosage: 100–1,000 mg/day.

No RDA.

No toxicity.

Synergies: A, B complex, linoleic acid.

Antagonists: alcohol, coffee, excessive sugar.

Natural food sources: green leafy vegetables, eggs, organ meats, fish, soybeans, wheat germ, nutritional yeast.

Natural vitamin sources: soybean powder, yeast.

Folic Acid: Water soluble, small amount stored in liver, 75 percent of intake excreted in urine within 24 hours, a member of the B complex.

Body parts nourished: blood, bone marrow, liver, kidneys, lymph nodes.

Body functions aided: appetite, body growth, maintenance of sex organs, hydrochloric acid production, protein metabolism, red blood cell formation.

Deficiency symptoms: anemia, birth defects, digestive disturbances, graying hair, growth problems, inflamed tongue.

Therapeutic uses: alcoholism, anemia, atherosclerosis, baldness, diarrhea, dropsy, fatigue, menstrual problems, mental illness, stomach and leg ulcers, stress.

Therapeutic dosage: 1,000–10,000 mcg.

RDA: 400 mcg/day.

No toxicity.

Synergies: B complex, C, E.

Antagonists: alcohol, coffee, stress, sulfa drugs, tobacco.

Natural food sources: whole grains, root vegetables, green leafy vegetables, organ meats, tuna fish, oysters, salmon, dairy products, nutritional yeast.

Natural vitamin sources: yeast.

Inositol: Water soluble, a basic constituent of lecithin, also combined with other ingredients in the liver to produce lecithin; a member of the B complex.

Body parts nourished: brain, eyes, hair, heart, kidneys, liver, muscles, stomach.

Body functions aided: retards hardening of the arteries, reduces cholesterol formation, promotes hair growth, stimulates intestines, contributes to lecithin formation, fat metabolism.

Deficiency symptoms: arteriosclerosis, atherosclerosis, high cholesterol count, constipation, eczema, eye abnormalities, hair loss.

Therapeutic uses: arteriosclerosis, atherosclerosis, cirrhosis of the liver, high cholesterol, constipation, heart disease, glaucoma, obesity.

Therapeutic dosage: 100–1,000 mg.

No RDA.

No toxicity.

Synergies: B complex, linoleic acid.

Antagonists: alcohol, coffee.

Natural food sources: whole grains, nuts, milk, meat, citrus fruits, nutritional yeast.

Natural vitamin sources: soybean powder, corn flour, yeast, lecithin.

Niacin (Nicotinic Acid, Vitamin B3): *Niacinamide is the synthetic form.* Water soluble, stored in liver, most abundant vitamin in the human body, 33 percent of intake excreted in 24 hours, a member of the B complex. Niacin ingestion is related to ingestion of the amino acid tryptophan, which can be converted to niacin in the body. The conversion rate is one milligram niacin per 60 milligram tryptophan.

Body parts nourished: brain, eyes, heart, liver, nerves, skin, soft tissue, tongue.

Body functions aided: circulation, growth, hydrochloric acid production, metabolism of protein, fat carbohydrate, reduction of cholesterol count, production of sex hormones.

Deficiency symptoms: appetite loss, canker sores, depression, fatigue, halitosis, headaches, indigestion, insomnia, muscular weakness, nausea, nervous disorders, skin eruptions, vomiting in severe cases, pellagra.

Therapeutic uses: acne, baldness, diarrhea, halitosis, high blood pressure, leg cramps, migraine headaches, night blindness, hypertension, poor circulation, stress, tooth decay.

Therapeutic dosage: 50–5,000 mg.

RDA:
Children, 8–15 mg/day
Adult male, 18 mg/day
Adult female, 13 mg/day; pregnancy, 15 mg/day; lactation, 20 mg/day.

No toxicity, but there are temporary (15 minute) side effects: tingling and flushing, both harmless. The synthetic form, niacinamide, does not have the tingling and flushing side effects but acne and migraine headaches do not respond as well to niacinamide.

Synergies: B complex, C, phosphorus.

Antagonists: alcohol, antibiotics, coffee, excessive sugar and refined carbohydrate—but very stable to heat, light and oxygen.

Natural food sources: whole wheat, green vegetables, legumes, nuts, fish, poultry, lean meat, milk, nutritional yeast.

Natural vitamin sources: yeast, bran.

Pantothenic Acid (Calcium Pantothenate): Water soluble, an average of 25 percent of daily intake is excreted, but deficiencies are rare as it is widely distributed in foods, a member of the B complex.

Body parts nourished: adrenal glands, brain, digestive tract, heart, liver, kidneys, nerves, skin.

Body functions aided: adrenal function, antibody formation, energy production via conversion of fat and protein, fat synthesis, regulates water metabolism, growth stimulation, vitamin utilization.

Deficiency symptoms: blood imbalance, diarrhea, duodenal ulcers, eczema, hypoglycemia, intestinal disorders, kidney trouble, loss of hair, muscle cramps, premature aging, respiratory infections, restlessness, nerve problems, sore feet, vomiting.

Therapeutic uses: Addison's disease, allergies, arthritis, baldness, cystitis, diabetes, fatigue, depression, alcoholism, digestive disorders, hypoglycemia, tooth decay, stress, vertigo, postoperative shock, wound healing.

Therapeutic dosage: 50–200 mg.

Protects: against radiation.

RDA: 10–15 mg/day.

No toxicity.

Synergies: B complex, C.

Antagonists: alcohol, coffee, up to 45 percent lost in cooking.

Natural food sources: whole grains, eggs, legumes, organ meats, oranges, peas, mushrooms, salmon, molasses, nutritional yeast.

Natural vitamin sources: yeast.

Para Aminobenzoic Acid (PABA): Water soluble, stored in body tissue, synthesized by intestinal flora under favorable conditions, a member of the B complex.

Body parts nourished: glands, hair, intestines, skin.

Body functions aided: blood cell formation, intestinal flora activity, protein metabolism, restoration of color to gray hair, skin health.

Deficiency symptoms: constipation, depression, digestive disorders, fatigue, gray hair, headaches, irritability, nervousness.

Therapeutic uses: Internal: baldness, graying hair, overactive thyroid, parasitic diseases (Rocky Mountain spotted fever), rheumatic fever, stress, infertility.
   External: burns, dark skin spots, dry skin, sunburn, wrinkles.

Therapeutic dosage: 10–100 mg.

No RDA.

Toxicity: continued high doses (over 30 mg) can be toxic to liver, heart, and kidneys; symptoms are nausea and vomiting.

Synergies: B complex, C.

Antagonists: alcohol, coffee, sulfa drugs.

Natural food sources: green leafy vegetables, organ meats, yogurt, wheat germ, molasses, nutritional yeast.

Natural vitamin sources: yeast.

Pangamic Acid (Vitamin B15): Water soluble, little is known about absorption and storage, excreted in urine, feces and sweat, the common form is calcium pangamate; a member of the B complex.

Body parts nourished: glands, heart, kidneys, nerves.

Body functions aided: cell oxidation and respiration, metabolism of protein, fat and sugar, stimulation of glandular and nervous systems.

Deficiency symptoms: diminished oxygenation of cells, heart disease, nervous and glandular disorders.

Therapeutic uses: alcoholism, asthma, atherosclerosis, emphysema, headaches, high cholesterol, insomnia, poor circulation, premature aging, rheumatism, shortness of breath, hypertension.

Therapeutic dosage: 5–10 mg (?—research not highly advanced).

Protects: against carbon monoxide and oxygen deficiency of polluted air.

No RDA.

No known toxicity.

Synergies: A, B complex, C, E.

Antagonists: alcohol, coffee.

Natural food sources: nuts and seeds.

Natural vitamin sources: apricot kernels.

Vitamin C (Ascorbic Acid)

Water soluble, a small amount stored in the adrenal cortex, otherwise most is eliminated within four hours of ingestion by urine and perspiration, therefore it is better taken in frequent small doses.

An unorthodox view of this vitamin is that it should be considered a complex, as vitamin B is, since C is always found naturally complexed with bioflavinoids (vitamin P). From this viewpoint, ascorbic acid would refer to the synthetic form, vitamin C the natural, including vitamin P within it. In any case, most nutritionists agree that the efficacy of ascorbic acid (synthetic) is enhanced by the accompaniment of natural C.

Body parts nourished: adrenal cortex, adrenal glands, blood, capillaries, collagen (connective tissue—skin, ligaments, bones), gums, heart, pituitary, ovaries, liver, teeth.

Body functions aided: absorption of iron; bone and tooth formation; collagen production; digestion; iodine conservation; healing; maintenance of capillaries; resistance to colds, infections and shock; protection against oxidation of nutrients.

Deficiency symptoms: anemia, bleeding gums, fragile capillaries, dental cavities, low resistance to colds and other infections, nosebleeds, poor digestion, poor lactation, tendency to bruise easily, swollen or painful joints, slow healing, in extreme cases scurvy.

Therapeutic uses: alcoholism, allergies, atherosclerosis, arthritis, baldness, carbon monoxide and heavy metal poisoning, colds, cystitis, drug addiction, hypoglycemia, heart disease, hepatitis, insect bites, obesity, prickly heat, sinusitis, stress, tooth decay.

Therapeutic dosage: 250–5,000 mg.

Protects: vital organs and glands against nitrates and nitrites, radiation, and acute infections.

RDA:
Children, 40 mg/day
Male adults, 60 mg/day.
Female adults, 55 mg/day, pregnancy and lactation, 60 mg/day.
Needs increased by infection, stress, trauma, allergies, old age, increased protein consumption.

Toxicity: no toxicity, but more than 5,000 mg. may produce unpleasant side effects.

Synergies: all other vitamins and all the minerals.

Antagonists: antibiotics, aspirin, cortisone, high fever, stress, tobacco, oxidation in food while in storage, leaching while soaking, cooking, copper utensils, baking soda.

Natural food sources: tomatoes, citrus fruits, peppers, alfalfa sprouts, papaya, greens, cabbage, berries, cantaloupe, broccoli.

Natural vitamin sources: acerola cherries, rose hips, citrus fruits.

Vitamin D

Fat soluble, stored in liver, brain, spleen, skin, manufactured by the interaction of the sun's ultraviolet rays and a form of cholesterol in the skin.

Body parts nourished: bones, heart, kidney, liver, skin, teeth, thyroid gland.

Body functions aided: calcium and phosphorus metabolism (bone and tooth formation), heart action, blood clotting, maintenance of nervous system, skin respiration.

Deficiency symptoms: burning sensation in mouth and throat, diarrhea, insomnia, myopia, nervousness, poor metabolism, softening of bones and teeth, in extreme cases rickets in children.

Therapeutic uses: acne, alcoholism, allergies, arthritis, cystitis, colds, eczema, eye disorders, psoriasis, stress.

Therapeutic dosage: 500–1,500 I.U.

RDA: 400 I.U./day.

Toxicity: 25,000 I.U.

Synergies: A, choline, niacin, C, F, calcium, phosphorus.

Antagonists: mineral oil.

Natural food sources: butter, eggs, organ meats, herring, sardines, salmon, tuna, bone meal, (sunshine).

Natural vitamin sources: fish liver oil.

Vitamin E (Tocopherol)

Fat soluble, small amounts stored in liver and fatty tissue, 65 percent of ingested dose appears in feces. There are seven forms of tocopherol, alpha tocopherol being the one of most nutritional value.

Body parts nourished: blood vessels, genitals, heart, bone marrow, muscles, nerves, pituitary gland, skin.

Body functions aided: enhances oxygenation of blood, reduces cholesterol, increases fertility and male potency, facilitates blood flow to heart, strengthens capillaries, protection of lungs, maintenance of muscles and nerves.

Deficiency symptoms: dry, dull, or falling hair; enlarged prostate gland; gastrointestinal disease; heart disease; impotency; miscarriages; nephritis; premature birth; sterility; wasting muscles.

Therapeutic uses: allergies, arthritis, atherosclerosis, baldness, cystitis, diabetes, heart disease, high cholesterol, menstrual problems, menopause, migraine headaches, myopia, obesity, phlebitis, sinusitis, stress, thrombosis, varicose veins. Applied to skin: burns, scars, warts, wrinkles, wounds.

Therapeutic dosage: 50–800 I.U.

Protects: against poisons in air, food, and water, radiation, and drugs that interfere with oxygenation.

RDA:
Children, 15 I.U./day
Female adults, 25 I.U./day
Male adults, 30 I.U./day

Toxicity: more than 2,000 I.U.; amounts in this range can be fatal to sufferers of chronic rheumatic heart disease. It is advisable for people with chronic heart ailments to start with small amounts, gradually increasing the dosage into the therapeutic range.

Synergies: A, B complex, C, F, K, manganese, selenium, phosphorus.

Antagonists: birth control pills, chlorine, mineral oil, rancid fat and oil.

Natural food sources: whole grains, dark green vegetables, unrefined vegetable oils, eggs, nuts, sweet potatoes, organ meats, wheat germ.

Natural vitamin sources: wheat germ oil, other vegetable oils; "mixed tocopherols" and "d-alpha tocopherol acetate" indicates a mixture of natural and synthetic sources; all sources identified with the prefix "dl" are synthetic.

Vitamin F (Unsaturated Fatty Acids)

Fat soluble, small amount stored in the liver; there are three essential unsaturated fatty acids: linoleic, linolenic, and arachidonic. Sufficient linoleic acid will provide for the synthesis of the other two.

Body parts nourished: adrenals, thyroid, hair, mucus membrane, nerves, skin.

Body functions aided: blood coagulation, reduces cholesterol, prevents hardening of the arteries, normalizes blood pressure, glandular activity, growth, respiration of organs.

Deficiency symptoms: acne, allergies, diarrhea, dry skin and hair, eczema, gall stones, nail problems, underweight, varicose veins.

Therapeutic uses: allergies, baldness, bronchial asthma, high cholesterol, eczema, gall bladder problems, heart disease, leg ulcers, psoriasis, rheumatoid arthritis, weight regulation.

Therapeutic dosage: four tablespoons of vegetable oil.

Protects: against x-rays.

No RDA.

No toxicity.

Synergies: A, C, D, E, phosphorus.

Antagonists: radiation, x-rays.

Natural food sources: butter, nuts and seeds and their butters, unrefined vegetable oils.

Natural vitamin sources: unrefined vegetable oils.

Vitamin K

Fat soluble, small amount stored in the liver, necessary to promote blood clotting, usually synthesized in adequate amounts by intestinal flora.

Body parts nourished: blood, liver.

Body functions aided: blood clotting.

Deficiency symptoms: diarrhea, excessive bleeding, miscarriages, nosebleeds.

Therapeutic uses: bruising, eye hemorrhages, gall stones, hemorrhaging, menstrual problems, preparation for childbirth.

Therapeutic dosage: 300–500 mcg.

No RDA.

No toxicity in natural form, but over 500 mcg. in synthetic form is toxic.

Synergies are unknown.

Antagonists: aspirin, antibiotics, mineral oil, radiation, rancid fats, x-rays.

Natural food sources: alfalfa, green leafy vegetables, unrefined vegetable oil, fish liver oil, cauliflower, soybeans, eggs, milk, yogurt, kelp, molasses.

Natural vitamin sources: alfalfa.

Vitamin P (Bioflavinoids, Rutin, Hesperidin)

Water soluble, occurring with natural food sources of Vitamin C, acting in conjunction and thereby increasing the effectiveness of C.

Body parts nourished: blood, capillaries, connective tissue.

Body functions aided: same as vitamin C.

Deficiency symptoms: same as vitamin C.

Therapeutic uses: same as vitamin C.

Therapeutic dosage: 500–3,000 mg.

No RDA.

No toxicity.

Synergistic with vitamin C.

Antagonists: antibiotics, aspirin, cortisone, fever, stress, tobacco.

Natural food sources: buckwheat, cherries, grapes, black currants, green peppers.

Natural vitamin sources: citrus skins, green peppers, black currants.

MINERALS

Whereas vitamins are organic in the purely chemical sense of having carbon incorporated into their molecular structure, minerals are inorganic. They are generally thought to be inert, though future science will probably identify a hitherto unrecognized level of activity. Once incorporated into the human system, minerals become highly active, participating in all biochemical processes. Due to faulty agricultural practices, mineral deficiencies are common to our farmland; therefore, nutritional mineral deficiencies are commonplace in our people—even more so than vitamin deficiencies, in themselves all too ubiquitous.

Calcium

The most abundant mineral in your body, 99 percent found in bones and teeth, 1 percent circulating in the bloodstream. It is the most difficult mineral to assimilate, 70–80 percent of ingested calcium being excreted in feces.

Body parts nourished: bones, teeth, blood, heart, connective tissue.

Body functions aided: formation of bones and teeth, blood clotting, contraction of heart and other muscles, nerve transmission and tranquilization.

Deficiency symptoms: tooth decay, irregular heartbeat, muscle cramps, insomnia, nervousness, numbness of arms and legs, depression, irritability, retarded growth, brittle bones, tetany.

Therapeutic uses: dental problems, arthritis, rheumatism, backache, bone and muscle pain, sleeplessness, trembling hands, menstrual cramps, nerve and menopause problems.

Therapeutic dosage: 1,000–2,000 mg.

RDA:
Children, 1,000–1,400 mg.
Adults, 800 mg.
Pregnant or nursing women, 100–1,400 mg.

Protects: 2 to 1 ratio calcium to magnesium (100 mg/50 mg) protects against heavy metals and radioactive metals.

Toxic level: Unknown, but excessive calcium intake probably has harmful side effects.

Synergies: vitamins A, D, F, C, iron, magnesium, phosphorus (ratio of 1 to 2.5 calcium), manganese, hydrochloric acid.

Antagonists: lack of exercise, hydrochloric acid, vitamin D, and excessive stress.

Natural food sources: dairy products, deep green leafy vegetables, sea vegetables, the cabbage family, carob, almonds, sesame seeds.

Note: The general difficulty of assimilation of calcium is associated with the strength of the bonds it establishes with other minerals in order to be structurally strong enough to become teeth and bones. Calcium is the key element in strong structures throughout the natural world, including the earth, as limestone and dolomite rock. Whenever we ingest calcium in the complex form—that is, bonded with other minerals—our digestive processes are able to split apart very little of it for assimilation into our blood, bones, teeth, and other cells. In other words, the strength which is so precious to us is also an obstacle. Calcium can only be truly easy to assimilate in the ionized (uncombined) form, of which little is found in nature. Looking to calcium supplements, dolomite, oyster shell, bone meal, and calcium lactate are all complex forms of calcium, with lactate the easiest to assimilate, dolomite the hardest. Perhaps the easiest of all supplemental forms of calcium to assimilate is *amino acid chelated calcium*, in which the ionized mineral is bonded with protein instead of other minerals.

Copper

Facilitates iron absorption and formation of red blood cells, RNA, and many enzymes involved in protein and vitamin C metabolism. Also involved in formation of myelin, the protective sheath of nerve fiber, and elastin, chief component of elastic muscle fibers. 70 percent of ingested copper is excreted in the feces.

Body parts nourished: blood, bones, muscle, brain, nerves, hair, skin.

Body functions aided: healing; formation of hemoglobin (oxygen-carrying element of red blood cells); maintenance of muscle tone; hair and skin coloring.

Deficiency symptoms: anemia, faulty breathing, general weakness, graying of hair, skin sores.

Therapeutic uses: anemia, leukemia, osteoporosis, baldness, bedsores, edema.

Therapeutic dosage: 2–4 mg.

RDA: 2 mg.

Toxic level: 40 mg.

Synergies: cobalt, iron, zinc.

Antagonists: excessive zinc.

Natural food sources: whole grains, green leafy vegetables, legumes, liver, fish, raisins, prunes, and pomegranates.

Iodine

Essential to development of the thyroid gland and its hormone, thyroxin, which promotes growth, prevents goiter, and regulates energy production. 70 percent of ingested iodine is excreted in the urine.

Body parts nourished: thyroid gland, hair, nails, skin, teeth.

Body functions aided: energy production and prevention of anemia; normal growth and development.

Deficiency symptoms: enlarged thyroid (goiter); dry hair; dry, rough and wrinkled skin; obesity; slow pulse; low blood pressure; cretinism in babies born to iodine-deficient women.

Therapeutic uses: angina pectoris, arterio- and atherosclerosis, hyper- and hypothyroidism, arthritis, hair and skin problems, lack of vigor.

Therapeutic dosage: 100–1,000 mcg.

RDA:
Women, 100 mcg.
Men, 130 mcg.

Protects: against radioactive iodine and reduces absorption of strontium 90 (as 2 t. or 10 tablets of kelp daily).

No known toxicity at therapeutic levels, but more may be dangerous.

No known synergies.

No known antagonists.

Natural food sources: fish and sea vegetables.

Iron

The "anti-anemia" mineral, it combines with copper and protein to form hemoglobin, the red coloring element which transports oxygen in the blood, and myoglobin, which transports oxygen in muscle tissue. Very little iron is destroyed by metabolism; most of it is recycled. But only about 5 percent of ingested iron is absorbed.

Body parts nourished: blood, bones, nails, skin, teeth.

Body functions aided: oxygen delivery to cells for efficient metabolism and muscle contraction.

Deficiency symptoms: difficult breathing, brittle and ridged nails, constipation, pale skin, fatigue.

Therapeutic uses: anemia, alcoholism, colitis, diabetes, nephritis, menstrual difficulties, peptic ulcers.

Therapeutic dosage: 15–50 mg.

RDA:
Women, 18 mg.
Men, 10 mg.

Toxic level: 100 mg.

Synergies: vitamins B12, folic acid, C, and E, cobalt, copper, calcium, hydrochloric acid.

Antagonists: coffee, tea, excess phosphorus, and zinc.

Natural food sources: organ meats, lean meat, fish, eggs, molasses, wheat germ, green leafy vegetables.

Magnesium

The "tranquility mineral," deficiencies due to food refining are widespread. About 70 percent is combined with calcium and phosphorus in the bones.

Body parts nourished: nervous and circulatory systems, bones and teeth, muscles.

Body functions aided: promotes absorption and utilization of carbohydrates, fats, protein, vitamins B, C, and E, and other minerals. Aids blood sugar metabolism and acid/alkaline balance.

Deficiency symptoms: confusion, disorientation, apprehensiveness, muscle twitching and tremors, rapid pulse, short temper.

Therapeutic uses: alcoholism, nervousness, kidney stones, osteoporosis, arthritis, backache, excessively acid stomach, convulsions.

Therapeutic dosage: 300–500 mg.

RDA:
Women, 300 mg.
Men, 350 mg.

Protects: 1 to 2 ratio magnesium to calcium (500 mg/1,000 mg) protects against heavy metals and radioactive metals.

Toxic level: 30,000 mg.

Synergies: vitamins B6, C, and D, calcium, phosphorus, and protein.

No known antagonists.

Natural food sources: green vegetables, whole grains, lima beans, almonds, corn, figs, apples, celery, seeds, unrefined oils.

Phosphorus

The second most abundant mineral in the body, in the ratio of 2.5 parts calcium to 1 part phosphorus, present in every body cell. Most ingested phosphorus is absorbed, roughly 90 percent found in bones and teeth; solid brain matter is phosphorized fats (although 85 percent of your brain is water).

Body parts nourished: bones, teeth, brain, nerves.

Body functions aided: cell division and reproduction, heredity, heart and other muscular contractions, transference of nerve impulses, growth, repair, bone and tooth formation.

Deficiency symptoms: stunted growth, nervous disorders, loss of appetite, irregular breathing, fatigue, dental disease (phosphorus is the least common mineral deficiency).

Therapeutic uses: stunted growth, tooth and gum disorders, arthritis, backache.

Therapeutic dosage: 800–1,000 mg.

RDA: 800 mg.

No known toxicity.

Synergies: vitamins A, D, F, calcium, iron, manganese, protein.

Antagonists: aluminum salts from cookware, excessive iron, magnesium, sugar.

Natural food sources: all protein-rich foods are also rich in phosphorus, as are raisins, whole grains, and mushrooms; deficiencies are rare—which is not the case with other minerals.

Potassium

The fourth most abundant mineral in the body—following calcium, phosphorus, and magnesium—it is 5 percent of your total mineral content.

Body parts nourished: blood, heart, kidneys, nerves, muscles, skin.

Body functions aided: responsible for transmitting electrical impulses, potassium with magnesium controls the heartbeat; working with sodium, it controls the balance of fluid between bloodstream and cells; aids in conversion of glucose to blood sugar, enzyme reactions, kidney function, and synthesis of muscle tissue from amino acids.

Deficiency symptoms: slow, irregular heart beat; nervousness; insomnia; continual thirst; poor reflexes; constipation; acne; muscle paralysis; dry skin. Due to excessive salt intake, deficiencies are widespread.

Therapeutic uses: angina, congestive heart failure, myocardial infarction, alcoholism, arthritis, diabetes, impaired muscle activity, acne, hypertension, dermatitis.

Therapeutic dosage: 100–300 mg.

No RDA.

No known toxicity.

Synergies: vitamin B6, sodium.

Antagonists: alcohol, coffee, cortisone, laxatives, diuretics, stress, excessive sugar and salt.

Natural food sources: green leafy vegetables, whole grains, oranges, sunflower seeds, bananas, nuts, molasses, milk, potatoes (skins).

Sodium

Found in all body fluids, sodium is after phosphorus the least likely mineral deficiency. About 90 percent of ingested sodium is generally excreted in the urine.

Body parts nourished: blood, lymph, muscles, nerves.

Body functions aided: regulation of fluid balance, muscle contraction, nerve stimulation, acid/alkaline balance (all with potassium); keeping other minerals soluble, hydrochloric acid production.

Deficiency symptoms: intestinal gas, weight loss, vomiting, neuralgia, muscle shrinkage (sodium deficiencies are rare).

Therapeutic uses: dehydration, fever, heat stroke, muscle cramps.

Therapeutic dosage: 100–300 mg.

RDA: 200–600 mg.

Toxic level: 14,000 mg.

Synergies: vitamin D, potassium.

No known antagonists.

Natural food sources: plant and animal seafood, celery, carrots, beets, asparagus, chard, romaine lettuce, apples.

Sulphur

Known as "the beauty mineral" because it keeps hair glossy and complexion clear, found in all plant and animal cells.

Body parts nourished: skin, hair, nails, nerves.

Body functions aided: cell formation and respiration, synthesis of collagen, keratin, insulin, and bile.

No known deficiency symptoms.

Therapeutic uses: topically in ointments for skin disorders.

No RDA or known toxicity or antagonists.

Synergies: B complex, biotin, pantothenic acid.

Natural food sources: protein foods, bran, cabbage, kale, brussel sprouts.

Zinc

"The enzyme mineral" because it is a constituent of so many enzymes and is active in so many processes. Stored in organs, muscles, bones, blood, skin, hair, nails, prostate gland, and sperm.

Body parts nourished: blood, liver, prostate.

Body functions aided: glycogen production, wound and burn healing, vitamin absorption, enzyme action, alcohol and other carbohydrate digestion, protein and phosphorus metabolism, prostate function, growth and development of reproductive glands.

Deficiency symptoms: delayed healing of wounds, delayed sexual maturity, sterility, retarded growth, fatigue, lost sense of taste and smell, poor appetite, decreased alertness and learning ability, white spots on fingernails.

Therapeutic uses: wounds, cholesterol deposits, prostatitis, diabetes, alcoholism, infertility, atherosclerosis.

Therapeutic dosage: 20–100 mg.

RDA: 15 mg.

Protects: against toxicity of marijuana.

No known toxicity.

Synergies: vitamin A, calcium, copper, phosphorus.

Antagonists: alcohol, birth control pills.

Natural food sources: whole grains, pumpkin seeds, nutritional yeast, liver.

Minor (Trace) Minerals

Some authorities classify copper, iodine, iron, and zinc as trace minerals. I have described them as major minerals because so much is known about their roles in human nutrition. Less is known about the other essential trace minerals. A partial list (43 trace minerals have been identified in tooth enamel alone):

boron	molybdenum	strontium
chromium	lithium	tin
cobalt	selenium	tritium
fluorine	silicon	vanadium
manganese		

THE TOP TEN MINERAL-RICH FOODS

Food	Excellent Source of
Calves liver	magnesium, zinc, copper, iron, selenium, chromium, cobalt
Beef liver	zinc, copper, iron, selenium, chromium, cobalt
Chicken liver	zinc, iron, selenium, chromium, cobalt
Oysters	zinc, copper, iron, selenium, cobalt
Sardines	calcium, potassium, selenium, cobalt, fluorine
Crab	zinc, selenium, cobalt, fluorine
Salmon	calcium, potassium, selenium, fluorine
Cod	selenium, iodine, fluorine
Mackerel	selenium, cobalt, fluorine
Shrimp	selenium, iodine, fluorine

(Source: *The Complete Book of Minerals for Health*, Faelten, Rodale Press).

Appendix Four A Cost Analysis of America's Most Popular Fast Foods—Hamburger, Fried Chicken, Pizza—and How to Do Them Better

THE BURGER

Fast Food

1 Big Mac	$1.20
2 Quarter Pounders	2.20
1 Cheeseburger	.60
3 Fries	1.35
4 Shakes	2.60
4 Pies	1.60
Total	$9.55

Convenience Food

1 lb. ground chuck	$1.88
4 enriched white burger buns	.30
Extras: 4 oz. jack cheese, .57; ½ lb. tomatoes, .40; ½ head lettuce, .17; 1 med. onion, .12; pickles, .08	1.34
24 oz. frozen french fries	.90
4 shakes (1 qt. milk, .54; 1 qt. ice cream, 1.45)	1.99
frozen pie for four	1.09
Total	$7.50

Preparation time: approximately 30 minutes	
Dollar difference against *Fast Food*:	$2.35
Saving:	25%

Natural Homemade

1 lb. lean ground beef, naturally fed	$1.98
4 whole wheat burger buns	.28
extras: 4 oz. jack cheese, .47; ½ lb. tomatoes, .30; ½ head lettuce, .15; 1 med. onion, .08; pickles, .08	1.08
1½ lbs. potatoes	.38
¼ cup veg. oil (oven fries)	.12
4 shakes (1 qt. milk, .47; 1 qt. honey ice cream, 1.85)	2.32
Pie for four	.77
Total	$6.93

Preparation time: approximately 50 minutes	
Dollar difference against *Convenience*:	$ .57
Saving:	8%
Dollar difference against *Fast Food*:	$2.62
Saving:	27%

Note: The beef would not be available in many natural food stores. Some supermarket-sized natural foods stores have full service fresh butcher departments. Smaller natural food stores generally carry only frozen meat and this is invariably more expensive; if it were 50% higher, which would not be unusual, the natural from scratch version of this meal would be virtually the same as the convenience version. In a case where fresh, naturally fed beef were not available and the frozen considered too expensive, conventional ground chuck would be the logical choice.

This comparison could also be invalidated by higher produce prices. I have made a hypothetical comparison with the natural food store being 50% higher on both meat and produce. In such a case, the natural homemade version would be more expensive than the convenience version but less than the fast food version: $8.31.

Dollar difference against Convenience:	−.81
Saving:	−11%
Dollar difference against Fast Food:	1.24
Saving:	13%

I have started with the most problematical and least impressive comparison. Even so, it shows that significant savings are possible for home preparation with natural foods compared to both fast and convenience foods. The case will become more dramatically clear.

FRIED CHICKEN

Fast Food

12 piece Family Banquet, including
2 pts. salad
1 pt. mashed potatoes
1 pt. gravy

5 rolls		$8.75
4 pies		2.60
2 cokes		.90
1 punch		.60
1 coffee		.45
	Total	$13.30

Convenience Food

2 lbs. assorted precooked frozen fried chicken		$2.59
2 14 oz. containers of salad—coleslaw		.93
2 pts. frozen potatoes with cheese sauce		2.20
5 rolls		.40
pie for four (1 lb. frozen apple)		1.09
2 cokes		.66
2 punch		.70
	Total	$8.57

Preparation time: approximately 20 min.

Dollar difference against *Fast Food:*	$4.73
Saving:	36%

Natural Homemade

2 lbs. fresh fryer chicken pieces	$1.58
½ cup whole wheat flour	.07
⅓ cup vegetable oil (.16) or butter (.21)	.21
(wheat and oil or butter for oven frying)	
coleslaw for four: 1½ lbs. cabbage, .23;	
1 carrot, .08; ½ cup mayonnaise, .25	.56
3 cups mashed potatoes: 1½ lbs. potatoes, .38;	
½ cup milk, .06; 2 T. butter, .10	.54
1 cup chicken gravy: chicken fat; 1 T.	
wholewheat pastry flour, .01; ½ cup milk, .06;	
½ cup water	.07
5 wholewheat rolls	.53
4 natural sodas	1.44
pie for four	<u>.77</u>
Total	$5.77

Preparation time: approximately 1 hour	
Dollar difference against *Convenience*:	$2.80
Saving:	33%
Dollar difference against *Fast Food*:	$7.53
Saving:	57%

Note: Again, many natural food stores will only have frozen chicken and again, this could cost as much as 50% more than fresh. Even so, in this case, the natural homemade version would be much cheaper than either the convenience or fast food versions. Even if the vegetables were 50% higher, this version would still be cheaper.

PIZZA

Fast Food

sausage, pepperoni, peppers	$9.14
2 salads	2.62
2 beers	1.50
2 sodas	<u>1.00</u>
Total	$14.26

Convenience

sausage, pepperoni, peppers 2 lb.	$4.38
2 salads (14 oz. ea. coleslaw & potato)	1.78
2 beers	.70
2 sodas	<u>.66</u>
Total	$7.52
Preparation time: approximately 20 minutes	
Dollar difference against *Fast Food*:	$6.74
Saving:	47%

Natural Homemade

sausage (nitrate free) and peppers pizza	
topping: ¼ lb. sausage	$.43
1 large pepper	.20
1 cup tomato sauce	.21
¼ lb. jack cheese	.47
¼ lb. mozzarella cheese	.59
dough: 2 cups wholewheat flour	.28
1 T. oil	.03
½ package yeast	.11
½ t. salt	.01
sausage and peppers pizza total	2.32
salad for two (coleslaw)	.28
4 natural sodas	1.44
Total	$4.48
Preparation time: approximately 1 hour 15 minutes	
Dollar difference against *Convenience*:	$3.04
Saving:	40%
Dollar difference against *Fast Food*:	$9.78
Savings:	69%

SUMMARY

Burger Meal: Homemade Version	
Saving vs. Convenience version:	8%
Saving vs. Fast Food version:	27%
Fried Chicken Meal: Homemade Version	
Saving vs. Convenience version	33%
Saving vs. Fast Food version	69%
Pizza Meal: Homemade Version	
Saving vs. Convenience version	46%
Saving vs. Fast Food version	72%

When all meal costs are averaged, natural homemade versions save 27% against convenience versions and 51% against fast food versions.

At the point at which hamburgers, fried chickens, and sausage pizzas are the mainstays of their diets, people still have some basic changes to make in order to participate fully in the New American Cuisine. Nevertheless, cooking from scratch is the first step; once it is mastered for these kinds of foods, other steps invariably follow. Here is how they are done.

MAKING THE BIG THREE NATURALLY

The Burger

Preheat oven to 425°.
Start with your potatoes: Wash, and, leaving the skins on, cut lengthwise into ½″ strips. Place on a cookie sheet, single layer, and coat with vegetable oil or melted butter (about ¼ cup). Bake 35 to 40 minutes. Turn them over with a spatula after 20 minutes.

Make hamburger patties.
Slice up the cheese, tomatoes and onions. Wash and drain lettuce. Arrange on a plate with pickles.

In the blender, mix up the milk shakes (raw milk, natural honey-sweetened ice cream, fruit, and/or natural flavors and spices). When done, place in the freezer if you like them icy, in the refrigerator if you like them just plain cold.

  After the potatoes have cooked for ½ hour, start frying the burger patties. When the potatoes and burgers are done, serve.

Preparation time: approximately 50 minutes.

Note: The biggest qualitative improvements above result from using whole wheat hamburger buns (or bread) and by making French fries from whole potatoes, using a minimum of good quality vegetable oil or butter. The next big step would be in using naturally fed or grass fed beef. After that, you might further improve by finding organically grown lettuce and tomatoes and cheese made from raw milk. The ultimate quality improvements result from making your own pies, ice cream, mayonnaise, and catsup from scratch.

Fried Chicken

Preheat oven to 400°.
Rinse chicken pieces and dust with whole wheat flour (season if you like). Place chicken pieces in a large baking pan. Dot with butter or drizzle oil over the pieces. Put in oven. After 10 minutes, turn down oven heat to 325° and cook 45 minutes to 1 hour until done.

Wash and cut potatoes into medium sized chunks. Do not peel. Preferably steam, otherwise cook in very little water, covered, until tender (approximately 15 minutes).

Meanwhile, grate the cabbage and carrot, add mayonnaise and seasoning. The coleslaw is done; refrigerate.

Back to the potatoes. Remove from water. Mash, and add ½ cup hot milk slowly, plus 2 T. butter. Cover and place bowl or pot in hot water. If too cool, place potatoes in the oven when you remove the chicken, leaving the oven on low until you are ready to serve the potatoes.

For gravy, pour off 1 to 2 T. chicken fat from the chicken you have just removed from the oven. With a wire whisk, stir and heat in a frying pan. Gradually stir in 1 to 2 T. wholewheat pastry flour. Then add the milk and water, also gradually, until well mixed. Heat slowly until the gravy bubbles and thickens. Season, and serve your meal.

Preparation time: approximately 1 hour.

Note: A great qualitative improvement can be made if you are fortunate enough to find naturally fed chicken. Many times I have heard people exclaim about it, "This chicken really *tastes* like chicken!" But if your purpose is to duplicate or improve on the taste of fast-food fried chicken, look to the seasoning. Remember that Kentucky Fried Chicken ascribes their taste to a "secret blend of eleven herbs and spices." Your own secret blend should be mixed with the whole wheat flour used to coat the chicken before cooking. Experiment with salt, black pepper, cayenne pepper, parsley flakes, marjoram, sage, chervil, rosemary, oregano, thyme, basil, cumin, powdered garlic, powdered onion, fennel, anise, ginger, cloves . . . not all at once, certainly, but mixing according to what you know you like, what smells good to you, and the advice of spice and herb charts. You can replace up to one third of the flour with seasonings.

Pizza

Mix up your pizza dough. This is good practice for bread making, and even if it doesn't rise very well, your pizza will still taste great. Put ½ package of baker's yeast in ⅔ cup warm water. Gradually add 2 c. whole wheat flour and 1 T. vegetable oil, stirring vigorously to mix thoroughly. Knead for 10 minutes. Cover in a warm place and let rise until double (about 2 hours). Don't let it rise a second time as you would for bread.

Meanwhile, you can prepare your topping. Chop and sauté the sausage and peppers in a little vegetable oil for about 10 minutes. Add 1 t. each of oregano, sweet basil and marjoram if you wish while you sauté. Then add the tomato sauce for the final minute.
Grate the mozzarella and jack cheese as the sausage and pepper are sautéing.

Preheat oven to 400°.
When the pizza dough is ready, sprinkle a 12″ pizza pan with cornmeal. Spread out the dough to cover the pan, curling the dough over the edge. Lightly cover with vegetable oil; this will prevent the tomato sauce from making the crust soggy. Cover dough with topping, finishing with the cheese. Let stand for 10 minutes, then bake for ½ hour or until the top is bubbly and light brown.

Preparation time: about 1 hour 15 minutes preparation time, plus 1½ hours of waiting while the pizza dough rises.

Note: An important point in this recipe is that even a *sausage* pizza can be improved with the methods of the New American Cuisine. But the fact is that sausage fit to eat is truly hard to find. Most of it is made with parts of the carcass that would otherwise be considered inedible, loaded with fat, salt, and nitrates. Unless you're really stuck on the notion of sausage and ready to throw dietary prudence to the wind, consider substituting lean ground beef or tofu seasoned with soy sauce. No matter which you use, this pizza will be much thicker and heavier than anything available commercially.

It is practical for single people to make the Big Three naturally, even the pizza. If only one fourth of the recipe is consumed fresh from the oven, the other three quarters can be individually wrapped and refrigerated or frozen for three subsequent meals.

Observe that any kind of food you have learned to like in fast food restaurants can be made at home with natural ingredients, transforming dubious food into unquestionably good food. "But I

APPENDICES

don't know how to cook," I've heard people protest. Learning to cook is like learning to ride a bicycle: you learn to do it by doing it and the more you do it the better you get. Soon you are about as good at it as most everybody else. Making meals like the three above is analogous to discovering how it feels to sit on a bicycle seat and get your balance; in cooking you begin simply, learning how food acts, how to time and coordinate things, getting the feel of the manual tasks involved.

All the above recipes have been kept plain in order to keep my comparison with fast foods and convenience foods valid. But there are few cost constraints restraining you from making things taste more lively with the wide variety of herbs, spices, and condiments at your disposal—we are just talking about pinches here, dashes there, squirts somewhere else.

Appendix Five Natural Foods by Mail

Arrowhead Mills
Box 866
Hereford, TX 79045

One of the original natural foods manufacturers, founded by Frank Ford in 1960. When I first visited Arrowhead Mills in the mid-sixties, Frank had a stone mill, an old railroad car for an office, and a product line of eight. Returning my visit not long afterward in San Francisco, Frank asked me if I thought a company could become large and still maintain its integrity. I said yes and have had the pleasure of seeing Frank, a devout Christian, make that dream come true. Arrowhead Mills now has a modern twenty-acre manufacturing and storage facility and over 250 products accomplished with exacting quality standards. Although they ship mail order, the minimum is 300 pounds. Arrowhead Mills is also the manufacturer of the only completely natural home food storage program, known as The Simpler Life.

Bob Cooperrider
Rt. 1, Box 308
Sheridan, OR 97378

Butte Creek Mill
402 Royal Avenue N
Eagle Point, OR 97524

Deer Valley Farm
Guilford, NY 13780

Diamond K Enterprises
Rt. 1, Box 30
St. Charles, MN 55972

East West Journal
17 Station St.
Brookline, MA 02146

Edwards Mill
School of the Ozarks
Point Lookout, MO 65726

Fangorn Organic Farm
Rt. 3, Box 141B
Rocky Mount, VA 24151

Fruits to Nuts
7205 Kenosha Pass
Austin, TX 78749

Golden Acres
Rt. 2, Box 115
Brentwood, CA 94513

Great Valley Mills
101 S. West End Blvd.
Quakertown, PA 18951

The Grover Co.
2111 S. Industrial park Ave.
Tempe, AZ 85282

Homestead Flour
911 W. Camden Rd.
Montgomery, MI 49255

Jaffe Brothers
P.O. Box 636
Valley Center, CA 92082

Lamb's Grist Mill
Rt. 1, Box 66
Hillsboro, TX 76645

Millstead Farm
RFD #2
Rushford, MN 55971

Moore's Flour Mill
1605 Shasta St.
Redding, CA 96001

New Hope Mills
R.R. #2
Moravia, NY 13118

Nichols Garden Nursery
1190 North pacific
Albany, OR 97321

Northern Health Foods
Box 66
Moorehead, MN 56560

Old Mill Co.
5314 Broadmoor
Greensboro, NC 24410

Old Mill of Guilford
Box 623, Rt. 1
Oak Ridge, NC 27310

Organic Farms and Mission
Rt. 1
Henning, MN 56551

Organic Food Research Farms
Rt. 3, Box 304
Dayton, OH 37321

Paul's Grains & Vegetables
Rt. 1, Box 76
Laurel, IA 50141

Shiloh Farms
P.O. Box 97
Sulphur Springs, AR 72768

Sunnyland Farms
Rt. 1
Albany, GA 31702

Vermont Country Store
Weston, VT 05161

Tom Vreeland
5861 Gedes Rd.
Ypsilanti, MI 48197

Walnut Acres
Penns Creek, PA 17862

Whole Earth Catalog calls Walnut Acres "the best, most reputable source in the U.S." I call Walnut Acres the most beautiful business I have ever seen: a lovely, 500-acre organic farm in the Pennsylvania hills; factory, mills, and store on the farm; employees share ownership and ship hundreds of freshly made products daily. Visit if you can—it will bring peace to your soul.

Wolf's Neck Farms
Freeport, ME 04082

Additional sources are listed in The Organic Directory, *published by Rodale Press.*

Appendix Six   *Herbs & Spices*

Herbs and spices have been used medicinally and in cooking for at least 4,500 years, early Assyrian and Egyptian records tell us. It is only during the last 500 years that pure chemicals have been included in pharmacopoeias. The modern pharmocopoeia still retains a large number of herbs and herbal extracts.

Herbs are defined as flowering plants whose stems above ground do not become wood. Spices are pungent, aromatic parts of plants, including woody plants. But even though herbs and spices are not synonyms, in therapy the term "herbal medicine" is used in the broader sense to include both these members of the plant kingdom.

Since all herbs and spices contain chemical compounds, they can alter body chemistry—that is, they have a possible medicinal effect. However, since they are generally used in minute quantities in cooking, the medicinal effect is generally negligible. It is when the herb/spice is used in larger quantities that the effects can be powerful—*medicinal*. If you want to treat yourself with herbal medicine, it is best to do so with the assistance of an experienced herbalist.

Because contemporary American medical schools teach only chemical medicine, medical doctors with a knowledge of herbs are extremely rare. Doctors of naturopathy and chiropractic are more apt to know and appreciate herbs, but in any case, it is not easy to find experienced herbalists. When you do, you are usually told that herbs are slower than chemicals while less apt to cause side effects. You are also generally told that herbal medicine is unlikely to be effective unless right food choices and eating practices are followed.

Without a consulting herbalist, the only real alternative is a good book on herbology. Such a book typically describes what herbs are good for what conditions, suggesting dosages in the traditionally used forms of teas, tinctures, and extracts. The major problem with this traditional approach is that it does not inform us regarding powdered herbs in capsules, which are found in abundance in modern health and natural foods stores. The following table was designed to remedy this situation.

TRANSFORMING TEAS, TINCTURES, AND EXTRACTS DOSES INTO HERB CAPSULE DOSES

Traditional Preparation	Herb Capsule Dose (Usually taken 2-3 doses/day)
Teas (Standard decoction or infusion of one ounce herb per pint of water:)	
1 fl. oz. (2 T.)	2–3 caps
Wineglass (2–3 fl. oz.)	4–9 caps
Half cup (4 fl. oz.)	8–12 caps
Teaspoon of herb in cup of water	2–3 caps
Tablespoon of herb in cup of water	6–9 caps
Tinctures (Standard tincture of four ounces herb per pint of alcohol)	
1–2 drachms (1–2 tsp.)	3–6 caps
Fluid Extracts	
1–2 drops (1–2 minims)	1–2 caps
5–6 drops	5–6 caps
Powders (Fine powdered herb taken in a small amount of water)	
5–10 grains	1–2 caps
10–20 grains	2–3 caps
20–60 grains	3–10 caps

Note: This is for 'O' (the small size) capsules, which are the size usually sold pre-filled. Always begin with a smaller first dose to check for sensitivity to the herbs. Note that when taking three doses per day, the number of capsules may be a dozen or more. The numbers given here are approximate since herbal powders vary in their strength. The estimated number of capsules is conservative and a larger number may be needed in some cases.
(Source: Subhuti Dharmananda, "Herbal Concentrates—A gift from China," *Bestways Magazine*, January, 1982.)

HERB BOOKS

Back to Eden, Jethro Kloss. Santa Barbara, CA: Woodbridge Press, 1975.

Herbs & Things, Jeanne Rose. New York: Grosset & Dunlap, 1972.

The Herb Book, John Lust. New York: Bantam Books, 1974.

A Modern Herbal, Vols. 1 & 2, M. Grieve. New York: Dover Publications, ND.

People's Desk Reference, "Traditional Herbal Formulas", Joseph Montagua—2 vol., 1500 page set, available from Alternative Medical Association, 7915 S.E. Stark St., Portland, OR 97215.

School of Natural Healing, John Christopher. Orem, UT: Bi World Industries, ND.

Using Plants for Healing, Nelson Coon. Emmaus, PA: Rodale Press, 1979.

The Way of Herbs, Michael Tierra. Santa Cruz, CA: Unity Press, 1980.

CULINARY HERBS AND SPICES

Anise. * Licorice-like flavor. Chopped leaves can be used in salads, to season vegetables. Seeds are used in breads and pastries.

Basil (Sweet Basil; Bush Basil). * Clove-like flavor, one of the most versatile herbs. Complements tomato sauces, salad dressings, stews, stuffings, herb butters, meat loaf, fish, eggs. Aids digestion.

Bay (Bay Laurel; Sweet Bay). * With a pungent resin-like flavor, it is an essential ingredient of *bouquet garni.* (Bouquet garni is literally "a bunch of herbs"—the classic mix being parsley, thyme, and bay, tied together or wrapped in cheesecloth, used to flavor soups, stocks, braises, and stews.) Use the whole leaf in meat, fish, and bean dishes; in all sorts of soupy, multiple-ingredient dishes. Use sparingly to avoid bitterness and remove leaf before serving. Aids digestion.

Capers. Pickled flower buds of a Mediterranean bush, with a lemon-tart flavor. Complements cold egg and fish dishes.

Caraway. * Distinctive seeds used to flavor rye bread, cheese, and vegetables in the cabbage family, in which they offset the propensity to create flatulence. Leaves can be used as salad green, root as boiled vegetable.

Chervil. * A member of the parsley family with a delicate anise-like flavor. Complements all vegetables; eggs; fish; chicken; should be added at the last minute in cooking to avoid killing the fragile flavor.

Chives. * Like miniature green onions. Mince and use raw to add zest to salads; soft cheeses; cheese, egg, and vegetable dishes; baked potato; tomato soup.

Cilantro (Chinese Parsley). * The leaves of the coriander plant, a member of the parsley family. Powerful flavor. Use sparingly with squash, eggplant, snow peas.

Cumin. * The small seed of a member of the parsley family native to North Africa and the Middle East. With its powerfully aromatic flavor, it is the major ingredient of chili and curry powders, and gives a unique flavor to grains, beans, and sauces.

Dill. * The leaves ("dill weed") have a sweeter flavor than the seeds, complement yogurt, eggs, tomatoes, potato salad. The seeds contain the same volatile oils as caraway seeds, but in different proportions. Use in pickling, cook with members of the cabbage family. Aids digestion.

Fennel. * Roots, leaves, and seeds all have a licorice-like flavor. Chop and cook with meat or fish. Sprinkle raw on food as a powerful aid to digestion.

Garlic. * The most powerful member of the onion family, the most medicinal of foods. A proven bacteriacide, it has been recognized for thousands of years as a blood purifier. Peeled and split, chopped, minced, crushed, or squeezed in a garlic press for its juice, garlic enhances almost everything, cooked or raw.

Ginger. * Piquant flavor of the finely minced fresh root adds zest to curries, eggs, fish, and meat, especially when paired with garlic. The dried root loses much of its piquancy and is powdered to use as a spice in baking.

Horseradish. * Medicinally powerful in the raw form, it loses most of its effects when cooked. Mince or puree, use as a condiment to aid the digestion of rich dishes.

Lovage. * Little-used yet useful herb with a musky, celery-like flavor. Cooking leaves, stems, and roots enhances vegetables; chopped leaves enhance potato salad, crushed seeds add flavor to bread.

Marjoram (Sweet Marjoram; Pot Marjoram). * The domesticated version of oregano, which is more pungent. Pot marjoram is easier to grow; sweet marjoram, as the name indicates, is sweeter. Mixes well with other herbs to flavor a wide variety of dishes: meat, fish, egg dishes; soups; salads; beans. Aids digestion.

Mint. * The most popular of the thirty varieties are spearmint and peppermint. Complements carrots, cucumbers, tomatoes, peas, fruit salads, as well as making excellent tea, jelly, and sauce to accompany lamb. Stimulates appetite, aids digestion, relieves nausea and flatulence.

Paprika. * Made from dried, red (ripe), sweet (not hot) peppers. Faint flavor, mostly useful as bright coloring for vegetables and sauces.

Oregano. * The wild version of marjoram, it is more pungent. It is a dominant flavor in many Italian dishes made with tomato sauce. A good flavoring for eggs and grains. Aids digestion.

Parsley. * Curly leaf and flat leaf (Italian); flat leaf is slightly stronger. Adds tang to almost everything, cooked or raw. Highly potent nutritionally, usually more valuable than the food it garnishes. Mixed with garlic, it will neutralize the odor. An ingredient of the classic version of *fines herbs*: fresh parsley, chives, tarragon, and chervil, finely chopped and mixed.

Pepper (Black Pepper; White Pepper; Red Pepper*). Black and white peppers are berries of the same tropical vine, which is unrelated to pepper plants. Black, the stronger, is the whole, dried, immature berries; white is the inner core of the ripe berries. Red pepper is most commonly known as "cayenne," "cayenne pepper," sometimes as "capsicum." Cayenne is made from the dried seeds and pods of hot red peppers. Black and white peppers irritate the mucus membranes and stomach. Cayenne, on the other hand, is nonirritating and a highly valuable stimulant and digestive aid.

Rosemary. * Resinous, pine-like flavor. Its astringent effect complements rich meat and fish dishes, poultry, soups, stews, sweet sauces, pickling. It is reputed to be an overall body tonic.

Saffron. * The dried stigmata of Spanish crocuses. Extremely expensive because of scarcity, but a small amount accomplishes much. Adds a rich orange color and delicately musky flavor to grains and sauces.

Sage. * Strong eucalyptus-like flavor complements other strong flavors. Good for meats, stuffings, beans, soft cheeses, mixes well with other strong herbs such as rosemary, thyme, and oregano. Aids digestion.

Savory (Summer Savory; Winter Savory). * Of the two types, winter savory is stronger. Since its piquant flavor particularly complements legumes, it is known as "the bean herb." Also complements cabbage, squash, string beans; stuffings; meat dishes. Aids digestion.

Tarragon. * With a licorice-like flavor, tarragon-infused vinegar is important in French cuisine, where it is used in sauce Béarnaise, mayonnaise, mustard, and salad dressings. Good with chicken and casseroles, to flavor butter for asparagus and artichokes. Aids digestion.

Thyme. (Common or Garden Thyme; Lemon Thyme). * One of the most versatile cooking herbs, thyme has a mint-like flavor, lemon thyme adds a hint of citrus. Adds distinction to grain dishes, vegetables, soups, stuffings, picklings, and meats. Said to be an overall body tonic.

*Can be grown in North American gardens.

Summary of Herb Uses

Beans: bay, cumin, garlic, marjoram, parsley, cayenne, sage, savory.

Bread: anise, caraway, garlic, lovage, parsley.

Cheese dishes: caraway, chives, garlic, parsley, cayenne.

Cheese, soft: chives, garlic, parsley, sage.

Eggs: basil, capers, chervil, chives, dill, garlic, ginger, marjoram, oregano, parsley, cayenne.

Fish: basil, capers, bay, chervil, fennel, garlic, ginger, marjoram, parsley, rosemary.

Grains: basil, cumin, garlic, oregano, parsley, saffron, thyme.

Herb butters: basil, garlic, parsley, tarragon, thyme.

Meat: fennel, garlic, ginger, marjoram, cayenne, rosemary, sage.

Meat loaf: basil, fennel, garlic, marjoram, parsley, cayenne, rosemary, sage, thyme.

Pickling: dill, garlic, rosemary, tarragon, thyme.

Poultry: chervil, garlic, parsley, cayenne, rosemary, tarragon.

Salad: anise, caraway, chervil, chives, dill, fennel, lovage, mint, parsley.

Salad dressings: basil, chives, dill, garlic, marjoram, cayenne, tarragon.

Sauces: dill, ginger, horseradish, mint, parsley, garlic, rosemary, saffron.

Soups: bay, garlic, parsley, cayenne, rosemary, thyme.

Stews: basil, bay, garlic, parsley, marjoram, cayenne, rosemary.

Stuffings: basil, garlic, parsley, cayenne, sage, savory, thyme.

Tomato sauce: basil, garlic, parsley, cayenne, oregano, rosemary, thyme.

Vegetables: anise, chervil, chives, garlic, lovage, mint, parsley, cayenne, thyme.

Fresh herbs are always more flavorful than dried, but, due to their moisture content, twice as much should be used when measurements are cited in terms of dried herbs.

Two methods for keeping herbs fresh after picking: (1) Wrap loosely in a dampened cloth and store in refrigerator. (2) Clip ends of stems, place in jar with an inch or two of water, store in refrigerator.

Fresh Spices

The little spice jars with powdered spices nested in racks in most supermarket are generally free of additives. But the most flavorful and least expensive way to buy them is whole. The oils responsible for their flavor are volatile and dissipate rapidly after grinding; a powdered spice will generally be flavorful when the jar is first opened, but become progressively flatter sitting in your kitchen. To get the "new jar" flavor every time, grind your whole spices fresh as needed.

Appendix Seven Food Supplements and Supplementary Foods

The essence of using health foods lies with the practice of supplementing ordinary foods with extraordinary ones in order to obtain high potencies of particular nutrients. When the extraordinary food is really just a part of a whole food, it is a *food supplement*; when the extraordinary food is in the whole form, it is a *supplementary food*.

FOOD SUPPLEMENTS

Wheat germ typifies food supplements perfectly. The germ is removed from wheat in the process of refining. Among other essential nutrients, the germ contains all the wheat's vitamin E. So using wheat germ as a supplemental food, you have an extraordinarily concentrated source of vitamin E. Taking the oil from the germ, you have an even greater concentration, since all the E is in the oil. You can concentrate even further by isolating the E from the oil. Of course, the further you go in steps of concentration, the more you leave behind in variety and balance. Going back up the line, wheat-germ oil is also a good source of vitamin F. Next, wheat germ is also a good source of B vitamins and protein. Finally, when you get back to the beginning, to the wheat itself, you have something balanced enough to be a reliable, staple food rather than a special-purpose supplement.

Wheat germ exemplifies another aspect of health foods: Great care must be taken to obtain the best quality; otherwise, what should be good for you will instead be bad. In the case of wheat germ, much of what is available is rancid. Rancidity occurs because most wheat germ is rolled into flakes, which breaks open the sac containing the wheat germ oil. Exposed to air, oxygen begins to work on the oil: oxidation equals rancidity. Since vitamin E is an antioxidant, there is a brief period of grace. But you can be almost certain that if the wheat germ flakes were not vacuum packed within the day they were rolled, they will be rancid.

I never buy wheat germ flakes that have not been vacuum packed. When opened, they should have a sweet smell; if rancid, they will have an acrid odor. After opening, they should be stored in the refrigerator. But the best way of all to guarantee that wheat germ will not be rancid is not to buy it in the flake form at all; rather, buy it unrolled. Unrolled wheat germ is variously known as "embryo," "chunk," or "unflaked" wheat germ. The only problem with this alternative is that it is hard to find.

Octacosanol: Selected by *Prevention* magazine as one of the food supplements most likely to succeed in the future, octacosanol is the active ingredient in wheat germ responsible for its proven

462

ability to increase vigor, stamina, and endurance. Some other possible benefits: it may quicken reflexes, increase fertility, prevent miscarriages, lessen the severity of muscular dystrophy and multiple sclerosis, cure pregnancy toxemia, and strengthen the heart muscle. (*Prevention*, June 1980).

Bran is usually taken to mean wheat bran, though rice bran (alternately called "rice polishings") is also used as a source for vitamins B1 and B12, in vitamin-mineral formulas. Bran is usually taken for its high fiber content, to establish regularity of the bowel; it is also a good source of minerals, especially iron.

Molasses, a by-product of sugar refining, is an excellent source of iron, a good source of seven other minerals, and six of the B vitamins. For some people it is also helpful in establishing regularity.

"Blackstrap" is the type of molasses with the most sugar removed and the greatest nutrient density. Molasses with higher sugar content is known as "Barbados" or "light" molasses, which some people prefer because of its milder flavor.

Lecithin, a waxy substance derived from soybeans, is an emulsifier of fats. That means if you have oil floating on water and add lecithin, it will attach itself to the oil in a way that will allow the oil to be dispersed throughout the whole volume of water. It is one of the most ubiquitous food additives; as a supplement it is taken to prevent the formation of fatty deposits in the bloodstream.

There are two common forms of lecithin: liquid and granular. The liquid is the most unprocessed form, but is used less frequently as a supplement because it is a bit hard to handle. Liquid lecithin is so thick it barely pours, making it less convenient to use than the dry lecithin granules. Being extremely high in phosphorus, each tablespoon of lecithin should be augmented with four tablespoons of spray-dried skim milk to preserve calcium-phosphorus balance.

Evening primrose oil: The evening primrose is familiar in several varieties, common names of which are king's cure-all, rockrose, night willow, fever plant, sun drop, and sandlily. The oil of evening primrose has been found to be the only known rich source of a rare nutrient called GLA (*gammalinoleic acid*). GLA is essential for the body's manufacturing of *prostaglandins*, hormone-like compounds vitally involved in the functioning of all organs and systems. Some of the effects of evening primrose oil reported by Richard Passwater (*Evening Primrose Oil*, Keats Publishing, Inc.) are: reduced obesity without dieting; lowered blood pressure and blood cholesterol; improved eczema, acne (with zinc), and hyperactivity in children; relief of moderate rheumatoid arthritis. GLA supports the immune system, so it is hoped that evening primrose oil will help prevent a wide range of health problems, from heart disease to schizophrenia to cancer.

EPA and DHA (eicosapentaenoic acid and docohexaenoic acid) are two long-chain unsaturated fatty acids (also known as *Omega-3* fatty acids, referring to double bonds in their molecular structure). EPA and DHA are found in the greatest concentrations in the body oils of such oily fish as salmon, mackerel, herring, sardines, and pilchard. Fish *liver* oils are not used as sources of EPA and DHA in order to avoid vitamins A and D overdoses. Research indicates that the greater the concentration of EPA and DHA in the blood, the less the incidence of heart attacks and associated circulatory disorders.

The most notable example of a high-EPA-DHA, low-heart-attack ratio is the traditional fatty-fish-eating Eskimo. EPA and DHA most often appear under the trade name "MaxEPA," which is exported to the U.S. by Seven Seas Health Care, an English company, which processes oily fish body oils to maximize EPA and DHA concentrations and remove undesirable fatty acids.

Homoeopathic Tissue Salts: "Through the like, disease is produced and through the like, it is cured," wrote Hippocrates around 400 B.C. A German medical doctor named Samuel Hahnemann established this principle as the corner-stone of homoeopathic medicine in the early 1800s. Called the "law of similars," this first law of homoeopathy states that "a remedy can cure a disease if it produces in a healthy person symptoms similar to those of the disease."

The second law of homoeopathy is the "law of proving." Proving is accomplished by dividing a group of healthy people in half, giving one half daily doses of a substance and the other a placebo (the double-blind method). The common symptoms produced by the substance become the remedy objective and the substance then becomes a remedy for that particular set of symptoms.

The "law of potentization" is homoeopathy's third major principle. It refers to the method by which homoeopathic remedies are made. The active substance is ground (triturated), then goes through successive dilutions and shakings. Each dilution *increases,* rather than decreases, the medicinal effect of the substance. Dilutions are identified successively as 3X, 6X, 12X, with the highest number, or greater dilution, representing the greatest strength. Homoeopathy does not concern itself with the substance but with the *emanations* of the substance. Therefore, in homoeopathy *less is more,* because the more the emanations are freed from the substance, the finer and more penetrating they become.

There are over six hundred proven remedies in the homoeopathic *Materia Medica.* Twelve of them are known as "tissue salts," being minerals vital to human nutrition. These and a few remedies for common illnesses such as colds and headaches are sold in many natural foods and most health food stores. The rest can be prescribed by a homoeopathic physician and obtained at a homoeopathic pharmacy. Homoeopathic tissue salts and remedies are completely nontoxic, and therefore do not produce side effects. Let the tablets dissolve under the tongue in a clean mouth and eat or drink nothing for at least fifteen minutes afterward. (Quotes from *Homoeopathic Medicine at Home,* Panos, M.D., and Heimlich, J.P. Tarcher, Inc.)

Bach Flower Remedies: In the 1930s, Edward Bach left a lucrative practice as a London physician for the English countryside. He had come to believe that "There is no true healing unless there is change in outlook, peace of mind, and inner happiness." He identified seven negative states of mind, seeing them as the primary causes of ill health. He discovered that extracts of wildflowers had powerful effects on inharmonious states of mind. The rest of his life was devoted to the development of extraction methods and to researching the effects of the extracts on negative personality traits. The best extraction method was found to be soaking blossoms in pure water in sunlight. Dr. Bach discovered remedies for thirty-eight distinct negative moods. These remedies are sold in little vials by many natural foods stores. (We who have grown up thinking in terms of more density and more weight equaling more power can have a great deal of trouble crediting water potentized by wildflowers as having strength enough to do anything at all, let alone create mood changes. For greater understanding of the kinds of forces at work here, read *Heal Thyself* and *The Twelve Healers and Other Remedies,* Bach, and *The Secret Life of Plants,* Tompkins and Bird, Avon Books.)

SUPPLEMENTARY FOODS

Used in their whole forms, supplementary foods are also sometimes called "specialty" foods, or "special purpose" foods.

Acidophilus: The name of one of a strain of bacteria often added to yogurt, it is also the generic name for a liquid product containing a far higher concentration of this bacteria than is present in yogurt. Acidophilus can greatly speed the intestinal recovery from antibiotics, which destroy the small intestinal flora responsible for proper digestion and B vitamin production.

Alfalfa: used in powder and tablet form as a source of vitamin K and a wide variety of trace minerals. Alfalfa leaves are also steeped for tea.

Aloe vera: A desert succulent of the lily family, whose thick leaves contain a translucent gel. Aloe vera gel, or the juice from the gel, has antibiotic, astringent, antimicrobial, and coagulating agents. It inhibits pain and prevents scarring by stimulating tissue growth. It is used externally for burns and all sorts of skin disorders, and internally for conditions such as ulcers, colitis, and hemorrhoids. Potted aloe vera—often called "the medicine plant"—is often kept as a house plant for first-aid emergencies. (See *The Aloe Vera Handbook*, Skousen, Universal Concepts, Huntington Beach, CA.)

Bone meal: Made from cattle bones ground into powder, it is a good source of calcium and phosphorus in the same ratio (2.5:1) as they occur in human bones and teeth. Bone meal is also a good source of trace minerals. There is, however, a problem with bone meal that is similar to the problem with dessicated liver. In this case it is because heavy metals such as lead, arsenic and mercury are deposited in the bones. Bone meal is a good supplement, then, only if it is certified to be free of heavy metal contamination.

Cider vinegar: Approximately 5 percent malic acid, similar to the hydrochloric acid manufactured by the stomach for digestive purposes, makes it a highly effective digestive aid, particularly for meat. Cider vinegar is also widely used in folk medicine (See Chapter 13).

Dessicated liver: the dried and powdered form. Liver *should* be ranked a "super food" because it is so rich in B vitamins, especially B12, and minerals, especially iron. I emphasize the word *should* because the liver is the main organ of detoxification and that, in view of current farm and feed-lot practices, creates a special problem: pesticides and antibiotics. It is routine to spray crops destined to be fed to cattle and poultry with pesticides and to feed cattle and poultry antibiotics. Their bodies treat these substances as toxins, so it is also routine to find pesticide residues and antibiotics in beef and chicken liver. Dessicated liver is—or should be—inspected to ascertain that it is free of pesticide and antibiotic residues.

Garlic: Taken in capsules, as well as eaten raw and cooked, garlic is used for its powerful medicinal properties. It has more than thirty active compounds, giving it antibiotic, antibacterial, antioxidant, and detoxifying qualities. A partial list of conditions that have benefitted from treatment with raw garlic or garlic extracts includes high blood pressure, atherosclerosis, diabetes, arthritis, hypoglycemia, colds, allergies, intestinal parasites, and dysentery. (See *The Miracle of Garlic*, Airola, Health Plus Publishers.)

Kelp and dulse: two types of seaweed commonly used in powder or tablet form for trace minerals, particularly iodine. High in sodium chloride, they are nutritious salt substitutes. Dried dulse leaves make a savory snack.

Nutritional yeast: This comes closer than anything else to being a "super food." Brewer's yeast, a by-product of brewing, is sometimes incorrectly used as the generic name. Other types of yeast are "primary grown"—that is, they are not by-products but are grown specifically for food purposes, on media such as wood pulp and molasses. Nutritional yeasts of all types are excellent sources of B vitamins and protein (50 percent) and good sources of minerals. They are suitable for both vegetarian and omnivarian diets but be warned: if you are unaccustomed to it, nutritional yeast may cause flatulence, due to the high concentration of B vitamins. To prevent this, begin with small portions and increase gradually. The best general approach is to start with ¼ teaspoon for several days, increasing every few days by ¼ teaspoon, up to a level of one or two tablespoons a day. Having followed the gradual introductory approach, if flatulence persists into the second month, it may be due to insufficient stomach acid to handle the protein. This can be corrected by taking hydrochloric acid tablets. (See also *Spray Dried Skim Milk.*)

Pollen: Colors and flavors vary greatly according to what kind of blossoms it was gathered from. Bees bring it to the hive in tiny pellets attached to their legs; to gather it, a trap is set at the door to the hive which knocks the pollen pellets from their legs. Touted as a super food, the noted herbalist Dr. John Christopher calls it "the most perfect food in the world." It contains vitamins A, B, C, D, and E, a wide variety of minerals and enzymes, and complete protein. Pollen is frequently used by athletes as an energizer and rejuvenator.

Propolis: The buds of certain trees exude a sap rich in nutrients and a natural antibacterial agent, *galangin.* Bees collect this sap and add their own secretions to it, making propolis, which they spread throughout the interior of the hive to keep it free of harmful germs. The action of propolis destroys bacteria, viruses, and fungi. It is said to strengthen the human immune system by stimulating the thymus gland. Propolis is a semi-waxy substance with an astringent taste, which can be used topically or taken internally.

Spray dried skim milk: milk solids precipitated when milk is sprayed into a column of heated air to drive off the water, a more natural form of milk powder than the instantized variety. Spray dried skim milk powder is a good source of calcium. *Nutrition Almanac* recommends supplementing each tablespoon of nutritional yeast, which is high in phosphorus, with four tablespoons of spray dried skim milk, to maintain calcium/phosphorus balance.

Rose hips: the berries of wild roses and some domestic varieties. A rich source of natural vitamin C (the complex), used in powder form or made as tea. (As tea, however, it is no longer rich in vitamin C, since C is partially destroyed by heat.)

Yogurt and kefir: generally speaking, the best ways to consume milk. The milk protein is predigested by the yogurt-making process and the lactic acid encourages digestion, so that even some people who can't tolerate milk find yogurt agreeable. Yogurt is made by culturing milk with a combination of beneficial bacteria (*lactobacillus bulgaricus* and *streptococcus thermophilus*), then incubating it at the best temperature (see page 305) for encouraging the intense multiplication of the bacteria. These bacteria are beneficial because they find their home in the small intestine where they participate in protein digestion and manufacture B vitamins.

When antibiotics are taken, they destroy *all* kinds of bacteria, not discriminating between beneficial and harmful. Therefore antibiotic consumption is usually accompanied by disturbances of digestion, assimilation, and elimination. Because of this side effect, and because we can build tolerances to antibiotics that reduce their effectiveness, their use should be limited to serious conditions. If antibiotics become necessary, their use should be accompanied by copious yogurt consumption, which should continue for weeks after discontinuing the antibiotics.

Kefir (KEY-fur) is not nearly as widely known as yogurt but just as beneficial. It has a thick, creamy consistency, a mildly sour taste, most often flavored with fruit and sweetened with honey. In this form it is like a tangy milkshake—but a healthy one—which some people who don't like yogurt thoroughly enjoy.

Yucca: a family of desert plants including the Joshua tree, with thick, needle-tipped leaves. Tablets made from yucca leaves have proven about 50 percent effective for relief from both osteo- and rheumatoid arthritis. (See *The Desert Yucca*, by Bellow, M.D., and Bellow, National Arthritis Medical Clinic, Desert Hot Springs, CA 92240)

PROTOMORPHOGENS

Protomorphogens are animal glands and organs used in human nutrition (*proto*, earliest form of; *morphogen*, developmental part of an organ). The use of protomorphogens as supplementary foods is known as *glandular therapy*. Some medical observers scoff at glandular therapy as unproven and farfetched theory, but German medical research has proven otherwise. Dr. A. Kment used radioactive isotope tracing to demonstrate that active nutritional factors from glandular tissues are absorbed from the bloodstream by the corresponding glands of the consumer. This explains why hunting animals and even primitive man instinctually consume the organs of fresh-killed prey before consuming muscle meat. Many of the nutrients in the organs and glands are known only as "unidentified food factors" or "intrinsic food factors." Whatever these mystery nutrients will turn out to be, it is important to note that most of them are destroyed by cooking.

The intrinsic factors of the organs and glands do not necessarily have to come from the same species, but are "organ specific." This means that even though you are not a cow, eating the liver of a cow will stimulate and support your liver, particularly if the cow's liver is uncooked. Since raw organs and glands are a singularly unpopular food, the freeze-dried tissues pressed into tablets are the common form consumed, and cattle are the most common source.

Protomorphogens and Metabolic Balance

Consistent with his many years of studying everything that influences metabolic functioning, Dr. Kelley has learned which protomorphogens have what effects on the different metabolic categories. The following protomorphogens can help balance sympathetics because they "turn on" the glands and organs in which sympathetics are characteristically weak, thereby creating an alkalinizing effect on their usually acidic body chemistry:

posterior pituitary	liver
anterior medial hypothalamus	gall bladder
thymus	spleen
parotid	stomach
lungs	duodenum
adrenal cortex	intestines
pancreas	lymph

The following protomorphogens can help balance parasympathetics because they stimulate the glands and organs in which parasympathetics are characteristically weak, thereby creating an acidifying effect on their usually alkaline body chemistry:

anterior pituitary	kidneys
posterior lateral hypothalamus	uterus
thalamus	prostate
thyroid	ovaries
parathyroid	testes
heart	bone marrow
adrenal medulla	

When pituitary, hypothalamus, or adrenals are taken in their entirety, instead of split according to function, they are neutral (as is brain tissue).

Other Nutritional Influences On Metabolic Balance

Chapters 8 through 10 on foods and Chapter 12 on supplements linked to the material above on protomorphogens make the point that everything you consume has some effect on your metabolic balance. Any unsuccessful experiments you may have made with supplements and supplementary foods may have been failures because you had no way of knowing that it favored your autonomic nervous system strengths instead of its weaknesses. You should have been supplementing with nutrients that would have made you less sympathetic or parasympathetic, rather than more so. *Balanced function leads to efficient function.* It is by supporting and stimulating the weaker aspect of your autonomic nervous system that you encourage balance. Too much support and stimulation of the stronger aspect of your autonomic nervous system leads to imbalance.

In the summary below, most of the materials listed have their balancing influence due to pH values, a few because of the stimulation of hormone production or some other metabolic process such as protein or carbohydrate metabolism. The summary is taken from Dr. Kelley's training manual, *Metabolic Technology II* and various readings on acid-alkaline balance.

SUMMARY OF
FOOD SUPPLEMENTS & SUPPLEMENTARY FOODS
AND THEIR INFLUENCES ON
METABOLIC BALANCE

Balancing Sympathetic Metabolisms (Alkalinizing)	*Neutral*	*Balancing Parasympathetic Metabolisms (Acidifying)*
vitamin B1	vitamin A	vitamin B12
vitamin B2	vitamin E	vitamin B15
niacin (B3)	vitamin F	pantothenic acid
vitamin B6	aloe vera	niacinamide
biotin	bentonite clay	inositol
folic acid	bran	choline
PABA	gelatin	calcium ascorbate
vitamin D	wheat germ oil	sodium ascorbate
vitamin K		bioflavinoids
calcium*		RNA
potassium		phosphorus
magnesium		chlorine
manganese		sulphur
iron		lecithin
chromium		wheat germ
sodium		apple cider vinegar
ascorbic acid		nutritional yeast
zinc**		dulse
chlorophyll		phosphorus drops
alfalfa		most protein powders
kelp		
pollen		
propolis		
most laxatives		
most herbs		

*Calcium is also highly recommended for parasympathetics. Dr. Kelley: "Due to weak parathyroid function and the overall alkaline condition, parasympathetics have very poor calcium utilization. They also have a real problem maintaining calcium levels, for they are constantly excreting it. We try to replace it and get it assimilated into the cells to strengthen cellular integrity."

**Zinc would also be recommended for parasympathetics in cases where its pronounced effects on healing would be desirable.

It should not be construed that sympathetics do not need the nutrients of the right-hand column or parasympathetics those of the left. Rather, they sould de-emphasize them. Ordinarily, balanced metabolizers should supplement across the spectrum, sympathetics should emphasize the left and center columns, parasympathetics the right and center columns.

Appendix Eight Recommended Reading List

If you were limited to one source for books about natural foods, health, nutrition, and related topics, the obvious choice would be Rodale Press. Best known as publishers of *Prevention*, with a circulation of over two million, they also publish *Organic Gardening*, *New Farm*, and *New Shelter* magazines, as well as a long list of books, available in health food, natural foods, and book stores.

Rodale Press was founded by J. I. Rodale more than forty years ago and continues under the direction of his son, Robert. Rodale Press is a model public-spirited corporation, supporting a large research farm and staff. They have also sponsored the Cornucopia Project, a nonprofit educational partnership with consumers dedicated to, in Robert Rodale's words, ending "the waste of soil, food, and energy that is going to cause the price of food to shoot towards the stratosphere." Rodale Press, 33 East Minor Street, Emmaus, PA 18049.

ADDITIVES

The Chemical Feast, James S. Turner. New York: Viking Press, 1970.

Consumer Beware, Beatrice T. Hunter. New York: Simon and Schuster, 1972.

A Consumer's Dictionary of Food Additives, Ruth Winter. New York: Crown Publishers, 1978.

Eater's Digest: The Consumer's Factbook of Food Additives, Michael F. Jacobson. New York: Doubleday Anchor Books, ND.

Eating May Be Hazardous to Your Health, Jean Carper and Jacqueline Verret. New York: Simon and Schuster, 1975.

COOKBOOKS

The Book of Whole Meals, Annemarie Colbin, ed. Nahum Stiskin. Brookline, MA: Autumn Press, 1979.

Bread Winners, Mel London. Emmaus, PA: Rodale Press, 1979.

Cooking with Care and Purpose, Michel Abehsera. Swan House.

Cooking with Sea Vegetables, Sharon A. Rhoads. Brookline, MA: Autumn Press, 1978.

Deaf Smith Country Cookbook, Marjorie Winn Ford, Susan Hillyard, and Mary Faulk Koock. New York: Macmillan, 1973.

The Dione Lucas Book of Natural French Cooking, Marion Gorman and _____De Alba. New York: Dutton.

The Do of Cooking, Herman Aihara. San Francisco, CA: Georges Ohsawa Macrobiotic Foundation, ND.

Feasting on Raw Foods, Charles Gerras ed. Emmaus, PA: Rodale Press, 1980.

Future Food: Politics, Philosophy, and Recipes for the Twenty-First Century, Colin Tudge. New York: Crown Books, 1980.

Laurel's Kitchen, Laurel Robertson et al. Petaluma, CA: Nilgiri Press, 1976 (hardcover). New York: Bantam Books, 1978 (paperback).

Moosewood Cookbook, Molly Katzen. Berkeley, CA: Ten Speed Press, 1977.

The Natural Foods Primer, Beatrice T. Hunter. Los Angeles, CA: Cancer Control Society, ND.

The Natural Healing Cookbook: Over Four Hundred Ways to Get Better and Stay Healthy, Mark Bricklin and Charon Claessens. Emmaus, PA: Rodale Press, 1981.

Naturally Delicious Desserts and Snacks, _____ Martin. Emmaus, PA: Rodale Press, ND.

Naturally Great Foods Cookbook, Nancy Albright. Emmaus, PA: Rodale Press, ND.

The New French Cooking: Minceur Cuisine Extraordinaire, _____Aulcino. New York: Grosset and Dunlap, ND.

The New York Times Natural Foods Cookbook, Jean Hewitt. New York: Avon Books, 1971.

One Bowl, Don Gerard. New York: Random House/Bookworks, ND.

Recipes for a Small Planet, Ellen B. Ewald. New York: Ballantine Books, 1973.

Salads, Time/Life Good Cooks Series. Alexandria, VA: Time-Life Books, 1980.

Sunburst Farms Family Cookbook, Susan Duquette, ed. Santa Barbara, CA: Woodbridge Press, 1978.

Tassajara Breadbook, Edward Espe Brown. Boulder, CO: Shambhala Publications Inc., 1970.

Tassajara Cooking, Edward Espe Brown. Boulder, CO: Shambhala Publications Inc., 1973.

Ten Talents Cookbook: Vegetarian Natural Foods, Frank J. and Rosalie Hurd. Chisholm, MN: Ten Talents Press, 1968.

The Vegetarian Epicure, Anna Thomas. New York: Knopf, 1980.

Vital Foods for Total Health, Bernard Jensen. Solana Beach, CA: Bernard Jensen Products, ND.

GARDENING AND FARMING

Alan Chadwick's Enchanted Garden, Tom Cuthbertson. New York: E.P. Dutton, ND.

An Acres U.S.A. Primer, Charles Walters and C.J. Fenzau. Raytown, MO: Acres USA, ND.

The Basic Book of Organic Gardening, Robert Rodale, ed. New York: Ballantine Books, ND.

Rodale Press is the foremost publisher of books on organic gardening and farming. Some of their books are:

An Agricultural Testament, Sir Albert Howard.

How to Grow Vegetables and Fruits by the Organic Method

The Encyclopedia of Organic Gardening

Composting: A Study of the Process and Its Principles

Companion Plants and How to Use Them, Helen Philbrick and Richard B. Gregg. The Devin-Adair Co., 1966.

Gardening for Health and Nutrition. John and Helen Philbrick. New York: Harper and Row, 1980.

Gardening without Poisons, Beatrice T. Hunter. Los Angeles: Regent House, 1980.

Growing Food the Natural Way, Ken and Pat Kraft. New York: Doubleday, ND.

How to Grow More Vegetables Than You Ever Thought Possible On Less Land Than You Can Imagine, John Jeavons. Berkeley, CA: Ten Speed Press, 1982.

The Living Soil and the Haughley Experiment, E. B. Balfour. Universe Books, 1976.

My Garden Companion, Jamie Jobb. New York: Scribner, 1977.

Organic Farming: Yesterday's and Tomorrow's Agriculture, Organic Gardening Magazine, ed. Emmaus, PA: Rodale Press, 1977.

The Organic Gardener, Catharine Osgood Foster. New York: Knopf, 1972.

The Organic Method Primer, Bargyla and Glyver Rateaver. Pauma Valley, CA: Rateaver Press, 1975.

The Secret Life of Plants, Peter Tompkins and Christopher Bird. New York: Avon Books, ND.

The Self-Sufficient Gardener: A Complete Guide to Growing and Preserving All Your Own Food, John Seymour. New York: Doubleday, 1979.

Booklets

Write for a list of booklets on gardening and related subjects to Garden Way Publishing Co., Charlotte, Vermont 05445.

Magazines

Acres USA, Raytown, MO 64133
Natural Food and Farming, Natural Food Associates, Atlanta, TX 75551
The New Farm, Rodale Press
Organic Gardening and Farming, Rodale Press, Emmaus, PA 18049

The following magazines about country living frequently run articles on organic gardening:

Country Journal, 205 Main Street, Brattleboro, VT 05301
Farmstead Magazine, P.O. Box 111, Freedom, ME 04941.
Harrowsmith, Camden East, Ontario, Canada K0K 130.

[HERBS—SEE APPENDIX SIX]

MACROBIOTICS

If these books are not available at your local health or natural foods store, write *East West Journal*, Dept. G, 17 Station St., Brookline Village, MA 02147.

The Book of Macrobiotics, M. Kushi

The Cancer Prevention Diet, Eastwest Foundation

Healing Miracles From Macrobiotics, Kohler and Kohler

Macrobiotic Cooking for Everyone, Esko and Esko

How to Cook with Miso, A. Kushi

NATURAL FOODS

The Book of Macrobiotics, Michio Kushi. Scranton, PA: Japan Publications, 1977.

The Book of Whole Foods, Karen MacNeil. St. Paul, MN: Vintage Books, 1981.

Diet For a Small Planet, Frances Moore Lappé. New York: Ballantine Books, 1971.

Food for Thought, Saul and JoAnne Miller. Englewood Cliffs, NJ: Prentice-Hall, Inc., 1979.

Supermarket Handbook: Access to Whole Foods, Nikki and David Goldbeck. New York: New American Library, 1974.

Whole Foods, Natural Foods Guide, Whole Foods Magazine, ed. Berkeley, CA: And/Or Press, 1979.

NUTRITION

Are You Confused?, Paavo Airola. Phoenix, AZ: Health Plus Publishers, 1971.

"Civilized" Diseases and Their Circumvention, Max Garten. Los Angeles, CA: Cancer Control Society, ND.

The Complete Book of Minerals for Health, _____ Faelten. Emmaus, PA; Rodale Press, 1981.

The Complete Book of Vitamins, Prevention Magazine. Emmaus, PA: Rodale Press, 1977.

The Complete Handbook of Nutrition, Gary and Steve Null. New York: Dell Publishing Co., 1973.

Diet and Disease, E. Cheraskin and W. Ringsdorf. Los Angeles, CA: Cancer Control Society, ND.

Diet and Nutrition, R. M. Ballentine. Honesdale, PA: Himalayan International Institute, 1978.

Eat Well, Get Well, Stay Well, Carlton Fredericks. New York: Grosset and Dunlap, 1980.

Everything You Always Wanted To Know About Nutrition, David Reuben. New York: Avon Books, 1979.

Feed Your Kids Right, Lendon Smith. New York: Dell Publishing Co., 1980.

Food for Naught, Ross Hume Hall. Vintage Books.

Food Is Your Best Medicine, Henry Beiler. Los Angeles, CA: Cancer Control Society, ND.

How to Be Healthy and Live Longer, John Tobe. Don Mills, Ontario, Canada: Greywood Publishing, ND.

Jane Brody's Nutrition Book, Jane Brody. New York: W. W. Norton and Co., ND.

Let's Stay Healthy, Adelle Davis. Los Angeles, CA: Cancer Control Society, 1981.

Live Longer Now, Jon N. Leonard et al. New York: Charter Books, 1981.

Meganutrition, Richard Kunin, M.D. New York: New American Library, 1981.

A New Breed of Doctor, Alan Nittler, M.D. Perry, IA: Pyramid Publications, ND.

A New Way to Eat, Linda Clark. Milbrae, CA: Celestial Arts, 1980.

Nutrition, _____ Hauschka. London: Stuart and Watkins, ND.

Nutrition Against Disease, Roger J. Williams. New York: Bantam Books, 1971.

Nutrition Almanac, John D. Kirschmann, ed. New York: McGraw-Hill, 1979.

Nutrition and Vitamin Therapy, Michael Lesser, M.D. New York: Bantam Books, 1980.

Nutrition and Your Mind, George Watson. New York: Bantam Books, 1974.

Own Your Own Body, Stan Malstrom. New Canaan, CT: Keats Publishing Inc. 1980.

Preventive Organic Medicine, Kurt W. Donsbach. New Canaan, CT: Keats Publishing Inc., 1976.

Psycho-Dietetics, E. Cheraskin and W. Ringsdorf. Los Angeles, CA: Cancer Control Society, ND.

Super-Nutrition for Healthy Hearts, Richard Passwater. New York: Jove Publishing, 1978.

The Vegetarian Alternative, Vic Sussman. Emmaus, PA: Rodale Press, 1978.

The Vegetarian Handbook, Roger Doyle. New York: Crown Publishers, Inc., 1979.

The Way of the Skeptical Nutritionist, Michael A. Weiner. New York, MacMillan Publishing Co., 1981.

The Wonderful World Within You, Roger Williams. New York: Bantam Books, ND.

You're Younger Than You Think, Lelord Kodl. New York: Popular Library, 1979.

Periodicals and U.S. Government Publications

Alternatives, P.O. Box 330139, Miami, FL 33133.
American Health, 80 Fifth Ave., N.Y., NY 10010.
Bestways, P.O. Box 2028, Carson City, NV 89701.
Brain-Mind Bulletin, P.O. Box 42211, Los Angeles, CA 90042.
East-West Journal, P.O. Box 1200, Brookline Village, Boston, MA, 02147.
Health Facts, Center for Medical Consumers and Health Care Information, 237 Thompson Street, New York, NY 10012.
Healthview Newsletter, P.O. Box 6670, Charlottesville, VA 22906.
Health World News, P.O. Box 4228, Westlake Village, CA 91359.
Let's Live, P.O. Box 74908, Los Angeles, CA 90004.
Macrobiotic Review, 6209 Park Heights Ave., Baltimore, MD 21215.
Medical Self Care, Box 717, Inverness, CA 94937
National Health Federation Bulletin, Box 688, Monrovia, CA 91046.
Natural Perspectives, P.O. Box 22424, San Francisco, CA 94122-Fred Rohé, Publisher & Editor.
New Age, 32 Station St., Brookline, MA 02146.
New Health, 1680 S. Main St., Springville, UT 84663.
New Realities, 680 Beach St., San Francisco, CA 94109.
Nutrition Action, Center for Science in the Public Interest, 1755 S St., NW, Washington, DC 20009. Also publishers of books, pamphlets, and posters.
Prevention, Rodale Press.
Price-Pottenger Nutrition Foundation Quarterly Journal, Box 2614, La Mesa, CA 92041.
U.S. Government Printing Office, Washington, D.C. 20402:
Dietary Goals for the United States
Global 2000, vols. 1 and 2
Ideas for Better Eating
Nutrition and Your Health.
Whole Life Times, 18 Shepard St., Brighton, MA 02135.

PROCESSING

Eating Better for Less, Ray Wolf. Emmaus, PA: Rodale Press, 1977.

Home Food Systems, Roger B. Yepsen, ed. Emmaus, PA: Rodale Press, 1981.

The Kitchen Almanac, Stone Soup Company. New York: Berkeley Publishing Co., 1977.

Old Fashioned Recipe Book: The Encyclopedia of Country Living. Carla Emery. New York: Bantam Books, 1977.

Stocking Up, Carol H. Stoner, ed. Emmaus, PA: Rodale Press, 1977.

SOYFOODS

The Book of Miso, William Shurtleff and Akiko Aoyagi. New York: Ballantine Books, 1976.

The Book of Tempeh, William Shurtleff and Akiko Aoyagi. New York: Harper and Row, ND.

The Book of Tofu, William Shurtleff and Akiko Aoyagi. New York: Ballantine Books, 1975.

All are available from the authors at the Soyfoods Center, P.O. Box 234, Lafayette, CA 94549.

Home Soyfoods Equipment, Ray Wolf. Emmaus, PA: Rodale Press, ND.

SUGAR

Body, Mind, and Sugar, E.M. Abrahamson. Los Angeles, CA: Regent House, 1981.

Sugar Blues, William Dufty. New York: Warner Books, 1976.

Sweet and Dangerous, John Yudkin, M.D. New York: Bantam Books, ND.

THERAPY

Cancer Therapy: Fifty Cases Reviewed, Max Gerson. Los Angeles, CA: Cancer Control Society, ND.

Cancer and Its Nutritional Therapies, Richard A. Passwater. New Canaan, CT: Keats Publishing, Inc., 1978.

The Complete Book of Natural Medicines, David Carroll. New York: Summit Books, 1980.

Dr. Mandell's Five-Day Allergy Relief System, Marshall Mandell and Lynne W. Scanlon. New York: Thomas Y. Crowell, 1979.

Earth Medicine—Earth Food, Michael A. Weiner. New York: MacMillan Publishing Co., 1980.

Folk Medicine, D.C. Jarvis. New York: Fawcett Crest Books, 1978.

The Handbook of Alternatives to Chemical Medicine, ⸻ Jackon and ⸻ Teague. Oakland, CA.

Health Secrets From Europe, Paavo Airola. New York: Arco Publishing Co., 1971.

High Level Wellness, Donald B. Ardell. Emmaus, PA: Rodale Press, 1977.

Hypoglycemia: A Better Approach, Paavo Airola. Phoenix, AZ: Health Plus Publishers, 1977.

Linda Clark's Handbook of Natural Remedies for Common Ailments, Linda Clark. New York: Pocket Books, ND.

Metabolic Ecology, Fred Rohé. Winfield, KS: Wedgestone Press, 1982.

Miracle Medicine Foods, Rex Adams. New York: Warner Books, 1981.

Nature Has a Remedy, Bernard Jensen. Orem, UT: Bi World Industries, ND.

Nature's Medicine, Richard Lucas. Los Angeles, CA: Cancer Control Society, ND.

The Practical Encyclopedia of Natural Healing, Mark Bricklin. Emmaus, PA: Rodale Press, 1976.

There is a Cure for Arthritis, Paavo Airola. Englewood Cliffs, NJ: Prentice-Hall, Inc., 1982.

The Well Body Book, Hal Bennett and Michael Samuels. New York: Random House/Bookworks, 1977.

Wholistic Dimensions in Healing: A Resource Guide, Leslie J. Kaslof, ed. New York: Doubleday Publishing, 1978.

The Wholistic Health Handbook, Bauman, Brint, Piper, and Wright. Berkeley, CA: Ten Speed Press, ND.

The Woman's Encyclopedia of Health and Natural Healing, Emrika Padus, ed. Mark Bricklin. Emmaus, PA: Rodale Press, 1981.

MISCELLANEOUS

An Edgar Cayce Health Anthology, ARE Press. Virginia Beach, VA: ARE Press, 1979.

The Annual Directory of Vegetarian Restaurants, Loren K. Cronk. Angwin, CA: Daystar Publishing Co., 1981.

Biological Transmutations, C.L. Kervran. Beckman Publications, 1980.

Dr. Schuessler's Biochemistry, J.B. Chapman. Great Britain: Thorsons Publishers Ltd., 1973.

Food First: Beyond the Myth of Scarcity, Frances Moore Lappé and Joseph Collins. New York: Ballantine Books, 1977.

The Food Inflation Fighter's Handbook, Judith L. Klinger. New York: Fawcett Columbine Books, 1980.

Fresh Vegetable and Fruit Juices, N.W. Walker, ed. Phoenix, AZ: O'Sullivan Woodside and Co., 1970.

Guidelines for Food Purchasing in the U.S., Nick Mottern. Available from the author, 129 Woodland, Sherborn, MA. 01770 ($5.00).

How to Keep Slim, Healthy, and Young with Juice Fasting, Paavo Airola. Phoenix, AZ: Health Plus Publishers, 1971.

The Nature of Substance, _____ Hauschka. London: Vincent Stuart Ltd., ND.

Talking Food pamphlets: sugar, oil, water, flour, etc.: Phil Levy, Talking Food Co., Gifford Court, Salem, MA 01970.

CREDITS

Quotations within are reprinted from the following sources:

Consumer Beware, © 1971 by Beatrice Trum Hunter. *Diet and Disease* by E. Cheraskin, M.D., D.M.D., W.M. Ringsdorf, Jr., D.M.D., M.S., and J.W. Clark, D.D.S. Copyright © 1968 by E. Cheraskin, W.M. Ringsdorf and J.W. Clark. Published by Keats Publishing, Inc., New Canaan, CT. Used with permission. *Diet and Nutrition,* Rudolph Ballentine, M.D., © 1978 by Himalayan International Institute of Yoga Science and Philosophy, Honesdale, Pennsylvania. *Digestive Diseases* by Ron Kotulak, Copyrighted, 1980, Chicago Tribune. Used with permission. *Eater's Digest* by Michael F. Jacobson. Copyright © 1972 by Michael F. Jacobson. Reprinted by permission of Doubleday & Company, Inc. *Eating Better for Less,* © 1977, 1978 by Rodale Press, Inc. Chart compiled by Anna Gordon, dietician at Columbia-Presbyterian Medical Center in New York. Permission granted by Rodale Press Inc., Emmaus, PA 18049. *The Food Inflation Fighter's Handbook* by Judith Klinger, © by Judith L. Klinger and Mary Anne McLean. *Future Food* by Colin Tudge. Published in the USA by Harmony Books, a division of Crown Publishers Inc. © Mitchell Beazley Publishers. *Guidelines for Food Purchasing in the United States* by Nick Mottern, Sherborn, MA 01770. *Harvard Medical School Letter,* December, 1980, (about crash diets). Used with permission. *Hypoglycemia: A Better Approach,* by Dr. Paavo Airola, Ph.D., published by Health Plus Publishers, P.O. Box 22001, Phoenix, AZ 85028. *Laurel's Kitchen: A Handbook for Vegetarian Cookery and Nutrition,* copyright 1976 by Nilgiri Press, Petaluma CA 94953. Authors Laurel Robertson, Carol Flinders, and Bronwen Godfrey. *The Living Soil And The Haughley Experiment* by E.B. Balfour, Universe Books, New York, 1976. *Nutrition and Physical Degeneration* by Dr. Weston Price, © Price-Pottenger Nutrition Foundation, P.O. Box 2614, La Mesa, CA 92041. Used with permission. *The Oxford Book of Food Plants,* © Oxford University Press, Oxford, England. Used with permission. *PCBs and Breast Cancer,* by Mosher and Moyer, from *Nutrition Action,* the monthly journal of Center for Science in the Public Interest. *One Answer to Cancer* by Dr. W.D. Kelley, Valenkel Press. *Revolutionary Letters,* by Diane DiPrima, © 1971, 1974, 1979 by Diane DiPrima. Reprinted by permission of City Lights Books. *The San Francisco Examiner,* column by Kevin Starr on March 17, 1980. Used with permission. *Storing Grain* and *Sugar and How it Got That Way* by Phil Levy, © Talking Food Company, Salem, MA. *The Tassajara Bread Book,* by Edward Espe Brown, © 1970 by the Chief Priest, Zen Center, San Francisco. Reprinted by special arrangement with Shambhala Publications, Inc. *The USDA Chickens Out on Food Poisoning,* by Jennifer Cross, February 25, 1981. © 1981 by The San Francisco Bay Guardian Co., Inc. Reprinted by permission. *Wheat,* by Paul C. Mangelsdorf, © Scientific American, July, 1953. Used with permission.

Index

Abrams, H. Leon, Jr., 110
acid-alkaline balance, 102, 105-106
    colds and, 149
acid indigestion, 150-151
acidophilus, 465
acidosis, 102
additives:
    in alcoholic beverages, 262-263
    in baby food, 267, 271
    New American Diet and, 14-15
    salt as, 13
    summary of, 423-426
adenine, 104-105
adult onset diabetes, 47, 49
adzuki beans, 225, 227
agar agar, 62, 63, 165, 364
aging, diet and, 85-86
Ahrens, Richard, 49
Airola, Paavo, 30, 31
alcoholic beverages, 261-263
alfalfa, 279, 299-300, 465
algae, blue-green, 166-167
alkalosis, 102
Allen, James, 264
allergies, food, 155, 258, 265, 267, 269
almonds, 231, 234
aloe vera, 465
alpha tocopherol, 35
Alta Dena Dairy, 60
aluminum:
    anodized, 393
    in baking powder, 315-316
    in cookware, 215, 393
amaranth, 168
amino acid chelates, 142
amino acids:
    in animal vs. vegetable protein, 29, 237
    in eggs, 67-68
    essential, 29

ammonia, meat consumption and formation of, 31
anabaena, 166
anemia, chlorine and, 41
Aoyagi, Akira, 162, 163, 164
aphanizomenon flos-aquae, 166
apple juice, 257, 384
apples, 282, 384
apricots, 283
arame, 53, 165
arrowroot, 165, 316, 324
ascorbates, 142
ascorbic acid, 138-139
    in canning, 366
    in freezing, 375
    minerals combined with, 142
asparagus, 280
aspirin:
    in canning, 366
    for colds, 149
atherosclerosis:
    chlorine and, 35
    milk consumption and, 61
athletes:
    beverages for, 89
    diet and, 86-90
    protein requirements of, 88
    special foods for, 87-88
Atkins, Robert, 73
ATP (adenosine triphosphate), 104
avidin, 67-68
avocados, 283

babies:
    food allergies in, 265, 267, 269
    New American Diet and, 264-271
Bach flower remedies, 464
baking powder, 315-316, 323
baking soda, 316, 323

balanced metabolic profile, 98-99
    diet and, 99-101, 103-104
Balfour, Lady Eve, 406, 408-409
Ballentine, Rudolph, 59, 77, 79
bananas, 283
barley, 178
    flour from, 347
bartering, 185
beans, 223-231
    as baby food, 268
    cooking directions for, 223-227
    glossary of, 225-226
    green, 280, 385
    purchase of, 277
    for sprouting, 226, 279, 298-300
beef:
    drying of, 388
    feedlot vs. grass fed, 32-33
    grades of, 32, 284-285
    hamburger, 239-240, 452
roasts, 240-241
    for stew, 240
beefalo, 284
beef jerky, 388
beer, 262-263
beets, 280, 385
Benditt, Earl, 71
Berchy, Hans Peter, 411-413
Bergland, Robert S., 402
berries, 283
Bertrand, Anson, 402
beta cells, 45, 47
beverages, 256-263
Bieler, Henry, 72
biological value (BV), 167
biotin, 67, 431
bitterns, 56
black beans, 225, 227
black-eyed peas, 225, 227
blackstrap molasses, 46, 463
Bland, Jeffrey, 135
blood pressure:
    interpreting readings of, 55
    microwave radiation and, 392
    see also hypertension
blue-green algae, 166-167
body types, 122
bone meal, 465
Borgstrom, George, 398
botulism, 201, 268, 367

bouillabaisse, 248
bran, 153, 154, 168, 463
brazil nuts, 231
breads, 274-277
    for breakfast, 198-199
    corn, 315, 347
    nonbread vs., 275-276
    nonwheat, 315, 346-347
    pita, 314-315
    purchase of, 274-275
    sourdough, 317
    sponge method, 312-314
    sprouted wheat, 317
    substitutions in recipes for, 318-320
    unleavened, 316
    unyeasted, 315-316
    weight control and, 130-131
    see also flour
breakfasts, 193-200
breast milk, 264-265
brewer's yeast, 297, 466
Bricklin, Mark, 158
broccoli, 280, 385
Brody, Jane, 80, 89-90, 125, 130
Bromfield, Louis, 400
broth, 296-297
Brown, Lester, 416
Brussels sprouts, 280
buckwheat flour, 199, 347
bulgur, 319
bulk buying, 182-183
butter:
    clarified, 79
    fruit, 363-364
    homemade dairy, 310
    nut and seed, 332-334
butterfat, 61
buttermilk:
    homemade, 309-310
    raw vs. pasteurized, 60
butter oil, 79
buying clubs, 183, 185-186

cabbage, 279, 385
caffeine, 258-261
cakes, 328-330
calcium, 440-441
    deficiency of, 31, 38, 85
    sources of, 62-63, 271
Calli, Vincent, 49

calories:
    activity and expenditure of, 125-127
    body fat and, 125
    see also overweight
cancer:
    of colon, 154
    DES and, 264
    nitrite and, 201
    of pancreas, 258-259
    warning signs of, 160
candida albicans, 49
candies, 331-332
canning, canned foods, 353-367
    common questions about, 365-366
    economizing by, 353
    freezing of, 358
    hot pack vs. cold pack, 355
    in oven, 365
    pressure method of, 362-363
    selecting produce for, 355
    spoilage and, 367
    supplies for, 354
    of sweet spread, 364-365
    water-bath, 358-362
canning bees, 353
carbohydrate loading, 87-88
carbohydrates:
    complex, *see* complex carbohydrates
    refined, 128-129
    simple vs. complex, 44
    see also sugar
carbon tetrachloride, chlorinated water and
    production of, 34
Carlson, C.W., 68
carob, 254-255
carrageen, 165
carrot juice, 336-337
carrots, 279, 385
Casserole Mixmaster, 117-118
catsup, 362
cauliflower, 280, 385
celery, 279, 385
centrifuge juicers, 339-340
cereal beverages, 261
cereal creams, 197-198
cereals:
    cold, 193-195
    hot, 195-196
    see also grains

cheese, 64-66
    raw-milk, 64-65
chelates, 141-142
Cheraskin, E., 43, 49
cherries, 283
chia seeds, 231, 236
chicken, 241-244, 286
    as baby food, 269-270
    fried, 452-453
    see also poultry
children:
    food portions for, 114
    kitchen responsibilities of, 187-189
    New American Cuisine and, 271-273
    overweight, 125
chlorella, 166
chlorine:
    deficiency of, 52
    health hazards of, 34-35, 41
    in water treatment, 34-35, 41
chloroform, in water supply, 34
chocolate, 254, 264
cholesterol, 70-72
    cattle grazing and, 32-33
    eggs and, 67-68
    natural production of, 71
    whole milk and, 61
choline, 67, 431-432
cider presses, 341-342
citric acid, 258
citrus fruit, 257-258, 283
clarified butter, 79
clay cookware, 394
Clough, William, 92, 94
cobalamin concentrate, 137, 430-431
coffee, 120, 258-261
cold-pressed oils, 75-76
colds, 149-150
colitis, 154-155
colon:
    cancer of, 154
    spastic, 154-155
complex carbohydrates:
    heart disease and, 10
    New American Diet and increased
        consumption of, 11-12
conserves, 363
constipation, 152-154
    milk and, 59
convection ovens, 392

convenience foods:
    natural, 291-297
    relative cost of, 179-180, 448-451
converted rice, 178
cookies, 330-331
cookware, 215-216, 393-394
copper, 215, 393, 441
corn, 280, 385
corn bread, 315, 347
corn germ, 168
corn meal, degerminated, 178
corn syrup, 46, 50
coronary disease, see heart disease
Costill, David, 42
Costle, Douglas, 34
cottage cheese:
    as baby food, 269
    homemade, 309-310
    crash diets, 131-132
    crockpots, 394-395
crops, declining nutritional value of, 134-135
Cross, Jennifer, 286
crystalline vitamins, 137
cucumbers, 280
cuisine, diet vs., 5
cyno-cobalamin, 137

dairy products, see milk, milk products
dal, 226
date sugar, 46
Davidson, Stanley, 56
Davis, Adelle, 148, 240
decaffeination, 259-261
dehydrators, 382-383
DES (diethylstilbestrol), 264
desertification, 401
desserts, 253-254, 323-332
dextrose, 45, 51
DHA (docohexaenoic acid), 463
diabetes, adult onset, 47, 49
diarrhea, 150
diastolic blood pressure, 55
diet, cuisine vs., 5
diets, dieting, 21-22
    crash, 131-132
    exercise vs., 88, 124
    macrobiotic, 25
    moderation in, 131-133
    see also New American Diet/Cuisine
digestion rates, 107

dinner, 204-209
Di Prima, Diane, 14-15
disaccharides, 50
disease resistance, sugar and, 44, 49
distilled water, 39
diverticulitis, 154-155
dry ice, 380
drying, dried food, 381-388
    of beef, 388
    of fruit, 234, 254, 332, 383-384, 386-387
    of herbs, 385-386
    methods of, 381-383
    nutrient loss in, 381
    package and storage of, 383
    of salmon, 388
    storage life of, 381
    of vegetables, 384-385
Dufty, William 47
dulse, 53-62, 166, 465
durum wheat, 207-208
dysplasia, 99

Earsman, Max, 410-411
earthenware, 394
eating habits, 128-130
eggplant, 280
eggs, 66-69
    allergies to, 269
    amino acids in, 67-68
    as baby food, 269
    bread and, 198-199
    food value of, 67-68
    grades of, 68
    judging quality of, 68-69
    as leavening, 323
    production of, 66-67
Ehret, Arnold, 153
Ellis, William, 61
enamel cookware, 393
endocrine glands, 45
enriched flour, 8, 275
EPA (eicosapentaenic acid), 463
Esselbacher, Kurt, 60-61
evening primrose oil, 463
excipients, 143
exercise:
    diet vs., 88, 124
    eating before, 88-89
    kidney stones and, 156
    salt and, 89-90

extractions, natural, 137

fast foods, relative cost of, 179-180,
    relative cost of, 179-180, 448-451
fats:
    beef grades and levels of, 32
    cold pressed, 75-76
    hydrogenated, 73, 74-75
    New American Diet and, 12-13
    polyunsaturated, 71-72, 73-74
    rancid, 76-77
fava beans, 225, 227
Fertur, Alex, 411
fetal development, nutrition and, 80-82
fibrocystic breast disease, 259
figs, 384
fish, 245-250
    as baby food, 269-270
    cooking directions for, 247-249
    freezing of, 377-378
    individually quick frozen (I.Q.F.), 245
    purchase of, 287
    raw, 250
    in soups, 248, 295
    testing freshness of, 245
    thawing of, 379
flatulence, 150
flax seeds, 153, 231, 236
flour:
    barley, 347
    coarse vs. fine, 352
    combustibility of, 349-350
    home milling of, 343-352
    refrigeration of, 350
    stoneground, 311
    white wheat, 8-9, 318-319
    whole wheat, 311, 318-319
fluoridation, 40-41
folic acid, 91, 432-433
folk medicine, 148-159
food affinities, 104-105
food allergies, 155, 258, 265, 267, 269
Food and Nutrition Board, 27, 30
food concentrates, 137
food co-ops, 183, 185-186
food groups, 112-114
food processors, 390-392
food supplements, 462-469
foraging, 185
Ford, Barbara, 166
fortified vitamins, 137-139

Fouad, Taher, 141
Freeman, Sally, 389
free radicals:
    chlorine and, 35
    in rancid oil, 76
freezers, 368-369
    loading of, 372
freezing, frozen foods, 368-380
    of canned foods, 358
    containers for, 369-371
    dry vs. brine pack method of, 376-377
    economics of, 368
    fresh foods vs., 368
    of fruits, 369, 372-375
    of meat, fish and poultry, 377-378
    packing food for, 371-372
    power failures and, 380
    of TV dinners, 379
    of vegetables, 369, 375-377
    vitamin loss and, 368
French fries, 207
fructose, 45, 50-51
fruit butter, 363-364
fruit jerky, 386-387
fruit juices, 257-258, 337-338
    canning of, 360
    freezing of, 374
    for infants, 265
fruits:
    affinity for, 104
    as baby food, 267
    citrus, 257-268, 283
    crushed, 374
    darkening of, 355, 375
    dried, 234, 254, 332, 383-384, 386-387
    frozen, 369, 372-375
    grades of, 279
    purees of, 257, 360, 374
    refrigeration of, 284
    seasonal, 283-284
    for snacking, 252-253
    sulphuring of, 383
    sweet spreads from, 363-365
    year-round, 282-283

garbanzo beans, 225, 227, 299
gardening, 185, 396-397
    indoor, 298-303
garlic, 279, 465
gas, 150
Geesy, Reinhard, 411-412

gelatin, 63
General Accounting Office, water pollution
    report by, 35
generic foods, 287-288
genetotrophic theory of disease, 91-92
Georgakas, Dan, 261
ghee, 79
ginger, 303
gingivitis, 157
ginseng, 157
glass, 394
glucose, 44, 47
goats' milk, 63, 265
Goldbeck, Vikki and David, 266
gomasio, 236
Goodwin, Mary, 180
Gordon, Anna, 117
gorp, 234-235
gout, 105
grain/meat cycle, phases of, 23-24
grains:
    affinity for, 104
    as baby food, 268
    coffee made from, 261
    home milling of, 343-352
    rancidity of, 277
    recipes for, 205-207
    peanuts combined with, 233
    as protein source, 27-29
    sprouted, 226, 276
    storage of, 343-345
granola, 194
granular activated carbon (GAC), 35-36
grapes, 381, 384
great northern beans, 225, 227
green beans, 280, 385
greens, 280-281
group buying, 183, 185-186
guar gum, 63
gums, bleeding, 157-158, 257-258

Hall, Ross Hume, 73
halogens, 40
halophytes, 168
hamburger, 239-240, 452
Hamilton, Thom, 148
hash browns, 200
Haughley experiment, 406-408, 416
HDLs (high-density lipoproteins), 71-72, 73
headaches, 158-159

heartburn, 150-151
heart disease:
    complex carbohydrates and, 10
    meat consumption and, 31
    milk consumption and, 60-61
    saturated fats, and, 70
    sugar and, 48
Hegsted, Mark, 9-10, 13, 22, 173
hemorrhoids, 155
hepatitis, 155-156
herbs, 457-461
    drying of, 385-386
    fresh vs. dried, 214, 303
    indoor growing of, 301-303
    for kidney stones, 156
herb teas, 258, 261, 266
Hess, John, 274, 276
hijiki, 53, 62, 165
Hippocrates, 148
home fries, 200
homesteading, 397-398
homoeopathic tissue salts, 464
homogenized milk, 60-61
honey, 48-50, 268, 318-319, 324
    in freezing, 373-374
honey botulism, 268
horseradish, 385
Hough, Lindy, 369
hummus, 225, 227
humus, 401-402
Hunter, Beatrice Trum, 392, 393
hydrogenated fats, 73, 74-75
hyperglycemia, 47
hypertension:
    diseases associated with, 54
    salt consumption and, 54
    sugar consumption and, 49
hypoglycemia, 47, 49

iatrogenic diseases, 159-160
ice cream, 255-256, 325-326
immune system, sugar and, 44, 49
impotency, 157
Indian Pudding, 197-198
inositol, 67, 433
insulin production, 44-45, 47
interconnections, 398-399
iodine, 54, 441-442
Irish moss, 165
iron, 442

Irons, Earl, 137
irrigation, 401

Jacobson, Michael, 417
jam, 363
Jarvis, D. C., 49, 148, 158
jelly, 363
jerky, 386-388
juicers, 338-341
juices, juicing, 335-342
    fruit, 257-258, 265, 337-338
    nutritional value of, 337-338
    orange, 257-258
    vegetable, 336-338
    wheatgrass, 337

kefir, 308-309, 466-467
Kelley, Suzi, 93
Kelley, William Donald, 92-97, 99, 102,
    105-106, 147, 467-468
kelp, 53, 62, 465
Keough, Carol, 35, 37-38
kidney beans, 225, 227, 299
kidney stones, 156-157
    water hardness and, 38
kidney stress, meat consumption and, 32
kitchens:
    as family rooms, 188-189
    self-reliance in, 184
Klinger, Judith, 33
kombu, 62, 166
kudzu, 165
Kunin, Richard, 35, 73

lactation, 82
lactobacillus bulgaricus, 307, 466
lactose, 45, 51
lactose intolerance, 58
lamb, 285
Langerhans, islands of, 45
Lappé, Francis Moore, 29, 33, 237, 416
larder, stocking of, 177-179, 183
laver, 166
laxatives, 85-86, 153-154
    natural, 153-154, 236
LDLs (low-density lipoproteins), 71-72, 73, 168
leavening, 315-316, 323
lecithin, 67, 463
lentils, 226, 227, 299
lettuce, 281

Levy, Phil, 46
lima beans, 226, 227
lipoproteins, 71-72
listening, 110-111
liver:
    as baby food, 270
    chicken, 286
    dessicated, 465
    nutritional value of, 285
    in sugar metabolism, 44-45
    toxins in, 270, 285
livestock, 185
Livingstone, Churchill, 56
Lockhart, Leland, 65
Love Canal, 35
lunch, 201-204

MacNeil, Karen, 10, 64, 252
macrobiotic diet, 25
magnesium, 442-443
    heart relaxation and, 38
    kidney stone treatment and, 38
maltose, 45, 51
Mangelsdorf, Paul C., 109
Mann, George, 61, 70
margarine, 75
Margen, Sheldon, 88
matté, 261
Max Planck Institute, 30
mayonnaise, 214
measurement equivalents, 294
meat:
    as baby food, 269-270
    evolution of consumption of, 23-24
    freezing of, 377-378
    hazards of overconsumption of, 31-32
    kidney disease and, 156
    processed, 287
    purchase of, 284
    as secondary food, 12, 25, 26, 237, 396
    tenderizing of, 238-239
    thawing of, 379
    veal, 285
    see also beef; poultry
melons, 283
Megro supermarket chain, 410-413
Mervyn, Len, 141
metabolic profiles, metabolism, 91-101
    food selection and, 106-108

self-testing of, 94-97
vitamin/mineral supplementation and,
    146-147
Mickelsen, Olaf, 130-131
microwave ovens, 392
milk, milk products, 58-66
    allergy to, 155, 265
    constipation and, 59
    from goats, 63, 265
    grades of, 65
    homogenized, 60-61
    intolerance to, 58, 61, 63, 66
    low-fat, 61
    mother's, 264-265
    over-growth and overconsumption of, 61-62
    pasteurized, 59-60
    raw, 59-60, 64-65, 265
    spray dried skim, 466
    symptoms of sensitivity to, 58, 61
    ulcers and, 152
    underpasteurized vs. raw, 65
    vegetables cooked in, 220
millet:
    for breakfast, 198
    for dinner, 205
    flour from, 347
mills, milling, 343-352
Milton, R. F., 407-408
Mindell, Earl, 136
minerals, 140-143, 439-446
    ascorbic acid combined with, 142
Mirkin, Gabe, 89-90
miso, 163-164, 297
molasses, 46, 463
monosaccharides, 50
Moody, Mary, 306
Mosher, Marcella, 264
Mottern, Nick, 174, 180-181
Moyer, Greg, 264
muesli, 194-195
muffins, muffin mixes, 199, 292-293
mung beans, 226, 227, 279, 298
Munro, Hamish, 9
mushrooms, 281, 385

National Academy of Sciences, Food and
    Nutrition Board of, 27, 30
natural extractions, 137
natural foods:
    as convenience foods, 291-297

defined, 4-5
by mail, 455-456
relative cost of, 179-180, 448-451
see also New American Diet/Cuisine
navy beans, 226, 227, 299
nectarines, 283, 384
nectars, 257
New American Diet/Cuisine:
    aging and, 85-86
    for athletes, 86-90
    babies and, 264-271
    children's adaptation to, 271-273
    children's servings in, 114
    daily food guide framework for, 115-116
    economizing with, 33, 173-175,
        222-223, 235, 353
    equipment for, 179, 390-395
    food groups in, 112-113
    as food selection system, 21
    foods to avoid in, 176
    habits to break in, 128-129
    health care and, 22
    internationalism in, 116-117
    meal planning in, 112-118
    nursing mothers and, 82
    omnivarians and, 24-25
    phases of, 5-6, 173-176, 335
    pregnancy and, 81-82
    recipe substitutions in, 323-325
    seasonal variations in, 108, 184-185
    sex roles in, 187-188
    shopping for, 176-177, 182-183
    summary of, 11-16
    teenagers and, 83-84
    time allocation for, 173-175, 187-189
    variety in, 116-117
niacin, 433-434
nicotine, 264
nigari, 56, 162
nitrite, 201
Nittler, Alan H., 150, 151
non-stick finishes, 394
nori, 53, 62, 166
NPK farming, 408
nucleoproteins, 104
nursing mothers, 82
Nutrition Foundation, 12
nuts, 231-236
    butters made from, 232-234
    in gorp, 234-235

purchase of, 277
roasting of, 232

oat bran, 168
oat flour, 347
obesity, *see* overweight
octacosanol, 87, 462-463
Ohsawa, George, 25
oils, 76-79
    rancidity of, 76-77
    recommended amount of, 78-79
    selection of, 78
    storage life of, 77
omnivarians, omnivarianism, 24-25, 110
omnivores, 24-25
onions, 279, 281, 385
orange juice, 257-258
organic farming, 276-277, 312, 400-416
organ meats, 270, 285
osteoporosis, 85
Oster, Kurt, 60-61
ovens:
    canning, in 365
    convection, 392
    drying food in, 382
    microwave, 392
overweight:
    in children, 125
    defined, 121-123
    as disease, 121
    New American Diet and avoidance of, 11
    vegetarianism and, 131

PABA (para aminobenzoic acid), 434-435
pacifiers, 266
Palmer's grass, 168
pancakes, pancake mixes, 199, 291-292
pancreatic cancer, 258-259
pangamic acid, 435
pantothenic acid, 91, 135, 434
papain, 238
Papazain, Charlie, 262
parasympathetic metabolic profile, 98
    diet and, 99-100, 103
parboiling, 216
parsnips, 281
Passwater, Richard, 38, 41, 70, 463
pasta, 207-208, 277
    egg, 320
    homemade, 320-322

sauces for, 208-209, 293-294, 307
pasteurization, properties destroyed by, 59
PCBs (polycholrinated biphenyls), 264
peaches, 283, 384
peanut butter, 232-233
peanuts, 231
pearl barley, 178
pears, 283
peas, 385
    split, 226, 227
pectin, 257, 364
Penn, J. B., 398
peppers, 281, 282, 385
Pfeiffer, Ehrenfried, 135
pH, 105-106, 159
phosphorus, 443
phytates, 317
Picker, Robert, 259
pickleweed, 168
pickling, 360-361
pies, 326-328
piima, 308
Pimentel, David, 398-399
pineapples, 283-284
pink beans, 226, 227
pinto beans, 226, 227
pita bread, 314-315
pizza, 453-454
plaque, arterial, 70-72
plums, 283, 384
polarization, 135
polenta, 197
pollen:
    as food, 50, 466
    for prostate treatment, 157
polysaccharides, 44
polyunsaturated fats, 71-72, 73-74
pork, 285
porridge, 195
potassium, 443-444
potassium chloride, 56
potatoes:
    for breakfast, 200
    for dinner, 207
    purchase and storage of, 279
    sweet, 282
poultry, 241-244
    butchering technique for, 241
    cooking of, 243-244
    freezing of, 377-378

grades and classes of, 285-286
thawing of, 379
power failures, freezing and, 380
pregnancy, 80-82
    coffee consumption during, 259
    New American Diet for, 81-82
    weight gain during, 80-81
Pregnancy Cocktail, 82
preserves, 363
pressure cookers, cooking, 228-229, 362-363
Price, Joseph, 41
Price, Weston, 7
processed foods, 8-9
    see also refined foods
produce:
    grades of, 279
    purchase of, 277-281
    see also fruits, vegetables
propolis, 466
prostate enlargement, 157
protein:
    affinity for, 104-105
    amino acid structure of, 29
    biological value (BV) of, 167
    from brewer's yeast, 297
    complementarity and, 29-30
    completeness of, 29
    conservation of, 32-33
    cooked vs. raw, 31
    cost comparison of sources of, 223
    deficiency of, 30-31
    grains as source of, 178
    required amounts of, 30, 88
    sources of, 27-29, 166-168, 233
protomorphogens, 467-468
psyllium seeds, 153, 231
purees, 257, 360, 374
purines, 104-105
pyorrhea, 157-158, 257-258

quiche, 218
quickbreads, 315-316

raffinose, 223
raisins, 381
rancidity:
    of grains, 277
    of nut and seed butters, 234
    of oils, 76-77
Randolph, Theron G., 136

raw milk, 59-60
    cheeses made from, 64-65
    for infants, 265
RDA's (Recommended Daily Allowances), 9
red beans, 226, 227
refined foods:
    class associations with, 10
    constipation and, 152-153
    disease linked to, 7
    nutrients lacking in, 8-9
refreezing, 380
rennet, 66
restaurants, dining in, 119-120
Reuben, David, 70-71
reverse osmosis (RO), 37, 39
riboflavin, 430
rice:
    brown, 9, 178, 198, 204-205, 277, 347
    converted, 178
    white, 9
Ringsdorf, W. D., 49
roasts, 240-241
Rodale, J. J., 48, 414
Rodale, Robert, 168, 414
Rohé, Fred, 93
Rohé, Jason, 40, 84
rose hips, 466
Rossant, Colette, 390
Roth, Dick, 396-397
rye, 346

St. John's Bread, 254-255
salads, 211-215
    dressings for, 212-214, 307
salmonella, 286
salmon jerky, 388
salt, 51-57
    in baby food, 267, 268
    in bread, 312
    in common foods, 14
    current intake of, 13
    iodized, 54
    New American Diet and, 14
    as nutrient, 52-54
    recommended amount of, 13, 56-57
    strenuous exercise and, 89-90
    substitutes for, 55-56
saltbush, 168
salt tablets, 89-90
sandwiches, whole grain, 201-203

Sasaki, Naosuke, 54
sashimi, 250
sauerkraut, 361
sautéing, 361
Schroeder, Henry A., 8
Scitovsky, Tibor, 180
Scott, Jimmy, 133
sea salt, 51-52
seasons, dietary adjustment to, 108, 184-185
sea vegetables, 52-53, 62, 165-166
seeds, 231-236
    butters made from, 232-234
    in gorp, 234-235
    purchase of, 277
    roasting of, 232
    for sprouting, 279, 298-300
Self-Leveling Activated Carbon Column, 37
Sellier, Claus W., 274
Senate Select Committee on Nutrition, U.S.,
    9-14
sesame salt, 236
Sesanaise, 214
seviche, 250
Sheldon, William, 99
shepherd's pie, 241
shoyu, 164
Shurtleff, William, 162, 163, 164
sloke, 166
Smith, Dori, 167
snacks, snacking, 251-256
    desserts as, 253-254
    fruits as, 252-253
    guidelines for, 48
    nuts and seeds as, 235
soba, 208
sodium, 444
    in baking powder, 315-316
    hidden sources of, 53
    see also salt
sodium chloride, *see* salt
sodium-potassium balance, 52-54
soft drinks, 256-257
Solomon, Neil, 72
soups:
    fish in, 248, 295
    homemade, 295-297
    liquid in, 296-297
    seasonings for, 295
    solids in, 296
sour cream, 309-310

sourdough, 317
soybeans, 226, 227, 229-231, 279
soy foods, 162-165
soy milk, 164, 265
soy sauce, 164, 296-297
spirulina, 166-167
split peas, 226, 227
spreads, sweet, 363-365
spring water, *see* water, spring
spring wheat, winter wheat vs., 345-346
sprouters, 300-301
sprouts, sprouting, 226, 276, 279, 298-301
squash, summer, 281
squash, winter, 280
stachyose, 223
stainless steel, 393
Stanley, Edith, 149
starch blockers, 132
Starr, Kevin, 274
Steinbeck, John, 401
stew beef, 240
stir-frying, 217-218
stoneground flour, 311
storage, principles of, 183-184
streptococcus thermophilus, 307, 466
sucrose, 45-46, 47, 50-51
sufu, 164
sugar, 43-51
    adult onset diabetes and consumption of, 47
    aliases of, 45-46
    average consumption of, 13
    in baby food, 267, 268
    in blood, 43, 45
    in common foods, 13
    date, 46
    as dietary thief, 43-44
    disease resistance and, 44
    diseases produced by, 47-48, 49
    food value of, 43, 44
    honey vs., 48-50, 318-319, 324
    naturally occurring, 11
    New American Diet and reduced intake of,
      11-12
    tooth decay and, 49, 158
    weakness caused by, 44
    in yogurt, 63-64
sulphur, 383, 445
sulphur dioxide, 120
sweet potatoes, 282
sweet spreads, 363-365

Switzerland, organic produce in, 410-413
sympathetic metabolic profile, 97-98
    diet and, 99, 103
synthetic vitamins, 139
systolic blood pressure, 55
Szent-Gyorgyi, Albert, 138

tahini, 213, 214, 234
tamari, 164
teas, herbal, 258, 261, 266
teenagers, diet of, 83-84
teething, foods for, 270
tempeh, 163
theobromine, 254, 264
thiamine, 429-430
thirst, 42
THMs (trihalomethanes), 34, 35
thyroid gland, toxins eliminated by, 149
tocopherol, 35, 437-438
tofu, 162-163
    cooking with, 229-231
tomatoes, 282
    canning of, 358-360
    freezing of, 369
tomato juice, 360
tooth decay:
    calcium deificiency and, 31
    fluoridation and, 40
    sugar and, 49, 158
trace minerals, 446
trichlorethylene, 259
triticale, 347
Tudge, Colin, 24, 25, 131, 311
turkey, 241-243, 286
TV dinners, 379

ulcers, 151-152, 259, 337

veal, 285
vegetable gels and thickeners, 165
vegetable rennet, 66
vegetables, 210-221
    affinity for, 104
    as baby food, 267
    baked, 219-220
    broth from, 296-297
    cookware for, 215-216
    dried, 384-385
    frozen, 319, 375-377
    grades of, 279

    juices from, 336-338
    parboiling of, 216
    rehydration of, 385
    sauces for, 217
    sautéing of, 217-219
    seasonal, 280-282
    spoiled, 367
    steaming off, 216
    stir-frying of, 217-219
    year-round, 279-280
vegetable shortening, 75
vegetarians, vegetarianism, 24-25, 94, 109-110
    overweight and, 131
viilia, 308
vitamin A, 427-428
    mucus membranes and, 153
vitamin B complex, 428-429
vitamin B_1, 429-430
vitamin B_2, 430
vitamin B_3, 433-434
vitamin B_6:
    hemorrhoids and, 155
    kidney stone treatment and, 38
vitamin B_{12}, 430-431
    natural extraction vs. crystalline, 137
vitamin B_{15}, 435
vitamin C, 436
    in canning, 355, 366
    colds and, 149
    fortification of, 138
    in freezing, 375
    metabolism and, 146
vitamin D, 436-437
vitamin E, 437-438
    chlorine and elimination of, 35
    endurance and, 87
    natural vs. synthetic, 135
    rancidity prevented by, 76
vitamin F, 438
vitamin K, 438-439
vitamin P, 439
vitamins, vitamin/mineral supplements,
    82, 88, 427-439
    crystalline, 137
    excipients in, 143
    fat-soluble, 144
    fortified, 137-139
    natural extractions of, 137
    natural vs. synthetic, 135-140
    shopping for, 144-146

sources of, 139-140
synthetic, 139
time release, 144
water soluble, 144
see also minerals
VLDLSs (very low-density lipoproteins), 71-72

wakame, 53, 62, 165
Waldbott, George, 40-41
water, spring, 36-37
distilled water vs., 39
sources of, 421-422
water, water supply:
chlorine in, 34-35, 41
distillation of, 39
fluoridation of, 40-41
hard vs. soft, 38
home treatment of, 36-38
for infants, 266
municipal treatment of, 35-36
pipes and, 39
recommended consumption of, 42
water-bath canning, 358-362
altitude adjustment for, 360
water pollution, 34-38
Watson, George, 91, 92, 110
weights, ideal, 122-123
wheat:
allergy to, 155
bulgur, 319
cracked, 319
durum, 207-208
selection of, 345-346

spring vs. winter, 345-346
wheat germ, 167-168, 462
wheatgrass juice, 337
white beans, 225, 227
Williams, Roger, 61, 70, 73-74, 91-92, 135
wine, 120, 261
winter wheat, spring wheat vs., 345-346
Wright, Jim, 35
Wulzen factor, 43

xanthine oxidase (XO), 60-61

yams, 282
yeast, 315
in bread, 312
brewer's, 297, 466
nutritional, 466
yoga, 154-155
yogurt, 63-64, 466-467
as baby food, 269
frozen, 64, 326
homemade, 304-308
in recipes, 307-308
in salad dressing, 213, 307
starters for, 306-307
sugar in, 63-64
yuba, 164
yucca, 467
Yudkin, John, 48

zinc, 157, 445
Zwerdling, Daniel, 410-413

About the author

Fred Rohé lives in San Francisco, where he conducts seminars and publishes a newsletter about natural foods (*Natural Perspectives,* P.O. Box 22424, San Francisco, CA 94122). His other books include *The Zen of Running* and *Metabolic Ecology: A Way to Win the Cancer War.*